GOVERNMENT
AND POLITICS
IN LATIN AMERICA

A Reader

Peter G. Snow

State University of Iowa

GOVERNMENT AND POLITICS IN LATIN AMERICA

A Reader

HOLT, RINEHART AND WINSTON, INC.

New York · Chicago · San Francisco · Toronto · London

To Jeanne and Steven

Preface

IN PUTTING together a book of readings, the major problems concern the selection of material. First one must decide what general areas to cover and then whether to use case studies or general works. One soon discovers that in some areas there are so many excellent studies that the job of selection is quite difficult; some fine pieces have to be omitted, and by no means can all Latin Americanists be represented. In other areas the selection process is also difficult, but for a different reason. Some aspects of Latin American politics—which should be included in any text—have been virtually ignored by scholars. This scarcity of materials may well mean than an editor must include pieces that are not altogether satisfactory. Then all these problems must be worked out within the space restrictions imposed by the publisher.

Originally I hoped that each of the chapters in this book could include a general treatment of the topic plus a case study. However, it soon became apparent that acceptable case studies are rather few in number and that this plan would result in a much longer book. Thus, only selections dealing with Latin America as a whole have been included. The decision to use works of a general nature instead of case studies was based upon three factors: (1) the editor's belief that they are the better point of departure for the beginning student, (2) the greater availability of these works, and (3) the ease with which they may be supplemented by the instructor's favorite case studies.

Although this book is intended primarily as a text for introductory courses in Latin American government and politics, the selections used here are certainly not limited to those written by political scientists. There are also studies by historians, journalists, sociologists, anthropologists, and economists. About a fifth of the selections were written by Latin Americans.

The book has been divided into four parts. The first, The Cultural Background, is an attempt to place the governmental and political systems within their cultural context and to point out some of the cultural differences between the United States and Latin America. Part 2, The Governmental System, emphasizes the formal structure of government: the constitution, president, congress, and courts. The Political System— Part 3—deals with groups such as the armed forces, organized labor, students, the church, and political parties. The last part, Major Political Issues, is an attempt to analyze some of the issues now dominating the political scene in Latin America.

At the beginning of each of the four parts of the book are very brief essays, whose purpose is to introduce alternative approaches to each of the four topics. Part I is introduced by a brief description of the concept of political culture; Part 2, by a functional approach to the making, applying, and adjudicating of authoritative rules; Part 3, by a functional typology of groups and their methods of articulating interests; and Part 4, by a discussion of political development or the drive to create a modern nation-state, which may well be *the* political issue in much of Latin America.

BUENOS AIRES
JANUARY 1967   *P. S.*

Contents

Part 2 / The Governmental System

Part 3 / The Political System

List of Contributors

Alba, Victor (21)*
>   Editor of *Panoramus* (Mexico City); author of *Historia del comunismo en América Latina* (1954), *El militarismo* (1958), *Las ideas sociales contemporáneas en México* (1960), *Historia del movimiento obrero en América Latina* (1964), and others.

Alexander, Robert J. (22, 24, 32)
>   Professor of economics, Rutgers University; author of *The Peron Era* (1951), *Communism in Latin America* (1957), *Prophets of the Revolution* (1962), *Today's Latin America* (1962), *Venezuela's Democratic Revolution* (1964), and others.

Anderson, Charles W. (13)
>   Associate professor of political science, University of Wisconsin; author (with William P. Glade) of *The Political Economy of Mexico: Two Studies* (1962).

Carroll, Thomas F. (26)
>   Chief of the Agricultural Development Group, InterAmerican Development Bank; author of numerous studies of agrarian reform in Latin America.

Clagett, Helen L. (12)
>   Chief of the Hispanic Law Division of the Law Library of Congress; author of *The Administration of Justice in Latin America* (1952).

Figueres, José (30)
>   Former president of Costa Rica (1953–1958).

---

* The numbers in parenthesis refer to the selections written.

Fitzgibbon, Russell H. (15)

Professor of political science, University of California, Santa Barbara; author of *Uruguay: Portrait of a Democracy* (1954); editor of *The Constitutions of the Americas* (1948).

Germani, Gino (18)

Professor of political science, Harvard University; author *Estructura social de la Argentina* (1955) and *Política y sociedad en una época de transición* (1962).

Gil, Federico G. (11)

Professor of political science, University of North Carolina; author of *The Political System of Chile* (1966) and (with William W. Pierson) of *Governments of Latin America* (1957).

Goldrich, Daniel (14)

Associate professor of political science, University of Oregon; author of *Radical Nationalism: The Political Orientations of Panamanian Law Students* (1961).

Gomez, Rosendo A. (10)

Associate professor of government, University of Arizona; author of *Government and Politics in Latin America* (1960).

Harris, Marvin (4)

Professor of anthropology, Columbia University; author of *Town and Country in Brazil* (1956).

Johnson, John J. (28, 33)

Professor of history, Stanford University; author of *Political Change in Latin America* (1958), and *Military and Society in Latin America* (1964); editor of *Continuity and Change in Latin America* (1964).

Johnson, Kenneth F. (15)

Assistant professor of international relations, University of Southern California; author of numerous articles on Latin American politics.

Kennedy, John J. (20)

Professor of political science, University of Notre Dame; author of *Catholicism, Nationalism, and Democracy in Argentina* (1958) and (with Rafael Caldera) *Christian Democracy in Latin America* (1966).

Kling, Merle (1)

Professor of political science, Washington University, St. Louis; author of *A Mexican Interest Group in Action* (1961).

Lieuwen, Edwin (17)
   Professor of history, University of New Mexico; author of *Arms and Politics in Latin America* (1960), and *Venezuela* (1961) and *Generals vs. Presidents: Neomilitarism in Latin America* (1964).

Lleras Camargo, Alberto (29)
   Former president of Colombia (1958–1962).

Martz, John D. (25)
   Associate professor of political science, University of North Carolina; author of *Central America: Crisis and Challenge* (1959), *Colombia* (1962) and *Acción Democrática: Evolution of a Modern Political Party in Venezuela* (1966).

McAlister, L. N. (16)
   Professor of history and director of the Center for Latin American Studies, University of Florida; author of *The "Fuero Militar" in New Spain* (1960).

Mecham, J. Lloyd (8)
   Professor emeritus of government, University of Texas; author of *Church and State in Latin America* (1934), *The United States and Inter-American Security* (1963), and *A Survey of United States-Latin American Relations* (1965).

Murena, H. A. (2)
   Argentine essayist, novelist, and poet.

Pierson, William W. (11)
   Former professor of political science, University of North Carolina; author (with Federico G. Gil) of *Governments of Latin America* (1957).

Pike, Frederick B. (19)
   Professor of history, University of Pennsylvania; author of *Chile and the United States* (1963); editor of *Freedom and Reform in Latin America* (1959) and *The Conflict between Church and State in Latin America* (1964).

Poppino, Rollie E. (31)
   Professor of history, University of California, Davis; author of *International Communism in Latin America* (1964).

Segundo, J. L. (7)
   Director of the complementary Christian Seminar of Montevideo.

Silvert, Kalman (18, 23, 27)
   Professor of government, Dartmouth University; author of *A Study in Government: Guatemala* (1954) and *The Conflict Society* (1961); editor of *Expectant Peoples: Nationalism and Development* (1963).

Stokes, William S. (3, 9)
   Professor of political science, Claremont Men's College; author of *Honduras: An Area Study in Government* (1950) and *Latin American Politics* (1959).

Tannenbaum, Frank (6)
   Professor emeritus of Latin American history, Columbia University; author of *Peace by Revolution* (1933), *Whither Latin America* (1934), *Mexico: The Struggle for Peace and Bread* (1950), *Ten Keys to Latin America* (1963) and others.

Vekemans, Roger (7)
   Director of the Bellarmino Center for Research and Social Action (Santiago, Chile).

Vera, Oscar (5)
   Assistant director of the UNESCO Regional Center for the Western Hemisphere.

Wagley, Charles (4)
   Professor of anthropology and director of the Latin American Institute, Columbia University; author of *Amazon Town* (1953); editor of *Race and Class in Rural Brazil* (1952) and *Social Science Research on Latin America* (1964).

GOVERNMENT
AND POLITICS
IN LATIN AMERICA

A Reader

Introduction

The State of Research on Latin America:

POLITICAL SCIENCE*

Merle Kling

Political research on Latin America resembles the area which is the object of its study. It retains underdeveloped and traditional features; it is under both internal and external pressures to modernize.

Little capital (funds, talent, or organizational experience) has been invested in political studies of Latin America, and as a result the returns have been relatively meager. Personnel with adequate training and appropriate technical competence have been in scarce supply, research techniques adapted to Latin American studies have been of a relatively primitive nature, and the level of productivity has been low. Political scientists conducting research on Latin America, like some landowners, have been reluctant to introduce advanced tools and machinery and to extend the intellectual acreage under cultivation—that is, to acquire new skills, to accept technical assistance, to encourage methods designed to diversify the crop of research findings, and to consider a redistribution of disciplinary properties. Political scientists specializing in Latin America have not reached, to borrow Rostow's familiar metaphor, the take-off stage. Like the large segment of the population functioning on the output side of Latin American political systems, they often have been content to play the role of consumers rather than creators of the newer conceptual products of modern political science. They therefore have enjoyed few of the rewards and exposed themselves to few of the hazards of participation in more recent experimental trends in political science.

* Merle Kling, "The State of Research on Latin America: Political Science," in Charles W. Wagley (ed.), *Social Science Research on Latin America* (New York: Columbia University Press, 1964), pp. 168–207. [Footnotes in the original version have been omitted.]

With the aim of encouraging a program of political research on Latin America, this paper will describe some of the studies published in the past, analyze the nature of the current transitional phase in the evolution of political studies of Latin America, and point to some of the research opportunities and needs in the field of Latin American political studies.*

TRADITIONAL STUDIES OF LATIN AMERICAN POLITICS

Elements of traditional cultures inevitably survive in modernizing environments. The style of living of a single individual may, indeed, incorporate both the heritage of an ancient Indian community and the complex rituals of a modern industrialized metropolis, for at a specific point in time the congeries of traditional values are not totally displaced by the distinctive patterns of behavior attributed to a modern culture. Likewise, traditional political studies of Latin America have not been relegated to an abandoned past. They continue to be carried on by meticulous and sometimes sophisticated, research workers, and their contributions are not merely anachronistic and dysfunctional. Modern political science does not discard its Indian heritage when it exchanges the *huaraches* of constitutional documents for the shoes of IBM cards. And the same scholar, of course, may—even must—wear the footgear of both intellectual cultures when he conducts research. Neither chronological time nor personality completely differentiates the past from the present. Traditionalism in political science, rather, is distinguished by its content and methods.

[The accumulation of data has been the major preoccupation of traditional political research on Latin America, the failure to construct explanatory theory (on the basis of generalizations derived from systematic observation) has been its major shortcoming, and the generous distribution of prescriptions for public policies has been its major diversion.] A general survey of political literature might yield the same set of judgments for the entire discipline of political science, for the term "traditional" is not used in any pejorative sense. Rather, as indicated below,

* The fields of international relations, international organization, and international law, as they impinge upon the study of Latin American political processes, are construed as falling outside the boundaries of this paper. Accordingly, the paper omits comment upon such works as L. Lloyd Mecham, *The United States and Inter-American Security, 1889–1960* (Austin, Texas), C. Neale Ronning, *Law and Politics in Inter-American Diplomacy* (New York, 1963), Bryce Wood, *The Making of the Good Neighbor Policy* (New York, 1961), and John C. Dreier, *The Organization of American States and the Hemisphere Crisis* (New York, 1962).

[it indicates an approach often basic and necessary before other research can be carried out, and it reflects the status of the discipline of political science at the time most such studies were carried out] By the same token, the term "modern" does not connote any ideal approach to the problems of political science. It is used to suggest a more general awareness of the full range of methods and concepts that have come into the forefront in recent years, such as the comparative, the behavioral, and the quantitative or mathematical.

Since the days of James Bryce, political literature dealing with Latin America has been composed predominantly of an amalgam of reports of personal observations, commentary on the discrepancies between formal governmental structure and effective practice, speculative explanations (there has been a shift from a racial to an economic emphasis) of the "causes" of violence and instability, and expressions of regret that the Spanish conquerors neither personified nor propagated the democratic faith. Sometimes the data and opinions have been organized on a country-by-country basis, sometimes the chapters have been arranged topically and references to conditions in particular countries have been inserted for illustrative purposes (in a "for example" spirit), occasionally a monograph has been devoted to a single country or specialized topic. But boundary lines among journalism, history, law, and social science often have been blurred and value preferences liberally interlarded.

Although Bryce's (1926) work, originally published in 1912, did not inspire many political scientists to turn their attention to Latin America, it served as a recognizable antecedent, if not a prototype, for the general volumes on Latin American governments and politics that were published after World War II. Bryce's treatment was both topical and country by country. Despite his professed "curiosity to learn the causes which produced so many revolutions and civil wars in Spanish America" (p. xvii), he refrained from engaging in systematic political analysis or elaborate political reporting. He included chapters on the history and races of Latin America, he described in some detail geographical and social conditions in the seven South American republics that he had visited, and he concluded with "Some Reflections and Forecasts." While his lengthy sections on geography sometimes resemble a travel guide and his misunderstanding of concepts of race can only alarm a generation that has endured Hitler, his perception of Latin American problems lingers on in contemporary political science: after all, one of his chapters is entitled, "The Rise of New Nations"!

[After World War I, political science in the United States became self-consciously cosmopolitan. It turned its attention to western Europe, eastern Europe, international relations, and the League of Nations; but it could scarcely have displayed greater indifference to the internal politics and governments of the Latin American countries. Under the auspices of the Carnegie Institution of Washington, however, several monographs were published: specifically one on Argentina (Rowe 1921), on Brazil (James 1923), on Peru (Stuart 1925), and on Bolivia (Cleven 1940). As the titles suggest, these studies were cast largely, though not exclusively, in a legalistic framework. In addition, the interwar period was marked by the publication of Mecham's massive study, *Church and State in Latin America* (1934), with its focus indicated by its subtitle, *A History of Politico-Ecclesiastical Relations.* Also prior to active participation by the United States in World War II, an issue of the *Annals* of the American Academy of Political and Social Science was devoted to a symposium on the topic, "Mexico Today" (1940). We search in vain, however, for a comprehensive treatise on political conflict in a single Latin American country or a textbook on the area written from the perspectives of political science. Before World War II, it was left largely to journalists and a few heterodox historians (since immersion in Latin American colonial history has been the orthodox source of status awards for historical scholarship) to cope with such dramatic political movements as the Mexican revolution.

Nor did political scientists vigorously respond to the stimuli of official expressions of interest in Latin America on the part of the U.S. government during World War II. By any standards the scholarly yield of the war effort must be regarded as meager, yet the analytical boundaries set by the Carnegie-sponsored studies were enlarged. Stevenson (1942), utilizing documents and interviews (but, of course, not sample survey techniques), published a historical account of the Chilean popular front, which stressed the nature of party alignments. The same year saw the appearance of Macdonald's *The Government of the Argentine Republic,* which sought to describe party programs and electoral practices as well as governmental structure in the pre-Peron era. A volume on Brazilian government and politics (Loewenstein 1942), however, provoked a reviewer, perhaps unfairly, to complain that "only a political philosopher could have devoted a large and learned book to a constitution that does not exist except upon paper" (Tannenbaum 1943).

Only after World War II did the first more or less conventional textbook appear. In the absence of rich deposits of monographic literature susceptible to synthesis and analysis, Macdonald (1949) also may be regarded as a research contribution. Besides an opening chapter attempting to identify common features of Latin American political life (such as *caudillismo*), this volume, in a country-by-country sequence, described

governmental institutions and reviewed party conflicts in the twenty
Latin American republics. Except for its brief descriptive sections on
the geography, economy, and general social structure of most Latin
American countries and its historical synopses, Macdonald's textbook
sought to shape Latin American materials into the familiar mold of textbooks on the government and politics of the United States.

Subsequent textbooks, such as Jorrin (1953), Pierson and Gil (1957),
Davis (1958), and Stokes (1959), have assembled political data under
such chapter headings as "The Executive Power," "The Legislature,"
"The Judiciary," "Political Parties and Elections," "Revolutions," "The
Army," "Constitutional Developments," and "Municipal Government."
They have commonly included lengthy chapters on education, demography, and economic development in Latin America. The authors frequently have compiled larger masses of data than Macdonald, sometimes
have exploited the taxonomic potentialities of a topical organization,
and sporadically have posed explanatory problems; but they have not
exhibited a sustained concern for systematic political analysis. The presentation of data, ordered without special reference to explicit conceptual
schemes, has been their chief preoccupation.

Traditional studies of individual states have likewise retained a descriptive, historical, and normative focus. Such volumes as those by
Stokes (1950), Fitzgibbon (1957), Tucker (1957), and Taylor (1960a)
reflect diligent research and a capacity for the tenacious pursuit of elusive data. All these writers are sensitive to the limited clues to political
behavior offered by the content of constitutional documents. Implicitly
at least, they reveal a concern with problems of prediction. Nevertheless,
large portions of these studies trace, in the spirit of the historian, the
political and constitutional development of Honduras, Mexico, and
Uruguay and describe, in the spirit of the lawyer, the formal procedures
of government. They approach most closely some of the emphases of
modern political science in their analyses of party organization and electoral practices. In conformity with the ethos of traditionalism they, of
course, shun neither reification nor value judgments:

> There is much to admire in both the structure and the functioning
> of Honduran government. . . . Authority without responsibility, however,
> is objectionable in both the theory and practice of government (Stokes
> 1950: 298, 300).
> Thus far Uruguay has been made to seem, by and large, a paragon.
> There are debits to be recorded, however—fortunately neither numerous
> nor fatal (Fitzgibbon 1954: 271).
> Mexico can be regarded as a developing democracy because of its repre-
> sentative governmental structure and its recent progress in the direction
> of responsibility to the people (Tucker 1957: 419).

In Uruguay,

> The State clearly has promised more than it has been able to de-
> liver. . . . Although its leaders know . . . that the State misuses the ser-
> vices of a shockingly large percentage of the productive population, there
> has been no slightest effort made to encourage either narrow or broad-scale
> improvement within the bureaucracy (Taylor 1960a: 156–57).

Among works primarily devoted to the synthesis and organization
of data on a single Latin American country, Blanksten's *Ecuador: Constitutions and Caudillos* (1953a) is notable on at least three counts:
its value judgments are inserted with extreme restraint, its literary style
does not impose an obstacle for the reader, and its conclusion that in
Ecuador "the Indian must die . . . in a cultural sense" (Blanksten
1953a: 176) anticipates a later stress among political scientists on cultural
change as a corollary, if not a prerequisite, of political change.
[The collection of constitutional documents with accompanying commentary is, I suppose, the most widely recognized manifestation of traditionalism in political science.] This facet of traditionalism in Latin American studies is registered chiefly in Fitzgibbon's useful reference work,
The Constitutions of the Americas (1948). In addition, the legal documents, along with brief descriptions of their historical context, providing
for the formal structure of Colombian governments from 1811 to 1945,
have been brought together by Gibson (1948).
[Latin American scholars, as might be anticipated, have made contributions largely from the perspectives of public law.] The academic structure
of Latin American universities tends to assign the study of government
to the law faculties, and political studies originating in Latin America
accordingly incline in the direction of formal description of administration and constitutional exegesis. Falling into these categories are such
works as Gonzalez Calderon (1930, 1931), Lazcano y Mazón (1942),
Linares Quintana (1946), Miranda (1957), Mendieta y Nuñez (1942),
Lopez Rosado (1955), Lanz Duret (1947), and Fabregat (1949).

When Latin American scholars have allowed their attention to wander
from governmental institutions, they have not embraced empirical research. Their academic culture and tradition, rather, apparently has provided a congenial environment for speculative and philosophical excur-
sions into nonlegalistic subject matter. The brief essay on political parties
by Mendieta y Nuñez (1947) adheres to the format of an early phase
of sociological and political thought, and U.S. students will recognize
citations to Max Weber and R. N. MacIver. Echaiz (1939) reviews,
without the distracting apparatus of footnotes, the development of
Chilean parties in the context of Chilean history. The thick volume

on *Los partidos politicos: Instrumentos de gobierno* (1945) by Linares Quintana approaches the study of political parties from the point of view of comparative law and comparative legislation. Political science as carried out by Latin Americans has been mainly oriented toward "filosofia" (Holt 1963) and formal legal studies.

Despite the current ubiquity of "readers"—books composed mainly of other people's writings—the legacy of traditional political science includes only one substantial book of readings in the Latin American field, *The Evolution of Latin American Government* (1951) by Christensen. This volume probably accurately reflected the state of Latin American studies immediately following World War II. It did not seek to point instruction and research on Latin American politics in new directions. Incorporating selections chiefly from North America historians, sociologists, economists, and political scientists, the book foreshadowed the topically-organized textbooks of the next decade in both its form and its content. As compared with the Christensen volume, *Political Behavior* (1956), a book of readings edited by Eulau, Eldersveld, and Janowitz, enlarged the audience for the findings and methods of a more self-conscious and empirically-oriented political science and thus could influence at least somewhat the tilt of the research effort in American politics.

CONCOMITANTS OF TRADITIONALISM

Fastidious concern with methodology can frustrate students of the "substance" of Latin American politics and exasperate the harassed policy maker, for they demand "facts" and up-to-date analyses of political trends and events. Sets of conceptual premises, nevertheless, have consequences. Unavoidably they establish standards of relevance for research and interpretation of the political scene. What have been the consequences of traditionalism for research on Latin American politics and government? what generalizations can be made about the quantity and nature of the products of traditional research in this field?

Initially, the positive contributions of traditional research should be acknowledged. Thanks to the products of traditionalism, we have available studies in some depth of the formal governmental heritage of a number of Latin American countries. The monographic studies of Honduras, Ecuador, Uruguay, and Mexico illuminate the institutional environment of political conflict in these countries. Textbooks have made considerable quantities of available facts readily accessible. Traditional studies have richly documented such relevant characteristics of political behavior in Latin America as instability in the tenure of governmental personnel, *caudillismo,* and the dominance of the executive; and they [have suggested and often stressed, especially since World War II, that numerous cultural factors, both social and economic in content, cannot be ignored] by political scientists in quest of an understanding of Latin American politics.

The yield of traditionalism, however, has failed to satisfy many political scientists of varied conceptual persuasions and policy makers of diverse partisan loyalties. In the first place,[the rate of obsolescence in traditional research is relatively high] Latin American society is changing rapidly. Latin American political regimes are often short-lived. The formal governmental structure of a nation, including the constitutional-legal bases of its government, may change before a book is through the press. Research concentrating exclusively on the description of formal governmental structure in Latin America quickly can acquire a dimension that endows it with greater relevance to the historian than the political scientist.

Second,[scholarly productivity under conditions of traditionalism has been extremely low. Few political scientists have been recruited] into the Latin American field, and embarrassing gaps in scholarship have persisted. Only recently have a handful of young North American political scientists begun to specialize on Brazil! In fact, as yet there is no book-length manuscript dealing with Brazilian politics since the suicide of Vargas in 1954. And this almost incredible gap exists despite popular forecasts that Brazil, as a concomitant of its size, population, and social ferment, is destined to exert significant weight in the international political conflicts of the future. Although Argentina regularly finds a place on lists of "advanced" and "important" countries in Latin America, no political scientist has completed a book-length study of Argentine politics since Peron was deposed in 1955. Quite apart from questions of methodological elegance, political scientists have not provided us with comprehensive studies of countries in Latin America with prima-facie claims to our attention.

Third, traditionalism in Latin American political studies, as in other sectors of political science, has been[characterized by conceptual vagueness and semantic ambiguity.] Criteria for the inclusion or exclusion of data in particular studies often appear to reflect relatively casual interests of authors and some of the conventional categories of political science. What is the relationship between the geographical data, frequently introduced, and the manner in which the legislature operates (or, rather, does not operate)? Why does a volume on Mexican government include the sentence, "Petroleum was used for medicinal and specialized purposes by the Aztecs" (Tucker 1957: 251)? Traditionalism, in other words, does not appear to have imposed an obligation upon investigators to define specific problems and to offer explanations derived from the systematic correlation of pertinent evidence. In these studies relationships between one kind of data and another are assumed or asserted rather than demonstrated or verified.

Since, moreover, the vocabulary of the politics of the western world—sufficiently deceptive when the usage is confined to the world of its origin—has been transferred without purification to the study of Latin America, attempts at the kind of explanation that is directed toward prediction either do not take place or lead into an analytical cul-de-sac. For the designation of men and groups in Latin America as "democrats," "socialists," "fascists," "nationalists," and "communists" provides unreliable clues to their political behavior. If we are in search of indices to political action by groups in Latin America, the normative language of western political science serves the purpose of neither accurate description nor heuristic classification. The language identifies the groups of which the author approves and disapproves, but it does not differentiate among the political interests in conflict or the decisions that will be made by those in a position to exercise power.

The main source of data for traditional research has been the written word. Political scientists anchored in traditional research methods have relied chiefly upon documents and books stored in libraries and acquired in foreign travel to provide them with the raw materials for their studies. In addition, they have drawn upon their observations while traveling in Latin America and have tapped residents of Latin America for information and opinion to supplement written sources. But they have not engaged in fieldwork with the passionate intensity of the anthropologist, and they have not conducted interviews with the sociologist's eye to quantification.

Finally, traditionalism has been characterized by the relative isolation of Latin American studies from the field of comparative politics. While there may be some difficulty for an area specialist in remaining intellectually alert to experimental departures in his discipline, the ties between traditional Latin Americanists and the discipline of political science, especially the field of comparative politics, seem unusually tenuous. Symptomatically, virtually no general treatises in comparative politics incorporate Latin American data whereas data on the Soviet area regularly are introduced, and the inclusion of materials on Asia in textbooks devoted to comparative politics no longer signifies radical innovation.

On the negative side, therefore, we conclude that traditional research has failed to provide adequate data—regardless of the methodological criterion invoked—on important countries in Latin America, has been analytically careless, and has suffered from incomplete assimilation into the discipline of political science.

SYMPTOMS OF TRANSITION

Traditional political research on Latin America, it perhaps should be stressed, has not disappeared. Traditionalism continues to survive in the current environment of rapid change within the discipline of political science. Under prevailing circumstances, the same individual may concurrently carry on both traditional and nontraditional research. Despite the persistence of traditional features, however, contemporary political science may be regarded as predominantly transitional in its nature. In concepts, emphases, and methods, it tends to challenge traditionalism. It is less concerned with formal procedures, written prescriptions, interesting anecdotes, governmental structure, recommendations for public policy, and normative judgments. It is somewhat more concerned with power, interests, parties, groups, elections, processes of decision-making, operational rules of the game, conceptual self-consciousness, analytical devices, methodological rigor, and the potentialities of quantification. In the Latin American field, it is represented in some of the work of Alexander (an economist), Blanksten, Brandenburg, Fitzgibbon, Gil, Johnson (a historian), Kantor, Kling, Lieuwen (a historian), Lipset (a sociologist who is not a Latin American specialist), Padgett, Scott, Silvert, Stokes, and Taylor and in some of the reports of the American Universities field staff. These men, of course, are not united by a common disciplinary ideology; some, indeed, view modernizing trends in research with anything but enthusiasm, some appear indifferent to the divisions within the discipline of political science, and some who profess to embrace nontraditional objectives probably would not escape a blackball if they applied for active membership in the club of behavioral political scientists. Their research, nevertheless, seems motivated by a desire to shift the traditional focus of political studies of Latin America.

The outstanding contributions of the transitional phase of political science to Latin American studies, in the opinion of this writer, are Scott's *Mexican Government in Transition* (1959) and Silvert's *A Study in Government: Guatemala* (1954). The attempt to apply an explicit scheme of political analysis and to integrate that scheme into a general model of political change sets off Scott's achievement from the bulk of research on Latin American politics. Not content with "simple empirical data-gathering," he deliberately aims for generalization and justifiably claims that "The principal difference between this and other studies of Mexican government, at least with regard to substantive materials, is that the data is presented within a particuar frame of reference, based upon what is hoped to be an internally consistent and logical method." He conscientiously and successfully executes a research design which draws inspiration from interest group analysis (as developed by Bentley and Truman) and the model of differences between non-Western and Western systems of politics elaborated by Kahin, Pauker, and Pye in their report on comparative politics in non-western countries (1955). Within his conceptual boundaries, Scott organizes and presents a significant body of Mexican political data, with special attention to the party system and the presidency. The book, appropriately for a work illustrating research in a culture in transition, does not sever links with the past: value judgments are not absent, democracy is retained as a relevant criterion for assessing change, and the research procedures are sufficiently conventional to reassure defenders of the traditional culture.

Although Silvert (1954) does not subscribe to as specific a research strategy as Scott, his work on Guatemala is distinguished by its conceptual sensitivity, its seizure of opportunities to generalize (especially with regard to the phenomenon of nationalism), its appreciation of the links between cultural norms and political practices, and its wealth of detail.

Aside from Scott's study of Mexican government and politics and Silvert's study of Guatemala, which manifest numerous features of political science in transition, research associated with the current transitional phase can be grouped under the following headings: studies of parties, interest groups, and elections; analyses of (political) system's traits; improvements in the quality of political reporting and data collection; experiments in quantification; and evidence of assimilation into the field of comparative politics.

Studies of parties, interest groups, and elections

The largest volume of transitional research in Latin American politics falls into this category, and the yield in this sector of Latin American studies has been a relatively rich one. Political scientists, perhaps relying upon a somewhat plastic interpretation of interest groups, have not been deterred by the pessimistic implications of Silvert's conclusion (1959:77) that "Interest or pressure groups are few in Latin America. Where caudillistic one-party rule holds sway, there is insufficient complication to give much room to variegated pressure groups."

Published studies concerned with the role of groups, parties, and elections in Latin American political systems include: Blanksten (1959), which classifies a variety of groups that compete for power and influence, distinguishes among the kinds of party systems operating in Latin America, and persuasively argues for the comparative analysis of groups in order to facilitate theory construction; Fitzgibbon's (1957) review of "The Party Potpourri in Latin America"; Abbott (1951) on the contemporary political parties of Chile; Lieuwen (1961), a substantial analysis of the diverse effects of military organizations upon Latin American politics; Johnson (1958), a strikingly successful effort to establish and support a consistent thesis about the relationship between the rise of a social group and the contemporary patterns of politics in Uruguay, Chile, Argentina, Mexico, and Brazil; Johnson (1962), in a chapter contributed to a book on *The Role of the Military in Underdeveloped Countries;* Kantor (1953), a study of the Peruvian Aprista movement; Kantor (1958), on the Costa Rican election of 1953; Gil (1962), on the political parties of Chile; Schneider (1958), on Communism in Guatemala; Taylor (1963), on Uruguay; and Alexander's (1949, 1957, 1958) prolific and policy-oriented work.

Political scientists stimulated by the group approach have showered more attention upon Mexico than upon any other Latin American country. In addition to Scott's book, there are Brandenburg (1958), a useful compilation of business organizations in Mexico, originally prepared as a report for the Committee on Comparative Politics of the Social Science Research Council; Kling (1961), a study confined to a single business association; Padgett (1960); and Taylor (1960b).

Analyses of political systems

Contemporary methodological ferment in political science has been marked by, among other things, a quest for comprehensive frameworks of analysis, and a by-product of this quest has been the passage of the phrase "political system" into the stream of discourse of the discipline While only a limited amount of empirical research reflects the application of the "systems model," the terminology has rapidly established its status in the vocabulary of political science.

Perhaps the most influential version of this approach has been formulated by Almond, in a paper ultimately republished as the introductory chapter to *The Politics of Developing Areas* (1960). To this volume, Blanksten (1960) has contributed a substantial section which seeks to adapt Almond's concepts to Latin American phenomena and to recast a considerable quantity of the available data on Latin America within

Almond's categories. Conforming to the present stage of development of political science, Blanksten, rather than offering a novel explanation of behavior derived from the exploitation of newly discovered raw materials, introduces a fresh synthesis of Latin American social, economic, and political data.

Several writers, without self-consciously utilizing an overarching scheme of political analysis or a uniform vocabulary, have attempted to identify and explain aspects of political behavior which appear widely distributed in Latin America. To a degree they have engaged in the analysis of traits of an ideal type—the usage is Weber's and carries no utopian connotations—of political system in Latin America, although they have not explicitly and deliberately organized their findings and interpretations within a framework of systems analysis. Their unit of analysis consequently may not achieve the levels of generality required for comparative political analysis pointed in cosmopolitan directions. But their studies of the nature and functions of violence, instability, and nationalism in Latin America may be regarded as exercises in analysis of a system's traits. Illustrations of such research and interpretation focusing on widely diffused political traits in Latin America include Stokes (1952), a study which emphasizes the pervasiveness and integral quality of violence in Latin American political systems and provides a taxonomy of violence in this area; Kling (1956), which argues a particular thesis to account for the chronic replacement of leading personnel by methods not authorized by written constitutional documents; and Silvert (1961b), which discusses implications of nationalism for the area and recognizes the diverse perspectives inherent in the concept of nationalism.

Improvements in the quality
of political reporting and data collecting

Specialists in Latin American affairs are accustomed to deplore the treatment of Latin American news in the mass media. They are disposed to describe news coverage of the area as shallow, inadequate, distorted, and spasmodic. Latin American events, they complain, are not accorded equal space with other geographical areas in the columns of newspapers. In their view, journalistic accounts often cater to the popular stereotype of Latin American politics as an entertainment composed of recurring acts of inexplicable violence. Specialists inevitably have expressed regret at the absence of reliable sources which might provide a steady flow of relevant information.

The problem of creating an abundant supply of accurate information for analysis has not been solved, and newspaper headlines continue to be monopolized by accounts of recent and impending outbreaks of violence in Latin America. But some publications, perhaps inspired by the vision of a less traditional climate for Latin American studies, have contributed a dimension of depth to the reporting of selected Latin American conditions and have made a serious effort to improve and stabilize the gathering and presentation of certain kinds of data. Thus, the *Reports* of the American Universities field staff devoted to Latin America incorporate analyses by scholars with prolonged field experience. The *Reports* do not embrace the entire Latin American area and they are not a substitute for a comprehensive file on the sequence of events in Latin America. These *Reports*, nevertheless, comprise brief, readable, and authoritative interpretations of politically relevant developments which have engaged the attention of their authors. Among the subjects of the *Reports* have been "The Peruvian Elections of 1962 and Their Annulment" (Patch 1962a); "Personalities and Politics in Bolivia" (Patch 1962b); "Political Universes in Latin America" (Silvert 1961d); and "The Annual Political Cycle of Argentina" (Silvert 1961c). Such essays not only draw upon firsthand experiences but also reflect a level of training, depth of knowledge, and sophistication of orientation that ordinarily cannot be assimilated into the mass media. While not constituting exhaustive or orthodox scholarship, they usually manage to avoid emphasizing the transient and ephemeral. They may not qualify for space in scholarly journals, but they are more durable than the daily newspaper or the weekly periodical.

Two other publications, with more regular publication schedules than the *Reports* of the American Universities field staff, now systematically attempt to collect and organize Latin American data of interest to political scientists: the *Hispanic American Report*, established in 1948 and published monthly by the Hispanic American Society of Stanford University,* and the *Statistical Abstract of Latin America*, compiled annually since 1955 by the Center of Latin American Studies, University of California, Los Angeles. The editors of the *Hispanic American Report*, believing that the political sector dominates Latin American society today, concentrate on printing summaries of political events in Latin America, particularly as reported in U.S. and Latin American newspapers; the periodical consequently performs some of the services of a press-clipping agency for Latin American scholars. The *Statistical Abstract*, which progressively has expanded the range of topics on which it collects and

---

* Unfortunately, the *Hispanic American Report* ceased publication in November, 1964. [ed].

tabulates data, is an extremely valuable and readily accessible source of quantified information. The *Abstract* not only prints statistics on population, education, and economic developments which are relevant as background and explanation (in the form of independent variables) for political analysis, but has begun to print election statistics and other data of a directly political nature.

Thanks to the vagaries of status considerations, probably few political scientists wish to compete with journalists. To describe a product of their research as a contribution to the elevation of the standards of journalism, therefore, is not to invite an expression of effusive gratitude. Yet, as has been pointed out, much of traditional political science, in its implicit definition of task as well as techniques of research, has not been sharply differentiated from journalism. And the transitional period has witnessed the appearance of at least one volume by a political scientist that raises a standard to which journalists of good will, talent, and high aspiration might repair. Blanksten's *Peron's Argentina* (1953b), written with considerable literary skill, brings together a mass of factual material on the Peron regime which was hard to come by. As his Preface suggests, he encountered and overcame the kinds of obstacles and restraints which political groups hostile to the public dissemination of uncensored information are likely to impose. Blanksten's study is without the apparatus of hypotheses, concepts, and generalizations attributed to modern social science, but in this writer's opinion it represents a notable contribution to elevating the quality of political reporting on Latin America. (See also Alexander 1951.)

Experiments in quantification

There is a good deal of evidence to suggest that the thrust towards science as an appurtenance of modernization carries with it a commitment to the goal of quantification. If political science follows in the methodological footsteps of the natural sciences and of such social sciences as economics, sociology, and psychology, with a corresponding slackening of its bonds with history and public law, then we can anticipate the substitution of quantitative measurements wherever feasible for impressionistic, qualitative appraisals.

In general, during the present transitional phase the few modest attempts at quantification in Latin American political studies deserve commendation for their good intentions rather than for their accomplishments. While they demonstrate sensitivity to the cues emanating from the culture of modern social science, their methods and procedures with few exceptions are extremely vulnerable to adverse criticism.

Fitzgibbon has made a heroic effort to subject an important concern of traditional political science (the state of democracy in Latin America) to statistical analysis. In a series of studies, he has sought to determine rankings according to the scoring of items included in a scale of democracy among the countries of Latin America and fluctuations at intervals in relative rankings (Fitzgibbon 1951, 1956a, 1956b; Fitzgibbon and Johnson 1961). Utilizing a panel composed of specialists on Latin America in both academic life and journalism, Fitzgibbon requested members of the panel to rank (with the letters A, B, C, D, and E) the individual countries of Latin America with respect to fifteen criteria, for example, educational level, standard of living, freedom of press and speech, freedom of elections, and civilian supremacy over the military. The letter grades were then translated into numerical scores, and the resulting computations were subjected to a variety of statistical analyses. The tables prepared on the basis of accumulated scores indicated the relative rank of each country in accumulated total scores (and hence rank in the "democratic" scale). The surveys were conducted in 1945, 1950, 1955, and 1960 and consequently register changes in assessments made by members of the panel during these intervals.

Fitzgibbon reports his findings with considerable caution, but the obvious limitations of the surveys should be appreciated. In the first place, each participant in the polls responds on the basis of individual, subjective judgments; the application of uniform standards by the judges cannot be assumed. Secondly, the criteria of democracy evaluated by each participant contain unavoidably large components of ambiguity. While the ultimate findings are reported with mathematical precision, the figures originate in subjective responses to a relatively ambiguous field of questions. Finally, as Lipset has observed, "The judges were asked not only to rank countries as democratic on the basis of purely political criteria, but also to consider the 'standard of living' and 'educational level.' These latter factors may be conditions for democracy, but they are not an aspect of democracy as such" (1959: 74).

Notwithstanding these substantial reservations, Fitzgibbon's surveys remain one of the most elaborate efforts at quantification of Latin American phenomena by a political scientist. While a few other political scientists have introduced quantified data and have appropriated some of the language of mathematics, the scope of their studies ordinarily has been modest and their statistical methods have been much less complex and sophisticated than Fitzgibbon's. Thus, Kling (1959) has attempted to test the hypothesis that a shift from *caudillismo* to interest-group politics is accompanied by a decline in the proportion of governmental revenues derived from the "external" sector; but his analysis rests on an impressionistic appraisal of conformity to *caudillismo* in the political behavior of Latin American countries, and the data gathered on the sources of revenue in Latin America are not complete. Silvert (1961a) has conducted a limited survey of two Guatemalan communities in an attempt to determine varied intensities of nationalistic sentiment. Regrettably, a planned survey including the capital city, which might have provided a basis for broader generalization, was not completed.

Perhaps Lipset, a sociologist, has made the most successful marriage between quantified technique and categories of continuing relevance to political scientists. In a study not confined to Latin America (1959: 69–105), Lipset has attempted to ascertain possible relationships between selected social and economic conditions and the stability of democratic political systems, and he establishes a correlation between indices of wealth, industrialization, education, and urbanization, on the one hand, and the countries which, on the other hand, he groups together under the heading of "democracies and unstable dictatorships" in Latin America. Collectively, the countries classified by Lipset as "democracies and unstable dictatorships" (Argentina, Brazil, Chile, Colombia, Costa Rica, Mexico, and Uruguay) rank higher on his social and economic indices than countries classified as "stable dictatorships" (the remaining thirteen states of Latin America). Whereas the social and economic indices rest on an impressive foundation of statistical data, the political taxonomy, unfortunately from the point of view of the development of greater precision in political science, largely depends upon qualitative judgments. Hence, Lipset, in classifying a Latin American country as democratic, employs the criterion "whether a given country has had a history of more or less free elections for most of the post-World War I period"; and even this standard is stretched in order to accommodate Mexico, on the ground that the Mexican system "does introduce a considerable element of popular influence." In conceding that "the judgments of experts and impressionistic assessments based on fairly well-known facts of political history will suffice for Latin America," he provides additional disturbing evidence to support the conclusion that we have not solved the problem of evolving quantified indices for important political variables.]

Thus far, Silvert and Bonilla have mounted the most direct attack on the problem of quantifying politically relevant variables in Latin America, and they have also conducted the most elaborate experiment in the application of quantitative and survey techniques to an intra-area comparative study. In *Education and the Social Meaning of Development: A Preliminary Statement* (1961) they seek to determine the relationship of class position, social mobility, and national identification to processes of social modernization. By administering questionnaires to groups in

Brazil, Chile, Argentina, and Mexico, they sought to ascertain class position, extent of political participation, degree of religiosity, and attitudes toward nation-oriented values and development values among their respondents. The results, not yet published in final form, have been reported with elaborate statistical tables constructed on the basis of the replies to the questionnaires. More than any published work, comparative or monographic in nature, devoted to the analysis of Latin American politics, this intra-area comparative study consistently relies upon quantitative and survey methods.

It is both ironic and admirable that Latin American scholars, despite the historic bias in favor of philosophical, speculative, and polemical literary enterprises in their academic environments, have assumed leadership in the quantitative study of voting behavior in Latin America. Although some would argue that the most impressive achievements of modern political science lie in the field of voting behavior studies, U.S. scholars apparently have been dubious of the value of conducting such studies in Latin America. (Or have political scientists interested in Latin America lacked adequate statistical training?) But some Latin American social scientists have responded promptly to the challenge of adapting the techniques of voting behavior studies to the Latin American milieu. Thus, modeling his work on ecological studies of voting patterns in France and relying upon aggregate statistics, Germani (1955, 1960) has attempted to establish correlations between membership in occupational groups and vote secured by various political parties in the Argentine federal capital during several elections. The journal *Revista Brasileira de Estudos Políticos* has devoted a special issue to analyses by Carvalho (1960) and cooperating scholars which also stress the geographical distribution of the vote among political parties in the election of 1958 in Brazil. And Soares (1961, 1962) is engaged in testing, by means of a comparative study employing advanced statistical techniques, a highly original and stimulating hypothesis regarding possible relationships between economic development and political radicalism as manifested in voting behavior.

Evidence of assimilation into the field of comparative politics

The relationship between Latin American studies and political science in general, and comparative politics in particular, remains awkward. No political scientist concentrating on the Latin American area seems to be so centrally situated professionally as, for example, Lucian Pye (an Asian specialist) or David Apter (an African specialist). Political research on Latin America, rather than flowing into the somewhat turbulent mainstream of modern political science, often appears to drift in an isolated channel of its own, with its sponsors perched along the banks of the more swiftly moving waters of the discipline. Authors of textbooks and treatises in the field of comparative politics therefore ignore Latin American data without evident pangs of remorse or expectations of censure for failure to recognize conspicuously pertinent research.

During the transitional phase, nevertheless, there has been some seepage of Latin American materials into two types of books in comparative politics: anthologies (or readers) and symposia on underdeveloped countries. Thus, *Comparative Politics: Notes and Readings,* edited by Macridis and Brown (1961), and *Foreign Policy in World Politics* (1958), edited by Macridis, include selections dealing with Latin American countries. Likewise, Kautsky (1962) reprints articles on Latin America and Johnson, ed. (1962), incorporates chapters on militarism in Latin America contributed by himself, Edwin Lieuwen, and Victor Alba. In addition, Blanksten (1960), as has been noted, is the author of the Latin American section in the influential volume on *The Politics of Developing Areas,* edited by Almond and Coleman (1960).

Scattered and fragmentary evidence also encourages the conclusion that closer integration between Latin American studies and the field of comparative politics may take place in the not-too-distant future. Lipset's analysis of the concomitants of democracy, embracing Latin America as well as other areas of the world, is included in his systematic treatise on comparative politics (Lipset 1960), which, incidentally, may be the most rigorously executed major work in the field. Almond and Verba (1963) include survey materials on Mexico; and Scott is scheduled to contribute a volume on Mexico to the comparative politics series of books to be edited by Almond, which will attempt to adhere to a common conceptual framework.

TOWARD MODERNIZATION

There is some disenchantment among social scientists with the preparation of elaborate agenda for research. The unstructured character of much of academic life, the traditional value attached to the scholar's prerogative of determining his own research priorities and pursuing his own idiosyncratic interests, militate against the fulfillment of collectively promulgated research plans. The frequent gap between announced, grandiose intention and modest result also breeds a wariness, if not an outright distrust, of enterprises with the professed aim of shaping the directions of scholarly research. Hence, Lane probably reflects the prevailing mood when, in reviewing *Essays on the Behavioral Study of Politics* (Ranney, ed., 1962), he praises the book because its "programs for future research—until recently so large a portion of the literature—are economical and useful" (Lane, 1963: 163). In the light of Lane's comment, we should strive at least for economy, even though usefulness may be beyond our grasp.

Although we cannot rely upon a unique intellectual or financial panacea to produce rapid modernization in political studies of Latin America, we can seek to obtain benefits from our exercise in self-conscious appraisal. Subject to the constraints of the properly hallowed principle of scholarly self-determination, moreover, we can attempt to identify elements in a program of research that might accelerate the trend in the direction of modernization. At the sacrifice of nuance and qualification, I should submit the following recommendations, in summary form, designed to improve the state of research in Latin American political affairs. That these suggestions are offered in the imperative tense is a testimonial to their author's quest for economy and not to his confidence in their merit.

Increase productivity

Measured by virtually any relevant standard, the *quantity* of serious research on Latin American politics is inadequate. Modernization, among other things, simply requires an increase in the volume of research conducted on Latin American affairs. Doubtless many will be gratified if an expanded program of research yields products of uniformly high quality, reflecting the application of modern methods and theory. But the requirements for personnel capable of adding to our store of knowledge of Latin American politics along almost any dimension are so great that we cannot be overly fastidious in setting boundaries of methodology. When we can turn to no post-World War II monographic studies of many Latin American countries (ranging from El Salvador to Chile in political importance) by political scientists, when existing monographic studies (of Honduras and Ecuador, for example) are not updated and analytically refined by successive generations of scholars, we can only echo the alleged demand of Samuel Gompers for labor: "More!" Any developed subject matter incorporates an underbrush of research of indifferent quality, but one symptom of development is the availability of abundant supplies of goods—in this case, research goods—for consumption or possible reprocessing. The experience of Russian area studies in the United States, moreover, indicates that an expansion in quantity need not inhibit improvements in quality. (And Russian area studies, we might note parenthetically, have confronted and surmounted a more formidable language barrier than Latin American studies.) There is, then, a compelling need to recruit a much larger number of able scholars to the Latin American field and to allocate appreciable resources for the support of their research. Academic norms still dictate that scholars be allowed to exercise maximum choice in the selection of fields of specialization, but there seems to be some correlation between the distribution of funds by governments and foundations in the post-World War II era and the fields of specialization elected by graduate students.

An exhaustive list of concrete research proposals cannot and probably should not be compiled, but members of the Seminar on Latin American Studies (of which this volume is a result) identified the following problems, by way of illustration, as deserving the attention of political scientists:

1. Contemporary analyses of Latin American constitutions as sources of relevant political symbols and values, the function of constitutions in setting limits to expressions of political opposition.

2. Political leadership—the recruitment and socialization of elites, rigidity and flexibility among elites, a taxonomy of political leadership.

3. The changing nature and role of the Church in Latin America.

4. Sources of cohesion, consensus, and national integration in Latin America.

5. Modifications in the nature and role of interest groups in the light of rural-urban migration, efforts at national unification, and movements toward international integration (common markets, for example) among Latin American states.

6. The content and influence of communication, including mass media, in Latin America.

7. The social correlates of political radicalism and democratization in Latin America, bases for initiation of drastic social and political change in Mexico.

8. The construction of theoretically oriented typologies of political actors and regimes in Latin America; a classification of regimes on the basis of their response to general problems, including economic development.

9. Studies of the process of political socialization. How are political values and attitudes acquired in Latin America? How may they be modified? How may techniques of governmental engineering be employed to promote effective democratic procedures?

10. The changing political role of women in Latin America.

11. The scope and functions of voluntary associations in Latin America, including an analysis of factors encouraging their prevalence or absence.

12. The content, functions, and domestic and international effects of ideology and political thought in Latin America.

13. The influence of new election procedures upon political participation.

14. The role of the army in the process of development.

15. The politics of diplomatic appointments, the composition of foreign office personnel, and perceptions of role by foreign policy officials.

16. The relationship between resource allocation, especially investment in education, and the development of political participation and democratization.

17. The prevailing rules of the political game in Latin America.

18. Intra-area comparative studies of political parties.

19. Relationships between the type of violence employed and the nature of a political system; the possible influence of guerrilla warfare, for example, in shaping the character of the Castro regime in Cuba.

20. The significance of area-wide movements, such as Christian Democracy, for Latin American political behavior.

21. Personality and party politics in Latin America.

22. The relationships between economic stagnation and political change.

23. The impact of United States policies, international politics, and international institutions upon decision-making in Latin America.

24. Private enterprise and governmental policies in Latin America.

25. The foreign policies of the major powers in Latin America.

26. Studies of the termination of regimes, particularly the conditions accompanying the demise of leaders who have exercised power for prolonged periods.

27. Problems of diplomatic and military intervention.

28. The effect of the emergence of new social and political groups upon foreign policy decisions in Latin America.

29. The political consequences of the norm of diplomatic asylum. Does the observance of this principle inhibit the evolution of techniques of political compromise?

30. Problems in the development of national character and national identity in Latin America.

31. The relationship between styles of decision-making and social and economic development.

32. The political worlds of Latin American intellectuals.

33. Comprehensive, insightful treatises on subjects of large significance, as distinct from intensive explorations of relatively minor topics.

34. The translation into English of basic documents and books prepared by Latin Americans.

35. Monographic treatments of individual countries in Latin America which have been neglected by contemporary political scientists, including Brazil, Paraguay, and the Central American republics.

36. A study of transnational politics. In the words of Samuel P. Huntington:

> Latin America is a political community, and . . . events in one country frequently have effects on other countries. Lieuwen . . . brought this out clearly in his book on the Latin American military; a radical (or conservative) coup in one country will often trigger off similar coups in other countries. A broad analysis of how transnational revolutionary, reform, and conservative movements operate on a continental basis would be most illuminating. The model for such a study exists in R. R. Palmer's *The Age of the Democratic Revolution* [1959]. Palmer conclusively shows how similar political currents ebbed and flowed and interacted with each other throughout the western world from Williamsburg to St. Petersburg in the late 18th century. Someone should do a similar job for Latin America in the mid-twentieth century.

Plug the widest gaps

Certain omissions in the literature dealing with Latin American political life verge on the scandalous. There are no book-length studies by political scientists of Brazil since Vargas or of Argentina since Peron. There is no book-length study of Chilean politics since World War II. Despite the dramatic emergence of a professedly Marxist-Leninist government in Cuba, there is no book-length study by a political scientist of contemporary Cuban politics; in fact, the best book on the Castro regime is by a journalist: Theodore Draper, *Castro's Revolution: Myths and Realities* (1962). The research opportunities offered by these important segments of Latin America would appear unusually inviting. Systematically organized data, interpretations, and analyses are so scarce that a political explorer of these territories is under no obligation to equip himself with methodologically impeccable instruments of investigation; the work of a Tocqueville on Brazil or Argentina will be warmly welcomed!

Specify the dependent variables

The dependent variable, for a political scientist, is an aspect of politics which he seeks to explain. Thus, for some students of North American politics, voting behavior may serve as the dependent variable. What are political scientists working in the Latin American field trying to account for? Among the multitude of "factors," "forces," and "conditions" in Latin America, which aspects of Latin America life do political scien-

tists describe with a view toward explanation? Presumably political scientists utilize political variables as their point of departure; but the
encyclopedic approach, inherent in many studies, incorporates a miscel-
lany of social, economic, and political facts and often fails to identify
clearly the political phenomenon under analysis. Are we trying to explain—that is, correlate with other relevant variables—instability? Or
caudillismo? Or the emergence of a one-party system? Or centralized
decision-making? Or the prevalent means for the selection and recruitment of politically active personnel? Or democracy? Or the legitimation
of procedures for solving problems of succession? Whichever it is, let
us be specific. We then can enlist social, economic, psychological, and
possibly other political data to function as independent variables for
purposes of explanation. Adherence to the research convention of speci-
fying the dependent political variables is a relatively simple device for
improving the symmetry of research, but heretofore it has not been
absorbed into the main currents of political research on Latin America.
Yet the regular application of this convention would facilitate comparison between one study and another, circumvent the limitations of a
purely descriptive report, possibly introduce a much-desired element
of cumulativeness into Latin American studies, and perhaps add to the
durability of each separate research effort.

Exploit the area approach in order to control for selected variables

Political scientists concentrating in Latin American studies have not
taken sufficient advantage of the potentialities of an area focus to contribute directly to the conversion of the study of foreign governments
into a field eligible for the label "comparative politics." By assisting
in this transformation, incidentally, Latin American specialists also can
create a more favorable intellectual environment for the growth of empirical political theory. As Eulau (1962: 397) has pointed out,

> Comparative analysis, truly to deserve its name, might have fared better,
> and done so earlier, if all students of government—the domestic brand
> as well as the foreign—had been concerned with a method which comes
> closer to the laboratory experiment than any other we have in controlling
> a few variables. For . . . "control" is the *sine qua non* of all scientific
> procedure.

While Eulau, drawing upon his experiences in a comparative study of
state legislative systems, argues the merits of utilizing the controls inherent in a single, albeit heterogeneous, culture, such as that of the
United States, the area approach makes it possible to impose controls
over a larger terrain. If we seek to ferret out the combinations of vari-

ables that warrant generalizations about political behavior, an area orientation enables us quite readily to isolate and identify those attributes which are widely distributed among the units we wish to compare. By the same token, the area approach quickly may lead us to discard, for explanatory purposes, other variables that do not discriminate between one system and another. Thus, if political activists in a number of countries share a common language and racial background, but in some of these countries a high degree of instability in the selection of key governmental personnel prevails while in other countries a mode of peaceful accession to office has evolved, we are justified in concluding that language and race cannot function as exclusive explanatory variables of instability. Likewise, the popular hypothesis that susceptibility to the appeals of Communism or political radicalism correlates with such variables as low income and low levels of literacy can be subjected to fairly rigorous testing in the Latin American milieu. (The case of Cuba, while not providing conclusive evidence, indicates that a relatively high per capita income and a relatively high literacy rate do not by themselves immunize a population against Communism.)

In so far as a number of Latin American societies share common linguistic, racial, religious, economic, and institutional traits, some variables can be held "constant" in a comparative study of politics within the Latin American area. By deliberately exploiting the possibilities of "controlling" for these selected variables in area-centered research, Latin American specialists can demonstrate a constructive role for area studies in the development of theoretical propositions derived from comparative analysis. As Silvert noted almost a decade ago, in the Preface to his monograph (1954: ix) on Guatemala, "A general awakening of awareness among area specialists of the importance of relating their geographical interests to broader trends is of special significance to the political scientist. . . ."

Establish empirical referents
for distinctive concepts employed
in Latin American studies

Political scientists have inherited a language comprising numerous concepts which lack precise empirical referents. Such terms as "democracy" and "dictatorship," for example, do not convey identical meanings to diverse audiences.

Specialists on Latin America obviously cannot assume responsibility for the elimination of all semantic ambiguity from the vocabulary of political science, but they may appropriately undertake the task of clarifying such concepts as "instability," "violence," and *caudillismo,* which are regularly applied to the analysis of Latin American political data. Thus, "instability" is not a unidimensional phenomenon in Latin America, and the goal of "operationalizing" its meaning involves both taxonomic and analytical problems. Instability assumes a variety of complex forms in Latin America, with differential consequences for Latin American political systems. Some kinds of instability merely rotate governmental personnel; other kinds of instability are accompanied by shifts of power among competing social and economic groups. If we propose to speak of some countries as "more unstable" than other countries, we require a more elaborate taxonomy of instability than we now possess, and we could profitably develop measurements for differentiated types of instability.

Although Stokes (1952) has developed a useful classification of forms of violence in Latin America, political scientists have been slow to locate violence in Latin America within a broader framework of studies of violence. In recent years, research on "internal wars," "unconventional warfare," and "revolutions" has proliferated. There would appear to be value in attempting to integrate research on violence in Latin America with such studies and to consider the multiple functions performed by violence in Latin American political systems.

The concept of *caudillismo* especially is susceptible to greater refinement. In an effort to develop more precise connotations for the term, political scientists might raise questions posed in studies of leadership in the United States: How are individuals socialized and recruited into roles of political leadership in Latin America? What elements are common in the backgrounds of Latin American political leaders? What changes, if any, have taken place in the nature (including personality characteristics and styles) of Latin American political leaders, and what are the accompanying characteristics of such changes? Under what circumstances do persons assume or lose power in Latin America? What are the rewards of the exercise of leadership? Such studies, by systematically collecting data on a large sample of Latin American political leaders and going beyond such biographical works as Alexander (1962b), could present results in a quantified form that might serve to provide an empirical referent for *caudillismo*.

Probe in new directions for the nature and origins of politically relevant values, attitudes, and allegiances

Traditionally, documents, constitutions, proclamations, and speeches have been consulted as statements of Latin American political values. But alternative techniques, applying somewhat different concepts, have been developed in the study of political attitudes and loyalties in the United States. Hence, the concept "political socialization" seems to have emerged as a powerful tool for the analysis of North American political behavior; it is a concept which apparently can account for the attitudes of children toward authority (Greenstein 1960; Easton and Hess 1962) and the voting behavior of most adults (Campbell *et al.* 1960: 147). An observation of Bryce regarding Uruguay suggests that the concept also may shed light on party affiliations in Latin America: "The parties have become largely hereditary; a child is born a little Blanco or a little Colorado, and rarely deserts his colour" (Bryce 1926: 359). It would seem particularly relevant to investigate how processes of political socialization work to produce both continuity and change in a Latin American political system, since internalization of the norm of violence would appear capable of either perpetuating or modifying the pattern of decision-making in a Latin American country.

The adaptation of interview techniques to the Latin American environment should provide an especially rich yield of fresh generalizations and insights. Almond (1954) has demonstrated that a comparative study, unfortunately not including Latin American respondents, can be conducted to determine the social and psychological characteristics of those who respond to and ultimately reject Communist appeals and that the results can be presented in statistical form. Lane (1962), assisted by a tape recorder, has conducted prolonged, intensive, depth interviews with a small number of respondents in an effort to discover "Why the American Common Man believes what he does." Lewis, in *The Children of Sánchez* (1961), reports in massive detail the results of taped interviews with a family in Mexico, but Lewis' research reflects his orientation as an anthropologist. Similar potentially exciting and original work utilizing such techniques remains to be carried out by political scientists.

Nor have library materials been exhausted as sources for clues to the motivation and values of political man in Latin America. Political scientists thus far have not examined political novels, such as those of Mariano Azuela, Carlos Fuentes, and Luis Spota, with a view toward securing insights, illustrations, confirmatory evidence, or "emotional closure" for their propositions about political behavior.

In any event, since there is general agreement that the written constitutions and laws do not, in Carl J. Friedrich's phrase, constitute "effective regularized restraints" in Latin America, we advantageously can employ new weapons in order to attack the problem of "legitimacy" and "the rules of the game" in Latin America. If the constitution does not prescribe the effective rules of the game, what are the operating rules governing political conflict in Latin America? Needler (1962) recently has argued the thesis that a "legitimacy vacuum" accounts for the instability and violence of Latin American politics. But may not violence itself become an accepted, and therefore "legitimate," value within a culture? Procedures for reaching decisions, including decisions on the selection of government personnel, do become institutionalized in Latin America, but they may not be the procedures formulated in a written document. To discover the effective rather than the formal rules of the political game in Latin America represents a continuing challenge to political scientists.

Explore the feasibility of studies of public policy formation

Although some social scientists have popularized the model of decision-making by a "power elite" in the United States, intensive studies of specific governmentally determined decisions at the national and local level tend to indicate that public policies in the United States reflect the interplay of complex interests and a pluralistic model of power. In the case of Latin America, political scientists continue to ascribe "power" to abstract, evidently monolithic, entities—the landowners, the army, the president. Yet, we have not made a series of empirical studies to determine the process by which specific decisions have been reached. What groups and individuals, exercising what degrees of power, have participated in decisions to initiate programs of land reform or modifications in tax legislation? By what process has a decision been reached to nationalize a public utility? Is there anything distinctive about Latin American policy-making processes? A comprehensive analysis of existing case studies is needed to see if any common patterns exist in the policy-making process. In general, who takes the initiative in pushing policy measures and in generating support (consensus building)? What are the veto groups on different types of policy? Are the patterns of negotiation and bargaining different from those in the United States? How have they changed in Latin America over the years? It is true that public decision-making in Latin America seems characterized by lower visibility than in the United States; but studies of the formation of specific public policies, if feasible, might make it possible to associate the concept of "power" more meaningfully with particular groups and institutions in Latin America.

An economist rather than a political scientist is responsible for the only substantial comparative study of public policy formation in the Latin American area, namely, Hirschman (1963). Drawing upon detailed studies of land reform in Colombia, attempts to introduce change in Brazil's Northeast, and the problem of inflation in Chile, Hirschman generalizes about the processes of development. Although he is an economist with a pronounced policy orientation, Hirschman continuously is concerned with the behavior of public decision-makers. [With notable sophistication and subtlety, he analyzes the semantics of public problem-solving and coins the term "reform-mongering" to describe the process by which economic development takes place.] The centrality of the concepts of power, conflict, political style, and decision-making in his work, the sustained concern with evolving models and theories which can facilitate prediction and at least partially control solutions, and the integration of concepts from multiple disciplines (including history and social psychology) make *Journeys toward Progress* an outstanding and highly stimulating contribution to the study of the formation of public policies.

Examine institutions and behavior in the light of the concept of functionalism

Clearly, parties, legislatures, and constitutions do not perform similar functions in different political cultures. In the United States and Great Britain, political parties may be significant vehicles for carrying on electoral contests. In the Soviet Union, the Communist Party functions as the center of decision-making and the principal arena of conflict. But what functions are discharged by one-party and multiple-party systems in Latin America? What functions are performed by legislatures in Latin America, and if the functions differ between one country and another, what are the correlates of such differences?

Edelman's concept of "symbolic reassurance" (1960), I believe, will prove a useful adaptation of the functional approach for political scientists concerned with Latin American behavior. Whereas Lenin advocated that revolutionary theory (symbols) should serve as a guide to revolutionary action, Edelman points out that in certain contexts symbols produce political quiescence. The symbols, in other words, may gratify certain personality needs and maintain some groups in a state of inactivity or quiescence, while the tangible resources, nominally the stakes of political competition, are awarded to other groups. Although numerous facets of political behavior in Latin America may be subjected to clarifying analysis through the application of Edelman's concept, I shall confine myself to one illustration—the functional role of opposition parties in Mexico. On the basis of Edelman's thesis, for example, we may hypothesize that support for opposition parties in Mexico, at least on the part of some Mexicans, is not intended to challenge the authority of the regime or to register dissatisfaction with the distribution of tangible rewards but to reassure some individuals that they have not violated

values acquired early in life, even though those values no longer correspond to their "tangible interests." Certainly, we also are warranted
in hypothesizing that the "leftist" and "revolutionary" declarations by
Latin American political leaders likewise often function as symbolic reassurance and are designed to induce political quiescence.

Adapt the concepts of community power studies to studies of local politics in Latin America

Silvert has emphasized the importance of the village and the hacienda
in Latin American political life. Huntington, in his memorandum quoted
above, suggested comprehensive studies of local decision-making:

> The study of political systems in villages and cities has leapt forward
> in the United States in the past decade. The trigger book here was Floyd
> Hunter's 1953 study of Atlanta's *Community Power Structure*. Hunter's
> research seemed to show a fairly monolithic and concentrated local power
> structure. His findings have been challenged as to their methodology and
> general applicability, most notably in the writings of Robert Dahl and
> his disciples. Other studies have compared the power structures existing
> in American and English cities. Others have analyzed the changes in the
> distribution of power in a single city over time. These studies have shown
> the effects of modernization in the breakdown of narrow oligarchical rule
> and the rise of a more pluralistic elite structure. The techniques, methods,
> categories, and theories developed in this rich and extensive literature
> might easily be applied to the study of medium-sized Latin American
> cities. Two studies have been made of cities just south of the border:
> namely, those by Form and D'Antonio (1959) and by Klapp and Padgett
> (1960).

Studies of local decision-making, moreover, could provide a focus
for collaboration between anthropologists and political scientists.

Move toward resolution of the problem of research priorities by clarifying the choice of reference groups for political scientists specializing in Latin American studies

The problem of research priorities is a problem in the choice of reference groups. To the members of which groups do we wish to look
for standards to guide our research? To those who encourage political
scientists to utter banal pleas for good will in the Western Hemisphere?
To those who seek to maintain a clientele for Latin American studies
by stressing the quaint, the deviant, and the exotic? To those who demand a prompt identification of friend and foe in Latin America? To
those who pressure political scientists to provide simple capsule solutions

to complex, enigmatic problems? (On behalf of pursuing alternative values, political scientists, in fact, might consider the declaration of a moratorium on premature prescriptions of public policy.) To those who merely wish political scientists to contribute a large fund of facts to an interdisciplinary area program? To those who believe that the development of empirical theory about Latin American political behavior, within the framework of comparative political analysis, holds out the greatest promise for contemporary political science? Although this paper has not repudiated eclecticism, it has tried to imply that political scientists who would study modernization in Latin America must not resist the modernization of themselves.

BIBLIOGRAPHY

Abbott, Roger S.
    1951   The role of contemporary political parties in Chile. American Political Science Review 45 (No. 2): 450–63.
Alexander, Robert J.
    1949   The Latin American *Aprista* parties. Political Quarterly 20 (No. 3): 236–47.
    1951   The Peron era. New York.
    1957   Communism in Latin America. New Brunswick, N.J.
    1958   The Bolivian national revolution. New Brunswick, N.J.
    1962a Today's Latin America. New York.
    1962b Prophets of the revolution: profiles of Latin American leaders. New York.
Almond, Gabriel
    1954   The appeals of communism. Princeton, N.J.
Almond, Gabriel, and Sidney Verba
    1963   The civic culture. Princeton, N.J.
Almond, Gabriel, and James S. Coleman (eds.)
    1960   The politics of developing areas. Princeton, N.J.
Amadeo, Santos P.
    1943   Argentine constitutional law. New York.
American Academy of Political and Social Science
    1940   Annals 208 (March): 1–186.
Blanksten, George I.
    1953a Ecuador: constitutions and caudillos. Berkeley and Los Angeles.
    1953b Peron's Argentina. Chicago.
    1959   Political groups in Latin America. American Political Science Review 53 (No. 1): 106–27.
    1960   Latin America. *In* The politics of developing areas, Gabriel A. Almond and James S. Coleman, eds. Princeton, N.J.
    1961   Fidel Castro and Latin America. A paper prepared for the 1961 annual meeting of the American Political Science Association.
Brandenburg, Frank R.
    1958   Organized business in Mexico. Inter-American Economic Affairs 12 (No. 3): 26–50.
Bryce, James
    1926   South America: observations and impressions. New York. (New edition corrected and revised.)

Campbell, Angus, *et al.*
✓ 1960   The American voter, [by] Angus Campbell, Philip E. Converse, Warren
          E. Miller, and Donald E. Stokes. New York.
Carvalho, Orlando M., *et al.*
  1960   [Analysis of election of 1958.] Revista Brasileira de Estudos Políticos,
          No. 8 (April).
Christensen, Asher N.
  1951   The evolution of Latin American government. New York.
Clagett, Helen L.
  1952   The administration of justice in Latin America. New York.
Cleven, Andrew N.
  1940   The political organization of Bolivia. Washington, D.C., The Carnegie
          Institution of Washington.
Dahl, Robert A.
  1961   The behavioral approach in political science: epitaph for a monument
          to a successful protest. American Political Science Review 55 (No. 4):
          763–72.
✓ 1963   Modern political analysis. Englewood Cliffs, N.J.
Davis, Harold Eugene (ed.)
  1958   Government and politics in Latin America. New York.
Draper, Theodore
  1962   Castro's revolution: myths and realities. New York.
Easton, David
✓ 1957   An approach to the analysis of political systems. World Politics 9 (No.
          3): 383–400.
  1962   Introduction: The current meaning of "behavioralism" in political science.
          In The limits of behavioralism in political science. Philadelphia, American
          Academy of Political and Social Science (October), pp. 7–8.
Easton, David, and Robert D. Hess
  1962   The child's political world. Midwest Journal of Political Science 6 (No.
          3): 229–46.
Echaiz, René León
  1939   Evolución histórica de los partidos políticos chilenos. Santiago, Chile.
Edelman, Murray
  1960   Symbols and political quiescence. American Political Science Review 54
          (No. 3): 695–704.
Eulau, Heinz
  1962   Comparative political analysis: a methodological note. Midwest Journal
          of Political Science 6 (No. 4): 397.
  1963   The behavioral persuasion in politics. New York.
Eulau, Heinz, Samuel J. Eldersveld, and Morris Janowitz
  1956   Political behavior. New York.
Fabregat, Julio T.
  1949   Los partidos políticos en la legislación uruguaya. Montevideo.
Fitzgibbon, Russell H.
  1948   The constitutions of the Americas. Chicago.
  1950   Pathology of democracy in Latin America. American Political Science Re-
          view 44 (No. 1): 100–49.
  1951   Measurement of Latin American political phenomena: a statistical experi-
          ment. American Political Science Review 65 (No. 2): 517–23.
  1954   Uruguay: portrait of a democracy. New Brunswick, N.J.
  1956a   How democratic is Latin America? Inter-American Economic Affairs 9
          (No. 4): 65–77.
  1956b   A statistical evaluation of Latin-American democracy. Western Political
          Quarterly 9 (No. 3): 607–19.

✓1957   The party potpourri in Latin America. Western Political Quarterly 10 (No. 1): 3–22.

1961   The revolution next door: Cuba. Annals of the American Academy of Political and Social Science 334 (March): 113–22.

Fitzgibbon, Russell H., and Kenneth F. Johnson
1961   Measurement of Latin American political change. American Political Science Review 55 (No. 3): 515–26.

Form, William H., and William V. D'Antonio
1959   Integration and cleavage among community influentials in two border cities. American Sociological Review 24 (December): 804–14.

Germani, Gino
1955   Estructura social de la Argentina: análisis estadístico. Buenos Aires. Chap. 16.

1960   Política e massa. Belo Horizonte, Minas Gerais, Brasil, Faculdade de Direito, Universidade de Minas Gerais.

Gibson, William Marion
1948   The constitutions of Colombia, Durham, N.C.

Gil, Federico G.
✓ 1962   Genesis and modernization of political parties in Chile. Latin American Monographs No. 18. Gainesville, Fla.

Gomez, R. A.
1960   Government and politics in Latin America. New York.

Gonzales Calderon, Juan A.
1930–31   Derecho constitucional argentino. Buenos Aires.

Greenstein, Fred I.
1960   The benevolent leader: children's images of political authority. American Political Science Review 54 (No. 4): 934–43.

Hirschman, Albert O.
✓ 1963   Journeys toward progress: studies of economic policy-making in Latin America. New York, The Twentieth Century Fund.

Holt, Pat M.
1963   United States political science and Latin America, p. 3 (mimeo, dated April 5).

James, Herman G.
1923   The constitutional system of Brazil. Washington, D.C., The Carnegie Institution of Washington.

Johnson, John J.
✓ 1958   Political change in Latin America: the emergence of the middle sectors. Stanford, Calif.

✓1962   The Latin America military as a politically competing group in a transitional society. *In* The role of the military in underdeveloped countries, John J. Johnson, ed. Princeton, N.J.

Johnson, John J. (ed.)
✓1962   The role of the military in underdeveloped countries. Princeton, N.J.

Jorrin, Miguel
1953   Governments of Latin America. New York.

Kahin, George McT., Guy J. Pauker, and Lucian W. Pye
1955   Comparative politics in non-western countries. American Political Science Review 69 (No. 4): 1022–41.

Kantor, Harry
✓1953   The ideology and program of the Peruvian *Aprista* movement. Berkeley, University of California Press. (A Spanish version also has been published: Ideología y programa del movimiento Aprista. Mexico City, 1955.)

1958   The Costa Rican election of 1953: a case study. Latin American Monographs No. 5. Gainesville, Fla.

Kantor, Harry, and Eugenio Chang-Rodríguez
1961   La América Latina de hoy. New York.

Kautsky, John H.
✓ 1962   Political change in under-developed countries: nationalism and communism.
          New York.
Klapp, Orrin E., and L. Vincent Padgett
  1960   Power structure and decision-making in a Mexican border city. American
          Journal of Sociology 65 (No. 4): 400–06.
Kling, Merle
  1956   Towards a theory of power and political instability in Latin America.
          Western Political Quarterly 9 (No. 1): 21–35.
  1959   Taxes on the "external sector": an index of political behavior in Latin
          America? Midwest Journal of Political Science 3 (No. 2): 127–50.
  1961   A Mexican interest group in action. Englewood Cliffs, N.J.
  1962   Cuba: a case study of a successful attempt to seize political power by
          the application of unconventional warfare. Annals of the American Acad-
          emy of Political and Social Science 341 (May): 42–52.
Lambert, Jacques
  1953   Le Brésil, structure sociale et institutions politiques. Paris.
Lane, Robert E.
✓ 1962   Political ideology: why the American common man believes what he does.
          New York.
  1963   *Review of* Essays on the behavioral study of politics, edited by Austin
          Ranney. American Political Science Review 57 (No. 1): 163.
Lanz Duret, Miguel
  1947   Derecho constitucional mexicano. Mexico City.
Lascaño y Mazón, Andrés María
  1942   Constituciones políticas de América. Havana.
Lewis, Oscar
✓ 1961   The children of Sánchez. New York.
Lieuwen, Edwin
✓ 1961   Arms and politics in Latin America. New York. Revised edition.
Liñares Quintana, Segundo V.
  1945   Los partidos políticos: instrumentos de gobierno. Buenos Aires.
  1946   Gobierno y administración de la República Argentina. Buenos Aires.
Lipset, Seymour Martin
  1959   Some social requisites of democracy: economic development and political
          legitimacy. American Political Science Review 53 (No. 1): 69–105.
✓ 1960   Political man: the social bases of politics. New York.
Lipson, Leslie
  1956   Government in contemporary Brazil. Canadian Journal of Economics and
          Political Science 22 (No. 2): 183–98.
Loewenstein, Karl
  1942   Brazil under Vargas. New York.
López Rosado, Felipe
  1955   El régimen constitucional mexicano. Mexico City.
MacDonald, Austin F.
  1949   Latin American politics and government. New York. (Revised edition,
          1954.)
Machado Horta, Raul, *et al.*
  1958   Perspectivas do federalismo brasileiro, [by] Raul Machado Horta, Gerson
          de Britto Mello Boson, Orlando M. Carvalho, Onofre Mendes, Jr., and
          Washington Peluso Albim de Souza. Belo Horizonte, Minas Gerais, Brazil,
          Universidade de Minas Gerais.
Macridis, Roy C.
✓ 1958   Foreign policy in world politics. Englewood Cliffs, N.J.
  1961   Comparative politics: notes and readings. Homewood, Ill.

Marx, Fritz Morstein (ed.)
1949 Foreign governments. New York.
Mecham, J. Lloyd
1934 Church and state in Latin America: a history of politico-ecclesiastical relations. Chapel Hill, N.C.
Mendieta y Nuñez, Lucio
1942 La administración pública en México. Mexico City.
1947 Los partidos políticos. Mexico City, Biblioteca de Ensayos Sociológicos, Instituto de Investigaciones Sociales, Universidad Nacional.
Miranda, José
1957 Reforma y tendencias constitucionales recientes de la América Latina (1945–1956). Mexico City, Instituto de Derecho Comparado, Universidad Nacional Autónoma de México.
Needler, Martin
1962 Putting Latin American politics in perspective. Inter-American Economic Affairs 16 (No. 2): 41–50.
Ogg, Frederic, and Harold Zink
1949 Modern foreign governments. New York.
Padgett, L. Vincent
1957 Mexico's one-party system: a re-evaluation. American Political Science Review 51 (No. 4): 995–1002.
Palmer, Robert Roswell
1959 The age of the democratic revolution: a political history of Europe and America, 1760–1800. Princeton, N.J.
Patch, Richard W.
✓ 1962a The Peruvian elections of 1962 and their annulment. Reports, West Coast South America Series, Vol. 9: No. 6 (September).
1962b Personalities and politics in Bolivia. Reports, West Coast South America Series, Vol. 9: No. 5 (May).
Peaslee, Amos J.
1950 Constitutions of nations. Concord, N.H. (2nd ed., The Hague, 1956.)
Pierson, William W., and Federico G. Gil
1957 Governments of Latin America. New York.
Ranney, Austin (ed.)
1962 Essays on the behavioral study of politics. Urbana, Ill.
Rowe, L. S.
1921 The federal system of the Argentine republic. Washington, D.C., The Carnegie Institution of Washington.
Schneider, Ronald M.
1958 Communism in Guatemala, 1944–1954. New York.
Scott, Robert E.
1951 Argentina's new constitution: social democracy or social authoritarianism? Western Political Quarterly 4 (No. 4): 567–76.
1959 Mexican government in transition. Urbana, Ill.
Silvert, Kalman H.
1954 A study in government: Guatemala. New Orleans, Middle American Research Institute, Tulane University.
1959 Political change in Latin America. In The United States and Latin America. New York, The American Assembly, Columbia University (December): 77.
1961a The silent voices: the nation and the village. In Reaction and revolution in Latin America: the conflict society. New Orleans, pp. 35–46.
✓ 1961b Nationalism in Latin America. In Latin America's nationalistic revolutions. Annals of the American Academy of Political and Social Science 334 (March): 1–9.
1961c The annual political cycle of Argentina. Reports, East Coast South America Series. Vol 8: No. 6 (December 12).

1961d Political universes in Latin America. Reports, East Coast South America Series, Vol. 8: No. 7 (December 17).

Silvert, Kalman H., and Frank Bonilla
1961 Education and the social meaning of development: a preliminary statement. New York: American Universities Field Staff, Inc. (mimeographed).

Soares, Glaucio Ary Dillon
1961 Economic development and political radicalism. Boletim do Centro Latino-Americano de Pesquisas em Ciências Sociais. Rio de Janeiro, UNESCO. Vol. 4 (No. 2): 117–57.
1962 Desenvolvimento econômico e radicalismo político: o teste de uma hipótese (Chile). America Latina 5 (No. 3): 65–83.

Stevenson, John Reese
1942 The Chilean popular front. Philadelphia.

Stokes, William S.
1950 Honduras: an area study in government. Madison, Wis.
1952 Violence as a power factor in Latin-American politics. Western Political Quarterly 5 (No. 3): 445–68.
1959 Latin American politics. New York.

Stuart, Graham
1925 The governmental system of Peru. Washington, D.C., The Carnegie Institution of Washington.

Tannenbaum, Frank
1943 A note on Latin American politics. Political Science Quarterly 58 (No. 3): 415.

Taylor, Philip B., Jr.
1960a Government and politics of Uruguay. New Orleans.
1960b The Mexican elections of 1958: affirmation of authoritarianism? Western Political Quarterly 13 (No. 3): 722–44.
1963 Interests and institutional dysfunction in Uruguay. American Political Science Review 57 (No. 1): 62–74.

Tucker, William P.
1957 The Mexican government today. Minneapolis.

Vanorden Shaw, Paul
1930 The early constitutions of Chile 1810–1833. New York.

Wallace, Elizabeth
1894 The constitution of the Argentine republic and the constitution of the United States of Brazil. Chicago.

Whitaker, Arthur P.
1956 The Argentine upheaval. New York.

	THE
Part 1	CULTURAL
	BACKGROUND

The student of comparative politics should first learn something about the culture of the region to be studied. If nothing else, he must be careful not to judge another area by the cultural standards of the United States; he must look instead at political systems as parts of over-all cultural systems and keep in mind the judgments, orientations, and values of the local culture. It is for this reason that a section on the cultural background precedes the selections devoted to the governmental system, the political system, and major political issues.

The selections in Part 1 analyze the educational system, the role of the church, social classes, subcultures, and give some indication—in the case of the first piece—what Latin Americans think culture is. Omitted is any reference to "political culture." This omission is not based on choice but rather on the fact that there does not appear to exist a study of this topic in terms of Latin America as a whole. In order not to neglect the political culture altogether, there follows a very brief introduction to this concept.

"The political culture of a society consists of the system of empirical beliefs, expressive symbols, and other values that define the situation in which political action takes place. It provides the subjective orientation to politics."[1] This concept "assumes that the attitudes, sentiments, and cognitions that inform and govern political behavior in any society are not just random congeries but represent coherent patterns which fit together and are mutually reinforcing."[2] There are three such attitudes

[1] Sidney Verba, "Comparative Political Culture," in Lucian W. Pye and Sidney Verba, *Political Culture and Political Development* (Princeton, N.J.: Princeton University Press, 1965), p. 513.

[2] Lucian W. Pye, "Introduction: Political Culture and Political Development," in Pye and Verba, *Political Culture and Political Development*, p. 7.

and beliefs that are of fundamental importance in the study of political culture: those involving political identity, the decision-making process, and governmental output.

The first of these can be divided into attitudes toward national identity and horizontal identification. In the case of each—indeed it is true of virtually all aspects of political culture—there is a great deal of variance from one nation to another, and within individual nations from one area to another. In many of the Central American and Andean nations there are large numbers of Indians whose identification with their nation—if such exists at all—is neither deep nor unambiguous; these persons may physically be Guatemalans, Ecuadorians, or Bolivians, but psychologically such is not the case. Also, it seems quite likely that national identification is stronger in urban rather than in rural areas and in metropolitan areas rather than in towns and cities of the interior. In every Latin American nation, national identity is impeded by a degree of localism, but this would appear to be less true of nations such as Argentina, Uruguay, and Chile, which have highly urbanized and racially homogeneous populations.

Closely related to national identification is horizontal identification with one's fellow citizens. A crucial aspect of this horizontal identification is trust and confidence, without which individuals will be quite reluctant to turn over governmental power to their opponents. This has been a major problem in Latin America for $1\frac{1}{2}$ centuries. While the reluctance to relinquish power peacefully is in part a desire to retain the spoils of office, it is also based upon a fear of what one's opponents will do with that power, that is, a total lack of trust or confidence in the opposition.

In relation to attitudes toward governmental input and output, Almond and Verba categorize cultures as parochial, subject, participant, and combinations of these (parochial-subject and subject-participant). The parochial political culture is said to be characterized by "the comparative absence of expectations of change initiated by the political system."[3] The parochial individual—best exemplified in Latin America by the Indian of the Chaco or the headwaters of the Amazon tributaries[4]—is totally removed from the political process. He does not perceive of himself as a political actor, nor does he even realize that there are input and output aspects of the political process. Today no Latin American

[3] Gabriel A. Almond and Sidney Verba, *The Civic Culture* (Princeton, N.J.: Princeton University Press, 1963), p. 17.
[4] This type, labeled the Tribal Indian, is discussed below by Charles W. Wagley and Marvin Harris in "A Typology of Latin American Subcultures."

nation could fairly be termed parochial in political culture—although Haiti is certainly not far removed from this stage. At the other end of the spectrum is the participant political culture where "the members of society tend to be explicitly oriented toward . . . both the input and output aspects of the political system."[5] While all the Latin American nations have progressed beyond the parochial political culture, none have yet reached the stage of the participant political culture.

The political cultures of Latin America all fall into the middle three categories: parochial-subject, subject, or subject-participant. Beginning toward the more traditional end of the spectrum, the parochial-subject political culture is one where "a substantial portion of the population has rejected the exclusive claims of diffuse tribal, village or feudal authority and has developed allegiance toward a more complex political system."[6] The nations of Central America—with the exception of Costa Rica—plus perhaps Ecuador, Peru, and Bolivia would seem to fit this characterization; that is, a very large majority of the citizenry in these nations is either completely ignorant of the political process (parochial) or aware only of the output aspect of government while retaining a relatively passive self-orientation (subject).

At the next level is the subject political culture, where "there is a high frequency of orientations toward a differentiated political system, but orientations toward specifically input objects and toward the self as an active participant approach zero."[7] The subject's orientation toward the political system is almost entirely toward the administrative or output process wherein policies are applied; government to him may well mean the bureaucracy and the courts. Subject political cultures in Latin America would probably include Brazil, Venezuela, and Colombia, and perhaps Mexico and Chile as well.

Last, there is the subject-participant political culture, where "a substantial part of the population has acquired specialized input orientations and an activist set of self-orientations, while most of the remainder of the population continue to be oriented toward an authoritarian governmental structure and have a relatively passive set of self-orientations."[8] In other words, the participant is aware of the flow of demands from society to government and the conversion of these demands into policies; he is thus oriented toward pressure groups and political parties as well as bureaucracies and courts. The Latin American nations most closely

[5] Almond and Verba, *The Civic Culture*, pp. 17–18.
[6] Almond and Verba, *The Civic Culture*, p. 22.
[7] Almond and Verba, *The Civic Culture*, p. 22.
[8] Almond and Verba, *The Civic Culture*, pp. 24–25.

resembling the subject-participant political culture would appear to be Uruguay and Argentina.[9]

[The student should bear in mind that the above is just a brief introduction to political culture. Due to limitations of space, many facets of this concept—political values, political style, patterns of cultural change, relations among political beliefs, and political socialization—have not even been mentioned.]

---

[9] It should be pointed out that within all these nations there are differences between the political cultures of the rulers and the ruled, and also that even in the participant political culture there exist parochials.

Latin American Culture: To Be or Not To Be*

H. A. MURENA

Being: That is the question. It echoes uninterruptedly throughout Latin American history, and anyone with ears can hear it. It is Latin America's real sore point.

It was first the problem of political independence—an innocent formulation that for a brief period of enthusiasm allowed us to be optimistic. If one considers that the wars of independence were won by a handful of men poor in arms, ammunition and money fighting against a great power rich in a brilliant military tradition *in partibus barbarorum,* one senses that there was an energy disproportionate to the aim and therefore—so to speak—abnormal. Naturally, then, political birth did not exhaust this energy. And the question (unresolved) of *being*—the source of this singular energy—turned into a ghost that appears in every act. A ghost that colors our actions, sometimes with the blue tinge of ideals but sometimes, unexpectedly, with the tragic color of blood. And those demoniac characters who hardly seem human until they have disappeared (Rosas, Melgarejo, Santa Anna, Doctor Francia and their contemporaries in the black Latin American pantheon), do they not perhaps have in common an anxiety about *existing?* Even if their anxiety manifests itself as xenophobia which for years has led them to isolate and persecute their own peoples out of hatred for what is foreign, that is, for what seems about to throw the various and still contradictory national realities back into chaos again.

Indeed, if certain starved Latin American peoples today hate the hand that holds out economic aid, plainly they do so because the aid does not stem from an ideal of equality but is only a mouthful thrown to a half-crazed animal. And it is the final and unbearable confirmation of their nonexistence.

To cite examples would be to give in to pathos. I will limit myself to asserting that if one ignores the question of *being,* one cannot hope to shed light on any of the mysteries of the haunted soul of Latin America. . . .

* "Latin American Culture—To Be or Not To Be" by H. A. Murena, originally in COMUNITA, Milan, as translated in ATLAS, The Magazine of the World Press, August 1963. © 1963 Worley Publishing Company, Inc. Reprinted by permission.

In Latin America there is only one great literary tradition—and this, paradoxically, is the tradition which subordinates the art of writing to the art of politics. At least a hundred of the hundred and fifty years' existence of these republics confirm this tradition. Latin America has gone through these hundred years so hypnotized by the Gorgon of politics that she did not feel the need for other forms of culture, such as music, painting, etc. But her literature is a wild horse that must be ridden for dear life (or death) and so leaves no time for concern with style. This kind of horsemanship robs riders of their composure and wrings curses from them. Two illustrious Argentines, Sarmiento and Alberdi, ended up calling each other "a dog to be kicked" and "an intellectual peasant": an exchange of courtesies that gives us a pale idea of the Latin American *Zeitgeist*. The political attitude of other major figures—say Francisco Bilbao, Hostos, Rodó, Justo Sierra, Montalvo—is no different, though they have their individualities and varying degrees of patience, culture or compassion. With the exception of a few works (e.g., Sarmiento's *Facundo*) in which inspiration has won out over political passion, their writings are too concerned with the conflicts of the time to be interesting from any but the historical point of view. And in addition, they possess no originality, for every Latin American political notion is only an exaggerated and distorted echo of European thought.

With all their limitations, however, these writings exude a feeling that may one day be considered Latin America's principal contribution to the Western order of things and that, in any case, may even now be considered prophetic—the profound and intense aspiration for concord among men. Indeed, in spite of verbal violence, rhetoric and intellectual debts of all kinds, one feels that these works voice a desire for universal brotherhood that is perhaps unprecedented as a tendency. This yearning, which transcends the chaotic life of the Latin American republics, is expressed by such positive facts as the overcoming of racial conflicts, the uncommon willingness of the republics to submit their differences to international arbitration, the pacifist programs solidly supported by the Latin American states in international organizations, and so on. This obstinate (even if intermittent) desire to build a single "city of just men" *for all* is the fruit of a harrowing and, in a way, exceptional experience: namely, exile from history and the lightheaded feeling one gets when one becomes aware of how fragile the institutions of the civilized world are. This desire not only expresses one of man's basic impulses but forewarns us of what one day the world (which is becoming Latin Americanized with unexpected rapidity) will perhaps consider urgent and fundamental.

However, a feeling is obviously only a *feeling*, and a feeling is never culture, since culture is expression—or, better, the elements by which the subjective is objectified. Culture, in short, is the expression of what we are. But what *are* we? Once again the question of *being*.

Are we Europeans? Yes and no. Are we indigenes? Yes and no. Do we represent something new? Yes and no. Do we represent something old? Yes and no. Do we look toward the country of our origin? Yes and no. Or toward that of our exile? Yes and no.

Whence derives our strabismus. The existence of the resplendent culture of Europe has turned one eye outward. Or perhaps the New World turned the other eye inward. It comes to the same thing.

The fact remains that our culture plods doggedly on, one eye on the distant ideal and the other on the ground, in order not to stumble. Obviously, progress is difficult. When the strabismus spreads from the eye to the spirit, the diagnosis becomes more serious: schizophrenia. Yes, schizophrenia: our culture pretended to be what it was not, while actually it was only American. But what does American mean?

In 1909, several months before he was killed, Euclydes da Cunha wrote from Rio to his friend Oliveira Lima: "I do nothing but waste away in this poor land of ours." The reference to the land seems to suggest cause and effect. Was da Cunha pining away because of the fate of his land? Seven years before he had published a work of grandeur and horror, *Os Sertões* ["The Forests"]. I will not relate the plot: I only wish to emphasize that the protagonists of the story are *nature* and Antonio Conselheiro, a being who is scarcely distinguishable from nature and in whom it is impossible to see anything human. But where is the sensitive and most lucid Euclydes da Cunha? He is absent. In this work the human element does not appear, and the author is dissolved in nature. Either in that nature called mountains and rivers and deserts or in that nature called Antonio Conselheiro. Understandably, the author was wasting away in that wretched land that did not allow him to express himself. Da Cunha, therefore, pities himself, even though pitying a man in this way really means pitying a land that is opposed to all things human.

About a quarter of a century earlier and further south, another eminent man of letters gave his fiancée a portrait of himself photographed from the back: this man was José Hernandez. In *Martín Fierro* the surrender to nature—as seen in the gaucho—is pushed almost to the point of unintelligibility. This poem, which cannot be translated without changing its meaning and which can only be understood by someone immersed in a specific time and place, embraces the silence of nature. Martínez Estrada has written that *Martín Fierro* is a revolt against culture and literature. I would add that it is a poem *against the word*.

In our own day, the Uruguayan Horacio Quiroga would often leave his wife, with whom he lived in the forest of Misiones, to spend entire weeks completely alone in the top of a tree, subsisting on raw meat. He thus finally came to resemble the mask which he had once donned for writing. His only characters were animals, and in the end he himself was led by his creations to give up a humanity which had absolutely no meaning in his own inner world.

Such is the fate of Indigenism. "If we are not Europeans," warns the Indigenist, "then we should not be Europeans in anything." And so the terrifying trap of nature is sprung. What is serious is that we are not even nature *tout court*. And meanwhile literary Indigenism leads to suffocation because it does not completely express American man; and it does not express him because the American is not brute nature. In fact no sooner does the West (that is, History) break into the autochthonous habitat than the Indigenist is disindigenized. At the most, therefore, Indigenism gives us a portrait of American man taken from the back.

Interlude: what is happening meanwhile with the other forms of culture? Annotation on the score: *largo desolato.* A glance at the South American cities is sufficient. The alleys of Lima and Santiago, the avenues of Buenos Aires, the uninspired architecture of Montevideo: in the best cases, an ugly copy of European styles from which all style has vanished when they are not absolute monstrosities. What, then, is the common denominator of the builders? The inability to see. By some mysterious contrivance, in fact, the geography of this continent, which lacks all sense of proportion, causes the human eye to recoil in terror or to focus in a special way. Like the eyes of a man at the edge of an abyss that search only for things to hang on to and ignore the beauty or ugliness of those things. This, the unseeing eye, gave rise to the sprawling South American cities. The humblest European dwelling promotes life because, in addition to giving shelter, it expresses something. A Latin American mansion induces death just as much as a hovel does; neither expresses anything and consequently both depress the inhabitant and cause him to wither. The eyes of a man at the edge of an abyss obviously perceive only the abyss.

But painting, sculpture, architecture, city planning, how can they get along with such eyes? Only by chance does some solitary figure emerge—and in any case he will be able to overcome inertia only for a few exceptional moments. . . .

The Ecuadorian Juan Montalvo—ignoring for a moment his role as political publicist—demonstrates another quality, one destined to bring him great fame: style. Around 1870 he published *Capítulos que se le olvidaron a Cervantes* ["Chapters Omitted from Cervantes"]. A contemporary historian of American literature has expressed surprise and enthusiasm for this continuation of *Don Quixote,* and Montalvo, in fact, displays a complete mastery of the Cervantesque atmosphere, a great knowledge of the classics and an extraordinary command of the language.

If we now pass on to novels in the "Montalvo formula," we get Jorge Isaacs' *Maria* (a romantic pastiche that might have been subtitled *Paul et Virginie en Colombie*) or Carlos Reyles' *El embrujo de Sevilla* ["The Enchantment of Seville"] or Enrique Larreta's *La Gloria de Don Ramiro.* I am citing extremes, or rather archetypes of the so-called "artistic current" of Latin American literature. Don't forget, these are the works that have had the greatest public acclaim. *Maria* and *La Gloria de Don Ramiro* are in fact best-sellers. The mass public is deeply moved by them. Which shows once again that culture matters little to the mass.

The authors of these works have applied the teachings of the Indigenists the other way round. "If we are Europeans," they say, "then let us be real Europeans." Flowery language, symbolism, "Arielism," "Spanishisms," sublime flights of spirit: this is what their works offer. But what do they reveal of the dramas, anxieties, joys and frustrations of their readers?

In fact, if culture really resembles anything they taught us in school, it must, in a sense, be maieutic, that is, must contribute to one's self-knowledge. And yet the motto of the "artistic current" (at present hidden and disguised but not yet dead) is levitation. If Indigenism has its feet firmly on the ground as a result of its *sacrificium intellectus,* Europeanism is way off in the clouds because of its *sacrificium phalli.* Completely absorbed in form, it ends up disregarding content: therefore, anything at all is permitted so long as the formless American reality can be transcended.

Yet from the Frenchifying of culture, from the worship of things foreign, there comes—at least as a tendency—the germ of sincerity that goes under the name of modernism. What is the reason for this phenomenon?

1. Latin America has no original culture;

2. This lack produces a cultural anxiety that is translated into an abnormal accumulation of information about other cultures. Even a cultured European can seem like a provincial when confronted by the morbid quantities of information that any Latin American man of letters has on European culture;

3. Modernism implicitly accepts this cultural proverty and, by venturing to create with an *Ersatz* culture, changes poverty into riches.

What, then, is the difference between modernism and Europeanism? The Europeanist pretends to be European and shows that he is nothing. The cosmopolitan modernist recognizes, instead, that he is nothing and thereby *is*. This commitment to truth—which operates precisely where the Latin American spirit most directly senses its own lack of genuineness—has become an enormous force. I will cite only two examples of the radical changes it has brought about in Latin American culture.

The first is that for the first time the Latin American intelligentsia acquired self-confidence. With this confidence it embarked on a revolution in language (especially in poetry) that influences even the Spanish mother tongue.

The second change is seen in the strength injected into Latin American culture; the strength that allows self-examination without hypocrisy. It is what we have for instance, in Leopoldo Lugones, hellenist and gaucho poet, who can use the vernacular without feeling he must *forget* or condemn European culture. . . .

1910, 1920, 1930, post-modernism, swifter communications, World War, the splendor of the last European avante-garde—all gave an unprecedented stimulus to creativity. The Mexican revolution seemed to revitalize a whole society. Argentine university reform shot like lightning throughout Latin America, producing basic changes in the relationships between communities and the centers of learning. Serious music found expression in Villa-Lobos and Chavez. American painting moved the hand that had remained inert for so many centuries and, thanks to Mexico, there came a grandiose and horrifying vision of reality which found expression in a respectable body of work even in Rio de la Plata. Finally even the written word seemed to have found its destiny: the poets (Cesar Vallejo, Pablo Neruda, Manuel Bandeira, Ricardo Molinari, Leopoldo Marechal) made their voice universal; the thinkers (Gilberto Freyre, Ezquiel Martínez Estrada, José Carlos Mariátegui) did their utmost to understand the world about them; the novelists (Mariano Azuela, Graciliano Ramos, Roberto Arlt, Eduardo Mallea, Romulo Gallegos) expressed their poetic worlds. And then there are those who defy classification such as Alfonso Reyes and Jorge Luis Borges. Of course accents can still be discerned: fawning European imitation, shortlived folkloric raptures and political passions that, in principle, have little to do with culture: but these are only a kind of counterpoint against which the true American accent is heard even more distinctly.

And what about today? *Where is Latin American culture heading today?*

In its January–February 1961 issue the magazine *Mito* ("Myth") of

Bogotá published a telling letter sent from Madrid by a Colombian, Darian G. Ruiz. Here are several sentences that give the gist of it: "*Mito* has recently completed its fifth year, but it is still difficult to say: *It exists,* for up to now it has done nothing more than scare the bead-counters. Indeed, *Mito* wanted to start its revolution with sex. It thought that it was being universal and getting in step with the most modern cultural tendencies: instead it stopped at Genêt, de Sade and Durrell. *Mito* does not seem to realize that the path of history can be straightened. But sex is neutral, in the sense that both Catholics and Communists not only share it but feel the same way about it." Here is a synthesis—perhaps even too bland and tidy—of the present cultural climate in Latin America.

Mito's correspondent regards revolution as inevitable and in so doing expresses a general feeling we all have, for we consider it unavoidable. But revolution against what? And for what?

The Uruguayan critic Emir Rodriguez Menegal called the Argentine literary generation that emerged in 1950 "The Parricides." He took the appellation from an essay by one of its exponents. The "Parricides" at first referred to the relationship between the new literati and their predecessors, but it soon expanded to include their attitude toward reality in general. It was not by chance that the "Parricides" came to the fore long before the angry young men and the beatniks. In fact, Spanish-American culture is so weak that we felt the convulsions that were to shake the West before anyone else. In order better to clarify the meaning of this pathetic and confused rebellion, let me recall that a Brazilian of this generation, José P. Moreira de Fonseca, published a long poem in 1956 entitled *La Tempestada* ["The Storm"], which was nothing if not a prefiguration of the Last Judgment. Of course, Latin American culture was not really on the verge of the Last Judgment but rather at the end of an era—that is, of a style of life that had lasted for a thousand years. And today this very feeling is spreading throughout the West. But in Latin America the universal bitterness reached apocalyptic proportions, aggravated as it was by Latin America's spiritual and historical segregation as much as by its sense of estrangement, like a helpless bystander or an unwanted guest. This bystander, however, has not yet stopped his march toward the zero zone. Ultra-nihilism—that is, the acceptance of the nihilistic environment in order to effect a vertical reform of society—is a prominent characteristic of present-day Latin American literature. Another is the watchful sensitivity of this literature to world problems. For many reasons (particularly the deficiencies and weaknesses of its own origin) Latin America has perceived almost immediately that the present-day situation (swift communications, universal ideologies, long-range weapons) has now wiped out nations and made all men stateless. . . .

Doubtless the correspondent of *Mito* was referring to the ultra-nihilistic and stateless character of Latin American literature when he reprimanded the magazine for having wanted "to start the revolution with sex" and "to be universal." The change is correct; but he is wrong in thinking that "sex is neutral," for it is not so at all, although "both Catholics and Communists not only share it but feel the same way about it." Sex, in fact, is revolution; and when we reduce such a complex literary movement to sex we have only to go back to the classic sexual concept of the Occident to understand why it is an innovator. For two thousand years—that is, ever since the Christian *Weltbild* was forged— Western life and thought have been dominated by a dualistic concept of man according to which everything connected with the body ("the tomb of the soul") was the object of repressive censure because it was shameful and contemptible. This dualism, which makes man a scarcely conceivable hybrid of two irreconcilable elements, body and soul, constitutes the backbone of Western philosophy. . . .

Literary men preoccupied with the sexual problem also demand— consciously or not—a thorough renovation of man. Moreover, in regions like South America, spiritually contaminated by the censures and suffocating sermons that are the great black of the Catholic Church, the battle is not only more difficult but more urgent and revolutionary. In spite of this the correspondent of *Mito* does not feel satisfied: he wants a different kind of revolution. What kind? . . .

History rights itself, then. Meaning, evidently, that once it went off the track and is now back on it. But *what* is the right track? And *who* decides? As far as I know, history has always followed tortuous paths in its deplorable as well as in its glorious moments. Perhaps because it lives and therefore follows the path of life; perhaps because in order to produce saints (or assassins) it must proceed willy-nilly, that is, tortuously. Otherwise it would not produce human beings but robots. History rights itself: ultimately the sentence gives one a physical sensation which, frankly, does not encourage optimism. Uneasiness supervenes. Who is to right it? According to what plan? The answer is obvious: *man.* But what man? Man-subject-of-history, man-maker-of-history, man-master-of-history: Karl Marx. The revolution the correspondent of *Mito* wants is the Marxist revolution. . . .

Latin America has always preferred its cultural influences to be anything (French, English, etc.) other than Spanish. Spain was too close not to arouse fear and humiliation. Moreover, non-Spanish influences could be accepted as an anti-Spanish expression. Today Latin America is oriented toward political influences that are as remote as possible from the West (which is forever preoccupied with Latin America) and from the United States (which represents something too close). And this means Marxism.

Latin American Marxism is more anti-United States than pro-Marxist. But in any case Marxism is a tide that is swelling visibly, especially in intellectual circles. Mariátegui said that Indigenist literature had a definite "revolutionary" and "emancipating" objective and compared its role to that of Populism, which helped unleash the Russian Revolution of 1917.

The truth is, instead, that the writings which express Indigenism would actually like to wipe it out—and, sometimes, even the individuals who personify it. "Don't try to spare the blood of the gauchos," said Sarmiento to General Mitre before the battle of Pavon. "It is a fertilizer our country needs." And Sarmiento wrote *Facundo!* . . .

The Indigenist's only interest in literature is to pose a problem and then resolve it: the problem eliminated, the literature becomes superfluous. Indigenism, in short, is cultivated to the point where it liquidates literature itself, for it is only a political view of culture and as such becomes an offshoot of the larger Latin American literary tradition (which, as was said earlier, has anti-literary characteristics). And the Marxism which today is spreading throughout the Latin American intelligentsia is all the more appropriately grafted onto this tradition, since it implies the same subordination of culture to politics. Marxism can accept the Indigenist path and in fact usually favors cultural forms that reflect autochthonous and nationalistic demands: the final objective, however, from the point of view of power, always remains society.

Culture, according to our brand of Marxism, is only a weapon to be used to seize the power necessary to reform society and therefore to "right history." If we look in the direction indicated by Mariátegui, we can discern in the decline of the Russian culture after 1917 a foreshadowing of what could happen to weak Latin American culture if Marxism really did succeed in "righting" its history. Marxism, a veritable sorcery, advances today along a thousand roads, is present in every vision of the future and gains ground with every expedient. A religion more than an ideology, it is embraced in a careless rapture, or out of inertia, or because of group pressure; and you find it in universities as well as in professional circles, in schools as well as in worldly gatherings. Anyone who glances at Latin American cultural reviews knows that culture takes a back seat not only to political considerations but to a violent pamphleteering whose only purpose is to stir to action. Instead of causing one to examine his thinking, this peculiar brand of Marxism usually provokes a mechanical acceptance or rejection depending on the various official credos. This virulent dogmatism stimulates equally dogmatic answers from the pusillanimous oligarchical or ecclesiastical circles, with the result that we do not have polemical discussion but positional war in which culture disappears.

In the face of the Marxist advance the partisans of the ultra-nihilist revolution—that is to say those who fight for a culture in which Marxism is accepted as a philosophic methodology—constitute a minority. After the sudden brilliance of the last ten years, is Latin American culture destined to slip back into its hundred-year-old a-cultural tradition—that is, into a conformity dominated by politics and therefore more or less synonymous with absolute silence?

Another question troubles me. Since the nineteenth century, Latin America has shown through its bloody *caudillos* what can happen when chaos takes hold of weakened democratic structures. Does Latin America today again foreshadow what may happen to culture in communities broken down by the inhumanity of politics and technology? We have asked where Latin American culture is going: but . . . where is Western culture going?

For centuries the anonymous artists who left their testimony at Altamira, Lascaux, etc., fulfilled a basic function in their respective communities. Suddenly other needs press the tribes, other challenges animate them. The tool maker appears, *homo faber,* who possesses the answer to new problems and becomes the hero of the hour. With the triumph of *homo faber, homo pictor* slowly disappears. It almost seems that mankind can be creative in only one area at a time. Perhaps we, too, are on the threshold of a similar era. Will *homo pictor* have to accept a role so insignificant that it is tantamount to extinction?

It is now past ten in the evening. In a Latin American city a man of letters goes out to eat after his day's work. He looks up at the sky, and all the solitude of the universe weighs down upon him. He reflects that he has spent an entire day working on pages that perhaps no one will read, that will probably awaken no echo, that hostile hands may tomorrow toss in a fire: and he wonders what sense there is in going on with this seemingly useless work. He wonders why he doesn't succumb to the temptation of throwing everything over, of taking refuge in placid vegetating.

But deep inside he knows that these are useless questions. He knows that there is something stubborn within him, something that will withstand any catastrophe, any dark age. He knows that within himself there is that conscience indifferent to success and failure which has always made it possible for *homo pictor* to rise up again after millennia in spite of his terrible enemies. And he knows that whether he wants to or not, this conscience will compel him tomorrow to bend once more over pages whose fate each day becomes more uncertain.

Translated by ANNE McGHEE

*Social Classes in Latin America** | WILLIAM S. STOKES

DEMOCRACY AND SOCIAL CLASSES

As democracy is a system of popular sovereignty, it follows that the doctrine of the equality of all men is essential. One reason, however, so few systems of political democracy have existed in Western Civilization is because the doctrine of equality seems not to be supported by facts and experience. Observation and tests show that men are not born with equal physical or mental equipment. If men are born with different personal qualifications, it becomes difficult if not impossible to argue that equality of opportunity exists in any given country. Personal qualities determine opportunity to a large extent.

Furthermore, study of large and small societies invariably shows that some men have more power and influence than others. Men's differences in social standing range from minimum status to maximum status. When such factors as family, race, profession, economic position, political privileges, and defined social values are found in one segment of society, a class exists. When a class system is firmly established, the superiority of one class and the inferiority of another or others is generally agreed to upon some widely accepted basis of rational justification.

General characteristics of ruling classes frequently include the following: wealth, finer housing and clothing, different food, physical symbols of status such as the "Chinese claw" of "soft hands" (to demonstrate lack of association with contemptible employment), marriage within class, chastity of girls, distinct burial customs, veneration of distinguished

* William S. Stokes, *Latin American Politics* (New York: Thomas Y. Crowell Co., 1959), pp. 1–9, 13–25. Reprinted by permission.

ancestry, and a belief in a "natural" right to expect servility from inferior individuals. When an individual is born into a class from which he cannot advance by his own efforts, a caste system exists. A caste system, of course, inhibits the development of democracy more than a class system.

Even though it cannot be shown that men are in fact equal mentally or physically nor in their environment, no one knows exactly what are the mental or physical potentialities of each individual. It is conceivable that the doctrine of equality might some day be proved scientifically, despite existing evidence to the contrary. Whether the doctrine of equality is a fact or a myth, however, it is imperative that it be unquestioned in a democracy.

Therefore, every citizen in a democracy must belive that he has an equal right to participate in the affairs of the state. He cannot develop this psychological attitude easily in a social system characterized by rigid class lines. Democracy does not and cannot demand the absence of classes. If men are born unequal, except as to worth in the sight of God, and if their environment is unequal, social classes become inevitable. Democracy does demand a psychological climate which permits men to move easily from one class to another in accordance with their individual merit and ability.

If it is found that in Latin America relatively rigid class lines exist, democracy is impeded. If it is found that the doctrine of inequality is accepted, democracy is impeded. To function effectively, democracy requires a large class of people whose material possessions, educations, and social values are roughly similar. This aids in developing the psychology of equality. Thus, the larger the middle class the better the chance for democracy. If it is found that a middle class exists in Latin America but that it is small and tends to associate itself with the upper class, democracy is impeded.

THE CLASSES ON THE EVE OF THE DISCOVERY

By the beginning of the sixteenth century, Spain was an oligarchy of military, clerical, and landowning interests. The aristocratic class was divided into three groups: (1) *hombres ricos* or grandees; (2) *hidalgos* or *infanzones;* and (3) *caballeros.* The *hombres ricos* were members of families of ancient and honorable lineage whose power and influence sometimes rivaled that of the monarchs themselves. They enjoyed civil and criminal jurisdiction within their estates; they could levy taxes and were themselves exempted from most direct taxation; they could raise armies; and in general their person and property were not subject to seizure or control by the royal authority. When an *hombre rico* was also a bishop or other high official in the Church hierarchy, his authority was almost absolute. The *hidalgos* made up the rank and file of the nobility with less status and privilege than the grandees but considerably more than the *caballeros*. The *caballeros,* the lowest category of the aristocracy, were supposed to be men of noble birth.

Great social distance separated the classes, yet there was a working relationship among them. The great grandees protected the lesser nobility in return for military aid when needed. The nobility protected and defended the small class of landowners, skilled artisans, and free laborers in return for service, agricultural produce, or money. The rural masses were bound to the soil as serfs. The class system in Spain and Portugal encouraged a superior-inferior psychology among men which was not conducive to the development of political democracy.

What happened to the Jews and Moors is relevant to an understanding of the social attitudes of the aristocracy in Spain and Portugal. The Iberian peninsula has long been known for its many geographic, ethnic, and cultural contrasts. Under Visigothic domination, however (about 476 A.D.–711 A.D.), Spain achieved a degree of religious, cultural and political unity. This unity was broken by the Saracen invasion of 711. For eight centuries Christian-Visigothic Spain attempted sporadically to reconquer territories seized by the Moors. The Moors were dominant in Portugal from 711–1244. The reconquest or *reconquista* exaggerated the role and importance of the *caballero* or knight. It created the cult of the chivalrous man on horseback. In addition, the Church took on military functions. Religious leaders led troops into battle. Monasteries were fortresses and staging centers for forays against the Moors. Finally, the *reconquista* strengthened the large landholder who increased his properties as territory was retaken from the Moors. These were, then, centuries in which the rôles of the knight, the priest, and the soldier were glorified.

During the Middle Ages large numbers of Jews emigrated to the Iberian peninsula to take advantage of what was then a relatively tolerant environment. They entered commerce, industry, banking, and the professions. The Moors distinguished themselves in the same general areas and were particularly known as traders. By the middle of the thirteenth century, the *Siete Partidas,* one of the greatest of all codes of law, regulated the social, political, and economic relations of Jews, Moors, and Christians. The policy of the Castilian monarchs was to isolate the Jews and Moors from the Christians. Jews could not legally eat, drink, or have sexual relations with Christians. The laws provided

that both Jews and Moors should exhibit distinctive symbols so that
Christians could easily recognize them and avoid their company.

The tolerance that existed dissipated in the fourteenth and fifteenth
centuries. Galling restrictions to the Jews, such as the revoking of the
usury laws, became characteristic. Spaniards and Portuguese accused
Jews of responsibility for the black death and other catastrophes and
massacred thousands of them. As the *reconquista* reached its climax
in the fifteenth century, Jews and Moors came increasingly to be regarded as enemies of Spain. A few months after the reconquest of
Granada in 1492, Jews were ordered to accept Christianity or leave
Aragón and Castilla. Although some became Christians (to become
known as *conversos* or *marranos*), much larger numbers emigrated.
Persecution of the Moors began within a decade and in 1609 they were
expelled.

The expulsion of the Jews and Moors was symbolic of the superiority
of the values of the nobleman over the values of the bourgeoisie. Some
scholars believe that Spain at least developed a middle class despite
the expulsion of the Jews and the Moors. In Cataluña, there was a
shift to industry, commerce, and navigation which resulted in the decline
of the old nobility and the development of a middle class. This group
united with the free rural landowners and actually came to dominate.
There was also a middle class in Castilla but at a lower level of development than in Cataluña. Another scholar claims that the members of
the guilds comprised what we today would call a middle class.

THE SOCIAL CLASSES IN THE COLONIAL PERIOD

Social position in the colonial period was determined largely by birth,
rather than by individual merit or achievement. As a general rule, one
had to be born a white, Catholic Spaniard or Portuguese to qualify
for membership in the elite. Social stratification was produced in most
cases by the various shades of epidermis.

The Spanish monarchs attempted to exclude Jews and Moors from
the New World by requiring all emigrants to prove "limpieza de sangre"
(purity of blood). This was, of course, more of a religious than a racial
prohibition. Stratification based on birth and race was furthered in the
New World by carefully recording the racial parentage of each child
in his baptismal record. The people were classified by race and each
had a different legal status. Portuguese law recognized four social
classes: the donataries, *fidalgos* (gentry), *peões* (plebeians), and
Indians.

Social class stratifications were as follows in the colonial period:

peninsulares (whites born in the Iberian peninsula)
criollos (whites born in the New World—called *mazombos* in Brazil)
mestizos (in Brazil, whites and Indians were called *mamelucos* and whites
  and Negroes were called *mulattos*)
Indians
Negroes. . . .

By 1823 the racial groups were estimated to be as follows in Spanish America:

Whites	(*peninsulares* and *criollos* combined)	3,276,000	19.4%
Mixed		5,328,000	31.5
Indians		7,530,000	44.5
Negroes		776,000	4.6

The "whites" constituted a social aristocracy during the colonial period with a dominant position in the Church, army, economic system, and government. The *peninsulares* made up the elite of the aristocracy. Out of 166 viceroys and 588 captains-general, governors, and presidents who held office during the colonial period (754 posts in all), *peninsulares* held 736. *Peninsulares* held 357 of the 369 bishoprics up to 1637. Of the 706 bishops in America prior to 1812, 601 were *peninsulares.* When the intendant system was established late in the eighteenth century, it was provided that only *peninsulares* would be eligible to hold the new posts.

The elite were given *fueros,* which were exemptions from uniform application of the law or statements of special privilege. Among those who were eligible for *fueros* were the nobility, those with decorations from the Crown, military officers, Church dignitaries, mine owners, merchants, and Indian *caciques* (chiefs). Some of the special privileges which *fueros* provided included: tax exemptions, freedom from imprisonment for debt, preference in public offices, and ceremonial honors.

The *peninsulares* demonstrated their social superiority through "conspicuous consumption." They tried to outdo each other in acquiring land; they took pride in their patriarchal "big house"; they wore expensive clothing and personal adornments, had many servants, and ostentatiously proclaimed their lack of association with manual, productive labor. They expressed contempt for the lower classes, including the *criollos.* They believed in the theory of inequality of the social classes and insisted that they had a natural right to rule. They believed in class privileges, not individual rights.

The *criollos* (or *mazombos* in Brazil) constituted the lesser nobility in the colonial aristocracy. They were "white," which meant being of pure European descent (born in the New World) or one-eighth Indian or one-sixteenth Negro. There were approximately ten times as many *criollos* as *peninsulares* in Spanish America by the beginning of the wars of independence early in the nineteenth century. Nevertheless, *criollos* found but few honorable posts open to them in the civil service, the army, the Church, or the universities. Of the 706 bishops in America prior to 1812, 105 were *criollos*. Of the 170 viceroys prior to 1813 there were four *criollos* (their fathers were government employees in America). Out of the total of 754 high-ranking colonial officeholders, 18 were *criollos*. However, *criollos* were a dominating influence in the *cabildos* (municipal councils), at least in the years immediately preceding the wars of independence. The *mazombos* dominated the *câmaras* (town councils) in Brazil. All but one of the substitute representatives chosen to attend the Cortes of 1810 in behalf of the New World and the Philippines were *criollos*. In addition, *criollos* were able gradually to enter the professions. Many became lawyers, physicians, and notaries. Some of the wealthy *criollos* were able to purchase titles of nobility and commissions in the army. It was in the economic field, however, that the *criollos* were permitted their greatest opportunities. Many became landowners, mine operators, and tradesmen.

Miscegenation (*mestizaje* is the word used most frequently in Latin America) was common. The indiscriminate sexual activity of Spaniards and Portuguese with Indians and Negroes produced such mixtures that racial castes became impossible. What were the reasons for the *mestizaje* that took place everywhere in the Latin American area? The reason most frequently advanced was the scarcity of white women in the colonies. This was a factor, but white women did emigrate early to the New World. It is possible that the existence of the Moors as ruling peoples for centuries on the Iberian peninsula encouraged Spanish and Portuguese men to put a premium on dark-skinned women. The universalism of Christianity with its emphasis on the brotherhood of man helped to create an attitude of tolerance. Gilberto Freyre, the great Brazilian sociologist, emphasizes the importance of a relaxed sexual morality which permitted seduction of Indian and Negro women without loss of social prestige.

It is logical to suppose that men develop tolerance or even affection for women with whom they have illicit sexual relations. It does not follow necessarily that they consider such women worthy of equality in social relations. The initiative in *mestizaje* rested with the Spanish and Portuguese men. One scholar asserts that the white Portuguese men were "master of the virginity" of all the Negro girls at puberty. Indian and Negro men were not invited to marry or consort with white women during the colonial period. It rested with the white men to legitimize their relationship with Indian or Negro women. If they decided to marry Indian or Negro women, which occurred, especially with the Indian nobility, then they would be advancing the doctrine of equality. On the other hand, the conquerors felt free to sire "naturales" (bastards) with little or no institutional restraints.

The fact is that [the colored groups had less dignity and influence in the community than other classes.]

For example, the social gulf separating the more than five million *mestizos* from the white aristocracy was great. The *mestizo* was legally prohibited from receiving academic degrees. Until some time before 1588, *mestizos* were excluded from the priesthood. They never achieved high places in the Church nor were they to be found in the upper echelons of the army. Some did fill minor posts in the parishes, convents, and missions. Some became small proprietors. A majority of the *mestizos* lived in the cities and worked as skilled and unskilled labor. Theoretically, *mestizos* could serve as apprentices to guild masters and be admitted to the guilds. They were permitted to dress as whites and were recognized as *gente de razón* (rational people).

The Indians were for the most part a servile, inferior, exploited class. The first studies of the Indians in the New World uncovered so much evidence of mistreatment that Spain in particular was cast in the rôle of a villain. It has been more common for scholars in recent years to revise the "Black Legend." It is said that the Spanish and Portuguese were not unusually cruel for the period. Furthermore, the monarchs were responsible for humanitarian programs designed to benefit the Indians.

Definitive studies of the theory and practice of government among the major Indian civilizations have not yet been written. The existing evidence does show that aristocracy, serfdom, and slavery were characteristic. The Indians believed in the divine right of their rulers to rule. Their societies had social classes in which inequalities were marked. Their economic systems were more collectivistic than individualistic. There were therefore some similarities between what the Indians were used to and what the conquerors introduced.

The Indians were generally exploited for their labor and treated socially as an inferior class in the colonial period. They were not regarded as *gente de razón*. Legally they were minors. It was unusual for them to be admitted to the clergy. They were prohibited from dressing like Spaniards. They could not bear arms nor own nor ride horses. It was the policy of the Crown from 1546 on to keep them in their own towns or villages (*reducciones* and *congregaciones*). They were not subject to military service and did not have to pay taxes (except for a small yearly personal tax). They were free from the Inquisition, and lawyers were supposed to be provided to defend them without charge.

There were literally volumes of laws which were designed to protect and defend the Indians. Such laws were at best only partially effective. Many laws attempted to abolish slavery, such as those of 1526, 1530, 1532, 1542, and 1548. The famous New Laws of 1542 declared that the Indians were free men and equal in practically all ways to subjects of the King. But the New Laws were never fully enforced. The most complete study of the laws of the Indies is that of Juan de Solórzano Pereyra, *Política indiana* (Madrid: 2 volumes, 1736; first published in 1648). The *Recopilación de Leyes de los Reynos de las Indias* as published in 1791 makes up three heavy volumes.

Negroes and those with a preponderance of Negro blood made up the social class with the least prestige in the community. The Negro slaves were at the very bottom. Slavery is a denial of the doctrine of equality. Its master-man, superior-inferior relationship remains in the minds of people for a long time and hinders the development of democracy. Negroes were brought into the New World as slaves from about 1502. The great importations of slaves did not come until the eighteenth century, however.

The word "casta" (literally, caste) was used to designate free men of color. Their inferiority in the social framework can be seen in the following prohibitions: (1) they were compelled to marry among themselves; (2) they were not permitted to be *gente de razón;* (3) Spanish law forbade the granting of academic degrees to them; (4) they were permanently barred from the priesthood; (5) they could not be admitted to the craft guilds; (6) they could not hold public office; (7) they could not appear on the streets after dark; (8) they could not carry arms; (9) they could not have Indians as servants; (10) Negro and mulatto women could not possess or wear luxurious clothes nor adorn themselves with gold or pearls. Colored men were, however, permitted to join the militia.

There were several ways by which colored men could rise in the social hierarchy. One was "passing," by which lighter mulattos claimed to be *mestizos* or even whites. Some were reported to have acquired status through "intrigue, bribery, perjury, and falsification of public books and registers." The Crown could grant Negroes a *cédula de gracias al sacar* by which they were given the legal rights and privileges of whites. The authority on this subject concludes, however, that only a

small numerical portion of the colored classes were "advanced to white-
ness" by the system. [When the independence period began, there was
much class bitterness over discriminations based upon color.]

SOCIAL CLASSES IN LATIN AMERICA TODAY

[The casual tourist and the serious student alike notice immediately
the importance of class in Latin America.] Latin American society is
marked by pronounced contrasts and inequalities. Particularly conspicuous is the great social distance that separates the ruling elite from
the masses of the people.

An aristocracy dominates this class system. It may be an aristocracy
of "whites," of culture, of wealth, or of all three. In this respect the
class system of present-day Latin America is strikingly similar to that
of the colonial period and even to that of Spain and Portugal before the
discovery of the New World.

FACTORS DETERMINING SOCIAL STATUS

[Three factors—race, culture, and economic position—are the chief
determinants of an individual's position in Latin American society.]

RACE   Although Latin America is thought of as being relatively free
from racial prejudices, two general truths must be noted: [(1) in every
Latin American country the ruling classes are whiter than the lower
classes, and (2) at any given point in the social hierarchy the whiter
the individual is, the higher is his social status.]

These truths hold even in Brazil, which is considered to have the
smallest racial problem of all the Latin American countries. Class distinctions associated with color characterize every aspect of Brazilian life.
The upper classes are predominantly white, the middle classes are mixed
bloods, and the darkest-skinned Negroes occupy the lowest class. The
whites and lighter-mixed bloods inhabit the more comfortable, more
healthful, more convenient areas in the city. The blacks and darker
mixed bloods live in the less convenient, less healthful, less expensive
areas. In the employment field, whites are dominant in such positions
as: bank employees, priests, businessmen, cabaret entertainers, professors,
lawyers, politicians, physicians, teachers, commercial employees,
and government functionaries. Mulattoes appear to be predominant over
blacks in these positions: barbers, musicians, street sweepers, streetcar
conductors, firemen, taxi-drivers, bus-drivers, and soldiers. The relatively

unmixed blacks are concentrated in the low-pay, low-status employments, and they are seldom found in the upper levels. Employment in which blacks appear to be predominant include: *carregadores* (porters and baggagemen at the ports), laundresses, *carroceiros* (men with mules and two-wheeled carts who transport goods), masons, stevedores, truck helpers, domestics, street laborers, candy-peddlers, cobblers, venders, newsboys, shoe-shiners, streetcar motormen, and truck-drivers.

Although there is no segregation in Brazilian schools, white and light students predominate, particularly in the secondary and university levels. Black teachers are rare and with few exceptions are limited to the elementary ranks.

A recent study of the seaport of Bahia reveals that of 46 members of the state legislature, only one was black, although 11 per cent were mulattoes. Of 14 aldermen, only two were mulattoes; none was black. In labor unions the leadership is white or near-white, even in those unions in which the membership is composed of black and darker-mixed bloods.

[Clearly racial prejudice exists in Brazil. Belief in the superiority of the white and the inferiority of the Negro is common.] The whites dominate the exclusive social clubs. Negroes are rarely, if ever, to be found in the major social clubs, hotels, better restaurants, barber shops, government offices, or party headquarters. There is an organization in Brazil called the União dos Homems de Cor whose purpose is similar to that of the National Association for the Advancement of Colored People in the United States.

This pattern persists, with variations, throughout Latin America. In Colombia one finds a "small, wealthy, highly intelligent, white, aristocratic elite" and a "great mass of humble, poverty-stricken, disease-ridden, uneducated, colored or mixed-blood *campesinos* at the bottom of the social scale." Colombians place such a high premium on "pureza de sangre" that racial discrimination appears to be an institution, and a person with Negroid or Indian physical characteristics cannot rise above the middle class despite his cultural accomplishments or material possessions. Similarly, the "gente de color" are at the bottom of the social scale in Venezuela.

The Andean states of Peru, Bolivia and Ecuador are Indo-mestizo countries, although each has some Negro peoples, and here, too, the same premium on Spanish blood is to be found. The almost black Negro (*retinto*) cannot enter a salon, be mayor of a town, an official in the army, or a priest. He cannot look at a white woman or even a *mestiza*. Even if he becomes wealthy, the Negro cannot improve his status. In Chile, such status attaches to being white that Chileans often claim the country is white, when in fact it is largely *mestizo*. Although it is estimated that no fewer than 90 per cent of all Chileans are of mixed blood, the population in the major cities seems European, akin to Spaniards and Italians. It is these European types who dominate the social and political life of Chile. As one leaves the cities and travels into the rural regions, frequently the people seem darker and more nearly like the *mestizos* of other countries. However, because Chile does have a relatively homogeneous racial type (Andalusian and Basque men—Araucanian Indian women), cultural and economic criteria are more important than race in determining class.

Argentina is thought of even more frequently than Chile as a "white" country. Nonetheless, Negroes, Indians and *mestizos* have contributed to the racial make-up of the country, and the rural Argentine lower-class people are a "criollo brown" as contrasted to the European whites who make up the ruling aristocracy.

Race is equally a class factor in the Middle American and Caribbean areas. In Mexico, although the Mexican Revolution has made some changes, the whites continue to dominate social life. Inasmuch as not more than about one per cent of the population in Mexico is Negroid, it is the relations among the "whites," *mestizos* and Indians which are important.

In Central America, *mestizos* dominate numerically in Honduras, Nicaragua, and El Salvador. Indians are in the majority in Guatemala. Costa Rica is thought of as a "white" country. Let us look for a moment at Costa Rica. Costa Rican writers frequently claim that their country enjoys white racial homogeneity throughout the entire country. Anyone who has visited the several regions into which Costa Rica is divided will question this generalization. The population which is concentrated around the cities of San José (the capital), Alajuela, Cartago, and Heredia admittedly is European in appearance. On the other hand, the people who live in the alluvial plains of the east coast (the Atlantic side) are Negroes. These Negroes have a low standard of living and are of a low class position. Indeed, it is reported that until recently these Negroes were forbidden by law to migrate from the Atlantic Coast. The people who live on the Pacific Coast are *mestizos* in appearance. Costa Rica, therefore, has some Negroes and *mestizos* in addition to the "whites" who dominate the social and political life of the country.

And in Guatemala, an "Indian" country, a small "white" aristocracy has for long governed the country and enjoyed the highest social class position. The *ladinos* are considered superior to the Indians. A *ladino* is one whose mother tongue is Spanish and who accepts the values of Spanish culture. An Indian is an individual whose mother tongue

POPULATION BY RACES*
1. PERCENTAGES

	POPULATION	WHITE	MESTIZO	INDIAN	NE-GROID	ORIENTAL
1. Brazil	47,460,000	39	20	3	37	1
2. Mexico	22,500,000	9	61	29	1	T
3. Argentina	16,108,000	89	9	2	T	
4. Colombia	10,580,000	20	59	12	9	
5. Peru	7,990,000	13	37	49	1	T
6. Chile	5,530,000	25	66	9		
7. Cuba	5,250,000	30	20		49	1
8. Venezuela	4,430,000	12	68	10	10	
9. Bolivia	3,750,000	12	31	57		
10. Guatemala	3,660,000	3	30	67	T	
11. Ecuador	3,360,000	7	32	58	3	
12. Haiti	3,300,000				100	
British W.I.	2,610,000	2	T		90	8
13. Uruguay	2,480,000	90	8	T	2	
American W.I.	2,150,000	20	20		60	
14. Dominican Rep.	2,100,000	5	14		81	
15. El Salvador	2,030,000	8	52	40	T	
16. Honduras	1,260,000	10	45	40	5	
17. Nicaragua	1,190,000	10	77	4	9	
18. Paraguay	1,160,000	5	30	65		
19. Costa Rica	760,000	48	47	2	3	
20. Panama	720,000	8	50	10	31	1
French W.I.	640,000	2			94	4
Guianas	640,000	3	5	12	39	41
Dutch W.I.	120,000	6	5		85	4
Belize	65,000	4	16	32	48	
Panama C.Z.	60,000	9	20	1	70	T
Falkland Is.	3,000	100				

* Arranged in order of absolute population, with the 20 Latin-American republics in order of population. The figures under the racial headings represent percentages of the total national population. The various races are defined as follows:

White—76 to 100 per cent Caucasian.

Mestizo—Indian-White breeds with not more than 75 per cent of either White or Indian blood.

Indian—76 to 100 per cent Amerindian, and including other persons recognized or accepted as Indians.

Negroid—All individuals with perceptible Negro blood.

Oriental—Eastern Asiatics such as Chinese, Japanese, Indo-Chinese, East Indian, etc.

Fractional percentages have been converted to the nearest whole per cent, consequently totals may not be exactly 100 per cent. "T" represents between .3 and .9 of one per cent; "—" may mean absolute absence or less than .3 of one per cent. Donald D. Brand, "The Present Indian Population of Latin America," Institute of Latin American Studies, University of Texas, *Some Educational and Anthropological Aspects of Latin America* (Austin: University of Texas Press, 1948), p. 51.

is Indian and who accepts the values of Indian culture. These terms refer more to culture than to race. The *ladinos* tend to think of the Indians as ignorant "brutes," "people without reason," who, because of their inferiority, should be used for the benefit of their superiors. If they treated the Indians well, it was as one would treat a dog or a horse. They did not apply the concept of the brotherhood of man to them. Holleran and many others have found much the same relationships of *ladinos* and Indians to exist in the major regions of Guatemala.

In the *mestizo* states of Nicaragua, El Salvador and Honduras, the familiar pattern prevails: we find that Negroes and Indians rarely occupy high social class, and that Spanish origin is prized. In Panama, the "whites" rank highest, the *mestizos* next, and the Negroes lowest in the social scale. Although intermarriage and intermating are permitted, the upper class discourages marriage of Negroes into their group, and discrimination is common. Furthermore, Panamanians of all racial types oppose further immigration of West Indian Negroes.

In Cuba, social relations tend to be either all white or all Negro with the mulattoes acting as go-betweens. The whites are again the ruling class, and the mulattoes and Negroes are generally to be found in the lower classes. There is discrimination against and even segregation of the Negro. The Negro population is not proportionately represented in government positions or other employment to which a high status attaches. The clubs, for example, which are so important in the social life of Cuba, are segregated strictly on a color basis. The yacht clubs are exclusively white. The colored people establish their own clubs, also on an exclusive basis.

In Haiti, the struggle of the "authentiques" (pure Negroes of undiluted African blood) to gain some or all of the power of government from the lighter-skinned mulattoes who have dominated Haiti during most of the twentieth century is well known.

[The common Latin American belief in the superiority of certain races receives support from many Latin American intellectuals.] Eminent men such as Jorge de Lima and Euclydes da Cunha are sometimes referred to as "devotees of Aryanism." Oliveira Vianna, well-known Brazilian sociologist, is quoted by Pierson as believing that there is an "irreducible" difference between the mentality of the Caucasian and that of the Negro. Pablo Cárdenas Acosta argues that "superior" races degrade and weaken themselves by crossing with "inferior" races and that the progeny of such unions never inherit the physical or moral qualities of the "superior" parent. . . .

CULTURE AS A DETERMINANT OF CLASS

Culture is another determinant of class. All evidence indicates that culture is even more important than race in determining an individual's status *within* a class. The following cultural factors help to establish class position: (1) family and friends; (2) occupation; (3) profession; (4) education; (5) language and religion; (6) location and type of residence; (7) type of clothing worn; and (8) manners and social ceremonials. The weight of each of these criteria in determining class is uncertain, but probably the first four factors are more significant than the last four. Colored peoples can sometimes advance to the "white" position if they acquire all or a majority of the above cultural qualifications.

THE FAMILY AND CLASS   In the Latin American countries, the family is one of the most important of all social institutions. An individual's rank in the community is derived in large part from his family. In the United States, one derives status and recognition as an individual rather than as a member of a family, but in Latin America it is the family that is more important. Throughout Latin America, position at the top of the social pyramid comes largely as a birthright rather than through individual effort and ability. Family is so important that upper-class families who lose their money do not immediately drop to the middle class.

Can a colored man rise to the social level of a white? Because status depends more on the family than upon the individual, class lines in Latin America are relatively rigid. A rise from the lower to the middle class is more frequent than any movement into the upper class.

Colored peoples can sometimes marry into "whiter" families if they have education, wealth, and other evidence of status. When an Indian in Guatemala marries a *ladino* woman and adopts as much *ladino* culture as he can, he gradually comes to be looked upon as a *ladino* by everybody, although a lower-class one. Conversely, when a *ladino* man marries an Indian woman in Guatemala, he may jokingly refer to himself as *muy indio* ("very Indian"), but he considers himself a superior individual among his Indian friends and married relatives.

Illicit sexual relations is a major characteristic of Hispanic culture among the male members of the elite families. Men who can afford to do so frequently keep mistresses. Concubinage is common in Brazil and is called *mancebia*. There are many sayings in Latin America to the effect that a white woman is best for marriage, a black one for work, and a mixed-blood for sexual relations. Upper-class families employ many servants, most of whom are colored. If men of upper-class white families have sexual relations with colored female servants, the offspring will usually be lighter than the mothers. Apparently a colored lower-class woman gains status by having a lighter colored child. In any event, the children of illicit unions sometimes are accepted into the family of the father. The illegitimate children ("naturales") ordinarily take the mother's name. When the father recognizes them and gives them his name, they may enjoy upper-class status. So much miscegenation is taking place in Latin America that one authority considers it possible that Indian cultures will disappear into *ladino* cultures in about 150 years.

OCCUPATION AND CLASS A common saying in Brazil is "Trabalho e para cachorro e negro" ("Work [i.e., manual labor] is for Negroes and dogs"). This is typical of the Latin American attitude that work is debasing, leisure ennobling. [Ostentatious use of leisure (travel, patronage of the arts, conspicuous consumption) is a symbol of upper-class status.] Everyone has contempt for the kind of labor described in the following terms: "manual, productive labor"; "menial labor"; "physical labor"; "labor with the hands"; "mechanical labor"; and "vile employment."

PROFESSION AND CLASS It follows logically from the general principle that work is debasing, leisure ennobling, that the highest status is accorded those who live in ostentation without labor of any kind. It is logical also that the professions which are obviously dissociated from manual, productive labor should have high status. Professions with high status are: lawyer, doctor, poet, priest, general, and high level bureaucrat. At a somewhat lower level of status are professions which are associated with the management of labor, such as foremen, engineers, white collar employees, and managers of business establishments. "Labor" jobs, of course, have the least status. Urban labor probably has a higher status than rural labor.

EDUCATION AND CLASS Education is without doubt one of the most important criteria of class and status in Latin America. Indeed, education is essential to upper-class position in social life and in government and politics almost everywhere.

Chile provides an exception to this generalization. In Chile, the children of elite families frequently do not attend the university. They travel and seek an education through personal contact with great thinkers and artists all over the world.

The cult of the "doctor en filosofía" (doctor of philosophy—"doutor" in Portuguese) pervades higher education in Latin America. The symbols of education are revered. Those who have them use them constantly on their calling cards and stationery, on name plates, on their front doors, and in salutations and in the conversation of government and politics. Some of the symbols are "Dr.," "Ing." (for engineer), "Lic." (for licentiate or lawyer), and "Arq." (for architect). Education is sought more for purposes of prestige than for its values in utility and training. The most popular curriculae are those producing lawyers, medical men, writers, poets and others who demonstrate by the titles of "doctor" that they have nothing to do with the inferior, producing classes.

SECONDARY CULTURAL CRITERIA

Secondary cultural criteria of status are language and religion, location and type of residence, type of clothing worn, and manners and social ceremonials. In each of these categories, it is the cultural values of the "white" class which count. Spanish and Portuguese are languages of high status. French has a higher prestige value in Haiti than the creole patois most of the people speak. If the Indian or Negro wants to rise in influence in the community he must give up his native language or dialect. Catholicism is everywhere the religion of high status. Although the Church as an institution has lost influence in the community, a lower-class man advances his position by becoming a priest. The "white" classes concentrate in the urban areas. The *mestizo* and Indian classes are mainly in the rural areas.

The cities are frequently laid out on the "plaza plan" in Spanish America rather than the "main street" plan (as in the United States). In the plaza plan, there is a central plaza or square with streets running from the square on a gridiron basis. The plaza and the arterials leading into it command the highest status and prestige in the city. On the plaza are located the cathedral, government buildings, principal businesses, and residences of the people with the greatest power and influence. The plaza is also the principal social center. It is there that the Sunday night promenades, fiestas, and religious activities take place. The lower classes live clustered around plazas located some blocks from the central plaza. The plaza plan is not characteristic of Portugal or Brazil.

When an Indian or a *mestizo* endeavors to break into the upper-middle classes, he copies the values of the white man. Indians and *mestizos* have opportunities to learn the methods of dressing and social ceremonials of the ruling classes. They learn about Hispanic culture if they go to school, are sent to the penitentiary, attend mass, work for "whites," or if they happen to be brought up in homes of the elite. An Andean Indian can often qualify as a *cholo* if he abandons Indian clothing, stops chewing coca leaves, learns Spanish, and can give up menial labor, such as carrying bundles for hire or working as *peón*. The Indian or *mestizo* needs also to master the elaborate ceremonials in Hispanic culture, such as polite language and proper conduct in courtship, marriage, mourning, holidays, and in Church and political activities. Formalism is extremely important in Hispanic culture.

ECONOMIC POSITION AND CLASS   Wealth is a third powerful determinant of class in Latin American society. In the United States it is difficult to differentiate among social classes on the basis of such things as clothing, food, means of locomotion, housing and the like. The uniformity of men's dress may be observed by standing on a street corner in almost any American city, large or small. A Hickey Freeman suit might cost a good deal more than a Foreman and Clark, but one has to have a sharp eye or an expert's training to detect readily the differences. A drive in an automobile from the center of a large city, such as New York, Chicago, or Los Angeles, to the suburbs will show cars of all kinds stretching out on the highway as far as the eye can see. In a grocery store or restaurant one can observe that much the same food is purchased and consumed by all classes of people. Regardless of how much money or social position a person has, household conveniences such as hot and cold running water, gas or electric stoves, telephones, washing machines, and radios are found virtually everywhere. The high unit cost of television sets is not prohibitive to any large number of people in the cities at least. About 65 per cent of the nation's families own automobiles and more than 50 per cent own homes.

[In Latin America there is a sharply stratified class society in which the differences between rich and poor are both extreme and obvious. The rich aristocrats tend to think of the poor as members of a class that is by nature poor, though deserving mercy, charity and justice. Thus begging is almost an institution, schools are established for the poor as such, and the president or first lady designates times during the year for awarding gifts and gratuities to the poor. Correspondingly, the poor feel that they have a right to the friendly aid, assistance, and guidance of the rich.]

From the economic standpoint, of course, a middle class exists in every Latin American country. Figures on possession of wealth and distribution of income show that there is always a group far above the masses of the people and far below the one to five per cent or so of people with a great deal of property and income. The middle class varies from an estimated 8 per cent in Venezuela to an estimated 50 per cent in Argentina and Uruguay.

These figures are rough estimates at best; they are not developed from a uniform definition of the middle class. Small landowners and businessmen and salaried employees, of course, exist in the Latin American countries just as they do in all other countries. From the economic standpoint, they are a definite unit. However, it is important to note that the middle classes in Latin America always adopt the values of the upper classes. They are not generally a cultural or political unit.

The most universal characteristic of the middle class in Latin America is its contempt for manual, productive labor. No one who works with his hands is middle class. People of the middle class avidly seek education in order to qualify for a government post or a white collar position—any "respectable" job in which they will not be required to work with their hands.

The middle classes in Latin America slavishly ape the aristocracy in many ways. They try to send their children, particularly the girls, to private schools (elementary and secondary) where the rich people send theirs. They must have servants in their houses or apartments. Although they often can't afford the Cadillacs, Lincolns, and Buick Road-masters of the elite, they like to be seen using taxis. Many "middle class" professional people who could afford a cheap car but not one with high prestige value prefer to do without a car altogether.

Middle class people are careful to dress formally. They scrupulously avoid carrying packages of any kind which would demean them. One will see middle class men promenading, buying lottery tickets ostentatiously, rolling the dice at bars and casinos, sending runners from their box at the track to place bets on horses they have selected, sitting in sidewalk cafes. Conspicuous consumption is characteristic. Middle class people spend all the money they have or can borrow on such things as marriages, baptisms, birthdays. They follow the old formalistic traditions of the upper classes in each case. They try to get into upper class social clubs to associate with the elite, and they stay away from lower class social centers.

Economically, then, there is a middle class in Latin America. Psychologically or culturally, with some few exceptions, there is not. It is, therefore, more accurate to think of an upper-middle and lower class division in Hispanic society. The term "middle class" is used only infrequently in most of the countries. Instead, one hears terms which show a psychological or cultural division: "gente decente" and "gente cualquiera"; "ricos" and "pobres"; "terratenientes" (landholders) and "campesinos"; "gamonales" and "campesinos"; "alta clase" and "baja clase"; "us poor people" and "the rich people"; "alguien o nadie"; "Hay que ser Dr. o peón." In Brazil similar terms are commonly heard. Some are "os bons" (the big shots) and "os pobres" (the poor people); "povo baixo" (common people) and "chefoes" (big shots).

CONCLUDING REMARKS

[The evidence is clear that a pronounced class system exists in Latin America. Between social classes there is rigid separation, great distance and little mobility.] This is not the sort of society that generates many democratic ideas. Democracy is more likely to come of a culture in which there are many and diverse criteria for evaluating an individual, and many ways in which dignity and influence may be acquired. In a democratic culture men have an incentive to examine critically the values of their society. However, a class system characterized by a rigid formalism permits only one set of criteria of evaluating human worth. In such a restrictive culture, ideas are important for their own sake; it is not conceivable that they should apply to day-to-day living. The object of the spoken word is beauty, grace, logic and force—not applicability. The values for "practical living" are already established. They are firm, fixed, virtually immutable. Thus we understand why Latin Americans publish lyric defenses of democracy but do not feel impelled to work for democracy in their own immediate neighborhood; why Latin American laws are the most progressive in the world and the administration of the laws frequently the most regressive; why democratic constitutions and oligarchy exist complacently and sometimes comfortably, side by side.

For several reasons, then, the Latin American class system hinders the growth of popular government:

1. When the means of acquiring dignity and power in the community are the monopoly of one class, citizens learn to the core of their being what privilege means. Privilege and favoritism in government become deeply understandable.

2. Although the frequency of sexual relations between the white and colored peoples helps to create an atmosphere of tolerance, it is still true that the colored peoples can advance to influence in the community only through acquiring values of the white group.

3. The colored peoples are still predominantly the "hewers of wood and the drawers of water" for the "whites." Ambitious colored peoples are encouraged to repudiate democratic methods of acquiring power and to resort to extremist measures. Furthermore, there is open or latent bitterness and hostility among the races in a number of the countries which makes national unity—working together to solve common problems of government—difficult if not impossible.

4. The hierarchical nature of the class system, the fact that a tiny upper-middle group exercises an influence in politics far out of proportion to its numbers, ensures that no reform may be made except from the top downwards. [People are encouraged to look up (*lo de arriba*) to authority to solve problems.] By contrast, in the liberal-democratic state the individual citizens assume responsibility for the things the state is to do.

5. Although a large middle class will not automatically produce democratic institutions, as some scholars seem to believe, experience does show that democracy frequently thrives when the middle class is large and dominant.

A Typology of Latin American Subcultures*

CHARLES WAGLEY
and
MARVIN HARRIS

One of the most perplexing problems in the study of complex national or regional cultures such as those of Latin America is the diversity of pattern and institution which they contain. There are a series of institutions, values, and modes of behavior which constitute throughout Latin America a "cultural common denominator" and which distinguish Latin American culture from other major culture spheres of the Western world. But the "common denominator" of modern Latin America does not consist simply of those institutions, values, and behavior patterns held in common by most of the Latin American population. Regular cultural differences within the complex and heterogeneous national so-

* Charles Wagley and Marvin Harris, "A Typology of Latin American Subcultures," *American Anthropologist*, vol. 57 (1955), pp. 428–451. (Notes and references in the original version have been omitted.)

cieties must also be considered. A conceptual framework based on these differences is much needed to provide a context for the extant data and to guide future research. This is especially true with respect to the numerous anthropological community studies, whose contribution to our knowledge of a national culture is often lessened by an inadequate definition of just what variety of the national culture is being considered—or, in other words, what segment of the diverse population they treat. The purpose of the present article is to suggest a taxonomic system of subcultures which we hope will have operational utility throughout Latin America.

This attempt to provide a classificatory system for ordering cultural data on Latin America is obviously not unique. As we shall discuss in more detail below, Redfield, by implication at least, distinguished four types of communities for Yucatán, although only the folk and urban types were emphasized. Steward and his associates in the Puerto Rican project isolated a series of significant Puerto Rican subcultures for study. And recently, there has been published a series of articles, dealing mainly with Latin America, aimed at refining and extending Redfield's folk-urban concepts. Most of these discussions of Redfield's classification and most attempts to develop a socio-cultural taxonomic system have dealt with varieties of whole local communities treated as whole societies. This is to be expected from a discipline whose traditional research methods involved prolonged, sedentary, and intimate contact with a restricted locale and the analysis of local sociocultural wholes. But it is apparent that many of the communities studied in Latin America by anthropologists have an internal heterogeneity of culture pattern depending upon class differences, differences between rural and urban residents of the same community, and other factors, too numerous to list. It is therefore often difficult to classify the culture of a whole local community as "folk culture" or as "urban culture"—or as "Indian," "mestizo," or "creole." The present taxonomy of subcultures attempts to distinguish between culture and society and to take into account not only the differences among communities but also internal cultural heterogeneity within communities.

We distinguish nine significant Latin American subculture types. They are called "subcultures" because they are variations of a larger cultural tradition and represent the way of life of significant segments of the Latin American population. They are called "types" because their content differs according to the environment, history, and distinctive local traditions of the nation or subregion in which they are found. Thus, the subculture types we have called "Peasant" differ in content in the western countries of Central and South America, with their strong American

Indian tradition, from the same type as found in the West Indies and lowland Brazil, which have felt strong African influences. Yet it seems to us that Peasant subcultures throughout Latin American share certain basic features which makes it possible to include them in the same typological category.

At least in a preliminary fashion, the following subculture types would seem to be useful for ordering the universe of Latin American cultural materials: (1) *Tribal Indian,* comprising the cultures of the few remaining aboriginal peoples; (2) *Modern Indian,* resulting from the fusion of aboriginal and, in the main, sixteenth- and seventeenth-century Iberian institutions and culture patterns; (3) *Peasant,* carried by the relatively isolated horticultural peoples of Latin America (and frequently by the lower classes of small isolated towns), who are called variously *mestizos, cholos, ladinos, caboclos,* or other local terms; (4) *Engenho-Plantation,* the subculture of the workers on family-owned estates; (5) *Usina Plantation,* the way of life on the large modern corporation-owned agricultural establishments; (6) *Town,* the way of life of the middle- and upper-class inhabitants of the numerous settlements serving as administrative, market, and religious centers throughout Latin America; (7) *Metropolitan Upper Class,* characteristic of the highest socioeconomic strata in the large cities and of the owners of plantations; (8) *Metropolitan Middle Class,* characteristic of an emerging group of big-city professional and white-collar workers and owners of medium-size business, and (9) *Urban Proletariat,* characteristic of a mass of unskilled and semiskilled industrial and menial workers in the larger cities.

Undoubtedly there are many other important Latin American subcultural types, and it is hoped that the present taxonomy will be refined and extended—or that it will stimulate others to formulate a more useful system.

TRIBAL INDIAN TYPES

In 1500, when the Europeans came to that part of the New World which is now Latin America, the natives of the lowlands (except for certain parts of the circum-Caribbean) lacked true tribal or political organization. There were innumerable "tribes" made up of villages or bands united only by a common language, common custom, and the consciousness of forming "a people" as against all outsiders. The power of chiefs seldom extended beyond one or more villages or bands; and the "tribes," sometimes even the villages or bands of the same tribe, were generally at war with one another. The population was sparse in aboriginal times, and disease, slavery, and European warfare against these highly divided groups rapidly led to the decimation and extinction of the native peoples in many localities. Nowadays, only an insignificant few of these tribal groups persist in localities such as the Chaco, the headwaters of the Amazon tributaries, and on isolated reservations and mission stations. Such tribesmen constitute an insignificant segment of the modern Latin American population, and as long as they retain their aboriginal cultures and their identity as tribesmen they are, in reality, carriers of distinct cultures within the geographic boundaries of Latin America and not subcultures of modern Latin America. However, the process of acculturation now taking place among these tribal groups does pertain to the study of Latin American culture, and, as Foster recently pointed out in his discussion of the folk culture concept, it is important to distinguish between tribal cultures and the mixed rural cultures of Latin America.

MODERN INDIAN TYPES

The Indians of the highland regions of Latin America must be included in any study of modern Latin American culture. Although their way of life differs strikingly from that of the nationals of the countries in which they live, they share many patterns and institutions, mainly of European origin, with the other inhabitants, and numerically they are an important segment of the population. Unlike the lowlands, the highland region was inhabited by a dense aboriginal population organized into native states. After the initial shock of armed conquest and disease, these peoples were brought under the control of the Spanish colonials. Through mechanisms such as the *encomienda, repartimiento, mita,* and other forms of forced labor, they were made to work for their conquerors and were integrated into colonial society. Missionaries taught them Catholicism and, in many cases, they were concentrated into Spanish-type villages and a European form of community organization was forced upon them. They borrowed freely from the European culture of the sixteenth and seventeenth centuries—a culture which in many respects contained as many "folk" features as their own. By at least the beginning of the eighteenth century, a new culture had taken form among these peoples out of the fusion of aboriginal and colonial Spanish patterns. This culture persists today, unchanged in its main outlines, and constitutes an important variant of national patterns in many highland countries.

Modern Indians generally speak an aboriginal language, although they may also be bilingual. Some of them work in mines, on coffee *fincas,* or on large *haciendas,* but most characteristically they are horticulturalists planting native American crops, although many European plants have also been adopted. Despite the tendency to individualize landholdings which began in the nineteenth century, among many Modern Indian groups the community is still the landholding unit. Community cohesion generally persists at a high level despite the encroaching power of the national states. Indian *alcaldes, regidores,* and other officials are often maintained alongside the national, bureaucracy. While the Modern Indian is nominally Catholic, it is characteristic that a large segment of aboriginal belief has been fused with Catholic ideology. In addition, Catholic saints are endowed with local characteristics and powers. The Indians of each community generally think of themselves as ethnic units separate from other Indian groups and from the nationals of the country in which they reside; they are the people of Santiago Chimaltenango, of Chamula or of Chucuito, rather than Guatemalans or Peruvians. Frequently they wear a distinctive costume which identifies them as Indians of a particular *pueblo,* and it is characteristic for the Indians of each community to be endogamous.

Numerous examples of this subcultural type have been studied in Latin America by anthropologists. The Indians of Santiago Chimaltenango, of Chichicastenango, of Panajachel, of Quintana Roo, Yucatán, of Kauri and of Chucuito in Peru, to mention but a few, are carriers of Modern-Indian-type subcultures. Yet, as noted above, few of these communities contain only carriers of the Modern Indian subculture type. In most of these communities, there are also a few non-Indians, carriers of a Peasant type subculture, who form an integral part of community life. Any full community study must treat not only the two subcultures of these communities but also the "caste-like" relationship between them. As Gillin has written, "Each group [*ladino* and Indian] has culture patterns more or less exclusive to itself, but the two castes are part of a reciprocal pattern which characterizes the community as a whole." Too often our community studies have treated Modern Indian subcultures as if they were isolated tribal groups.

PEASANT TYPES

Throughout Latin America, the people who inhabit rural farms and the numerous small and isolated agricultural villages have a way of life which is analogous in many respects to that of peasants in other parts of the world. Latin American peasants may be physically American

Indians, Negroes or Europeans, or mixtures of these racial stocks. They are the people who are called *mestizos* (Mexico and other countries), *ladinos* (Guatemala), *cholos* (Peru), or *caboclos, tabareus, caipiras,* and *matutos* (Brazil). In some respects, their way of life is similar to that of the Modern Indian. They are generally horticulturalists using essentially the same "slash-and-burn" techniques of farming as the Modern Indians, and they frequently depend primarily upon native plants such as maize, manioc, and potatoes. As stated earlier, Peasant-type subcultures are strongly flavored with aboriginal traits in some areas as for example in the Amazon Valley, where native shamanism is an integral part of peasant religion. In other areas, such as the West Indies and the Guianas, African traits persist in varying degrees among the Peasant subcultures just as American Indian traits do elsewhere. But everywhere Peasant-type subcultures are characterized by a predominance of archaic European patterns, which survive alongside the American Indian or African patterns and which are slowly giving way to new national patterns and institutions. Unlike the Modern Indians, Peasants generally consider themselves to be nationals of the country in which they reside. Although they tend to be regional in their loyalties and to have but a vague idea of what it means to be a member of a nation, national patterns and institutions play a larger role in Peasant than in Modern Indian subcultures. Peasant subculture economies are closely tied in with regional and national economies. There is fairly extensive participation in commercial transactions through the medium of markets, to which Peasant farmers regularly go to sell their surplus for cash. Peasants maintain accounts at stores and trading posts from which they receive goods of nationwide circulation such as kerosene, steel tools, cloth, thread, and sewing machines.

Peasants characteristically speak the national language (i.e., Spanish or Portuguese), although sometimes an aboriginal tongue (e.g., the Tarascan of the Michoacan *mestizos*), or, as in Haiti, a *créole,* is spoken. Peasants participate to some extent in political life, voting if there are elections and if they have the franchise. Catholicism in Peasant subcultures tends to be more orthodox than that of the Modern Indian. Peasants share national fashions, values and aspirations, although in all of these they are generally "behind the times" since they tend to be isolated from the centers of diffusion. Thus young men may play soccer if it is the national sport, as it is in Brazil. Peasants often celebrate national holidays and perhaps know something of their national heroes. Literacy is valued as an aid in social and economic improvement. Nowadays, Peasants tend to dress after the style of the city as soon as such styles are known and when people can afford them. Because such people are generally poor, illiterate, and isolated, they have little in the way of modern technological facilities such as electric lights, motor-driven vehicles, and modern housing.

Again, it is not difficult to cite examples of this type of Latin American subculture which have been studied by anthropologists. Both Modern Indian- and Peasant-type subcultures tend to be carried by relatively small and simply organized social units which thus lend themselves to investigation by the traditional field techniques of ethnology. The rural agriculturalists living in the environs of Moche in Peru, those of the community of Tzintzuntzan in Mexico, those of Cruz das Almas in southern Brazil, those of Itá in the Brazilian Amazon and those of Marbial Valley in Haiti are carriers of subcultures which correspond to the Peasant type. The Small Farmer subculture of Puerto Rico would also seem to correspond to this category.

But it must be emphasized that most of the communities mentioned above also contain people who are not peasants, not even rural, but townsmen with urban aspirations and urban patterns of behavior. The subculture of these people will be considered below as the Town type. Due to the tendency to regard "folk culture" as a way of life characteristic of a type of community, the folk subcultures (or in our terms, Peasant subcultures) of such communities have often been emphasized to the exclusion of the nonfolk elements. The restudy of Redfield's Tepoztlán by Lewis is an example of how the concept of a homogeneous folk community needs to be qualified in view of the internal heterogeneity of cultural patterns found in rural communities.

The fact probably is that the carriers of Peasant-type subcultures live everywhere in communities which also contain carriers of Town-type subcultures—whose ties with national life are the intermediate bonds by which the peasant is also tied into national life. Indeed, many peasants are actually town dwellers who have their domiciles in town and their farms in the nearby area. Although settlements inhabited exclusively by people who have a homogeneous Peasant subculture are extremely common, it is a distortion to view them as isolated communities, or even as total communities. Since the Peasant subculture is distinguished from the Modern Indian precisely on the grounds of greater identification with and participation in national patterns and institutions, it is clear that a group of peasants can only be *part* of a community, and that the terms "folk society" and "folk culture" are misleading when applied to a community which actually and necessarily contains more than one subculture. It may perhaps help to clarify the matter if the communities in which peasant households, hamlets and villages occur are thought of as larger Town-Peasant communities, implying that Town and Peasant subcultures must be considered together if a proper understanding of either is to be attained. This symbiotic relationship between Peasant subcultures and Town subcultures (i.e., "folk and nonfolk") has been recently emphasized by Foster.

ENGENHO PLANTATION AND USINA PLANTATION TYPES

The Europeans who settled in the Caribbean and in the lowland parts of northern South America did not find the riches in gold and silver nor the large aboriginal labor force which their contemporaries encountered in the highlands. But by the middle of the sixteenth century sugar cane had become an important commercial crop in Brazil and in parts of the West Indies. For a time, the great wealth which sugar brought to this lowland region was comparable to that derived from minerals in the highlands. From the Old World the planters brought a commercialized version of large-scale agricultural enterprise, which had its roots in sixteenth-century Europe and even earlier in the ancient Mediterranean world. In the New World this agricultural system was modified by the massive use of slave labor, by the exigencies of sugar as a commercial crop, and by the physical and social environment of the New World colonies. The result was the New World plantation—the *hacienda,* the *finca,* the *estancia,* the *fazenda,* or whatever it happens to be called in the various countries.

Such plantations came to form veritable communities, or neighborhoods of larger communities, with their own variety of Latin American culture. Although large-scale agricultural establishments differ from one part of Latin America to another and in accordance with the crop to which they are dedicated (i.e., sugar, coffee, bananas, cotton, cacao, henequen, etc.), there are numerous social and cultural similarities among them. Furthermore, some fundamental changes in the way of life on Latin American plantations have followed essentially the same developmental process throughout the whole area, despite differences in the commercial crops.

The general characteristics of the *Engenho* Plantation subculture type may best be illustrated by reference to plantations dedicated to sugar cane, which was for centuries Latin America's most important commercial crop. Although there were local differences, sugar-cane plantations during the period of slavery seem to have followed a similar pattern throughout the area. The center of the plantation, and of the community or neighborhood which it formed, was the mansion in which the owner, his large family, and the many domestic servants lived. A chapel, which was either attached to the mansion or situated near it, served as the church for the owners and for the slave workers. Behind the mansion were the slave quarters—a street of huts. Nearby there were the sheds used to store tools and equipment and to house the oxen and other animals. A storehouse, where the food and other supplies for the field hands were kept and periodically distributed, was also a common feature. Then, nearby, there was the *engenho* (Spanish *ingenio*), which was a small sugar factory containing a mill driven by hand, by animal traction, or by water power. Such plantations were generally situated on waterways which furnished easy transportation to market centers. Characteristically, the plantation settlement pattern was a concentrated one resembling that of a small village.

The number of people on such plantations was generally not large during the slave period. On the average, no more than 200 to 300 people lived on a relatively large sugar plantation, and within this small "village-like" society social relations tended to be intimate and highly personal. The members of the owner's family were tied together into a large, extended patriarchal group. Between these aristocrats and the slaves there was a stable set of relations often accompanied by personal intimacy and intense loyalty. It was, in other words, a "caste" society made up of Negro slaves and European owners in which each "caste" was conscious of the rights and obligations of the other. Leadership was provided automatically by the dominant European group, and economics, religion, and almost all aspects of life were directed and controlled by the aristocratic owner or his administrators.

The abolition of slavery, the vagaries of the international market, and finally the industrialization of sugar refining brought about important changes; in the old colonial sugar plantations. However, many plantations may still be found throughout Latin America which strongly resemble the old *engenho* despite the substitution of wage labor for slavery and other innovations. Such plantations are still owned, and often administered, by descendants of the same aristocratic slave-owning families of the nineteenth century. The workers, some of whom may actually be descendants of former slaves, show much the same dependency and loyalty toward their employers as the slaves are said to have shown for their masters. Each of these *engenho*-type plantations, with its cluster of houses and sheds and its small chapel, forms, as in the past, a small concentrated village or neighborhood. Economic life is still focused upon monoculture, and little land or time is left for the workers to grow their own gardens. Today, the sugar factory itself is no longer a part of the *engenho*-type plantations. The *engenho*-type plantations have become, instead, suppliers of sugar cane to large mechanized sugar mills, or *usinas,* which do the processing and marketing. But in many respects the way of life on these old-style plantations has changed remarkably little since the nineteenth century.

Here again, the community unit consists of the carriers of two distinct subcultures, that of the workers and that of the owners. Although it would be tempting to make the *engenho* plantation community unit and the *Engenho* Plantation subculture coincide, the fact is that the plantation owner is generally also an urban Latin American cosmopolitan who is found in the upper strata of the principal large cities. Since early colonial times he has had both a "town house" and his place in the country, and has alternated his residence, sometimes seasonally, between one and the other. His employees, formerly his slaves or peons, including his domestic servants in town as well as the workers in the country, are treated by him with characteristic patriarchal, intimate, and usually benevolent concern. To this treatment the *engenho* plantation worker responds with loyalty and attitudes of dependence. It is this dependence and allegiance to the *patrão* (boss), together with the distinctive land tenure, occupational and communal arrangements peculiar to the monoculture regime, which distinguish *Engenho* Plantation subcultures from Peasant subcultures.

Throughout Latin America, a transition from the *engenho* plantation to the modern industrialized agricultural enterprise has occurred or is now taking place. We have called the newer form the *usina* plantation, from the term used for the modern industrialized sugar mill. Speaking again in terms of sugar plantations, as steam-driven mills were introduced capital came to play a more important role than land. The central-power-drive *usina* could process and distribute far more efficiently than the smaller installations, and so the small plantations came more and more to depend upon the *usina* to process the cane. Gradually, great corporations have bought out the smaller properties and welded them together into large agricultural factories. There is a transitional phase, however, in which each *engenho* plantation is administered as a separate unit by employees of the corporation. During this phase much of the old way of life continues. This period of transition is one which is particularly vulnerable to social tension and economic instability. The workers have lost the security provided by the traditional *patrão,* and the new system of social welfare and social security of the national government has not as yet been extended to cover them.

Then, as industrialization progresses, it becomes more efficient to fuse these smaller properties into one large centralized commercial farm. Where this process has been completed, as in Cuba, Puerto Rico, and Brazil, the result is a type of Plantation subculture which differs profoundly from that of the old-style *engenho* plantation. The traditional pattern of intimacy and mutual dependence between the workers and their employers is replaced by a more strictly economic relationship between the workers and the administrators and officials of the corporation. The local group becomes larger as the number of workers increases and the social unit is more heterogeneous as new specialized occupations appear. The workers, without the old emotional ties to their fellows and to their employers, are more mobile than before, often leaving the plantation to seek higher wages elsewhere. The *usina* plantation is more closely integrated with national institutions and culture patterns. Labor unions are sometimes active among the workers, and social welfare legislation is enforced more often than in the *engenho* plantation. There may be electric lights, modern housing, schools, medical clinics, public health facilities, and excellent communications with the metropolitan centers. The workers on such establishments seem to have a way of life more similar to that of the growing urban-industrial proletariat of Latin America than to that of the workers on the *engenho* plantations. Mintz has recently characterized the workers on these large commercial plantations as the "Rural Proletariat."

The discussion of these two types of Plantation subculture has been based on plantations involved in sugar production. Large-scale agricultural estates that grow other kinds of commercial crops for export are of course also found in Latin America. Such crops as cacao, coffee, maté tea, henequen, and cotton are also produced on large-scale mono-culture plantations. It is probable that the regime of exploitation of each different crop determines distinctive sociocultural conditions. Thus when more data become available it may be convenient to formulate a series of additional subtypes for *Engenho* and *Usina* Plantation subcultures based on crop specialties. Livestock ranches, for example, with their small number of workers, their exclusion of female laborers, and their saturation with a kind of horse complex, clearly merit treatment as a subtype.

From another point of view, the widespread occurrence of share-cropping suggests an additional sector of refinements for our categories. Share-cropping of a commercial crop as a substitute for wages can probably be subsumed under the category of *Engenho* Plantation subcultures. Relationships between the owner and his workers approach the highly personal ones characteristic of *engenho* plantations, with the employer offering assistance in a crisis and in many instances being the sole purchaser of his tenants' produce. The individual share-cropping regime, however, may act to reduce the community cohesion characteristic of nucleated wage laborers on other *engenho*-type plantations.

For the purpose of this paper, it seems sufficient to set forth the hypothesis that at least two broad types, the *Engenho* Plantation and the *Usina* Plantation subcultures, may be found throughout Latin America. No matter what crop the plantation produces, there has been a transition from the old traditional enterprise to the modern industrialized establishment analogous to that which has taken place in sugar production. Everywhere this transition has involved a shift from a more personal and stable set of relations between the classes to a mobile, impersonal one based on economic values and urban standards. It has involved a change from a small and relatively homogeneous society to a larger and more variegated one; and it has led to a more important role for national institutions and patterns on all levels of plantation life.

It is surprising that so few examples of the Plantation subcultures of either type have been studied by anthropologists, especially in view of the obvious numerical importance of plantation workers in the Latin American population and in view of the importance of plantation production in the national economies of the Latin American nations. A study of an *Engenho* Plantation subculture has been carried out by Hutchinson as part of a community study in the Recôncavo region of Bahia in Brazil. A study of a government-owned sugar plantation was made by Elena Padilla Seda in Puerto Rico, and on the same island Mintz studied a large sugar plantation owned and operated by a commercial corporation. Loomis and Powell have studied a Costa Rica *finca* producing sugar and coffee, and have given us a comparison of a *hacienda* and a peasant community in rural Costa Rica. A study of a community in Brazil in which there are cacao-producing plantations has been carried out by Anthony Leeds. If the present classification of Latin American subculture types serves no other purpose, it indicates that a large segment of the Latin American population—and an important variant of the culture of the area—has been relatively neglected in our field investigations.

TOWN TYPES

Towns where periodic fairs are held and which serve as the administrative and religious centers for rural districts are old in Latin America. They have their roots both in the European and in the aboriginal traditions. With the improvement of transportation (especially with the use of trucks), many of these towns have become regional markets similar to the market towns that serve the rural United States. As these market centers enlarge their range of trading, the rural population no longer produces only for local consumption but comes to plant by more modern methods cash crops that are sold on the national market. The towns thus become more closely integrated with national economic and political life. Their populations increase, and new concepts and patterns are introduced from the cities. Life in these larger towns is more like that of the great urban centers, by which they are more directly influenced, than like that of the surrounding countryside.

Yet in Latin America today there are still innumerable small towns serving only an immediate rural area and preserving many traditional patterns. Such towns cannot be understood without reference to the whole community of which they are the centers. For it is characteristic of Town subcultures that their "city folk" look down upon the "country people" as "hicks," and that behavior patterns, values, standards of dress, speech and etiquette differ for the upper-class townspeople as opposed to both the lower-class townspeople and to the inhabitants of the rural countryside.

As we have already indicated, such towns are part of communities which include two strongly contrasting subcultures. The contrast between the two corresponds to a marked schism in socioeconomic class status between a nonfarming, landlord, business-owning, bureaucratic, "white-collar" group and a farming, manual-laboring group. Within the town itself, there are a small number of people who are craft specialists, like shoemakers, blacksmiths, and carpenters, who are permanent residents of the town, and who do not engage in agricultural activities. From the point of view of the local upper class these people may be "hicks" just as much as the town-dwelling and country-dwelling farmers. Although these artisans themselves often regard the rural people with condescension, the fact is that they are generally more closely related (by kinship, by marriage, by social and cultural values, by economics, and by social intercourse) with the rural farmers than with the town upper class. The stigma of poverty, of illiteracy, and of manual labor is on both groups. Thus in isolated areas, town-dwelling farmers, town-dwelling artisans and laborers, and domestic servants can generally be classed as carriers of a Peasant subculture. But such people represent a gradient of contact between isolated semisubsistence farmers and the upper-class townspeople who are carriers of Town subculture.

The life of the upper-class townsman differs radically from that of the carriers of the Peasant subcultures. The small-town upper-class "urbanite" manifests in many respects an archaic version of the ideals and patterns of the big-city cosmopolitans and the plantation gentry of bygone days. Although upper-class townspeople are often more familiar with the geography of the nearest large city than with the geography of the rural areas of the community they live in, and although they seek to emulate cosmopolitanism with respect to dress, manners, and outlook, they are often thwarted in these ambitions by the incompleteness and inaccuracy of their notions of the contemporary standards of sophistication. Thus, in most Latin American small towns, culture patterns persist which are today considered "old-fashioned" in the metropolitan cities. Courting, for example, is closely chaperoned, and it is a common sight to see a young man quietly conversing with his fiancée from the street while she looks down at him safely from the window of the house. And in the plaza there is often the *paseo,* during which the young men circulate in one direction as the young ladies go in the other.

Except in regions where there are large plantations owned by a rural gentry, upper-class townsmen control most of the political and economic power in the community. Their political life is intense, and there is great competition for the support of lower-class peasant electors. Upper-class social life frequently revolves around clubs which sponsor dances and other forms of entertainment from which the peasants are excluded. Upper-class Catholicism is more orthodox in Town subcultures than in Modern Indian and Peasant subcultures. More emphasis is placed upon church-going and on formal sacraments as against household saints and unorthodox cults. Where deviations from Catholic tradition occur, they are apt to take the form of Protestantism or spiritualism. Upper-class townsmen have radios, receive mail, magazines, newspapers, and send their children to be educated in big-city high-schools and colleges. They own fashionable clothing and often have servants to cook, wash, carry water, and take care of their house for them.

The existence of Town subcultures in isolated communities furnishes the key to the problem of the relationship of Peasant subcultures to lines of national political and economic integration. Local standards are set and maintained by this sociocultural segment, and it is through the upper class of the town that changes emanating from national legislation and metropolitan influences must filter before reaching the peasant stratum.

Many studies of local variations of Town subcultures have been made in Latin America by anthropologists as part of the study of communities which also include Peasant or even Modern Indian subcultures. But frequently, in such studies, it is difficult to know which data pertain to the Town subculture as distinguished from the subculture of the community's rural population. The town of Cunha in São Paulo, Brazil, and the town of Moche in Peru—as against the rural peasants of both communities—seem to have subcultures of this type. Two community studies recently carried out in Brazil, namely, Monte Serrat in the arid northeast and Minas Velhas in the central mountain region, both distinguish between the Town and Peasant subcultures. In general, however, anthropologists have tended to emphasize the Latin American peasants or Modern Indians. A large portion of the population in countries such as Argentina, Uruguay, Paraguay, Brazil, Chile, and Colombia live in small towns. Not until we know more about the way of life distinctive of these small urban centers will our knowledge of Latin American culture be anything more than relatively superficial. It is not, in our opinion, the so-called *mestizo* or *creole* patterns (i.e., in our terms, Peasant subcultures) which, as Gillin maintains, are the emergent culture patterns of Latin America. Rather, the predominant trend in contemporary Latin America would seem to be toward Town subcultures which are closely identified with the urbanized and industrialized world.

METROPOLITAN UPPER CLASS, METROPOLITAN MIDDLE CLASS, AND URBAN PROLETARIAT TYPES

Little research has been carried out, either by sociologists or by anthropologists, on the modern Latin American city. As far as anthropology is concerned, such cities pose a difficult problem in research methodology, since the traditional field methods are best applied to relatively small populations and relatively homogeneous societies. The problem of class differences in the Latin American urban centers presents one of the most pressing and difficult challenges to students of Latin American culture. There is a critical lack of information about socioeconomic stratification as well as about the basic subcultural differences which attend the various levels. Accordingly in this paper we can do little more than speculate about the subcultures to be found in the great metropolitan centers of Latin America.

It is quite clear to all who have visited Latin America that while the metropolitan centers share much with cities throughout the Western world, they have their own peculiar characteristics. Caplow has pointed out two distinctive features of Latin American cities:

> . . . those traits which are common to metropolitan cultures everywhere in the modern world are most concentrated in groups of high status, whence they are diffused rather raggedly down through the social system of each community; second, that there is more cultural variation within the Latin American city than within most cities of the United States or Europe.[1]

[1] Theodore Caplow, "The modern Latin American city," in *Acculturation in the Americas,* ed. Sol Tax. Proceedings of the XXIX International Congress of Americanists (Chicago: University of Chicago Press, 1952), pp. 255–260.

These two differences between the cities of Latin America and those of the United States and Europe explain why the population of the Latin American city often seems, in a sense, to be smaller than the census data indicate. For the number of people who participate effectively in city life (i.e., buy newspapers, attend the cinema, have electric lights and telephone service, and so forth) is exceedingly small as compared with the actual population. The largest proportion of the population lives, in one sense, outside the stream of city life, differing little in many respects from inhabitants of rural areas; as a matter of fact, a large number of these Latin American city dwellers have but recently migrated from the rural zones.

The people of the metropolitan upper class attempt to maintain, as far as possible, the traditional patterns and ideals of an aristocratic landed gentry. It is this group which participates in and generally dominates local and national politics. Its members are absentee landlords, high-level government employees and officials, owners of industry and large commercial enterprises, and many well-to-do doctors, lawyers, and other professionals. No matter whether such people are the actual descendants of the landed gentry of the nineteenth century or descendants of immigrants or others who have recently achieved wealth and position, they tend to adopt many of the ideal patterns of nineteenth-century agrarian society. There is an emphasis among them upon widely extended kinship ties which is strongly reminiscent of nineteenth-century aristocratic society. They have a disdain for manual labor and admiration for courtly manners, and a love of luxury. But, at the same time, it is this group in Latin America that permits its daughters to have "dates" and allows them to enter the professions, thus breaking the old traditional patterns of highly chaperoned courtship and the confinement of women to purely domestic realms. At least the better educated and the wealthier members of this group are in close touch with Europe and the United States. Until the last two decades, it was France to which they looked for innovations, and French tended to be their second language. Recently, however, the United States has come to supplant France in this respect, and English has become the preferred foreign language. Hence the metropolitan upper class tends both to preserve old traditional forms and to be the innovator, accepting new forms from abroad, diffusing them down to the lower class of the city, outward to the people of the towns, and ultimately to the peasants and to the workers on plantations. To a large extent, therefore, many of the ideal patterns common to the other Latin American subcultures derive from Metropolitan Upper Class patterns.

Studies specifically pertaining to the subculture of the Metropolitan Upper Class have not been carried out by anthropologists except for one by Raymond Scheele, as yet unpublished, which was part of the Puerto Rican Project directed by Steward. To date most of our information comes from data acquired by anthropologists and others during their casual relations with Latin Americans of this group, and from what Latin Americans write about themselves. It is suggested that the ethnographic method should be used in the study of representative local segments of the Latin American upper class. Until this is done, much of what we say about this important segment of Latin American culture will remain entirely hypothetical.

Even less of a concrete nature is known about the Metropolitan Middle Class and Urban Proletariat subcultures. The middle class in the large cities of Latin America is made up of a rapidly increasing group of first-generation professionals and of white-collar workers in business and government. Most observers tend to agree that this middle class maintains standards of material consumption and prestige closely patterned after those of the metropolitan upper class. Its members place a high value on freedom from manual labor and in matters of housing, clothing, and etiquette consciously strive to reduce the gap between themselves and their wealthier models. The presence in the cities of a vast substratum of marginal wage-earners, constantly replenished by rural emigration, permits the metropolitan middle class to employ domestic servants and to avoid the stigma of menial labor. But there is intense competition for white-collar positions, and salaries are often insufficient to maintain leisure-class standards in other respects. One result noted by many observers has been the multiplication of the number of jobs held by each middle-class wage earner. Some high-school teachers in Rio de Janeiro, for example, teach in as many as five or six different schools and have to rush from one place to the next with split-second precision in order to arrive at their classes on time. Caught between low incomes and high standards of consumption modeled after those of the upper class, the middle class is forced to devote a large part of its income to items of high display value such as fashionable apartments, stylish clothing, and greatly overpriced automobiles. Thus, in contrast to the middle classes of other world areas, the Latin American metropolitan middle class appears not to have developed an emphasis on savings nor as yet to have a distinctive "middle class ideology."

Although the urban proletariat is numerically the dominant segment of the metropolitan centers, it is the least well known of all. The phenomenal growth of Latin American urban centers in the last generation, mainly as a result of migration from rural zones, indicates that a large percentage of the urban proletariat may actually be carriers of Peasant, Plantation, or Town subcultures. A recent study by Lewis of migrants from Tepoztlán to Mexico City indicates that their ideological culture remains basically unchanged despite the urban setting. Only empirical research will answer the question whether there is a type of Latin American subculture distinctive of the urban proletariat and different from the subcultures of small towns and rural areas.

Whether or not the present typology of subcultures will be of any value in controlling variations and differences in the complexity of Latin American culture, and whether it will provide a useful frame of reference for research, depends on its operational utility in concrete situations. Its final usefulness over such a large area as Latin America as a whole will, of course, depend upon considerably more research and upon whether or not the available data can be ordered meaningfully within this framework. But an illustration of the use of this typology in a specific research project may indicate its possible value in the study of complex modern cultures. The research in question was carried out in the State of Bahia in Brazil in 1950–51 and comprised the study of three communities, each in a different ecological zone of the state. The communities studied were: Vila Recôncavo, in the sugar-planting area near the coast; Minas Velhas, an old mining center in the central mountain zone; and Monte Serrat, a community in the arid semidesert of the northeast. An analysis of the subcultures present in these communities and in the State of Bahia seemed to be most meaningful in describing this sociocultural diversity.

Not all subculture types outlined in this paper will, of course, be present in any particular area of Latin America. In the State of Bahia, the indigenous population was quickly exterminated or assimilated. Thus, the subculture types called Tribal Indian and Modern Indian are not present. But throughout the state there are numerous rural agriculturalists, many of whom are descendants of Indians, whose subculture is of the type identified above as Peasant. Throughout the state there are also small towns which are essentially trading and administrative centers with Town subcultures. The coast of Bahia, especially around the Bay of Todos os Santos, where it is known as the Recôncavo, was one of the earliest sites of sugar plantations in Latin America. Here are found both the old-style *engenho*-type and the new *usina*-type sugar plantations. And finally, in the city of Salvador, the capital and largest metropolitan center of the state, there is a culturally conservative urban upper class preserving many old Brazilian traditions, as well as a large metropolitan proletariat.

Each of the communities in which field research was carried out contains at least two subcultures. The old mining town of Minas Velhas is a trading, manufacturing, and administrative center for a larger community encompassing a number of satellite villages inhabited by simple peasant farmers. Monte Serrat contains these same two subcultures: a religious, administrative, and trading town which is visited periodically by the surrounding scattered peasant population. The third community, Vila Recôncavo, contains a town which is inhabited by traders, government employees, a group of fishermen, a few artisans, manual laborers, and a variety of marginal wage-earners. It also contains in the rural zone a series of *engenho*-type plantations, a small *usina* which still administers its various plantations as separate units (in transition between the *engenho*-type and *usina*-type plantations), and a number of metropolitan upper-class families, owners of plantations and of the *usina*, who participate in community life. The other Metropolitan subcultures (Middle Class and Urban Proletariat) are found in the city of Salvador but were not studied by this research project. Thus, of the major subculture types found within the State of Bahia, four are represented in the communities of research.

Despite differences deriving from the degree of isolation, from different environments and different local historical circumstances, there are many crucial similarities in the Town subcultures of Monte Serrat, Minas Velhas, and Vila Recôncavo, on the one hand, and in the Peasant subcultures of these same communities, on the other hand. Likewise, there are crucial differences between the Peasant and Town subcultures of each community as well as between these subcultures and the Plantation and Metropolitan upper-class subcultures of Vila Recôncavo. The broad sociocultural differences between subcultures of different type in the Bahia area conform to the criteria upon which this taxonomy of Latin American subcultures had been based and have therefore been described above. But a specific illustration may help to clarify how such a typology can be used to explore additional categories of patterned behavior.

During the period of field work general elections were held throughout Brazil. There was considerable regularity in the communities being studied in regard to political behavior during the campaigns and during the election.

PEASANT SUBCULTURES There was little or no interest in the elections among the peasant segment of population in both Minas Velhas and Monte Serrat. On election day in Monte Serrat, political parties sent trucks out to the rural zones to bring peasants to town to vote. The day was treated as an outing by peasants who came to town with their families dressed in their best clothes. They were served free meals by the political party which claimed their vote and whose truck had transported them to town. They voted according to the dictates of an influential townsman, motivated by personal loyalty and economic bonds (i.e., debts) rather than by strong political feelings or beliefs. Similar behavior was reported also for the peasants in Minas Velhas as well as for other communities with Peasant type subcultures in which more casual observations were made during the political campaign and the elections.

TOWN SUBCULTURES   The political campaign in both Minas Velhas and Monte Serrat (communities with Peasant and Town subcultures) was intense among the townspeople, yet their interest was focused upon local and state rather than national issues. In both Minas Velhas and Monte Serrat, the townspeople were split by allegiances to opposing political parties. In Monte Serrat each of the principal bars was frequented by men belonging to but one political party and anyone known to have any sympathy for the opposing party would not dare enter the bar of the other. Two public address systems blared forth each day competing with each other in sheer volume and in political promises and accusations. Practically all conversation revolved around the coming elections. In both Minas Velhas and Monte Serrat almost everyone had something at stake; municipal, state and federal employees were anxious for their jobs, and commercial men and artisans stood to gain favors from being on the winning side. Even the parish priests were intensely active in the campaign and their sermons were not free of political propaganda. During the campaign, normal social life (i.e., visiting among families, dances, and the like) was almost entirely suspended. Election day was a tense and active occasion for the townspeople, most of whom were busy attempting to influence the peasant voter until he actually walked into the polls. Short visits during this period to other Bahian communities made it clear that this intense political activity was typical of Town subculture political behavior.

In the third community which contained a Town subculture, namely Vila Recôncavo, the political behavior of the town dwellers was deviant from that described above as typical for Town subcultures. In Vila Recôncavo, the political scene was dominated by metropolitan upper-class families. The local candidate for mayor was a member of one of these families rather than of the town upper class as in the two communities described above. Because of the powerful personal and economic hold which this landed gentry exerted on local affairs, the townspeople were not able to organize an effective opposition and the candidate ran virtually unopposed. The townspeople (i.e., commercial men, bureaucrats, artisans, etc.) put on a weak imitation of the political campaign which took place in Minas Velhas and Monte Serrat, but it was a foregone conclusion that the party of the metropolitan upper class (i.e., landed gentry) would win. Thus, in regions or areas, such as the Recôncavo of Bahia State, where the town is overshadowed by the surrounding plantations and the communities dominated by a landed gentry, the criteria of intense political activity for Town type subcultures will be regularly absent.

ENGENHO PLANTATION SUBCULTURES   As stated above, the community of Vila Recôncavo contained family-owned, *engenho*-type sugar plantations. During the political campaigns of 1950 little was heard about politics from the workers on these plantations. When the question was asked as to how they might vote, they were apt to answer, "I don't know, I haven't found out how the *patrão* will vote," or, "With the *patrão*, Senhor." For them, election day was a day without work when those who were literate (i.e., able to sign their names) went to town to vote as did the plantation owners. Such behavior seemed to be typical of workers on Engenho plantations throughout the State of Bahia.

USINA PLANTATION SUBCULTURES   Although as stated above there was not a large Usina plantation in any of the communities studied intensively in the Bahia area, we were able to observe political behavior in nearby highly industrialized sugar plantations. Simply from the messages painted on walls in red and black paint at night urging the election of one candidate or another (especially of left-wing groups) and from the numerous political posters, it was obvious that political activity was intense among the Usina workers. Far from voting with the administrators, these workers on large industrialized plantations supported the opposing political party. Labor unions exerted considerable influence and in general the workers were much interested in politics. Furthermore, since much of their political education came from national organizations such as labor unions and Vargas' Brazilian Labor Party (Partido Trabalhista Brasileiro), their interest focused more on national elections than local and state elections.

METROPOLITAN UPPER CLASS SUBCULTURE   Representatives of the upper class were present in only one of the communities studied, Vila Recôncavo. For this group, political activity on a high level is characteristic and traditional. Most individuals in this class had friends or relatives to whom success or failure at the polls was of the utmost importance. Cousins of important families in Vila Recôncavo were candidates for federal deputy, while one of the candidates for governor was a life-long friend of most of the members of the same families. In Salvador large, united families from this group were pitted against each other for political control of the state and city. But, as stated above, in Vila Recôncavo, since the metropolitan upper-class families have intermarried, they presented in a sense a united front. Thus, the outcome of the election in Vila Recôncavo was easily predicted.

METROPOLITAN MIDDLE CLASS AND URBAN PROLETARIAT SUBCULTURES
Little can be said regarding the political behavior of these groups during the 1950 campaigns and elections. It was obvious that political reactions of both groups were emotional and intense but large-scale quantitative techniques would be necessary to study the political behavior of this large mass of people.

A great number of subcultural differences and similarities which are valid for the area studied might also be pointed out. Material culture, technology concepts of the cause and cure of disease, work patterns, occupational specialization, settlement patterns, housing, etiquette, speech habits, social ranking, and many other items are variable within the communities but constant within the subcultures of the area. Even the use made of tobacco is regular according to subculture type rather than community: peasant women smoke pipes, town women do not smoke, while metropolitan upper-class women smoke cigarettes. Thus a typology of subcultures is an indispensable tool for relating the community to its larger sociocultural context. Such a typology not only lends order to research materials and directs attention to the need for additional comparative data, but it also provides a basis for predicting with reasonable accuracy the reactions of certain segments of the population to new social stimuli. It is therefore of utility for both theoretical and applied purposes.

Through a comparison of four Yucatán communities—Tusik, a "tribal" village of Quintana Roo; Chan Kom, a "peasant" community; Dzitas, a town on the railroad; and the city of Merida—Redfield concluded in his *The Folk Culture of Yucatán:*

> . . . the peasant village as compared with the tribal village, the town as compared with the peasant village, or the city as compared with the town is less isolated, is more heterogeneous; is characterized by a more complex division of labor; has a more completely developed money economy; has professional specialists who are more secular and less sacred; has kinship and godparental institutions that are less well organized and less effective in social control; is correspondingly more dependent on impersonally acting institutions of control, is less religious, with respect to both beliefs and practices of Catholic origin as well as those of Indian origin; exhibits less tendency to regard sickness as resulting from a breach of

moral or merely customary rule; allows a greater freedom of action and choice to the individual; and . . . shows a greater emphasis upon black magic as an ascribed cause of sickness.

Except as these differences relate to the regional culture of Yucatán they are also implied in the present taxonomy of subcultures, and it should be noted that six of the subculture types discussed above are carried by the local societies or by segments of the societies studied by Redfield in Yucatán. Thus, Merida would presumably contain subcultures of all three Metropolitan types. Dzitas seems to have both a Town and a Peasant type of subculture. Chan Kom, in our terms, would be a community with a Peasant subculture and Dzitas would be representative of our Modern Indian subculture. Although neglected by Redfield, Plantation subculture types are also present in the henequen-producing areas of Yucatán. Tribal Indian subcultures, as defined above, are no longer present in the peninsula. Thus the present classification is clearly related to Redfield's folk-urban gradient. A fundamental difference exists, however. If the present taxonomy were to be used as the basis of a study of the urban-folk continuum in Latin America, the lines in the gradient would have to consist not of whole communities but of segments of whole communities. In this way one of the most serious defects in the use of the "folk culture" concept can be circumvented, for, as Lewis has shown for Tepoztlán, the homogeneity of a rural community with respect to its folk characteristics is easily overemphasized when it is the whole local society which is the subject of characterization.

Redfield was primarily interested in culture change, especially the effects of modern urbanization upon "folk culture" and the resulting "disorganization of the culture, secularization, and individualization," to use his well-known terms. The primary purpose of the present taxonomy is not to analyze the direction and effects of culture change but to establish categories which may help to orient many additional problems. Many of the subculture types we have been describing are more or less stable features of the Latin American scene. Although individual settlements or large segments of their populations may change rapidly from carriers of one subculture type to another (e.g., "Indians" become "mestizos") and while new subculture types have appeared, most of these subculture types have been part of the cultural scene of Latin America since the sixteenth century. They have changed in culture content and in their relative importance to the wider cultural scene, but they have constantly maintained their distinctiveness as variations of Latin American culture and their essential relationship to one another.

Soon after 1500, when the distinctive culture of Latin America began to take form, at least Modern Indian, Peasant, Town, *Engenho* Plantation, and Metropolitan Upper Class types were already present in the New World. The European conquerors brought with them a strong tradition of urbanism. In their European homelands there were cities, towns, and peasant villages. Large agrarian estates, similar in some ways to the New World plantations, were also present. Furthermore, as is well known, the native civilizations of America also had their cities, their market centers, and their villages and hamlets. The Europeans transplanted to the New World a culture which was already characterized by a number of subcultures analogous to those described for modern Latin America, but in the New World they were modified in content and in the form of interaction between them.

The Spanish and Portuguese (also the other nationals who controlled more limited areas of Latin America) who were given land grants, *encomiendas,* or other economic rights in the New World soon established a colonial aristocracy with its traditions derived from the feudal aristocratic patterns of their homeland. In the region of native American civilization, these colonial aristocrats supplanted the native ruling class, and in lowland Latin America they came to dominate the segmented tribal groups and became the owners of African slaves. Although only small numbers of European peasants came to the New World to work the land as they had done in Europe, a few did come, transposing their way of life almost intact. Before long, however, a distinctive Latin American Peasant subculture took form as the various tribal groups of the lowland region came under the influence of missionaries and colonial governments, lost their identity as autochthonous peoples and borrowed or had forced upon them European culture patterns. Under the impact of Spanish rule, the Indians of the highland regions acquired numerous Spanish culture patterns which fused with aboriginal patterns to form the subculture type called herein Modern Indian. The content of each of these subculture types differed, of course, from that of today, but those of 1600 were the historical antecedents of the contemporary types.

The transition of populations from one subculture type to another still goes on. The Tenetehara, a Tupí-speaking tribe of northern Brazil, for example, still have a culture which is essentially aboriginal and distinct from the culture of the Brazilian nation within the borders of which they happen to live. But the Tenetehara are slowly adopting Brazilian culture patterns; they are being brought into the orbit of the Brazilian commercial system through the sale of palm nuts and the increasing necessity to purchase imported and manufactured supplies. The Tenetehara might now be classed as a Modern Indian subculture and, as the process of acculturation continues, they will lose their identity as "distinct people" and their culture will be transformed into that of a Peasant subculture of modern Brazil. Likewise, in Ecuador, Guatemala, Mexico, Peru, and other countries where there are large numbers of people living by Modern Indian subculture patterns, there is a noted trend for such Indians to adopt Peasant patterns (i.e., *mestizo, ladino,* or *cholo* patterns) and to lose their identity as Indians. In many localities of Latin America both Indians and peasants are still being drawn upon as plantation workers, especially as communal forms of land tenure break down and as commercial agricultural enterprises expand their holdings. In other localties, many isolated areas inhabited by peasants are being connected with national markets by roads and other means of communications, and towns are taking form where a small local marketplace once existed. Under similar impulses, small towns are growing in size and in complexity to become veritable cities. And, as noted earlier, there is a continuing trend for family-owned *engenho*-type plantations to be welded into large industrialized *usina*-type plantations.

All Latin American subcultures are certainly changing under urban and industrial influences, and yet the differences between some of them may remain great for many years to come. The content of Peasant and Metropolitan subcultures in Europe has in both cases changed profoundly during the last five hundred years, but the differences between city folk and peasants in almost any European nation are still striking. In the future, certain subcultures may diminish in importance or entirely disappear as the people who carry them adopt other culture patterns. Tribal Indian subculture types will probably disappear well within the next hundred years, and *Engenho* Plantation types are becoming extinct with at least equal rapidity. Modern Indian types, on the other hand, especially where enlightened policies of government assistance prevail, are likely to endure for much longer. Barring wide political upheaval, Peasant, Town, *Usina* Plantation, and Metropolitan Upper Class subculture types also appear to have long futures ahead of them, while the Metropolitan Middle Class and Urban Proletariat types are just now beginning to emerge.

The changes in content which all these subculture types are undergoing are adequately embraced by the folk-urban transition suggested by Redfield. But any such picture of progressive urbanization must take into account the possibility that as the subculture types change toward greater urbanization, most of them do not merge in content, but remain as distinctly defined as ever within the national context. This is true because throughout all the stages of the urbanization of a nation, the city subcultures are not static but rather continue to be the innovators of most of the new features. Furthermore, although the rural-urban concept provides us with excellent hypotheses for the general direction of diffusion of new cultural items on a national scale, it does not prepare us for the problem of fundamental structural changes such as the emergence of new subcultures or the realignment of power. To describe the structure of a complex nation and the changes it is undergoing we need a taxonomy of parts such as that which has been tentatively developed in this paper. The emergence of new and the extinction of old sociocultural segments is an aspect of cultural change which the student of complex national cultures cannot afford to neglect.

The Educational Situation and Requirements in Latin America*   OSCAR VERA

INTRODUCTION

This paper proposes discussing the more important quantitative and qualitative aspects of the educational situation in the countries of Latin America to help promote a clearer understanding of the way in which it is linked with their social and economic development. . . . The great diversity of conditions existing, not only among the 20 countries, but also within each of them, is obvious to all those familiar with Latin American problems in any field. Nevertheless, it will not be amiss to stress again the limitations inherent in any generalization applied to the region as a whole—and the classification of the Latin American countries into three groups according to their educational situation adopted in this paper should be regarded in the light of this observation.

In spite of the persistent efforts of international organizations to encourage and improve the collection of statistical information, up-to-date, complete, reliable and comparable data on education in the different countries, particularly in the field of technical and higher education,

* Oscar Vera, "The Educational Situation and Requirements in Latin America," in Egbert de Vries and José Medina Echavarría (eds.), *Social Aspects of Economic Development in Latin America* (Paris: UNESCO, 1963), pp. 279–307. Abridged by permission.

and of finance and costs of education, are, for the most part, very limited, and make the problem of assessment more difficult.

The first part of this paper deals with illiteracy and access to the different levels within the educational systems in Latin America. It is largely concerned with the quantitative aspects of the educational situation, aspects which are changing rapidly as a result of the efforts being made by nearly all the countries in the region to extend their educational facilities.

It then studies briefly certain important qualitative aspects, common, in general, to all the countries, on the basis of official publications and first-hand knowledge of the national educational systems and their problems. It is difficult to assess objectively progress made in these qualitative aspects, but it is certainly not outstanding; indeed, in certain cases, some of the conditions which largely determine the quality of education appear to have deteriorated during the last few years.

Finally, the most important conclusions arising from the study are summarized to provide a tentative basis for the discussion of existing educational needs in Latin America and of the measures required to meet these needs in view of the prospects of its social and economic development.

ACCESS TO EDUCATION IN LATIN AMERICA

Legislation in the Latin American countries invariably emphasizes the universal right to education without discrimination, and establishes the responsibility of the State to provide primary education, which is free and compulsory, between the ages of 6–7 and 12–15 years of age. Public secondary, technical and higher education is also practically free, and students belonging to low-income families are usually exempted from the payment of the generally small enrolment fees levied. However, the extent to which people avail themselves of the educational opportunities provided, at least in principle, by legislation, including compulsory attendance at primary school, varies very considerably from country to country and in some is extremely limited. Indeed, according to available figures it can be stated that in 1950 approximately 49 per cent of the population of 15 years of age and over in Latin America had either not attended school or had left school before completing the first grade; 44 per cent had received some primary education, but only about 8 per cent had completed the period of compulsory primary school attendance; 6 per cent had received some secondary or technical education but no more than 2 per cent had completed or nearly completed it; and only 1 per cent had begun or completed any form of higher education.

Illiteracy

Before studying the characteristics of access to the different levels of education in Latin America, it may help to examine the relationship between the number of illiterates—that is to say, those who presumably had no access to formal education—and other indices relating to economic and social conditions, such as *per capita* income, and the proportions of rural population and population of 15 years of age and over. This will help to see the educational situation in Latin America within its social and economic framework and, above all, to appreciate the marked way in which it differs from one country to another. Table 1, in which the Latin American countries are listed in order of prevalence of illiteracy according to information available in 1950, has been prepared for this purpose.

Of course, merely to give the degree of illiteracy, or of literacy, is not sufficient an indication of the educational level in a given country or region; it must be accompanied by other information of the kind given later in this paper. On the other hand, the definitions of literacy such as the ability to read and write, or just to read, used in national censuses of population (which, with all their limitations, represent virtually the only source of data available to calculate educational levels) are not only vague and inconsistent, but are inconsistently applied. If the criterion for functional literacy (the ability to read and write at the level equivalent to fourth grade primary school) had been unerringly applied, there is not the slightest doubt that the educational situation in this respect would be more serious than that indicated in Table 1. Probably no more than 30 per cent, rather than 58 per cent, of the population of 15 years of age and over (which in 1950 amounted to 93,000,000) would have qualified as literate, and thus the total number of adults who could be termed functionally illiterate in that year was not 40,000,000 but 65,000,000.

Table 1 shows a close correlation between literacy, *per capita* income and the proportion of urban population, as well as between illiteracy and the proportion of population of 15 years of age and over, with two notable exceptions: Costa Rica, with a *per capita* income and a demographic structure corresponding to its high proportion of rural population, has a relatively low percentage of illiteracy, and Venezuela, with the highest *per capita* income in the region and a relatively low

proportion of rural population, has a relatively high percentage of illiteracy. In the case of Costa Rica, the concentration of more than half
its population in less than 8 per cent of the total area of the country
(the 'intermountain' valley with an average of 142 inhabitants per square
kilometre as compared with less than 10 in the rest of the country),
the great importance which the Costa Ricans attach to education, and
the fact that the country does not have to bear the cost of maintaining
a large regular army, no doubt help to explain this situation. However,
a study of the development of education in relation to social and economic development in Costa Rica would be of great interest and might
help to show to what extent these and other factors have counteracted
the influence of the high proportion of rural population and the relatively
low *per capita* income, and to explain the educational progress made
in this small country. As for Venezuela, the nature of the main source
of its national income and the way this is distributed among the different
social strata, are probably important reasons for the relative backwardness
of its educational situation in 1950, and also suggest the need for detailed
historical studies and investigations into social structure.

The case of Costa Rica, moreover, confirms that a high proportion
of rural population is not necessarily accompanied by a high percentage
of illiteracy. According to Table 1 illiteracy in countries with 60–70
per cent rural population and a *per capita* income of less than $150
may vary from 20 per cent to 68 per cent, which shows clearly that
other factors in addition to a large rural population and a low national
per capita income exert an influence upon the educational level of Latin
American countries. . . .

Level of education

A clearer indication of the level of education in a country or region
than that given by the index of illiteracy, is the distribution of the
adult population according to the number of years spent in school. Table
2 gives relevant figures as in 1950 for the population of 15 years of
age and over in 16 Latin American countries, representing 80 per cent
of the total population of the region, as well as similar figures for Puerto
Rico, the U.S.A. and Japan.

While the average educational level of the population of 15 years
of age and over in 1950 was 9 school years in the U.S.A., 7.2 school
years in Japan and 4.5 school years, in Puerto Rico, it only reached
2.2 school years in the 16 Latin American countries taken as a whole,
ranging between 3.6 school years in countries belonging to the first
group (see Table 1) and 1 school year in countries belonging to the
third group, the level being just under 2 school years in countries belong-

TABLE 1. POPULATION, ILLITERACY AND *PER CAPITA* INCOME: LATIN AMERICA, 1950

| COUNTRY | POPULATION | | ILLITER-ATES 15 YEARS AND OVER | PER CAPITA INCOME | RURAL POPULATION |
	TOTAL	15 YEARS AND OVER			
	(000)	%	%	U.S.$	%
Argentina	17 189	69	[1]13.6	300–449	37.5
Uruguay	2 407	69	*15.0	300–449	
Chile	6 073	61	19.9	150–299	40.1
Costa Rica	801	57	20.6	100–149	66.5
Cuba	5 508	64	22.1	300–449	43.0
(5 countries with 20% of total pop.)	(*31 978*)	(*66*)	(*16.6*)	(*300–449*)	(*40.0*)
Panama	797	58	30.1	150–299	64.0
Paraguay	1 397	56	34.2	100	65.4
Colombia	11 334	57	37.6	100–149	63.7
Mexico	25 826	58	*38.0	100–149	57.4
Ecuador	3 197	57	44.3	100	71.5
Venezuela	4 974	58	47.8	300–449	46.2
Brazil	51 976	58	50.6	100–149	63.8
Peru	8 521	56	*53.0	100–149	64.6
(8 countries with 70% of total pop.)	(*108 022*)	(*58*)	*(*45.7*)	(*100–149*)	(*62.0*)
Dominican Republic	2 131	56	57.1	100	76.2
El Salvador	1 868	59	60.6	100–149	63.5
Nicaragua	1 060	57	61.6	100–149	65.1
Honduras	1 428	59	64.8	100	71.0
Bolivia	3 019	60	67.9	100	66.4
Guatemala	2 805	57	70.6	100	75.0
Haiti	3 112	61	89.5	100	87.8
(7 countries with 10% of total pop.)	(*15 423*)	(*59*)	(*69.9*)	(*100*)	(*74.0*)
GRAND TOTAL	155 423	60	*43.0	100–149	58.4

[1] Population of 14 years of age and over.
* Estimated.
Sources: United Nations, *Demographic Yearbook*, 1955, 1956, 1957, 1958; and *Informe preliminar sobre la situación social en el mundo*, New York, 1952. Unesco, *World Illiteracy at Mid-century*, Paris, 1957.

ing to the second group. For the adult population who had had an opportunity of attending school (51 per cent of the total), the average educational level was 4.4 school years, very few differences existing between the three groups—about 4.4 school years for the first and second groups and 3.8 school years for the third group.

A careful comparison of the way in which the population of the Latin American countries is distributed among the different educational levels confirms, as far as educational issues are concerned, the relationships suggested in Table 1. Note, for example, that in the U.S.A. and Japan a very large proportion of the population having attended school have spent between 10 and 12 and between 7 and 9 years in school—that is to say, have completed the second and first cycles respectively of secondary schooling, an essential prerequisite for the preparation in sufficient numbers of the technicians and skilled workmen necessary to achieve an advanced state of industrial development.

In Latin America, on the other hand, the longest period of time spent in school by a sizeable proportion of the population is 4–6 years (second cycles of primary schooling) and that in four countries only: Argentine, Cuba, Chile and Panama. In all the remaining countries the educational level of the main body of the population having attended school does not go beyond the first three grades of primary education. The proportion of those who have had the opportunity of pursuing their education beyond the primary school stage, being 81 per cent of the population in the U.S.A. and 58 per cent in Japan, scarcely goes beyond 7 per cent of the population of the Latin American countries taken as a whole, and varies between 11 per cent of the population of the countries belonging to the first group and 3 per cent in those belonging to the third group—the proportion in the case of those countries belonging to the second group being little more than 6 per cent.

If, on the basis of the information contained in Table 2, the number of people who have received post-primary education for every 100 of those who have received primary education only is calculated, the number reaches 513 in the case of the U.S.A., and 161 in the case of Japan, and only 16 in the case of Latin America, with only slight differences existing between the averages for the three groups of countries, but with considerable variations between the individual countries—a situation which would be extremely interesting to analyse in the light of the peculiar social and economic circumstances which obtain in each case.

It is worth noticing that even in the most developed countries of Latin America the average educational level of the total population does not go beyond the fourth primary school grade and that in very few does it go slightly beyond the fifth grade for those having attended school. Among these is the apparently paradoxical case of Haiti which, with an educational level which does not reach half of the first grade for the population taken as a whole, has, nevertheless, a level of slightly more than five primary school grades in the case of the selected 10

TABLE 2. DISTRIBUTION OF POPULATION, 15 YEARS AND OVER, BY EDUCATIONAL LEVEL: LATIN AMERICA, U.S.A., JAPAN, PUERTO RICO, 1950

COUNTRY	PERCENTAGE OF SCHOOL YEARS COMPLETED							AVERAGE EDUC. LEVEL POP. WITH SCHOOLING		POP. WITH POST-PRIMARY EDUC. PER 100 POP. WITH PRIMARY EDUC.
	TOTAL	NONE OR LESS THAN ONE	1–3	4–6	7–9	10–12	13 AND OVER	TOTAL	ING	(Number)
								(School years)		
Argentina[1]	100.0	15.1	23.2	53.1	3.7	3.8	1.2	3.9	4.6	11.4
Chile	100.0	21.1	56.9		20.1		2.2	4.2	5.3	39.2
Costa Rica	100.0	19.4	41.2	31.2	4.2	2.4	1.6	3.2	4.0	11.0
Cuba	100.0	23.9	28.1	42.0	2.4	2.2	1.4	3.3	4.3	9.0
(4 countries)	*100.0*	*18.4*	*70.7*		*9.5*		*1.5*	*3.6*	*4.4*	*15.6*
Panama	100.0	32.2	20.4	32.4	8.4	5.2	1.4	3.5	5.1	28.4
Paraguay	100.0	33.5	42.9	16.8	6.1		0.7	2.4	3.6	11.4
Colombia	100.0	42.0	30.4	18.2	4.8	3.9	0.7	2.4	4.2	19.3
Mexico[2]	100.0	46.0	48.4		2.9	1.6	1.1	2.3	4.2	11.6
Ecuador[2]	[3]100.0	46.0	24.1	23.2	3.7	2.2	0.8	2.3	4.3	14.2
Brazil	100.0	62.7	16.0	15.7	1.7	3.1	0.7	1.7	4.5	17.4
(6 countries)	*100.0*	*55.4*	*38.4*		*5.4*		*0.8*	*2.0*	*4.4*	*16.1*
Dominican Republic[4]	100.0	68.9	20.5	9.2	0.8	0.3	0.3	1.0	3.2	4.7
El Salvador	100.0	64.2	21.9	10.3	3.3		0.4	1.3	3.7	11.5
Nicaragua	100.0	64.0	20.1	12.8	1.7	0.9	0.5	1.4	3.8	9.4
Bolivia[5]	100.0	72.2	14.5	8.6	2.6	1.5	0.6	1.2	4.3	20.3
Guatemala	100.0	70.6	17.6	9.0	1.6	0.9	0.4	1.1	3.7	10.9
Haiti	100.0	89.6	3.7	4.1	1.5	1.0	0.2	0.5	5.1	34.6
(6 countries)	*100.0*	*73.3*	*15.4*	*8.3*	*2.7*		*0.4*	*1.0*	*3.8*	*13.1*
Total 16 countries	*100.0*	*49.3*	*43.8*		*6.0*		*0.9*	*2.2*	*4.4*	*15.8*
U.S.A.	100.0	3.0	16.0		33.0	35.0	13.0	9.0	9.3	512.6
Japan	100.0	7.0	4.0	32.0	36.0	16.0	6.0	7.2	7.8	161.0
Puerto Rico	100.0	26.7	19.6	41.8		7.8	3.2	4.5	6.1	48.0

[1] 20 and over. [2] 25 and over. [3] Includes persons with educational level not stated. [4] Total population. [5] 5 and over.

Source: United Nations, *Demographic Yearbook 1956.*

TABLE 3. POPULATION AND ENROLMENT IN PRIMARY, SECONDARY AND UNIVERSITY EDUCATION: LATIN AMERICA, 1956

COUNTRY	POPULATION			NUMBERS ENROLLED					
		5 TO 14		PRIMARY		SECONDARY		UNIVERSITY	
	TOTAL	NUMBER	PER CENT	NUMBER	POP. 5–14	NUMBER	POP. 5–14	NUMBER	PER 10,000 INHAB.
	(000)	(000)		(000)	%	(000)	%	(000)	
Argentina	19 493	3 820	19.6	2 623	68.6	777	20.3	145.5	74.6
Uruguay	2 650	504	19.0	296	58.7	64	12.7	*12.0	*45.3
Chile	6 944	1 667	24.0	1 026	61.5	*167	*10.0	*26.0	*37.4
Costa Rica	988	260	26.3	155	59.6	26	10.0	2.2	22.3
Cuba	6 261	1 484	23.7	787	53.0	69	4.6	22.4	35.8
(5 countries—20%)	36 336	7 735	21.3	4 887	63.2	1 103	14.3	208.1	57.3
Panama	940	239	25.4	141	59.0	30	12.6	2.6	27.6
Paraguay	1 601	439	27.4	275	62.6	*19	*4.3	3.5	21.9
Mexico	30 538	8 062	26.4	4 106	50.9	270	3.3	66.2	*21.7
Ecuador	3 800	980	25.8	490	50.0	48	4.9	6.1	16.1
Colombia	12 939	3 351	25.9	1 312	39.2	155	4.6	14.3	11.0
Venezuela	5 953	1 494	25.1	647	43.3	52	3.5	8.8	14.8
Brazil	59 846	15 380	25.7	6 094	39.6	830	5.4	78.7	13.1
Peru	9 651	2 567	26.6	1 154	45.0	133	5.2	17.0	17.6
(8 countries—70%)	125 268	32 512	26.0	14 265	43.9	1 535	4.7	197.2	15.7
Dominican Republic	2 608	702	26.9	422	60.0	20	2.8	3.2	12.3
El Salvador	2 268	581	25.6	236	40.6	23	4.0	1.5	7.3
Nicaragua	1 288	352	27.3	128	36.3	*10	*2.8	1.1	8.5
Honduras	1 712	430	25.1	136	31.6	10	2.3	1.1	6.4
Bolivia	3 235	773	23.9	307	39.7	41	5.3	4.5	13.9
Guatemala	3 347	857	25.6	229	26.7	20	2.2	3.4	10.2
Haiti	3 344	866	25.9	214	24.7	15	1.7	0.8	2.4
(7 countries—10%)	17 802	4 561	25.6	1 672	36.6	134	2.9	15.6	8.8
TOTAL	179 406	44 808	25.0	20 824	46.5	2 772	6.2	420.9	23.5

1 Universidad Nacional Autónoma, Mexico, and 29 polythechnic schools of the Instituto Politécnico Nacional.   * Estimated.
Sources: United Nations, *Demographic Yearbook 1958.* Unesco, *Basic Facts and Figures, 1958,* Paris, 1959. Official national sources.

per cent of its population that attended school—a situation which corresponds to the characteristics of the social structure of this country. The case of Haiti, as well as the fact that in no country does the average educational level of the population having attended school fall below three grades, suggests that the Latin American educational systems, if the results of their efforts to provide educational facilities for all are not considered, have operated with a certain degree of efficiency. . . .

Private school education

From the educational point of view, the proportion of pupils enrolled in private primary and secondary schools reflects in the main the social structure of the Latin American countries. In general, pupils attending private primary schools belong to families with sufficient means to meet the cost of an education which, for a variety of reasons, they prefer for their children to that offered in the public primary schools. Such pupils generally go on to secondary education, also in private schools, which, in many countries . . . cater for a considerable proportion of the total number of pupils following this type of education.

It must be pointed out that the great majority of private secondary educational establishments offer an academic type of secondary education in preparation for university studies and that only very few of them offer a technical or vocational education.

Premature school leaving

Premature school leaving is rife in Latin America and is one of the reasons underlying the average low educational level of the population already indicated. Table 4 illustrates this from the point of view of the proportion of pupils who complete their primary or secondary school course, in the case of a few countries for which relevant data corresponding to different periods are available.

It can be seen from this table that in most of the countries the number of pupils completing primary or secondary school studies increases as time goes on. Nevertheless, the highest rate of increase at the primary school level registered in Chile during the period 1951–56 shows that scarcely 25 per cent of the pupils reached the sixth grade in 1951; three-quarters of those who began the course in 1946 left school before completing it. The figures for Colombia show a considerable difference between the proportion of pupils staying on in urban schools, more than 30 per cent, and the proportion of those staying on in rural schools, less than 1 per cent.

TABLE 4. PERCENTAGE OF PUPILS COMPLETING PRIMARY AND SECOND-
ARY SCHOOL COURSES IN CERTAIN LATIN AMERICAN COUNTRIES

COUNTRY	LENGTH OF COURSE YEARS	PERIOD	PERCENTAGE OF PUPILS COMPLETING COURSE
Primary education			
Brazil	4	1946–49	17.0
		1956–59	18.7
Colombia	5	1954–58	14.2
(Urban)			(32.4)
(Rural)			(0.5)
Costa Rica	6	1946–51	18.1
		1950–55	22.2
Chile	6	1946–51	19.6
		1951–56	24.8
Peru	6	1945–50	19.8
		1950–55	18.4
Venezuela	6	1949/50–1954/55	15.3
		1953/54–1958/59	22.7
Secondary education			
Costa Rica	5	1952–56	56.2
Chile	6	1945–50	22.6
		1951–56	26.6
Peru	5	1951–55	27.6
Venezuela	5	1949/50–1953/54	26.6
		1954/55–1958/59	30.1

At the secondary level, among the countries studied, Costa Rica stands out with 56.2 per cent of its pupils staying on to complete the school course. It is worth noting, however, that in this country, between 1952 and 1956, only 52 per cent of the pupils enrolled in the sixth grade of the primary school in the preceding year began the secondary school course, while the corresponding percentage rose to 91 per cent and 98 per cent in Chile between 1950 and 1951 and between 1955 and 1956 respectively and to 76 per cent in Peru between 1950 and 1951. . . .

CHIEF PROBLEMS
IN LATIN AMERICAN EDUCATION

It is now proposed to examine briefly, within the limits laid down for this paper, the more important qualitative aspects of education in Latin America and the main problems that this has to face.

School systems

In all the Latin American countries a clear distinction is made between the primary school, which generally lasts for six years, with four years in Brazil, five years in Colombia and seven years in the Argentine, and secondary education or *bachillerato* which lasts five years in eight countries (Argentine, Costa Rica, El Salvador, Guatemala, Honduras, Nicaragua, Peru and Venezuela) and six years in the remaining countries, with the exception of Brazil, in which it is divided into two cycles, the *ginasio* lasting four years, and the *colegio* lasting three years. This distinction, as well as the small proportion of pupils leaving public primary schools who go on to secondary schools, corresponds to the conception of the primary school as the school for the people, by means of which the obligation concerning compulsory school attendance can be honoured; it also corresponds to a certain extent to the relative importance already noted of the private primary schools and of the primary preparatory classes attached to the public or private *liceos*, colleges or institutes providing secondary education, which exist in many countries and whose pupils usually come from socio-economically well-placed families.

The division of secondary education into two cycles, of which the first *común* or basic is intended to complete general education begun in the primary school and rounded off by a period of vocational guidance, and the second *diferenciado* or optional, aims at offering a pre-university, professional or technical training, is beginning to spread in the various countries but is still a long way from being generally established.

The public primary schools, which in towns of 2,000 or 3,000 inhabitants and over, generally offer the full appropriate educational cycle, seldom go beyond the third grade in rural areas, although from the technical point of view, even in the remotest areas with a very small school-age population, this limitation and the serious effects it has on the level of education might quite easily be avoided by developing the one-teacher all-grade primary school.

Sufficient data do not exist to give a rough idea of the extent to which the adult population is receiving formal education. In all countries literacy campaigns have been organized and in all, in one form or another, there exist Adult Educational Services and a number of evening schools and night schools offering primary, secondary and vocational education. A careful study of the situation in this respect and of the results so far obtained is urgently required in that a determined effort to develop the systematic education of adults is the only short-term way of raising the general level of education.

Another characteristic of Latin American school systems, is the underdevelopment of vocational or technical education. The total number of pupils enrolled in schools offering this type of education does not exceed in the majority of the countries a quarter of the number enrolled in the traditional secondary schools, and is limited, apart from the teacher training schools, to commercial schools, some of which are privately owned and run for profit, to girls' technical schools and to a small number of trade or industrial schools, generally not of a very high standard. As for education in agriculture this bears no relation whatsoever, in either quality or quantity, to the fact that agriculture is the main activity of the majority of the countries.

Only recently has university education begun to add to the traditional fields of study (law, medicine, humanities, engineering, etc.) other fields essential for social and economic development.

Co-ordination between the various types and levels of education and the transfer of pupils from one to the other, as well as the number, quality and distribution of educational institutions are unsatisfactory and present varied problems. In general, it can be said that Latin American school systems have developed haphazardly rather, under the influence of pressures of one kind and another, than as the result of plans based upon the careful study of educational needs and of the best use of available resources.

Teaching personnel

If it is agreed that the efficiency of any school system depends in the main upon the quality of its teaching staff, what is known about the composition and professional training of teaching personnel in Latin America indicates that this is one of the gravest problems in the educational situation in the region.

In effect, about 1957 out of a total of 436,000 primary school teachers in 16 countries, representing about 80 per cent of the total population of the region, only 221,200, or 51 per cent, had received any specific training for teaching.

Although the valuable contribution made to teaching by many untrained teachers must not be underestimated, nor the possession of a teaching diploma be considered as a sufficient guarantee of competency, since there are usually many excellent teachers among those without diploma and some very mediocre ones amongst those with diploma, the gravity of the situation revealed by these figures cannot fail to be recognized. The truth is that a large number of these teachers not only lack professional training but have scarcely completed their own primary education. Their powers of teaching are thus very limited, their work inefficient and uninspiring and responsible to a certain extent for the high degree of premature school leaving already referred to.

Even though the level of professional training imparted by the teacher training schools in the majority of the countries is adversely affected by the large number of inadequately qualified members on their teaching staffs, the teachers who graduate from them are usually capable of doing a reasonable teaching job. The most serious thing is that the number of trained teachers they produce, except in one or two countries, is quite insufficient to meet the growing needs of primary education and to replace the unqualified teachers in the schools.

Salaries earned by primary school teachers are usually meagre, and in only a few countries does the teaching profession enjoy the advantages of social welfare and statutory protection of their professional rights. It is not surprising, therefore, that so few wish to train as teachers and that many leaving teacher training schools turn to more remunerative forms of employment.

So far as secondary school teachers are concerned a similar situation exists. In those few countries, where a specific professional training exists for this level of teaching, the number of unqualified teachers is considerably higher than in primary education. Secondary school teaching posts are usually entrusted either to university graduates—lawyers, pharmacists, doctors, engineers, priests, who for one reason or another, are interested in teaching—or to teacher training school products, *bachilleres* and even to people without a complete secondary school education. Furthermore, low salaries, and payment according to the number of teaching hours put in, oblige many teachers to exercise their profession in several establishments and to work under conditions which not only impair the efficiency and quality of their work but also restrict very considerably the possibility of their professional improvement. The situation as it affects vocational or technical school teachers is even more serious in that appropriate specialist training establishments exist in two countries only.

The possibility of devoting full time to university teaching is a comparatively recent development which is only beginning to spread throughout the countries in the region. University faculties are still made up in the main of outstanding professional men who deem it an honour or mark of prestige to engage in university teaching, from which they derive only a small fraction of their income. It is not surprising, therefore, that as a whole little research work is undertaken in the Latin American universities.

This brief résumé would be incomplete if it omitted to recognize the enthusiasm, competency and desire for self-improvement characteristic of so many teachers at all levels, and if it failed to point out the growing preoccupation in the majority of the countries with the need to raise standards in selection and training of teachers and to improve the conditions under which they work, as well as the increasing influence of teachers' organizations in this effort. . . .

School curricula and courses of study

The task of preparing school courses and schemes of work is usually entrusted in Latin America to committees of specialist teachers in the different subjects who, although competent enough from the academic point of view, do not always succeed in interpreting satisfactorily the true educational needs of the pupils, of the communities to which these belong, and of the nation. Moreover, school courses and schemes of work are usually uniform for all the country and, although in many of them it is recommended in principle that they must be flexible and adaptable to the peculiar characteristics of localities and the differing needs of pupils, the scanty professional training of many of the teachers and the demands made by examinations based upon the content of official schemes of work, of necessity limit the implementation of this recommendation.

The criticisms most frequently levelled against primary and secondary school curricula in national and international conferences are that they are encyclopedic, overladen with material, excessively ambitious and rigid; that, quite remote from the daily lives and experiences of the pupils, they tend to lose sight of the basic aims of general education and encourage memorization, verbalism and intellectualism rather than the development of personality, initiative, powers of observation, the acquisition of the habit of scientific inquiry and the application of skills and knowledge to the problems met in everyday life; that they include topics of doubtful value and exclude others which would be of greater use and efficacy educationally; that the grading in subject matter does not always correspond to the ages of the pupils, that there is little co-ordination between subjects, or between the content of primary education and the first years of secondary education, that they are repetitious and enter into too much detail, thereby limiting the initiative of the teacher; and finally, that they fail either to express clear and realistic aims or to offer constructive suggestions on teaching method calculated to help achieve these aims.

It seems clear that, in spite of the continued attempts at their reform, school courses and schemes of work still retain many of the features which characterized them many years ago when access to schools, and particularly to secondary schools, was limited almost entirely to the socio-economically well-placed sectors of the population. Whatever the deficiencies, however, in school courses and schemes of work in Latin American schools, they constitute the one factor among those which help to determine the quality of education that can be most readily and quickly changed; another decisive factor, the competency of the teacher, is not so easily changed. . . .

CONCLUSIONS

The educational situation in Latin America, as outlined in this study, may, if compared with the situation in North America and Europe, present a rather depressing picture; but if the comparison is made with other regions of the world such as Asia, Africa or the Near East, or, as it should be, with the educational situation as it was in Latin America thirty or forty years ago, the picture is frankly encouraging.

From the brief survey of the quantitative and qualitative aspects of education in Latin America just presented, the following main conclusions emerge:

1. The average level of education in the region was, in 1950, 2.2 school years for the whole of the population of 15 years of age and over, with a maximum of 4.2 years in Chile and a minimum of 0.5 years in Haiti, and of 4.4 school years for the mass of the population which had had the opportunity of attending school, with variations ranging from 5.3 years in Chile to 3.2 years in the Dominican Republic. The results of the censuses of population being carried out in 1960 and 1961 will no doubt reveal an appreciable increase in the level of schooling among adults in all the countries, corresponding to the expansion of educational services that has taken place during the last fifty years.

2. There exist great differences in the level of education of the population between the different countries as in within each country; these correspond in the main, to existing differences in social and economic conditions.

3. Having regard to these differences, the Latin American countries can be classified into three groups, clearly distinguishable by the state of development of their education, by the size of their most pressing educational needs and by the problems to be solved in order to meet these needs.

4. The great efforts to expand their educational services which nearly all the countries have made differ according to which of the three groups they belong and are particularly noteworthy in those countries that are trying to carry out comprehensive and systematic economic, social and political development plans.

5. In all the countries the sectors of the population with a high social and economic status enjoy educational opportunities comparable very often with those existing in more developed countries in other regions of the world; for the great majority of the population, however, such opportunities are very limited, particularly in rural areas.

6. The primary schools which existed in 1956 attended to the educational needs of little more than 20,000,000 out of the 36,000,000 children of 7 to 14 years of age, that is of only 58 per cent of the school-age population. In the group of most developed countries the lack of schools prevented about 20 per cent of the children of school-age to initiate or complete their primary education; this deficit was about 45 per cent and 55 per cent respectively in the other two groups of countries.

7. The development of post-primary education, particularly vocational, technical and university education, is very limited. The number of pupils enrolled in 1956 in secondary schools and university departments reached 13.4 per cent and 2.2 per cent respectively of the total number of pupils enrolled in primary schools; these figures were 22.6 per cent and 4.3 per cent in the case of the group of countries with the highest educational level; 10.8 per cent and 1.4 per cent in the case of the middle group, and 8.0 per cent and 0.9 per cent in the case of the group of countries with the lowest educational level.

8. The degree of premature school leaving is very high. A few years ago, even in the most developed countries in the region, it was roughly 75 per cent in the case of primary education and 68 per cent in the case of secondary education; but only 5 per cent of the pupils who began primary education went on to complete secondary education.

9. The educational opportunities for women are generally less than for men but tend to become equal and slightly greater as the average educational level of the population rises.

10. The mere creation of more primary and secondary schools would not suffice to counteract the influence of the low socio-economic level of the population upon school absenteeism and premature school leaving. Moreover, it would be essential to increase and intensify the various types of indirect and direct financial assistance for schoolchildren if it is desired that they should avail themselves effectively of opportunities for education. On the other hand, the spread of group schools (núcleos escolares) and the general adoption of the all-grade one-teacher school in districts with a sparse school-age population, in addition to this finan-

cial assistance, would bring about a considerable increase in educational opportunities in rural areas.

11. Available data make it difficult to judge the results of literacy campaigns and adult education in Latin America; there is no doubt, however, that the development of such programmes, technically well devised and executed, is the only short-term method of raising the educational level of the population, in view of the fact that it is only at the end of a few decades that the expansion of normal school services begins to have an appreciable effect upon the adult level of education.

12. The structure, contents and tendencies of education at all levels are derived in the main from the conception of educational needs implicity maintained by small sectors of the population, rather than from a careful and well-balanced analysis of the universal demands of culture and present-day life, and the characteristics and requirements peculiar to the country and its different areas, as seen from the point of economic, social and political development.

13. Regulations relating to the length of the school year and school day are not always strictly obeyed, particularly in rural areas; in the large cities in some countries they have been so reduced as to provide but a fraction of the minimum time required to impart an acceptable education.

14. The pupil-teacher ratio reaches such extremes as to be frequently incompatible with conventionally accepted standards in this respect. Realistic considerations suggest that in Latin America this ratio should never exceed 40 in the case of primary education and 35 in the case of secondary education, ratios 20 per cent higher than those usually regarded as normal.

15. Standards in teacher training, salary levels and other conditions under which teachers and executive and administrative personnel in education have to work are, in general, unsatisfactory in the majority of the countries. About 45 per cent of those engaged in teaching in primary schools are unqualified; this percentage is very much higher in secondary schools. Some countries have suitable secondary school teacher training establishments, but very few countries have adequate facilities for training the staffs for technical, vocational and teacher training schools and for the formation of heads of schools and inspectors required for the efficient organization and control of an educational system. As for the training of high-level specialists needed to undertake educational research and the administrative and executive control of educational services, the first steps are being taken to ensure this with the aid of international organizations. Moreover, increasing efforts are being made to improve conditions for teachers, and in many countries the development of professional teaching organizations can be noted.

16. Sums of money for financing education are clearly insufficient to ensure satisfactory standards in educational services and to allow for the expansion of these services. It is estimated that the average annual cost per primary school pupil in the region is equivalent to U.S.$20.

17. The control and administration of educational systems present, in general, very serious deficiencies. These derive principally from the lack of planning and continuity in educational policy and the little relation this bears with other basic features of national development policy; from the influence of considerations often incompatible with technical requirements in administrative structure, in the selection of personnel and in the running of educational services; from the lack of specialists in research, inspection and administration and of technical advisers. However, in an increasing number of countries, great attention is being paid to the application of the principles of systematic planning in education, and some have already embarked upon careful studies of their educational needs in order to ensure more efficient and rational use of resources and the co-ordination of educational development plans with over-all plans for national development.

From these conclusions can be deduced the most important educational needs in Latin America, as well as some of the measures required to meet these needs within a reasonable period of time. Naturally, a suitable and efficient plan of action demands a careful and detailed study of the situation in each country not only so as to be able to state basic aims to be followed in determining educational policy, but also to be able to define the specific goals that can be attained within a certain number of years. . . .

*Religion in Latin America**

FRANK TANNENBAUM

The American Indian at the time of the discovery was a profoundly religious and mystical human being. A great part of his daily existence was bound up in religious rites, in propitiating his many gods, in finding

* Frank Tannenbaum, "Toward an Appreciation of Latin America," in The American Assembly, *The United States and Latin America*, 2nd. © 1963. Reprinted by permission of Prentice-Hall, Inc., Englewood Cliffs, N.J.

grace, justification and peace. Every act had its religious significance; every wind, every change in the color of the moon, every appearance of the unexpected had its religious portent. In the highly developed cultures such as the Aztec and the Inca, a large priesthood served to interpret the will of the gods, and a profound mystic philosophy and a questioning of the essence of human existence informed and disciplined their attitude toward life and death.

The Spanish conquest was insensible to the spiritual and moral values that ruled the lives of the American Indians. The conquistador, whatever his virtues of courage and fealty, was no philosopher, no mystic; and he was obtuse—in most cases—to the values inherent in this strange world he found himself in.

The greatest shock to the American Indian civilization was the complete denial of its existence by the soldiers of Spain, a denial manifest in indifference or in brutal destruction of ancient gods, their objects of worship and their temples; pulling the gold off the walls in the Temple to the Sun in Cuzco was merely one of a thousand instances of an irreverence for the spirit of a culture that centered in its religion. And in destroying the religious temples and the religious leaders the soul of Indian civilization was also destroyed. Its values, its beliefs, its pattern of existence and its great art and artists were scattered by the wind that blew across the ocean.

What was left of the Indian as a human being with a belief in God and the burden of the sudden tragedy that had overtaken his world, found refuge in the Christian Church. That is the true meaning of the conversion of millions of Indians in so short a time. The Catholic Church saved what meaning there was left to existence, after all had been taken from him by men he could not understand and whose motives were completely incomprehensible to him. And in the Church the Indian could rebuild a faith in the forces that govern the world, that bring day and night, sunshine and rain, life and death. And the Church wisely built where the old temples were, and the saints in the Church gave the Indian full scope for his attachment to a particular mystery, a special symbol, a unique identity with the forces that lay beyond human reach and were all powerful. The Church did something in addition. It in some way brought the conqueror and the conquered into the same Church. It gave the Indian identity with the European, a sense that they were both mortal, and gave the conquistador a conscience that he was dealing with human beings who had souls and who were inside his Church and children of the same God as himself. It required a papal bull to make that point for the conquistador. For the strangeness of American culture, the ways of the Indians, the bitterness of the conquest, and the belief in the devil working his evil designs through strange beings made it easy to deny to the Indian his claim to human fellowship.

The Church was the Indian's salvation here and now by giving him a place where he could feel free in spirit, and where he could reweave the threads that had always bound him to the world beyond his immediate senses—and that service the Church has continued to perform for the Indian through the centuries that have changed both the original zeal of the early friars and raised problems and difficulties of a political and social nature. But these are secondary to the great spiritual role in the life of the Indian, that of giving a meaning to existence in a world ruled by men who have remained strange and incomprehensible.

It is useful in trying to unravel the mysteries of Latin American culture to remember that during the colonial period the Church ruled while the State governed. While the State in its paternal preoccupation was meddling with the public and material aspects of life, the Church ruled the most intimate and personal needs and preoccupations of the individual from the cradle to the grave and beyond. The Church in the large city, small town, village, and even on the pathway over the mountains was ever present, for there would be a cross or small chapel at every difficult passage, at the top of every hill one climbed. The Church was everywhere—even when the priest was absent. But so it had been before the conquest and before the white man. Every mountain, every stream, every strange and marvelous thing (and to the unpretentious, the humble and the pious, simple things are marvelous and strange) had its own *huaco* (shrine, holy place) and continued to have it in the new faith by identification with a favorite and miraculous saint.

The Church was everywhere and with every individual all of his life and filled all of his days. The day began with early morning Mass and ended with an Ave Maria, and every occasion, every sorrow, every joy, every holiday had its own special religious symbolism to be acted out in church. During the colonial period the Church was also the school, the university, the hospital, the home of the aged, the sick and the abandoned. It served the individual and the community in many ways. In the absence of newspapers, libraries, museums, theaters, the religious exercise and ritualism in the churches, the orders, the monasteries and the convents filled the role of giving the individual his place in an enchanted and meaningful world. And everything that happened from a bull fight to the arrival of a new Viceroy, an earthquake, or the king's birthday always required public manifestation, processions, prayers, masses and sermons in which the Church was active, perhaps the chief actor in the drama, or better, the chief embodiment of the symbolism that endowed every activity with meaning. It surrounded life at all turns and all times. The church or cathedral bell dominated the community, and daily life was disciplined and ordered to its sound.

In cities like Lima, Quito, Mexico, the church buildings, the monasteries dominated all buildings, and the profession of priest or membership in an order, belonging to a monastery or convent, was a high calling and a privilege. The few diaries that have come down from the colonial period reveal preoccupation with the ever present Church. The daily record is filled with religious processions, with the celebration of the saint's day in this or that monastery, church, convent, or ward, with gossip, scandal and even riot, because of the great popular interest in the election of a prior or prioress in monastery and convent.

The independence movement brought so many difficulties to the Church that it has not to this day fully recovered from them. For one thing the hierarchy being largely Spanish were less friendly to the independence movement than the lower clergy. And as a result the American churches were to considerable extent without bishops during and for a period after the conflict was over. And during the conflict the Papacy sided with Spain against the independence because of the pressure of the powerful Spanish Embassy in Rome. After all, Spain had been the great Defender of the Faith since the Reformation. The ideas of the French Revolution which were not unknown or unspoken in Latin America made the claims of Spanish sovereignty also seem on the side of justice, morality and faith.

The resulting rift between the American leadership and Rome was aggravated by the claim of the new governments to the rights of the patronage which had been exercised by the Spanish Crown and by the insistence of the Church that the patronage had been personal with the king and that now when the king was gone from America the Church was free. This question remains in fact unsettled and variously compromised in different countries.

But more serious perhaps than the above was the struggle that emerged between Church and State when the new governments attempted to pattern themselves on French and American constitutional precepts. It became evident, and quickly, that trouble lay ahead for the Church from the modern State with its claim to the control of education, to the equal enforcement of the same law against all citizens; with its opposition to corporate privileges, i.e., *fueros*, in a special law enforceable in ecclesiastical courts; and with its opposition to exemption from taxation of the Church for its properties. In fact, the revolutionary lawyers trained in the Roman law and imbued with French anti-clericalism on one side, and the priests traditionally identified with the corporate Church and its claims on the individual on the other, found it most difficult to abide in the same world. The quarrel between the anti-clerical lawyer steeped in concepts of absolute sovereignty and the priest, who looked upon all matters that might touch the soul and affect human salvation as the special responsibility of the Church, ended in a conflict often bitter and bloody. And the lawyer won the battle. The Church in most countries lost its land, its wealth, its monopoly over education, its censorship over the literature and the press, over the hospitals, over public charity, over the universities, over marriage (for civil marriage became legal), over the registration of birth, over the burial grounds and over the right to exclude other faiths from the country. It came out of the struggle much poorer, much less influential, and in most places on the defensive against continuing threats to its remaining power.

A hundred years of conflict have gradually attenuated the bitterness, and the Church has recovered a measure of the prestige it had lost by taking sides in recent years against the dictatorship in Argentina, Colombia, Venezuela and less openly in Cuba. It has also taken a definite position on behalf of land reform and has slowly come to voice the social doctrines expressed in the *Rerum Novarum* of Pope Leo XIII and most recently in the *Mater et Magister* of Pope John XXIII. In some measure the Church's political position is therefore better than it has been since independence. It is more independent of the State and perhaps closer to the social movement sweeping Latin America than it was a few years ago. But these changes vis-à-vis the State and public policy have had little to do with the role of the Church as a religious institution. The people have remained Catholic, and the Latin-American anti-clerical often dies in the faith, is married in church and his children are baptized as if he had never fallen under the influence of French philosophers or the more recent Marxists.

The role of the Church in Latin America is therefore very different from what it is in the United States. There is personal or family identity with the favorite saint which to this day has a quality of intimacy. The city, the town, has its patron or patroness: Santa Rosa in Lima, the Virgin of Guadalupe in Mexico, etc. Every parish in turn has a saint of its own: St. Francis, St. Dominic, St. John. All guilds—the gold-smiths, the seamen, the carpenters—used to have their own saints with their own *corfradia* inside the church, their own chapel in their corner. Every large hacienda had, and mostly still has, a chapel or sometimes a church—which occasionally connects with the main house, so that one goes from one part of the house to the other by passing through the chapel. And this chapel has its own saint that in some intimate way belongs to the family. He is the family patron who looks after its members and protects them. His name is invoked on every occasion. He has a familiar presence in family affairs as if he were a living member of it—and the children are baptized and married inside this family chapel and in the presence of the family patron. And in this chapel the members of the family used to be buried. The patron of the plantation is the patron of the plantation community, and the entire life of the plantation community is lived and in some measure ordered by the sound of the chapel bell. This is true of the smaller towns, the smaller cities and to some extent of the larger ones.

Not so much as a hundred years ago, travelers tell of the cathedral bells in Quito ringing for vespers and the entire city becoming quiet, the people kneeling down in the streets, taking off their hats and saying their prayers. But in essence it is still true—more of the women than of the men, of the unsophisticated, the poor, the illiterate (much more for these than the others), and it is true for the country folk and for the Indians very much indeed.

This personal sense of intimacy with the mysteries is seen in the family in another way. Each member old or young has a patron saint. The big occasion is not the birthday but the saint's day after whom the child was named—St. Francis, St. John, St. Peter, St. Katherine— depending on the name one received when baptized. The day is like Christmas. It begins with going to mass with one's friends, all in their best dresses. There are presents, music, visits. It lasts all day and sometimes with dancing late into the night. As the families are large, there are numerous occasions for such festivities, for each member of the family; for each of the grandparents, the parents, the children, and the grandchildren has his own particular patron saint who when his day arrives is celebrated in a similar fashion. Then there are the numerous first, second, third and fourth cousins, the aunts and uncles, the school friends, the companions and associates in business or the professions and last but not least, the "compadre"—the godfathers and godchildren—and these may literally run into the dozens. The life of the family and of the individual is greatly and continuously involved with the Church.

This is the most continuing influence in the life of the individual, especially as one gets away from the large urban center. It begins at birth and terminates only in the burial ground. One must not exaggerate the implications of this relationship of the individual, the family and the community to the Church. But one need be careful not to underestimate it. It gives life a certain quality and adds something to the meaning of daily activities which is lacking in our community—for going to church is not just a Sunday affair—it is a part of daily life. And the priest and the bishop are present on every important occasion—personal, family or community. There are few gatherings of intellectuals where some member of a religious order does not take an active part. And there are certainly few public affairs where the members of the Church are not active participants. This participation is uneven and varies with the community, but there is added colorfulness and solemnity. And a certain emphasis upon eternal verities on even the least religious occasions is added by the presence of Franciscan or Dominican brothers, or when the Bishop of Ibara takes part in a conference on history and illustrates a point in popular folklore by playing the song on a piano.

*Essay of a Socio-Economic Typology of the Latin American Countries**	ROGER VEKEMANS and J. L. SEGUNDO

It is a significant fact that *Latin America* uses the all-inclusive term developing countries' to arouse the interest of the more developed parts of the world and seek their help, but it often rejects that interest or help, on the grounds that it does not take sufficiently into account the fact that there is no *Latin America,* but 20 nations, 20 profoundly different sovereign States.

As a matter of fact, although this term may be adequate to draw attention to, and enlist help for, the underdevelopment that affects, to a greater or lesser extent, the entire Latin American continent, it is obvious that the term does not explain the actual situation of the Latin American countries, just as the term 'more developed' does not explain what is happening in the European countries—especially since the differences between the various underdeveloped Latin American countries are more pronounced than those existing between the 'developed' countries of Western Europe.

* Roger Vekemans and J. L. Segundo, "Essay of a Socio-Economic Typology of the Latin American Countries," in Egbert de Vries and José Medina Echavarría (eds.), *Social Aspects of Economic Development in Latin America* (Paris: UNESCO, 1963), pp. 67–94. (Footnotes in the original version have been omitted.)

We cannot therefore apply to the group of Latin American countries universal economic, demographic, or social terms, even by dividing that group vaguely into geographic regions. It is necessary to study the actual unit represented by each country, a political independent unit coping with its own problems.

However, since every intelligible idea is related to the universal, very real problems of development that go beyond national limits, these can and should be identified and measured in some manner. It is a matter, in a word, of establishing a typology replacing the variables that are insignificant in themselves, such as geographic proximity, or the over-simplified ones, such as *per capita* income, by a sufficiently complex correlation of variables to permit us to approach the actual situation of each country without losing ourselves in each individual case.

We were thereby faced with the preliminary task of taking the most significant variables and preparing, on the basis of each variable, a partial typological table of the complex Latin American situation. The following five variables were selected: economic variable, social stratification index, cultural variable, including in the next column data on public health, ethnological-demographic variable, and the political variable. These five basic studies constituted the essential preliminary task. The present paper is merely a synthesis, an attempt to correlate the data obtained by these studies.

It is therefore natural that, for an explanation or verification of the figures presented herein, the method used to obtain them, their margin of error, and the accompanying comments, etc., we refer the readers to the above-mentioned studies.

To give those readers unfamiliar with Latin America an overall picture of the differences existing in the continent, we can sum up in a table (see Table 1 at the end of this paper), with the reservations indicated below the table, the indexes we obtained from the five basic studies.

GENERAL REMARKS

There are three possible ways of clarifying the figures for the 25 indicators used in this tentative typology.

The first would be to place in each column the relevant absolute percentages. This method was obviously unsuitable for our particular purpose, which is not merely to reproduce or assemble already familiar statistical data, but to explain a typology, in other words to shed the fullest possible light on certain sets of factors singled out from the complex situation of the Latin American countries. A further special difficulty is inherent in this method, in that the highest do not always reflect the most favourable situation as, for instance, in the case of the death rate. And so, if our object is to obtain a speedy yet correct overall view, on which a typology can be based, it is not helpful to find a high figure (e.g., for *per capita* income) alongside a very low figure (e.g., for the death rate). In one way or another, the table had to show clearly for each indicator the level attained by the individual countries.

A second course which could then be adopted would be to give the 20 Latin American countries a mark, from 1 to 20, for each indicator, the figure 1 denoting the most favourable situation and 20 the least favourable. Yet this method, too, is unsatisfactory for the establishment of a typology. We feel it to be most unscientific for our purposes since it disregards one vital factor for gaining an exact idea of the various groups and types, namely, the relative distances between the separate countries. For instance, if it is known that countries 1, 2 and 3 are very close together but that there is a big distance between countries 3 and 4, this is obviously a very strong reason for placing the first three countries in one group and beginning another group with country 4.

For the above reasons, we had to choose the third course which, though not without its drawbacks, combines the advantages of the first two methods. It involves a very simple calculation taking into account both the relative positions of the countries and the distances between them. The absolute figures are taken for each indicator, and the distance is measured between the most and the least favoured country. This difference is divided by 10 so as to make 10 levels, and each country receives a mark for its particular level, from 1 to 10. For instance, supposing that Venezuela has the highest *per capita* income in Latin America ($540) and Haiti the lowest ($64), the difference between the two is $476. This difference, divided by 10, gives us the distance between each level ($47.60). And so countries whose *per capita* income varies between $540 and $492.40 (540 — 47.60 = 492.40) will be placed on the first level (1); countries ranging between $492.40 and $444.80 (492.40 — 47.60 = 444.80) will be on the second level (2); and so on to level (10), on which countries whose *per capita* income ranges from $111.60 to $64 (111.60 — 47.60 = 64) will be placed, $64 being the lowest limit, that of Haiti.

Using this method, several countries can be placed on the same level. For instance, we find, on level (7) for the *per capita* income, ranging from $206.80 to $254.40, Mexico (220), Brazil (230), and Colombia (250). Moreover, as already mentioned, we can readily gain an idea of the differences between the various groups by observing, for instance, that there is no country on level (6)   (from $254.40 to $302.00). The mere fact that this particular level is unoccupied brings home to us the very appreciable difference between one group of countries which approach or exceed $300 and the following, which barely reaches $250.

In contrast to the first method, the one adopted enables us to place the most favoured countries on the high levels, no matter whether the aboslute figures are high or low. For example, the lowest figure for the death rate and the highest for the *per capita* income would constitute the most favourable index and would both be placed on level (1). It is thus easy to gain an overall view of the problems that have to be faced by various countries or regions and to grasp the relative acuteness of these problems [from their proximity to level (10)]. In actual fact, in columns f, m, v, w and y, the lowest absolute figures denote the top level, while in the remaining columns the highest figures go on the top levels.

However, the following three fundamental reservations limit the validity of the findings in Table 1.

1. We wish to point out the impossibility of drawing scientific conclusions from this table by calculations or estimating averages without first studying the value of these figures, hence, without referring to the corresponding basic studies, it would be especially dangerous to strike averages without knowing the relative importance of each column. Thus, for example, it would first be necessary to know whether cement consumption or the number of doctors per 100,000 inhabitants is the more significant index of economic development. Similarly, account must be taken of the fact that while certain columns cannot change without making fundamental effects in the others, others can be modified easily without changing the general structure of the country. An example of the first case would be the column on *per capita* power consumption, and of the second, the column on the percentage of foreigners, or, according to many demographers, the column on infant mortality.

2. But even if an attempt be made to ascertain the relative value of the different columns, an average would be without value unless account be taken of the highly exceptional nature of certain extreme figures that somewhat distort the classification by decils, especially with respect to the next highest or next lowest countries. For example, among the uniform figures for Argentina, we find a 5 and a 6 in the second and third columns, respectively. These high figures are actually due to the exceptionally heavy consumption of electric power and cement

by Venezuela with respect to all other Latin American countries. This heavy consumption used as a basic figure for classification in decils places the two following countries, that is to say, Argentina and Uruguay, in the fifth and sixth decil, when as a matter of fact they are far ahead of the other countries. The opposite occurs with regard to the number of foreigners. This number is so high in Argentina and Uruguay that Venezuela appears with number 8, and yet it is one of the Latin American countries with the largest number of foreigners.

3. Finally, it must be remembered that the distance between the extreme figures varies. It is not the same to be in the tenth decil when the distance between the highest and lowest is between one and two as when it is between 1 and 100. Thus, for example, in the columns for the economic variable, the distances are from 1 to 7 in the first, 1 to 3 in the second, 1 to 50 in the third, 1 to 27 in the fourth, 1 to 14 in the fifth, and 1 to 78 in the sixth.

Lastly, it should be pointed out that several indicators refer to two, three, or even all sectors of social life. For instance, the indicator for the birth rate could equally well be included in the economic, demographic, cultural, political or social stratification sectors, since it is an important constituent of them all. Much the same could be said of the number of doctors per 100,000 inhabitants, the paper consumption and so on. Thus the fact that an indicator is placed in one sector of social life does not mean that it is used for basic analyses in this sector only. It may be analysed for several sectors, although in the general table it is placed in the most appropriate one for obtaining an overall view. Sometimes columns for obviously interrelated indicators have been juxtaposed; for example the proportion of the population employed in agriculture, will be found under the economic index, but near the indicators of social stratification on which it has a special bearing.

SPECIAL REMARKS

The columns on economic typology, as is evident, indicate the current situation. Neither in this sector nor in the political is there the notion of speed of progress noted in the other sectors. It is clear that there are no cyclical movements in social stratification or in demography, but there are some of considerable importance in the economic and political fields. Therefore, the present status of the economic factor alone, for example, cannot indicate whether it is in a period of expansion or facing an economic recession. Thus, in three of the countries that are in a better position in this sector, a recession is noted, while two of those that are situated in the middle of the table have flourishing economies, as we shall see in detail in the paragraphs below.

The middle and high sectors have to be put together, which deprives these statistics of much of their meaning. It is more illuminating to compare the manpower employed in industry proper (establishments with more than five workers) with the manpower employed in industry in the broad sense of the term.

We have added a few indexes on consumption and health to give a general idea of the standard of living of the various countries. Very few of the figures under this heading include all the countries of the Latin American continent. Among others that are missing are those that indicate the sum of various elements, such as the figures on calories, which, as can be seen in the table, have been given for only 7 of the 20 countries of which Latin America is composed. In this special case, taking into account the fact that other statistics that are not very reliable for a country in Central America give a caloric total of only a little less than that of Mexico, we have made the division in decils, taking Argentina and Mexico as extremes, although, of course, none has to have figures lower than those of Mexico.

With respect to the political sector, it is only too evident that no statistics can be found there. However, if one examines the basic study on political typology, it will be seen that it would be possible to establish, up to a certain point, a development index that takes into account the various factors of political maturity examined in the study: (a) developments in the use of force; (b) actual representation and integration of influence groups; (c) complexity and realism of political ideas; and (d) effective representative of the entire electorate in the system of political parties. On the basis of these factors, a numerical classification can be attempted that will lack scientific value, but that can be useful in the general table to indicate the countries that have serious problems in this sector of social life. . . .

GROUP I.
MOST OF THE CENTRAL AMERICAN COUNTRIES:
EL SALVADOR, GUATEMALA, HAITI, HONDURAS,
NICARAGUA AND THE DOMINICAN REPUBLIC

The situation of these countries is, generally speaking, the basic situation analysed in the preceding section. As a matter of fact, they are the countries that, because of serious difficulties, are kept at a very primitive level, which is aggravated, rather than alleviated by the invasion of elements from the modern western world.

Economically, these countries depend on agriculture which is the occupation of a very high percentage of the active population, ranging from 63 per cent in El Salvador to 83 per cent in Honduras and Haiti. The agricultural economy is of the monocrop type (coffee, bananas), and has a great influence on the rural social structure. Coffee gives rise to a kind of national feudalism, while the banana industry is in the hands of foreign companies, especially the United Fruit Company.

From the viewpoint of their economy, this group of countries could be divided into two, one consisting of El Salvador and Nicaragua, and the other of the remaining countries. The reason for this division is neither the *per capita* income index nor the electric power consumption, but rather the existence of certain factors that are closer to the human level and that indicate a predisposition to greater economic development. This is shown directly by a greater consumption of cement, an index closely related to saving and investment ability, and is indirectly confirmed by factors that are largely cultural, such as the low percentage of illiteracy, the larger urban population and consequently, larger paper consumption and more health facilities (doctors and hospital beds). But despite this better situation in the first sub-group, we should not forget that in both cases the level is one of severe underdevelopment.

The *per capita* income varies in these countries from $165 to $64 while that of Venezuela, for example, is $540. The *per capita* consumption of electric power varies between 0.12 (tons) to 0.03, while, even excluding the exceptional case of Venezuela (with 1.65), the Argentine figure is 0.90.

But the greatest difficulties and the indexes that need specially to be taken into account are the ethnological-demographic, social, and standard-of-living indexes of these countries.

Ethnically, Haiti is 95 per cent Negro. The Dominican Republic has a Negro population of 15 per cent and a mulatto population of 75 per cent of the total population. In the other countries, the purely Indian element (in so far as it possible to calculate it) varies from 5 per cent in Nicaragua to 54 per cent in Guatemala, with 10 per cent in Honduras and El Salvador. But account must always be taken of the large proportion of mestizos that varies between 65 per cent and 85 per cent (with the exception of Guatemala), who have a high percentage of Indian blood.

This ethnic composition is complicated by the difficulties it causes in cultural integration. Illiteracy ranges from 55 per cent in the Dominican Republic to 90 per cent in Haiti. And the influence of these two factors is expressed demographically in a great population expansion that is producing in this area the highest population density in the hemisphere, 122 inhabitants per square kilometre in Haiti, and 118 in El Salvador.

Moreover, these ethnic, cultural and demographic factors contribute to a maximum immobility of social stratification. It can be said that in these countries there is no middle class properly speaking, but only middle-class groups in the islands of modern living constituted by the cities. These middle-class groups are composed of a small number of small businessmen and professional people. In Haiti, which is an extreme case, they can be considered a sub-group of the proletariat, differing from it only in having primary education and in being engaged in business rather than agriculture. The extraordinarily low indexes of domestic consumption give an idea of the extremely primitive standard of living of the urban and, even more, the rural proletariat.

This total human situation leads one to the logical deduction that there exists in these countries a serious lack of political coherence and stability. They are actually province-countries, whose lack of [national] coherence has been the principal factor since their political independence. This lack of political coherence and stability makes any foreign aid or advice difficult, for we have to find first what the French call *l'interlocuteur valable*, that is to say, the political power that will truly represent the interests of the entire country. We cannot hope in this case for the guarantee that would be constituted by the operation of democratic institutions representing national opinion. This is a case where negotiating with *caudillos* can be justified (since these countries have not really advanced beyond the stage of the *caudillo*) on condition that they use their power to work toward the cultural, social, and political integration of their own countries instead of using it to protect foreign interests as well as their own.

However, the fact that there is no nation-wide political opinion does not mean that the country is without any kind of political unity. We have already indicated that such unity at the lowest level is based on feelings of national dignity and pride in the internal balance of the country, which will always have to be taken into account—especially since the small size and lack of organization of these countries makes any kind of foreign intervention appear excessive. The investment of large amounts of foreign private capital is especially dangerous, since the private interests having such capital can easily appear to be anti-national.

GROUP II.
THE CENTRAL COUNTRIES OF SOUTH AMERICA:
BOLIVIA AND PARAGUAY

Most of the indexes we have before us in the various sectors of economic and social life would lead us to include these countries in the preceding group.

Actually, both Bolivia and Paraguay have the lowest *per capita* income and electric power consumption indexes, and their economies are based on their export trade, with Bolivia exporting mineral raw materials, and Paraguay agricultural products. From the ethnological standpoint, they are also very similar to the countries in Group I, since 63 per cent of Bolivia's population is Indian, while 74 per cent of Paraguay's population is mestizo, with a large proportion of Indian blood.

However, despite all these similarities, we have separated these two countries from Group I, and not only because of their different geographical location.

What distinguishes them is that these two countries have begun to overcome the social stratification immobility found in Group I.

In Paraguay, this is being carried out by progress in the cultural field. The proportion of illiterates, constituting between 30 and 35 per cent of the country's population, places it in the third decil of the Latin American continent, while the proportion of persons enrolled in primary education (62 per cent) is one of the highest, coming after Argentina and equal to Chile and Panama. It can be foreseen that by these means the country can achieve greater social mobility, the creation of a cultural middle class, and after that a national political unity, all of which are factors that can have a favourable effect on its economic development.

Bolivia, with more serious ethnic problems, has followed a different path, that of social revolution to integrate into the life of the nation a very large Indian population, which until recently was held in a state resembling slavery. It is still too early to calculate the results obtained in the face of such great difficulties.

It can be said in general that, although in many aspects these countries are similar to the preceding group, they differ from it in that they have put in motion the body politic.

It can also be added that the much larger territorial dimensions of the two countries and the sources of wealth (petroleum and others) not yet exploited that are found in them, give greater hope of a more accelerated development.

However, we should also apply to them the observations we made concerning the preceding group in respect of political matters. The social revolution and the fact that they possess a certain culture promotes nationalism, and the economic and political fragility of the two countries tends to increase their vulnerability to everything foreign. The land-locked position of these countries which, up to a certain point, makes them dependent on more powerful neighbours (especially in the case of Paraguay), aggravates rather than alleviates this difficulty.

[Nor is it possible, in either of these two countries, to count on any reliable authority that really represents the political opinions of the country, since neither of them has as yet attained national unity, although Bolivia is acquiring it more rapidly.]

GROUP III.
THE PACIFIC ANDEAN COUNTRIES:
COLOMBIA, ECUADOR AND PERU

The composition of this regional group may present difficulties. As we see immediately, Colombia occupies, in several respects, a higher place than the other two countries. From the ethnological-demographic, as well as the economic standpoints, the difference is great, particularly as regards the more universal factors. But the cultural, political and, in some aspects, demographic, and social situation of Colombia is closer to that of her neighbours to the south than to that of her gigantic south-eastern neighbour, Brazil (with which it shares, however, several economic factors). Let us leave Colombia in this group, therefore, although we shall establish for it a sub-group above that of the other two countries.

Economically, in Colombia the *per capita* income exceeds $200 (250), while in Ecuador and Peru it exceeds only 100 (150 and 120). This places Colombia two decils from the other two countries in the general table for the Latin American countries. Within that gap are found almost all the countries of the first two groups studied (with the exception of Haiti, Paraguay, and Bolivia, which are below Peru). In the index for electric power consumption, Colombia occupies the eighth decil (0.47), Peru, the ninth (0.33) along with Brazil and Costa Rica, and Ecuador, the tenth (0.14) along with the countries of Groups I and II.

However, when we go on to factors more directly related to human life and the future outlook, the differences narrow. The cement consumption figure as an indication of the saving and investment capacity, places Colombia (107) and Peru (97) almost together, while Ecuador is two decils below (50). In contrast, in the agricultural occupation factor,

Ecuador is slightly above Colombia (53.2 per cent against 53.9 per cent), while Peru is two decils lower with 62.5 per cent. Finally, Colombia is only one decil above Ecuador and Peru in medial services, and is in the same decil as they are in *per capita* paper consumption, with a figure twice as high as the average for the countries in Groups I and II.

This similarity is also seen in important demographic indexes, such as birth and death rates, which are very high in the three countries in this group.

[This tendency for the countries to show similar indexes in spheres more directly related to the people's way of life, and serious differences in the universal economic index, makes us suspect great social imbalances.]

For it is important to take into account ethnic and cultural factors. The Peruvian population in 1940 was 46 per cent Indian and 52 per cent white or mestizo, the latter having a large proportion of Indian blood. To this we must add the fact that 35 per cent of the population does not speak Spanish but only Indian languages, and that between 50 and 55 per cent of the population apparently is illiterate. The population of Ecuador appears to be 30 to 40 per cent Indian and the rest white or mestizo, 40 to 45 per cent of them being illiterate. The ethnic composition of Colombia is based on guesses that give the following figures: 5 per cent Indian, 5 per cent Negro, 65 per cent mestizo, mulatto, and zambo (Indian and Negro) and 25 per cent white. But it has an illiteracy rate of 38 per cent, which is lower than that of Ecuador or Peru.

When these powerful factors of differentiation and social immobility operate as in this case over large territories with an inadequate communication system, [they become divided geographically in regions that are very heterogeneous socially and economically. So much so that this heterogeneity between the various regions of these countries constitutes the outstanding characteristic common to the group and the greatest obstacle to progress of any kind.]

For example, in Peru the number of persons employed in industry and in services in the tertiary sector are concentrated in three provinces: Lima, Callao and Arequipa. The coastal departments occupy an intermediate position, and those of the mountains (other than Junin) have a large Indian population and are very backward. In Colombia, Medellin, Cali, Bogota, and Barranquilla are four outposts of modern life situated in four different regions and profoundly different from the rest of the country.

The greater size of the city population of these countries, and hence of the outposts of modern life, help to establish an urban middle class that is much more coherent and much larger than that of the countries in the above groups. However, entire regions are still practically outside the framework of a true market economy.

And, with the migration of the lower classes to the capital, a phenomenon is beginning to be noted here, namely that instead of contributing to progress, these urban centres are having a disrupting effect.

Politically, these countries are quite different from those of the preceding groups because they appear to have emerged recently, but with resolution, from the *caudillo* stage. Political institutions give a certain guarantee of national integration. But this does not decrease, but rather increases, the possibility of social revolutions that endeavour to solve the problem of the great social inequalities. Only rapid progress could prevent this more or less violent solution. However, such progress in the economic field would require heavy investment, especially investment that could provide these countries with communications, coherence, and homogeneity.

GROUP IV.
WITHOUT GEOGRAPHIC PROXIMITY:
MEXICO AND BRAZIL

The final possibility mentioned for the preceding group is precisely what is beginning to become a reality in this group, which enables us to single out these two countries that belong to the most interesting ones in Latin America. Despite the fact that Mexico and Brazil are extremely dissimilar, they appear to have entered into a period of continuous development whose economic results are being well distributed throughout the country, and are contributing to the establishment of basic structures for future improvements.

This outlook for the future makes these countries one of the most representative groups of Latin America. If only current figures are taken into account, the difference between them and the countries in the preceding group is minimal in the case of Mexico, and practically non-existent in the case of Brazil.

As a matter of fact, both countries have practically the same *per capita* income as Colombia (Colombia, 250; Mexico, 220; and Brazil, 230). Mexico has a higher consumption of electric power than Colombia (0.65 and 0.47, respectively), but Brazil has less (0.35). Both have a lower cement consumption than Colombia and Peru (Colombia, 107; Peru, 97; Mexico, 85, and Brazil, 62). And something similar occurs with respect to the other economic indexes.

From the ethnological standpoint, the same geographically localized heterogeneity exists. Mexico's population is 15 per cent white, 30 per cent Indian, and 55 per cent mestizo, with little white blood. The statistics on Brazil are subject to controversy, but they appear to be as follows: 62 per cent white, 26 per cent mulatto and mestizo, and 11 per cent Negro. As we indicated, the great social differences that develop from such ethnic heterogeneity, have been localized in widely different regions. In Mexico, development is concentrated in the capital and in the northern States bordering on the United States of America, while the central and southern Pacific States are characterized by a very low level of development. In Brazil, the State of São Paulo accounts for 31 per cent of the national income; the Federal District, 14 per cent; the State of Minas Gerais, 11 per cent, and Rio Grande do Sul, 10 per cent. Therefore, a study of that continent known as Brazil has to be divided into two chapters: the old Brazil and the new Brazil.

If, up to this point, everything would seem to suggest a situation identical to that of the countries in the preceding group, how can we explain the constant rate of progress peculiar to this group?

The principal causes may be the following:

1. From the demographic viewpoint, Brazil and Mexico have large urban centres and a rather high proportion of urban population. Moreover, large numbers of foreigners are often found in these urban concentrations of population, as in São Paulo or Rio in Brazil; while very many of their inhabitants are familiar with life abroad, as in the Mexican States that border on the United States of America. The large cities cease, to a certain extent, to be isolated centres of modern life.

2. This effect is accentuated by the urban industrialization, which is characteristic of these two countries. Through industrialization the entire country is better organized, and the large cities that before, owing to their isolation, had rather a disturbing effect, are now doing more to spread the modern way of life and are providing a greater opportunity for social mobility.

3. These effects are noted at the political level and at the same time are conditioned by it. While in the countries of the preceding group there has not yet been any political opposition to the sectors that are unbalanced, in this group we find reactions that have been violent in the case of Mexico, and slower in Brazil, with the dictatorship of Vargas and the action of leftist parties. This political opposition gives a guarantee that the national income will be invested in structures of national interest, which guarantee is lacking in the countries examined earlier.

4. Finally, at the cultural level, the two countries of this group have carried out a serious project and have had gratifying results, if account

is taken of the above-mentioned difficulties. In Mexico, illiteracy dropped from 74 per cent in 1900 to 51 per cent in 1940, and the figures for 1950 show 43 per cent for those above 15 years of age. For all over 15 years of age in Brazil, the percentage of illiteracy was 65.3 in 1900, 64.9 in 1920, and 56.1 in 1940.

GROUP V.
SEVERAL CARIBBEAN COUNTRIES:
CUBA, VENEZUELA,
COSTA RICA AND PANAMA

This group, like Group II consisting of Bolivia and Paraguay, is made up of countries that have developed, or are developing, irregularly owing to one exceptionally favourable factor that is unable to make the other factors equal to it. This factor is, in the case of Venezuela, the exploitation of petroleum; in the case of Costa Rica, the great basic homogeneity of its white population; in Panama, the Panama Canal; and in Cuba, the social revolution added to an uneven economic development.

With respect to Cuba, it is obvious that the figures we have do not tell us anything regarding the reforms introduced by the revolutionary regime. The economic indexes can be valid only to describe the previous situation, because, being the most sensitive indexes, they are affected profoundly by the political changes. However, the ethnological-demographic and cultural figures give us the basis on which the revolution is operating today, and as such we offer them here.

Suffice it to say then that the economic indexes placed Cuba in the middle upper group with Venezuela and immediately below Group VI, composed of Argentina, Uruguay, and Chile. This favourable, though unbalanced, economic situation applies to a population of which a considerable number are foreigners, 72.8 per cent are white; 12.4 per cent Negro; and 14.5 per cent mulatto. If to this is added a good literacy index (an illiteracy of only 20 or 25 per cent), the Cuban situation at the time of the revolution appears favourable.

The causes of the revolution are to be sought, first of all, in the social imbalance existing between the urban and the rural population. Cuba is a monocrop country (sugar cane), and the vast majority of the farm workers have only seasonal work. Moreover, in the early stages of the Cuban revolution political motives characterized as democratic opposition to the dictatorship of Batista were just as great, if not a greater, force. Also, in the political field, the excessive amount of visible foreign private capital and economic dependence on the United States of America must be added to the causes of the revolution and their effect on the masses. Also to be borne in mind is the fact that this factor of economic dependence on the United States, which also exists in Venezuela and Panama in this group, can have a great political influence on the development of these countries.

Venezuela is an even more typical example, if possible, of uneven development. Economically, it has the highest *per capita* income in the American continent (540) which only Argentina approaches (460) and an electric power consumption that is almost double that of Chile, which is second in the continent (1.65 against 0.98). In the *per capita* consumption of cement, it far surpasses the second country, which is Uruguay (270 as compared with 166).

On the other hand, in the indexes that reveal more directly the standard of living of the majority, its position is markedly lower, which is consistent with its ethnic, cultural, and social characteristics.

Its ethnic composition appears to be 20 per cent white, 7 per cent Indian, 8 per cent Negro, and 65 per cent mestizo. Illiteracy is high: from 45 to 50 per cent of the population. There is a sharp social differentiation between the classes, which is localized in various regions. All these elements remind us of the countries in Group III, which Venezuela resembles certainly far more than the countries in Group VI.

This imbalance between the purely economic and the human, suggests that up to now the oil wealth of Venezuela has not been evenly distributed throughout the country. It is not surprising to find, therefore, a serious political instability, although the country appears to have progressed beyond the *caudillo* stage to a more advanced social policy whose effects will be seen later. It may be said that Venezuela, despite this disproportionately high economic factor, is on the dividing line between the countries of Groups III and IV, and that its best course would be to join the latter countries, practising a more accentuated national policy.

Like Venezuela, Costa Rica and Panama appear to belong at the same time to different types of countries.

On the one hand, they have a high *per capita* income, especially Panama (250), although Costa Rica's is slightly higher (181) than that of the first three groups. The difference is less as regards the consumption of electric power: Panama, 0.36 and Costa Rica, 0.32. Panama's unusual index in cement consumption (157) shows the factor that favours its economy tremendously, that is, the canal installation. On the other hand, the high cultural levels that favour Costa Rica (illiteracy: Costa Rica, 21.0 per cent, Panama, 30 per cent) point to the tremendously favourable factor of this country—a homogeneous white population with no great social imbalance and considerable political maturity.

The limitations of these countries are also shown in a correlative manner. In Panama, the ethnic composition is not favourable: 10 per cent white, 65 per cent mestizo and mulatto, 10 per cent Indian, and 15 per cent Negro and other. The same thing may be said of the impermeable social stratification outside the Canal Zone, which is both urban and modern. The limited development of Costa Rica is due to its small size and consequent lack of resources, both strictly economic and human.

GROUP VI.
THE SOUTHERN CONE OF THE CONTINENT: ARGENTINA, URUGUAY AND CHILE

In a certain sense, this last group of countries at first glance does not exhibit any exceptional characteristics, but a medium rate of development if compared with other countries of the western world. But if account is taken of the fact that the countries of this group have progressed from a basic situation very similar to that of the other countries, the fact of their greater development is of interest in itself for an understanding of the continent, and introduces the problems that occur in Latin America when a certain development level is reached.

Economically, these countries have a high *per capita* income of around $400. Argentina registers 460 on our index, while Chile has 360 and Uruguay 440. The other economic indexes show a high, balanced level among the other continental levels. The low percentages of the farming population (although with a high income in the first two countries)— Argentina 21.7 per cent, Uruguay 25.2 per cent, and Chile, 29.6 per cent— clearly distinguish them from all the other countries, since, except for Cuba and Venezuela (41 per cent), the other countries have a farming population of 50 per cent or more. In the *per capita* consumption of electric power, Chile surpasses Argentina (0.98 compared with 0.90) owing, not to its industry, but to its mining production, and Uruguay follows with 0.78. Moreover, Uruguay's cement consumption (166) is second only to Venezuela, and is followed by Argentina, with 131, and Chile, with 130.

The other indexes most closely related to the human situation also show levels that would be considered anywhere in the world as fairly well developed. This is, moreover, consistent with the large proportion of white population in these countries. In Chile, there are mestizos with a large percentage of white blood, and in Argentina and Uruguay, the population can be considered as almost completely white. Moreover, these two countries have been practically invaded by a recent wave of immigrants from Europe, which gives them a modernistic stamp different from that of the other Latin American countries. In this sense, it would not be entirely correct to say they have developed from the same basic situation we analysed in the introduction.

As regards the cultural aspect, we find the illiteracy indexes here the lowest of the Latin American continent: 14 per cent in Argentina, from 15 to 20 per cent in Uruguay, and 20 per cent in Chile, which has the highest index for enrollment in primary, secondary, and technical schools (17.9 per cent), while Argentina and Uruguay have the highest percentage of university enrolment (0.48 and 0.47 in 1948).

But what most clearly characterizes these countries and places them in the top level in Latin America, although it also creates its own problems is, in the social aspect, a greater equalization of classes, with the development of a genuine urban middle class, and even a rural middle class in the first two countries. We say a true middle class, and not simply more or less numerous middle-class groups, because there is a class consciousness at the national level, and that consciousness is expressed in powerful political parties with their own ideologies. Moreover, the existence of a true middle class goes hand in hand with the importance from the economic standpoint, of the domestic market that characterizes these countries.

[All of this notwithstanding, a certain stagnation is to be noted in these countries. The explanation of this reveals two important facts in the more developed Latin American world. In general, there is no question but that these countries took advantage of the especially favourable economic conditions of the post-war period to advance their economic development. When these conditions disappeared at the end of the Korean war, they were unable to adapt themselves to the new and less favourable situation; this caused an imbalance in their economies which led to the present recession.]

[The first cause of this failure to adapt must without doubt be laid at the door of the political sector] [The influence of political opinion on policies that are well organized to express it, has become exceptionally strong, rendering difficult the adoption of restrictive measures of any kind, especially those that threaten to affect the working classes.] Moreover, the need to industrialize has entered into the political ideology of the man-in-the-street. Although these countries have domestic markets, they are incapable of absorbing large amounts of manufactured products, to which must be added the high cost of manpower in countries determined to safeguard the interests of the popular classes. Hence, the industrialization demanded by public opinion in its political struggle is paid for out of the proceeds from agricultural exports, and when this is not enough, with continued inflation.

The second cause, which is intimately related to the first, is that international market requirements necessitate—if a suitable standard of living is to be maintained—an industrialization that includes mechanization of agriculture. 'It is therefore under pressure (and this did not affect preceding generations) that Latin America must accelerate the mechanization of agriculture and its industrialization process. However, an attempt is being made to introduce modern agricultural techniques in areas where the land tenure system does not meet the economic and social development needs and in countries whose present industrial activities (limited as they are by narrow national markets) are not able even now to absorb all the available manpower.'

It is precisely these countries, whose development has been checked by the above-mentioned conditions, that have tended most strongly to the realization that a solution to these problems might be found in the common Latin American market, the initial steps of which were taken in the Montevideo Treaty.

On the incidence of the problem Dr. Galo Plaza, former President of Ecuador, made the following statement: 'Latin America is experiencing the beginning of a social revolution because the need for a growing middle class and the expectations of the masses are exerting strong pressure on an economic system that is not capable of carrying out its task. Unless we can bring about an economic revolution to meet the needs of this social revolution, our problems will go beyond the political field, with dire consequences for the entire Hemisphere.'

The group of countries we are studying is the one most aware of this problem, because their structures and their own economic situation make them aware of it. That is why they are so vital to a complete understanding of the Latin American continent.

To sum up, a study of the socio-economic typology of Latin America reveals six types of countries in the continent.

Three of these groups, Groups I, III, and VI show three balanced situations, or three levels of slow development: the lower (which includes the group of Central American countries), the middle one (which includes the Pacific Andean countries), and the upper one (which includes the countries of the southern tip of the continent).

The lower level is practically that of the primitive situation we described as the basic situation in Section II. The middle level is characterized by the presence of modern structures side by side with residual and antiquated structures, which are regionally localized. The highest

TABLE 1[1]

COUNTRY	ECONOMY						SOCIAL STRATIFICATION				
	PER CAPITA INCOME	PER CAPITA ELEC. CONSUMP.	CEMENT CONSUMPTION	NEWSPRINT CONSUMPTION	CALORIE INTAKE	% OF LABOUR FORCE IN AGRICULTURE	% URBAN POPULATION	% INTERMED. AND SENIOR GRADES OF EMPLOYMENT IN SEC. SECTORS	% LAB. FORCE IN PRIM. SECTORS	% LAB. FORCE IN SEC. AND TERT. SECTORS	% EMPLOYED IN INDUSTRY PROPER
GROUP I	(a)	(b)	(c)	(d)	(e)	(f)	(g)	(h)	(i)	(j)	(l)
Haiti	10	10	10	10		10	10	10	10	10	10
Guatemala	8	10	10	10		9	8	9	10	8	6
Honduras	9	10	10	10		10	9	10	10	10	9
Dominican Rep.	8	10	7	10		8	9				6
Nicaragua	9	10	9	10		8	7				10
El Salvador	9	10	9	9		7	8	8	10	7	5
GROUP II											
Paraguay	9	10	10	10		5	8	7	9	6	9
Bolivia	10	10	10	10		5	7	9	10	8	8
GROUP III											
Peru	9	9	7	9	10	7	7				7
Ecuador	9	10	9	9		5	8	8	10	4	10
Colombia	7	8	7	9		5	6	5	5	5	7
GROUP IV											
Brazil	7	9	9	9	7	7	7	7	10	7	3
Mexico	7	7	8	8	8	6	5	6	9		2
GROUP V											
Panama	7	8	5	6		5	6	7	10	5	5
Costa Rica	8	9	8	8		6	8	5	6	5	5
Venezuela	1	1	1	8	8	3	4	6	9	3	1
Cuba	5	7	6	4		3	5	5	10	4	3
GROUP VI											
Chile	4	5	6	5	5	1	3	5	10	1	4
Uruguay	3	6	5	2	1	1	1	1	1		2
Argentina	2	5	6	1	1	1	3	1	1	1	2

[1] For reference sources of each column see pages 138–139.

[2] Various problems are involved in showing the ethnic make-up of a country in summary, quantitative form, owing to the lack of any exact definition of the concept and to the difficulties of obtaining satisfactory statistics. For this reason, and in view of the purpose of this study, it was decided to analyse, for the ethnodemographic variable, two ethnic components—the proportion of foreigners and the proportion of Indians and/or Negroes in the Latin American countries. It was

TABLE 1. (Continued)

	CULTURE						STANDARD OF LIVING				ETHNOGRAPHY[2]		POLITICAL SECTOR
% ILLITERACY	% PRIM. SCHOOL ENROLMENT	% SEC. SCHOOL ENROL.	UNIVERSITY ENROL. PER 10,000 INHABS.	NEWSP. CIRC. AS % OF POP.	% RADIO SETS	% CINEMA SEATS	DOCTORS PER 100,000 INHABS.	NO. INHABS. PER HOSPITAL BED	% BIRTH RATE	% DEATH RATE	% FOREIGNERS	% INDIANS AND NEGROES	
(m)	(n)	(o)	(p)	(q)	(r)	(s)	(t)	(u)	(v)	(w)	(x)	(y)	(z)
10	10	10	10	10	10	10	10	10	10	10	10	10	(10)
8	10	10	10	9	10	8	10	4	9	10	10	2	(10)
7	9	10	10	9	10	8	10	5	8	7	9	2	(10)
6	2	10	9	9	9	9	10	2	10	9	10	2	(10)
7	8	10	10	6	10	4	9	3	9	8	10	6	(10)
7	7	9	10	8	10	8	10	3	8	9	10	2	(10)
3	2	9	8	9	8	9	7	4	8	7	8	1	(9)
8	7	9	9	9	8	9	9	3	8	8	10	8	(9)
6	6	9	8	6	7	9	9	3	8	9	—	7	(7)
4	5	9	9	8	10	6	9	3	8	7	10	5	(8)
4	7	9	9	7	2	6	8	2	8	5	10	2	(6)
5	7	9	9	7	8	6	8	2	8	8	9	2	(6)
4	5	10	8	—	7	3	8	6	7	6	10	4	(4)
3	3	5	7	4	6	3	9	1	8	7	7	3	(8)
1	3	6	8	5	8	3	8	1	8	5	8	1	(4)
5	6	9	9	5	6	2	7	1	8	7	8	2	(5)
2	4	9	6	3	5	1	3	1	4	4	8	2	(5)
1	2	6	6	3	7	3	7	1	6	4	10	1	(2)
1	3	5	5	1	1	5	4	1	1	1	1	1	(1)
1	1	1	1	1	4	3	1	1	1	1	1	1	(3)

felt that these factors, though important from the social viewpoint, do not necessarily reflect fully and exclusively the ethnic make-up. Although the two variables meet the requirement of being expressible in figures, it should be pointed out that the figures, especially those giving the number of Indians and Negroes, are no more than rough estimates. The lack of objective criteria makes any strictly accurate classification impossible.

level is that of the development of modern structures within the limitations of the entire Latin American situation.

In addition to these three types of more or less balanced situations of slow development, we find three types of rapid development. Two of them, the second and fifth, exhibit an uneven development, and one, the fourth, exhibits a strong, balanced development, starting from a rather low basic situation.

The second type presents us with the case of two countries that are making a serious although unilateral effort to rise above the lower group by means of social or cultural policies. The fifth type exhibits countries where an especially favourable economic, political, or demographic factor produces a relatively artificial progress, which it is hoped will spread to the other sectors in order to attain a rapid, balanced development. Finally, the two countries that constitute Group IV exhibit this rapid, balanced development in the various sectors, although they began with a situation where great ethnic, social, and geographical imbalances existed, which they are endeavouring to correct.

REFERENCE SOURCES TO TABLE 1

(a) Per capita *national product of fifty-five countries 1952–1954.* Statistical Office of the United Nations, New York, 1957. Estimates of *per capita* net national product of 55 countries expressed in U.S. dollars. Annual average 1952–54.

For Costa Rica, Bolivia, El Salvador, Nicaragua, Haiti, F.A.O. *Perspectivas de la industria de papel y celulosa en la América Latina.* 1955, p. 49, Table 10.

(b) *La Variable Económica,* Roberto Maldonado and J. Claudio Araya, p. 19, Table 2. *Per capita* power consumption in terms of the number of tons of coal used per head of population in Latin America, 1954.

(c) *La Variable Económica,* Roberto Maldonado and J. Claudio Araya, p. 28, Table 1. *Per capita* cement consumption for each country (expressed in kilogrammes).

(d) *La Variable Económica,* Roberto Maldonado and J. Claudio Araya, p. 38, Table 1. *Per capita* newsprint consumption in the Latin American countries (kilogrammes of paper per inhabitant in the period 1946–50).

(e) *Informe sobre la Situacion Social en el Mundo,* New York, 1957, p. 60, Appendix C. Calorie rations as compared with needs (daily consumption of calories per inhabitant).

(f) *La Variable Económica,* Roberto Maldonado and J. Claudio Araya, p. 12, Table 1. Percentage of agricultural workers in the labour force of the Latin American countries for the years covered by the table.

(g) *Estudio preliminar de la Situación Demográfica en América Latina,* CEPAL, ninth year, May 1961, p. 37, Table 11. Urban, rural and total population, 1950 and 1960 (unofficial mid-year estimates).

(h), (i), (j) and (l) *Estudio Comparativo de la Estratificación y de la Movilidad Social en los Países de América Latina,* Federico Debuyst.

(m) 'Report of the Meeting of Experts on Development of Information Media in Latin America', 1–13 February 1961, Unesco/MC/41.

For Peru and Uruguay, *World Illiteracy at mid-Century,* Unesco, 1957, p. 38–43.

(n), (o) and (p) *Aspectos de la Situación Educativa en América Latina,* Oscar Vera. Report submitted to the meeting on the social aspects of economic development, Mexico, 1960, Table IV. Population and enrolment in primary and secondary schools and universities, Latin America, 1956.

(q), (r) and (s) 'Report of the Meeting of Experts on Development of Information Media in Latin America', 1–13 February 1961, Unesco/MC/41.

(t) *La Variable Económica,* Roberto Maldonado and J. Claudio Araya, p. 33, Table I. Consumption of special services in Latin America (number of inhabitants per doctor).

(u) *Informe sobre la Situación Social en el Mundo,* New York, 1957, p. 43, Table 9. Hospital beds.

(v) and (w) *Tipología Socio-económica de los Países Latinoamericanos, la Variable Etno-demográfica,* J. H. van der Boomen, p. 47a, Table 2.2.1. Latin America: Vital statistics, illiteracy, industrialization and urbanization.

(x) *Tipología Socio-económica de los Países Latinoamericanos, la Variable Etno-demográfica,* J. H. van der Boomen, p. 11, Table 1.2.1. Latin America: Percentage of births abroad and in Europe.

(y) *Tipología Socio-económica de los Países Latinoamericanos, la Variable Etno-demográfica,* J. H. van der Boomen, p. 27, Table 1.3.2. Latin America: Ethnic composition.

(z) *Tipología Socio-económica de los Países Latinoamericanos, la Variable Política,* Renato Poblete B., S. J., J. Luis Segundo Diaz, S. J.

| Part 2 | *THE*
GOVERNMENTAL
SYSTEM |

The selections in this section emphasize the organizational structure of the governments of Latin America; to a lesser extent they also analyze the functions performed by various governmental institutions. This topic may be approached from the other end as well. Instead of seeking to determine the functions of certain institutions (such as presidencies, legislatures, and judiciaries), one may begin with a set of authoritative functions (rule-making, rule-application and rule-adjudication, for example) and attempt to determine what institutions perform these functions.[1] What follows is a very brief introduction to such an approach.

Latin American constitutions expressly delegate the rule-making function to legislative assemblies, but in fact this function is more often exercised by other bodies—Presidents, the military, the church and even constituent assemblies. Seldom have the Congresses of Latin America acted as major rule-makers; instead they have adopted altogether different functions, chief of which is the legitimizing of rules made by others. In the enactment of major legislation, for example, seldom is the initiative taken by a Congress; it will usually await the introduction of an administration bill, and then give the President's rules legitimacy by means of the formal legislative process. Congresses may also serve as a forum for the expression of hostilities and aggressions, and to some extent they may perform a representational role; few, however, serve as their nation's main rule-maker.

Normally it is the chief executive who performs the rule-making function in Latin American nations. In a great many instances, however,

[1] This is the approach used by each of the contributors to Gabriel A. Almond and James S. Coleman (eds.), The *Politics of the Developing Areas* (Princeton, N.J.: Princeton University Press, 1960).

141

the President is forced to share this function with others—most frequently with the leaders of the armed forces. The military may actually make the rules in some instances, while at other times it simply wields a veto power over rules made by the President. The church has also performed a rule-making function at times, although it usually has done so in a passive, veto-wielding, sense. Even this is less often the case today than in the past. If there is such a thing as a typical case in Latin America, it may be one where the President makes most of the authoritative rules (some of which may require military approval) and then sends them to Congress for legitimation.[2]

In each of the Latin American nations the application of rules is primarily a function of the President. Here there exists far less difference between the formal structures and the authoritative functions of government. The constitutions of this area uniformly give the President primary responsibility for the application of rules, and in most instances he does in fact exercise this function—but not always exclusively.

The armed forces traditionally have played an important role in the application of rules; this is especially true of rules made by the military. For example, a major rule made and applied by the Argentine armed forces is that the Peronists must not be allowed to regain any appreciable amount of power. To a lesser extent, the church also plays a role in the application of rules. Blanksten says that in this respect "the function of the clergy is to endow the rules with legitimacy and provide them with moral and political sanctions."[3] It should be emphasized, however, that the role of the church in the application of authoritative rules is decidedly secondary to that played by Presidents and leaders of the armed forces.

In spite of the fact that the rule-adjudication function constitutionally is granted to judicial systems, it is not the courts which in actuality perform this function. Instead, primary responsibility falls to the President, with the military again playing a major role and the church a relatively minor one. It is true that in some nations there is a trend toward the creation of an independent judiciary, but nevertheless in important controversies final adjudication seldom takes place in the courts.

Given the degree of personalism still prevalent in most of Latin America, it is only natural that the President, as the personification

[2] Constituent assemblies also play a role in the making of rules due to the frequency with which some of the Latin American nations change their constitutions (which, of course, contain many of the basic rules).

[3] George I. Blanksten, "The Politics of Latin America," in Almond and Coleman, *The Politics of the Developing Areas,* p. 526.

of the government, should have a major adjudicatory role. The church may also enter this realm because of its ability in some controversies to endow one side or the other with legitimacy. The final arbiter is, of course, the military, which in many instances considers itself a sort of national conscience.

In summary, it may be assumed that the making, applying, and adjudicating of rules are all functions that traditionally have been performed by the President. The church has played a role, but within a rather limited sphere; the role of the armed forces, on the other hand, has been very important—and in many cases even dominant. This should not be taken to mean that legislative and judicial branches are meaningless, but rather that they perform functions that differ appreciably from those described in national constitutions.[4]

---

[4] There is, needless to say, a great deal of variation from one Latin American nation to another (as is pointed out in the selections that follow). For instance, in a few nations—such as Chile and Uruguay—legislative assemblies do perform a large part of the rule-making function, and judiciaries are important in the adjudication of rules. Such cases are far from typical, however.

Latin American Constitutions*

J. LLOYD MECHAM

If the drafting of democratic constitutions serves as preparation for practice in the art of popular government then, indeed, Latin Americans are well prepared. Since gaining independence the twenty republics have essayed a grand total of 186 *magna cartae,* or an average of 9.3 each. A breakdown per country reveals the following: Argentina 4; Bolivia 14; Brazil 5; Chile 7; Colombia 6; Costa Rica 7; Cuba 2; Dominican Republic 22; Ecuador 16; El Salvador 10; Guatemala 5; Haiti 18; Honduras 10; Mexico 5; Nicaragua 8; Panama 3; Paraguay 4; Peru 12; Uruguay 4; and Venezuela 24. Today thirteen of the Latin American republics are governed by constitutions adopted since 1940, and only two antedate World War I. There seems to be no end to constitution making.

[This points up an anomaly: on the one hand apparent devotion to constitutionalism as a cure for national problems, and on the other, lack of respect for constitutional mandates. Nowhere are constitutions more elaborate and less observed.] Politically, Latin Americans seem to be unqualified optimists, for the long succession of constitutional failures has never dampened hopes that the perfect constitution—a cure-all for national ills—will be discovered eventually.

THE NOMINAL CONSTITUTION

Since it is the objective of the present inquiry to show how widely government in operation departs from constitutional mandate, we first note the constitutional norm, *i.e.,* a composite or average constitution of the Latin American republics.

THE COMPOSITE CONSTITUTION This constitution is a lengthy instrument of about 35 pages, in contrast to 13 pages for the Constitution of the United States. Cuba's constitution is the longest with 68 pages; Mexico

* J. Lloyd Mecham, "Latin American Constitutions: Nominal and Real," *Journal of Politics,* Vol. 21: No. 2 (May 1959), pp. 258–275. (Footnotes in the original version have been omitted).

144

and Venezuela tie for second at 54 pages each. The excessive length results in part from a distrust of government, particularly the executive; hence the elaborate provisions to prevent abuse of power.

The composite constitution contains no preamble. It sets about forthrightly to declare that the nation is sovereign, independent, and unitary or federal as the case may be; that the government is republican, democratic, and representative; that sovereignty is vested in the people who express their will be suffrage which is obligatory and secret for all citizens, male and female, over 20 years of age. No literacy or property tests are required. This is universal suffrage in its most liberal sense.

The guarantees of individual liberty, the familiar rights of man, are spelled out in great detail. These include: the freedoms of speech, press, assembly, and petition; equality before the law; *habeas corpus;* no unreasonable searches or seizures; due process; no retroactive penalties; and no capital punishment. Religious freedom is guaranteed, and all cults receive the equal protection of the state. [The minute enumeration of the inalienable rights of the individual is inspired by a desire to erect a constitutional barrier to tyranny.]

[The effectiveness of this barrier is weakened, however, by provisions for the suspension of the individual guarantees in times of stress.] This device is called "declaration of state of siege," a temporary annulment, by presidential decree, of all constitutional guarantees and privileges. This important presidential power is restricted only by the formality of securing congressional approval before the act if the Congress is in session, and after the act when that body is convened. The easy suspension of the constitutional guarantees is evidence of the fact that they are considerably less than absolute.

One of the most detailed and lengthy sections of the constitution deals with "social rights and duties," a recent addition to Latin American constitutional law. Conforming to contemporary conceptions of social justice, social rights and duties are enumerated *in extenso* under the subheads: labor, family, education, and the economic order.

[Labor is declared to be both a right of the individual and a social obligation.] The state recognizes a special responsibility to protect the worker. The labor section, a veritable labor code, guarantees maximum hours of work and minimum wages, equal pay for equal work without regard for sex, compensation for industrial accidents, special protection for women and children, annual holidays with pay, medical assistance, collective labor contracts, and the right to strike. A labor jurisdiction is established to which all controversies between capital and labor are to be submitted.

The social guarantees relating to the family are based on the principle that the family, motherhood, and marriage are under the protection of the state. It is the duty of the state to safeguard the social development of the family, to preserve its integrity, and to assume responsibility for neglected children. All children are equal before the law whether born in wedlock or not.

[Education also receives special mention. It is the right of everyone to receive instruction and is the responsibility of the state to provide educational facilities.] Primary education is obligatory; that provided by the state is free. Secondary and higher instruction imparted by the state is also gratuitous.

The guarantees relating to the economic order are inspired by considerations of social welfare and national consciousness. Thus, [although the right to private property is recognized, its use and retention are conditioned by social need.] Private property cannot be expropriated without just compensation. The subsoil belongs to the state which may make concessions for its exploitation. [Many of the social and economic guarantees find their inspiration in the nationalistic aspiration to abolish or bring under greater control foreign enterprises.]

The supreme powers of government are divided for their exercise, by application of the principle of the separation of powers, into the legislative, the executive, and the judicial. Two or more of these powers shall never be united in one person or group of persons, for by counterbalancing and checking each other they will prevent the establishment of a tyranny.

The legislative power is vested in a Congress composed of two houses, a Chamber of Deputies and a Senate. Both deputies and senators are chosen by direct popular vote, for terms of four and six years respectively. The deputies are apportioned according to population, whereas each province or principal political subdivision is arbitrarily assigned an equal number of senators. In the federal unions each state enjoys equal representation in the Senate, and the Federal District is given representation in both of the houses. Vacancies in the Chamber of Deputies are filled by alternates elected at the regular elections. In general both houses of the national legislature possess the same powers and perform the same functions. They are equal partners in the legislative process. Although each chamber possesses certain special powers these are of no particular consequence.

It should not be necessary in centralistic states to delegate powers to the national Congress, for it is understood to possess the power to legislate on all subjects which are not denied to it. Why then the delegation of such obvious powers as: tariff duties, taxation, creation and abolition of public offices, and appropriations? This is because in the colonial period all of these powers belonged to the king and his viceroy; and because of the persistence of the tradition of the strong executive it is felt necessary, by these constitutional delegations, to erect barriers to the establishment of a dictatorship.

The powers of the national government in the federal states of Latin America are considerably broader than in the United States. In addition to virtually all those powers delegated to the United States Congress, [the Latin American federal Congress is authorized to enact general codes of civil, penal, procedural, and commercial law for the whole nation. The federal Congress is also authorized by express constitutional grant to enact necessary legislation dealing with labor, education, public health and natural resources.] Most significant of all these exceptional federal powers, because of its use to convert constitutional federalism into actual centralism, is that of intervention into the affairs of the states "for the preservation of the republican representative form of government." As with respect to the declaration of a state of siege, the president plays the leading role in intervention; the Congress ratifies the presidential initiative.

An interesting feature of the legislative branch found in the composite constitution, and of course unknown to the American Constitution, is [the Permanent Committee of Congress.] Composed of senators and deputies chosen by their respective chambers, [this body functions during the recess of Congress. Its principal task is to keep a watchful eye over the executive branch of the government,] and, in the event of gross abuse of power, to summon the Congress in special session. Here is another of the numerous paper barriers to dictatorship.

The executive power is exercised by the president with a council of ministers. The president is chosen by direct vote of the people (even in the federal states), serves for a term of four years, and is not eligible for reelection until after one term intervenes. There is no provision for a vice-president because this heir apparent might become the magnet for conspiracies against the constituted government.

The powers of the Latin American president are relatively greater than those of the president of the United States, for, [in addition to the customary executive grants, he is authorized to directly initiate legislation in the national Congress, expel foreigners on his own authority, suspend the constitutional guarantees, and in federal states impose his will on state administrations by exercise of the power of intervention.] [His decree-making power is so broad as to be quasi-legislative in character; indeed, the constitution authorizes the Congress to delegate, in emergencies, extraordinary legislative powers to the president.] Constitutional checks on dictatorship are thus cancelled out by contrary constitutional delegations.] The end result is that dictatorships are possible within the terms, if not the spirit, of the Constitution.

The composite constitution provides that the president shall be assisted by ministers of state, the superior chiefs of their respective departments. The number and nature of these departments are to be determined by legislation. The ministers are appointed and removed by the president. All regulations, decrees, and orders of the president must be countersigned by the minister to whose department the matter pertains. This too is intended to operate as a check on the chief executive. It might be effective were not the minister the creature of the president. Ministers have the right to attend the congressional sessions and to participate in the debates, but without a vote. Although the Congress can summon a minister for a report or questioning (called interpellation) it has no power to impose political responsibility. Thus the Latin American cabinet, although not parliamentary, is rather distinct from that of the United States.

The judicial system, independent and coordinate, is composed of a hierarchy of courts; a supreme court, appellate courts, and inferior courts or courts of first instance. In the federal unions the state constitutions provide for a separate system of courts as in each of the states of the United States. The supreme court in the unitary states exercises supervisory jurisdiction over the entire court system, and in the federal unions over all the federal courts. The justices are appointed and serve for limited terms. The Latin American countries base their legal system on the Roman Law and so do not make use of trial by jury. United States influence is discovered however, in the constitutional provision conferring on the supreme court the power to declare laws unconstitutional.

In addition to the regular courts there are a number of special courts, notably the administrative tribunals and the electoral tribunals. The former have jurisdiction over suits involving the infringement of private rights by public officials, and the latter have jurisdiction over all cases involving the application of the electoral laws. The members of the electoral tribunal are recruited from the regular judiciary.

In its organization of local government the composite constitution for the unitary state provides a highly centralized system as in France. The nation is divided, principally for administrative purposes, into departments, and each department has a governor appointed by the president, and directly responsible to the minister of interior. There is no departmental assembly. Insofar as self government exists on the local level it is found in the municipalities which have their own elected mayors and councils. It should be recognized however, that neither mayor nor councilman actually has much to do. The various national ministries, particularly the *gobierno* or ministry of the interior which controls the police, absorb most of the local jurisdiction. Local self-government functions under highly restrictive limitations both in law and custom. Within the respective states of the federal unions the organization of local government conforms rather closely to that of the unitary nations.

Reflective of the prominence which the military assumes in the political life of the Latin American nations, a separate constitutional chapter is devoted to "the armed forces." In addition to national defense the military are assigned the role of "guaranteeing the constitutional powers." This provides a basis for political intervention despite the injunction that the armed forces are "essentially obedient and not deliberative." This is another of the numerous but ineffective constitutional word-barriers to the rule of force.

The constitution is easily amended. The proposed amendment must receive a two-thirds vote in two consecutive legislative sessions. The executive cannot object. This is meaningless, however, since the amendment would have little chance of adoption if the president opposed. There is no popular ratification of constitutional amendments; indeed, the original constitution itself was not popularly ratified.

VARIATIONS FROM THE NORM   Such is an average Latin American constitution. Of course there are many interesting departures from this composite instrument. Included in these exceptions to the rule are the following: the National Council of Government or plural executive in Uruguay; the unicameral congress in four of the Central American republics, also Panama and Paraguay; functional representation in the Senate in Peru and Ecuador, and modified parliamentarism or ministerial responsibility in Cuba, Ecuador, Guatemala, Panama, Peru and Uruguay.

But by no means exceptional in Latin American constitutions are unique and extraordinary provisions gauged by any constitutional standard. In the first place are those broad idealistic declarations, such as, in the Paraguayan Constitution (Art. 22), "Every Paraguayan home should be located on a piece of [privately] owned land," and "All inhabitants of the Republic [Paraguay] are obliged to earn their living by legitimate work"; also, the Venezuelan Constitution (Preliminary Declaration) consecrates "labor as the supreme virtue and as the supreme claim to human betterment." In the second place are those provisions that elaborate the obvious such as: "All usurped authority is ineffective and its acts are null" (Dominican Republic, Art. 89); and "There will be no public officials in Nicaragua the functions of which are not determined by law or regulation" (Art. 316); and "Public officials are not masters but trustees of authority" (Costa Rica, Art. 19). And in the third place there are numerous constitutional provisions which reflect an awareness of instability and inevitability of *coup d'état* and revolution, such as: "All usurped authority is ineffective and its acts are null. Every decision agreed to because of the direct or indirect application of force or the assemblage of people with a subversive attitude is similarly null" (Venezuela, Art. 87). Some constitutions even sanction the right of revolution; for example that of El Salvador (Art. 36) reads: "The right of insurrection shall in no case produce the abrogation of the laws, its effects being limited to the removal, as may be necessary, of persons discharging governmental office"; and the fundamental charter of Guatemala (Art. 2) recognizes the right of the people to "revert to rebellion" when the principle of "alternability in the exercise of the office of the President . . . is dared to be violated." The final article (136) in the Mexican Constitution achieves the utlimate in naiveté; it reads: "This Constitution shall not lose its force and vigor even should its observance be interrupted by rebellion. In case a government the principles of which are contrary to those it sanctions be established through any public disturbance, as soon as the people recover their liberty, its observance shall be re-estáblished." An identical article appeared in the Mexican Constitution of 1857.

In spite of these constitutional curiosities, which in fact have been inconsequential in contributing to or detracting from the effective operation of governments, the contemporary Latin American constitutions measure up quite well, compared with other world constitutions, as advanced instruments of democratic government. Latin American framers of constitutions are generally keen scholars of political theory and bring to the constituent assemblies a high level of competence. Nor can it be fairly held that this competence is purely theoretical. One need but read carefully the debates and proceedings of constitutional conventions to realize that they reflect not only an intimate acquaintance with the literature of political science and with constitutional development and trends around the world, but also with their own national deficiencies. Latin Americans are unsparing in self-criticism; thus there is little that a foreign political scientist can tell them of which they are unaware.

The Latin American's attitude toward constitutional law differs radically from that of the Anglo-American in that whereas to us the constitution is the fundamental law and must be observed, to the Latin American it is, in many respects, merely a declaration of ideal objectives.

[To us the constitution is almost sacrosanct, for we subscribe to the principle of a government of law; to the Latin American the constitution, generally a useful and convenient guide and program, must bend to the principle of a government of men.]

THE OPERATIVE CONSTITUTION

The foregoing, in broad outline, is the composite "paper" constitution of the Latin American republics, together with certain distinctive variations. It is now in order to describe that constitution as actually operative. With the exception of Uruguay, and the doubtful addition of Costa Rica, Chile and Mexico, democratic government does not exist in Latin America. A majority of the countries are either undisguised personalistic dictatorships or pseudodemocracies. In either case the proud constitutional assertions that these are popular, representative, democratic states, and that all governmental authority derives from the people in whom sovereignty resides, are mere verbiage, or at best declarations of ideal aspirations.

DIVERGENCES IN ACTUAL PRACTICE [Universal suffrage, provided by more than half of the constitutions, is actually exercised by only a fraction of those qualified, even in countries where voting is supposed to be compulsory] These few votes must then run the gamut of [the "official count."] It is a well-known fact that a requisite more important than honest voting is the honest poll of the votes. Since governments in power are usually in control of the voting and the tabulating of the vote, it is a commonplace that Latin American administrations never lose elections. On the rare occasions when this happens, as in Cuba in 1944 when Batista "allowed" the election of Dr. Grau San Martin, the shock of the unusual event reverberated throughout Latin America.

What shall we say about the observance of those fundamental guarantees of individual liberty: the freedoms of speech, press, assembly and conscience? What of the guarantees of domicile and all of the components of what we know as due process of law? Since from the earliest days of their independence, Latin Americans have been so profoundly engrossed in the constitutionalizing of an ever expanding enumeration of civil liberties, it seems that they should, by this time, have attained a status of sanctity and respect. This however is not the case. The [guarantees are respected only at governmental convenience and by sufferance.] The constitutions generously supply the executives with the means to be employed in emergencies, to suspend the guarantees. This device, known as "state of siege," is abused by overuse for it is the customary resort to overwhelm opposition and entrench dictatorship. It is ironical that democratic constitutions bestow so lavishly on the executive the means to destroy the feeble manifestations of democracy. With respect to the status of the individual guarantees, therefore, much depends on the attitude of the president.

A principle of the "paper constitution" which is transformed beyond recognition in the operating constitution is the separation of the powers. Theoretically the three powers—executive, legislative and judicial—are separate, coordinate, and equal. Numerous safeguards, many of which are found in our own constitutions, are provided to prevent wanton exercise of authority by any one of these powers. Because of the well-founded belief that it is the executive which will be most prone to irresponsibility and be acquisitive of power, the most numerous constitutional limitations are those imposed on the presidents. Despite all this, and responsive to the strongman tradition in Latin governments[the executive overshadows the other two powers. Latin American governments are emphatically of the strong presidential type.]

That the president is the dominant power in the government is never doubted. His supremacy derives from his dual position as constitutional chief-executive and as extra-constitutional *caudillo*, chief or boss. From the earliest days of their independence Latin Americans have shown a strong disposition for *caudillos*, preferably for those with a military background, for the magnetic attraction of the man on horseback can always be expected to reinforce the lure of demagogues. The *caudillo* embodies the program of his political partisans; he is the platform of his pseudo-party. That is what is called *personalismo* in Latin American politics, which means placing emphasis on individuals rather than on public policies. The *caudillo* because of his hold on the popular imagination, but more significantly because of his control of the army, meets with docile acceptance.[Neither the disguised dictatorship, nor the pseudo-democracy is a government of laws, all are governments of men.] One of the least effective of the constitutional checks on ambitious presidents is the no-reelection provision. *Caudillismo* and *personalismo* have transformed the constitutional office of the presidency beyond recognition.

In consequences of the dominance of the executive it is hardly necessary to indicate the position of the congress and the courts. Both are subordinate to the executive. Since the president usually controls the electoral machinery and since the members of congress are elected with

his approval, or certainly without his disapproval, they are almost completely amenable to the executive's pleasure. Although they put on a
show of heated debate, these histrionics are usually intended for the
edification of a gullible public. Since most of the congressmen are the
president's men and can be counted on to go down the line for him,
the president gets the kind of legislation he wants. Rare indeed are
the occasions when he must exercise the veto power.

Freedom and equality of the courts is also a fiction, for the judiciary,
like the legislature, is subordinate to the executive, numerous constitutional provisions to bulwark the power and independence of the courts
to the contrary notwithstanding. In fact, the courts of Latin America
are even less effective than the legislature in limiting the authority of
strong presidents. Although a number of the constitutions give to the
courts the power of judicial review, rare, indeed, are the judges who
will tempt fate by invalidating acts of congress or presidential decree
laws. It simply is not good form or good sense.

It is not necessarily because the presidents have ways of getting rid
of objectionable judges which accounts for their surrender of independence; rather it is because of a long standing tradition of Spanish origin
that there must be no interference by the judiciary with the policies
of the chief executive. The old principle that the king can do no wrong
is observed by the deference paid by the courts to the wishes of the
president. However, routine matters in the lower courts, and other cases
in which the executive manifests no interest, are usually free of political
interference.

The constitutions of the centralistic states give to the president and
his Minister of Interior sufficient power to maintain a firm grip on local
government. Therefore it is seldom necessary to resort to extra-constitutional means to impose the will of the executive on all strata of local
government. In the federal states however, the imposing of the will
of the national government on the individual states and their subdivisions, resulting in the converting of theoretical federalism into actual
centralism, is accomplished by violating the spirit, if not the letter, of
the constitution. This is the notorious interventionism, a common practice
in all of the so-called federal states of Latin America: Argentina, Brazil,
Mexico and Venezuela.

As if it were the manifest purpose of the federal constitution to nullify
the very federalism which those instruments established, they give the
federal authorities, actually the president, exceptional power to intervene
in and control state governments. The power usually invoked is to preserve the republican form of government. The vagueness of the meaning

of "republican form of government" gives to the president ample latitude for action, an opportunity, needless to say, which he seldom neglects, particularly when the opposition seems to have won an election, for it is intolerable that a state government should be controlled by elements distasteful to the national administration. On such occasions the election is declared to be fraudulent (as, indeed, it was) and, since for this reason the republican form of government ceased to exist, it accordingly is the duty and responsibility of the president to order an intervention. An executive decree brings the state government under federal control. An interventor appointed by the president takes full charge of state affairs supplanting both the governor and the legislature. In due time, when the president is disposed to restore autonomy to the state, his interventor supervises an election and makes certain that only officials acceptable to the national administration are successful at the polls. Certainly, if there is a constitutional principle which is rendered meaningless by actual practice, it is that the states are autonomous entities in the federal unions of Latin America.

[Equally as fictitious as Latin American federalism is the constitutional mandate that the army does not deliberate, i.e., intervene in politics.] Any practical discussion of Latin American politics which omits reference to the political role of the army would be sadly unrealistic, for the most significant feature of Latin American politics has always been the predominance of the military authority over the civil. It is an old story dating from the independence period when the possession of governmental authority became the prize of contesting arms. None of the countries has escaped the blight of military political intervention, and today [the military are in control, openly or disguised, in most of the nations of Latin America.]

[The very nature and purpose of the army invites political activity, for it is designed more to preserve internal order and support the regime than to defend the frontiers against foreign invaders. Several of the constitutions impose on the army the responsibility of guaranteeing the fulfillment of the constitution and the laws.] The militarists do not shirk this obligation for they regard themselves as the most competent, unselfish, and patriotic interpreters of the national interest. Moreover, it is a well-established fact that a presidential candidate is severely handicapped unless he bears a military title. There is a feeling, shared by more than just the militarists, that the nature of the executive office calls for the qualities and experience generally associated with military command. Today military men preside over several of the countries. But [whether the president be an army officer or a civilian he never forgets that his tenure is dependent on the continued support of the

army.] Accordingly, he showers favors on the officers and men to keep
them happy, for dissatisfaction breeds revolt, the over-indulged resort
of the political opposition.

VIOLENCE INSITUTIONALIZED One of the most patent facts of Latin
American government, and certainly the best-known to Anglo-Americans,
is recurring *revolution*. The term is a misnomer, for it usually refers
to nothing more than a *coup d'état* or a *cuartelazo* (barrack revolt),
the classic "substitution of bullets for ballots," the ousting of the "ins"
by the "outs," or perhaps the enforcement of the principle of "alternability of public office." These are not popular movements, for relatively
few people participate, outside the military. The rabble, of course, assem-
bles in the main plaza to acclaim impartially each succeeding *caudillo*.

Since the great revolution for independence early in the nineteenth
century there have been few authentic revolutions in Latin America,
that is if we restrict the term to those deep-seated popular movements
aimed at fundamental change in the political, social, and economic
orders. Only a limited number of the demonstrations of force so common
to the political scene are worthy of designation as revolutions; this,
notwithstanding the crying need in most of the countries for a thorough
revamping. What Latin America needs, paradoxically, is not less but
more revolutions. Fundamental revolution may be the specific for the
cure of chronic pseudo-revolution.

[So frequently employed is the *coup d'état* (hereafter referred to as
revolution in italics), and so ever-present is it in the calculations of
government and practicing politicians that it would not be amiss to
regard it as a component of the functioning constitution.] It has already
been noted that some of the formal constitutions accept the inevitability
of *revolution* and try to provide accommodations for that eventuality.
One of these is the prohibition of capital punishment for political offenses
(in those few countries that still allow capital punishment). [Another
is the recognition of the right of asylum to political fugitives.] With
the exception of the Haya de la Torre case, Latin American governments
have been most scrupulous in recognizing the right of political offenders
to enjoy immunity in foreign embassies and legations, and to leave the
country under safe conduct. Or, as a recent writer puts it, "If their
[the oppositions'] effort fails they are never denounced as traitors by
the triumphant administration, but under the *noblesse oblige* of the
system, are allowed to retire quietly into exile." The same punishment,
exile, is meted to the ousted president and his principal ministers in
the event the *revolution* is successful.

Why so tolerant of the offense of taking up arms against the consti-

tuted government? In the first place, since constitutions are regarded
as inevitably ephemeral, the violation of the constitutional order, being
more or less expected, is regarded as one of the lesser offenses. And
in the second place a government should not be too severe in the punishment of its unsuccessful revolutionaries, for inevitably there comes the
time, however secure a regime may seem, when it will find itself outweighed in the scales of fortune How convenient then that the late
incumbents be allowed to depart quietly into exile which by the law of
averages will be of short duration. It may be argued that leniency begets
revolutions, but on the other hand it makes them less dangerous.

Revolutions might be regarded more seriously were not their sham
revealed by the sad experiences of history. Despite extravagant promises
to achieve democratic government and social justice, the shameful exploitation of the people is continued by each new group of "liberators."
Revolutions bring new forces into the government, but the basic political
and social systems remain the same.

[Since Latin American administrations seldom lose elections, the justification of *revolution* as the only cure for *continuismo* is worn thin,
for all too often the opposition, realizing its inability to win an election
even if honestly conducted, cries fraud and coercion and resorts to its
natural right of rebellion. It is significant that a large percentage of
these forcible "transfers of power" occur during the incumbent's first
term of office, after only a few months. Take Ecuador for example:
the average time vouchsafed the twenty presidents during the period
1925–1948 was thirteen and a half months each. Of these, and a multitude of similar cases in other countries, it can hardly be held that governments tenacious of power left the opposition no alternative but resort
to force. On the contrary they are indicative of the mercurial temper
of Latins and a strong indisposition to wait for scheduled elections.
Dissatisfaction with a current administration calls for immediate ouster
action.

Honestly conducted elections, although a prime requisite, will not
alone insure orderly and stable government. Equally as important is
the willingness of the defeated minority to accept the will of the majority. This does not come easily to Latins for it calls for a measure of
self-discipline which they do not possess.

ADJUSTING THE CONSTITUTIONS TO REALITY   In view of the considerable
divergences of actual practice from the constitutional norm, the question
arises: how can the fundamental charters of Latin America be regarded
as "acceptable examples of the constitution makers art" since they are
merely nominal or paper constitutions? Does not the fact that they are

observed in the breach prove their artificiality? No, this is not necessarily so, for the validity of the cliché that Latin American constitutions are "divorced from reality" needs to be examined.

It can be conceded that these constitutions are divorced from reality in that they ostensibly establish democracies on the insecure foundation of a citizenry lacking in the tradition of freedom and undisciplined in democratic processes. However, it should be recalled that Latin American constitution makers do not delude themselves that they are building upon achieved democracy, but rather are setting their nations upon the road to democratic achievement. When viewed in this light Latin American constitutions are actually in considerable harmony with reality.

The critics of these alleged "exotic" and "artificial" constitutions fail to develop their arguments to any reasonable conclusion. They appear to hold for the incompatibility of the Latin American and the democratic constitution. Yet it is a fair surmise that these very critics would be the last to argue for the abandonment of all democratic pretense in Latin American constitutions. This must mean then, that they believe that the materials for democratic government are at hand in Latin America, and all that is needed is a rational arrangement of these parts.

This we find impossible to accept. How indeed are these so-called artificial and exotic constitutions to be modified to conform to the realities of the Latin American scene and still retain their democratic character? What provisions which they do not already contain in profusion will curb *caudillismo*, the *cuartelazo*, and the rigging of elections? Who can suggest constitutional formulae which will broaden and strengthen the bases of popular government and usher in political, social, and economic democracy?

The simple truth of the matter is that there are no constitutional formulae which, however well-suited to any practical situation or peculiar environment, will of themselves inaugurate a democratic regime. The road to popular and responsible government is a long and difficult way. There are no easy shortcuts. Those requisites of a democratic society: fair play, tolerance, self-discipline, responsibility, human dignity, majority rule but respect for the minority, a spirit of compromise, and respect for the rule of law, are the qualities of a democratic citizen which have deep roots in his historical past. These qualities which are of the inner man and so cannot be legislated into existence have not unfortunately prospered in the soil of the Latin American's historical past. Nor after 140 years of tortured experience in self-government does the present status of democratic achievement in Latin America auger much improvement in the forseeable future.

Latin American Federalism* | WILLIAM S. STOKES

Introduction

Most Latin Americans are conditioned by their historical traditions and social and economic institutions to understand and accept concentrated, centralized power, usually of a highly personal sort. The strong, frequently exalted rôle of the father in the family, the importance of the elite in the class system, the honor, dignity, power, and influence of the *doctor* from the *aula* (lecture hall), the significance of centralized leadership in the Church, the paramountcy of the "general" in politics, and the position of the public and private monopolist in the economic system—[these characteristics of Hispanic culture all suggest powerful, centralized government] In addition, the political experience and tradition of hundreds of years was with a powerful monarchy operating by means of a centralized administrative hierarchy. The modern constitutions all provide for "interventionist" states.

In a unitary state, all the power that government can have is concentrated in a single organization. Centralization is, therefore, a natural, cardinal principle in the unitary state. The values of Hispanic social, economic, and political life suggest the plausibility—perhaps inevitability—of unitary organization. Sixteen of the 20 Latin American states are in fact organized formally along unitary lines. On the other hand, individual participation in decentralized local units of government is largely foreign to Hispanic culture, and there is practically nothing in Latin America comparable to the "home rule" of the states and local governments in the United States. . . .

In order to show how powerful is the predisposition to centralization in Hispanic culture, consideration should be given to what has happened in the instances in which the Latin American countries have sought decentralization through federalism. . . .

THE CENTRALIZED ARGENTINE FEDERAL REPUBLIC

Government by the First Junta, the Second Junta, the First Triumvirate, and the Second Triumvirate followed the May Revolution. There was a good deal of experimentation in the drafting of constitutions or organic statutes in the period 1810–1816, but no government or organic

* William S. Stokes, "The Centralized Federal Republics of Latin America," in *Essays in Federalism* (Claremont, California: Claremont Men's College, 1961), pp. 93–160. (Footnotes in the original version have been omitted.)

158

law was effective throughout the entire area. The great issue was monarchy or republic, and many of the most distinguished military and civilian figures favored monarchy. When no monarch could be found, and the republic became inevitable, the issue was now the unitary or federal state. Again, many of the important figures favored the unitary form. General José de San Martín, for example, is quoted as saying, "I die every time I hear federation mentioned."

The Congress of Tucumán of March, 1816 finally broke all ties with Spain by issuing a Declaration of Independence on July 9, 1816. The Congress drafted the country's first constitution on April 22, 1819. It set up "The United Provinces of South America" with a unitary form of government. The provinces repudiated the 1819 document, however. Not a single one was willing to accept a system which would make Buenos Aires centrally dominant. When the Congress adjourned on February 2, 1820, and the Supreme Director at Buenos Aires resigned, central government disappeared. The provinces seceded, drafted their own constitutions, and set up independent states. Several signed treaties of alliance among themselves.

The unitary constitution of 1819 was followed by the Constitution of 1826. This constitution offered modest concessions to local autonomy by permitting the provinces to elect their own "Administrative Councils." But the constituent assembly of 1824 which framed the 1826 constitution was dedicated to unitary principles. Bernardino Rivadavia was elected president without consulting the provinces or even waiting for their action on the constitution. Provincial autonomy was in fact destroyed by making the provincial governors "responsible to the president."

The country was plunged into civil war. The man who eventually restored order was Juan Manuel de Rosas. Rosas became one of the hemisphere's greatest despots. Although a federalist, he advanced centralization by subduing all rival *caudillos* in the provinces. . . . Rosas' long dictatorship was finally terminated by military defeat at the hands of General Urquiza at the Battle of Monte Caseros on February 3, 1852.

Despite the centralizing effect of the "federal" *caudillo,* there were 30 treaties among the provinces dealing with military, commercial, and other matters in the period 1820–1846. The last important agreement was the Treaty of El Litoral signed by Buenos Aires, Santa Fé, and Entre Rios on February 15, 1831. It became known as the Federal Pact of 1831.

On April 8, 1852, General Urquiza invited the governors to meet at San Nicolás de los Arroyos on May 20. He made reference in his invitation to the Federal Pact of 1831. The governors of 12 provinces attended the meeting and signed the "Agreement of San Nicolás."

The Constitutional Convention of November, 1852 included representation from 13 of the 14 provinces. However, Buenos Aires, the most important province, rejected the San Nicolás agreement and refused to attend the convention. Although the prospects for a federal system appeared dismal, the Committee on Constitutional Affairs submitted a draft on April 18, 1853.

The 1853 constitution was not submitted to the provincial legislatures for approval or rejection, nor was it voted upon by the people in conventions or in plebiscites. The federation attempted to function, but it faced conflict—and at times war—with Buenos Aires. Buenos Aires finally agreed to ratify (November 9, 1859), subject to certain conditions which were put in the form of amendments at the constitutional convention held on January 5, 1860. The Congress of the Confederation called a national convention on June 23, 1860 to consider the reforms. It accepted all of them with minor modifications on September 14, 1860.

This historical background serves to demonstrate that the Argentine federal system grew out of genuine conflict and was designed to be more than a paper organization of government. The provinces, however, have succumbed to centralization under the Constitution of 1853. Professor Rosendo A. Gómez, in a remarkable study, explains in detail how this came about. The practice of direct intervention by the federal government in the affairs of the provinces is a dramatic part of the explanation, but there are other factors which must also be taken into account.

The enumerated powers of the federal government were considerably greater in the Argentine Constitution of 1853 than in the United States Constitution of 1787. For example, the Argentine federal government was given the power in Article 67 to draw up civil, commercial, penal, and mining codes for the entire nation. Article 67 also contained broad authority to promote and develop the prosperity and well-being of the provinces. The 1949 constitution expanded the powers of the federal government in both of these fields and compelled the provinces (in Article 5) to cooperate in whatever the federal government saw fit to initiate. Scott concluded that " . . . the new constitution makes it clear that in practice even limited provincial sovereignty is moribund in the country." The 1853 constitution concentrated power in the federal executive. The 1949 constitution added even greater authority to his strong, centralized position.

Article 6 of the 1853 constitution provided that the federal government could intervene in the provincial governments in order to: (1) guarantee a republican form of government; (2) repel foreign invasion; or (3) restore order on the request of provincial authorities.

The central government began to intervene directly in the provinces right from the beginning of the federal system. It has continued the practice to the present time. Gómez has found that there were 20 interventions from 1853 to 1860, 101 interventions from 1860 to 1930, and 145 interventions up to the *cuartelazo* of June, 1943 which ultimately brought *peronismo* to power. In recent years, especially from about 1946 to 1955, when the great executive, General Juan Domingo Perón, was president, there was almost continuous intervention in the entire republic.

Although there were some 25 attempts made up to 1932 to enact legislation to regulate the power of the federal government to intervene in the provinces, the Congress has not debated the issue seriously since the 1860's and 1870's. The courts have refused to restrain the federal president and congress on the grounds that the issue is a "political question."

Gómez has found that many pretexts have been used for intervention. The president usually decides whether republican government has been threatened, although he may refer the question to the subservient congress. The procedure is simple. The president appoints an *interventor* to govern the province, sends troops to back him up, makes the necessary political changes in the province, usually through supervising an election, and turns power over to the governor and legislature of his choice at the time he deems appropriate. The president governs under *estado de sitio* (state of siege) during the entire period if he so desires. *Estado de sitio* was used 36 times from 1853 to 1946. The provinces are compelled to accept intervention. They lack force to resist. In addition, they are accustomed to the procedure. There is evidence that many expect it as a normal concomitant of federal-provincial relations.

It must not be assumed that only authoritarian presidents who have seized power by force have used intervention to effect centralization. President Hipólito Irigoyen is usually regarded as the most "liberal" and "democratic" president Argentina has ever had. President Irigoyen intervened 24 times in the provinces in his two administrations (1916–1922; 1928–1930), more times than any other president up to the administration of General Perón. Irigoyen did not even go through the formality of arranging for some provincial authority to request intervention. He simply moved in with federal troops.

So effective has been intervention, along with fiscal and financial controls and domination of the political parties by Buenos Aires, that Dr. Gómez was led to conclude that, "The provinces have become little more than election districts."

In conclusion, one can say: The founders of Argentine federalism advocated division of powers as a restraint upon the exercise of arbitrary power in the center, and they recognized the value of federalism in adjudicating the intense economic conflict between Buenos Aires (as capital, principal city, rail center, major port) and the provinces in the interior. The evidence indicates clearly that neither the masses nor the classes have insisted that federalism perform either or both of these rôles. Instead, centralization became almost instantly a major characteristic of government, not only in federal-provincial relations but in provincial-local relations as well.

Although Argentina is usually regarded as culturally and economically the most advanced of the Latin American countries, it has not been immune to political problems of the most serious nature. Even in the face of centralization and increasing centralization, many Argentine *pensadores* and men in public life continue to urge federalism as the most logical and satisfactory method of establishing and utilizing public power. However, the relative failure of federalism to perform the functions for which it was created raises questions as to the value of the form in a country of Hispanic culture, such as Argentina. It is certain that the cumulative effect of hundreds of years of experience with governmental centralization plus the conditioning impact of the class system, family, church, education, army, and economic organization—all of which are strongly centralized—have created a subtle but powerful, recognizable predisposition to support great personal concentrations of political power at the center. The more completely that power has become centralized, however, the more prone it has become to abuse. The culmination of misuse and abuse of power occurred in the tyranny of Perón's planned state. However horrible *peronismo* might have been, it was popular, especially with the lower class, organized labor groups in the urban centers. The reform administration of President Frondizi has restored the Constitution of 1853 without reforming federal-provincial relations. The basic problem is that Argentine society is not conducive to the development of attitudes of individualism, voluntarism, and participation. If governmental policies would lead to an environment in which such attitudes could develop, one of the immediate concomitants would be demand for more independent provincial and local government. But, attitudes and values develop slowly and change slowly. Even though one may believe personally that men everywhere will ultimately perceive that only individual liberty and freedom advance their interests and those of the community, the scholar is compelled by fact and reason to conclude that profound changes in the nature of Argentine federalism will not occur in the immediate future.

THE CENTRALIZED MEXICAN FEDERAL SYSTEM

Ramos de Arizpe submitted his famous "Report on the Natural, Political and Civil Condition of the Provinces of Coahuila, Nuevo León, Nuevo Santander and Texas of the Four Eastern Interior Provinces of the Kingdom of Mexico, with an Exposition of the Defects of the System in General, Especially the Government, and of the Reforms and Improvements Necessary to their Prosperity" to the Cortes of Cádiz on November 7, 1811. "Doctor," lawyer, and priest, Ramos de Arizpe was a man of culture and prestige who had spent some 36 years on the frontiers of northern New Spain. He languished six years in Spanish prisons as a reward for his *Report*. By the time Mexico achieved independence, however, his ceaseless efforts in behalf of local and provincial self-government had resulted in a series of popularly-elected councils, which he called "provincial deputations." Nettie Lee Benson, in manuscripts published in 1950 and 1955, describes Ramos de Arizpe's ideas in detail and evaluates accurately his influence in the development of the federal Constitution of 1824.

Ramos de Arizpe, the principal author of the constitution, adopted the United States model of division of powers. The states were burdened with limitations, however. They were obliged to model their constitutions on the federal document, and any disputes they might have with the federal government or among themselves were to be adjudicated by the federal congress. Dr. Ramos de Arizpe undoubtedly understood federalism, abhorred the tyranny of centralized power, and advocated local self-government. Apparently many Mexican supporters of federalism did not, however. The new government almost immediately became strongly dominated by centralized, executive power. For example, the Constitution of 1824 contained a provision which stated that the president could be granted extraordinary powers in times of emergency. The congress promptly delegated such powers to President Victoria, although there was less of an emergency than at any time in the next several decades.

To most Mexicans in public life, federalism seemed to be more of a political slogan than a structural form of government with real meaning in practical politics. There was a genuine struggle between those who yearned for the restoration of monarchy and the reestablishment of the traditional values of Hispanic culture and those who wanted a republic and a fundamental break with the past. Federalism, local autonomy, and even individual participation in government were not major objectives in themselves. Certainly it is accurate to say that few of the ideals and aspirations of men like Ramos de Arizpe were realized under the Constitution of 1824.

The centralist Constitutions of 1836 and 1843 abolished federalism, restored directly or indirectly many of the privileges of the elite groups, and made possible personal dictatorship under the colorful Santa Ana. The reform movement of the 1850's, led by men like the great Benito Juárez and Miguel Lerdo de Tejada, culminated in the drafting of a new constitution in 1856, which was promulgated on February 5, 1857.

The Constitution of 1857 reestablished federalism on the United States model of division of powers. Justo Sierra, writing late in the nineteenth century in his magazine, *La Libertad,* and Emilio Rabasa in his famous book, *La constitución y la dictadura* (1912), both criticized the Constitution of 1857 because it made the presidency too weak. In fact, however, power became centralized in the hands of the chief executive. The states were made subservient to the federal government. This was made possible in part by Article 74, Part B, Sections V-VI, which conferred on the federal Senate the power to adjust all political disputes arising among state officers or authorities when one of them appealed for such aid or in cases of armed conflict. In addition, if the Senate declared that all the constitutional powers of a state had disappeared, the president was empowered to intervene and appoint a provisional governor.

It was under the federal Constitution of 1857 that Porfirio Díaz established executive dictatorship and destroyed any semblance of effective state or local self-government in the long period of his domination (1876–1911). The Revolution of 1910–11 resulted eventually in the Constitution of Querétaro of 1917.

[Federalism was not an issue at the constitutional convention at Querétaro. It was neither challenged, defended, debated, or even discussed at any length whatever. The impression one gets is that federalism was inextricably associated with liberal, republican ideals and was, therefore, an indispensable part of the new system. But it is doubtful that the framers of the 1917 document contemplated that it would be a working principle of government. Article 124 guaranteed reserved or residual powers to the states, but the enumerated powers of the federal government in the "interventionist" state were so numerous and all-embracing that few areas of importance were left to reserve.]

Although the constitution established separation of powers, in fact the Mexican chief executive has completely dominated the legislative and judicial branches. As head of the central government, he has made use of certain constitutional powers to control state and local government. Article 76 restates the provisions of the 1857 constitution relating to the power of the Senate to adjudicate political questions or disputes among state officials and to declare that all state constitutional government has disappeared. This provision, of course, permits federal intervention in and control over the state governments. In the most complete and detailed analysis yet made of this form of federal intervention, Scott found that the Senate declared disappearance of powers 45 times in period of 1918–1948. Although some of the interventions could be justified in terms of constitutional provisions, Scott concluded that at least 25 of the instances were "arbitrary."

It is possible that writers on Mexican federalism have over-emphasized the importance of Article 76 in destroying the federal system. Scott demonstrates that its use has been limited since 1935 and is now confined almost entirely to instances of clear emergency. The reason for its decline, however, is not that the states have become stronger but rather that the federal government has found more effective methods of maintaining and expanding centralized control.

The *Secretaría de Gobernación* is, in Scott's opinion, " . . . of much greater importance in breaking down true federalism." *Gobernación,* acting under the personal direction of the president, is the intermediary between the federal government and the states. Since about 1921, it has built up a detailed record of the political histories of the states. It early organized a group of confidential investigators who studied the backgrounds and political positions of state candidates and officers. It watches over state elections. In addition, *Gobernación* receives the petitions and complaints of state officials, political parties or factions, and private citizens. The president permits *Gobernación* to adjudicate most of the day-to-day political difficulties of state governments and federal-state relations. Its function is to know who are the individuals and groups in each state who will work amicably with the federal government and who will not. *Gobernación* sees to it that the friends are in office while the enemies are denied political power.

Article 105 provides that the federal Supreme Court shall have exclusive jurisdiction in all controversies between state officials or branches of government as to the constitutionality of their acts. This permits the Supreme Court to decide in favor of those state officers whom the president supports. In addition, the record of state appeals to the Supreme Court for protection against federal interference is almost completely unsuccessful. Scott uses the term "futility" to describe state efforts to achieve protection from the Supreme Court "against the depredations of the national government."

In the area of functions, the federal government has maintained its great grant of enumerated powers and has increased its jurisdiction at the expense of the states. For example, the evidence is overwhelming that the federal government has gradually whittled away the tax base of the state and local governments. Indeed, a monopoly of taxation by the federal government may well develop in the foreseeable future. Of all income or revenue taken in by all levels of government in 1956, the national government and the Federal District (Mexico City) received 85.9%, the 29 states, 11.1%, and the 2,349 *municipios,* 3%. The constitutions of 1857 and 1917 did not allocate taxes or tax sources among the federal, state, and local governments. There is overlapping and duplication at the present time. However, the central government has contrived to seize the important sources of revenue for itself. The federal *Secretaría de Hacienda* has had the task of delimiting the tax fields, and some of the methods it has used have unquestionably been unconstitutional.

The most interesting method the federal government has used is called *participaciones* or shared taxes. Under this method, the federal government collects the taxes and returns a portion of the tax to the state in return for the exclusive right to tax in the field concerned. A number of National Fiscal Conventions have been held, beginning August 10–20, 1925, in which problems of federal-state use of taxes have been discussed. It is fair to conclude that the device of *participaciones* and the fiscal conventions have had a centralizing effect. The states borrow from the central government on anticipated *participaciones* and thus become even more susceptible to control. Such debts sometimes are forgiven if the states willingly accept federal tutelage. In addition to *participaciones*, the federal grant-in-aid is also used. Writing in 1959, Scott concludes that there is a ". . . very high degree of hierarchical control of finances."

[The federal government seeks aggressively to achieve centralization, yet Scott and Mecham point out that the states are apathetic and do not defend their constitutional rights of self-government] The psychological attitudes and values, of course, are all-important in explaining this seeming paradox. There is a predisposition toward strong, centralized, personal power in Hispanic affairs. The states do not even object when the constitution is formally amended in ways that obviously result in further federal centralization. Scott found that the constitution had been amended 110 times up to January 1, 1949. He concluded in 1949 that federalism is "indeed defunct" in Mexico. Instead, ". . . the constitutional and political systems have never represented and probably never will represent a federal system of government." After ten years of additional research, Scott published an important book on Mexican government (in 1959) in which he makes crystal clear that the 1949 conclusions on federalism remain valid.

Professor Spain published a revisionist study in 1956 in which he contended that the critics of Mexican federalism had perhaps overemphasized the centralizing tendencies of the federal government and underestimated the vitality of state and local government. His argument seems to be based on the following points: (1) geographical remoteness of the states and local governments from the central authorities often means that these units can formulate interim policy; (2) the facts show that "the scope and quality of state activity vary from one region of the country to another;" (3) the state constitutions define and describe their reserved powers; (4) there are instances on record in which the Senate has failed to declare "disappearance of powers" and instances in which the federal government could not intimidate a state government; (5) an important instance of state independence occurred in the 1920's and 1930's when the state of Sonora decided to expel certain Chinese for allegedly exploiting Mexicans in the banking and commercial fields. The state defied federal court orders and expelled the Chinese. The federal government failed to send troops or to intervene in any other way. Professor Spain concludes that the remains of state autonomy are "substantial."

Dr. Spain's research merits careful study. Time may reveal that his judgments are more accurate with respect to Mexican federalism than, for example, the devastating critique of Scott. Many of Professor Spain's illustrations in support of federalism, however, also characterize the operation of government under unitary structures in Latin America as well. Federalism requires a dividing of sovereignty through some form of division of powers in which the central and local units respect each other's independence and in which the units are in fact able to operate in their respective spheres without invasion from the other. No federal system functions precisely in accordance with the theory of division of powers under which it is established. The evidence is strong indeed that the Mexican federal system deviates almost totally from the legal and constitutional pattern.

THE CENTRALIZED BRAZILIAN FEDERAL SYSTEM

The adoption of the United States model of division of powers was artificial to some degree in all the Latin American countries which established federal systems, with the possible exception of Argentina. The division between federal delegated or enumerated powers and state reserved or residual powers was particularly artificial in the case of the Brazilian Constitution of 1891. By the time the constitution was adopted, Brazil was as unitary a state as almost any that could be cited in the world at that time. The beginnings of state autonomy and local self-government had largely been extirpated.

The influence of the United States was strong in the sections of the constitution dealing with federalism. There were some differences, however. The federal government was given the exclusive power to regulate foreign and interstate commerce and navigation, to establish or change the boundaries of the states, and to draft uniform law for the entire republic in the civil, commercial, and criminal fields. On the other hand, the states were given the exclusive power to tax exports, real property, transfers of property rights, and industries and professions. The states and local governments were permitted to establish and control their political branches, subject to federal intervention, and they were empowered to create their own judicial systems.

Division of powers functioned instantly in such a way as to preserve most of the characteristics of traditional centralization. Article 6 permitted the federal government to intervene in the states in order to repel foreign invasion or invasion of one state by another, to maintain the republican form of government, reestablish order in the states on the request of the political authorities, and to insure execution of federal laws and court decisions.

The federal government intervened on November 3, 1891, and like the central governments of Argentina, Venezuela, and Mexico, it continued to intervene throughout the entire life of the Constitution of 1891. Efforts were made from time to time to curtail or control the power of intervention, but they were never strong enough to effect serious changes. For example, an amendment to the constitution was adopted in 1926 which prohibited federal intervention in matters which were "peculiar" to the states. The federal government continued, however, to have power to intervene to repel invasion, guarantee the integrity of the nation and respect for the country's laws and constitutional principles, such as the republican form of government, municipal autonomy, the right to vote, and non-reelection of political officials as prescribed by law.

The new constitution, which the National Assembly accepted on September 18, 1946, maintains the federal system with 20 states, a Federal District, and four territories. The 1946 constitution restores to the states their flags, hymns, and other symbols. The states can unite, divide, or dismember themselves to form new states. They have a share of the taxing power. Article 18 guarantees reserved powers to the states. Anyone who examines the enumerated or delegated powers of the federal government, however, is likely to conclude that there is very little left to reserve. The traditional power of the federal government to intervene in the states is maintained in Articles 7–14, but the power is worded negatively. The central government cannot intervene unless there is foreign invasion or civil war or unless it is necessary to prevent reelection of governors or mayors to consecutive terms or unless federal power is needed to enforce court decisions. Whether the power is worded negatively or not, the federal government has seen fit to intervene in the states with armed force in recent years.

[Neither the states nor the people have anything to do directly with amending the constitution.] Article 217 permits the national legislature to propose and ratify amendments.

Nevertheless, it was the intention of the farmers to strengthen the powers of the states with relationship to the federal government. The most populous states were deliberately under-represented in the National Chamber of Deputies in an effort to increase the importance of the less-developed states. Although the federal government is clearly favored in the collection of taxes and other revenue, Article 15 provides that the central government must share the proceeds of certain designated taxes with the state and local governments. These provisions, although undoubtedly superior to the relationships that existed from 1930–1945, still greatly encourage centralization.

Ocelio de Medeiros, who has compared the status of the *município* under the constitutions of 1891, 1934, 1937, and 1946, creates the impression that the present period is one which might permit a resurgence of local autonomy. If the comparison is made with the 1930's, using Carvalho's research on the *municípios* for this period, such as inference is unquestionably justified. The 1947 basic law on municipalities strengthens this position, as Arruda Viana's work makes clear. On the other hand, Rafael Xavier, writing in 1946, pointed out that the *municípios* were receiving only about 8 per cent of public revenues, and most of these funds were collected and spent by the capitals of the states. Xavier argues, quite rightly, that local governments must have an adequate tax base in order to achieve any important degree of autonomy and self-government.

All the Brazilian scholars and men in public life the author talked to in São Paulo and in Rio de Janeiro in 1955 spoke in terms of centralized planning for local, state, and regional development. A dynamic, progressive, hard-working state like São Paulo, nourished by a steady flow of ambitious European immigrants, can be expected to challenge the federal government and win from time to time. Most of the other states and local governments cannot and must, therefore, submit to centralized tutelage and control.

The conclusions one can draw from the experience of Brazil in attempting to secure decentralization through federalism are similar to those one is compelled to reach for Argentina, Mexico, and Venezuela. Political tradition and the nature of the social and economic institutions have produced a strong centralizing effect, which perhaps reached a climax in the period of Getúlio Vargas' tenure (1930–1945; 1950–1954).

It has often been argued that Brazil's great size and the fact of ethnic and cultural heterogeneity will forever guarantee an effective federal system. The facts belie the contention, for Brazil has never achieved the decentralization that federalism contemplates. In addition, one must not forget the case of the Soviet Union with great area, ethnic and cultural diversity, and an avowedly federal constitution, but with a strongly centralized system of government.

But whereas the scholar is likely to conclude that centralized governmental direction of economic and social as well as political affairs is likely to continue in the foreseeable future in Argentina, Mexico, and Venezuela, there is somewhat less certainty that this will be the case in Brazil. This attitude derives from the vitality, initiative, and spirit of independence of the people of the state of São Paulo. It would require detailed analysis to explain why São Paulo has been able to achieve what other states and provinces in Latin American federal systems have been unable to achieve. At the risk of over-simplification, one can suggest that the impact of energetic European immigrants employing traditional principles of private initiative and enterprise have won for themselves such economic success—largely without governmental aid, direction, or control—that a new set of values, emphasizing individualism, localism, and independence, has developed. Although centralizing trends are still dominant in Brazilian politics, it is certainly fair to conclude that São Paulo is difficult to control and will continue to be difficult to control. What has occurred in this one state may well occur in others, with the result in time that some of the principles of federalism may become generally operative.

THE CENTRALIZED FEDERAL SYSTEM OF VENEZUELA

Less research has been conducted with respect to Venezuelan federalism than has been the case with the other federal republics of Latin America. Enough work has been done, however, to permit certain things to be said.

Venezuela is a large country which has always had well-defined geographical regions which created, in theory at least, the bases for federal structure. There are four major regions, and in the important Highlands, geographers usually recognize four subdivisions.

The provinces of the Captaincy-General developed a spirit of localism during the colonial period which was reflected in demands for autonomy. These demands became insistent during the independence period. The extent to which such factors influenced the adoption of the federal system of 1811, the quasi-federal structure of 1830, and the federal Constitution of 1864 cannot be measured accurately. That they had some influence cannot be doubted.

The Constitution of 1864 established a federal system based upon the United States model of division of powers. Lott quotes a distinguished Venezuelan scholar, however, to the effect that by this time, division of powers was purely theoretical. The states were not in fact sovereign and had nothing to reserve.

The principle of division of powers has been modified formally again and again in favor of the federal government. In 1925, for example, both the federal and state governments were given enumerated or delegated powers. This weakened the reserved powers of the states. In 1953, the provision guaranteeing reserved or residual powers to the states was omitted entirely. Furthermore, the central government has gradually usurped almost every field in which government can operate. For example, the central government acquired from the states the following powers: Maritime, coastal, and fluvial fields in 1881; secondary education in 1901; postoffices, telephones, and telegraphs in 1914; and health in 1922. In 1925, a whole series of powers were transferred from the states to the federal government. The fields included credit, banks, social welfare, conservation of forests, natural resources, labor, expropriations, and public registry. The Constitution of 1936 removed elections from state control. In 1945, the states lost their judicial systems. In 1953, the federal government acquired the exclusive power to regulate hotels, recreational resorts, tourism, and lotteries.

The Constitution of 1953 asserted that Venezuela was a federal republic with 20 states, two federal territories, a Federal District, and Federal Dependencies. The states, however, no longer had any reserved powers, and there were practically no powers left to enumerate for them either. The states still had power to draft constitutions as long as they were not in conflict with the traditional constitution or laws. They could change or modify their internal boundaries. They could spend federal funds allotted to them or tax monies which they might be able to collect. This exhausted the list in the 1953 constitution.

The political controls of the federal government are so great that state resistance to centralized domination is impossible. For example, the states have never acquired the power to elect their own governors. The federal president appoints them. Then 1953 constitution provided most clearly and unequivocally that the president could freely appoint and remove all state governors. There apparently are no restrictions whatever on the use of this power. Lott found for the period 1936–1953 that there were 262 governors, out of which 207 were in office less than 15 months each and 106 held power less than six months. The president can even appoint men to head the state governments who are not residents of the state to which they are assigned.

The states have also lost so much of their revenue base to the central government that they have become servile dependents on federal largesse. The *situado* or grant-in-aid developed because the federal government took from the states their chief source of revenue, which was income from the salt and metal mines, unappropriated lands, and the fishing and pearl industries. The states had control of such sources from 1864 to 1881.

Tax and other revenue sources are now almost completely centralized. The federal government collects the monies, holds yearly meetings to consider what to give the states, and then doles out the amounts it deems appropriate. The states are usually permitted to spend from 10–25 per cent of the total amount collected by the federal government. In 1949–1950, according to Lott, over 90 per cent of all state revenue came from the *situado*. The states cannot even spend their *situado* as they see fit, however. They are subject to the tutelage of the Minister of the Interior. The socialist-"liberal" government of *Acción Democrática*, which seized power by force in 1945, even demanded that the states submit "detailed plans leading to the wiser investment of these funds."

There is not much that the states can do to free themselves from economic bondage to the federal government. It is a principle of the Venezuelan federal system that all fields which the federal government taxes or which it has power to tax are absolutely prohibited to the states and local governments. The 1953 constitution removed the states' last important source of revenue—the sale of sealed paper for legal documents.

One is forced to agree with Professor Lott's conclusion that Venezuelan federalism is a case study in "frustration."

CONCLUDING REMARKS

Whether one defends centralization or decentralization as a method of achieving political ideals depends upon each individual's philosophy and upon interpretation of the evidence. Dr. Herminio Portell Vilá, eminent historian of Cuba, declared emphatically in 1956 in a paper prepared for the use of specialists in Latin America, that ". . . local government is the foundation for the regular structure of the state and if such foundation is rotten, it will affect the whole structure." The author's own personal feeling is that not only democracy but progress in social and economic fields as well depend to a very large extent upon creating an environment which starts with the dignity, worth, and importance of the single, solitary individual. If permitted freedom and a reasonable amount of equality of opportunity to develop their talents and abilities, individuals are able to govern themselves and to cooperate voluntarily with others in achieving common ends, such as the protection of life and property and the preservation of knowledge and values which the group has found indispensable.

The other point of view, which is more popular and which has powerful arguments in its support, is that the superior few at the center can best decide what is in the interests of the many below. Students of Latin American culture know that centralization in general and concentration of centralized power in the great cities in particular has long been characteristic of most of the Latin American countries, including the federal republics. To what extent has centralized control resulted in the rapid development of political democracy or of progress in social and economic fields? One thing is absolutely certain. Latin America's experience with centralization has not produced virtuous, efficient, economical, democratic government. Politics in Latin America tends to be the sophisticated art of calculated hypocrisy, combined, when necessary, with uncompromising, intolerant, barbarous violence. Some countries have made determined efforts to break the circle of social, economic, and political authoritarianism, the heritage of Hispanic culture. There have been leaders of the most valiant courage and the greatest virtue and integrity in every Latin American country who have attempted to make politics the reasoned art of democratic compromise. When such men have relied upon centralized power, they have invariably fallen short of their ideals. When they have permitted such principles as individualism, voluntarism, and decentralization to operate, as in Uruguay, Argentina, Chile, and Costa Rica in certain periods of the histories of these countries, better results have been achieved.

The evidence here presented indicates that although not all the effects of centralization are evil, nevertheless progress toward the realization of commonly-accepted goals has been slow, even negligible in some instances. But there is no way of proving that development would have been more rapid if the federal republics had permitted a greater degree of individualism, voluntarism, and decentralization to prevail.

What lessons can the United States learn from the experience of centralization in the federal republics of Latin America? Perhaps none at all. However, it is at least fair to say that what has happened in the Latin American federal republics merits serious scrutiny by those many Americans who desire to increase the power of the federal government at the expense of the states and the power of the federal executive at the expense of the other branches of government.

*Latin American Executives: Essence and Variation** | ROSENDO A. GOMEZ

The most widely-professed fact in the field of Latin American politics is unquestionably the dominant role of the president. The task facing Latin Americanists is not the defense of this theme but the elaboration of it. One of the most confining factors—so often lamented at conferences where these matters are discussed—is the lack of information in depth concerning all of the revelancies of power structure. This is particularly evident in appraising cultural factors although it must be admitted that much excellent work is now being done. A very challenging problem in the area of comparative government is involved, a problem admitting of some of the methodological uneasiness associated with the branch of political inquiry. Obviously, in the study of Latin American politics one may proceed with greater assurance with the "variations on a theme" technique than would be possible in many other areas; however, some disillusionment and appreciable inaccuracies lie in wait if one submits to this temptation too extensively.

It would appear that there are two assignments in the analysis of executive power that should be accepted and carried out, pending the results of more plodding tasks of fact-enrichment. The first assignment is to consider more sweepingly the executive power in Latin America in its relationship to the broad matter of executive power in general. The second assignment is to classify our existing observations in more meaningful ways. Both of these assignments may be described as attempts to frame hypotheses, in the future investigation of which we may channel our efforts to significant findings.

* Rosendo A. Gomez, "Latin American Executives: Essence and Variation," *Journal of Inter-American Studies*, III, No. 1 (January 1961), 81–96. Reprinted by permission of the *Journal of Inter-American Studies* and of the author. (Footnotes in the original version have been omitted.)

NEW-WORLD AUTHORITARIANISM

At the risk of summoning the obvious, one should first consider the essence of executive power. [The organization of the modern responsible executive is the outcome of a long struggle between the temptations and demands of power, and the restraints, of public or self-imposed character, that have become operable upon the holder of such power.] This struggle has built our modern institutions of representative government. For all but a short modern period, authoritarianism has been the prevailing (and some would still say, the natural) pattern for the application of power. So many for so long have phrased the nature of this running battle that it encompasses the whole sweep of political literature that has become available to us—from "philosopher-kings" to Lord Acton's frequently-quoted observation on the insidiousness of power. It is held to be very remarkable, indeed, as evidenced in modern democratic systems, that the executive power has been constricted to the degree observable in our time. It has involved not merely the notion of responsibility—responsibility is after all a very old idea of the portfolio of political scientists—but, more significantly, the reduction of executive power to the concept of *managership*.

The prescription for executive power in a system, and the application of it in practice, together comprise a crucial aspect of politics. Jacques Necker, who observed the organization of power in revolutionary France following the events of 1789, wrote of this:

> The executive power is the moving force of government. It represents, in the political system, that mysterious principle which, in moral man, unites action to the will. In the meantime, so various are its relations, so extensive is its influence, and so great the place, thus to express itself, which it occupies in the social order, that the adjustment of its limits, and the accurate adaptation of its means to its ends, offer to the human mind one of the most comprehensive subjects of reflection.[1]

One finds in this description all the ingredients that have combined to form our modern representative institutions. It is, from the political scientist's point of view, an acceptable version in capsule form of the framework within which Western democratic systems have developed. The executive power has always suggested motion and action; and the central problem, among moral men, is to adjust the limits of this raw force to the requirements of society.

The organization of executive power in the United States and Great Britain represent major examples of the delicate balancing of action

[1] *An Essay on the True Principles of Executive Power in the Great States*, (London: Robinson, 1792), I, p. 1.

and restraint. These examples have very remarkably combined power with sensitivity to mandate and opinion. By contrast, the French system has been characterized by excessive preoccupation with shackling executive power to the point where the terms "assembly government" and "*immobilisme*" are commonly used to describe that tendency. Curiously, the French and American revolutions, although often coupled together as expressions of the confidence in rational man in a revolutionary age, did not develop similar institutionalizations of executive power. In each case, the initial reaction was the same—a shift of emphasis from the *ancient régime* to assembly government. In the short space of approximately a decade, however, the United States dipped into its genius to fill the void, replacing the assembly-oriented Articles of Confederation with the strong executive of the U.S. Constitution; the French have struggled with the problem almost constantly and are at the moment launching an attempt at a strong executive superimposed upon the cabinet system. It is too early to say whether this development is fastened securely or whether it is dependent upon the personality of General De Gaulle for its existence. In any event, the French experience of approximately one hundred and seventy years well attests to the uneasiness expressed by M. Necker who watched the throes of organization.

Latin-American independence from Spain was fought in the name of the same ideals that spearheaded the French and American revolutions. The presidential system was adopted throughout Latin America with high aspirations. The experience of the years since the revolutionary movement has been somewhat disenchanting. The delicate balance between action and restraint has not been found in many Latin American republics. The Latin-American colonies vaulted into independence with a great strain of authoritarianism in their culture and with little opportunity to erase the past.

The delicacy of the problem of organization of executive power is clearly illustrated by the observations of some of the Latin American revolutionary leaders. Those who led the revolution had undergone intellectual ferment in the years preceding the action; they were familiar with the writings of the patron saints of the French and American struggles. What more logical thing than strong consideration of the presidential system since it was believed to be the product of revolutionary ideas? [Bolívar, whose thought ranged widely, believed essentially in recognizing Latin America's authoritarian antecedents and was supposed to have said that the "new states of America, once Spanish, need kings with the title of President."] Monteagudo, the brilliant Argentine journalist, who favored monarchy, wrote that Argentines were "not able to be as free as those born in that classic land, England . . . nor as free as the democrats of North America." Charles Darwin, from the "classic land," and not averse to adding observations on politics to his experiences, upon viewing affairs in Santa Fé province in the Argentina of 1833, wrote in his journal that "tyranny seems as yet better adapted to these countries than republicanism." A practitioner of politics, President of Argentina from 1868 to 1874 and also a great admirer of the United States, Domingo Sarmiento, very wistfully expressed the problem: "Would that a people could be free by the same sort of *ad hominem* arguments that can bring about independence!" Many decades later, this was summed up by Leo S. Rowe who pointed out that Latin American countries were still engaged in a struggle "to bring their social organization into closer harmony with their political institutions."

THE NATURE OF NEW-WORLD AUTHORITARIANISM. The experience of the past two decades has brought to comparative government, and to social studies in general, a considerable emphasis upon authoritarianism. The spectacular and extreme versions represented by the Hitler and Mussolini systems undoubtedly gave great impetus to this emphasis. In addition to the investigation of the nature of this pattern, there have also been attempts to maintain distinctions; thus, it is necessary to realize that, while totalitarian systems are extreme examples of authoritarianism, highly-authoritarian systems can exist without all of the overwhelming machinery and oppressive techniques of the totalitarian state. The concern to maintain distinctions has been deepened by the increasing and alarming tendency in these postwar years to group rather too easily or to polarize into neat little ideological packages. In the study of Latin-American systems, it is vital to distinguish degrees of authoritarianism. Indeed, the first observation that must be made is that no Latin-American system, however loftily a leader may have ascended within it, has been classifiable as a totalitarian state.

There is no doubt concerning the deeply-ingrained authoritarianism of Iberian culture nor of its tenacious remnants in Latin America. But authoritarianism in the New World is significantly different from the old-world Iberian pattern. The distinctions do not lie in such cultural trappings as Church, family, or personalism; these tend to be very much the same. The real distinctions are historical in nature, functions of time and space, rather than of basic cultural patterns.

The basic difference between old and new-world Iberian authoritarianism centers on a vital factor in history—*revolutionary commitment*. In critical periods when national sentiment is directed to revolution, and particularly if important institutional changes are sought, the ideals and institutions for which the revolution is fought constitute a commitment which will dictate the form, if not always the substance, of the particular nation for a long period of time. Next to natural historical growth (such as custom's place in the growth of law), this may well be the most compelling institutional and ideological determinant. If the substance is appreciable (as in the United States), a high degree of consistency to the commitment may be maintained; if the substance is meagre, the form will nevertheless be employed to await the growth of substance. [The Latin-American republics, unlike the seats of old-world authoritarianism such as Spain and Portugal, have a revolutionary commitment to the ideals and institutions of responsible, representative democracy of the presidential type.] The consistency displayed varies considerably from republic to republic, but even in republics where substance may be long in developing the revolutionary commitment is compelling and is a major institutional determinant.

[One of the most common manifestations of Latin-American commitment is the compulsion to seek legality by constitution, even if power be won extra-constitutionally and be maintained in this way.] No Latin-American president rests comfortably in power without eventually seeking constitutional status, if he ascended to power without it. Much of the addiction to constitution-making in Latin America is attributable to this compulsion.

It would appear in the face of these observations that a significant factor in comparative government is often overlooked—the environmental impact of institutions *per se*. Generally speaking, most students of comparative government emphasize the necessity to immerse themselves in the particular culture in order to understand properly its political institutions. A corollary of this thought is that one wastes time inspecting institutions for any value in themselves. Yet, there is danger in over-emphasizing the lack of importance of institutions. For institutions *per se* may be influences as well as mere results. This is clear in Latin America where, if it may be argued that the presidential system was too abruptly adopted, generations of Latin Americans have stuck doggedly to the form—the commitment—until it has become a firm and continuous environmental influence.

Another distinction between old and new-world authoritarianism, another function of time and space, is the separation from the old order of Europe. [This, of course, has created a spirit of innovation, a feeling of creativity institutionally speaking.] It has accounted for a very decided sense of constructiveness, of society in motion; this sense can, of course, develop action both for progress or withdrawal. A Latin-American republic is always faced with a wide range of choices and nowhere is this more evident than in the activities of the executive power.

MAJOR TYPES OF LATIN-AMERICAN EXECUTIVES

In the foregoing paragraphs may be found an introduction to the essence of the relationship between Latin-American executive power and executive power in general. From this basis one may begin investigation of the differences in degree that have developed. The following paragraphs attempt a classification of Latin-American executives based upon patterns that have been distinguishable, particularly in the last twenty-five years.

Before investigating these classifications, it would be well to stipulate two assumptions upon which the approach rests. First, it should be assumed that the Latin-American presidencies are offices with historical depth in accordance with the principle of commitment mentioned above; we are not discussing useless and fleeting institutions. Second, it is assumed that standards applied with the United States in mind are unrealistic; all executives in Latin America are to some degree illustrative of authoritarianism in the Iberian tradition; all of the ordinary evidences of *personalismo* are taken for granted as characteristic of even the most responsible presidents.

CONSTITUTIONAL PRESIDENT Perhaps the most distinguishing feature of this type is that it has existed in greater numbers than is widely believed. One of the most commonly-used terms with reference to Latin-American politics is "dictator." To be sure, there have been many dictators through the years, but there have also been a great many presidents who have taken over official duties and conducted these duties within reasonable reach of constitutional directives.

A number of conditions are necessary for satisfaction of this classification. Election must be constitutionally acceptable, a reasonable reflection of the popular will (taking into consideration the retardation in such matters as suffrage and the reality of public opinion that exists in many republics). It must be understood that this condition does not bar the eventual constitutionality of a regime established initially by *coup d'état*. Establishment of power by force may be necessary for the fulfillment of constitutional conditions. At a suitable time thereafter, however, legitimization of proper sort must follow. It is not easy to assess the propriety of these steps in all cases. When is a *coup* legitimized properly and when is it legitimized under intimidation, for example? There is no sure formula widely applicable. One may perhaps safely judge that the legitimization of the National Revolutionary Movement in Bolivia in 1952, when Paz Estenssoro took over the presidency, reflected a genuinely-popular sentiment, since he had received a plurality of votes cast in the election at issue. On the other hand, Batista legitimized himself in 1954 under strong intimidation of Cuban opposition groups that left considerable doubt as to genuineness. A government of doubtful status itself can pave the way for a constitutional regime. For example, General Odría's government, established by force in Peru in 1948, and later supposedly legitimized by an election in 1950, made its way under the shadow of a suppressed popular party (the Apristas); by 1956, however, this party was allowed some freedom and the election of Manuel Prado qualifies, in the main, as a constitutionally-proper one.

To satisfy the requirements of this type, it is also necessary that the opposition be given freedom to contest elections reasonably effectively and to express its views regarding policy-making as well. Again, we encounter difficulty in interpretation and must resort to a realistic appraisal of local circumstances. Thus, in spite of the opposition's continuous cry of fraud and *imposición*, the *Partido Revolucionario Institutional* (PRI) in Mexico must be granted a place of legitimacy in these respects. The PRI must be viewed for what it is—a very large confederation of political groups within which the ordinary differences of politics are fought out, similar to the Democratic Party in some U.S. Southern states. There is considerable difference between the PRI and the *Colorados* of Paraguay or the *Partido Dominicano* of the Dominican Republic, to mention the other major examples of one party domination in the Latin-American area. It is a difference that touches upon aspects of the formation of opposition from effective party organization to the various phases of the electorial process, and including the effective pression of opposition in the various media of communication. A very crucial criterion is of course the application of laws affecting the freedom of expression in its many forms.

The fraternity of constitutional presidents does not include those executives who have unreasonably maneuvered constitutions to extend their tenure of office beyond the spirit of the constitution. The practice of *continuismo* is not in harmony with Latin-American constitutionalism and it is particularly at variance when it involves that version by which a president-dominated constitutional assembly, after drawing up a new fundamental law, proceeds to appoint the incumbent to serve as president under the new system. This disqualification does not extend, of course, to a proper constitutional amendment relating to extension of tenure if the incumbent then is elected to the office.

Finally, it should be observed that to occupy the post of constitutional president, personalism must be confined to constitutional limits. When a president, however legitimate originally, climbs to a pedestal and creates himself as an order above the constitution, particularly if he actively sponsors a cult centered on his person, he has violated the spirit of Western constitutionalism. The constitutional president must be conscious of his heritage in this respect and exercise restraint.

There is a strong correlation between republics supplying the larger number of constitutional presidents and the political awareness evident among the great mass of people in those republics. This awareness is in turn dependent upon well-known, economic, and educational advantages. The most constant of these have been Chile, Costa Rica, Mexico, and Uruguay. In the second rank may be placed Argentina, Brazil, Colombia, and Cuba. Ecuador, Guatemala, Peru, El Salvador, and Venezuela have shown occasional promise; Bolivia appears to be enjoying an introduction.

DEMAGOGIC CAUDILLO This type has not as yet appeared in quantity, but it is a highly-spectacular type that warrants attention because of the very modern touch involved. It bears some similarities to European Fascism, although it is not generally as such. There are a number of distinguishing features that serve to give this type a standing of its own. Argentina affords the best example during the years that Juan Perón dominated the scene.

The first characteristic of the demagogic *caudillo* is a very close relationship with constitutionalism. It emerges in a system that has had deep commitments to constitutional presidencies in the past. The demagogic *caudillo* can easily win legitimation by elections. He rises above constitutionalism not necessarily by violation of electoral laws but chiefly on other grounds. The proper habitat of this type is the republic with a high degree of political awareness founded on an economic order of considerable productivity. A key to the power structure created is a large industrial worker's movement of such massive power that it becomes an aggressive reflection of popular support. It must be constantly wooed and rewarded even to a point beyond the attention customarily given to the military. The demagogic *caudillo* realizes the harnessing of a force which supercedes the military and which, until the structure weakens, can be used effectively to stand off strong military opposition. The maintenance of such a system of mass approval calls for extraordinary powers of organization, diversion, and communication. One of the weaknesses of the system is the difficulty of keeping mass support alive, for the mass appetite grows and becomes increasingly difficult to satisfy. Since the leader has committed himself to the role of saviour of the worker and since increasing adulation of him soon transcends the more mundane spirit of the constitution, the cult of the Leader results. It is this characteristic that most closely resembles the European totalitarian systems of recent memory.

Excessive nationalism, with the implication that Latin-American leadership is involved, together with heavy doses of anti-Yankeeism, is very important to the pattern. One of the distinctive touches is ideological in nature. The Leader becomes the symbol of an ideology—preferably a "new way"—like the supposedly-new course by Perón's *justicialismo*. The demagogic *caudillo* takes the old complaints and declares that he has solved them by a quasi-messianic summoning of the greatness of the people.

The demagogic *caudillo* represents a curious combination of regressiveness and advancement. He is of both worlds, old and new. He is regressive in that he builds firmly upon ingrained authoritarianism and creates a gigantic monument to personal leadership; he is a symbol of advancement in that he has realistically appraised a modern industrial society, wooed and won mass support, and undertaken a social mission in keeping with the twentieth century's demands.

The prototype of this type of executive was, as mentioned, Juan Perón. Vargas of the 1930's merits some consideration but his claim to real legitimation was rather poorly-founded until his return in 1950. Perón was popularly-elected in 1946 and again in 1952 and it is clear that he would probably have been elected on both occasions even without the intimidations practiced by an enthusiastic party following. He was raised to heroic stature and from this eminence he clearly operated beyond the intentions of the constitution. It would not be correct to label Perón as the product solely of Latin American caesarism, or as the *duce* of a totalitarian system, or even as a military dictator. He was each of these in some measure but principally he represents a new departure—a leader with the characteristics of a constitutional president who, however, soared out of the constitutional cage into a personal venture so high as to allow for no safe return.

At the moment, there is no demagogic *caudillo* in any of the Latin-American republics. If one were to explore potentialities and engage the risk of speculation, there appears only one real possible candidacy and there are many reasons why it might not develop. This possibility is Fidel Castro of Cuba. Cuba fits the pattern fairly-well in terms of socio-economic pressures reflected in voluble mass sentiments. It lacks the major ranking that could justify pretensions to Latin-American leadership, but this could be outweighed by the image of Castro as a revolutionary leader already possessed of heroic stature. Castro could ascend to dizzy heights of personalism, particularly if there were added some of the provocations that attended the rise of Perón in Argentina.

MILITARY GUARDIAN   The setting for the military guardian is the republic of major or medium power in economic terms wherein an appreciable—if not substantial—political awareness has been generated. [Usually the political scene has been sufficiently-active to provide for a number of political parties. One of these parties may be the vehicle of considerable popular sentiment for reform; its strength is potentially great enough to make a bid for power and, indeed, it may have done so only to be thwarted by perhaps illegal methods. One of the sociological factors of this setting is invariably the lack of a large middle class actively seeking change. In such a sociological situation, the military has usually flourished as a political determinant.] In the period since the end of World War Two, excellent examples have been found in Colombia, Peru, and Venezuela.

Against this general background, there may be viewed the various thought patterns of the military officer intent upon political power. Military guardians may arise in an endless variety of combinations of local political considerations, but there are [two major justifications cited by intervening military leaders that demand particular attention: Order and Neutralism.] Ordinarily, these are found in combination and are closely related. Order is, of course, a major preoccupation of the military profession everywhere. In Latin-American republics, there occur many opportunities for using this as a justification, although often the intervention of the military goes well beyond the demands of the situation. One of the best examples of military guardianship established in the name of order was that of General Rojas Pinilla in Colombia in 1953. Colombia had for generations enjoyed comparatively-orderly government without military intervention. The bitter struggle between the Liberals and the Conservatives broke out into widespread violence following the assassination of a Liberal leader, Gaitán, in 1948. This soon assumed the magnitude of civil war with apparently little chance of bringing the warring political leaders to settlement. Breaking a tradition of long standing, General Rojas Pinilla stepped in and took over power. These were other personal motivations involved, but essentially some movement toward order was necessary. Once in power, General Rojas Pinilla was motivated by power itself and carried intervention to a point not justified by the situation.

More common in the ranks of military guardianship is the complicated motivation that might be said to result in a defensive military guardian. In this maneuver, neutralism is cited in order to protect the national dignity, honor, and traditions from the excesses of the masses. Stated more baldly, this is a last stand against popular government that threatens the old order. A large popular party presses forward with the electoral power to sweep into office; the language of reform fills the air. The military guardian comes forward to "save" the republic from this mass "chaos." The best recent examples were in Peru and Venezuela where the Apristas and Democratic Action, respectively, had demonstrated enough power to win elections. Accordingly, General Odría in Peru and Colonel Pérez Jiménez in Venezuela intervened and suppressed the parties battering at the gates. Both leaders stated that it was time to save the masses from their own ignorance, or words similar in meaning. General Odría, indeed, stated this most colorfully when he announced that "party politics poisons the hearts of the people and sickens their minds." One is reminded of Thomas the Cynic in Ignazio Silone's *School for Dictators* who stated that in socially-backward countries "the army constitutes the only barrier against the so-called 'anarchy' of the popular masses and the corruption of the politicians." This belief has been entertained by many Latin-American military guardians. The stated aim is "neutralism" but the result is suppression of popular will. A special version of this sort of guardianship took place in Guatemala in 1954 when Castillo Armas swept into Guatemala to combat the impact of Communism.

All military guardians are, of course, driven by some degree of personal yearning for power. The military-officer class in a typical Latin-American republic is a considerable reservoir for political ambitions. A leader of this class may be given an opportunity sooner or later to cite one of the ancient justifications for military intervention and thus launch a political career at the head of the republic. The military guardian, in our time, stands ultimately at the mercy of the popular movement he wishes to delay. Both Odría and Pérez Jiménez have given way to constitutional presidents, although the circumstances of their withdrawal differ considerable; Odría presided over an election and Pérez Jiménez was ousted from office.

PATERNALISTIC CAUDILLO   In the paternalistic *caudillo* we find a type that was more widely evident in the nineteenth century before the onset of industrialism and associated effects. At the present time, it is narrowed down largely to the Central American and Caribbean areas, particularly the Dominican Republic and Nicaragua. Although a special case, Paraguy belongs in this category. A decade or two ago, the paternalistic *caudillo* flourished in most of the Central-American republics in spectacular fashion. As the title of this type indicates, the system of government resembles a large *hacienda* with strong superimposition of the *patrón*.

[The paternalistic *caudillo* is, indeed, a national *patrón.*] He may in | fact possess large holdings in property and control a number of basic industries. Nepotism is especially evident in such a system; the total holdings of the *caudillo's* family connection will be staggering. The paternalistic *caudillo* carries to an extreme a long-entertained notion in Latin-American political life: the possession of political power is a concession and the concessionaire manages as large a return as possible (much of which may be quite legal, or "honest graft" as it is sometimes called in the United States). The republic is in great part a private preserve. The *caudillo* need not be overpoweringly oppressive, although he protects his system with tightly-controlled military forces. He may be viewed by many as a great national father who takes care of his own, at least to the extent he feels is good for them. The *caudillo* usually openly indicates that he is exercising a tutelage over ignorant and child-like people who are not ready for the bewildering machinery of a free system. Some of the major examples of recent years have been the follow-ing: Anastasio Somoza who, until his assassination in 1957, ruled Nicaragua for approximately twenty years (and left his "plantation" in the hands of two sons); Rafael Trujillo of the Dominican Republic who has dominated that country for twenty-nine years;* and Tiburcio Carías Andino who dominated Honduras for seventeen years until 1949. In Venezuela, the last of the larger republics to support a paternalistic *caudillo,* Juan Vicente Gómez managed to rule for twenty-seven years until his death in 1935.

There are two electoral features that characterize the administrations of paternalistic *caudillos.* The technique of *continuismo* is employed to excess in such circumstances—that is, the application of presidential domination to extend one's tenure beyond the intention of the constitu-tion. The other feature has to do with alternation in office. A paternalistic *caudillo's* position is usually so secure that he can occasionally afford the luxury of allowing someone else a turn in the presidential office, perhaps a member of the family (as Héctor Trujillo, brother of Rafael).

PROVISIONAL EXECUTIVE ARRANGEMENTS Since at any given time at least one republic has undergone a *coup,* or other interruption of the constitu-tional pattern, some brief mention should be made of a highly-significant Latin-American executive organization, the provisional government. The most common institution is the *junta,* a council of varying number of

* Trujillo was assassinated in 1961 [ed.].

revolutionaries, though usually not more than five. The *junta's* aim is to provide temporary leadership until the constitutional electoral process be reinstituted. It may be several years before the provisional government deems it proper to hold such an election. In the meantime, a constitutional assembly may be reworking the constitution which will serve as the banner of "the new era." Another provisional arrangement is simply to continue the use of the presidential office, the president being appointed by the successful revolutionary leadership. Cuba is at the moment employing the latter arrangement with a puppet president and Fidel Castro, the leader of the revolutionary movement, assuming the office of prime minister.

Since it may be said that provisional government is in great measure government exercised in a constitutional void, it must be observed that from this position the leader of a *coup* may go in any of several directions. He may, of course, simply provide for the resumption of constitutional activity in a short time without unnecessarily influencing the process, as appears to have happened in Argentina preceding the election of President Frondizi. He may employ his position to create electoral triumph for himself in due time, as witness Batista in the Cuban election of 1954. He may simply ignore the electoral process and establish himself arbitrarily in a presidential term of office either by a "plebiscite" as did Castillo Armas in Guatemala following the *coup* of 1954 or by arranging an appointment by a hand-picked constitutional assembly as demonstrated by Vargas on the occasion of the 1934 constitution.

CONCLUSIONS

Surveying the trends of recent decades, new-world authoritarianism has developed a pattern that warrants a number of observations. In the first place, the days of the paternalistic *caudillo* appear to be numbered. It is observable that popular dissent may be easily aroused even in very unlikely places in the Latin America of the mid-twentieth century. Educated Latin Americans find it more and more difficult to look the other way. Latin Americans are active in the United Nations and in the specialized organizations associated with it. They have, for example, felt compelled, in the spirit of the Declaration of Human Rights, to observe more closely their internal problems. It is significant that women's suffrage has swept practically all of Latin America. Other more exciting factors are at work, too. For example, at the moment there is considerable international recrimination raging in the intimacy of Caribbean life. The Castro triumph in Cuba has fired the imagination and the courage of disaffected citizens of such countries as the Dominican Republic and Nicaragua. An abortive attempt to emulate the Castro technique in the mountains of Nicaragua apparently failed. Trujillo of the Dominican Republic called for investigation by the Organization of American States of an alleged invasion force staged in Cuba with Castro's approval. Even if these events do not herald immediate success, the trend does not favor existing paternalistic *caudillos.*

Constitutional presidents are increasing and it is likely that the next few years will see a solidification of these in many cases and a wavering between these and military guardians in other cases. The military guardian waits in the wings for his cue practically everywhere. But out of this there emerges the conviction that Latin America may be entering the final phase toward solving the equation between constitutions and social institutions.

The only real doubt is one of time, not of promise. Latin-American constitutionalism is a revolutionary commitment that awaits fulfillment, not death.

*Legislative Assemblies**

WILLIAM W. PIERSON
and
FEDERICO G. GIL

Although the constitutional systems of Latin America have entrusted the legislature with the power to enact laws and to determine public policy, the congress, in reality, is not the center of the political life of these nations. As we have seen in the preceding chapter, the executive rather than the legislative branch holds a position of preeminence. Logically, the weakness of all legislative assemblies and their inferior prestige and authority as compared to those enjoyed by the president are the consequence of the almost omnipotent role that the legal systems and political customs have assigned to the executive branch. However, weak legislative bodies are also partly the result of such factors as the nature of the class system, defective electoral processes, and the fragmentation and fluidity of organized political groups. These factors combine to make the theory of legislative supremacy nothing more than fiction in Latin America.

Historical circumstances may also have contributed, to some extent,

* From *Governments of Latin America* by Pierson & Gil. Copyright © 1957 McGraw-Hill, Inc. Used by permission of McGraw-Hill Book Company.

to congressional weakness. The fact that there never existed important deliberative bodies in colonial days and the lack of any parliamentary tradition may, perhaps, account, in some measure, for this defect. It may also be true that, in many instances, the congress by its factional quibbling and lack of responsibility has incurred an unfortunate stigma and is regarded with good-humored contempt. This causes the people to look to the chief executive for order and leadership and to condone presidential usurpation of authority. Thus, the president often assumes a major role in the determination of legislative policy with the tacit consent of the people and of the members of the congress.

Despite the validity of these observations, it would be unjust to conclude that all Latin-American legislatures have failed to fulfill their constitutional mandates. Some congresses were not rubber-stamp bodies e.g., those of Chile in the period of the "parliamentary republic," 1819–1925; of Uruguay under the constitution of 1917; or even of Honduras from 1927 through 1931. On the contrary, they were independent, properly elected deliberative assemblies which challenged effectively the ascendancy of executive authority and participated actively in the determination of national policies.

The effectiveness of all Latin-American legislatures is handicapped by some common defects. The legislative powers of the president being so ample, the scope of congressional functions and authority is necessarily restricted. The relative brevity of the congressional sessions tends to lessen the efficacy of the legislative as a check upon the other two branches of government. In nine countries the executive alone has authority to call congress into special sessions. In many cases the legislature is to be concerned exclusively with such matters as might be included in the presidential summons. The lack of parliamentary experience frequently prevents the attainment of compromises and the ironing out of differences which are so necessary to all legislative chambers. Legislators engage in bitter controversies which often lead to personal encounters involving physical violence. A defeated minority sometimes chooses to abandon the floor rather than to accept compromise. In addition, there is always a strong tendency to depend upon direction from the executive in the enactment of legislation.

Latin-American political scientists have been well aware of these defects. In fact they have been, in general, more severe than foreigners in their criticisms, for they have indicted their legislatures not only for inefficiency and irresoluteness but also for acting too often against the public interest. Searching for correctives, some writers have stressed the need for a reform of congressional organization. Among the modifications that have been proposed are the reduction of the number of members; the establishment of advisory committees and technical counseling at the service of legislators; the determination of a fixed period for the approval of certain types of legislation; and the division of the legislative task into two phases—one session devoted to research, preparation, and drafting of projects, and another for the actual enactment of those projects into law.[1]

Many of the conditions generally ascribed to the congress in Latin America may vary sharply and distinctly not only between the various nations but within individual countries. In Argentina, for example, Carlos S. Viamonte refers to three distinct periods in the history of the congress: the first phase extends from the *cabildo* of 1810 at the outset of the independence to the Constitutent Congress of 1853, the second period from this date to 1912, and the third from 1912 to the present time. During the first period the Argentine assemblies reflected the restlessness and troubles caused by the revolution for independence and by the pressing problem of national organization. The great debate of the period was that of federalism versus unitarism. The second period, from 1853 to 1912, was an era of institutional development. The prestige of the legislature was increased by the enactment of the codes and the organic laws which gave the country a legal system. The legislatures of this era frequently demonstrated independence by resisting vigorously any encroachment of the executive branch, and in this they were generally supported by public opinion. The third period of development was significant by reason of the participation of the masses in the electoral process and the formation of new political parties which soon gained representation in the congress as a result of electoral reforms. The tone of the legislative branch was then set by the activity of parties of a popular nature, previously excluded as a result of corrupt electoral practices, and by the appearance of new problems of social and labor significance. Viamonte, on appraising the role of the congress in his native country, observes that toward the end of the second period this body was nearly always a subservient instrument of the executive, and further notes that it became finally a "courteous reunion of oligarchs who never debated ideas but who argued politely over their own private interests." The congress of the third period was a much less educated body but more representative of the elements of society than its predecessor. He noted, however, that after 1916 the legislature became again an "officialist" organ, inclined to complacency and insensitive to the feelings and the desires of the people. He finds, that, although there is popular representation, there may be now even greater subservience to the executive than in the past. The so-called "labor parliament" which swept into

---

[1] See, for instance, Jorge S. Oría, *Ficción y realidad constitucional* (Buenos Aires, 1946), pp. 213–216.

power in 1946 was certainly popular in composition, and yet it was a docile instrument in the hands of President Perón.[2]

Lawyers have traditionally been predominant in Latin-American legislatures, but there are also other professionals among their members such as physicians, engineers, journalists, and university professors. Generally speaking, one can distinguish several categories among legislators. There are, in the first place, the professional politicians for whom politics (*hacer política*) is just a way, if rough, of making a living. They are the political bosses, who, in large or insignificant scale, as the case might be, operate their own machine, and who change party affiliation with great ease and expediency. It is from this group that, in general, a president recruits the core of his supporters in the congress. There are also the wealthy landowner, the big industrialist, and the promoter, who aspire to sit in congress not because of political ambition but as a matter of business sense and convenience. They become perennial senators or representatives, and they are almost exclusively concerned with watching over their vast economic interests and those of their associates and protecting those interests from damaging legislation. As a rule, this type of "politico" encounters no difficulty in finding a safe place in the ballot. Most political parties are willing to hand him the nomination in return for a generous contribution to the party chest.

More recently a new type of legislator has appeared in most countries. He represents economic groups which only recently have become influential such as labor unions or farm organizations. The rise of new nationalistic parties and the increasing political significance of labor have thus affected the nature and composition of legislative assemblies. These parties, competing for power with the older traditional groups of conservatives and liberals, have gained legislative representation and, in some cases, control of the congress. This has not necessarily resulted in the much-needed development of legislative vigor and independence, but at least it has turned new congresses into bodies which are more representative of the popular will than their predecessors, which often represented only the interests of a ruling oligarchy.

CONGRESSIONAL ORGANIZATION

Four of the republics of Central America (Costa Rica, El Salvador, Guatemala, Honduras), Panama, and one state in South America (Paraguay) have adopted a unicameral legislature; all the others provide

[2] Carlos Sánchez Viamonte, *Historia institucional de Argentina* (Mexico, 1948), pp. 191–195.

for the bicameral form. In countries with a federal form of government, as in the United States, the upper chamber represents the major political subdivisions of the union, and the lower chamber represents the people. It is obvious, however, that the bicameral structure is not related to the federal system. In fact, the only reason for the use of .bicameralism in unitary countries is to provide for discussion and approval of laws at two distinct times and by different chambers. Those who advocate the adoption of the unicameral system contend that neither this feature nor the older age of the members of the upper chamber is any assurance that better legislation is attained. There no longer exists in Latin America, they further argue, the aristocratic type of society which would justify in unitary states the existence of the senate. It is also pointed out that even in those countries with a federal plan, bicameralism has not achieved its objectives. Often the states of the union have their interests defended more effectively by their deputies in the lower house than by those who represent them in the senate.

The lower and single house

ELECTIONS   Members of this branch of congress or of the unicameral legislatures are chosen by direct popular vote in all the countries. In some, a system of proportional representation is used. Representatives are elected by direct vote in Cuba from each of the six provinces which are given representation in proportion to their population. In Brazil, representatives are elected by the states, the territory of Acre, and the Federal District. They are chosen in a similar manner in Uruguay, by departments, with each of these having at least two representatives.

A feature of the Latin-American systems is the practice in Brazil, Mexico, Colombia, Venezuela, Uruguay, Paraguay, El Salvador, and Panama of choosing alternatives (*suplentes*) or substitutes at the same election.[3] In Honduras, in case of permanent absence of a deputy, a substitute is appointed by the congress to complete his term. In the Dominican Republic the law provides that vacancies be filled by the respective chambers which choose a substitute from a list of three names presented by the political party to which the former deputy belonged. If the party fails to submit a list the chamber is free to appoint any

---

[3] The institution of the *suplencia* seems to be of Spanish origin. It appeared for the first time in the Cádiz constitution of 1812. Its merits are questioned, since members of the lower house supposedly represent the entire nation and not just their districts. Election by districts is merely a technical device to maintain their number in proportion to the population.

TABLE 1. THE LEGISLATURE

COUNTRY	UPPER CHAMBERS*		LOWER OR SINGLE CHAMBER†	
	REPRESENTATION	TERM, YEARS	REPRESENTATION	TERM, YEARS
Argentina	2 for each province 2 for capital	6	1 for each 100,000 in- habitants	6
Bolivia	3 for each department	6	105 deputies	4
Brazil	3 for each state 3 for Federal District	8	1 for each 150,000 in- habitants	4
Chile	5 for each "provincial group"	8	1 for each 30,000 in- habitants	4
Colombia	1 for each 190,000 in- habitants	4	1 for each 90,000 in- habitants	2
Costa Rica			45 deputies	4
Cuba	9 for each province	4	1 for each 35,000 in- habitants	4
Dominican Republic	1 for each province 1 for Santo Domingo District	5	1 for each 60,000 in- habitants	5
Ecuador	2 for each province 1 for each of 2 Oriente provinces and the Galapagos Is- lands 12 "functional" mem- bers	4	1 for each 50,000 in- habitants	2
El Salvador			3 for each department	2
Guatemala			1 for each 50,000 in- habitants	4
Haiti	21 senators elected by departments	6	37 deputies elected by *arrondissements*	4
Honduras			1 for each 25,000 in- habitants	6
Mexico	2 for each state 2 for Federal District	6	1 for each 150,000 in- habitants	3
Nicaragua	16 senators-at-large	6	42 members-at-large	6
Panama			1 for each 15,000 in- habitants	4
Paraguay			1 for each 25,000 in- habitants	5
Peru	50 senators	6	150 deputies	5
Uruguay	31 senators-at-large	4	99 deputies-at-large	4
Venezuela	2 for each state 2 for the Federal Dis- trict	5	1 for each 40,000 in- habitants	5

* In all countries the upper chamber is the Senate or Chamber of the Senate.
† The lower chamber is known as the Chamber of Deputies or Representatives in states with a bicameral system. However, the single legislatures of the other six countries are known by various other titles.

person. Total membership of the lower house varies from 304 in Brazil, which has the largest body, to 34 in Nicaragua.

TERMS   The terms of members of the lower house range from one to six years. A term of four years is found in Brazil, Chile, Uruguay, Bolivia, Cuba, Haiti, Guatemala, Costa Rica, and Panama; two years in El Salvador, Colombia, and Ecuador; three years in Mexico; five years in Venezuela, Paraguay, Peru, and the Dominican Republic; and six years in Argentina, Nicaragua, and Honduras. In some countries, such as Brazil, Peru, Venezuela, or the Dominican Republic, the terms of representatives are not staggered and there is complete renewal of the lower house at every election. In others there may be partial renewal every second year, as in Cuba, Bolivia, Guatemala, or Argentina. In two countries, Mexico and Guatemala, reelection of any member of the legislature to the next succeeding congress is prohibited by constitutional provision.

QUALIFICATIONS   Citizenship and the full enjoyment of civil and political rights are common qualifications required for election to the lower house. Only native-born citizens are eligible in eleven countries,[4] but elsewhere naturalized citizens can be elected as deputies or representatives provided they have resided continuously in the country for a specified period counted from the date of naturalization. This residence period may extend from four to ten years. The minimum-age requirement is twenty-one years in Brazil, Costa Rica, Chile, Cuba, Venezuela, and Guatemala; while the rest of the countries establish a minimum of twenty-five, with the exception of the Dominican Republic where a deputy must be thirty years of age.

In the majority of the countries the constitution provides that certain persons are ineligible to serve in either branch of the legislature. Members of the armed forces and the clergy, government officials, citizens who hold contracts with the government, debtors to the Treasury, and close relatives of the president and of members of the cabinet are frequently excluded. A common provision is a declaration that the office of congressman is incompatible with any other office remunerated by the state, province, or municipality or related with any agency supported wholly or partially by public funds. However, in several countries this provision does not apply to university staff members with teaching functions. Thus, in Cuba, professors in an official institution may qualify for election to the lower house. Similar exceptions are also operative

---

[4] These are Bolivia, Brazil, Ecuador, El Salvador, Guatemala, Haiti, Honduras, Mexico, Nicaragua, Paraguay, and Peru.

in Chile, the Dominican Republic, Guatemala, Honduras, Nicaragua, Paraguay, El Salvador, and Uruguay. This exception is generally justified on the grounds that teaching positions are obtainable only by competitive examinations, a procedure which excludes risks of coercion or favoritism by the administration. Furthermore, it is argued that such persons possess technical and specialized knowledge which can be used by the congress in the public interest.[5]

The upper house

ELECTIONS At the present time, all fourteen countries with an upper chamber elect their members by direct popular vote. Those with a federal scheme of government and several countries with a unitary form provide for equal representation for each state or province. Another group of states apportions senatorial seats on the basis of population. It should be noted that the capital city and the federal district are always represented in the membership of the senate. Thus, in Argentina, Mexico, and Venezuela, two members for each state or province and two for the Federal District are elected; in Brazil, each state and the Federal District elect three senators.

In Nicaragua ex-presidents become lifetime members of the senate, and in Peru the outgoing chief executive becomes a senator for one term. The Venezuelan upper house includes four members chosen at large, who represent minorities which received a certain percentage of the total vote but which failed to elect any candidates by states. A distinction is made in Ecuador between "functional" and "provincial" senators. Thirty-three senators, popularly elected, represent the provinces and the Galapagos Islands. In addition, there are twelve "functional" senators, who are not popularly elected but chosen by economic, professional, and occupational groups and who represent these interests. Cultural groups such as the universities and labor unions, agricultural associations, and other similar organizations are given representation in congress by this device. The "functional" senators are in turn of two kinds: national and regional. Four of the twelve are "national functional" senators, and they represent the sectors of public education, private education, journalism, scientific and literary organizations, and the armed forces. The other eight are "regional functional" senators and are equally divided between the two major regions of the sierra and the coast. They represent the interests of industry, labor, agriculture, and commerce in each of those regions. They are chosen by electoral colleges

[5] Ramón Infiesta, *Derecho constitucional* (Havana, 1950), p. 225.

designated by the economic or occupational group entitled to representation.

"Functional" representation has existed in Ecuador since 1929, and is defended as an institution well fitted to political reality. It is claimed that it serves two fundamental purposes within the governmental scheme of that country: it gives an added protection to forces such as the land-owning class, the army, and state educational centers; and it contributes, in addition, to maintaining the necessary balance of power between the two major regions which compose the republic.[6]

In some of the countries, such as Mexico, Colombia, Venezuela, Ecuador or Uruguay, alternatives (*suplentes*) are also chosen for each incumbent senator, and these are called upon to fill a seat if it becomes vacant before the next election. In the upper chambers of Argentina, Bolivia, Brazil, and Chile, staggered senatorial terms are used, as in the United States. In the rest of the countries an entirely new senate is chosen at one time. The most numerous bodies are those of Brazil and Colombia, with sixty-three members each, and the smallest that of Nicaragua, with only fifteen senators.

TERMS   Senatorial terms range from four years (Colombia, Ecuador, Uruguay, and Cuba) to eight years (Chile, Brazil). A six-year term is used in Argentina,* Mexico, Peru, Bolivia, Haiti, and Nicaragua. In Venezuela and the Dominican Republic senators are elected for five years. Members of the senate can be reelected to the next succeeding congress in all the countries except Mexico.

QUALIFICATIONS   The requirements of citizenship are about the same as those provided for membership in the lower house, but the age requirements are higher, the usual rule being thirty or thirty-five years.

In Cuba in addition to the usual qualifications senators must not have belonged to the armed forces in active service during the two years immediately preceding their nomination. In Colombia, a senator is required to have occupied one of certain offices (president, *designado*, member of the congress, cabinet minister, chief of a diplomatic mission, governor of a department, justice of the supreme court, councillor of state, attorney-general, or comptroller-general), or to have been a university professor for five years, or to have practiced a liberal profession as possessor of an academic degree. In Nicaragua senators must be of "secular status." The Mexican list of qualifications is more extensive

---

[6] George I. Blanksten, *Ecuador: Constitutions and Caudillos* (Berkeley, Calif., University of California Press, 1951), pp. 105–107.

* The term of office for Argentine Senators has since been extended to 9 years.

than any other. In addition to the common conditions, the person may not be a member of the federal army or may not hold a command in the police or the rural constabulary in the district from which he is elected for at least ninety days preceding the election. A similar disqualification applies to heads of the executive departments and supreme court justices unless they resigned ninety days prior to the election. State governors cannot be elected in a district under their jurisdiction even if they resign their office. Ministers of any religious denomination are also excluded.

Officers of the house and the senate

As a rule, the officers of the lower chamber include a president, one or two vice-presidents, one or more secretaries, and in some instances, a treasurer and a comptroller. These officers compose the steering committee known as the *mesa directiva*. The presiding officer and the other members of this *mesa directiva* are generally chosen in the house by a plurality of votes for a term of one year, and they may be reelected. In Mexico, however, officers of both chambers are elected at the last meeting of each month to serve during the following month. This committee usually prepares the legislative calendar and exercises general supervision over the activities of the house. The presiding officer may in some countries have the important power of appointing the members of the permanent or standing committees. In nearly every republic the president also exercises the powers of recognition of speakers, restriction of debates, keeping of order, and decision of points of order.

The organization of the senate is very similar to that of the lower house. In countries where there is a vice-president, he invariably presides over the senate, but he has no right to vote except in case of a tie. In all other countries, a presiding officer and one or two vice-presidents, who serve in case of absence or disability of the president, are elected by the senators. An interesting innovation made in the new Uruguayan constitution of 1952 is that the president of the senate and of the general assembly (congress) shall be the member of the leading party who received the most votes at the election.

The steering committee of the senate usually determines the order of legislative business and names the members of the regular committees. In some countries, such as Uruguay, members of the standing committees are appointed by the president of the senate, but they are subject to approval of the total membership.

The congress of Honduras furnishes an example of the organization of unicameral legislatures. The Honduran congress elects a president, a vice-president, two secretaries, and two prosecretaries. The presiding officer may, if he chooses, exercise a great deal of control over the legislature by making use of such discretionary powers as those of regulating the duration of the sessions, recognizing speakers, and appointing the standing committees. The rule has developed of designating as president of the congress a person closely identified with the chief executive and his policies. The Honduran system does not allow the opposition any representation among the officers or the committees of the congress. The evils derived from this despotic control exercised by the majority party and by the presiding officer overbalance by far the advantages of expediting legislative business.[7]

Standing committees

There exist in every legislature a number of regular or standing committees created by the rules of the house and the senate. The role played by these committees in the legislative process is of great significance since, as a rule, the bulk of legislation originates in them. Only occasionally are major changes made before enactment of important bills as reported by these committees. The number and nature of the committees vary according to countries. There are nineteen in the chamber of deputies of Argentina and eleven in the senate, and in each committee political parties are represented in proportion to their strength. Committee members are appointed in the house by the presiding officer, but the real appointive body is in practice the party caucus. Committees are not required to report on any bill unless they so desire, except in the case of the budget bill which, the rules specify, must be discharged within one month.[8] On the other hand, in most other countries, committees are obligated by the rules to report on every bill, so as to prevent any "burying" of proposals.

In Mexico the number of committees is the same in both houses. Members are elected for three years by a special committee in which each state is represented by one member designated by the state's delegation (*diputación*). Bills must always be reported by the committees. In Bolivia, congressional committees must not only report on all bills, but on certain proposals a report must be made within a specified number of days.

[7] William S. Stokes, *Honduras: An Area Study in Government* (Madison, Wis., University of Wisconsin Press, 1950), pp. 271–275.
[8] Austin F. Macdonald, *Government of the Argentine Republic* (New York, Crowell, 1942), pp. 255–259.

The Ecuadoran "legislative committee"

In Ecuador, in addition to the regular committees of both chambers, a "legislative commission" is provided for by the constitution, which is authorized to prepare bills for amendment or interpretation of the constitution, and some general bills. Its bills are not referred to any of the regular committees of either house, but are presented directly to a joint session of congress for action, and upon passage go to the president for promulgation. The commission is composed of one senator named by the senate; one deputy chosen by the lower house; one representative of the executive department appointed by the president; one representative of the judiciary selected by the supreme court; and the dean of the faculty of jurisprudence at the Universidad Central of Quito, as an ex offico member. These persons and two alternates for each are named for a four-year term and may be indefinitely reelected. They must meet the same qualifications as those elected to the senate. Legislation prepared by this body is acted upon by a joint session of the congress and not by either chamber acting separately. Furthermore, such legislation requires approval by two-thirds of those present, but, once passed, it is not subject to presidential veto.[9]

Other committees

Investigating committees are also used, and their existence is recognized by constitutional or by statutory law. These are, of course, short-lived committees which disappear as soon as their report is made to the parent body. The authority, scope, and methods of such committees have been the subject of controversial debates in some states. In Argentina, for example, the chamber of deputies in 1941 passed a resolution creating a committee to investigate anti-Argentine activities, which was granted specially delegated authority to receive the assistance of the armed forces, to violate the home and the secrecy of correspondence, and to order the arrest of persons. It is of interest to note that when the investigating committee requested assistance of the police to enter and search homes, the chief executive refused to extend such aid on the grounds that such a request was unconstitutional. The chamber of deputies in turn declared that the committee had acted within its proper boundaries and recommended that it exhaust all actions before the other two branches in order to make possible the fulfillment of its mandate.[10]

[9] Constitution of Ecuador, Arts. 77, 78. See also Blanksten, *op. cit.*, pp. 115–116.

[10] *Diario de Sesiones de la Cámara de Diputados*, 1941, vol. II, p. 283. Cf. Segundo V. Linares Quintana, *Gobierno y administración de la República* Argentina (Buenos Aires, 1946), vol. I, p. 300.

All efforts of the committee, however, proved futile in view of the determined boycott of the executive branch.

In addition, a certain number of party committees are found in every congress. These may include congressional campaign committees, policy committees, patronage committees, and others.

Sessions of Congress

In most countries constitutional provisions fix time limits for legislative sessions. This is significant in view of the fact that all countries have attempted to strengthen the legislative branch of the government in recognition of the positive danger of domination by the executive and of the need of assuring a balance of power among the three "powers." In Cuba, El Salvador, and the Dominican Republic the congress meets twice in every year. In all the other countries there is one annual session. The duration of the legislative sessions ranges from two months in Ecuador and Nicaragua to nine in Uruguay. In most countries, however, legislative sessions may be extended. In Venezuela the congress may stay in session for another ninety days by a favorable vote of two-thirds of the members of congress on the initiative of either of the chambers or of the chief executive. In Mexico, on the other hand, the period of the legislative session may be shortened but never extended.

As has been mentioned previously, the constitutions also provide for the call of extraordinary or special sessions of the congress. In some of the countries the chief executive has the exclusive power to call congress in special session. In others, such a privilege may be exercised either by the executive or by the presiding officer of the congress upon request of the majority, as in Chile, or of two-thirds of the members, as in Ecuador and in Honduras. Some of the countries which use the permanent committee give this power to that body. In some countries the congress, whenever assembled in extraordinary session, is limited to dealing exclusively with those matters that have been the subject of the convocation. Such is the case in Argentina and in Nicaragua. It is also true in Chile unless the special session was called at the initiative of the congress itself.

Parliamentary procedure

Foreign precedents and customs, especially those of the United States and France, have exerted some influence on the development of Latin-American parliamentary practices. Often the writings of well-known North American, or British, or French authors are cited by congressmen in support of a certain parliamentary point. The rules generally declare that a quorum is constituted by a half plus one of the membership of the respective chamber. They also prescribe how often the chamber meets and impose penalties, in some countries, on those members who are absent from a certain number of meetings without proper authorization.

Joint sessions

Meetings in which both houses of congress sit together are held for various purposes besides those of a ceremonial nature. Joint sessions are required in Brazil to inaugurate the legislative session, to issue common rules of procedure, to receive the oath of office of the president and vice-president, and to consider a bill over the president's veto. Joint sessions have a special significance in Ecuador in view of the extensive list of matters which, by constitutional prescription, require consideration of the congress meeting as one body. This list includes the amendment of the constitution; the formal proclamation of the president-elect and vice-president-elect; acceptance or rejection of the president's resignation; the decision to declare the chief executive physically or mentally incapacitated; the election of justices of the supreme court and other high officials; the enactment of the national budget; the approval of presidential appointments requiring congressional consent; the grant of extraordinary powers to the executive or the withdrawal of such powers; and the examination of the actions of cabinet ministers and censure of such actions.

Congressional immunities

All countries recognize in general the inviolability of the legislators for their opinions and votes. Congressional rules usually place certain limitations upon language used in debate, and members may be reprimanded if they violate such regulations.

The scope of parliamentary immunity from arrest in some of the Latin-American countries is very broad, as stated by the supreme court of Argentina, "for peculiar reasons that are native to our own society and for motives of state."[11] It was felt by the drafters of these constitutions that ample safeguards were indispensable if the members of the

[11] Case *In re Tabanera, Fallos,* vol. 119, p. 305. See Linares Quintana, *op. cit.,* p. 291.

legislature were to be adequately protected against abuses of the executive branch.

One group of countries extends such an immunity over the entire congressional term of office; others limit this privilege to the duration of the legislative sessions and a period before and after; while a third group regulates the subject in a special manner. Countries of the first group, such as Argentina, Bolivia, Brazil, Costa Rica, Cuba, Haiti, Panama, Paraguay, Uruguay, and Venezuela, follow the principle that legislators are immune from arrest from the day of their election until the expiration of their terms unless surprised *flagrante delicto* (in the actual commission of the crime), and even in this instance notice must be given immediately to the respective chamber. Neither can legislators be indicted on a criminal charge except with the authorization of the body to which they belong. In such cases decision is made by the votes of two-thirds of the members.

Among the countries in the second group the Dominican Republic establishes congressional immunity only during the duration of the legislative sessions. The other countries extend the immunity for a period which varies in each case, before and after the legislative sessions.

Mexico is a good example of a third group of states. In this country the members of congress as well as supreme court justices, cabinet ministers, and the attorney general are liable for common crimes committed during the time of their office, and also for those that they may commit in the discharge of their duties. The chamber of deputies acting as a grand jury (*gran jurado*) decides, in cases involving a common offense, by an absolute majority, whether there are sufficient grounds for proceedings against the accused. If the decision is a negative one, such proceedings are discontinued. The so-called "official offenses" are tried by the senate, acting as a grand jury, upon previous accusation made by the lower house. The senate's decision in such cases requires a majority of two-thirds, and the only penalties that it can impose are those of loss of office and disqualifications for holding any other for a certain period.[12]

It is not surprising that the remarkably broad basis of parliamentary immunity has led to many misuses and abuses in almost every country of Latin America. Some have shown awareness of such dangers and in recently drafted constitutions have attempted to prevent abuses of congressional immunity by restricting such privileges. The earlier constitutions of Cuba, for example, vested in the congress the power to authorize the arrest or prosecution of any of its members, but they did not

[12] Arts. 108, 109, 111.

make it mandatory for the legislature to answer in any way the writ by which the courts request the authorization. The results of such a system were shown by the large number of cases in which each chamber had chosen to take no action on the judicial request and by the number of petitions which had been formally rejected. During the period from 1902 to 1920 the record shows that, of 372 writs received by the congress, in only one case was authorization granted.[13] This situation prompted the Constituent Assembly of 1940 to take a special interest in the matter. In the course of the debate one delegate stated that, in thirty-nine years, up to 1,261 crimes had been committed or presumably committed by legislators under congressional immunity. This figure included 2 murders, 9 homicides, and 265 libel cases, the rest being misdemeanors. With reference to libel suits, he pointed out that in many cases they had involved the use of a "delegated immunity," as when a congressman serves as nominal editor of a newspaper and in practice transfers his personal immunity to other persons who are writers or owners of the publication.[14]

The constituent convention, in order to remedy these abuses, voted that if the senate or the chamber of representatives fails to decide upon the requested authorization within forty days after the opening of the legislature such an authorization is understood to be granted. It was also provided that in all cases the decision of the congress must be taken for acknowledged cause. A similar action was taken by the Venezuelan Constituent Assembly of 1947, in deciding that the respective house will, in every case, reach a decision within five days counted from the session in which it received an account of the facts.[15]

Disciplinary power

This power is generally vested in each chamber by most of the constitutions. It may include measures ranging from reprimanding or calling a member to order, or censuring him, to the extreme disciplinary measures of expulsion. In some countries these actions may only be taken by a two-thirds vote of the members. Somewhat related to the disciplinary power is the authority of each chamber to compel members to attend its sessions. In Uruguay, where neither chamber may commence its sessions unless more than half its members are present, the

[13] Infiesta, *op. cit.*, p. 235.
[14] Andrés M. Lazcano y Mazón, *Constitución de Cuba* (*con los debates sobre su articulado y transitorias en la Convención Constituyente*), (3 vols., Havana, 1941), vol. III, p. 79. See also Evelio Tabío, *La inmunidad parlamentaria* (Havana, 1947), p. 22.
[15] Cuba (Art. 127); Venezuela (Art. 146).

minority may meet for the purpose of compelling absent members to attend under penalties which they may prescribe.[16]

In some countries the functions of senator and deputy are obligatory. Such is the case in Ecuador where, in addition, legislators cannot resign without permission of the respective house at the risk of losing their citizenship for two years. Other countries, such as Argentina, Cuba, or Chile, may expressly permit the resignation of members of the legislature. In general a simple majority is sufficient to accept voluntary resignations although a two-thirds vote is required in a few states.

FUNCTIONS OF CONGRESS

To carry out its functions the congress is endowed in all the countries with particular powers of a legislative, directoral, constitutive, electoral, and quasi-judicial nature.

In the determination of the general power to legislate there is usually included the authority or duty to enact codes and laws of a general character;[17] to levy and collect taxes, duties, imposts, and excises that may be necessary for the general welfare; to discuss and to approve the national budget; to approve loans, with the obligation in some countries of voting the revenues necessary for the payment of interests and amortization; to coin money and to fix the standard of weights and measures; to enact laws for the regulation and promotion of domestic and foreign commerce, and for agriculture and industry as well as for the protection of labor, old age, maternity, and employment; to establish uniform rules for obtaining citizenship; and to regulate the communication services. In some countries special majorities are required for the approval of those laws dealing with certain economic matters.

The power to declare war and to approve treaties of peace is also common to all the congresses. A vote of two-thirds of the total membership of the congress is required for approval of treaties in most countries, although in a few an absolute majority of the full membership is sufficient. A curious provision in Bolivia authorizes the legislative branch "to exercise the right of influence" over diplomatic actions or international commitments negotiated by the executive.[18] No occasion for an

---

[16] Art. 110.

[17] However, attention must be called to the fact that many constitutions have provisions empowering the congress to enact any other laws that it may consider necessary in the public interest, or that may be necessary to execute provisions of the constitution. Such clauses may be considered similar to the famous "implied powers" clause of the United States Constitution.

[18] Art. 58, cl. 16.

interpretation of this clause has ever arisen, and there is no evidence that the congress has ever attempted to interfere with the executive's conduct of foreign relations.

The power to fix the number of the armed forces or of the militia and of regulating its organization is generally included, as well as authority to permit the entry of foreign troops into the national territory. In Uruguay the congress has the power to refuse or to allow the sending of troops abroad. In such cases if authorization is given by the congress this body must also fix the time for their return to Uruguay.[19]

Among the electoral functions of the congress is that of scrutinizing the votes for president and vice-president. In many cases, however, the congress simply declares the election of each of these officials in view of the certificate transmitted by the supreme electoral body which exists in some countries. Of course, the task of electing a president or a vice-president may fall upon the congress under certain circumstances. It may be entrusted in some instances with other electoral powers such as the selection of supreme court justices and other important officers. In Honduras, the legislative and not the executive department has the power to appoint supreme court judges and members of the superior tribunal of accounts, although it has been noted that the electoral function in such cases is of a somewhat artificial character, since in practice the chief executive submits nominations to the leaders in congress.[20]

An important formal power of the congress is that of giving or witholding approval of appointments that are made by the president. Consent of the upper chamber is needed in many countries for appointments of ambassadors and ministers. Almost everywhere, approval is also required for appointments of high officers of the armed forces. It should be mentioned also that in countries where the state has the right of presentation in the filling of high ecclesiastical offices, as in Bolivia or Peru, the congress participates in the exercise of such functions.[21]

The quasi-judicial functions of congress relate to the impeachment proceedings against the president and other officials which have already been described. Other judicial powers assigned to the legislative department may include the authority to punish for contempt. In a majority of the countries the congress also participates with the president in the exercise of the pardoning power by passing bills of general amnesty.

Despite the strong "presidentialism" of Latin-American systems, the executive and administrative powers assigned to the legislative branch are always in theory, if not in practice, very significant. Congressional

---

[19] Art. 85, cl. 12.
[20] Stokes, *op. cit.*, pp. 283–284.
[21] Bolivia (Art. 71, cl. 8); Peru (Art. 123, cl. 14).

scrutiny of the president's actions has given theoretically to the legislature an important share in many executive functions. Aside from the participation in the appointment of high officials, in the making of treaties, the power to prescribe executive and administrative duties by the issuance of regulatory legislation, and the possibility of investigations, the Latin-American congresses may be vested by law with the power to call cabinet ministers and to question them about their activities or with authority to censure them for their actions.

In a majority of countries the congress can compel cabinet ministers to appear and answer questions. Without distinguishing at this time between countries which have some form of parliamentary responsibility and those which do not, it can be said here that such a power may be used by the legislatures of Argentina, Bolivia, Brazil, Colombia, Cuba, Ecuador, El Salvador, Guatemala, Honduras, Mexico, Nicaragua, Panama, Peru, Uruguay, and Venezuela. Ministers are permitted to attend the meetings of congress, in most countries on their own initiative, and they can participate in the debates. The general rule is, however, that they do not vote, since they are not members of the legislature. If they are legislators, their congressional rights are suspended by the fact of their appointment to the cabinet.

Other potential if not operative powers of congress to check executive control and to assure its share in policy making are illustrated by the case of the Dominican Republic. There the legislature may interpellate cabinet members and has the authority to examine and to approve each year all acts of the administration. The results of such interpellations or disapproval are not specified, and there are no instances on record of the use of such power.[22] Similar provisions establishing the right "to censure the conduct of the executive" exist also in Honduras and Nicaragua. It is well known, however, that in these republics the decisive influence of the president is so strongly felt through the whole legislative process that it renders such provisions inoperative.

THE LEGISLATIVE PROCESS

The Latin-American systems do not restrict the privilege of introducing bills to the members of the legislature, but rather they give ample opportunities to the other branches and organs of the government to participate in the initial phase of lawmaking. Proposals of laws may be introduced by any member of the legislative chamber or by the

[22] Art. 33, cl. 19, 20.

executive directly or through his ministers. In Ecuador bills may be introduced with the support of at least three members of either one of the three "functional" branches. Supreme Court members may represent the judiciary for the introduction of legislation. Resolutions and declarations may also be introduced by any member of the congress, and the procedure is much the same for any type of proposal. In Colombia, bills may be presented by any congressman or by a cabinet member, but the lower house has exclusive power to initiate legislation raising revenue, and bills dealing with the administration of justice are initiated by one of the special standing committees or by a cabinet member. In Uruguay, bills may be presented by any member of congress or by the executive, but the latter has exclusive initiative on matters concerning the national debt and the creation of public offices and services. In other countries the judicial branch is given authority to originate proposals dealing with justice and judicial procedure. In the group of states where the judiciary does not enjoy this privilege it still plays a significant part in lawmaking, e.g., in Honduras, where the congress often transmits bills to the supreme court and requests its advice on their constitutionality before assigning them to a committee.[23] Also in Colombia, justices of the supreme court may participate in debates on legislation concerning civil law and procedure. In Cuba legislation may be initiated not only by members of the legislature, but also by the executive, the supreme court, the supreme electoral tribunal, and the tribunal of accounts on matters within their competence. The Cuban system also includes the method of popular initiative and allows the introduction of bills by at least 10,000 qualified voters. The state legislatures have in Mexico the right to initiate laws or decrees in the federal congress.

The procedure regarding passage of a bill through the legislative chambers is usually to be found in the *leyes de relaciones* and the rules of those bodies. Bills must be presented in writing with the signature of the author or authors to the secretary, and the presiding officer proceeds then to assign them to the proper committee. As we have noted before, committees are in some countries forced to consider proposals or to report on them under special circumstances. Each house keeps a legislative calendar on which bills are placed as they are discharged by the various committees, but party leaders usually decide in informal conferences questions of precedence and indicate the preference to be given to proposals.

In Honduras a bill is discussed article by article in three separate readings, and members can speak a maximum of three times on any point, with the exception of the author, who is not under any restriction.[24] Proposals receive two readings in Argentina, and only on the second can items of the bill be discussed separately. As a rule, on presentation of the committee's report members representing the committee's majority and minority respectively are given an opportunity to present their views. In countries where three readings are prescribed, the second and the third are simply reduced to a reading of the bill by title only, and the real debate is confined in practice to the first meeting. There is also the possibility in most countries that the congress may, by a special majority, decide to discuss a proposal after only one reading. Although it is not a common occurrence, legislative rules in some countries permit either branch of the legislature to transform its total membership into a committee of the whole for specific purposes. This permits consideration of proposed legislation under less formal procedures.

Voting may be by voice or show of hands. It may also be by rising, or it may be each member answering yes or no as the role is called. The Cuban congress uses two additional ways of voting: secret voting by depositing written ballots, which is used in the lower house for the election of officers; and voting by white and black balls (*por bolas*), which is used by the senate when acting in judgment on the conduct of officials or whenever the decision requires a two-thirds vote. In addition to these conventional modes of voting, modern electric voting machines have been installed in several Latin-American legislative halls.

Approval of bills is by an absolute majority except when specified otherwise by law. In Cuba a distinction is made between ordinary and extraordinary laws. The organic laws,[25] those indicated as such in the constitution, and any other to which the congress may give this character are extraordinary. All other laws are ordinary. Extraordinary laws require for their approval a majority of the total number of members of each house. Ordinary legislation can be approved by a majority of those present.

In Honduras, a member of the congress may request that a bill be reconsidered after it has been approved by the majority. Concurrence of a two-thirds vote is necessary in such cases in order to reopen the debate and to take a new vote.

In countries with a bicameral system, after a bill has been approved by one chamber it passes to the other. In Cuba, once a bill is approved

---

[24] *Ibid.*, p. 276.

[25] Among the organic laws are those dealing with the civil service; the executive and judicial branches; the tribunal of constitutional and social guarantees; the electoral courts; the tribunal of accounts; and the municipalities.

in one house, it is referred to the committee on style for its final drafting. It is then printed and distributed among the members within twenty-four hours after its approval, and finally it is sent to the other chamber or to the president, as the case may be.[26] As a rule, no bill that has been rejected completely by either one of the legislative chambers may be introduced again during the same legislative session.

Compromises between the houses

A conflict arises when, after a bill is passed by one house, the other returns it with additions or amendments. This conflict may be solved by several methods. In Argentina, if the chamber in which the bill originated rejects the amendments proposed by the revising chamber, this body may insist on its modifications by a special vote of two-thirds, in which case, the other chamber may reject it only with a two-thirds majority. A similar plan is used in Chile, although there a mixed committee composed of an equal number of members of each house is appointed to work out a compromise. In Venezuela, Ecuador, Bolivia, and Uruguay the method of holding a joint session is used to decide the problem. A third method is employed by Cuba and also by Haiti, which consists of the use of conference committees to adjust disagreements between the two chambers. In Cuba, a conference committee composed of five senators and five representatives is formed in order to conciliate the divergent views of the two houses. If the committee fails to agree, the proposal is considered rejected. If, on the contrary, it agrees to a formula, its report is submitted for discussion and approval in both chambers, but no amendments can be made to it. The report must be approved by both houses.[27] The practice for solving legislative differences in Brazil is that of holding joint sessions of the appropriate standing committees of both chambers.

Approval and publication of the laws

Proposals, after having been approved in the form already described, are transmitted to the president. Two more steps must be taken before a bill becomes law: its promulgation or sanction by the president, and its publication. As we have seen in the preceding chapter, the president may, of course, reject the bill by using his veto power. If he approves it, he signs it and orders it to be published. The act passed by the

[26] Ley de relaciones (Oct. 25, 1946), Art. 20.
[27] *Ibid.*, Arts. 22 and 23.

congress and approved by the president is then printed in the official publication known as *Registro Nacional Registro, Oficial, Diario Oficial,* or *Gaceta Oficial,* according to the country. It is only after the bill has appeared in this official periodical that it becomes law. In Cuba, for instance, the civil code in Article 1 provides that "the laws will go into effect three days after their publication in the *Gaceta Oficial de la República* unless otherwise provided in their text." The Spanish civil code established a period of twenty days under the same conditions. In all cases, the law in question has no validity despite congressional and presidential approvals until this other requirement is fulfilled. Despite the frequency with which the terms "promulgation" and "publication" are indiscriminately used,[28] it can be said that both phases are invariably found in the legislative process of every Latin-American country. The legislative function is completed with the approval of the executive and the implied ordering of the law's enforcement, or promulgation; publication serves the purpose of making the law known to the people.

The Judicial Systems of Latin America*

HELEN CLAGETT

RELATION OF THE JUDICIAL TO OTHER POWERS OF GOVERNMENT

Since the Latin American nations, with the exception of Brazil and Haiti, inherited the Spanish system of administration of justice, it is not surprising to find in these countries a great many parallels in the basic structure of judicial organization and similarity in procedural legislation. As a matter of fact, any divergencies that exist may well be attributed to such factors as the degree of political freedom permitted

---

[28] See Linares Quintana, *op. cit.,* p. 308; Andrés M. Lazcano y Mazón, *Las constituciones de Cuba* (Madrid, 1952), pp. 327–329. For definitions of these terms see Rodolfo Rivarola, *Diccionario manual de instrucción cívica y constitucional argentina* (Buenos Aires, 1934).

* Helen Clagett, *The Administration of Justice in Latin America* (New York: Oceana Publications, Inc., 1952), pp. 11–40. (Footnotes in the original version have been omitted.)

in a particular country, the problems peculiar thereto, the force of public opinion, and the progressiveness of the nation in adapting new universal concepts to its own domestic conditions. North American influences in the matter of judicial organization, which were felt and acknowledged in the earlier days of some of the new southern republics, have disappeared, leaving but few traces, while European influences have prevailed and still exist with appropriate modifications.

[The importance of the judicial power, as well as the type of judicial organization, depends in general on the form of the political government of the individual countries.] Although self-labelled as "democratic republics," the Latin American nations cannot and should not all be placed in the same political category; in practice they range all the way from military dictatorships to democratic regimes. All claim constitutionally to derive their power from the people, and, except in the case of suspension or abolishment by *de facto* governments, all of the nations have a written constitution or political code, which assures the people of certain enumerated personal, political, and civil liberties and contains a varying number of economic and social guarantees. These charters also recite provisions on separation of powers.

A detailed exposition of the political differences existing among these countries would involve extensive research into historical and legislative backgrounds that could not be justified in this brief monograph. However, the development of judicial institutions cannot be entirely divorced from other institutions in the country, and for that reason a few paragraphs are devoted to a sketch of the governmental structure and the relations of the judicial to the legislative and executive branches.

At the hour of achieving independence from their mother countries, Spain and Portugal, the Latin American nations were wholly unprepared to adopt a democratic type of government, and indeed, it would have been most unsuitable at that time in their history. Among the unfavorable factors were a complex racial composition, including large illiterate Indian populations, and the almost complete absence of a middle class. Great areas of land with only a thinly spread population also were an obstacle. But one of the most important factors was the total lack of experience on the part of the people and their scant knowledge of democratic institutions. As we well know, a number of these countries still suffer today—one hundred and twenty-five years later—from the same ills that existed in their earlier history, and as a result, the form of government that was found to be more workable then still prevails to some extent. This form was either a benevolent dictatorship, a patriarchal administration, or a type of *caudillo* regime. In a few countries, however, great political strides have been made since the 1820's: A middle class is very slowly but steadily emerging, the common people have been given increasingly greater educational advantages, industries are growing apace, and notable improvements have been achieved in the transportation and communication systems. Such progress is bound to be reflected in a decrease in bloody revolutions, greater governmental stability, and the development of true democratic tendencies in government.

In the course of the evolution of public power in Latin America, history has noted that in a few of the American republics little progress has been made in so far as judicial authority is concerned. Although it may be true that many of the principles and freedoms stated in Latin American constitutions and laws have remained purely theoretical, it is not within the scope of the present work to go into any other aspects of the matter than legislation as it appears on the statute books.

In the written constitutions, the provisions with respect to the various powers of government and their relations to each other are usually limited to a mere pronouncement of general principles and broad concepts, leaving to complementary and implementary legislation the working out of necessary details. The balance and separation of public powers has been considered a fundamental necessity to prevent the usurpation of conferred authority, and consequently, the classical tripartite division of governmental powers into executive, legislative, and judicial has been adopted in Latin America. In its earlier history, Mexico as a new republic attempted to establish a four-power government consisting of executive, legislative, judicial, and the "Supreme Preservation" powers, but this was short-lived.

The majority of the countries to the south of us are constitutionally set up as "unitary republics," strongly centralized in all branches. Centralization is particularly apparent in the judicial area, for in the great majority of the countries the judiciary is composed of a single pyramid of courts and judges. Only four nations—Argentina, Brazil, Mexico, and Venezuela—have adopted a federated representative form of government similar to our own, resulting in a dual system of courts, federal and local. Unfortunately, recent political trends in Brazil and Venezuela have served to reduce and restrict local power generally in favor of centralization and nationalization; in the judicial branch this has been effected by the elimination of the lower federal courts and the substitution of the highest local courts to act as liaison between the lower state or provincial tribunals and the federal supreme court. In Brazil one intermediate appellate court still remains because, soon after the change was made, it became obvious that the burden on the Supreme Tribunal was too great without intermediate screening of some kind. In the chapter on "Judicial Systems" more detail has been included on these two systems.

The following paragraphs are devoted to a discussion of the relations between the three powers of government in Latin America, showing how the functions of each branch overlap to some extent into the affairs of the others, and to what extent control may be exercised by the Executive or Legislative over the Judicial Power, and *vice versa*.

Executive power

The executive power in the Latin American republics is exercised by a Chief Executive known as the President, aided generally by a cabinet of ministers and, as in Paraguay and Colombia, an advisory Council of State. A very recent change in Uruguay has installed in that country a nine-man National Council as the Executive Power, similar to the Swiss government. The functions of cabinet officers are similar to those in our country, the principal difference being that they may initiate legislation, and must countersign, with the President, executive decrees and regulations affecting their particular fields. It is generally conceded that in Latin America this branch of the government is by far the most powerful. Whereas the legislative power formulates the general rules of law, it is the executive power that puts them into actual practice, in relation to the objectives and purposes of the nation. In order to discharge this important function, the President may legislate to a certain extent, being authorized to issue regulatory decrees with respect to the laws passed by the legislature. This permits of broad interpretation, and, as a matter of fact, a law may frequently be practically unenforceable because of the absence of a presidential decree to implement it. In addition, the Executive may issue decree-laws at certain times, as for instance, when the legislature is not in session or during some emergency. Administrative rulings issued by the various executive departments in practice also have the force of law, and this makes available to the Executive an additional source of power.

Whereas the legislative power is vested in only one organ, which may sit in two or more chambers to carry on its functions, the executive power requires a complexity of instrumentalities or agencies for its exercise. These are generally Cabinet offices or administrative departments. Semi-autonomous agencies and government corporations, also to be found in many countries and apparently growing in popularity, likewise aid in carrying on executive duties. Local organs in the form of provincial, district, and municipal governments also represent the national Executive. When, under certain circumstances, a state of siege is declared, the Executive gains practically dictatorial powers for the period of the emergency.

In relation to the judicial power, the Executive in many countries has the authority to make judicial appointments, either alone or with the consent or approval of Congress or of one of its chambers, or of the Council of State. The Executive is specifically prohibited from interfering with the exercise of judicial authority, but he is generally granted the power to pardon or commute sentences imposed by the courts. In all the countries the executive and the judicial powers are most closely associated in the office of government attorney, denominated by various names, such as *ministerio público, ministerio fiscal, procuradortía geral,* and *procuradoria general.* In some respects it resembles the office of Attorney General of the United States, but the area of its activities is not so broad, because generally, in addition to this office, there is a Department of Justice headed by a Minister or Secretary of Justice, who is a Cabinet officer. In a few of the countries the government attorney's office is attached to the Ministry of Justice; in others it operates as a more or less distinct agency. Some countries have eliminated the Department of Justice.

This office may be said to form one of the strongest executive controls in the judicial field. It is the direct agent of the Executive in the courts, being vested with a mixture of judicial, administrative, and disciplinary powers with respect to the judiciary. Its representative appears in court in every criminal case and in those civil cases involving such matters as minors, rights of married women, expropriation, attachment of property. The representative of this office may appear as a party to the case or as an adviser, or his mere presence at the trial may be required without active participation. In addition, the government attorney represents the administration in all cases in which the nation or any political part or entity thereof is a party or may be directly affected by the decision rendered by court. In a few of the countries, the government attorney is empowered to correct abuses in the courts, though the latter may not, in turn, correct or censure the office of government attorney for any abuse or lack of discipline; indeed, it may not even criticize any member of this office who is engaged in performing his duties, except in a prosecution for misfeasance or malfeasance, or similar proceeding.

A further intervention of the executive power in the judicial field is the coexistence of administrative courts with the ordinary judicial organs. In addition to the dispensation of justice through the administrative departments and through special procedures in the ordinary courts, there are courts in the labor, military, electoral, and other areas that are responsible to the Executive rather than to the judicial power. Special courts are discussed fully in a later chapter.

Legislative power

In practice, the legislative power of the majority of the Latin American countries may probably be said to be the weakest of the three public powers. At the present time, the greater number of the countries have a bicameral legislative body denominated National Assembly, Congress, Legislative Assembly, or National Congress. Unicameral legislatures are found in Paraguay, and in five of the Central American nations—Costa Rica, El Salvador, Guatemala, Honduras, and Panama—Nicaragua being the sole adherent to the bicameral system in this region.

The principal function of the legislative organ is the enactment of general laws and precepts applicable to the entire nation. These rules of law are abstract and general in character, and can be made effective only if the other two branches of the government cooperate in implementing them and putting them into practice, as the executive branch does, or by interpreting and applying them to particular cases, as the judicial branch does.

With respect to the administration of justice, the Legislative wields some influence through its power to appoint and remove judicial officials, and to approve or consent to presidential appointments, as the case may be. The Legislative could conceivably bring much pressure to bear on the judicial branch through its power to enact legislation regulating the judiciary's powers, jurisdiction, salaries, conduct in office, and many other matters. In many of the countries the Supreme Court may draft legislation concerning itself or the court system in general, for submission to the legislature.

A judicial function of the legislature in practically every country is the impeachment of high officials. In a few instances, the legislature also has the power to pass upon the constitutionality or unconstitutionality of its own enactments or to limit judicial action in this field to executive decrees.

Judicial power

The judicial power of the government is the one in which we are primarily interested here, since the bulk of the work of administering justice falls within its scope.

In general, all civilized and free nations, including the twenty Latin American republics, have accorded the judicial power a position of great importance, principally because they consider justice to be closely linked to human liberty. The function of this branch of government fundamentally affects the relations between the government and the governed, and it is through its mediation that the latter's fear of abuse of power by the former has been mitigated. The administration of justice is not only a most important function of any government, but also the most difficult to discharge.

The history of the Latin American countries clearly demonstrates the tireless, though often frustrated, pursuit of an independent and unbiased judicial power. North Americans, more fortunate in their judicial inheritance and in the stability of their political institutions, often fail to appreciate the tremendous struggle in which their neighbors to the south have been engaged for many years in an effort to create a judicial power that would be a truly unfettered branch of their government. In practice it has proved impossible to realize the complete separation of powers—and this is equally true in our own country and in modern governments elsewhere—for circumstances have forced the exercise of judicial functions outside of the judiciary.

With respect to judicial power, the constitutions in most of the countries have been limited to the statement of basic concepts in general terms, defining the functions of the administration of justice, postulating the gratuitousness of justice and the independent nature of the judicial power, outlining the court system, to be later implemented by special legislation, enumerating the qualifications for justices of the highest court, and similar provisions.

It would seem that more effort has been expended in preventing the judicial power from encroaching on the legislative and executive power than vice versa. Judicial precedent and the doctrine of *stare decisis*, discussed more fully later in this work, are given little weight for fear of creating judge-made law, which would interfere in the legislative field. Among other restrictions and limitations on the judicial branch is the legislative power to repeal laws and decrees which have been declared unconstitutional.

JUDICIAL SYSTEMS

General

Organs for the administration of justice are generally known as courts or tribunals of justice, composed of judges, ministers, or magistrates. These organs act within a jurisdiction prescribed by law, and their competence extends to civil and or criminal cases arising within a prescribed territory. They may be unipersonal (a single judge carries on the judicial functions) or collegiate (*colegiado*) (two or more judges preside and act together). Usually, the lower courts are unipersonal, while the appellate courts are generally of the collegiate type; the highest court of the land is, without exception, collegiate.

In Latin America we find two systems of court organization, namely, the "unitary" and the dual. The former is by far the more common, for it is more compatible with the centralization of governmental power found in the majority of the countries there.

A unitary judicial system is composed of a single pyramid of courts, the apex of which is a supreme court, national in scope and jurisdiction. Courts and judgeships under it are organized bureaucratically in a series of superior and inferior ranks and categories. Division of the nation into judicial districts and subdistricts, within which appeals are permitted from one rank to the next, makes it easy for the highest court in the land to supervise and administer the entire system from the nation's capital city. The general pattern seems to be the establishment of superior courts locally in the capital city of each state, province, or department into which the country may be territorially divided. Consecutively lower ranks of courts or judgeships vary in number according to the importance of the city or town and the volume of litigation. Justice of the peace courts and mayors' courts (*alcadias*) are generally the lowest, both in unitary and dual systems. Four of the Latin American republics—Argentina, Mexico, Brazil, and Venezuela—have a federated form of government. Until recent changes were made in Brazil and Venezuela, a dual system of courts had functioned with apparent success in all four of these countries. Trends toward centralization and the creation of a national state in Brazil and Venezuela, resulting from changes in administration and policy, have caused the suppression of certain ranks of courts in these two states and the merging of federal and local judiciaries into practically a unitary system. In Brazil, this shift was initiated with the adoption of the Constitution of 1937, which eliminated all lower federal appellate courts (with the exception of one in Rio de Janeiro) and incorporated the state tribunals into the national system. This made the highest state courts appellate tribunals bridging the gap between the lowest state courts and the *Tribunal de Appellação* and the *Tribunal Supremo*. The new Constitution of 1946, though less nationalistic than its predecessor, left the courts untouched, and the system still remains definitely unitary.

In Venezuela the judiciary was nationalized in 1945 by a specific constitutional amendment, and a provision incorporated in the Constitution of 1947 states that the power to administer justice is an exclusively federal function, not a dual faculty. It was not until 1948, however, when a law, enacted on November 5, ordered the implementation of the constitutional precepts, that the actual elimination of dual characteristics was carried out.

In view of the above, it would appear that today Argentina and Mexico remain as the only true adherents to the federated system, patterned after that of our own country.

The fact that the lower courts in the majority of the Latin American Republics are unipersonal obliges the judge to weigh both questions of fact and questions of law. He should be a good lawyer, with keen insight into human problems and human behavior, possessing practical sense and broad general experience. Since this obviously represents a complex and difficult task for any one person, the higher courts, handling the more important problems and applying law on a higher level, are generally of the "collegiate" type, that is, pluripersonal. The use of expert testimony is general, and where obscurity exists, reliance is placed on doctrinal opinion rather than on judicial precedent in the interpretation of law. Juries are not popular in Latin America, but are authorized by law in certain types of cases. A few paragraphs describing the jury trials will be found in a later chapter.

Legislation on the judicial power in Latin America

The Latin American republics inherited from the mother countries not only court organization and procedural methods, but even the very form of the legislation enacted for the regulation of the administration of justice. Apart from the broad concepts and principles with respect to judicial power incorporated in the written constitution, great detail is found in statutory law. Constitutional precepts are generally limited to an outline of the judicial structure, a bare statement of requirements for eligibility to office on the highest court, the number of justices to complement the bench, the boundaries of jurisdiction and competence, and similar matters. In some of the charters we also find declarations as to the gratuitousness of justice for everyone, the independence of the judiciary, permanency of tenure for judges, and so on. Because generally a constitution is amendable only by a long and difficult process, it is considered too static in nature to contain other types of provisions that should be amenable to modification. Thus the details of administration of justice are left to more easily reformed legislation, usually consisting of basic organic laws, sometimes in the form of a code, which implement the constitutional precepts and vary greatly in length and detail from country to country. As a rule, these laws are gathered into separate chapters dealing with the various ranks of courts and judgeships. Included are provisions on the number of courts and their location, the number of judges on each bench, requirements for holding office, competence and jurisdiction of each court, administrative functions and internal regulations, and the appointment and functions of other court officials, among them the *fiscales* (advisers in court), public defenders, secretaries, reporters, court clerks, and notaries. Disciplinary matters, leaves, filling of vacancies, the hiring and dismissal of employees, the keeping of files and records, and many other related matters also are to be found in these organic laws. Where there is an integrated bar, as in Chile, the basic code pertaining to the courts includes regulation of the legal profession as well. The office of government attorney, or *ministerio público,* is generally the subject of a separate and special law.

In order to keep abreast of growth and development, current practices, and changes in policy, these basic regulatory laws and codes have in most cases undergone many modifications. Where this material has not been revised or codified, extensive research is necessary to find all amendments. In addition to examining the constitutions and the organic laws or codes of court organization, the investigator in this field must also consult internal regulations of the individual courts or ranks of courts for rules and administrative details. In the matter of procedure—civil, criminal, administrative, or special—it is necessary to consult the various procedural codes in these specific fields, both federal and local where the country has a dual judicial system.

The highest courts in Latin America

Among the Latin American republics, there is no uniform denomination for the highest tribunal of the land. We find such varied official titles as Supreme Court, Supreme Court of Justice, Supreme Court of Justice of the Nation, Supreme Tribunal, Supreme Federal Tribunal, Cassation Tribunal, Federal Court and of Cassation, High Federal Court, and there are others. The lower courts are also known by many names, including superior court, appellate court, circuit court, district court, *audiencia,* court of first, second or third instance, civil tribunal, criminal tribunal, peace court, justice-of-the-peace court, mayor's court, and municipal court. In addition to these organs of the regular judicial power, the research worker in this field will also find a great variety of organs in special jurisdictions administering justice outside the judicial power.

The number of justices or judges on the bench of the highest court of the nation varies from country to country, ranging from three to thirty-one. The number sometimes depends on the fact that much of the court business is accomplished in chamber or in court divisions based on subject-matter. In those countries where special courts are created to handle litigation in particular fields, the burden on the highest court of the judicial system is to that extent eased, and fewer justices are needed. . . .

Qualifications for office

The constitutional provisions dealing with the judicial power usually stipulate the qualifications for office on the bench of the highest court of the nation. Except for the age limits and the number of years of law practice, one finds little variation among the requisites for eligibility imposed in the twenty republics. In Chile, we find nothing in the text of the Constitution on this subject, aside from the statement that appropriate provisions will be incorporated in the organic law on the judiciary.

With the exception of Haiti, all the Latin American countries provide that candidates for the highest court must be native-born citizens, while in Costa Rica and Panama they may be either native-born or have been naturalized for a stated number of years. The minimum age limit for this high office varies between thirty and forty years. In Argentina, the Dominican Republic, El Salvador, Haiti, Honduras, and Venezuela the minimum is thirty years, while in Cuba, Ecuador, Nicaragua, Peru, and Uruguay the candidate must be over forty years. Bolivia, Brazil, Colombia, Costa Rica, Guatemala, Mexico, Panama, and Paraguay require that a candidate be "over thirty-five"; Chile, over thirty-six. We also find a maximum age limit set forth in some of the constitutions. Mexico, El Salvador, and Peru have fixed this at sixty-five, seventy, and seventy-five years, respectively, while in Brazil, it is mandatory that a judge retire from office at the age of seventy years. In the other countries, retirement of judicial officials is laid down in statutory law rather than in the constitutions.

With respect to candidacy for office in the inferior courts, the lower the court, the lower is the age limit.

The Latin American nations without exception insist that candidates for the highest judicial posts must be lawyers by education and profession; most of them also require that they shall have practiced law or held a judicial post in the lower courts for certain periods of time. The average term of law practice called for by the constitutions of many of the countries is ten years. In Peru twenty years is the minimum, in Chile, Ecuador, and Panama fifteen years. Several of the countries set shorter periods: Colombia, four years; Mexico, five; Haiti, seven; and the Dominican Republic, El Salvador, and Guatemala, eight years each.

The requirements that a candidate be of secular status, actively participating in civic affairs and exercising fully his political and civil rights are common to practically all of the republics. In addition, in Brazil candidates for judgeship must be of "outstanding good knowledge and spotless reputation"; Mexico and Nicaragua require of them irreproachable conduct and good reputation; while Paraguay demands that they be "blameless in public and private law." Apart from these prerequisites, a number of the countries provide for a competitive examination, or require that the candidate have seniority in office as a judge on an inferior tribunal before he may be considered or included in a panel of eligible candidates.

Disqualifications for office are likewise listed in some of the charters and in practically all of the organic laws. Common among these are such grounds as relationship to appointive officers or other persons on the bench, existence of a criminal record, that the aspirant is deaf or mute, that he has been received into an ecclesiastical order, that he has passed through bankruptcy, etc.

The appointment of judges

In the days of absolute monarchs, it was the natural prerogative of the king to appoint persons to administer justice in his name, since the function was his and not the State's. With the spread of democratic procedures, in some countries the judges are elected by the people, but this method apparently is little used in Latin America. Appointment by parliamentary bodies is a better-known practice, and it has the advantage of avoiding difficulties encountered in direct election. On the other hand, it suffers from the defect that the judicial power cannot then always be completely independent of the legislative power, as provided constitutionally. The same argument applies to designation by the Executive, for then the judiciary would be responsive to the administration. In Latin American countries, as elsewhere, appointment by one branch with the consent or approval of another, has been found to be the most satisfactory. Competitive examinations and the placing of eligibility on an intellectual basis would appear, perhaps, to have more merit than other methods, but this would not insure that intellectual superiority would be accompanied by other necessary qualifications for the office, such as moral integrity and experience. It would merely obviate the pressures that are present where the Legislative or the Executive has appointive powers.

In the Latin American nations appointment to posts on the highest courts of the land varies among three types: by the President; by the

President with the consent or approval of the Senate or the Congress; and by election of the legislative body. Some limitations are provided when there is a requirement that panels of candidates must be prepared and submitted by some other agency, which reduces appointment to a selection from among these names.

In Chile and Haiti, no restriction is placed on presidential authority to fill judicial vacancies on the Supreme Court, though in Chile, the candidates' names are placed on a panel or slate drawn up by the members of the Supreme Court itself, and the President makes his appointments from among these names. In Argentina, Brazil, Cuba, and Mexico, presidential nomination must have Senate approval. Paraguay, where Senate approval was required up to 1940 when the new Constitution was adopted, now requires consent of the Council of State, while in the five Central American countries possessing unicameral legislative bodies, consent must come from these organs. In Bolivia, the Chamber of Deputies makes judicial appointments, electing the judges from lists submitted by the Senate. One-half of the membership of the Colombian Supreme Court bench is appointed by the Senate, the other half by the Chamber of Deputies, selection being made from panels prepared and submitted by the President of the nation; if the number of vacancies to be filled is odd, the extra position is filled by the Senate. The Senate in the Dominican Republic is authorized to elect the justices of the highest court, while in Uruguay, Peru, and Nicaragua, vacancies are filled at a joint session of the legislature. In Peru the choice is made from a double panel of candidates. Until recent years the Venezuelan Congress made judicial appointments by majority vote, but at the time of writing this function has been taken over by the Military Junta in power.

Perhaps some details as to the drafting of the slates or panels may be of interest here. The number of names required to appear on the slates varies from country to country, ranging between three and twenty-five. In some of the countries the Chief Executive is responsible for preparing the lists, in others it is the function of one or both houses of the legislature or of members of the Supreme Court itself. In any case, it is done in accordance with certain rules. For example, a certain number of candidates may have to be selected from among incumbents of judicial offices in the lower courts or perhaps in the immediately lower tribunal, on the basis of seniority or merit, while others may be selected from outside the judicial profession. In some cases, inclusion depends on passing a competitive examination or some other test. In addition, all candidates must, of course, meet the prerequisites mentioned at the beginning of this section with respect to citizenship, a stated period of legal practice, and age limitations, as well as other qualifications set forth in constitutional and statutory provisions.

In comparatively few of the countries is the Supreme Court Chief Justice, or *Presidente,* as he is generally known, appointed directly. The method of selection varies, but the most popular manner seems to be election of one of the members of the court by his own colleagues. His term of office may be for one year or more, or for the entire term of his appointment, and there may or may not be the privilege of re-election. In some countries, the position of *Presidente* is rotative; in others it depends on seniority in office. In Bolivia the President makes this appointment, but only after the candidate has been suggested from among and by his own colleagues. In this case it is a permanent office.

A practice that differs from our own, but which is widely followed in the Latin American republics, is the appointment or selection of alternate or substitute judges at the same time as that of the judge himself. In some countries only a few alternates are named; in others, one for each judge is named. The purpose of this is to have someone who, in the absence of a judge for any reason, will be immediately available to take his place on the bench. These persons must possess the same qualifications for office as the regular judges. Another interesting practice is the appointment of *fiscales,* or advisers to the court, who in some of the countries are elected at the same time as the justices, and must possess the same or similar qualifications for office.

The manner of appointment, discussed above, varies not only from one country to another, but from one level of courts to another within the same country. In some countries the President or the legislature makes all judicial appointments to the lower courts in the same manner as to the Supreme Court. Some Latin American States provide that the panels or slates of candidates for the various courts are to be drawn up by different bodies though the President or the legislature or both together make all the appointments. In some countries these panels are drafted by each level of courts for the appointment of judges to the next lower rank of courts. In Honduras, the members of the Supreme Court make appointments to fill vacancies on all lower court benches. In Mexico, in so far as the federal courts are concerned, the magistrates of the circuit courts and the judges of the district tribunals are all appointees of the Supreme Court. Some countries, particularly those that have a dual hierachy of courts, confer the power of appointment to the lower courts on the governor of a state or province, for the judicial power of local entities, as distinguished from federal powers, is constitutionally allocated to the states. Municipal judges and justices of the peace are sometimes elective officers and serve without salary.

Tenure of office

Permanency in office, dependent upon good behavior and liability under law for corrupt administration of justice, is not widespread in Latin America, though it seems to be gaining acceptance. Such a policy would go far to promote the independence of the judiciary, as has been demonstrated in many other countries of the world. In view of their long history of political instability, however, it is not surprising that the majority of the Latin American countries have not been able, up to the present time, to make this institution effective in practice as well as theory.

Supreme Court justices are appointed for life and during good behavior in Argentina, Brazil, Chile, and Cuba. In the remaining countries, the terms vary from three to ten years, generally with the privilege of reappointment or relection for similar terms. Justices may hold office for ten years in Bolivia, Haiti, Panama, and Uruguay; for eight years in Costa Rica; and for six years in Ecuador, Honduras, Mexico, and Nicaragua. In Colombia, the term of office of Supreme Court justices is five years, as it is also in the Dominican Republic, Paraguay, and Venezuela. Guatemala limits appointments to four years, and El Salvador to only three years.

Tenure of office for incumbents in the lower courts and holders of judgeships on inferior levels varies from country to country as well as within each country. Good behavior is a general requisite, whether the term is for life or for years. The problem of *"inamovilidad"* (irremovability or permanence in office during term of appointment) has been a favorite topic of discussion by legislators and statesmen for many years. In the majority of the countries, an incumbent is guaranteed against being removed or transferred from his post without his consent, or demoted at the will of the Supreme Court or any other agency of the government. Promotion is, naturally, an exception, but removal from office for any other cause may be made only in accordance with certain regulations and after proper hearing and other steps required by law. The president of the republic sometimes is empowered to report judges or justices for misfeasance, malpractice, or corruption in office, requesting impeachment or removal. In the majority of the countries, however, in so far as courts and judges in a unitary system are concerned, the Supreme Court, and particularly the Chief Justice, is responsible for the behavior of judges and other officials in all the lower courts, and may take disciplinary measures of certain types or try them for more serious violations.

Administrative functions of supreme courts

As a general rule, the highest court of the land in the Latin American republics is the recognized head of the judiciary and supervisor of the entire system. In this role it is assigned various duties and functions in keeping with its status, in addition to its judicial functions and its supervisory tasks in seeing that the codes and laws are correctly applied and interpreted by the lower courts.

A number of the countries grant authority to the highest court, which extends even to appointment of all magistrates and judges of lower courts as well as other court officers; others merely impose the additional task of preparing a panel or slate of candidates from which selection is made by another person or branch of the government. In some instances the supreme court is empowered to transfer judges and cases from one court to another, and to make substitutions where necessary, in order to settle conflicts of jurisdiction or competence arising between two or more courts of the same or different ranks. Other duties include correction or reprimand for abuse of authority and corruptive practices on the part of judges and other officials, disciplinary action against them, or, if sufficiently grave reasons are present, the Supreme Court may recommend removal of these officials to the appropriate authority.

In the majority of the countries disciplinary action may take the form of private or public correction, oral or in writing, imposition of a fine, or even arrest in aggravated cases.

Leaves, vacations, financial matters, and so on are either handled by the Supreme Court or delegated by it to some inferior court. Visits of inspection to lower courts and penal institutions are mandatory in some countries, and in some cases, each judge on a bench may be assigned some particular district for which he is responsible.

The Supreme Court and its members issue reports of various kinds, such as annual reports, and it prepares an organ for the dissemination of its decisions and resolutions or of its *jurisprudencia* (fixed case-law). Court calendars and annual or periodical budgets for itself and the entire court system are also drawn up by the Supreme Court in its capacity as the head of the judicial hierachy. The Supreme Court, in a great number of the countries, also has authority to propose or draft legislation for the consideration of the legislature, generally in fields affecting its own work; some nations confer a broader power in this connection. Several of the republics permit the court to propose the amendment or repeal of legislation already on the books, because of unconstitutionality or disuse. In others the Court or its Chief Justice may be asked to review a bill already introduced in the legislature, but not yet approved, in order to determine its constitutionality.

The Supreme Court is also charged with compilation of judicial statistics and with the maintenance and indexing of court files; in some instances notarial registers and archives also fall within its jurisdiction. The maintenance of a library for its own use and for the use of lower courts is sometimes an assigned .function of the highest court of the land.

The Supreme Court of a country meeting in plenary session, or any one its members, may be asked to act as legal adviser to the executive or legislative branch, although the modern trend seems to be to consult special legal advisers outside of the judicial system.

	THE
Part 3	POLITICAL
	SYSTEM

This section is devoted primarily to interest groups and political parties. Since each of these groups is here dealt with in a somewhat isolated manner, this introduction is an attempt to tie them together by summarizing Gabriel Almond's analysis of the different types of political groups involved in the articulation of interests.[1] By interest articulation Almond has in mind the formulation and expression of political interests, that is, the flow of demands from society to polity. He identifies four types of structures involved in interest articulation: institutional interest groups, associational interest groups, nonassociational interest groups, and anomic interest groups.

Institutional interest groups are formal organizations which perform other political and social functions, but also articulate their own interests or those of other groups. In Latin America the most important of these groups are the armed forces and the Church.[2] Traditionally the armed forces have articulated the interests of the large landowners and the Church in addition to their own. While the alliance between these groups is not as strong as in the past, there can be little doubt as to the importance of the military as an interest group. In most of the

[1] Gabriel A. Almond, "A Functional Approach to Comparative Politics," *The Politics of the Developing Areas* (Princeton, N.J.: Princeton University Press, 1960), pp. 3–64 [especially pp. 33–45]. The following comes primarily from that piece and James S. Coleman, "The Political Systems of the Developing Areas," *The Politics of the Developing Areas*, pp. 532–576, George I. Blanksten, "The Politics of Latin America," *The Politics of the Developing Areas*, pp. 455–531, and Blanksten, "Political Groups in Latin America," *American Political Science Review*, Vol. 53: No. 1 (March 1959), pp. 106–127.

[2] It is quite likely that bureaucracies should be added to this list, but the almost total absence of serious research pertaining to this group makes it quite difficult to assess its significance.

227

nations to the south the Church has long played an important role in the political arena, even to the extent of having political parties formed around its basic tenets (the Conservative parties of Ecuador and Chile are examples).

Associational interest groups are formal organizations whose primary function is the explicit representation of the interests of particular groups. Examples in Latin America would include labor unions, student groups, and associations of landowners, businessmen, and professionals. The importance of organized labor has increased greatly in the last few decades, and this will probably continue to be the case as industrialization takes place at an ever increasing pace. Student organizations have far greater significance in the political systems of Latin America than do their counterparts in the United States; student-sponsored demonstrations and riots have frequently had important political consequences. Associations of landowners undoubtedly wield great political influence—the same is true to a lesser extent of business and professional associations—but this is difficult to analyze due to the nature of their activities.

Nonassociational interest groups are those without formal organization that articulate interests informally and intermittently (such as class, status, ethnic, kinship, and regional groups). Of these groups, class and regionalism are probably of greatest significance in Latin America. Within the relatively rigid class system the upper class traditionally has been the most articulate; also, it is the interests of this group which have been best protected. In a few nations (most notably Argentina, Brazil, Chile, Mexico, and Uruguay) the rapidly growing middle class has become quite articulate in recent years. Regionalism is mainly of two types: one involves the interests of the countryside pitted against those of a single dominant city (this is most pronounced perhaps in Uruguay), while the other is a manifestation of geographic isolation (as in Peru where the Andes divide the nation into three quite separate regions).

Anomic interest groups are defined as "more or less spontaneous breakthroughs into the political system from society . . ."[3] such as demonstrations, riots, and the Latin American brand of "revolution." Anomic movements vary greatly in type and scope. While most involve a minimum of violence such is not always the case; for example, the famous *bogotazo* of 1948 in Bogotá, Colombia, claimed upwards of 5000 lives. While this was an almost completely spontaneous breakthrough, it was more the exception than the rule. More typical would be demonstrations with

[3] Almond, *The Politics of the Developing Areas*, p. 34.

at least some organizational base—indeed, demonstrations may even be carefully planned by the government.

According to Almond, "the structure and style of interest articulation define the pattern of boundary maintenance between the polity and society, and within the political system affect the boundaries between the various parts of the political system."[4] A high incidence of interest articulation by either institutional or non-associational groups is said to be an indication of poor boundary maintenance, while a high incidence of interest articulation by associational interest groups is said to indicate good boundary maintenance.

Measured against such a scale the Latin American nations do not come off very well. According to *A Cross-Polity Survey* in Latin America institutional interest groups are the most significant in the articulation of interests, then come nonassociational groups, and last, associational groups.[5] Interest articulation by institutional groups is rated "limited" in none of the nations, and "moderate" in only three (Uruguay, Costa Rica, and Chile); in the remaining 17 states it is rated as either "significant" or "very significant." Articulation by nonassociational groups is said to be limited in about half the nations and moderate in the other half; nowhere in Latin America is it rated negligible, and only in Haiti significant. On the other hand, articulation by associational groups is rated negligible or limited in 14 nations, moderate in four, and significant in only two (Argentina and Brazil).

[4] Almond, *The Politics of the Developing Areas*, p. 35.
[5] Arthur S. Banks and Robert B. Textor, *A Cross-Polity Survey* (Cambridge, Massachusetts: The Massachusetts Institute of Technology Press, 1963), tables 115–129. All subsequent rankings also come from these tables.

Toward a Theory of Latin American Politics*

CHARLES W.
ANDERSON

For some, it may appear quite bizarre and quixotic to speak about the "political system" of Latin America. Social system refers to pattern, persistence, and regularity in human behavior. Latin American politics appear to be whimsical, unstable, crisis ridden, and unpredictable. It would appear that what is at issue in the political life of this region is failure to establish political systems, the hardening of a state of crisis when all rules are suspended, into a way of life.

However, though the patterns be unfamiliar to the observer who identifies political system with the processes of constitutional democracy, there do seem to be certain recurrent and persistent patterns in Latin American political life. The intervention of the military in politics, the technique of the *coup d'etat,* the use of violence and terror as political instruments, insecurity of tenure for constitutionally established governments, are all phenomena that appear over and over again in the political history of the region. As K. H. Silvert puts it:

> "Unpredictable" and "unstable" are the two adjectives most often applied to Latin American politics. The implications of both pejoratives are partially erroneous. First, to be "unstable" is not necessarily to be "unpredictable." As a matter of fact, one of the easiest things to predict is instability itself. And second, some types of revolutionary disturbance do not indicate instability. If the normal way of rotating the executive in a given country is by revolution, and there have been a hundred such changes in a century, then it is not facetious to remark that revolutions are a sign of stability—that events are marching along as they always have.

Still more enticingly, we are aware that certain patterns of Latin American politics, such as the generally respected rights of exile and asylum for losers in power struggles, may indicate that there are rules

* Charles W. Anderson, *Toward a Theory of Latin American Politics* (Nashville, Tennessee: Vanderbilt University, Graduate Center for Latin American Studies, Occasional Paper No. 2, February 1964). (Footnotes in the original version have been omitted.)

of political activity generally understood by the participants, which are effective in regulating political conduct even where formal, constitutional commitments do not apply. It may be that those versed in the skills of Latin American politics have not yet stated the nature of this art. Perhaps it is not that the term "political system" is inapplicable to Latin American politics, but rather, that we, the outsiders, do not yet know how that system operates.

A second objection to the effort to describe the "rules of the game" of politics in Latin America will be raised. I have been using the term "political system" in the singular. Surely, the same set of propositions cannot be applied to the heterogeneous circumstances of the twenty Latin American nations. Obviously, Costa Rica and Paraguay, Brazil and Uruguay, Bolivia and Mexico reflect quite different forms of political life. On the other hand, on close examination, it is clear that the simple label "constitutional democracy" does not account precisely for the political history of Costa Rica which has thrice had recourse to violent techniques of adjusting power relations in the twentieth century, nor does the appelative "military dictatorship" reflect the subtleties and complexities of the technique of rule of the Somoza family in Nicaragua. There would seem to be a need for a body of theory, a set of statements sufficiently general to enable us to compare Latin American governments in similar terms, and which could be adjusted to the characteristics of specific situations. Hence, what we shall say is not meant to refer only to the "typical" Latin American political situation, and to exclude such deviant cases as Uruguay or the Dominican Republic during the era of Trujillo. Rather, it is hoped that by adjusting the value of such variables as the "power capabilities" included in this theory, these statements can be applied generally to political life throughout Latin America.

A frequent point of departure for analysis of Latin American politics is to note that in this region there is imperfect consensus on the nature of the political regime, that the "legitimacy" of the formal political order is weak. Political legitimacy is that characteristic of a society which enables men to disagree vigorously over the policies that government should pursue or the personnel that should occupy decision-making posts, yet to support common notions of the locus of decision-making authority, the techniques by which decisions are to be made, and the means by which rulers are to be empowered. For the American student of Latin American politics, the sublime countertheme that ran below shock and grief at the assassination of the President of the United States was the sure knowledge that the system would survive, the republic would prevail. In lands where political legitimacy is weak, the end of a government brings into question not only the person of the successor, but the very form of government that will emerge.

However, imperfect consensus on the nature of political regime is not a problem of politics peculiar to Latin America, nor does it account for the distinctiveness of Latin American politics. Rather, it is on a further dimension of the problem of political legitimacy that we must concentrate. For in Latin America, no particular techniques of mobilizing political power, no specific political resources, are deemed more appropriate to political activity than others. No specific sources of political power are legitimate for all contenders for power.

Of course, this is to some extent the case in every society. In the United States, despite the fact that our own political ideology prescribes the aggregation and mobilization of consent as the only legitimate means of structuring power relationships, we do recognize that possessors of certain power capabilities, economic wealth, or control of armed force have particular influence in decision making. However, in democratic society, the organization of consent according to prescribed norms is generally reinforced by holders of other power capabilities, and, in the long run, democratic processes serve as a court of last resort in structuring power relationships. In contrast, in Latin America generally, democratic processes are *alternative* to other means of mobilizing power. The problem of Latin American politics, then, is that of finding some formula for creating agreement between power contenders whose power capabilities are neither comparable (as one measures the relative power of groups in democratic society by reference to votes cast) nor compatible. The political system of Latin America may be described as the pattern by which Latin American statemen conventionally attempt to cope with this variety of political resources used in their societies, and the way in which holders of these diverse power capabilities characteristically interact one with another.

In restructuring our frame of reference to cope with this unfamiliar state of affairs, we might begin by suggesting that the techniques used in advanced Western nations as means of ratifying power relationships more frequently appear in Latin America as means of demonstrating a power capability. The significance of this can best be seen by examining three prominent techniques which we commonly assume are means of ratifying power relationships (that is, or structuring a regime or government) and reflect on where they fit in the Latin American political scheme of things. These would be: election, revolution, and military dictatorship.

Elections are not definitive in many parts of Latin America. However, they are conscientiously and consistently held, and just as conscientiously and consistently annulled. Few Latin American nations can demonstrate an unbroken sequence of elected governments over any substantial period of time. In a sense, our real question is not that of why elections are ignored, but why they are held at all given their inconclusive character.

Latin American political instability is more comprehensible if we do not view election as definitive, but as part of an ongoing process of structuring power relationships, in which election is important to some contenders, but not to all. Democratic election is really only relevant to those who have specific skills and support, who rely on their capacity to aggregate mass consent through parties and movements and interest groups for participation in the political process. Insofar as such contenders cannot be ignored by other holders of power capabilities, election, which is the device that "demonstrates" this power capability, measures and confirms it, is part of the political process. But since there are other contenders in the political process, whose power is not contingent on this type of support, elections do not define political relationships. Rather, the results of an election are tentative, pending the outcome of negotiations between other power contenders and the groups that have demonstrated a power capability through election.

Thus, when a new political movement which has amassed sufficient electoral power that other contenders must take it into account appears in the political arena, judgments must be made by other political contenders as to whether, on balance, the threat posed by this movement to the position of existing contenders is greater than the cost of its suppression, whether the stability of the system would be better insured by accommodating the power contender into that circle of elites that negotiate for control of the resources of the state or by its suppression.

Similarly, it is conventional to distinguish between "real" revolutions and "typical" revolutions in Latin America. Again, the "real" revolution, in the Western sense of the term, is a technique of ratifying power relationships, of structuring a new regime. The "typical" Latin American revolution, on the other hand, does not demolish the previous structure of power relationships, but adds to it that of the revolutionaries, who may be said to have demonstrated a power capability that other power contenders had found it advisable or necessary to recognize and accommodate into the power structure of the society.

Finally, we generally say that Latin American military dictatorship is to be distinguished from European military totalitarianism. With the possible exception of Perón, political intervention by the military in Latin America does not seem to have the effect of overhauling the power system of the society. Rather, under military governments in Latin America, holders of important power capabilities in the society are assured that their position in the society will not be endangered, and are permitted some participation in the political process. (Certainly, military governments may brutally restrict entrance of other new power contenders into the political arena, and in some nations, they are supported by other power contenders for just this reason.) In general, [the effect of military *coup* in Latin America is to add a new power contender to the "inner circle" of political elites, but one whose control is not exclusive or definitive.]

[One may say that the most persistent political phenomenon in Latin America is the effort of contenders for power to demonstrate a power capability sufficient to be recognized by other power contenders, and that the political process consists of manipulation and negotiation among power contenders reciprocally recognizing each other's power capability.]

It is apparent that [it is often not necessary for a power contender to actually use a power capability, but merely to demonstrate possession of it.] For example, Latin American armies often prove incredibly inept when actually called upon to use armed force in a combat situation. One recalls the fate of Batista's well-equipped military force during the events of 1958. However, except in "real revolutionary" situations, Latin American armies are seldom called upon to actually use armed force. What is at issue is the demonstration and recognition of a *transfer* in the control of the military institution. This may be accomplished by the announcement of a shift in allegiance of certain critical garrisons. That one of the primary targets in a *coup* is control of a radio transmitter so that the insurgents can *inform* the populace of the change in loyalties is a vivid example of what is in fact going on.

Similarly, "manifestation" or "demonstration" is a means of demonstrating the implicit power capability of the mob. Seldom does mob action actually become manifest (as it did in the Bogotazo of 1948), rather, the presence of the multitude assembled before the national palace is generally adequate for existing power contenders to recognize and seek to placate or accommodate the new power capability that has emerged in their midst.

Even the use of noninstitutionalized violence and terror is often designed to show possession of a power capability rather than to use it directly for political ends. More true to the Latin American tradition in such matters than the political assassination or widespread destruction of property or life is the symbolic act of terrorism or violence. For example, the theft of an art collection in Caracas in 1962, the kidnapping and release unharmed of a U.S. Officer, as components of a rather consistent strategy of the FALN terrorists in Venezuela, were designed to produce the largest dramatic appeal and embarrassment to the regime, without large-scale devastation of property.

While the Latin American political process is becoming more complex, and such acts of civic disruption and violence are growing more serious and threatening in intent, in the classic pattern of Latin American political life, such techniques of demonstrating a power capability seem generally accepted as appropriate to the political system. Thus, when such techniques as manifestation, strike, and even violence are used symbolically, that is, as the demonstration and not the use of a power capability, there would seem to be an *a priori* case that the appropriate response of government leaders should be conciliation and bargaining. However, when use of such techniques actually degenerates into important destruction of life or property, it seems more generally felt that the rules have been transgressed, and that the use of sanctions is called for. Brutal police suppression, with the loss of life and widespread arrests, in the face of a student riot, even one that may have culminated in the burning of automobiles or the breaking of windows, may breed an ugly public mood. On the other hand, persistent agitation that actually disrupts the way of life of the society and is not dealt with firmly by constituted authority may lead quickly to agitation for a stronger, "no nonsense" government.

The characteristic political process of Latin America may then be described as one of manipulation and negotiation among power contenders with reciprocally recognized power capabilities. Seldom is this process overt or public. Often it does not consist of a formal situation of "negotiation" at all, but is rather implicit in the statements of a new government as it takes office, and carefully announces a policy format that accounts for the interests of all prominent elites, or as it delicately pursues a policy which takes account of dominant power contenders.

The character of the system is perhaps most strikingly illustrated in the "learning process" which Latin American reformist movements undergo when they come to power. While "outside" the effective political arena, they build consent on the promise of radical and sweeping reforms. The power of the military will be reduced, large foreign economic interests will be nationalized, a thoroughgoing agrarian reform will be carried out. Having created and demonstrated a power capability on this basis, having assumed political power perhaps on the basis of an election, their attitude changes. They become proponents of "evolutionary change," or "gradual, reasonable, reforms," in which "all social forces must participate and contribute to the welfare of the nation." The army is confirmed in its perquisites. Economic policy becomes more moderate. Strong action contemplated against existing elites is modified or abandoned.

[What is at issue is less political cynicism, or the difference between campaign oratory and actual statesmanship, than it is a process by which these newly accepted power contenders learn the conditions of their own rule.] In some cases, this learning experience is quite overt and apparent in public pronouncements made before and after entering office. In others, such contenders learn only by hard experience, by being deposed, and subsequently readmitted to power as more docile contenders. Of the former type, Arturo Frondizi of Argentina is a prime example. A fire-eating reformer out of office, committed economic nationalist, and defender of the rights of labor, he became an economic moderate in office, once instructed in the economic "facts of life" of post-Perón Argentina, quite eager to accept the stabilization recommendations of the International Monetary Fund, to invite in foreign petroleum firms, to hold the line on labor wage increases. Of the latter case, the *Acción Democrática* movement in Venezuela is revealing. Coming to power in 1945 on a program of reform, suggestions of action against both the military and foreign oil interests contributed to their replacement in 1948 by a harsh military government. The party returned to power in 1958 chastened and wiser, now seeking a "reasonable relationship" with the petroleum industry, and suggesting no diminution of the power of the army in national life.

The Latin American political system is "tentative." Unlike nations where constitutional provision and the legitimacy of election guarantees a specified tenure for any government, in Latin America, [government is based on a flexible coalition among diverse power contenders which is subject to revision at any time] if the terms under which the original government was formed are deemed violated. Revision occurs primarily when an existing holder of an important power capability feels threatened by action of government. Thus, in 1954, when the government of Jacobo Arbenz, the second consecutively elected government in recent Guatemalan history, attempted to carry out an extensive agrarian reform, diluted the army's power through creation of a "people's milimia," and permitted overt Communist activity in collaboration with the government, it was overthrown by threatened holders of important power capabilities. Similarly, in Argentina, the government of Arturo Frondizi was deposed when Frondizi appeared prepared to permit *Peronista* electoral participation, adjudged a serious violation of previous "understandings" by important power contenders.

The Latin American political system, therefore, accounts for change, and permits change, but only within a rather rigorous context. New contenders are admitted to the political arena of reciprocally recognizing elites in Latin America when they demonstrate a significant power capability, and when they provide assurances that they will not jeopardize the ability of any existing power contender to similarly participate in political activity. Thus, with the exception of "real revolutionary" situations, the normal rule of Latin American political change is that new power contenders may be added to the system, but old ones may not be eliminated.

It is this characteristic of the system that gives Latin American politics its distinctive flavor. While, in the history of the West, revolutionary experiences or secular change have sequentially eliminated various forms of power capability, contemporary Latin American politics is something of a "living museum," in which all the forms of political authority of the Western historic experience continue to exist and operate, interacting one with another in a pageant that seems to violate all the rules of sequence and change involved in our understanding of the growth of Western civilization. Politically pragmatic, democratic movements, devoted to the constitutional and welfare state ideals of the mid-twentieth century, stand side by side with a traditional, and virtually semi-feudal landed aristocracy. "Social technocrats" and economic planners of the most modern outlook confer and interact with an institutionalized Church which in some countries is favored with a political position not far removed from the "two swords" tradition of Medieval political thought. Military *caudillos* cast in a role set in the early nineteenth century, and little changed with the passage of time, confront an organized trade union movement, a growing middle class, a new entrepreneurial elite.

The rule that new power contenders will be admitted to the system only when they do not jeopardize the position of established contenders contributes to the tentativeness of the system in operation. Neither the accommodation of a new power contender (such as a reformist political party) nor its suppression is final. There is a marked reticence in the classic pattern of Latin American politics to define for all time who may and may not participate in the political process, illustrated by the rule that exile rather than purge is the appropriate way of coping with an antagonistic power contender. If a suppressed power contender can survive long years of banishment from the political forum, the chances are good that at some future date the patterns of coalition and alliance among established contenders will be revised in such a way that the contender will again be able to participate in political activity, to re-demonstrate its power capability in an environment more hospitable to its admission to that inner circle of forces that reciprocally recognize each other's right to be part of the political system. The long and tragic history of the Peruvian APRA party, suppressed and underground for long periods, yet recurrently admitted to the political arena by virtue of its capacity to demonstrate large-scale mass consent to its leadership and program, is illustrative.

New contenders are admitted to the political system when they fulfill two conditions in the eyes of existing power contenders. First, they must demonstrate possession of a power capability sufficient to pose a threat to existing contenders. Second, they must be perceived by other contenders as willing to abide by the rules of the game, to permit existing contenders to continue to exist and operate in the political system. If the first condition is not fulfilled, the power contender will be ignored, no matter what the merits of his case may be. (For example, a strike by a few hundred students over a penny increase in bus fares may bring on a full-scale governmental crisis and immediate concessions to the students, while a full-scale agrarian revolt in some remote province may merely be noted and deplored by decision makers in the capital city. Given the urban bias of the Latin American political system, the former affects the conditions of power in the system, the latter does not.) If the second condition is not fulfilled, efforts will be made to suppress the new power contender.

The ability of established elites to effectively suppress a new power contender depends on a variety of circumstances. Some established contenders are not loathe to support a new contender to strengthen their bargaining position in the political process. Hence, in recent years, some military leaders in Latin America, reading the handwriting on the wall, have adopted a "reformist" or "democratic" posture, seeking alliances with mass movements or middle class parties. Increasingly, the Catholic Church is abandoning its old bases of political alliance, and throwing in its lot with the "modern" political forces. In addition, the basic style of the political process, which resembles a complex game of chess between political forces with reciprocally recognized power capabilities, implies a certain level of conflict and competition between the established power contenders. When such inner circle elites are in conflict or stalemate, a new contender may enter the process by the back door. For example, in 1945 in Peru, the APRA party, for years suppressed by dominant elites, was permitted to participate in an electoral contest. The election itself was in many respects the outcome of a deadlock between the established elites.

When disunity or deadlock among established contenders threatens to admit a potentially dangerous power contender to the political arena, military dictatorship is often the most satisfactory remedy to preserve the system intact. Without jeopardizing the status of existing contenders, the *caudillo* replaces bickering, conflict, and "politicking" among the dominant political participants with order, firmness, and suppression of the threatening new political force. That this is often the basis for military rule in Latin America is well evidenced by the enthusiasm and relief felt by established political groups when an Odría in Peru, or a Rojas Pinilla in Colombia comes to power to end a "crisis" of enmity and conflict between those elites which dominate the political system, and in which a threatening political force is bidding to come to power in the vacuum thus created. Yet, like that of other contenders, the rule of the military dictator is tentative, contingent on his ability to maintain the coalition of agreements and imputed objectives that brought him to power. Should he fail to maintain his power capability, or to obey the rules of the game that existing contenders are to be permitted to act politically according to the rules of negotiation and coalition, should he, in short, violate the implicit "understandings" that led to his acceptance, he too may be turned out. The fate of Idígoras Fuentes in Guatemala, of Perón in Argentina (particularly in his relations to the Church, the economic elites, and the military), and for that matter, of Odría and Rojas Pinilla, is illustrative.

It is inappropriate to view this classic political system of Latin America as entirely static. Often, we suggest that the normal course of Latin American politics is designed to reinforce the power of the oligarchy against the forces of change at work in the society. This is not entirely the case, and put this way, is somewhat deceptive. The rule of the system is of course that established elites will be permitted to continue to operate and to maintain many of their political and socioeconomic prequisites intact. But the rule of the system is also that new contenders, new holders of significant power capabilities, will be able to partake in negotiation for a share of the resources and powers of the state if they do not jeopardize the right of established elites to similarly act. Hence, although the landowners, the Church, the military, continue as prominent political economic forces, the terms of their share in the perquisites which political involvement can offer has been adjusted by the accommodations of a burgeoning middle class, new types of interest groups and political parties, a working class elite of skilled, organized, industrial laborers, into political life. It is true that these "new" forces have not achieved as great a share of the political economic resources of the society as have their counterparts in the advanced nations because of the requirements of the system that a substantial part of available resources must be allocated to the "older" contenders, the landowners, the military, and the like. However, it is, in almost all Latin American nations, quite untrue to suggest that these new contenders have been denied any share in political economic rewards at all, for the system has accommodated new power contenders, the system has changed. [The conflict and crisis of contemporary Latin America is then more accurately described as one in which newer contenders feel that too large a share of social rewards is allocated to established contenders in fulfillment of the terms of the classic political system, rather than that the political system is one of complete rigidity and suppression,] in which the emerging forces of change are unable to participate and derive benefit from political economic life at all. The peculiar character of Latin American political economic change, then, would seem to be best analyzed not in terms of our conventional and oversimplified categories of "class warfare" and "resistance to change," but as product of the distinctive political system of the region, one that permits new power contenders to be added to the system but is so designed that older political factors are not eliminated, one that is—if one can accept a most surprising use of the term—more "tolerant" as to the types of power capabilities that are relevant for political participation than are the political systems of the advanced, Western nations.

[margin note: i.e. you may have a bite, but you must not ask for too big a one!]

Ironically then, Latin American politics are not characterized by "revolution" as we conventionally assume, but by the total absence of any historic revolution that could eliminate some power contenders from the political system, and legitimate certain types of power capabilities as exclusively appropriate in the mobilization of political power. The significance of the great democratic revolutions of the eighteenth century in Western Europe and North America, then, is seen as that of rejecting as legitimate power capabilities those based on the feudal control of groups of serfs and land, or sheer military power, or the divine right of monarchy in which Church and state mutually reinforced the other's claims to legitimacy. The significance of the great democratic revolutions was that they effectively eliminated all power contenders who could not, at some point, base their claim to power on the aggregation and mobilization of consent, electorally tested. Latin America never experienced this democratic revolution. Latin America never went through the process by which those whose skills and resources were appropriate to the mobilization and organization of consent (the middle class) became dominant in the society, and could deny political participation to all those who could not base their claim to power on a type of power capability which was, in fact, only one of many possible in organizing power, and which did, in fact, refer to the political resources available to only one part of the population. Latin America did not legitimate democracy, that is to say, it did not restrict political power to only those who could mobilize consent. In fact, Latin America, as a region, has not undergone a revolution that could legitimate any particular type of power capability. Hence the power systems of divine right monarchy, military authority, feudal power, and constitutional democracy all exist side by side, none legitimate, none definitive, and the political system that has emerged is one in which all of the political techniques that have been experienced by Western man continue as part of the system, and the system prescribes the rules for their interaction, and for the persistence of the system itself, by prescribing that none of these historic power capabilities may be eliminated entirely.

In saying this, we have implied a definition of revolution, which might be stated as follows: revolution occurs when some power contenders or some types of power capabilities are successfully eliminated from political participation. By this definition, some revolutions have occurred in Latin America, some political forces have chosen not to play according to the rules of the classic system just described, and have been successful in their endeavor.

what is a revol. in L.A. context.

Most students of Latin American politics agree that three regimes exist in modern Latin America that could properly be described as "revolutionary" in nature. These revolutions occurred in Mexico in 1910, Bolivia in 1952, and Cuba in 1959. Some note Guatemala from 1945–1954 as a revolutionary situation, and we will define it as a revolution that failed, or is temporarily in abeyance, perhaps going through a Thermidorian phase.

All three of these situations essentially fit our definition of revolution. In each, a large part of the thrust of revolutionary agitation was against foreign control of natural resources or economic institutions. It is to be noted that here the intent was to eliminate certain power contenders (the foreign owners) rather than the power capability (control of economic factors as a political resource). In two of the revolutionary situations, Cuba and Bolivia (the latter in relation to at least mineral resources), the objective was to add the power capability of economic control to other political resources of the revolutionary regime through the device of expropriation and nationalization. In Mexico, the economic power capability previously in the hands of foreign power contenders was eventually allocated both to the revolutionary regime (nationalization of some basic industries such as petroleum) and to a new private, but national, group of entrepreneurs (Mexicanization). In all three cases, a prime component of revolutionary ideology was "anti-imperialism," which we would define as the intent to eliminate external power contenders from participation in the political system, to "nationalize" the political process.

[Agrarian reform in all three revolutions was designed to eliminate both the power contenders and the power capability represented by the semi-feudal control of land and labor through the institution of the *hacienda.*] All three revolutions were to some extent successful in thus "modernizing" the political system (e.g., in eliminating an archaic power capability), but in all three, residual traces remained, and in each, there is some evidence that the power capability of traditional agrarian authority was in some areas merely transferred to the new administrator of the collective or state farm (Cuba) or the agrarian or *ejido* bank (Mexico).

[All three revolutions more or less successfully eliminated the traditional military as a prominent power contender.] (However, only Costa Rica, which constitutionally abolished its army, can be said to have abolished the power capability of semi-legitimate control of armed force.) In Cuba, this power capability has been incorporated into the other political attributes of the regime through the device of the militia. In Mexico, the military remains as a power contender, though its capacity to use its power capability has been substantially, though always tentatively, reduced by the increasing legitimacy of other types of political resources.

[In Mexico particularly, and to some extent in the other two nations, efforts were made, none completely successful, to eliminate the power capabilities of the Catholic Church.] In these situations, as throughout Latin America, it is primarily the secular attributes of the Church (the *hacienda* power capability) that have successfully been reduced, while other power capabilities (ideology, capacity to aggregate consent) have remained more intractable.

The revolutionary mystique in Latin America insists that the classic system of politics can be transformed by the elimination of specific power contenders and power capabilities. The revolutionary experience in Latin America suggests that in some instances the characteristics of the older system reemerge, though often in greatly revised form. Revolution may make a great difference in the course of Latin American political life, though generally not all the difference expected by its perpetrators. Thus, the anti-imperialist strain in Cuban revolutionary thought culminated not in the elimination of the foreign power contender, but in the replacement of one set of foreign contenders (the United States interests, public and private) with an alternative set (the Soviet bloc).

Similarly, the Bolivian revolution has been kept alive by giant infusions of United States aid, aid that has implied a prominent role for the U.S. in the decision-making processes of that nation. In Mexico, it is to be noted that foreign investors were eventually readmitted to the political economic system, though on terms that radically reduced their ability to use economic resources as a political capability.

[The present political regime in Mexico, which Mexicans like to refer to as the "institutionalized revolution" is remarkably suggestive of the tenacity of the classic system of Latin American politics.] Although the revolution of 1910 eliminated some power contenders, the eventual outcome of the revolutionary experience was the formation of a new set of elites, each recognizing, on the basis of demonstrated power capabilities, the right of the other to negotiate in the allocation of the resources available through the system. The interaction of the various sectors of the official party in Mexico—the campesino, popular, and labor sectors of the Party of the Institutionalized Revolution, or PRI—can only be described as manipulation and negotiation between mutually recognizing power contenders. The eventual inclusion of the new industrial and commercial elite of Mexico into the political system, though not into the official party, from which they are pointedly excluded, and the reconciliation of the revolutionary regime with the Church, in contradiction to a basic theme of revolutionary ideology, reflects the capacity of the informal system to survive and reshape the formal structure of the Mexican revolutionary regime, just as the informal system survives and describes patterns of political interaction not anticipated in the formal, constitutional, democratic structures of other Latin American nations.

Change is accounted for in the classic system of Latin American politics, but at a pace that is too slow for some of the newer power contenders. For some, revolution, by eliminating some power contenders and power capabilities promises to change the pace of change, to make the Latin American political system more compatible with those of advanced Western nations, which themselves eliminated certain archaic power capabilities through revolutionary techniques several centuries ago.

However, some Latin American elites see the possibility of increasing the pace of change without revolution, without the drastic elimination of power contenders from the system. The basic conflict between modern power contenders in Latin America concerns the relative merits of "evolutionary" or "revolutionary" change. For proponents of either course of accelerating the course of change, the conflict is with those who would preserve the "legitimacy" of the classic system of politics in Latin America.

The evolutionary route to accelerated change, embraced by such leaders as Rómulo Betancourt of Venezuela, José Figueres of Costa Rica, Fernando Belaunde Terry of Peru, and many others, may be described as the quest to⌊legitimate "democratic" power capabilities (those that rest ultimately on some form of aggregated consent)⌋through the conversion of non-democratic power capabilities into democratic ones. In other words, those whose power does not rest on consent will have their actions redirected through structural change of the system, their power capability converted and not destroyed. Hence, the military will be "professionalized," not eliminated from the political arena, but directed toward a role more appropriate to democratic states. The old *hacienda* owners will not be destroyed, but required to adopt modern means of production, and modern forms of labor relations. Traditional authority, binding the patron and peon, will gradually disappear to be replaced by bargaining between responsible employers and responsible representatives of organized labor. The effort, in short, is to revise the classic system in terms compatible with the classic system. Existing power contenders are assured that their position within the system will not be jeopardized, in fact, so the ideology of the evolutionary reformer goes, it will actually be enhanced. The power of the *latifundista*, for example, is on the wane, his economic importance diminishing. He can only preserve his power, and enhance it, by adopting more modern techniques of production and social and political interaction. Other evolutionary leaders argue that such change is essential if the system is to remain the same, that the alternative to reformed performances by existing power contenders is their elimination through a revolutionary movement.

The ideological framework of this approach appears under the aegis of many conventional categories of contemporary political thought, yet it is adequately described by none. The heritage of Marxism, continental Second International socialism, Christian democracy, and the "New Deal," may be invoked to define what these leaders are about, as well as such indigenous strains as Peruvian *Aprismo* and the experience of the Mexican Revolution. However, none of these describes what really is at issue for such evolutionist movements.

[Their prime appeal is to something that can only be described as a notion of the "national interest," made vivid by the awakening of nationalism as a relevant and meaningful notion of reference and interaction for increasing numbers of publics in Latin America. Their vision and context of action is that of the interrelationship of the various sectors of the nation in development] Hence, labor unions must moderate irresponsible wage demands, for investment essential to national industrial development can only be achieved with moderate labor costs, and industrialization is vital if the goal of productivity, welfare, national greatness, and a higher level of industrial employment is to be achieved. However, industrialists must accept extensive programs of education, public health, and social welfare if a "modern" domestic market and pattern of consumption is to be achieved. Agrarian reform is essential if a level of agricultural productivity is to be achieved that will be sufficient to feed increasing urban populations, aside from local subsistence food production, if scarce foreign exchange earnings are not to be wasted on imported foodstuffs, if export agriculture that will provide the wherewithal for industrial expansion is to be developed.

The educational mission of statecraft implied by this approach has made a certain impact. For the modern sector, in some nations at least, the classes seem less antagonistic, the interests of industrialists and workers less contradictory, than they did some years ago. The prospects of the evolutionary approach may be seen by an examination of Betancourt's Venezuela, Rivera's El Salvador, Lleras Camargo's Colombia. Its limitations are also apparent. The pace of change appears faster than that implied in the classic system, but for many, slower than that implied by revolutionary change, particularly that exemplified by the Cuban revolution. The economic shambles of Goulart's Brazil, the demise in frustration of Frondizi in Argentina, bring questions about the validity of the evolutionary approach in these nations. The collapse of Bosch's Dominican Republic and Villeda Morales' Honduras at the hands of the defenders of the "old order" frames the question clearly. The evolutionary style of reform may be undone either from the right or from the left.

Victor Raúl Haya de la Torre of Peru, the father of *Aprismo*, has said, "Latin America is not easy to govern." As this notion of the "system" of Latin American politics should make clear, the tasks of statecraft in this region are intricate, complex, and frustrating. Even the most skilled democratic political craftsman, a man of the stripe of Lyndon Johnson or Franklin Roosevelt, might pale before the task of "creating agreement" among the diverse contenders and forces as work in the Latin American political milieu. [In the classic or evolutionary styles of Latin American statesmanship, politics is supremely the art of the possible, the art of combining heterogeneous and incompatible power contenders and power capabilities together in some type of tentative coalition, one in which the various members feel no obligation to maintain the combination intact for any prescribed term of office.] George Blanksten, in his *Perón's Argentina*, likens the task of the Latin American politician to that of the juggler, who must keep a large number of balls simultaneously in the air, and is apt to be hit on the head by the one that he misses.

In view of the complexity and frustration of working within the system, it is no wonder that the apparent simplicity and malleability of revolution has an appeal in Latin America that itself adds to the complexity of government. But the attractions of the revolutionary alternative are often deceptive. Its simplicity is premised on the existence of a revolutionary situation, of a vivid and vital mass desire and capacity to start over again, on new terms, under new conditions, and that situation is exceptional rather than predictable. Certainly, there have been revolutions in Latin America, and there will be more, but there have been more insurgent movements that failed, that captured no following, that could not overcome and replace the going system.

Revolution requires exceptional leadership of a certain style to succeed, and those who have possessed it, the Maderos, Zapatas, Castros, and Bolívars and San Martíns, have entered the ranks of the vivid personal heroes of Latin American history. But there is another style of leadership which is relevant to the conduct of Latin American government, and there is no reason to believe that it is less available in this culture than that represented by the revolutionary politician in arms. The skills at the craft of politics, of working within the system to the end of transcending it, have been exemplified by men like Betancourt, Frondizi, Figueres, Lleras Camargo, López Mateos, and many others. They have their historic predecessors in such figures as Sarmiento and Juarez. Their skills and capabilities are not to be despised. In fact, set within the context of the system in which they have operated, and against the background of man's efforts to govern himself, they often appear as little short of incredible.

how does this account for phenomena such as personalism?

Toward the Comparative Study of Politicization in Latin America*

DANIEL GOLDRICH

THE PERCEPTION OF THE RELEVANCE OF GOVERNMENT: THE BEGINNING OF POLITICIZATION

There has been no systematic study of the phenomenon of politicization. Frequently in commentary on contemporary Latin American politics, for example, a high level of politicization throughout these societies is assumed, whereas I believe the matter to be a critically important variable to study in the process of political change.

Logically, a political decision-making process cannot be considered to have begun, nor people to have become involved in an attempt to exercise influence, until they have perceptually entered the political arena. Before people act politically, before they formulate protests or make demands or deliberate policies, they must be at least minimally politicized. I conceive of the politicization process as a continuum ranging from lack of perception of the relevance of government to one's life, through perception of it, to active involvement in politics. This seems obvious, and yet it is tremendously significant. One of the most profoundly revolutionary developments in the culture of a less economically advanced society is the emergence of the perception among tradition-directed or long-subjugated people that government is not, *sub specie aeternitatis*, unchanging and unchangeable, but can be modified and manipulated to meet their needs.

Perhaps the most important agent of initial mass politicization, the bridging of the gap between nonperception and perception of the relevance of government, is revolution. The genesis and development of revolution is imperfectly understood, but it seems clear that there is a variation in the extent of mass involvement during the earlier stages.

* Daniel Goldrich, "Toward the Comparative Study of Politicization in Latin America," in Dwight B. Heath and Richard N. Adams (eds.), *Contemporary Cultures and Societies of Latin America* (New York: Random House, Inc., 1965), pp. 361–375. (Footnotes in the original version have been omitted.) Reprinted by permission.

After a revolution has succeeded, however, new channels of communication and interaction between governors and governed are frequently established. After Castro came to power in Cuba, new revolutionary organizations were created that reached into communities and levels of communities that had never before been "touched" by government. For example, administrators were sent throughout rural Cuba to organize agricultural and fishing cooperatives and state farms. For many of the people affected it was their first experience of government intervention to ameliorate their living conditions. Similarly, early urban measures such as the slashing of rents and the inception of the island's first major low-cost public housing program probably stimulated a widespread perception of the personal relevance of government among the lower classes. Other later measures such as the block internal security system must have operated in the same direction.

The Bolivian Revolution of 1952 has been evaluated in this country largely in terms of how much that government's "inefficiency" is costing the U.S. taxpayer. Its efficiency in politicizing an inert mass of Indians to assume participant roles and egalitarian norms is but dimly comprehended. As Patch has written, "Until the revolution of 1952 they were serfs. Now they vote, send their children to school, participate in political rallies, form unions, and buy Italian accordions."

A similar case is the Guatemalan Revolution of 1944–54. K. H. Silvert has estimated the proportion of "national" Guatemalans as at most 10 per cent of the population, mostly resident in the capital city. But the Revolution initiated a process of politicization in the hinterlands, formerly "politically dead." Parties were organized that extended not only politics but competitive politics into the local community, local election of local officials was established, farm labor unions arose, etc. From all this came a general political awakening, the development of national consciousness, and an incipient sense of individual independence and personal dignity.

A particularly important aspect of this revolution was the politicization of the younger, progressive Indians. After the anti-Communist revolution of Castillo Armas in 1954, which in the countryside quickly became a systematic counterrevolution, a number of these younger, new leaders were shot while a great many others fled. This raised the important theoretical consideration of *depoliticization.* How enduring were the effects of the first revolution? What was the impact of the relatively brief terror on the newly politicized Indians? Has the reestablishment of the conservative oligarchy merely quieted the peasantry, or has the perception of the personal relevance of government actually disappeared?

While it is virtually definitional that repression or suppression can have the effect of deactivating the politically participant, it is much more difficult to imagine conditions under which people change from perception of the relevance of government to nonperception. In other words, politicization in its primary meaning of change from nonperception to perception would at first glance seem to be practically irreversible. And yet this is not at all a safe assumption. The peasant uprising in El Salvador some thirty years ago was met with wholesale massacre, and there has been no such manifestation of politicization by the peasantry since then. Extreme coercion may have deactivated or thoroughly depoliticized, and we do not know which. Furthermore, people who have hoped and waited in vain for governmental action for a long time may become cynical about the capacity of government ever to act as they wish, and such prolonged cynicism could lead to a gradual loss of the perception of the personal relevance of government. This could occur over a long period of time, across generations, or through a gradually changing process of political socialization. It must be remembered that there were a number of Indian revolts against the Spanish during the colonial period, while today it is assumed that the Indians are "traditionally" nonpoliticized.

Those interested in underdeveloped nations have made a cliché of "the revolution of rising expectations," of which an important aspect is the recognition that government can be organized and operated to meet newly recognized needs. Political-cultural revolution, however, of the kind mentioned above, is far from ubiquitous. In fact, what surprises me is its relative infrequency in circumstances that would seem likely to promote it. For example, in the cities of Latin America facilities such as housing, sewage, clinics, schools, electricity, transportation, and even water have been falling castastrophically behind population growth, yet mere politically oriented action, let alone revolution, is exceptional rather than normal among those who are objectively the most deprived. While there has been no systematic attempt to account for this, a number of separate studies made recently do indicate the manner in which certain factors retard politicization among such people as the urban mass of Latin America. A few of these studies will be briefly noted.

In extreme poverty and stress, with a continued inability to ameliorate it, people are more likely to become socially disorganized than impelled into political action as they concentrate on keeping themselves alive. As Eric Hoffer has written of the abjectly poor, "When people toil from sunrise to sunset for a bare living, they nurse no grievances and dream no dreams."

Very rarely, a person in such a state of misery reacts with outrage.

A São Paulo *favelada* (a resident of Brazil's urban slums, the *favelas*), Carolina Maria de Jesus, somehow developed a perspective on the life she was forced to lead and wrote a diary which was published in 1960 under the title *Quarto de despejo* (Garbage Room). Frank Bonilla quotes from it as follows:

> Too tired to do her family foraging through the city's trash in search of something to eat or sell . . . [she wrote] "When I am hungry, I want to kill Janio, I want to hang Adhemar and burn Juscelino. Hardship dims the affection of the people for the politicians."

But hers was an isolated protest, and her neighbors thought her diary writing was "putting on airs." When, thanks to the success of her book she moved from the *favela*, they showered her with stones, garbage, and curses. Her perception of her life as affected by government and politicians (if only through their inaction), her awareness that things as they are do not have to be, did not make her a leader among a people not ready for mass political action. In the swelling *favelas* of Rio de Janeiro, where observers have imagined politicization to be high, nearly half the residents interviewed in a recent study saw nothing to be gained through political action, and less than one fifth had discussed politics heatedly with a friend in the previous six months, even though over half of them said that things had gotten worse for them in the last five years. A recent Brazilian opinion survey found only the most rudimentary information or opinion on politics among the rural populace. The potential for politicization seems therefore extremely undeveloped.

Another factor that may retard politicization is the sense of community developed by rural immigrants into urban areas (the rural exodus accounts for much of Latin America's recent and accelerating urban explosion); this phenomenon has been noted in both Mexico and Brazil. Oscar Lewis has found it among rural immigrants in the *vecindades* of Mexico City, Richard Morse mentions the social cohesion that characterized some São Paulo proletarian neighborhoods, and Bonilla writes of his Rio *favela* respondents:

> Despite the conflict, frequent aggression, exploitativeness, and insecurity of personal relationships that according to the accounts of all observers are commonplace in the *favela*, the *favelado* himself feels that he is part of a fairly cohesive, solidary group. It is vis-a-vis the world outside the *favela* that he feels bypassed, forgotten, and excluded.

This sense of community seems to provide much security and may well retard any tendency to look to the government for the solution of daily problems.

A similar factor is the extended family and ceremonial kinship relationship. One survey indicates that a typical resident of São Paulo identifies from thirty to 500 relatives, many of whom live in the city. What Morse terms the "continued vitality of the extended family" is also mentioned by Lewis as characteristic of at least some *vecindades*. Other students of urbanization have similarly described the importance of kinship. Since most lower-class Latin Americans have had no direct relationship with their national or local governments, it is not surprising that traditional familial relationships continue to be the major source of personal security, rather than an alien government bureaucracy whose officials are generally neither committed to assistance nor equipped to provide much of it.

In addition to this comforting sense of community and dependence on the family among rural immigrants to urban areas, Victor Alba has remarked the close relationship maintained between such immigrants and their native villages. It functions as a safety valve in times of economic pressure:

> It explains why economic crises, unemployment, etc., have less severe repercussions in Latin America than elsewhere. The worker who loses his job can return to his village without much difficulty.

Some occupational factors that probably retard politicization include the very high proportion of Latin Americans who are engaged in service work and petty commercial activities such as street vending. Such people tend to form an atomized labor force, and their lack of regular contact with others like themselves, plus their exceedingly long working day, probably do very little to generate an orientation toward government and politics.

Nor can it be assumed, either, that industrial employment is the locus of a politicized labor force. Most of the factory workers of Latin America are employed in handicraft types of operations or are otherwise in very small firms. This kind of employment tends to maintain the traditional reliance on the boss as the protector, the *patrón*, once again in lieu of the development of a political orientation, a turning to the political process for protection or amelioration of conditions.

Strategic activities of businessmen and industrialists may also contribute to the relatively low politicization of the working class. Morse notes that São Paulo employers' groups have created social service organizations devoted to

> Resolving workers' domestic and legal problems, broadening their social horizons, giving job training, raising living standards, defending real wages—and, like the church, to subsidizing the education of promising

youths to key technical and managerial positions. In its first year [one
of these organizations] set up thirty-seven supply posts in São Paulo city
which undersold retailers by 30 to 50 per cent and forced general price
cuts in staple foods.[1]

These too may act to retard the development of political consciousness
among the urban poor, but even more significant than their safety-valve
function is the indirect control they exert on the future development
of such consciousness. By educating "promising" lower-class youths and
giving them relatively prestigious positions, the representatives of "the
establishment" in São Paulo may siphon off from each generation the
potential leaders of a political movement of the disadvantaged.

This resumé suggests a number of cultural, social, and economic variables that should be investigated in the search for conditions of politicization. For example, the politicization of the following contrasting
groups can be compared: slum dwellers integrated into family and community and those who are isolated; new urbanites with recourse to subsistence agriculture in time of economic crisis and those who lack such
recourse; people at various levels of poverty (for, as Oscar Lewis demonstrates, the culture of poverty is extremely complex, and the relationship
between deprivation and political orientation is almost completely unknown); service workers, petty merchants, handicraft workers, and workers in large manufacturing plants. Furthermore, since many of these
variables relate to the process of urbanization, the suggested inquiry
should be carried out on a longitudinal or at least quasi-longitudinal
basis. Given the relative infrequence of the perception of the personal
relevance of government among the Latin American working and lower
class, cases of people such as *favela* dwellers or the extremely destitute
who *do* exhibit this perception or more advanced states of politicization
should be recognized as having great significance for theory building
and for understanding the nature of the human response to deprivation,
and investigated through deviant-case analysis.

MODES OF POLITICIZATION

Among the minimally politicized, those who at least perceive the personal relevance of government, there are significant differences based
not primarily on the quantity of politicization, but its quality. This qualitative dimension will be termed the mode of politicization. In the following, I will present some modes which seem to occur frequently in Latin
America, but also elsewhere, perhaps in varying frequency, and give
consideration to the conditions which give rise to the particular mode.

[1] Richard Morse, *From Community to Metropolis: A Biography of São Paulo,
Brazil* (Gainesville: University of Florida Press, 1958), p. 213.

The defensive type

This mode seems characteristic of citizens who are socioeconomically marginal. The defensive approach politics not to make a demand but a counter-demand. In Latin America a common catalyst of this mode of politicization is an abrupt threat to the precarious standard of living of the lower class. One such threat is the austerity program adopted by several Latin American governments in recent years as an effort to control inflation, which control is a prerequisite for getting financial assistance from some international and other foreign lending agencies. "Austerity" has frequently meant wage stabilization and increased taxes on basic consumer goods. Demands by conservative governments for belt-tightening have sometimes been resisted by a congeries of union, student groups, and "the mass" who deny the possibility of further belt-tightening under conditions already at the bare survival level. One such case, for example, contributed to the overthrow of the Velasco Ibarra government in Ecuador late in 1961. The politicization triggered by the announcement of such austerity measures seems to be quite short-lived, however. Demonstrations are made, succeed or fail rapidly and politicization of the "mass" subsides. Other such threats are plans for slum clearance or the uprooting of squatters. Despite the squalor and physical inadequacy of most of the slum areas of the major Latin American cities, they offer a great deal of security to many of their residents. Housing is at the very least inexpensive, and many find that if they build their own shacks they can avoid rent payments; often it is possible to maintain a garden plot or keep animals. Thus the kind of settlement exemplified by the *favela* provides a way station for people coming in from the country (in Lewis' term, the urban peasantry), and allows relative independence in housing for other poor residents of the metropolis. Pearse says:

> The *favela* offered to the in-migrant a means of establishing himself and his family as an unbroken unit in the shortest possible time, and with the least possible outlay, in his own house, in conditions similar and sometimes superior to those of his country home. . . .
> What is significant, however, and what is overlooked constantly by the city commentators who weep over the *favelas,* is that though the house-type is "rural," the conditions of life which the *favela*-dwellers—by their illegal initiative—have secured for themselves, are rated higher by them in most respects than the conditions prevailing in the rural areas from which the great number of them have come.[2]

As suggested above, the residents of such areas frequently settle on

---

[2] Andrew Pearse, "Some Characteristics of Urbanization in the City of Rio de Janeiro," in *Urbanization in Latin America*, Philip Hauser, ed. (New York: Columbia University Press, 1961), pp. 195–196.

unused land that is privately owned or acquired legally by another owner after the squatter settlement has taken place. In one such situation, squatters reacted to confrontation by the owners with sudden politicization. In a study of Panama City's *barriadas brujas* (literally, witch quarters—the shack settlements which the very poor have thrown up around the city), Gutiérrez describes a people sufficiently aware of their common problem to join together in a common effort to organize associations "to defend what they considered to be their rights." Nevertheless, the squatters' action was apparently aimed entirely at preventing owners of the property from evicting them from their shacks and adjacent lands. It never became either programmatic or oriented toward other political action.

The margin-oriented

This concerns the desire to arrange a special margin of economic security in one's "normal" occupational relationships. Lewis' documentation of the life of the Mexican urban poor is replete with such phenomena. Similarly, there is the virtually universal "institution" of the petty *mordida* (literally, the bite), in which the agent of the public bureaucracy must be paid a "consideration" to perform his official function, or to perform it in other than a routine impersonal fashion according to statute or bureaucratic policy.

To the extent to which the poor man or the petty civil servant feels impelled to try to arrange a special margin in his human relationships, a sense of generality is impaired and may affect the whole orientation toward government and politics. If every transaction is special, politics may become a matter of private negotiation between individuals, and there can be no politics of protest, none based on planning, none aimed at a policy. Further, any general policy that threatens the whole carefully constructed system of margin through special relationships is likely to be resisted, even by those whom the policy is designed to benefit.

Margin orientation is probably promoted by the tendency of the Latin American urban poor to hold no regular job but a set of irregular jobs, or to move from job to job, as a "labor nomad." If one fails to identify oneself on the basis of a rather integrated occupational role, then one may well be less likely to develop a stable orientation toward politics based on one's occupational status, a factor that would retard the development of a sense of group or class consciousness and a set of interests related to it. This has been suggested for the urban migrant from Brazil's Northeast, who sees himself as only temporarily a city dweller, a worker only until the nest egg is accumulated that will allow him to return to his rural home. It matters little whether he returns home or not: with this as his orientation he will not develop a set of occupation-based demands on politics. The extent of service occupations in urban Latin America contributes to this kind of margin orientation, for the worker is wholly dependent on intermittent contacts with his patrons. Given the level of wages for the typical petty service, if he fails to develop margins in these relationships, he may well not survive.

Immediate gratification

In the Peruvian presidential election of June, 1962, the Lima vote went neither to the *aprista* Haya de la Torre, Latin America's foremost political ideologist, nor to Fernando Belaúnde, a rising populist ideologue, but to Manuel Odría, a former dictator without a program and without any promise of the capacity to organize Peruvian government to meet ominous problems. Odría was known primarily for the public works created during his previous presidency (1948–56), and otherwise benefited from the coincidental relative prosperity of the country during those years. Since most of the urban population is extremely poor, Odría's victory in Lima suggests that ideology and abstract intellectualized reformism meant less to a large number of economically marginal citizens than tangible products of government such as a stadium or a hospital, such direct benefits as employment under the public works program (even though the program was no part of an attack on basic national problems), or than the belief that "times were good" as a result of X's presidency.

It has been noted by Lewis and others who have dealt with the culture of poverty that under pressure of deprivation slum dwellers have little ability to defer gratification, and exhibit a sense of fatalism and resignation. Thus the *favelados* are reported to respond to political campaigns with hope and relative enthusiasm, because candidates come through the *favelas* distributing food or clothing or money—it is the only time politicians exhibit any interest in these people at all. But except for such infrequent occasions, living is so close to the edge of disaster that an orientation toward the future is not likely to develop. This suggests that when extreme poverty carries with it minimal politicization, the mode is one of immediacy, an alertness only to what is closely related to the needs of the moment. It suggests that the electoral process is unlikely to have meaning for the impoverished because its very nature is gradualist and abstract, and that the poor are unlikely to perceive constitutionalism as a whole as having a relation to their lives.

Personalism-paternalism

Personalism as a mode of politicization means reliance on personal relationships, personal guarantees in politics, rather than formal legal or contractual relationships. This is surely one of the most commonly observed characteristics of Latin American politics, though the extent of the phenomenon in Latin America as compared to the United States or other supposedly more "rational" political systems has never been empirically investigated. Personalism is so institutionalized in Latin America that in those rare instances where broad, relatively coherent programs have been enacted (for example, in Argentina under Perón or in Cuba under Grau San Martín and Prio Socarrás), they have tended to be rendered ineffective by the catastrophic waste associated with personalistic administration, characterized by graft, concessions, *botellas* (positions in the public bureaucracy filled by patronage, for which little or no instrumental work is expected), and the like. The formal legal requirements of the situation tend to fall before the demands of the friend, the family, the group responsible for placing the leader in power.

One type of personalist orientation toward politics is the reliance on the *patrón*.

> The patron, whether he is an estate manager or a political boss . . . , provides protection and special favors in exchange for loyalty and service. This relationship is founded upon mutual trust, not on legally defined obligations; in fact, it normally operates outside of, and to a great extent in conflict with, formally regulated social and economic (and political) structures. The benefits bestowed by the *patrón* are expected but not specifically required of him, and are looked upon as demonstrations of his generosity and magnanimity.[3]

To the extent that the culture stresses personalism and paternalism, one might also expect a focus on the specific in political orientations. These value orientations would seem to discourage a sense of political identification based on common circumstances, one form of which is class consciousness. Personalism and paternalism would likewise seem to discourage political organization based on a common conception of interest. Pearse has used the term "populism" in his description and analysis of the consequences of personalism and paternalism in urban Brazil, specifically to refer to the urban adaptation of the traditional rural dependency relationship between the lower class and the *patrão*.

[3] Wyatt McGaffey and Clifford R. Barnett, *Cuba* (New Haven: HRAF Press, 1962), p. 97.

> Populism does not favor the organization of common interest groups or co-operative groups, and power is usually delegated downwards rather than upwards. . . . Coming from a tradition of rural dependence . . . , the city masses still fit easily into this structure. The ordinary property-less man feels that he is in no position to improve his lot significantly since he does not know either how to obtain his legal rights or how to operate successfully even in the lower echelons of the power and influence structures.

While personalism seems from this example to characterize the relationship between the leader and a lower class following, this is not necessarily its only or even its major manifestation, for other students of Latin American culture have seen it as a characteristic primarily of the *middle* sectors, and still others as a general characteristic of "traditionals" wherever they may be found in the social structure. In this regard it is interesting to note that among the predominantly middle-class Cuban exiles in the United States, there are an estimated 200 "organizations" committed to particular approaches to the problem of *fidelismo*. The distribution of personalist and paternalist modes of politicization across the social structure is another major question on which research has scarcely begun. While personalism is ordinarily treated as a prohibitive barrier to the development of democracy, a more general conclusion is probably that this mode retards the institutionalization of *any* rules of the political game, so that the society is continuously thrown back on coercion as the only workable means of social control.

Radical efficacy

This mode of politicization is rarely studied, although it is critically important in political change. The radically efficacious have confidence in their ability to do "great" things, to bring about major changes, to destroy institutions or even societies and remake them in a new image. Radical efficacy seems to have been a salient characteristic of the leadership of the 26th of July movement in its struggle to overthrow the powerful Batista regime, the Castro government in its subsequent efforts to reconstruct national economic and social institutions, the Egyptian leadership in its decision to nationalize the Suez Canal, and the Cárdenas administration in its expropriation of foreign-owned petroleum industries in Mexico. Radical efficacy has come increasingly to occur in association with (or as a catalyst of) radical nationalism and social revolution, but it is also a characteristic of the (non-Black Nationalist) Negro sit-in movement in this country.

Radical efficacy seems to occur among relatively advantaged people who experience frustration. As such, the radically efficacious fall within the category identified by Crane Brinton as the stratum from which revolutionary leadership is recruited. The frustration may relate to drives for wealth, status, power, or self-respect. For example, Paul Kecskemeti has noted of the leaders of the Hungarian Revolution of 1956:

> . . . revolutionary activity originated with groups who were partly privileged and partly frustrated. The writers, who were the first to rebel, had a highly privileged social and economic position, but suffered acutely from the loss of personal integrity and professional satisfaction [after the disclosure of the atrocities committed by the previous government, a government that had been systematically praised and justified by these men]; the students who followed suit were nurtured by the regime and could expect to rise into relatively high social brackets, but they resented regimentation and forced indoctrination.

In my own work on the probable development of this mode of politicization among Panamanian students, I found the following pattern among radical nationalists:

> Though similar to the Moderates in socio-economic status and the frequency with which members of their families were involved in politics, the Nationalists' backgrounds were marginal in a few significant aspects which suggest that they may feel relatively deprived in status. Their expectation of success is high, and they seem to have a stronger motivation toward achievement than do the Moderates—radical nationalism may thus have been embraced because the success of the movement would mean the expansion of socio-economic opportunities and because the Nationalists have projected their drive for achievement onto the nation as a whole, particularly since the nation itself has also experienced relative deprivation in status in the international community.

The emergence and growth of radical efficacy is extremely important because even though the number of activists politicized in this mode is likely to be small, the symbolism they manipulate is highly dramatic and diffuse (nationalism, "Panama for the Panamanians"; equality; renunication of weakness the redressing of shame or humiliation, etc.), and they are capable of catalyzing major movements of political change. In Latin America and other colonial or quasi-colonial areas, radical efficacy is most likely to emerge among intellectual and student groups and, given their crucial and continuous role in educational policy making, the education system is likely to be strongly affected by it, as well as serving as the center of radical efficacious politics. In Mexico, for example, the Revolution was both a cause and consequence of radical efficacy, and intellectuals politicized in this mode created the rural cultural missions designed to educate the Indian masses and thus to transform the heterogeneous congeries of traditional subsistence communities into an integrated nation. Although the relative successes and failures of the missions are hard to define and assess, the program has been immensely attractive to groups in other countries who are charged with the task of modernization. It is quite possible that the task of economic development can only be accomplished in areas such as Latin America under political conditions which generate radical efficacy, and make it possible for the radically efficacious to attain power. With the scarcity of resources, the weight of traditions of fatalism and resignation, and the entrenched opposition of the privileged and those who aspire to privilege, only the commitment of the radically efficacious and the symbolism available to them can transform such societies.

CONCLUSION

Clearly, the foregoing has been an unsystematic presentation of various modes of politicization. Some seem to be mutually exclusive (for example, the defensive and the radical efficacious modes), and some may well occur in a syndrome (immediate gratification, personalism, defensive). One of the next steps toward a systematic typology is an elaboration of the polar opposites of the types already presented (the demanding versus the defensive, acceptance of delayed gratification versus immediate gratification, personalism versus impersonalism, etc.). Following this, the variables implicit in the definitions of these types must be abstracted and the typology systematically reformulated. The latter will, in turn, serve as the basis for a cross-cultural research program.

In summary, then, there are two major dimensions of politicization by which political systems can be compared: the extent of politicization and the mode. For example, a comparison of U.S. and Latin American politics might show the following:

1. Minimal politicization (perception of the personal relevance of government) has been attained by a larger proportion of the citizens of the U.S. than of Latin American nations.

2. Average politicization is higher in the U.S. than in Latin American countries; there are more high participants and fewer low participants in the United States.

3. The frequency of impersonal as compared to personalistic modes of politicization is higher in the United States.

4. Though the distribution of this mode is such that the U.S. is pre-

dominantly characterized by impersonal modes and Latin American countries by personalistic ones, the ranges overlap to the point that there are substantial minorities of personalistically oriented citizens in Latin America.

5. Personalism does not vary with extent of politicization in Latin America (equal proportions of the personalistic and impersonalistic are highly politicized), but personalism varies inversely with extent of politicization in the United States.

This hypothetical summation raises some interesting questions. What proportion of its citizens must be politicized in an impersonal mode (oriented toward the rule of law) before we can characterize the polity as operating by that mode? No meaningful answer can yet be given, but it seems quite possible that even where only a relatively few citizens are politicized in this mode, if they monopolize the ranks of the highly politicized the polity may function according to the rule of law and not personalism. Such a finding would accord with Stouffer's finding that the community leadership in the United States tends to value civil liberties more than the less-politicized citizens, and thus the polity functions as a relatively open society even though non-civil libertarian norms predominate in the citizenry.

What factors promote impersonal modes of politicization? It is usually assumed that modern value orientations, including impersonalism and achievement orientation, etc., vary with socioeconomic development. If this is so, Argentina should exhibit a higher frequency of such modes than less economically developed Latin American countries. If this proves not to be true for Argentina and yet the relationship seems generally to hold, Argentina should be analyzed as a deviant case. Why did the rule-of-law orientation fail to develop widely in its context of socioeconomic development? What special conditions account for the deviation, and what does this tell us about the general relationship? Is it possible that the impersonalistic mode did increase with economic development in nineteenth-century Argentina, but that the failure to integrate the nation politically and socially has since led to the rise of personalistic modes?

Under what conditions are personalistic modes transmuted into impersonalistic ones? Natural experimental situations abound in Latin America for this sort of inquiry. For example, the Dominican Republic changed temporarily from a situation of oligarchical regime and personalistic elite power structure to a much more democratic regime, a competitive leadership, and much greater mass participation in politics. It would have been a theoretically rather straightforward, simple endeavor to determine through survey methods the distribution of modes of politicization toward the beginning of this change, and to make new measurements after a period under the new system. Thus one might begin to analyze the effect of the change in the leadership's modes of politicization on the modes of the population-at-large.

What is the effect of class origin on the politicization of Latin American students? Where in the student body of the secondary schools and universities do we find the greatest incidence of impersonal modes of politicization? Does this mode characterize the upwardly mobile student of working-class origin, or the more established middle-class youth? This is critically important. If those who attain upward mobility are completely self-oriented and model themselves after the traditionally privileged, then they will exert no pressure toward reformation of the social system on a universalistic-achievement basis. If they do not reject their conditions of origin, they may exert some pressure for reform. What difference in this regard results from training in a classical curriculum as opposed to a more vocationally oriented one?

What happens to the defensively politicized as government changes from an emphasis on maintenance of its traditional scope (the provision of basic services to the upper social strata and control of the lower) to a focus on development through raising the general level of living? Does the government's definition of the situation of the impoverished as a state of need and its subsequent meeting of those needs lead the defensive-minded to perceive more and more needs in relation to government and produce ever-increasing demands? Does this lead to increasing support for the system or to increasing dissatisfaction, as the perception of needs outruns the capacity of the government to fulfill them?

What is the incidence of the mode of radical efficacy among the youth of the Latin American countries? Are there substantial numbers of equally highly politicized young people who exhibit other modes—for example, policy orientation but not radical efficacy? What ideologies are found in association with radical efficacy? Are the radically efficacious neutralized by differences in goals, means? Does acceptance of the use of violence increase or decrease with time as the radically efficacious become increasingly frustrated? (Though the answer seems obvious, it is apparently not so simple. The long-frustrated grew increasingly violent in Algeria, but the *apristas* in Peru grew increasingly moderate. Thus other explanatory variables must be introduced.)

These are a few of the crucial questions in the comparative study of political systems, economic development, and cultural modernization that can be investigated through the use of the concept of politicization.

Measurement of Latin American Political Change[*]

RUSSELL H. FITZGIBBON
and
KENNETH F. JOHNSON

Social scientists are finding an increasingly useful and stimulating tool in the application of statistical techniques to their problems. As in the employment of any new tool, both the utility and the limitations of this one must be learned. It seems beyond reasonable doubt, however, that quantification of data in the social sciences will become a more widely used and rewarding procedure as time goes on.

Prudence dictates that stress be laid on its limitations. The enthusiasm with which a new tool—toy, some would say—is adopted should not blind the user to dangers which may be implicit in its overuse. One cannot squeeze more juice from an orange than the orange contains, no matter how modern the squeezer. Care must be exercised, too, lest the bitter essence of the rind become mixed with the nourishing juice of the fruit itself.

The present analysis is an attempt, in not too complex a fashion, to make use of such techniques to organize and validate data which might otherwise permit only the broadest sort of generalizations by way of conclusion, conclusions unsatisfactory roughly in proportion to their breadth. The senior author of this article has for more than a decade and a half been interested in the problem of objective measurement of certain aspects of political change in Latin America with particular respect to the sum total of phenomena falling under the rubric of "democracy." On four occasions, 1945, 1950, 1955, and 1960, he conducted a survey among groups of specialists on Latin America to elicit evaluations which then, with the help of such statistical procedures as seemed useful, were summarized and analyzed. In the study of the most recent survey, undertaken on a more comprehensive basis than earlier ones, he was joined in the analysis and presentation of findings by the junior author, whose contribution has been such as to justify

[*] Russell H. Fitzgibbon and Kenneth F. Johnson, "Measurement of Latin American Political Change," *American Political Science Review*, Vol. 55: No. 3 (September 1961), pp. 515–526. (Footnotes in the original version have been omitted.)

coauthorship. Results of these surveys have previously been published, with a degree of response which indicates keen and widespread interest in the approach and methods. The present paper embodies an attempt to make a purely statistical analysis of the consensus of judgments by forty specialists; other sorts of analyses are possible and it is hoped can subsequently be made.

The objective of the successive surveys was to determine, with as much certainty as the necessarily subjective approaches by individuals to their respective evaluations would permit, trends of democratic or undemocratic change in the several Latin American states and the correlations and interrelationships among contributory factors. It was premised, as the preceding sentence suggests, on the assumption that democracy is a complex process, shaped and conditioned by many and diverse factors. It cannot be equated simply with, say, free exercise of the ballot. In ultimate analysis, of course, democracy can be said in large degree to be merely a state of mind; but to approach the appraisal on such a basis involves one in a subtle interplay of intellectual, spiritual, and other factors which scarcely lend themselves to any sort of precise expression, if indeed, they are wholly identifiable in the first place.

Another problem inherent in this brash undertaking is simply that of definition of terms to begin with. We shall not now attempt that, but rather simply point out that a definition of democracy which might be widely acceptable, perhaps even unconsciously, in, say, Great Britain, Switzerland, Belgium, and the United States might not find such acceptance or even recognition in states of Latin America. It is an oversimplification, but suggestive, to say that much public opinion in the first group of states mentioned above is inclined to regard the problem as one of political democracy, although the approach in much of Latin America is likely instead to emphasize social democracy. We know too little about the whole amorphous and involved problem to propose as more than a highly tentative hypothesis, that a shift to emphasis on the political aspects is a result of longer experience with self-government; the very complexity of the matter immediately suggests caution in making deductions.

It seemed necessary first to specify criteria which had an apparent relationship to the sum total of democratic attainment in a given country, with especial reference to states of Latin America. Some of these criteria were social, some economic, some cultural, some political in nature. Fifteen criteria, listed below, finally suggested themselves as having an important relationship, direct or indirect, to the determination of where State X in Latin America stood on a scale of political change relevant to democracy. They were:

1. An educational level sufficient to give the political processes some substance and vitality.

2. A fairly adequate standard of living.

3. A sense of internal unity and national cohesion.

4. Belief by the people in their individual political dignity and maturity.

5. Absence of foreign domination.

6. Freedom of the press, speech, assembly, radio, etc.

7. Free and competitive elections—honestly counted votes.

8. Freedom of party organization; genuine and effective party opposition in the legislature; legislative scrutiny of the executive branch.

9. An independent judiciary—respect for its decisions.

10. Public awareness of accountability for the collection and expenditure of public funds.

11. Intelligent attitude toward social legislation—the vitality of such legislation as applied.

12. Civilian supremacy over the military.

13. Reasonable freedom of political life from the impact of ecclesiastical controls.

14. Attitude toward and development of technical, scientific, and honest governmental administration.

15. Intelligent and sympathetic administration of whatever local self-government prevails.

The order of arrangement above is what appeared to be a logically contributory and developing order and not one which indicates the relative importance of the respective criteria. Obviously such a criterion as freedom of elections is more significant than some of the others in determination of ultimate results. Hence, it seemed desirable to weight the different criteria to indicate that degree of importance. Of those listed above, items 1, 2, 3, 4, 5, 9, 10, 11, 14, and 15 were weighted one; items 6, 8, and 12 one and one-half; item 7 (which appeared the most important of all) two; and item 13 (now partially of historical importance only), one-half. Respondents in the surveys were asked to rank the various states by the letters A, B, C, D, and E, indicating in general an individual judgment of excellent, good, average, poor, or insignificant (virtually no) democratic achievement, respectively, on the particular criterion. A rating of A was evaluated at five points, one of B at four points, and so on, to one point for E. The variation in ratings given to one country by a single respondent (taking into account the different weightings of the several criteria) could therefore range from 17 to 85 points.

Brief explanatory material regarding the criteria and the method of ranking was sent the respondents and in addition an evaluation form on which each person was asked to express 300 judgments—his evaluation for each of fifteen criteria applied to each of twenty states. In addition, in the 1960 survey, each respondent was asked, in a self-rating, to indicate his degree of familiarity, whether "considerable," "moderate," or "little," with each state and each criterion. The evaluation sheets used were in the form of a fifteen-by-twenty matrix, fifteen components of democratic practice listed to correspond to rows of cells for recording evaluations, and twenty states listed to correspond with the same cells in columns. The evaluation sheet also included an additional row and column of cells for indication of the respondents' "familiarity level" with the states and the criteria, respectively. This aspect of the analysis cannot be considered in detail at this time but it can be summarized by saying that the self-confident evaluations ("considerable familiarity") of the states did not usually differ significantly from the non-self-confident judgments ("little familiarity").

Although no sacrosanct quality is claimed for the phrasing of the criteria used, it seemed desirable to keep them identical in successive surveys in order to assure greater comparability of results. Each respondent was asked to view the scene in each state as of "recent months," though no specific time span was prescribed. It was also suggested that average conditions within a given country should be considered, though the difficulty of doing that for one as large and complex as, say, Brazil is immediately apparent. Given the somewhat exacting conditions laid down, the respondents certainly participated in the survey "above and beyond the call of duty" and the authors are deeply grateful for their collaboration. Replies were received in the early months of 1960; time since then has been spent in various sorts of analyses of the data, in part of which an advanced type of electronic computer was used.

A necessary first step in the analysis was the compilation of original or "raw" scores for the various states, determined simply by totalling the points for evaluations of the several criteria, taking into account their different weighting. "Raw" scores for the various states as shown in the four surveys are given in Table 1.

Use of the "raw" scores is open to serious statistical objection, however, because of the natural (and perhaps unconscious) optimism of this respondent and the pessimism of that. That is, one person will be inclined to view the Latin American states through rose-tinted glasses, another through lenses befogged with various smudges of prejudice. Then, too, the ranges of scoring varied widely for the respondents. Inasmuch as the ranges rather neatly straddled 1,000 points it seemed expedient and helpful to adjust or "normalize" the scoring of the various respondents by allotting each of them 1,000 points for all countries and

TABLE 1. RAW SCORES, BY COUNTRY

	1945		1950		1955		1960	
	POINTS	RANK	POINTS	RANK	POINTS[1]	RANK	POINTS[2]	RANK
Argentina	628	5	536	8	499½	8	704½	4
Bolivia	308	18	334	17	374½	15	439	16
Brazil	481½	11	605	5	633	5	648½	7
Chile	712½	3	732½	2	713	3	741½	3
Colombia	683½	4	597½	6	507	6	651½	6
Costa Rica	730	2	702½	3	746	2	768	2
Cuba	590½	6	659	4	504	7	452	15
Domin. Rep.	301	19	320½	19	307	19	315	18
Ecuador	379½	14	474	9	487	10	556½	10
El Salvador	411½	13	424	14	461½	11	508½	12
Guatemala	416	12	472½	10	393½	14	483½	13
Haiti	330½	16	329	18	367	17	309½	19
Honduras	328	17	379	15	418½	12	452½	14
Mexico	545½	7	569½	7	639½	4	664	5
Nicaragua	345½	15	354	16	329½	18	370½	17
Panama	528	8	471	11	498	9	519½	11
Paraguay	289	20	293½	20	291½	20	284	20
Peru	494	10	428	13	369½	16	562½	9
Uruguay	772	1	788½	1	820	1	785	1
Venezuela	504	9	451	12	397	13	611½	8

[1] Initial "raw" score divided by two and rounded to next low one-half point if necessary.

[2] Initial "raw" score divided by four and rounded to next low one-half point if necessary.

recalculating individual state scores correspondingly. This was done by calculating reciprocals of the total scores given by each respondent to all states on all criteria and then determining the adjusted score to be given each state by multiplying the reciprocal by the "raw" score for each state. This statistical adjustment meant, of course, a change in the total for each state but not a change in relative ranking. Adjusted scores, omitting fractions (which are statistically insignificant) are shown in Table 2; a graphic indication of the progressive changes is shown in Figure 1. Later aspects of the analysis are all based on adjusted scores.

Table 2, in addition to giving the adjusted point-score for each state in the first column of each year's tabulation, shows in the second column for each year the rank order of the state in that year's survey. Ranks are somewhat delusive, however, in that two states with immediately adjoining rank positions (i.e., fourth and fifth places or seventeenth and eighteenth places) may be close together or relatively far apart in terms of points. It is desirable, then, to determine percentage positions

TABLE 2. ADJUSTED SCORES, BY COUNTRY

	1945			1950			1955			1960		
	POINTS	RANK	PER CENT	POINTS	RANK	PER CENT	POINTS	RANK	PER CENT	POINTS	RANK	PER CENT
Argentina	634	5	63.9	542	8	53.3	513[1]	7[1]	47.8[1]	652	4	78.0
Bolivia	315	18	19.2	335	17	23.4	384	15	29.5	406	16	39.2
Brazil	495	11	44.4	612	5	63.4	651	5	67.4	600	7	69.2
Chile	745	3	79.4	740	2	81.9	735	3	79.3	688	3	83.7
Colombia	718	4	75.6	602	6	62.0	524	6	49.4	602	6	70.1
Costa Rica	765	2	82.2	713	3	78.0	773	2	84.7	713	2	90.8
Cuba	619	6	61.8	667	4	71.4	513[1]	7[1]	47.8[1]	422	14	41.7
Domin. Rep.	310	19	18.5	318	19	20.9	312	19	19.3	290	18	20.9
Ecuador	387	14	29.3	479	9	44.2	498	10	45.7	514	10	56.2
El Salvador	417	13	33.5	422	14	36.0	469	11	41.6	468	12	49.0
Guatemala	426	12	34.7	478	10	44.1	398	14	31.5	445	13	45.3
Haita	336	16	22.1	331	18	22.8	375	17	28.2	283	19	19.7
Honduras	331	17	21.4	378	15	29.6	426	12	35.5	414	15	40.4
Mexico	562	7	53.8	570	7	57.4	657	4	68.2	613	5	71.9
Nicaragua	349	15	23.9	351	16	25.7	336	18	22.7	341	17	28.9
Panama	537	8	50.3	468	11	42.6	505	9	46.7	478	11	50.6
Paraguay	304	20	17.6	293	20	17.3	297	20	17.1	261	20	16.3
Peru	505	10	45.8	425	13	36.4	378	16	28.7	518	9	56.9
Uruguay	804	1	87.7	804	1	91.2	850	1	95.6	767	1	96.2
Venezuela	518	9	47.6	448	12	39.7	404	13	32.3	564	8	64.1

[1] Tie.

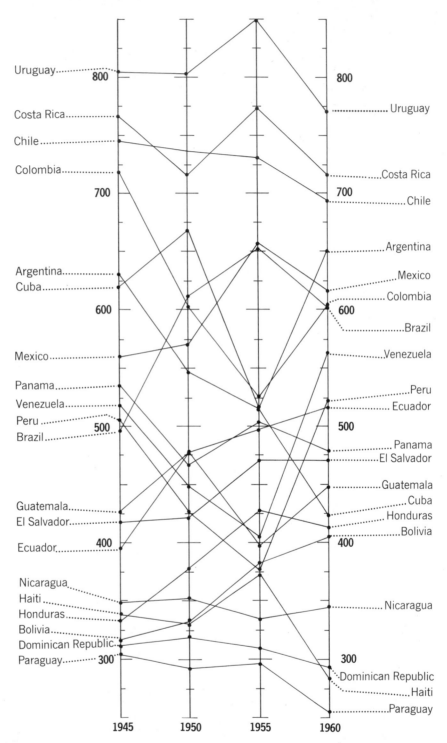

Fig. 1. MOVEMENT IN ADJUSTED SCORES, BY COUNTRIES, 1945–1960.

and shifts for the several states. It would not be feasible to do this on the basis of a perfect or even an optimum "democratic measurement"; but it can be done by assigning to the lowest possible score a percentage of zero, and to the highest possible a percentage of 100. If "raw" scores were to be used, the variation—in a ten-respondent survey—would be between 170 and 850 points; i.e., if a given state were rated *E* on all criteria by all ten respondents it would receive a total of 170 points, while if another state were rated *A* in similar fashion its total would be 850 points. Using adjusted scores, however, it was necessary similarly to adjust the minima and maxima employed for determining percentages. On this basis percentage achievement in the various years surveyed could be determined, and the results are shown in the third column of each year's tabulations in Table 2. Percentage positions are more revealing than rank positions in that they show up what would otherwise be occasionally concealed by "bunching."

Table 3 gives certain summary information extracted from Table 2. The first three columns show percentage changes by states from, respectively, 1945 to 1950, 1950 to 1955, and 1955 to 1960; the fourth column cumulates these and shows the net percentage change from 1945 to 1960. The fifth column indicates the maximum point fluctuation by states over the fifteen-year period, and the last column shows the net point change over that period.

In the broadest terms, a tentative conclusion might be reached that Latin America has gained somewhat in recent years in total democratic achievement. This may be determined by totaling "raw" scores of the four surveys, dividing the totals for 1955 and 1960 by two and four, respectively, because of the larger number of respondents. The resulting totals are: 1945, 9,763½; 1950, 9,943; 1955, 9,760; 1960, 10,827½. The considerable jump in 1960 may well be a reflection of the impression caused by the fall of various Latin American dictatorships in the late 1950s. Greater comparability and hence more validity might be gained by using only the totals of those seven respondents who participated in all four surveys. On this more limited basis the respective totals were: 1945, 6,452½; 1950, 6,995; 1955, 6,338; 1960, 7,132. In the shift from 1955 to 1960, the most marked of any of the three quinquennia available for comparison, the seven "veterans" are an even three per cent more liberal than the total of the forty respondents.

The monopoly of certain states on relative positions among the Latin American group in terms of democratic achievement is illustrated in part by Table 2. It can be further demonstrated by determining the respective number of ratings of excellent, good, average, poor, and insignificant given the several states in total. Each state in the four surveys

TABLE 3. PERCENTAGE AND POINT CHANGES, BY COUNTRY, 1945–1960

	% CHANGE 1945–50	% CHANGE 1950–55	% CHANGE 1955–60	% CHANGE 1945–60	MAXI- MUM POINT SHIFT	NET POINT SHIFT 1945–60
Argentina	−10.6	− 5.5	+30.2	+14.1	139	+ 18
Bolivia	+ 4.2	+ 6.1	+ 9.7	+20.0	91	+ 91
Brazil	+19.0	+ 4.0	+ 1.8	+24.8	156	+105
Chile	+ 2.5	− 2.6	+ 4.4	+ 4.3	57	− 57
Colombia	−13.6	−12.6	+20.7	− 5.5	194	−116
Costa Rica	− 4.2	+ 6.7	+ 6.1	+ 8.6	60	− 52
Cuba	+ 9.6	−23.6	− 6.1	−20.1	245	−197
Domin. Rep.	+ 2.4	− 1.6	+ 1.6	+ 2.4	28	− 20
Ecuador	+14.9	+ 1.5	+10.5	+26.9	127	+127
El Salvador	+ 2.5	+ 5.6	+ 7.4	+15.5	52	+ 51
Guatemala	+ 9.4	−12.6	+13.8	+10.6	80	+ 19
Haiti	+ .7	+ 5.4	− 8.5	− 2.4	92	− 53
Honduras	+ 8.2	+ 5.9	+ 4.9	+19.0	95	+ 83
Mexico	+ 3.6	+10.8	+ 3.7	+18.1	95	+ 51
Nicaragua	+ 1.8	− 3.0	+ 6.2	+ 5.0	15	− 8
Panama	− 7.7	+ 4.1	+ 3.9	+ .3	69	− 59
Paraguay	− .3	− .2	− .8	− 1.3	43	− 43
Peru	− 9.4	− 7.7	+28.2	+11.1	140	+ 13
Uruguay	+ 3.5	+ 4.4	+ .6	+ 8.5	83	− 37
Venezuela	− 7.9	− 7.4	+31.8	+16.5	160	+ 46

received a total of 1,200 ratings (the four were, chronologically, 150, 150, 300, and 600). If State X had received from every respondent in each survey a rating of A it then would have had 1,200 A's and no other ratings of any kind. The actual distribution of ratings is indicated in Table 4.

Similarly, 1,200 opportunities were offered in the four surveys for complete concentration of evaluations or a partial or complete spread among the respondents. That is, all respondents could evaluate criterion X for State Y as good, for example; or, on the other hand, their evaluations could wholly or partially cover the gamut from A to E, i.e., excellent to insignificant. Since the number of respondents increased in the third and fourth surveys chance would make it more likely that disagreement or spread rather than agreement or concentration would prevail; but curiously, of the seven instances (out of 1,200) when complete agreement was registered five occurred in 1955, with twenty respondents participating. In that year all twenty judged that attainment in freedom of party organization in the Dominican Republic was insignificant and that Uruguay's achievement in freedom of expression, freedom of elections, significance of party organization, and civilian supremacy should

TABLE 4. DISTRIBUTION OF RATINGS, BY COUNTRY

	EXCELLENT	GOOD	AVERAGE	POOR	INSIGNIFICANT
Argentina	342	465	214	91	88
Bolivia	29	127	318	452	274
Brazil	213	464	420	86	17
Chile	494	526	162	17	1
Colombia	205	458	417	94	26
Costa Rica	563	511	120	6	0
Cuba	127	336	383	220	134
Domin. Rep.	31	100	234	301	534
Ecuador	55	256	509	303	77
El Salvador	49	216	500	347	88
Guatemala	40	145	476	435	104
Haiti	14	72	226	453	435
Honduras	38	97	427	470	168
Mexico	248	511	339	77	25
Nicaragua	19	75	326	479	301
Panama	76	264	507	284	69
Paraguay	8	45	155	463	529
Peru	64	208	511	306	111
Uruguay	799	360	37	4	0
Venezuela	111	310	480	196	103

be regarded as excellent. In 1950 all ten respondents had agreed that civilian supremacy over the military was good in Cuba and that the Dominican Republic's progress toward free elections was insignificant. No instances of complete agreement occurred among the respondents in 1945 or in 1960.

Among the 1,200 ratings in the four surveys, 133 instances—more than half of them in 1960—showed the respondents evaluating particular criteria for given states all the way from excellent to insignificant; even specialists may disagree. A complete spread in evaluations was commonest with regard to Panama, where in fourteen instances the respondents registered clear across the spectrum from excellent to insignificant, and Cuba, El Salvador, and Honduras, where all gradations of judgment were represented in twelve instances. The degree of spread or concentration of evaluations is shown in Table 5. In it Column 1 indicates the instances, by states, in which all respondents agreed on a single evaluation, whatever it was. Column 2 shows the number of times in which all respondents concentrated their judgments on two evaluations, even though these might not be contiguous evaluations, i.e., excellent and good, good and average, etc. Columns 3 and 4 indicate the numbers of cases in which the spread was proportionately greater, and Column

5 shows the number of instances in which the spread was complete, i.e., representing all evaluations from excellent to insignificant.

Among the several criteria, it appeared that the respondents found it easiest to disagree on the status of internal unity and the absence of foreign domination. In the former case there were twenty instances of disagreement "across the board"; in the latter, twenty-one. An extreme illustration of divergence of views was presented by opinions on Cuba's freedom from foreign domination in 1960; for ten respondents its situation in that respect was excellent, for ten it was good, for ten it was average, for six it was poor, and for four its freedom from foreign domination was insignificant. Table 6 indicates, by criteria, the concentration or spread of judgments in similar fashion to Table 5.

The data are subject to analysis also from the point of view of the criteria used. In such an analysis it may be possible to determine tentatively, for one thing, the nature of the shifts taking place in the various components of democracy in Latin America. Totals of points in each survey for each criterion, the corresponding rank achieved by each, and the point changes for appropriate periods are indicated in Table 7. The same data are shown graphically in Figure 2.

Table 7 indicates the consensus of the specialists, that conditions affecting all components improved in the last half of the 1950s, sometimes

TABLE 5. EVALUATIONS, BY COUNTRY

	1	2	3	4	5
Argentina		11	21	22	6
Bolivia		6	25	22	7
Brazil		6	30	21	3
Chile		15	35	9	1
Colombia		10	25	20	5
Costa Rica		20	37	3	
Cuba	1	8	19	20	12
Domin. Rep.	2	12	19	17	10
Ecuador		1	23	28	8
El Salvador			11	37	12
Guatemala		3	26	20	11
Haiti		9	27	19	5
Honduras			23	25	12
Mexico		3	24	24	9
Nicaragua		3	25	27	5
Panama			15	31	14
Paraguay		9	37	10	4
Peru		4	24	29	3
Uruguay	4	35	17	4	
Venezuela		1	19	34	6

TABLE 6. CONCENTRATION AND SPREAD
IN EVALUATIONS, BY CRITERIA

	1	2	3	4	5
Educational level		19	44	17	
Standard of living		20	42	18	
Internal unity		5	20	34	21
Political maturity		16	27	30	7
Lack of foreign domination		5	23	31	21
Freedom of speech, etc.	1	16	30	25	8
Free elections	2	17	27	27	7
Free party organization	2	9	34	26	9
Judicial independence		6	34	33	7
Government funds		5	24	40	11
Social legislation		8	46	23	3
Civilian supremacy	2	15	28	25	10
Lack of ecclesiastical control		6	29	29	16
Government administration		6	32	37	5
Local government		3	41	28	8

strikingly (e.g., in regard to elections and civilian supremacy), and also registered a gain in each instance (even in freedom from ecclesiastical controls, which had always been considered good) over the whole period of a decade and a half. Changes of this sort are in general agreement, especially as regards the quinquennium 1955–60, with the shifts earlier mentioned in total point scores ("raw") for the half decade (i.e., from 9,760 to 10,827½ between 1955 and 1960). . . .

What sorts of substantive—not procedural—conclusions does the series of surveys seem to justify? These, it must be emphasized, are, and will doubtless continue to be, tentative. But, on the basis of the statistical analyses conducted, they have an impressive weight of consensus about the evidence behind them, a weight reinforced by the individual and collective expertise of the respondents.

Three of the states, Uruguay, Costa Rica, and Chile, regularly have occupied the first three rank positions for the past fifteen years—Uruguay uniformly in first place. A significant percentage gap has usually prevailed between the lowest of the three and the next highest ranked state. These three states may justifiably be segregated, then, as a top group which thus far has monopolized a premium position in terms of democratic achievement. That such a monopoly may not be permanent is perhaps indicated by the fact that the adjusted point score obtained by Colombia in 1945 exceeded that of the third-ranked state in 1950 and those of the second- and third-ranked states in 1960.

Turning to the bottom of the ladder, five states, Paraguay, the Domini-

TABLE 7. CHANGES IN EVALUATIONS, BY CRITERIA, 1945–1960

	1945		1950			1955			1960			
	POINTS	RANK	POINTS	RANK	CHANGE IN POINTS 1945–50	POINTS[1]	RANK	CHANGE IN POINTS 1950–55	POINTS[2] RANK		CHANGE IN POINTS 1955–60	1945–60
Educational level	521	15	586	6	+65	562	8	−24	590	13	+28	+69
Standard of living	525	13	563	11	+38	559	9	−4	571	15	+12	+46
Internal unity	623	4	639	3	+16	627	3	−12	666	4	+39	+43
Political maturity	561	8	576	8	+15	582	6	+6	617	10	+35	+56
Lack of foreign domination	659	2	669	2	+10	686	2	+17	724	2	+38	+65
Freedom of speech, etc.	650	3	609	5	−41	605	5	−4	689	3	+84	+39
Free elections	552	9	538	15	−14	541	12	+3	659	5	+118	+107
Free party organization	546	10	548	14	+2	533	14	−15	630	7	+97	+84
Judicial independence	574	5	581	7	+7	547	10	−34	620	9	+73	+46
Government funds	523	14	552	12	+29	544	11	−8	602	12	+58	+79
Social legislation	562	7	622	4	+60	609	4	−13	629	8	+20	+67
Civilian supremacy	567	6	568	10	+1	521	15	−47	632	6	+111	+65
Lack of ecclesiastical control	732	1	717	1	−15	722	1	+5	739	1	+17	+7
Governmental administration	539	12	569	9	+30	565	7	−4	612	11	+47	+73
Local government	542	11	551	13	+9	540	13	−11	583	14	+43	+41

[1] Initial score divided by two and rounded to next lower whole point if necessary.
[2] Initial score divided by four and rounded to nearest or next lower whole point if necessary.

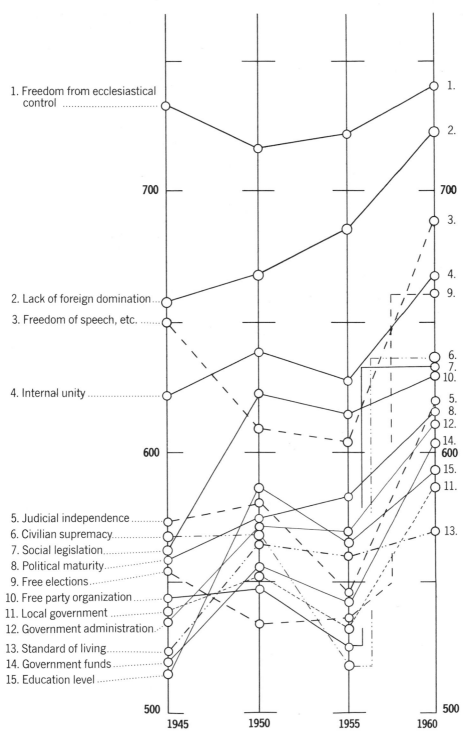

1. Freedom from ecclesiastical control ....

2. Lack of foreign domination ...

3. Freedom of speech, etc. ....

4. Internal unity ....

5. Judicial independence ....

6. Civilian supremacy ....

7. Social legislation ....

8. Political maturity ....

9. Free elections ....

10. Free party organization ....

11. Local government ....

12. Government administration ...

13. Standard of living ....

14. Government funds ....

15. Education level ....

700

600

500

1945   1950   1955   1960

700

600

500

1.
2.
3.
4.
9.
6.
7.
10.
5.
8.
12.
14.
15.
11.
13.

Fig. 2. MOVEMENT IN EVALUATIONS, BY CRITERIA, 1945–1960.

can Republic, Haiti, Nicaragua, and Bolivia, have regularly occupied rank positions among the lowest six in the four surveys, with Paraguay consistently holding lowest rank. Bolivia's continued place in this unenviable low group seems uncertain in view of its consistent and relatively striking gain over a period of fifteen years both in terms of point and percentage ranking. In three of the four surveys Honduras occupied the other position among the lowest six. It, too, however, like Bolivia, has shown a considerable improvement in respect both to points and percentages.

It is among a middle dozen, excluding a top three and a bottom five states, that the greatest and most interesting changes occur. These twelve are Argentina, Brazil, Colombia, Cuba, Ecuador, El Salvador, Guatemala, Honduras, Mexico, Panama, Peru, and Venezuela. Changes in them are, of course (as with all the states, for that matter), to be set against the backdrop of specific political change in the respective states during the decade and a half covered by the surveys. Substantial net percentage gains during the fifteen years were recorded by Brazil, Ecuador, Honduras, and Mexico; and a striking net loss by Cuba because of the combined impact of Batista and Castro. Average maximum point fluctuations (see Table 3) were substantially larger for this group than for either the top three or the bottom five; in the case of Cuba the pendulum swung through the fantastically wide arc of 245 points. The greatest net gainers (Brazil and Ecuador) and the greatest net losers (Colombia and Cuba) are also in this group. It is in this intermediate group, then, that the greatest flux appears; it is there that in the foreseeable future we may probably expect the most change, either upward or downward.

Turning to conclusions to be drawn from scrutinizing the data involving the criteria, the consensus is striking that conditions with regard to all criteria improved during the quinquennium 1955–60 and also during the total period covered by the four surveys. The impact on democratic attainment registered by the relative absence of ecclesiastical controls continued uniformly to be regarded as the most positive (or least negative) factor conditioning democratic achievement; by the same token, it reflected the lowest net gain during the decade and a half. It can similarly be concluded that foreign political domination of Latin American states—the controversial Cuban case apart—is not now significant: uniformly during the four surveys that criterion was given the second most favorable rating. Conditions surrounding free expression and internal unity have also been regarded favorably.

On the other hand, the educational level, the handling of governmental funds, the status of governmental administration, and conditions of local government have regularly been considered as leaving much to be desired. The toppling in the late 1950s of dictatorial regimes, so often supported by military props (beginning with that of Perón in 1955, *after* the 1955 survey was made) is reflected by the spectacular change in the consensus regarding civilian supremacy over the military: that criterion was put in last place in 1955 but in sixth in 1960, for a gain of 111 points. A roughly parallel improvement, for obviously related reasons, was shown in the consensus on freedom of elections: a gain of seven rank places and 118 points.

Freedom of elections, in the context described in the directive distributed to the respondents at the beginning of the surveys, is doubtless the most directly contributory of the fifteen criteria devised for the mensuration. Its close relationship to the other criteria is strikingly confirmed by the tabular material obtained from use of the chi-square and the coefficient of contingency correlation formulas. This is also true of the two other criteria thus tested: one, an essentially economic component of democracy (the standard of living) and the other a political or quasi-political component (civilian-military balance).

Democracy and political change in Latin America (or anywhere else, for that matter) are far more fluid and subtle phenomena than can be described and delimited simply by statistical data and techniques. But, the authors believe, the use of such tools gives a means of refining and confirming subjective and intuitive conclusions which must otherwise by their very subjectivity and intuitiveness remain partially unsatisfactory. The political scientist can probably, with profit, make more use of such tools.

Civil-Military Relations in Latin America*

L. N. McALISTER

It is hardly necessary to assert that the armed forces have been important factors in the historical development of the nations of Latin America. By bringing into association men from all parts of the national territory,

* L. N. McAlister, "Civil-Military Relations in Latin America," *Journal of Inter-American Studies*. III, No. 3 (July 1961), 341–350. Reprinted by permission of the *Journal of Inter-American Studies* and of the author.

by posing as the incarnation of the national spirit, and by teaching patriotism and exalting national virtues, they have been a significant influence in overcoming regionalism and localism.] By providing an avenue for advancement for members of lower social strata, they have encouraged social mobility.[In many countries they have contributed to the transition from traditional to modern societies through their work in constructing communications systems, their emphasis on general and technical education within their ranks, and by their demands for industrialization.[In the political sphere they have repeatedly overthrown the governments that created them; generals have employed the forces entrusted to them to make themselves heads of state; military factions have intervened in the political process in support of specific economic objectives or of broader ideologies. In a less spectacular fashion, the armed forces acting through political parties as in Mexico, or through officers occupying cabinet posts have exerted powerful influences on public policy.]

These facts are generally recognized and a great deal has been written about Latin-American "militarism." Existing literature, however, raises some serious conceptual and methodological problems. These may be defined by posing and commenting on a series of questions. In the first place,[do the interrelations between the military and society at large constitute a discrete sociological and historical problem susceptible to systematic description and analysis?] Some scholars concerned with general principles of social organization and with the history or sociology of regions other than Latin America have conceived of them in this fashion. Max Weber and later Gaetano Mosca recognized the importance of military factors in shaping societies and developed concepts and methods for dealing with the problem. Subsequently historians and social scientists have refined and expanded the ideas of Weber and Mosca and produced a substantial body of literature dealing with these interrelationships in general and with their manifestations in the United States, Germany, Japan, the Middle East, and Southeast Asia.

Perhaps because of their more obvious and immediate nature, the political and administrative aspects of this problem have been stressed; that is, the distribution of power within the state between civil and military elements. This area of study is commonly called "civil-military relations." The range of civil-military relations extends from situations in which civil authority is supreme to the direct and forcible usurpation of power by the military for nonmilitary ends.

The political role of the armed forces has likewise been stressed in Latin America. In general, however, Latin Americanists have been unwilling or unable to face up to the nature of interrelations between the military and civil elements of the state. The recent publications of Edwin Lieuwen, Víctor Alba, and Theodore Wyckoff are exceptions to this generalization. Much of Latin-American history has been written in terms of "Progress toward Democracy" or "The Struggle for Democracy." Within this teleological system the armed forces are regarded as "Obstacles to the Achievement of Democracy." Now no right-thinking person would deny that democracy is a desirable goal and it would be mean-spirited indeed not to wish the Latin Americans success in their struggle toward it. Yet, this conceptual framework encourages simplistic interpretations and explanations. The military is conceived of as a force external to and interfering with "normal" historical processes rather than as an integral element in them. In this position it can conveniently be regarded as a constant whose importance is recognized and accepted but which need not be described or analyzed systematically.

Second, if the importance of the military as a power factor in Latin America is accepted and the nature of its relations with the civil elements of the state can be regarded as a discrete historical and sociological problem, what is the scope of the problem and how may it be defined? The most commonly used term to describe the role of the armed forces in Latin America is "militarism." In the sense that it means the use of military force or threat of force to achieve nonmilitary ends, it is adequate. It has, however, two disadvantages. To many scholars it has a more specific usage; that is, a system or way of life which glorifies war, in which the military is a high-status profession, in which an entire nation is oriented toward military virtues and mores, and which has strong imperialist overtones. Such a system may have existed in Paraguay during the dictatorship of Francisco Solano López, and the G. O. U. in Argentina may have aspired to it. It has, however, been atypical of Latin America. Also, it does not cover instances in which armed forces have been nonpolitical and, if the problem is to be viewed broadly, such instances also require description and analysis. Another commonly-used expression is "the army in politics," but this term also excludes situations where the military has been nonpolitical. Moreover, it seems rather too mild an expression with which to describe the praetorian excesses of some Latin-American armies in the nineteenth century. "Civil-military relations" is also open to the latter criticism. It is, however, comprehensive enough to cover the range of phenomena involved in the problem and its accepted usage elsewhere is an argument for its adoption by Latin Americanists.

(3)   Third, [what is the structure of the problem?] As H. Stuart Hughes
remarks, historians are reluctant to make distinctions and tend to view
their problems as all of one piece. Thus *pronunciamientos, cuartelazos,
golpes de estado, machetismo,* militarism, praetorianism and all other
instances where armed forces transcend their purely military functions
tend to be viewed as phenomena of the same order and explainable
with more or less the same formula. Sometimes these phenomena are
even confused with military history. This is equivalent to regarding
the Assumption of Mary and the exercise of the ecclesiastical patronage
as belonging to the same order of things or of teaching surgery and
medical sociology in the same course. In fact a diversity of patterns
or systems of civil-military relations has existed in Latin America and
each pattern consists of complex interactions involving the structure,
status, and power of groups, both civil and military, and the motivations
of individuals, as these several elements are influenced by the political,
social, and economic environment. Thus the role of the Brazilian officer
corps in the overthrow of the Empire, the institutionalized gangsterism
prevailing in the contemporary Dominican Republic, and the *pronunciamientos* of Antonio López de Santa Anna are sharply different examples of civil-military relations involving different types of civil and military elements interacting in different environmental situations.

At a schematic level several types of civil-military relations in Latin
America may be defined. The first might be called the "Praetorian State."
[It is characterized by the frequent overthrow of governments by military
revolutions or *coups d'état* for nonmilitary purposes. It tends to be associated with a high degree of social and political disorganization and
a low degree of professionalism within the armed forces.] Examples are
Mexico during the first thirty years of the republic and Venezuela before
and after the dictatorship of Juan Vicente Gómez. The second might
be described as the "Gendarmist State." [It emerges when a single individual, generally but not always a military man, uses a mercenary army
to make himself master of the state, imposes social and political order,]
tames the army and uses it as a gendarmery to maintain himself in
power. The dictatorships of Gómez in Venezuela, and Anastacio Somoza
in Nicaragua are examples. The third type, after Harold Lasswell,
is the "Garrison State." [In it the military not only dominates or strongly
influences the political system but it attempts to militarize the state
and society at large. It occurs in connection with deep fears of aggression
from the outside or strong aggressive tendencies within and is associated
with a relatively high degree of political and social stability and a professionalized military establishment.] Paraguay under Francisco Solano

López might be taken as an example of this type. As noted above, it is atypical of Latin America. Fourth, is the "Civilist State." [It is characterized by civil supremacy over the military and exists in relatively stable societies with professionalized armed forces] Examples are Argentina between 1861 and 1930 and Uruguay since the turn of this century. [A fifth type may be emerging in Cuba but it is as yet difficult to identify.]

It should be added that these are ideal types in the Weberian sense. They do not exist in pure form and may shade or metamorphose into one another. Thus a strong *caudillo* may in certain circumstances transform a praetorian state into a gendarmist state as in the case of Porfirio Díaz and Rafael Trujillo, or the weakening or death of a leader or pressures within a society may turn a gendarmist state into a praetorian state as, for example, Mexico after 1910. Changes in the social or economic structure within praetorian or gendarmist states may result in the emergence of a civilist pattern as in contemporary Mexico, while conversely political, social or economic strains within a civilist state may result in the emergence of praetorian or gendarmist patterns as in the case of Argentina after 1930 or Colombia after 1949. These paradigms, it should be added, are not intended to present conclusions. They are devices to illustrate a point and to encourage the asking of pertinent questions.

The emphasis in the preceding paragraphs on the diversity of systems of civil-military relations in Latin America raises another question. Does Latin America itself constitute an adequate conceptual framework for the study of civil-military relations? Is it simply a convenient geographical and cultural delimitation or have civil-military relations in this region exhibited characteristic features or patterns? It is rather suggestive that Spain and Spanish America have had many similar experiences with their armed force. It might, therefore, be assumed that the Hispanic world is distinguished by typical patterns of civil-military relations. This assumption, however, is challenged by the fact that there seem to be greater structural and functional similarities between the Nasser regime in Egypt and the Perón regime in Argentina than between the latter and the dictatorships of Santa Anna in Mexico. It was recently suggested to the writer that there are certain "built-in" features of instability in the social and political organization of Moslem society which encourage military intervention in politics and that Hispanic civilization absorbed these features through its long contact and intermingling with the world of Psalm. The idea is challenging. Yet it does not account for the fact that armies in Burma and Thailand appear to have acted in much the same way in much the same circumstances as armies in Spain, Latin

America, and the Moslem world. This leads to the hypothesis that in general the patterns of civil-military relations in Latin America are typical of "developing areas." This might test out for the last decade when Latin America has undoubtedly shared many problems and aspirations with the emerging nations of the Middle East, Africa, and South and Southeast Asia. For earlier periods, however, it is not applicable. At the outbreak of World War Two, most of the latter nations were still dependencies or colonies of western powers while Latin America had enjoyed independence for over a century. Thus the argument comes full circle. It is quite possible that historically, Latin America or at least the Hispanic world provides a functional as well as a convenient unit for the study of civil-military relations.

If civil-military relations in Latin America can be conceived as a discrete problem of considerable diversity and complexity and if it is accepted that these relationships have been important factors in the historical development of the region, historians are confronted with a challenge and an opportunity. The problem, or perhaps it would be better to say, the complex of problems, may be redefined as follows: What are and what have been the patterns or systems of civil-military relations historically present in Latin America, why has one pattern prevailed at a particular time and place rather than another, and how and why have patterns changed? These questions pose others that are still more fundamental: What are the elements or ingredients whose interaction has produced patterns of civil-military relations in Latin America in general or in particular instances? How do these elements interact to produce a particular pattern and how do they and their interactions change in time to produce different patterns?

The statement of the problem in this fashion raises a final query: What methods will be most fruitful in providing answers to the preceding questions? It is not the purpose of this paper to lecture historians on their methods. We all know what they do and how they go about it. Without committing themselves to explicit assumptions and without explicit hypothesizing, they begin with empirical data and develop conclusions, interpretations, or generalizations in terms of how the data arranges itself or is arranged. Their normal procedure is, moreover, to work from the particular to the general, first the monograph, then the synthesis. Therefore it would seem that in view of the diverse character of civil-military relations in Latin America, a number of "case studies" dealing with particular countries and periods are needed before any convincing generalizations can be made. In undertaking such projects, the historian may use any one of several approaches: (1) he may describe and analyze a system or pattern of civil-military relations as it existed at a particular time and place in the past; (2) from this base he may "trace" and explain the process whereby this system changed to another; (3) without initially defining a system he may identify its elements and show how over a period of time they combined to form a system; (4) he may define a pattern as it existed at a particular time and place and then explain the process whereby it came to be what it was. In each case, if the method is narrative rather than analytical, patterns may remain implicit. These approaches and methods have and will yield sophisticated explanations and interpretations of civil-military relations as, for example, Gordon A. Craig's *The Politics of the Prussian Army, 1640–1945* and Yale C. Maxon's *Control of Japanese Foreign Policy; a Study of Civil-Military Rivalry, 1930–1945.* Without abandoning their humanistic and literary traditions, however, historians can profit from a selective and cautious use of the theory and methods of the social sciences. The potentials and dangers of this kind of borrowing have been explored at length by Social Science Research Council, *Bulletin 64* and by H. Stuart Hughes, Richard Hofstadter, Sir Isaiah Berlin, and others and it is unnecessary to review the argument and conclusions here. Instead certain general approaches and several specific methods will be discussed.

First, the sheer volume of sources now available and a growing awareness of the complexity of historical processes suggest that in many situations a more explicit definition of problems and assumptions would be a valuable aid to research. This entire paper is, in fact, an argument for such a procedure. Second, Lord Acton notwithstanding, it would be useful for research purposes to regard Latin-American armed forces "scientifically," that is, as social phenomena rather than as disasters and their relationships to civil society as a problem properly belonging to history and the social sciences rather than to demonology. It would, of course, be inhumane and illiberal not to deplore military excesses, but if "militarism" is to be regarded as a social disease, some knowledge of its pathology is necessary before remedies can be prescribed.

Third, the functional approach to political systems evolved by that new hybrid, the political sociologist, helps put the military in proper perspective. James S. Coleman *et al.* in their search for "a genuinely comparative and analytical approach" to comparative politics (*The Politics of the Developing Areas*) postulate that all societies from the primitive tribe to the modern nation state have political systems which perform the same set of functions although in different ways and through different structures; that is, associational and nonassociational interest groups, parliaments, bureaucracies and the like. These functions are: political recruitment and socialization; interest articulation, interest aggregation, political communication, rule-making, rule application, and rule adjudication. In this system, when armed forces cease to be neutral instruments of policy, they may be regarded as actively performing one or more of these functions, and civil-military relations involve how and to what extent they do so.

The trend of this discussion leads to an examination of the possible value to the historian of theoretical frameworks and models. Social scientists concerned with Latin America have by and large been of a traditional turn of mind and cannot provide us with models of political systems or of civil-military relations in that region. There are, however, some general models available for examination. Samuel P. Huntington in his *The Soldier and the State* identifies six elements that in various triangular combinations shape universal patterns of civil-military relations. These are: antimilitary ideology (within the society at large), promilitary ideology, low military political power, high military political power, high military professionalism, and low military professionalism. He states that the pattern most common to the Near East, Asia, and Latin America combines antimilitary ideology, high military political power, and low military professionalism. The systems of civil-military relations in Latin America which were constructed earlier in this paper are based extensively on Huntington's work and might themselves be regarded as primitive models. Stanislaw Andrzejewsky (*Military Organization and Society*) builds much more complex systems. He postulates various types of military organization deriving from triangular combinations of six elements: high military participation ratio (the ratio of the number of men under arms to the total population), low military participation ratio, high military subordination, low military subordination, high military cohesion, and low military cohesion. The several combinations are identified by neologisms. These models are then related to types of social organization. Although none of the examples given is drawn from Latin America, the type of military organization which appears to most closely fit that region is the Ritterian which is based on low M. P. R., low cohesion, and low subordination. The society in which such a type exists is characterized by steep social stratification and egalitarianism within the élite. The accompanying political form is a decentralized nobiliary republic.

This kind of conceptualization is uncongenial to most historians. It violates their highly particularistic and humanistic view of the social universe, and evokes among them emotions ranging from hilarity to deep hostility. These reactions derive in part, at least, from a misunderstanding of the use of models. They are intended not as the conclusions of prolonged and painstaking research but, as remarked above, are devices to facilitate the asking of pertinent questions and the ordering of data. It is not suggested that historians become model builders but those constructed by social scientists can be stimulating if employed with caution. For example, by pointing out the significance of military professionalism and ideology in any system of civil-military relations, Huntington's theoretical frameworks suggest lines of research that might illuminate this relationship in Latin America.

Finally, traditional historical methods are inadequate to eliminate the greatest single obstacle to the systematic study of civil-military relations in Latin America. As Huntington points out, the principal focus of any system of civil-military relations is the relation of the officer corps to the state. Without commenting on the adequacy of our knowledge of the structure of Latin-American states in general or particular, we have little except impressions based on random samples about those military groups in Latin America loosely and often interchangeably referred to as the 'officer corps,' the 'officer class,' and the 'officer caste.' Until more precise information is available about these elements, even the sociological validity of terms such as corps, class, and caste is doubtful. The techniques of group and élite analysis developed by social scientists can be of assistance in solving this problem. Morris Janowitz's careful study of the social origins, career motivations, career development, style of life, ideology, and self-image of the armed forces of the United States is an example of what can be done. If similar studies of Latin-American officer corps in several countries at different periods were available it would no longer be necessary to rely on vague generalities.

It would be convenient if Janowitz or others would do the job for us, but inasmuch as social scientists are concerned primarily with contemporary phenomena, it is likely that historians will have to strike out for themselves. It will be a difficult task. The successful use of social science methods depends to a large extent on the availability of large masses of quantitative data systematically arranged (such as censuses) and the use of interviews, questionnaires, field work, and the like. The historian has nothing but his documents written by persons who mischievously neglected to collect and systematize the data needed and which at best have been randomly collected and stored. His task, however, is not impossible, as Woodrow Borah and S. F. Cook, Sir Lewis Namier and Marc Bloch have demonstrated in their research on other types of historical problems.

The Military: A Revolutionary Force*

EDWIN LIEUWEN

Until well into the twentieth century, revolutions in Latin America were not social upheavals. They were political in nature, but they were not mass movements. The combatants were generally limited to rival military chieftains and their close adherents. Sometimes, in the background, interested members of the landed oligarchy or a small group of professional men would engage in the political intrigues, but the overwhelming majority of the population was not affected. The so-called revolutions were merely palace revolts, fights for the spoils of office amongst the military and civilian elite. When a revolt succeeded, the top personnel in government would be supplanted by the victors, but, for the masses, all that occurred was a change of masters.

Though extremely active in national politics, the Latin-American military, until very recently, did little to disturb the social order. On economic and social questions, the armed forces were generally cast in the role of preservers of the *status quo*. With the great majority of the population inarticulate, poverty stricken, and politically apathetic, the military leaders were under no pressure to change the existing social system nor did they show any inclination to do so. Throughout the nineteenth century they identified themselves with the propertied elite and often utilized their political office to amass fortunes and become landowners themselves.

During the twentieth century, however, the traditional social order—under which a praetorian military caste, a landed aristocracy, and a Catholic church hierarchy monopolized power, wealth, prestige, and influence—began to break down. Societies and economies began to undergo fundamental transformations which were reflected in the changing nature of politics. New constitutional forms began to reshape the environment. Though the extent and intensity of change were uneven, every nation in Latin America felt the impact of fundamental shifts in its own society and the world environment.

World War I marked the beginning of the end of the old system

* Edwin Lieuwen, "The Military: A Revolutionary Force," *Annals of the American Academy of Political and Social Sciences*, Vol. 334 (March 1961), pp. 30–40. (Footnotes in the original version have been omitted.)

under which Latin America's well-established economic and social organization was firmly tied to a stable old-world order. Fractures in the neat international system of trade and diplomacy precipitated by the 1914–1918 upheaval were compounded by such subsequent crises as the Great Depression, World War II, and the cold war. Added to this was the ideological impact of socialism, fascism, and communism, and the influence of the New Deal, all of which helped hasten the breakdown of the old order.

CONSERVATIVE ROLE

Until the time of World War II, the armed forces of Latin America generally played the role of defenders of the *status quo* in the face of the growth of popular pressures for social and economic change. When the war broke out in Europe, conservative generals were presiding in Bolivia, the Dominican Republic, Ecuador, Guatemala, Honduras, Nicaragua, Peru, El Salvador, Venezuela, and Paraguay. Traditionalist civilian regimes were maintained in office by the armed forces in Argentina, Panama, and Haiti. The army-backed Getulio Vargas and Fulgencio Batista dictatorships in Brazil and Cuba had lost much of their early radicalism, and had become, by this time, right-of-center regimes. Only in Chile, Colombia, Mexico, Costa Rica, and Uruguay were the military forces not playing an active and conservative political role.

Effect of World War II

The net effect of World War II was to freeze such traditionalist regimes in power. The wartime emergency provided dictatorial regimes with justification for outlawing all political experimentation and major social and economic reform for the duration. Also, the United States, whose overriding consideration was strategic, did its best to maintain stability and, accordingly, provided incumbent regimes with military and economic aid.

And yet the war produced pressures which made the maintenance of the *status quo* progressively more difficult. Trade disruption, as in World War I, gave great new impetus to industrialization and, when the transportation squeeze eased, to unprecedented exports of industrial raw materials and foodstuffs to the allies. But this wartime prosperity was not broadly based, for the traditionalist governments, despite inflation, often froze wages and prohibited strikes. The hardships suffered by the middle and lower income groups intensified social stresses and strains. It was merely a matter of time before popular pressure would break through the oligarchic dikes and bring in a flood of social change and reform.

The decade 1943–1953 was, in many Latin-American countries, one of revolt against the old order. Civilian foes of the *status quo* were joined by military ones, mostly young officers restless under a static armed forces organization that offered little opportunity for change and advancement. Toward the end of World War II, an assortment of disgruntled, patriotic, and ambitious colonels and majors began joining aspiring popular movements, and, as a result, there began to occur in Latin America a cycle of revolutions far more fundamental than the palace revolts of the past.

REVOLUTION AND REFORM

The first break-through came in Argentina in June 1943, when the Group of United Officers, a Fascist-inspired conspiratorial colonels' clique, seized control of the armed forces and toppled the traditionalist regime of President Ramón S. Castillo. Under the aegis of Colonel Juan Perón, who ultimately emerged as dictator, the military rebels made an alliance with labor and set up a radical, nationalistic regime whose announced aims were social justice and economic independence.

In Bolivia, another junior officers' movement, led by Major Gualberto Villaroel, came forward in December 1943 with a program very similar to Perón's. As in Argentina, the idealistic young officers led the proletarian masses against the domestic oligarchy and the foreign imperialists. The young officers had the firm backing of labor and middle-group elements represented in the popular National Revolutionary Movement (MNR). Villaroel and the MNR head, Victor Paz Estenssoro, made war upon the tin barons and the landlords by launching a revolutionary program of social reform and national reconstruction, until the whole experiment was stopped short by a counterrevolution which returned the old order to power in 1946.

In May of 1944, just before the scheduled presidential elections, the sociopolitical thaw came to Ecuador, where the oligarchy had been in firm control prior to World War II. Radical young-officer revolutionaries forced President Arroyo del Rio to resign, set up a military junta, then invited José María Velasco Ibarra, the people's choice, to take over the presidency.

Similarly, Guatemala's *ancien regime* came to an end in October of 1944 when young army officers made common cause with discontented civilian leaders and, in a successful revolution, deposed the *status quo* generals and the old oligarchy. A civilian-military junta was set up, and Juan Arévalo, a left-of-center intellectual, became the triumphant revolutionists' choice for president. His government promptly passed a rash of reform legislation directed toward expansion of education, protection of organized labor, improvement of social welfare, development of industry, and reform of agriculture.

The contagion of social revolution spread to Venezuela in October of 1945. Here, the traditionalist President, General Isaías Medina, whose legal term was about to expire, made plans for perpetuating Venezuela's customary political pattern under which senior army officers ran the government as their personal domain. These plans went awry, however, when a group of restless and disgruntled junior officers joined forces with the popular civilian opposition represented by the *Acción Democrática* (AD) party and, in a relatively bloodless coup, ousted the Medina regime. The new government, headed by AD's political and intellectual leader, Rómulo Betancourt, sharply increased taxes on the foreign oil companies and the larger Venezuelan businesses, encouraged labor to organize and assert its rights, thoroughly reorganized the educational system with an eye to reducing illiteracy, set in motion economic development and diversification programs, and drew up a blueprint for land reforms.

El Salvador's revolution, generated by young officers and popular forces, followed the familiar post-World War II pattern. It came in December 1948. Initially, this upheaval, spearheaded by vocally radical majors and colonels and backed by reform-minded middle-group intellectuals, appeared to signal the beginning of the end of militarism and feudalism in El Salvador, for the military-civilian provisional government made sweeping promises for honest government and social reforms.

Late liberal movements

A liberalizing revolution led by the military took place in Panama in 1952. In that year, Police Chief Colonel José Antonio Remón, with the obvious sympathy and backing of the hitherto ignored lower income groups in the society, seized control of the government which he promised to make the servant of all classes rather than only the privileged. He introduced social welfare measures, reduced corruption in government, thoroughly reorganized the country's finances, and promoted agricultural and industrial development.

Finally, in Colombia, the impetus to reform came in 1953. A general, Gustavo Rojas Panilla, led the movement, but his most enthusiastic support came from the junior officers. The background of the 1953 coup was five years of civil war growing out of the economic and political aspirations of the nation's newly awakened lower and middle income groups. The army's June 1953 coup aroused great popular enthusiasm, and most of the fighting in the countryside subsided as General Rojas promised to bring order and to hold elections as soon as possible. Like Perón, he began a program of broad social reform. He levied heavier taxes upon the upper income groups, adopted a social welfare program, sponsored government labor unions, and launched a "third force" political movement which appealed to the long neglected lower and middle groups in the society.

In four countries, social change proceeded apace either without positive encouragement or in face of outright resistance from the military. In Peru, in 1945, the armed forces temporarily adopted a neutral attitude when the middle-of-the-road candidate José Luis Bustamante won the presidency and the revolutionary *Aprista* party won control of Congress. Similiarly, in Brazil, the armed forces permitted labor-leftist candidate Getulio Vargas to assume the presidency following his victory in the 1950 elections. In Costa Rica, in 1948, the regular army was destroyed when it attempted to nullify the elections and prevent the winning reform candidate from taking office. The same thing occurred in Bolivia in 1952.

COUNTERREVOLUTION

Six years before the cycle of revolution and reform had run its course, it began to be overlapped by a new cycle of counterrevolution. As early as 1947, when the wave of social reform seemed to be carrying all before it and 85 per cent of Latin America's total population was living under broadly based, reform-minded regimes, political currents in some countries began to flow in the other direction. And, in this trend, as in the trend to the left, the armed forces were cast in a deciding role.

The reaction to popular reform governments began in 1947 and continued for an entire decade until nearly every government of this type had either been overturned or forced to adopt a more moderate course. The armed forces stepped in, either at the behest of the oligarchy or of the frightened middle class, to halt further leftward evolution. Reformist rulers lost a measure of popular support when they failed to deliver on demogogic promises, yet it does not appear that the people turned against them. Rather, the military was generally provoked to intervene by the middle and upper groups who reacted against deliberate efforts by leaders supported by labor to widen existing social cleavages. Often the military unmade the very revolutions they themselves had launched several years before.

In Ecuador, late in 1947, the armed forces decided the time had come to save the country from what they regarded as the demagogic rule of Velasco. He was unceremoniously ejected, whereupon a national unity coalition in 1948 elected the more moderate Galo Plaza Lasso to the presidency. Subsequently, the turbulence in Ecuador subsided, mainly because the social question, which loomed so important, was declared out-of-bounds as a political issue.

In Peru, the counterrevolution occurred in late 1948. Moderate President Bustamante, soon after his 1945 election, found himself caught between two extremist forces. The reformist *Aprista* party had a plurality in Congress, but the Conservative opposition brought the legislative machinery to a standstill by refusing to form a quorum. When the deadlock occurred, the oligarchy began conspiring with the armed forces. On October 27, 1948, the army overthrew the Bustamante government and outlawed the *Aprista* party. General Manuel Odría held power for eight years, during which time the armed forces increased their customary lion's share of the national budget and the oligarchy were made secure against such annoyances as land reform demands and labor agitation.

Similar to the October 1948 revolution in Peru was that which occurred a month later in Venezuela. Here the very young officers who had launched the popular and liberalizing revolution of 1945 began, after 1947, to become dissatisfied with the radical program of *Acción Democrática*. After several attempts had failed, a coup d'état succeeded in November of 1948. *Acción Democrática* was ousted, and the army once more took charge of the government. Clearly the army decided to halt the social revolution and to continue its long tradition of exclusive domination of Venezuela's politics. A military junta ruled till 1952, when Colonel Peréz Jiménez, after staging a notorious electoral farce, which clearly demonstrated popular antipathy to him, assumed the office of president. Thus, Venezuela once more returned to military dictatorship.

In El Salvador, too, the young officers of the popular, liberating revolution gradually began to turn their backs on social reform. By the early 1950's, the revolutionary movement had petered out. The colonels introduced modest welfare measures, but, faced by firm resistance from the planters, they no longer even mentioned agrarian reform or sweeping social changes. The net result of the 1948 revolution was the substitution of colonels for generals, and the introduction of slightly greater responsibility in the administration of government. The 1948 revolution, thus, did not turn out to be a revolution in any fundamental sense.

Carribbean movements

Resurgent militarism also hit the Caribbean at mid-century, but here the revolts were autonomous military movements rather than counter-revolutions; social questions were not paramount in the 1950 army coup in Haiti or in that of 1952 in Cuba.

The Guatemalan uprising of June 1954, however, was a genuine counterrevolution. Here, social questions were clearly important, but Communist participation and the international aspects of Guatemala's position confused the conflict. After Jácobo Arbenz won the presidency in 1950, the social revolution veered decidedly leftward; the energetic Communist minority got the ear of the new president and rapidly began to usurp control. However, the shipment of Soviet-bloc arms to Guatemala gave the exiled moderates under Colonel Castillo Armas, apparently with an indirect assist from the United States government, their opportunity to return in 1954.

In that same year, the armed forces of Brazil, backed by alarmed conservatives, intervened to oust the reform-minded regime of Getulio Vargas. Though the generals permitted Vargas to assume the presidency in 1950, they kept an extremely short rein on him. Faced with a moderate-conservative opposition majority in Congress, he was powerless, by constitutional means, to deliver on his campaign promises. As the country's economic deterioration and political stagnation continued, Vargas tried desperately to intrigue his way out of his constitutional limitations by manipulating strikes and by directing the pressure of the masses against existing institutions. But the generals became increasingly restless. Late in 1954, after an air corps major had been killed, apparently by one of the President's henchmen, the army stepped in and forced Vargas to resign, whereupon he committed suicide. Since then, constitutional order has been preserved in Brazil, but fundamental social reform has lagged.

Counterrevolution and reform

In the fall of 1955, the Perón regime in Argentina was brought to an end by the action of the military. Politically, the September 1955 revolution, inasmuch as it toppled a dictatorial regime, was a liberating action. Socially, however, since a heretofore labor-oriented government was now replaced by one supported by the middle and upper income groups in the society, it was a counterrevolution. In 1958 elections were conducted on schedule and normal constitutional processes were restored as the military junta transferred political control to a moderate regime headed by Dr. Arturo Frondizi. Since then, the military has not hesitated to use force to protect the incumbent government against any resurgence of Peronism.*

The last of the rightist-military reactions occurred in Colombia in 1957. When, after the 1953 revolution, the traditional parties recognized that General Rojas not only intended to perpetuate himself and the army in power but also that he wanted to lead a social revolution, they resisted, whereupon civil war again broke out. Politicians from both parties and their presses went into uncomprising opposition, and Rojas reacted by tightening his dictatorship. Political tensions came to a head in the spring of 1957 when Rojas made known his determination to continue in power beyond the expiration of his term of office in 1958. Early in May, violence broke out in the capital, whereupon the army, faced with the prospect of intensification of the nine-year-old civil war, turned against their leader. Rojas was ousted on May 10, 1957, and a new military junta took over. In 1958 a moderate civilian government headed by President Alberto Lleras Camargo assumed power.

In summary, then, it is clear that the armed forces have been playing a key role in Latin America's revolution of rising expectations. In the decade 1943 to 1953, they intervened directly to break the sociopolitical stranglehold of the traditionalist rulers in Argentina, Bolivia, Ecuador, Guatemala, Venezuela, El Salvador, Panama, and Colombia. However, none of the regimes resulting from these liberating revolutions lasted more than a decade. The armed forces' brief experiment as leaders of social reform had come to an end everywhere by 1957. In all the above countries they returned, at least temporarily, to conduct a holding action for the right against pressures from the left.

DECLINING ROLE OF MILITARY

The rapid disappearance of military rulers from the Latin-American scene over the past five years suggests that the armed forces' involvement in the Latin-American social crises may be waning. For example, in March of 1955, thirteen of the twenty Latin-American countries were ruled by military presidents who had originally come to power by force. Then, suddenly, in the space of less than four years, the great majority

---

* Indeed, when Peronists won several congressional seats and gubernatorial posts in about half the provinces in 1962, the military deposed Frondizi and annulled the elections. [ed.]

of these leaders were removed from power in a most spectacular fashion and with a degree of rapidity unprecedented in the entire history of the area. During 1955, Remón was assassinated in Panama and Perón, as already mentioned, was toppled by revolution in Argentina. The following year General Anastasio Somoza was assassinated in Nicaragua, General Paul Magloire was driven from power in Haiti by a general strike, and General Manuel Odría was obliged to retire in Peru following the failure of his candidate to win the elections. During 1957 Colonel Carlos Castillo Armas was assassinated in Guatemala, and General Gustavo Rojas Pinilla was driven from power, as mentioned, in Colombia. The year 1958 witnessed the downfall of General Marcos Pérez Jiménez in Venezuela by revolution and of General Carlos Ibáñez del Campo in Chile by constitutional means. In January of 1959, General Fulgencio Batista and the armed forces were overwhelmed by the revolutionaries in Cuba. In October of 1960, Colonel José María Lemus was ousted from the presidency in El Salvador.

Remaining military leaders

Accordingly, today the number of military officers in presidential chairs in Latin America has been reduced to just three: General Rafael Trujillo in the Dominican Republic, General Alfredo Stroessner in Paraguay, and General Miguel Idigoras Fuentes in Guatemala.*

Though there has been unmistakably a sudden, pronounced antimilitaristic trend underway in Latin America over the past five years, it is premature to attempt to draw any definite conclusions with respect to its duration and probable significance. However, it is well to bear in mind that repeatedly in the past there have been alternating trends toward and away from military rule in Latin America, and that, accordingly, there can be no assurance that the political pendulum which is currently swinging toward the civilian leaders will not again revert to army officers.

Military influence

Also, despite the recent disappearance of so many uniformed presidents, the sociopolitical influence of the military is still very pronounced

---

* As of March 1966 the number of military presidents had doubled; the list then included: Colonel Enrique Peralta Azurdia in Guatemala, Colonel Julio A. Rivera in El Salvador, General Osvaldo López Arellano in Honduras, Admiral Ramón Castro Jijón in Ecuador, General Alfredo Ovando Candia in Bolivia, General Alfredo Stroessner in Paraguay, and General Humberto Castello Branco in Brazil. [ed.]

in two thirds of the Latin-American republics. And, in all these countries, the armed forces are acting as a drag upon the area's social revolution. In Paraguay, under General Stroessner, there has flourished the most extreme case of predatory praetorianism ever since May of 1954 when the armed forces declared a moratorium upon all civilian political activity, set up an all-military regime, and, subsequently, helped themselves annually to more than half the government's total revenues. The Dominican Republic has an equally primitive and predatory, but more personalistic, military government which General Trujillo has maintained ever since 1930 by brutal dictatorial methods. The Somoza family—Luis Somoza is president—and the *guardia nacional*—Tachito Somoza is its commander—continues to rule and exploit Nicaragua in the manner to which they have been accustomed since 1933. In Haiti, the tenure of President François Duvalier, like that of his predecessors in office, depends not so much upon what he does for the welfare of the country as it does upon how well he looks after the army. In Panama, though the civilian oligarchy has, since 1955, returned to dominate the executive branch of the government, the police—now called the *guardia nacional*—remain, as they have ever since the 1930's, the key force behind the scenes and the ultimate political arbiter. Liberal President Ramón Villeda Morales' reform program for Honduras has been drastically watered down in the face of the traditional conservatism of the armed forces and their threats to intervene and assume their customary political monopoly. In El Salvador, the armed forces, ever since 1930, have dominated the nation's politics and administration. They are essentially instruments for the preservation of the *status quo*. In Guatemala, the strength and stability of General Idigoras' caretaker-type government today rests in the last analysis upon the support of the armed forces. Civilian government has prevailed in Peru since 1956 when the alliance between the military leaders and the civilian oligarchy collapsed, but the armed forces stand ready to check radical change, either at the instigation of the oligarchy or if their own traditional privileges and emoluments are put in jeopardy by civilian groups. Since the 1945 revolution, Venezuela has oscillated between traditionalist military dictatorship and civilian democratic government, and, although the latter has been in control since the beginning of 1959, the century-long political omnipotence of the armed forces prior to 1945 suggests that military reaction, though currently dormant, is far from dead in Venezuela.

In Argentina, the moderate Frondizi government continues to rely heavily upon the armed forces to protect it against the onslaughts of the outlawed *Peronista* party. In Brazil, the armed forces, in their role of guarantors of constitutional processes, may be expected to come forth whenever they feel it again necessary to save the country from leftist demagogy and radical social reform. In remains to be seen what attitude the Colombian armed forces will take as social tensions in that country once more intensify. In Ecuador where the past three presidential elections have taken place under civilian control, the noninvolvement of the armed forces in sociopolitical problems appears to be taking on an air of permanence.

In only one country can it be said that the armed forces are today active agents of social reform. In Cuba, this is the role now being played by Castro's liberation army, but even here the whole movement has been perverted by communism.

In only five countries are the armed forces definitely not involved in the area's revolution of rising expectations: in Chile and Uruguay, where they have become nonpolitical institutions; in Costa Rica, where the army has been eliminated entirely; and in Mexico and Bolivia, where the army has been effectively subordinated to the civilian leadership of the ruling revolutionary party.

MEANING FOR UNITED STATES

The profound military involvement in Latin America's social revolution has some very serious implications for United States policy, for the United States since World War II has been cooperating with and building up the Latin-American armed forces. On the eve of World War II, United States military missions began to take over the job of advising and training Latin America's armed forces. During the war itself, the Latin-American armed forces were built up with $400 million worth of lend lease military equipment. Military aid to Latin America was cut off in the immediate postwar period, but during the 1950's military assistance in an amount roughly equivalent to the World War II lend lease aid has been granted to twelve Latin-American nations, with whom military defense assistance agreements have been signed. In addition, the twenty Latin-American republics have thus far received about $200 million worth of military equipment under the reimbursable aid provisions of the Mutual Security Act.

Now the official explanation for such aid, since World War II, is to strengthen the hemisphere against Communist aggression both from within and without. Military aid is ostensibly designed not only to add to Latin America's limited military capabilities, but also to stimulate Latin-American nations to strengthen themselves, for, in exchange for such aid, the recipient government is obligated to increase its defense capacities.

As a strictly military proposition, however, the military assistance program for Latin America makes little sense. Despite the programs, the military power and war-making potential of the Latin-American states count for practically nothing in the world today. The fact is that United States military planners have no real desire, since the basic requirements are missing, to prepare Latin America's armed forces for a meaningful military role in the cold war, or in a hot one.

Political objectives

On close analysis, it becomes readily apparent that the real objectives of United States military programs in Latin America are primarily political. The political orientation of Latin America in the cold war is of vital importance to the United States, and the great importance attached to military assistance in securing Latin America's political co-operation flows in a large measure from the strong internal political role played by Latin America's armed forces and their great and continuous desire for more and more arms. Of course, the United States is not unaware, as it was in World War II, that military assistance helps keep friendly and co-operative governments in power. Military aid obviously improves the recipient government's ability to maintain internal stability, not only against Communist subversion but also against the threat of any violent social upheaval or ultranationalist revolution that might bring to power a government unfriendly to the United States.

Now a fundamental problem has arisen from the fact that while Latin America after World War II began undergoing sweeping political and social changes, the United States was fixing its attention almost exclusively on the cold war. Thus, while the United States believed that military security of the hemisphere against the Communist threat was the paramount problem, Latin Americans insisted that their internal problems and social problems, which the United States tended to ignore, were of greater importance.

APPRAISAL

United States military policies aimed at stability, security, and opposition to communism, may have inadvertently interfered with sociopolitical changes and held up Latin America's revolution of rising expectations.

In countries where the energies of the armed forces were traditionally devoted to internal politics, military equipment and support from the United States was probably to some degree converted into political power. Where civilian and military elements are vying for power, United

States military aid may have unwittingly tipped the balance in favor of the armed forces.

In Brazil, for example, following the receipt of nearly $300 million in lend lease equipment during World War II, the armed forces assumed the right to depose Vargas after the war. According to Lawrence Duggan, it was this military aid that inclined the officers towards politics. In Colombia, United States military aid and assistance in the 1941–1953 period must certainly be considered as one contributing factor that helped to tip the political balance, bringing the Colombian army back into politics in the 1953–1957 period after a half century of civilian rule. Also, insofar as the military aid programs have increased the political influence of the armed forces, democracy has generally suffered, for the military, far more often than not, resorted to nondemocratic procedures to achieve the internal order and stability which both they and the United States, for quite different reasons, so ardently desired.

The United States, of course, has little choice but to deal with the Latin-American armed forces as a military organization. However, while doing so, it should not fail to keep in mind that the military's role is primarily a political one and that as its physical power is strengthened so is its capacity to exert an influence on the social problem. What makes the problem particularly explosive is that the United States, with its military assistance programs, has entered the picture just at that juncture when the old order of society is at the point of breakdown. The old oligarchy, as well as the military allied with it, quite understandably exploit what the United States conceives to be its security needs in order to save themselves. Their solicitude for hemisphere defense springs from the use they hope to make of it, not to stop Soviet aggression, but rather to stop social change. The result is that opposing social forces, which comprise the majority of the population, rightly or wrongly tend to hold the United States at least partially responsible for preserving the order they felt they were well on the way toward destroying when the cold war began.

It is because of the pressing Latin-American social problem—that of finding new political and social institutions which will satisfy the demands of new groups and provide outlets for their energies without dissolving society into chaos—that United States military programs may be playing directly into the hands of the enemy against whom they are directed. Robert J. Alexander's recent study of communism in Latin America demonstrates that where the effect of military aid has been to underwrite backward societies and stifle reforms, as for example in Paraguay, the Dominican Republic, Nicaragua, Peru, and Venezuela, United States policies have unwittingly helped "to break down the barriers between the genuine advocates of the Latin-American social revolution and the Communists." This is because these policies provide the Communists, who are well aware of the potential of popular discontent, with the opportunity to co-operate and make cause with civilian resistance to militarism. The recent course of Cuban history sharply illustrates this point.

Now that the United States government has very recently agreed to participate in resolving Latin America's social problems and has promised greater economic assistance toward that end, new problems arise. Is there perhaps a basic conflict between the military and economic components of our foreign policy? Is it possible to continue to emphasize security and at the same time support social reform?

Certainly it would be unwise and fruitless to grant economic aid to military or military-backed regimes bent on preserving an outworn order. It would seem that in granting aid for social reform, preference ought to go to those countries with broadly based civilian governments. It would also seem that militarism can be discouraged to the extent that United States economic assistance is wisely used to relieve some of the pressures that exist among large groups of discontented people in the recipient nation.

Politics, Social Structure and Military Intervention in Latin America*

GINO GERMANI
and
KALMAN SILVERT

The recent politico-military events of Turkey, Pakistan, Egypt, and even France demonstrate that the application of unabashed armed might to the solution of civic problems is not peculiar to Latin America, nor indeed a phenomenon to be correlated only with economic underdevelopment. Public violence and political instability in Latin America have all too often been treated either as merely comic or else a manifestation of "spirit," "temperament," or "Latin blood." Riots in the streets of Buenos Aires are no less tragic than riots in the streets of Algiers—and

* Reprinted from the *European Journal of Sociology*, II (1961), pp. 62–81, by permission of the authors and the publisher.

no less related to the basic facts of social disorganization as they may be reflected in crises of political legitimacy and consensus.

Military intromission in the political power structure always indicates, of course, at least a relative inability of other social institutions to marshal their power effectively, and at most an advanced state of institutional decomposition. This is to say, if the armed forces are viewed as having a limited and specialized set of functions having only to do with internal order and external defense, then a widening of castrensic activities into other social domains implies a generally weakened and sick social system, no matter the country or even the special cultural conditions concerned. This premise suggests several ways of constructing typologies of civil-military relations: one possibility is to order the types of social pathology to be found, and then to relate them to the historical facts of politico-military action; another is to order types of public violence, and once again to relate these to the real types of military interventions; and still a third alternative suggests itself in the direct listing of the institutional arrangements between the military establishment and the political institution treated as a variable dependent upon other social factors. This article will employ the latter procedure as being of the most immediate analytical utility, even though direct correlations between military action and the general state of social and economic development are at best vague.

Most Latin American countries have reached their first century and a half of independent existence. However, their social development into national states lagged behind formal independence and it is only now that a few of them are reaching a stage of full nationhood. While in some countries the breakdown of the traditional structure began in the last quarter of the nineteenth century, in many others a similar process of structural change did not start until the last two or three decades of the present century. Furthermore, one must remember that nowhere, not even in the most "advanced" Latin American nations, may it be said that the transition is complete.

In this transitional process we shall distinguish a series of successive "stages" so that the degree of development reached by any single Latin American country can then be described and compared with others. It is hardly necessary to emphasize the intrinsic limitations of such a procedure: nevertheless, it seems the most convenient one to yield a short-hand description of the present situation, while at the same time retaining a clear awareness of the total dynamics of the process. It must be added that this "model" of the transition is the result of a schematization of the actual historical process as it has been observed to take place in Latin America.

TABLE I

[...] No data. *1940. (1950 circa) The typology

COUNTRIES	% MIDDLE AND UPPER STRATA	% IN PRIMARY ACTIVITIES	% IN CITIES OF 20,000 AND MORE INHABITANTS	% MIDDLE AND UPPER URBAN STRATA	% LITERATES	UNIVERSITY STUDENTS PER 1,000 INHABITANTS

Group A: (a) *Middle strata: 20% and more;* (b) *cultural, psychological and political existence of a middle class;* (c) *ethnic and cultural homogeneity; national identification and considerable level of participation in different spheres;* (d) *urban/rural differences and geographical discontinuity exist, but to a lesser extent than in other Latin American countries.*

COUNTRIES	% MIDDLE AND UPPER STRATA	% IN PRIMARY ACTIVITIES	% IN CITIES OF 20,000 AND MORE INHABITANTS	% MIDDLE AND UPPER URBAN STRATA	% LITERATES	UNIVERSITY STUDENTS PER 1,000 INHABITANTS
Argentina ⎫ urban predominance	36	25	48	28	87	7.7
Uruguay ⎬	...	22	50	...	95	5.2
Chile ⎭	22	35	43	21	80	3.9
Costa Rica rural predominance	22	57	18	14	80	3.9

Group B: (a) *Middle strata: between 15 and 20% (approx.) heavily concentrated in some areas of the country;* (b) *cultural, psychological and political existence of a middle class;* (c) *ethnic and cultural heterogeneity; pronounced inequalities in the degree of participation in national society and in other aspects;* (d) *strong regional inequalities with concentration of urbanization and industrialization in certain areas and rural predominance in the greater part of the country.*

COUNTRIES	% MIDDLE AND UPPER STRATA	% IN PRIMARY ACTIVITIES	% IN CITIES OF 20,000 AND MORE INHABITANTS	% MIDDLE AND UPPER URBAN STRATA	% LITERATES	UNIVERSITY STUDENTS PER 1,000 INHABITANTS
Mexico lesser survival of traditional pattern	17*	56	24	...	59	0.9
Brazil greater survival of traditional pattern	15	62	20	13	49	1.2

Group C: (a) *Middle strata between 15 and 20% (approx.);* (b) *emerging middle class (but there is no agreement as to its degree of auto-identification);* (c) *ethnic and cultural heterogeneity, pronounced inequalities in the degree of participation in national society and other aspects;* (d) *pronounced discontinuity between rural/urban areas and strong regional inequalities:*

COUNTRIES	% MIDDLE AND UPPER STRATA	% IN PRIMARY ACTIVITIES	% IN CITIES OF 20,000 AND MORE INHABITANTS	% MIDDLE AND UPPER URBAN STRATA	% LITERATES	UNIVERSITY STUDENTS PER 1,000 INHABITANTS
Cuba ⎫ urban predominance	22	44	37	21	76	3.9
Venezuela ⎭	18	44	31	16	52	1.3
Colombia rural predominance	22	58	22	12	62	1.0

Group D: (a) *Middle strata: less than 15%; emergent middle strata in some countries, but clear persistence in all, in varying degrees, of the traditional pattern;* (b) *ethnic and cultural heterogeneity in almost all;* (c) *vast sectors of the population still marginal;* (d) *rural predominance in general; regional inequalities.*

COUNTRIES	% MIDDLE AND UPPER STRATA	% IN PRIMARY ACTIVITIES	% IN CITIES OF 20,000 AND MORE INHABITANTS	% MIDDLE AND UPPER URBAN STRATA	% LITERATES	UNIVERSITY STUDENTS PER 1,000 INHABITANTS
Panama	15	55	22	15	70	2.6
Paraguay	14	54	15	12	66	1.3
Peru	...	60	14	...	42	1.6
Ecuador	10	51	18	10	56	1.4
El Salvador	10	64	13	9	57	0.5
Bolivia	8	68	20	7	32	2.0
Guatemala	8	75	11	6	29	0.1
Nicaragua	...	71	15	...	38	0.7
Dominican Republic	...	70	11	...	43	1.2
Honduras	4	76	7	4	35	0.7
Haiti	3	77	5	2	11	0.7

A tentative simple typology of the social structure of the twenty Republics has been summarized in Table I. In constructing it we have taken into account those traits which we consider most relevant to the problem at hand: namely, economic structure; the social stratification system (especially the existence of a self-identifying middle stratum); the degree of economic and cultural homogeneity and of participation in a common culture and in national life; the degree of national identification; and geographical discontinuities in the socio-economic level of the various regions within each country.[1] While we do not identify the successive "stages" of the historical scheme with the different "types" of social structure described in the Table, we suggest that various degrees of "delayed development" may have resulted in situations similar to those indicated in the typology.

STAGES 1 AND 2. PREDOMINANCE OF THE TRADITIONAL SOCIAL STRUCTURE. FORMAL NATIONAL INDEPENDENCE AND CIVIL WARS

The common trait of these first two stages of Latin American development is the persistence of the "traditional" society which maintained its essential features throughout the political upheaval and radical changes in formal political organization.

STAGE 1. REVOLUTIONS AND WARS FOR NATIONAL INDEPENDENCE

At the time when they gained their independence (in most cases *circa* 1810) the Latin American countries may be said to have approximated the "ideal type" of the "traditional society": subsistence economy

---

[1] The table appeared in a slightly modified form in Gino GERMANI, "The strategy of fostering social mobility," paper prepared for the Seminar on *The Social Impact of Economic Development in Latin America* (Proceedings publ. by the UNESCO, forthcoming). Only part of the basic data are shown in the table.

For the main concepts used in formulating the scheme, see: G. GERMANI, *Integración política de las masas* (Buenos Aires, CLES, 1956); "El autoritarismo y las clases populares," in *Actas IV Congreso Latino Americano de Sociologia* (Santiago, Chile, 1957); *Politica e Massa* (Minas Gerais, Universidade de Minas Gerais, 1960); K. SILVERT, "Nationalism in Latin America" in *The Annals of the American Academy of Political and Social Science,* 334 (1961), 1–9; of the relevant bibliography on this subject we took especially into account: S. M. LIPSET, *Political Man* (New York, Doubleday, 1960), and D. LERNER, *The Passing of Traditional Society* (Glencoe, the Free Press, 1958).

marginal to the world market and a two strata system characterized by little or no mobility and caste-like relationships. The Spaniards and Portuguese were the ruling group, and immediately below them we find the small élite of the *créoles*, of European descent and mainly urban, who while deprived of political power still belonged (subjectively as well as objectively) to the higher stratum and retained a dominant position from the economic and cultural point of view. It was this creole élite who brought about the revolutions and achieved national independence with support of the lower strata, including the *Mestizos* and even part of the outcast group of the Negroes and the Indians who filled the armies of the independence wars. The creoles were inspired mainly by the American model, the French revolution, and seventeenth century illuminism. They attempted to establish modern democratic states with their corresponding symbols: the "constitution," the "parliament," the elected rulers, and so on. There were, however, two basic limitations to their action. The first may be found in the creole élite itself: it was the expression of a traditional structure and in spite of its ideology, it still perceived itself as an aristocracy widely separated from the popular strata. The democracy they dreamed of was the "limited" democracy of the wealthy, the educated, the well-bred of proper descent. On the other hand, the prevailing state of the society was scarcely adequate to the establishment of a representative democracy: powerful geographical as well as ethnic, cultural, and economic factors made such an undertaking simply utopian.

STAGE 2. ANARCHY, "CAUDILLISMO," AND CIVIL WARS

The outcome of such a situation was simply that, even before the end of the long and cruel wars of independence against the Spaniards, the constitutional "fictions" created by the urban élites broke down. The political and institutional vacuum resulting from the disappearance of the colonial administration and the failure of the "constitutional fictions" resulted in the geographical fragmentation of political power: the rise of local "caudillos" often of *mestizo* or even Indian origin, frequent local wars, and a rapid succession of military coups.

The army of the "caudillos" was seldom anything more than an armed band, under the leadership of a self-appointed "general." At this stage we do not find in Latin America any professional army, but the political rule of the caudillos often adopted some symbols both of the army and of the democratic regimes: the geographical fragmentation took the form of a "federal" state, the absolute rule of the caudillo that of the "president" and, at the same time, "general" of the army. During this stage the social structure remained very much the same. This was especially true of the primitive state of the economy, the stratification system, and the isolation, both economic and social, of most of the population.

STAGES 3 TO 6. TRANSITION OF THE SOCIAL STRUCTURE FROM THE "TRADITIONAL" TO THE "INDUSTRIAL" PATTERN

While some countries show a clear succession of these four stages, in the majority of the cases there is much overlapping. Nevertheless the scheme is useful as a conceptualization of the transition towards a mature national state: that is, toward political unification and organization, attainment of certain preconditions of economic growth, changes in the social structure, and progressive enlargement of social participation (including political participation).

There is one very important and well known feature of this process which must be emphasized here; the unevenness of the transition, the fact that some groups within the society and some areas within each country remained unchanged and underdeveloped while others underwent great changes. This is a familiar fact in most countries, but in Latin America (as in other underdeveloped areas) it acquired a particular intensity. The typical *dual* character of the countries both from the *social* and the *geographical* points of view is expressed in the contrasts between the socially "developed" higher and middle strata and the "backward," more primitive, lower strata; the cleavage between certain areas in which most of the urban population, industrial production, educated people, wealth, and political power are concentrated, and the rest of the country, predominantly rural, with a subsistence economy, illiterate, and politically inactive and powerless. The transition, in Latin America, cannot be understood without taking into full account the repercussions of this dual structure.

Social development involves first the extension of the modern way of life to a growing proportion of the people living in the most favored areas (the emergence of an urban middle class and a modern industrial proletariat in the "central" sector of a country), and second the incorporation—by way of massive internal migration or by geographical diffusion of industrialization and modernization—of the marginal population living in "peripheral" areas. The circumstances of the process, and especially its speed, are of the utmost importance for the political equilibrium of the country.

STAGE 3. UNIFYING DICTATORSHIPS

The struggle between the caudillos within a given country was eventually replaced by the hegemony of one among them. The unity of the state was restored and a degree of order and stability achieved. However, the character of these "unifying dictatorships" differed very widely. For our present purpose they may perhaps be classified into two main categories: "regressive" dictatorships, which maintained completely intact the traditional pattern, and "enlightened" dictatorships, which introduced at least some modernizing measures. The most important difference between the two lies in the economic sphere. While the former maintained their countries isolated from the world market, and the old subsistence economy continued to predominate, the latter fostered at least a minimum degree of economic development, through the construction of means of transport and communication, some modernization of agriculture, some educational measures, organization of the public bureaucracy, and so forth.

Generally it was these relatively more enlightened authoritarian regimes, as well as the "limited democracies," which marked the beginning of the transformation of the Latin American countries into producers of raw materials and their integration into the world market. Foreign capital was introduced, the beginnings of industrialization took place, and these changes began to produce some impact on the social structure. While they left untouched the main features of the traditional pattern— the concentration of land ownership, the two class system, the isolation of the great majority of the population—they created certain dynamic factors which in time produced further changes making for transition. The integration of the country into the world market and the degree of economic modernization often fostered the emergence of new urban middle occupational strata. While they remained a relatively small proportion of the total population, and significantly, continued to be identified with the traditional upper class, these urban strata also represented an essential precondition for further changes.

One important feature of the enlightened dictatorships is the attempt at a "professionalization" of the army and the fact that while the dictators were often military men they tried to control the army itself, submitting the unruly military caudillos to the central political authority of the state.

STAGE 4. "REPRESENTATIVE DEMOCRACY WITH LIMITED PARTICIPATION"

The changes in the social structure under a "limited democracy" were often only slightly more pronounced than those induced by the "enlightened" dictatorships. In other cases, however, the modification was more substantial. This happened chiefly when the modernizing attitudes of the elites were bolder and the resulting economic and cultural changes more profound. In some cases the contribution of massive immigration from Europe—a part of the modernizing policy of the elite—was a decisive element in the transformation of the social structure.

The most significant feature of this stage is the formal functioning of democracy, the existence of a party system, the periodical replacement of the government through elections, freedom of the press and other "constitutional" guarantees. Another and no less essential feature is the "limitation" of democracy to only a fraction of the total population. This limitation is twofold. On the one hand the existing deep cleavage between developed and backward areas within a given country involved the almost complete exclusion of a substantial proportion of the population, practically all those living in the "peripheral" areas. On the other hand, a similar cleavage existed within the "central" areas, between the elites and the emerging middle strata, on the one side, and the lower groups on the other. Often the cleavage had also an ethnic basis even if we cannot speak of "racial" discrimination in Latin America. Both kinds of cleavage—geographical and social—meant the lack of a common basis for a real national identification on the part of a substantial proportion of the population, and of course a lack of cultural and economic participation. In consequence, the functioning of democracy was really limited in the sense that only the higher strata and the small newly formed middle groups (which identified themselves with the elite) living in the "central areas" did participate in one way or another in the political process (even at the lowest level of simple voting).

However, in those countries where the middle occupational strata could expand to a higher proportion of the total population and because of their immigrant origin, or their economic and cultural significance or some other causes, were able to acquire a greater psychological and social autonomy, strong political movements appeared which strove for a more real and enlarged democracy. In general such a situation was reached only in the most advanced areas of the country.

STAGE 5. "REPRESENTATIVE DEMOCRACY WITH ENLARGED PARTICIPATION"

The typical structure corresponding to this stage is still that of the dual society referred to previously, involving the geographical juxtaposition of a modern "central region" and "backward" peripheral regions. The former comprised most of the urban population, the industry, the literates, the middle strata and the modern urban proletariat, including, of course, the industrial workers. This region would contrast sharply with other regions which still remained—even though to a lesser degree—outside this development. Democracy, social, cultural and political participation, as well as national identification, included mostly people residing in the "advanced" areas. The difference from the previous stage of "limited" democracy is that now not only the middle strata would usually participate directly in the government or even control it, but the urban proletariat of the "central" region would also be included through the unions and political parties. The spread of nationalism—right and left—and of different "ideologies of industrialization" are characteristic of this phase.

STAGE 6 (A). "REPRESENTATIVE DEMOCRACY WITH TOTAL PARTICIPATION"

With the growing integration of previously marginal social groups and geographical areas into the cultural, economic and political life of the nation as a whole, with the acquisition of national loyalties and identification by all the inhabitants, and with the resulting higher degree of cultural and economic homogeneity of the various groups in society, we reach a new stage which we may call, for lack of a better term, that of "full nationhood." A high degree of urbanization, total literacy and a high average education, a high degree of occupational differentiation and a high proportion of the urban occupational middle strata which may now well be nearly 50% of the active urban employed population, are the other well known traits which characterize such a stage.

While in older nations, cultural homogeneity and national loyalty may not be accompanied by a high degree of economic development, in most instances "mass consumption"—that is, mass participation in the material culture of the industrial society—may also be regarded as one of the traits of the phase of "total participation democracy." From the political point of view it means effective full citizenship for the entire population, irrespective of area of residence or of socio-economic or ethnic affiliation. As a result, an important indicator of this stage is that of political participation at the level of voting of a substantial majority of the adult population of both sexes[2].

STAGE 6 (B). TOTAL PARTICIPATION
THROUGH "NATIONAL-POPULAR" REVOLUTIONS

This pattern, which is increasingly typical of many underdeveloped countries—either under the form of communist totalitarianism or under the form of nationalistic authoritarianism—has also appeared in Latin America. It is obvious that the kind of "political participation" which takes place in the framework of such "national-popular" regimes is quite different from that of "representative democracy." However, it would be a mistake not to recognize the tremendous change involved for the marginal strata of the "dual" underdeveloped society.

While the national popular regime negates the very values which are the basis of participation in "representative democracy"—such as civil liberties—it does incorporate the marginal strata into the economic, cultural and political life of the nation. It induces their forceful "national-ization," and results in a change from passive acceptance (through internalized norms) to "compulsory participation." In Latin America, perhaps more than in other countries, "national-popular" regimes appear to be the outcome of the failure to develop into a full "representative democracy." From this point of view such an outcome appears to be connected with the failure in the formation of adequate channels of political expression for the social groups which successively emerge from the isolation and marginality in which they lived within the traditional social structure.

Such seems to have been the role of both "limited" and "enlarged" democracy: to prepare the institutional means and adequate outlets for the political pressure of the emerging larger strata of the population,

---

[2] The phenomenon of "non-voting" and "political" apathy which appear in some developed countries (as the U.S.A., for instance) has a different meaning from the non-participation of the marginal and isolated sectors in underdeveloped countries.

within the framework of "representative democracy." Obviously, this is not only a political problem. The successful integration into such a framework also requires an expanding and modernizing economy, at least sufficient to give, even at a very modest level, an increasing degree of participation in the material culture of the industrial civilization, and this latter requirement is certainly more acute today than it was in the countries of Europe in which development occurred eariler.

If "limited democracy" is to succeed in the role we have mentioned, at least two conditions must be met. Firstly, the regime must be stable enough and last long enough to allow the establishment of a party system adequate for the expression of the increasing popular participation. Secondly, the "revolution in aspiration" must be to a certain extent synchronous with the economic and technical possibility of raising the level of living of the population. If both conditions are not satisfied, the chances are very high that political participation will be reached through one kind or another of "national-popular" revolutions. The marginality or the complete isolation of these larger strata of the population explains the greater stability achieved in the past by "limited" democracy both in Latin America and elsewhere. The chances of such stability are decreasing very sharply today and for a country whose socio-economic development has been retarded for one reason or another, political participation is more likely to take the form of a "national-popular revolution" than that of a "limited" or even "enlarged" democracy.

Considering now the present situation of the 20 Latin American Republics we find examples of most of the "stages" just described, with the obvious exception of the first, and (perhaps) the second, stage. The "contemporaneity of the non contemporaneous" certainly does apply to present Latin America, even if qualifications must be made for the peculiar historical circumstances of each country; and for the fact that certain changes would affect every country irrespective of their general socio-economic conditions. It is true, furthermore, that we do not find here a strict correlation between the political and the total social structure, or, as was pointed out earlier, with the type and extent of military intervention. But let us insist on the purely descriptive character of our typologies. They are no more than devices for introducing some order in a rather confusing and contradictory picture.

There can be little doubt that while "representative democracy" did reach—at least during certain periods of their history—a fairly high degree of stability in the countries we have classified at the top of Table 1 (Groups *A* and *B*), it never appeared or else it failed to attain a comparable duration and stability in the other two groups (*C* and *D*). But, of course, many inconsistencies both apparent and real appear

all along the continuum from minimum to maximum national and socio-
economic development as defined according to the criteria adopted.

With the possible exception of Colombia, and to a lesser degree and
more recently, of Venezuela, Peru and Ecuador, it can be safely stated
that most of the 14 countries included in the two lower groups have
failed to escape the vicious circle of dictatorships, brief attempts (or
none at all) at "limited" democracy, succession crises (in general under
the form of military "coups"), even if at one time or another some
more "enlightened" autocracy may have introduced a certain degree
of "modernization," at least in opening the country to foreign capital
and enterprises to exploit the local resources in raw materials. These
combinations have often proved to be stable enough—small groups of
big landowners, mainly military autocrats, and foreign investors. Such
is clearly the case of the Dominican Republic, Haiti, Nicaragua, Honduras, El Salvador, Paraguay, and we may note that their present social
structure is fairly consistent with their political history and actual situation. Of the other countries, Colombia—with a relatively high proportion
of middle occupational strata—has managed to maintain for a longer
time a more stable "limited democracy," but even so gravely perturbed
by the chronic civil wars between political factions. Venezuela showed
the first symptom of changes towards representative democracy after
the long dictatorship of Gomez. Its first freely elected government
(1946) had a short duration and only in recent years a new attempt
at a "representative democracy" is being made. Similar processes can
be seen in the other countries.

It is not surprising that it is precisely in this area that in the last
decade there have been at least three "national-popular" revolutions
(Bolivia, Cuba and Guatemala), and that presently the attempts at
"representative democracy" of the new civilian regimes of Peru, Ecuador,
Venezuela and Colombia encounter such great difficulties in the face
of the growing pressure of the previously marginal strata, which the
rapid urbanization and the growth in communication media are so
swiftly displacing from a passive to an active role. While the ruling
class may perhaps be ready to accept the functioning of a "limited"
democracy, they are certainly not disposed or prepared to accept an
enlarged participation with all its economic and social implications. The
chances of incorporating the new strata—statistically the great majority
of the population—into the framework of a representative democracy
are greatly impaired not only by this opposition, but also by the relatively politically "anomic" situation in which these vast social groups
find themselves because of the lack of adequate channels of expression

of their political aims within the existing party system. The legitimacy of the regime is frequently at stake and its stability greatly diminished.

The six countries of the first two groups fit rather closely into our scheme of the transition. All of them had their period of anarchy, centralizing autocracies, limited democracies and, now enlarged democracies. The modern urban proletariat and the urban middle strata form the human basis of such regimes. In Mexico and Brazil, while both groups only constitute a relatively low proportion of the total population, their heavy concentration in the cities and in certain regions within each country explains their dominant role in political life. But although with many peculiarities "representative democracy" can be said to function at present in these countries, they do offer contrasts as to the degree of stability and degree of interference of the military in civilian affairs.

Perhaps the contrast between Argentina and the other countries is the most disturbing fact. While Argentina may be considered as the most "advanced" as a national state on the basis of the usual indicators, it is also the most unstable and disturbed. After more than 60 years of continued functioning of a representative democracy, and having passed from a limited to an enlarged level without major troubles, it has relapsed in the last three decades into military revolutions, a decennial dictatorship and the very uneasy democracy of the post-Peronian périod. There is, however, a difference. While most of these countries are certainly to be considered as "enlarged" democracies, the situation of Argentina can be better described as one of recent transition into a—as yet unstable—"total participation" democracy. Its very instability as compared with the greater stability of the other countries can be interpreted, at least partially, as one effect of this difficult transition. The level of voting is certainly suggestive of such an interpretation. If we consider the proportion of voters in the total adult population we find a sharp contrast between Argentina on the one hand and Mexico, Chile and Brazil on the other. While in Argentina the percentage of voters in the total adult population (20 years and more) is over 80% (and if we take, according to the legal definition, persons of 18 years and older it is still 75%), in Mexico (1958) it is 48%, in Brazil (1960) 40%, in Chile (1958) 34%. We must also remember that if we discount the foreign residents, who in Argentina are around 15% (adult age groups), the proportion of participants would be even higher. In the remaining countries the foreign residents are a very low proportion and would not make any significant difference.

We are not assuming that the proportion of voters is a cause of instability; we are using it as an indicator of the level of functioning of democracy and of integration into national society: here it is sufficient to mention countries such as England (80%, 1951), Australia (86%, 1949) or Canada (74%, 1949). We have used as a uniform basis for comparison: percentage of voters in total population of 20 years and more. It cannot be denied that the low proportion of voters in countries such as Brazil, Mexico and Chile simply means that a considerable sector of the adult population is not yet integrated into the national body. The rural dweller, the peasant isolated in his small community, is certainly less politically relevant than the industrial worker in the cities, and his role continues to be more a passive than an active one. This integration is certainly a fact in contemporary Argentina and here we must take into account the historical circumstances which caused the partial failure of the "enlarged" democracy to create an institutional framework for the smooth functioning of a representative regime at a total level of participation, in order to understand the apparent "paradox" of this country, relatively so advanced (within the Latin American continent) and still in the grip of continuous military intervention.

While it would not be safe to make any prediction, it is reasonable to think that the greater stability enjoyed by both "limited" and, later on, "enlarged" representative democracy in Chile, the strong traditions which have been formed through its long political experience and the more firmly established party system (in comparison with Argentina) will be great assets in the transition from the present "enlarged" participation, to the coming level of "total" participation. But, in any case, in all the five countries, with their rapid rate of urbanization and the even more rapid spread of communication, the incorporation of the still marginal groups is imminent. It will involve a great strain on the present institutions and, as the cases of Vargas and Peron show very clearly, they will not be immune from the possibility of "national-popular" solutions.

The role of the military in Latin America must be understood in this rather complex picture. If we conceive it as related both to the kind of political system and to its *degree* of stability, then we must expect everywhere in Latin America and at all levels of socio-economic and national development the possibility of some intromission of the military into civilian affairs. In fact, some degree of stability can be reached in most of the transition stages, even at the "backward" one of centralizing autocracy; and conversely instability may appear even at the most "advanced" level of "enlarged" democracy if its corresponding social and political requirements are not adequately satisfied.

Let us formulate now a typology of institutional civil-military relations and relate them to the different particular situations of the Latin American countries.[3]

THE CLASSICAL MILITARY GARRISON STATE   This form develops typically in response to real or imagined external factors. No example of such Spartan organization is to be found in Latin America, where cases of truly serious and devastating wars of sufficient duration to work fundamental institutional change are extremely scarce. The major exception is the Paraguayan War of the last century, but social conditions in that country were insufficiently advanced to permit of the establishment of a truly centralized garrison state, despite the devastating nature of the armed conflict itself.

THE MODERN TOTALITARIAN GARRISON STATE   This phenomenon is still, fortunately, an evil dream of imaginative writers, for no historical examples are to be found anywhere. The low state of the technological arts everywhere in Latin America makes this development at present impossible for these republics.

THE TOTALITARIAN POLITICO-MILITARY RELATIONS   This pattern of relationships inextricably intertwines political and military functions within a monolithic public organization, as in Nazi Germany. Once again the insufficiencies of Latin America's technological state have to date prevented the formation of modern, totalitarian states, although such a country as Argentina is beginning to approach at least the material ability to include such a solution within its array of social possibilities. The "national-popular" revolutions have not attained so far this politico-military structure and one reason may be the technical underdevelopment of their bureaucratic organization. On the other hand, the rapid extension of radio, television, and other media of mass communication heightens this possibility as the unilateral dependence on weapons alone for social control in extreme cases thus becomes less necessary.

THE MILITARY AS INSTITUTIONALIZED GOVERNORS   This kind of authoritarianism is very common in Latin America, and is a persistent form from the earliest days of independence to the present day. The existence of the armed forces as an organized and ostensibly efficacious group

[3] For a narrower version of this typology and other suggested categorizations of Latin American politics, see K. H. Silvert, Political Change in Latin America, in Herbert MATTHEWS, ed., *The United States and Latin America* (New York, The American Assembly, 1959). Also refer to the March 1961 issue of *The Annals of the American Academy of Political and Social Science*, entitled *Latin America's Nationalist Revolutions*, for other pertinent and recent information.

in administrative affairs has tempted to the simple transposition of personnel from military to governmental functions and to subsequent rule as *de facto* and eventually *de jure* governors. Given the long-standing tradition of military privileges (from the colonial period) and military participation (from independence wars) in Latin America, such a pattern is likely to appear whenever the political instability reaches a point at which the social legitimacy of a regime or a government is no longer accepted by the major relevant groups within the society. Such a situation may happen, as we noted earlier, at every level of the transitional process. It is obvious why it would predominate during the early days of independence and the years of confusion and anarchy which followed the failure in establishing modern states in the liberated colonial territories. And it still predominates in the more retarded countries such as the Dominican Republic, Honduras, Haiti and Nicaragua, in all of which the structure of traditional society has changed very little. But it is small wonder that relatively more advanced countries such as Argentina from the early thirties and, in very recent years, Colombia and Venezuela have experienced the same phenomenon. Here the instability must be related, as we indicated before, to a different underlying situation. The crucial common ground of all these cases is an irreconcilable division among the various politically relevant groups, and the lack of shared norms regarding political activity. The military, clearly and loyally, has usually worked in conjunction with important civilian elements, serving as an arm for the maintenance of group interest. History belies the simplistic belief that such alliances have always been between the most conservative groups and the military. On many important occasions organized military might has been brought to bear to promote the interests of new industrial agglomerations against the pretensions of landed Conservatives and sometimes even the Church. During certain periods of Mexico's growth, for example, the military in combination with civilians contributed heavily to the social experimentation characterizing that country from 1917 until 1940 at least. This important category of events needs, thus, to be subdivided in accordance with the civilian allegiances and ideological orientations of the military, and the resultant effects on the total socio-economic and political structures.

THE MILITARY AS TRUSTEE GOVERNORS   As naked military intervention becomes increasingly viewed as shameful, this phenomenon has increased in incidence. There are two notable recent cases, that of the Provisional Government of General Pedro Eugenio Aramburu in Argentina (1955–1958), and that of Admiral Wolfgang Larrazabal in Venezuela (1958–1959). Both governments arose after the fall of dictators, both of whom had risen out of the ranks of the military and subsequently were deposed by the military in combination with civilian groups. Aramburu and Larrazabal committed themselves to "cushion" governments, *interregna* permitting the formation of parties, the holding of legal elections, and the installation of civilian authorities.

THE MILITARY AS ORIENTERS OF NATIONAL POLICY This very subtle manifestation involves the exercise of power not on the immediately visible scene but rather in the fashion of a grey eminence. The military in this situation attempt to establish the broad policy limits within which civilian activity may express itself, the sanction for disobedience obviously being deposition of the legally constituted authorities. The significant Mexican developments mentioned above are, in all their real complexity, a combination of this category with the two immediately preceding. Whether or not the Mexican armed forces still effectively limit the freedom of the Mexican Government is a matter of some debate, especially given the strength of the single official party of Mexico and the very wide distribution of the civilian sectors supporting this party system and the incumbent governors.[4] Perhaps the clearest, most evident case of tutelary military behavior can be seen now in Argentina, where the military overtly acts to contain the policies of the Government, openly threatens coups, publicly debates political policies, and on occasion even moves troops to back its demands on the civilian governors. Military budgets are holy, and officers of the armed forces in a limited retirement occupy many important administrative positions in the civil service.

THE MILITARY AS PRESSURE GROUP WITH VETO POWER This rather standard manifestation of military power in many developed countries is still little seen in Latin America, except possibly in the case of Chile. In this situation the military institution has the power to prevent antagonis-

---

[4] Oscar Lewis, in his "Mexico Since Cardenas," *in* Lyman Bryson, ed., *Social Change in Latin America Today* (New York, Harper, 1960), pp. 301–302, writes:

"*A comparison of the allocations of federal funds to the various departments over the four presidential administrations from Cardenas to Ruiz Cortines reveals* [. . .] *some highly significant trends Especially marked is the sharp decrease in the proportion of funds allocated to national defense, reflecting the demise of caudillismo as a serious factor in Mexican life. Adolfo Ruiz Cortines was the first president since the 1920's who did not depend heavily on either the national or a private army to maintain his control.*"

Professor Lewis then points out that between 1935 and 1940 defense expenditures absorbed 17.3 per cent of the national budget, dropping to 8.1 per cent in the period 1953–1956.

tic civilian action undertaken against it, but cannot initiate independent action or policy in fields outside of its range of professional interest.

THE MILITARY AS SIMPLE PRESSURE GROUP   This stage, the last before the military fades away into complete subordination to the civil authorities, is probably the status of the armed forces of Uruguay alone among the Latin American republics. The very special circumstances of Uruguay's past offer some apparently reasonable explanations of this phenomenon. A buffer state lying between two relatively powerful neighbors, Brazil and Argentina, Uruguay has never been able realistically to dream of armed exploits. Further, the country is politically a city-state, a fact which has contributed to the early development of what can truly be called a "bourgeois" society (in the primitive sense of the term). Moreover, a high degree of political involvement of the citizenry has created areas of civil power not conducive to military adventures.

THE MILITARY AS SIMPLE POLICE FORCE IN COMPLETE SUBORDINATION TO THE GOVERNMENT   Costa Rica prides itself on having this kind of civil-military pattern, and is even wont to deny the existence of an army altogether, stating that the civil force is in truth merely a police agency. If the situation is not really such a pure subordination of the armed forces to the civil authorities, still the case offers a reasonable approximation. Once more circumstances unique for Latin America have brought about this situation. Costa Rica was unattractive to early Spanish colonizers, for it had a small indigenous population and no readily available minerals. As a result the Costa Rican central valley was an area of slow and secondary settlement, peopled by persons who had to work the land themselves. This emergence of a landed peasantry permitted the development of a type of "bourgeoisie" (in the figurative sense of the word) which, as in the case of Uruguay, has had long experience in the organization and application of its power to the detriment of armed pretenders.

THE MILITARY AS POLITICAL ARM OF THE STATE   This pattern, obviously closely related to the idealized versions of the functions of the Red Army of the USSR and of the various "People's Armies" invariably tends to emerge from revolutionary situations of the left. The Arevalo-Arbenz Governments of Guatemala (1945–1954) and the present Governments of Cuba and Bolivia are the only three cases in Latin America of frankly leftist politics, albeit of different colors. In the Guatemalan case no serious attempts were made to turn the military into an active arm of the government; instead, especially during the interrupted term of

President (and Lt. Col.) Jacobo Arbenz Guzman, the design was to keep the army small and the officer corps highly contented. According to available report, the Castro Government has broken the professional army by investing civilian militias with great power and by politicizing the officer corps of the regular forces. This procedure was also used in Bolivia with the establishment some eight years ago of an armed civilian militia whose primary function was to counterbalance the regular army.

Military intervention in civilian affairs, as is suggested by this typology, clearly does not occur either in an ideational vacuum or in the absence of a sometimes very wide range of interests and pressures. Military politics inevitably and invariably involve identification with wider social interests and ideologies. The patterning of these identifications depends in important measure on the social origins of the officer corps and the social mobility functions which the military institution may serve. Unfortunately there are almost no reliable data available on these questions. From subjective evaluations and informal observation, however, one may suspect a considerable variation in the social origins of officer groups from country to country, and a consequent variation in the political identification of the military. It is also entirely evident that there must be great variation in the opportunities for upward social mobility offered by differing armed forces. Wide differences in budgets and in the sizes of the military establishments must affect mobility, of course, as do generalized social attitudes concerning the prestige of the military.[5]

COUNTRY	PERCENTAGE OF NATIONAL BUDGET	YEAR
Mexico	11,3	1958
Costa Rica	3,8	1958
El Salvador	10,2	1958
Guatemala	8,8	1958
Honduras	11,7	1957
Haiti	19,1	1957
Argentina	21,1	1958
Brazil	27,6	1958
Chile	21,9	1958
Colombia	5,7	1958
Ecuador	21,6	1958
Peru	23,2	1958
Venezuela	9,5	1959

These figures are admittedly tenuous, and probably err on the low side, of course.

[5] *The Statistical Abstract of Latin America 1960* (Center of Latin American Studies, University of California in Los Angeles), p. 32, offers some partial and tentative figures on the percentage of Latin American budgets devoted to defense expenditures. The data are incomplete for all countries.

A relatively safe generalization is that throughout Latin America the sons of middle class families are more attracted to the military than are the sons of the upper groups. The result often has been to split the ideological unity of the military, to create inter-service rivalries as well as intra-service discord. This growing fragmentation must be projected against the increasing complexity of Latin American society itself, affected as it is by economic development, changing world ideological currents, and rapidly growing industrial urbanization. Because nowhere in Latin America—even in famed Uruguay and Costa Rica—are the institutional patterns of secular and impersonal representative democracy fully established, many civilian groups are innately revolutionary in their attitudes and predisposed to the use of force as an inherent and thus desirable part of the social pattern. Both military schisms and military adventures are encouraged by the civilian groups soliciting armed aid for their political ambitions. Even though the following quotation concerns the Spain of the 1930's, it is valid for the Latin American arena as well:

> No doubt the generals in 1936 thought they were saving Spain [. . .] The State must be capable of embodying and responding to what Maura called the vital forces of the community. Otherwise, as he warned repeatedly, the army will claim to embody the national will in order to enforce changes which political institutions are impotent to encompass. Above all, no democrat, repeating the follies of the progressive and moderate minorities, can appeal to the sword rather than to conviction, however slow the educative process may be. Though the Republic of 1931 came in on a vote, many Republicans were willing to see it come in through the army. Repeating the tactics of Ruiz Zorrilla, they systematically undermined the loyalty of the army. Some saw the danger. 'I would prefer no Republic to a Republic conceived in the womb of the army.' Many did not. How could they complain when other forces tampered with the loyalty of the army in 1936?[6]

The military will be reduced to their barracks and their professional functions alone only when Latin American countries develop sufficiently complicated power structures and a society sufficiently flexible and integrated; when social and geographical discontinuities have been greatly lessened and isolated or marginal masses incorporated into the national body; when economic and social conflicts have found institutionalized expression within a common framework of shared norms.

[6] A. R. M. Carr, "Spain," *in* Michael Howard, ed., *Soldiers and Governments: Nine Studies in Civil-Military Relations* (London, Eyre and Spottiswoode, 1957), pp. 145–146.

The Conflict between Church and State[*]

FREDERICK B. PIKE

In 1947, José María Caro, then Cardinal-Archbishop of Santiago, Chile, denounced a Chilean political party because, in part, of its outspokenly critical attitude toward the Franco administration in Spain. In 1949, Costa Rica's Archbishop Víctor Manuel Sanabria y Martínez lashed out against a proposed article for the new constitution then being formulated which declared that education was essentially a function of the state. The archbishop's flat assertion that the Church would not accept this concept even if it were to be embodied in the new constitution helped bring about the defeat of the proposal. In 1954, the opposition of the Catholic Church was a contributing factor to the overthrow of Guatemala's communist-infiltrated Jacobo Arbenz administration. The following year the Church in Argentina gave its support to the uprising that toppled the régime of Juan Domingo Perón, a man whose presidential bid the Church had overtly supported in 1946. By the beginning of 1958, Marcos Pérez Jiménez and Gustavo Rojas Pinilla had been forced out of office in Venezuela and Colombia respectively, and in both instances Church opposition probably hastened the end of their dictatorial régimes. Perón had been engaged for some time in a bitter struggle with the Church. Both Pérez Jiménez and Rojas Pinilla, however, appeared to be anxious to maintain friendly relations between Church and state. Interestingly enough, both the Vatican and the State Department in Washington seemed to decide at about the same time that their respective interests might no longer be served by supporting friendly dictators who were intransigently dedicated to preserving the *status quo* against mounting pressure for social change.

In the above examples of recent participation in Latin American political affairs, as well as in others, the Roman Catholic Church has acted in accordance with its traditionally asserted right to serve as the final arbiter of issues which affect the moral and spiritual wellbeing of peoples who, either actually or nominally, are overwhelmingly Catholic. Church

[*] Reprinted with omissions by permission of Alfred A. Knopf, Inc., from *The Conflict Between Church and State in Latin America* by Frederick B. Pike. Copyright © 1964 by Frederick B. Pike.

insistence upon the exercise of this right has frequently led to difficulties in Latin America, where individualistic Catholic laymen are apt to consider themselves competent to make moral judgments free from clerical influence. Even if the lay faithful are willing to accept the authority of the Church in the spiritual realm, friction can result from the fact that churchmen claim the power to define what constitutes moral and spiritual issues. Matters which some churchmen regard as having moral and spiritual implications are often considered by lay political leaders as purely political and secular in nature and therefore removed from the Church's competence.

The roots of the long-enduring conflict between clerical and anticlerical forces in Latin America reach into earliest colonial times. From almost the outset of the Spanish conquest of America, relations between Church and state were governed by the *patronato real*, or the system of royal patronage. By 1508 the principal powers and privileges involved in royal patronage had already been bestowed upon the Spanish crown, primarily by a papal bull issued in that year by Pope Julius II. The most important power accruing to the crown from the system of royal patronage was the right of nomination to Church benefices in the "Indies."

The system of royal patronage, augmented by traditional Spanish patterns of royal control over ecclesiastical affairs as well as by the gradually expanding claims of royal authority which the Vatican was in no position to contend, produced unique results. The Church in Spanish America was, from an administrative point of view, more a Spanish, national Church, controlled from Madrid, than a Catholic Church, controlled from Rome. The "Catholic Kings" Ferdinand and Isabella were outraged when Pope Alexander VI in 1493 sent a papal *nuncio* to the island of Española and demanded his immediate recall. The Pope meekly capitulated, and not until the early nineteenth century did another direct agent of the papacy set foot in Spanish America.

The control which the Spanish kings were able to exercise over the Church in the Indies has been summarized in the following terms by the distinguished Mexican historian Joaquín García Icazbalceta:

> By virtue of the bull of Julius II and of other concessions subsequently secured, the Spanish kings came to exercise a power in the ecclesiastical government of America which, except in purely spiritual matters, appeared to be pontifical. Without the king's permission, no church, monastery, or hospital could be constructed and no bishopric or parish erected. No priest or friar might go to America without his express license. The kings named bishops and, without waiting for their confirmation by the pope, sent them out to administer their dioceses. The kings marked out the boundaries of the bishoprics and changed them at their pleasure. They could appoint to any religious office—even to that of sacristan—if they wished. They

had the power to reprove severely, to recall to Spain, or to banish any ecclesiastical official, including bishops who, even though they might often dispute with governors, never failed to listen to the voice of the king. The kings administered and collected the tithes, decided how and by whom they should be paid, without reference to bulls of exemption. They fixed the income of the benefices and increased or diminished them as they saw fit. They tried many ecclesiastical suits and, by the use of force, paralyzed the action of church tribunals or prelates. Lastly, no decision of the pope himself could be carried out in the Indies without permission of the king. And in the records of the early church in America are found a hundred laws or provisions emanating from the king or Council of the Indies for every bull or brief sent from Rome.[1]

Similar conditions prevailed in the Portuguese colony of Brazil. A bull issued by Pope Leo X in 1515 temporarily conferred powers of patronage upon the Portuguese crown. Then, in 1551, the Portuguese kings were denominated Permanent Grand Masters of the Order of Christ. As such, they were endowed with permanent rights of patronage.

In theory at least, the crown, whether Spanish or Portuguese, could control the secular clergy more completely than the regular clergy. Secular clergymen were directly under the control of archbishops and bishops, to whose authority they had vowed obedience. The prelates, in turn, had been nominated by and were to some degree beholden to the crown. The regulars, as members of a religious order, had taken a vow of obedience which subjected them to the discipline of a general in Rome and his subordinate representatives throughout the world. Prominent among the regular clergymen who served in the Ibero-American colonies were the Dominicans, Franciscans, Benedictines, Carmelites, Mercedarians, and Jesuits, the last of whom took, in addition to their other vows, a special one of obedience to the Pope. Concerned by the tendency of the religious orders to look to Rome rather than to Madrid for direction, King Philip II of Spain sought approval of a plan to establish a patriarchate of the Indies, centered in Madrid and endowed with virtually absolute power over all the clergy in the Spanish Indies, regular as well as secular. When the papacy denied its approval, Philip II and the able Juan de Ovando, president of the Council of the Indies, responded with the *Ordenanza del Patronazgo* of 1574. The purpose of this ordinance was to reduce the role of the regulars in the Spanish colonies and to bring about their gradual replacement by seculars. Owing in part to the scarcity of secular priests, this was never fully accomplished. The regulars continued to play an important part in the religious life of the colonies, a fact which often occasioned royal concern, particularly on the part of eighteenth-century Bourbon rulers.

[1] *Don Fray Juan de Zumarraga* (Mexico, D.F., 1881), pp. 128–129.

[While the state exercised extensive authority over the Church throughout the colonial period in Ibero-America, clergymen also enjoyed vast influence over affairs of the state. Frequently, clergymen were appointed to the highest political offices. This resulted in an overlapping of ecclesiastical and political authority.] It was impossible to know where one branch of authority ended and another began. Moreover, although the Church recognized the right of royal patronage, "in fact, it aspired to override political authority each time it could, and it was accustomed to make use not only of the prestige it enjoyed with the people, but also of the influence it possessed at Court and the threats of the Inquisition." This led inevitably to jurisdictional disputes between Church and state. As an example of such a dispute, the encounter between Archbishop Serna and Viceroy Gelves in seventeenth-century New Spain is described in one of the selections included in the first section of readings in this book.

The difficulty, given prevailing intellectual attitudes during colonial times, of distinguishing between the secular and the religious, contributed to jurisdictional disputes. The immanence of God in human society was overwhelmingly accepted as an article of faith. One need consult only a few of the early historians and chroniclers of colonial events, laymen or clerics, to become aware of the extent to which supernatural causation was ascribed to most human actions. Further, the explanations for natural phenomena were frequently sought in theological rather than in natural and scientific bodies of knowledge. Because of the manner in which God was assumed to infuse every aspect of human activity, churchmen who regarded themselves as God's servants naturally looked upon their mission as being very broad indeed. It was felt by them to extend beyond the duty of saving souls, and to include the legitimate function of creating the kingdom of divine justice on earth.

The administration of temporal justice in colonial Ibero-America extended the overlapping between secular and religious interests, and consequently led to jurisdictional disputes between civil administrators and churchmen. [As a special privilege or *fuero*, the Church was allowed to maintain its own system of courts. The Church insisted that all cases in which ecclesiastical discipline or the actions of churchmen were involved be tried in its own courts. Laymen, fearing they could not always expect impartial justice when dealing with ecclesiastical courts, desired to hail churchmen before civilian tribunals. Consequently, protracted debate often arose over what court enjoyed competence in a particular case.]

[The most important reason for chronic Church-state conflict in the Ibero-American colonies was the anticlericalism exhibited by so many of the laymen settlers.] The essence of this anticlericalism was an attitude of suspiciousness and even hostility toward the administrative organization of the Church and toward most clergymen. Generally, as has remained true to the present day, Ibero-American anticlericalism did not imply willful opposition to the Roman Catholic faith. Almost subconsciously, however, something of a theological rationale was adopted to justify anticlericalism.

The Mexican historian Silvio Zavala has suggested that an unwitting tendency toward heresy inhered in the creole mentality. Without realizing that their position was in any way heretical, creoles, and for that matter their Spanish-born contemporaries as well, inclined toward the beliefs that constituted the heresy of quietism, conceived by the Spaniard Miguel de Molinos (1640–1694). One of the main tenets of quietism, as described in the *Catholic Encyclopedia* (1911) is: ". . . they who have reached perfection, i.e., complete absorption in God, have no need of external worship, or sacraments, or of prayers; they owe no obedience to any law since their will is identical with God's will." This point of view would engender a rejection of the priestly class and the formal sacramental role of the organized Church itself. Throughout their history, Spanish—and Portuguese—American Catholics have often appeared to believe that salvation is achieved by faith alone and has no connection with the performance of actions prescribed by the positive law of the Church.

Contributing more directly toward an atmosphere of anticlericalism was the unedifying manner in which churchmen frequently quarreled among themselves: the creole and the peninsular churchmen were generally at odds, sometimes to the extent of violence. The regulars felt the seculars were too far removed from papal authority, and therefore not fit for the work of evangelization, and the various orders were consistently in conflict, as the pages of colonial history testify. In 1600, a group of seculars from Michoacán in New Spain actually invaded Nueva Galicia and put the regulars to flight. This may seem an extreme instance, but in reality such occurrences were rather commonplace. Somewhat more unusual was the action of Franciscans in sixteenth-century Chile in setting fire to an Augustinian convent.

Churchmen rarely presented a united front, and their internal bickering was bound to undermine the respect of the lay faithful. Not infrequently two different factions of churchmen maintained diametrically opposed positions, with each claiming that only its viewpoint represented the proper application of Church teachings to a particular situation. As an administrative organization concerned with practical problems, the Church was not at all a monolithic structure with a pat, party-line position in regard to the issues and problems confronting the colonists.

Another factor that nourished anticlericalism was the envy-arousing wealth of the Church. Enjoying a tax-exempt status, owning much of the finest land, controlling money-lending transactions, and with an important source of its revenue, the tithe, collected and delivered to it almost in its entirety by state officials, the Church occupied a highly privileged financial position and thus could exercise extensive temporal influence. Civilians often felt their own economic opportunities were stifled because of the unique advantages enjoyed by the Church. The Inquisition, during the seventeenth and eighteenth centuries, became a symbol to many laymen of the Church's excessive concern for and favored position in obtaining economic gain. Rumor, at this time, often had it that the Holy Office was interested less in preserving the purity of the faith than in condemning well-to-do individuals so as to confiscate their wealth.

The Inquisition in its various functions was a microcosm of the temporal and spiritual activities of the Church in colonial Latin America. The operations of the Holy Office were frequently marked by discord arising from the overlapping of ecclesiastical and civil authority, and on numerous occasions its activities led to bitter struggles among churchmen. Moreover, according to its critics, the Inquisition afforded a striking proof that the Church, which held virtually monopolistic control over education and the media of public expression, used its power to stifle curiosity, legitimate political expression, and freedom of intellectual inquiry. Referring to the consequences of the Inquisition, a nineteenth-century Argentine priest, Father Gregorio Funes of Córdoba, asserted: "In the colonial, Church-dominated period, thought was a slave and not even the soul of the citizen was his own." Conversely, defenders of the over-all accomplishments of the Spanish colonial system tend to deny or to qualify the charge that the Inquisition suppressed intellectual freedom. The vastly differing interpretations of the operation and effects of the Inquisition are revealed in the four opening selections of the reading materials in this book. Whatever the truth may be about this conflict of opinion, it seems certain that the Inquisition was well accepted and even popular when it was first introduced in the Spanish colonies. By the end of the colonial period, however, the Inquisition was opposed by many and hated by some; it had become an important factor contributing to anticlericalism.

The power of the Portuguese Inquisition, established in 1531, extended to Brazil, and the Holy Office first proceeded against a resident of that colony in 1543. However, no separate tribunal of the Inquisition was ever established in Brazil. The exercise of Holy Office powers was entrusted to bishops and other agents in Brazil, while persons accused of offenses were sent to Portugal for trial. Although it has been argued that "What was lost by not having a Tribunal on the ground was gained by the ardor with which the Familiars of the Inquisition denounced all whose acts, words or thoughts could make them prospective cases for the Holy Office," still the Inquisition in Brazil never rose to a level of importance comparable to that of the Holy Office in Spanish America. This moderate activity was characteristic of the general Brazilian religious scene. The Church in the huge Portuguese colony, so far as the exercise of power was concerned, was only a dim reflection of the ecclesiastical organization in the Spanish Indies.

.Nevertheless, the same sort of Church-state disputes which often erupted in the Spanish Indies occurred also in Brazil. Even as their Spanish counterparts did, Brazilian churchmen struggled to gain control over Indian affairs, justifying their actions on the grounds of their desire to protect the aborigines against the exploitation of greedy colonists. On their part, the colonists often accused churchmen of being anxious to control Indian labor in order to enhance the temporal wealth of the Church in general and of various religious orders in particular. A conflict over Indian policy between Jesuits and colonists in seventeenth-century Brazil led to virtual civil war, and one phase of the clash is described in the selection that concludes the first section of readings.

The rise of the independence movement in Hispanic America presented the Church with new difficulties, revealing that the clergy was more than ever divided among its own members, and just as inclined as always to regard political questions in a theological light. While some churchmen in Mexico prayed to the *Virgin de los Remedios* to hasten the success of the divinely-favored royalist cause, others invoked the intercession of the *Virgin de Guadalupe* to speed the providentially-preferred patriot victory.

The overwhelming majority of the hierarchy, which was born in Spain and which felt that the Church could not maintain its exalted position if deprived of the support of the Spanish crown, tended to regard favorable attitudes toward independence as impious if not downright heretical. A large number of native-born Spanish-American clergy, on the other hand, including both creoles and mestizos, favored independence and worked zealously to attain it. Fathers Miguel Hidalgo and José María Morelos, prominent among the early leaders of Mexico's struggle against Spain, Luis Beltrán, the great metallurgist and munitions maker in La Plata and Chile, and Camilio Henríquez, founder of Chile's first newspaper, were a few among the many leaders whom the clergy contributed to the patriot cause.

So far as the future position of the Hispanic-American Church was concerned, the period of the revolutionary wars was a particularly poor time for the clergy to divide, even more uncompromisingly than usual, among themselves. Independence, as an accomplished fact, was soon to present the Church with the greatest temporal challenge it had confronted in Hispanic America. During the colonial period, in spite of not infrequent clashes between representatives of royal and clerical interests, the crown consistently prevented civilian forces from striking genuinely crippling blows against the Church. On its part, the Church generally impressed upon the masses their duty to respect royal authority. At times, Inquisition officials seemed as concerned about stamping out signs of treason as extirpating heresy. There was a symbolic relationship between Church and state which worked to the advantage of both.

[With the coming of independence to Spanish America, Church-state relations underwent a dramatic transformation. Gone was the crown, the great political institution and the one power that had been able to control contending administrative agencies] The Church remained. But without the backing of the crown, its position as an unassailable bastion of privilege was in jeopardy. [Accordingly, the Church entered more directly into the political arena, hoping through political action to protect its customary rights and privileges. As often as not, the Church sustained defeat in its political ventures. When this occurred, civilian groups, at last able to give meaningful expression to their long pent-up hostility toward churchmen, moved quickly to strip the Church of its temporal power. Sometimes they even took advantage of the Church's political discomfiture to deprive it of the effective means to exercise its spiritual office. They proceeded to this extreme not only because of intellectual conviction, but because of the desire to stamp out any vestige of influence that the Church could conceivably find useful in staging a political comeback.]

Even while Latin American revolutions for independence from Spain were still in progress, heated dispute between Church and state officials had burst forth over the issue of patronage. The insurrectionary governments claimed that they had inherited the patronage rights once exercised by the Spanish crown. Patronage, they insisted, was one of the inalienable prerogatives of sovereignty. Therefore, when new groups acquired sovereign control over areas once ruled by Spain, they gained the rights of patronage that had inhered in the Spanish crown. On the other hand, many churchmen contended that control over patronage had been bestowed upon the monarchs as a special, temporary, and revokable privilege. The loss of sovereignty by the crown, they asserted, meant that the Church should reclaim authority over religious affairs and so begin to exercise directly the powers of patronage.

Independence had scarcely been won when political leaders and churchmen began to argue over taxation. Should, for example, the national government continue the colonial tradition of collecting tithes for the Church? Invariably, this question precipitated serious disagreements. The separate Church courts, provided for by the ecclesiastical *fuero* of colonial times, also came in for attack. Gradually, they were abolished by national administrations. Much Church property was also seized and a substantial number of religious communities were suppressed, occasionally against a background of violence.

The issues of patronage, Church taxes, separate ecclesiastical courts, and Church property had already been fought out to a large degree in various European nations, beginning as early as the eleventh century, and by 1800 had been substantially resolved. Although in the process the temporal power of the Church had been weakened, in general its rights to minister to the spiritual needs of its followers had not been denied. In Latin America, vexatious problems that had concerned Europeans for centuries were resolved in the course of a few short years.

Other disputes which had erupted generations and even centuries previously in Europe, and for which certain accommodations had been arranged, appeared in Latin America only after the attainment of independence. For a variety of reasons, many political leaders in the new republics sought to limit Church control over education and charity. In several Latin American countries cemeteries were secularized so as to deprive the Church of the formidable power to deny burial in the *campo santo* (consecrated ground) to those who had incurred its displeasure. Laws were also passed to remove marriage from the control of the Church by providing for the legality, sometimes the exclusive legality, of civil marriage contracts. In addition, some republics enacted laws of religious toleration during the nineteenth centruy. To these measures Church authorities often replied with massive excommunications. At other times, supported by large numbers of the lay faithful, they resorted to civil insurrection.

During this period Latin Americans did not develop indigenous intellectual movements, but looked to Europe for philosophical guidance. The anticlerical aspect of nineteenth-century European liberalism found fertile ground in an environment where hostility toward the clergy had long existed. Furthermore, particularly in Mexico, Chile, and Brazil, intellectuals were influenced by the positivism of Auguste Comte. Positivism proclaimed that the laws of progress for civilizations could be discovered only by scientific, empirical investigation. Positivists equated revealed truth with superstition and maintained that formal religions must be swept away so that allegedly obscurantist, unfounded views could not stand in the way of progress based upon scientific truth.

[The changes in status with which the Church was threatened during this period meant an inevitable reduction of its material and temporal strength. Churchmen, however, tended to interpret any attempt to alter the *status quo* as inimical to religion itself.] They were largely justified in this alarmist viewpoint, precisely because most champions of change and reform believed that the Church, *per se,* was incompatible with modern progress. Clerical fear of novelty sprang also from the manner in which many churchmen of the previous century had indiscriminately welcomed the ideas of the Enlightenment. This movement had led to notable scientific and economic progress in Latin America, as well as to a remarkable freedom of intellectual activity. However, in Latin America the Enlightenment in its ultimate effects also spawned a lack of respect for authority, a religious relativism, and a secularism which redounded to the serious disadvantage of the Church and the values it defended. Because they had once been beguiled by what had appeared to be ideas that were useful and yet not opposed to formal religion, churchmen became hyper-cautious and consistently opposed manifestations of the new.

Church authorities and their lay partisans in the late nineteenth century insisted that the only unifying, constructive tradition from which Latin Americans could establish order and achieve progress was the Catholic tradition of colonial times. To depart from it, they contended, would produce chaos and political institutions that were distorted and unnatural because they were not rooted in the past. Diego Portales of Chile (the dominant political figure from 1830 to 1837), Gabriel García Moreno of Ecuador (sometimes the president and always the main political power from 1860 to 1875), and Rafael Núñez of Colombia (the president or president-maker from 1880 to 1894) were among those controversial statesmen who felt it necessary to preserve the traditional power and influence of the Church as a means of attaining national unity and stability. Similar viewpoints have been championed by many Latin American intellectuals down to the present time, and are reflected in the selection from the writings of Aurelio Espinosa Polit. On the other hand, anticlerical leaders insisted that the Catholic tradition was one of sterility and oppression. Their viewpoint is succinctly described in the selection by William Rex Crawford. It is manifested also, in extreme form, by a statement of the nineteenth-century Chilean journalist Domingo Arteaga Alemparte: "So deplorable has been the record of the Church in regard to political interference that it is impossible for a Catholic to be a good citizen."

The struggle between liberal, anticlerical forces and conservative, proclerical groups was violent and protracted in Guatemala, Ecuador and Colombia. The passion with which Colombians of these two respective camps assailed each other during the nineteenth century is reflected in the works of many national historians. Writing in 1938, Colombia's liberal author Jorge Espinosa Londoño referred to the origins of the Church-state dispute in the national period:

> The fanaticism of the population was the polar star for the leaders of the reactionary movement. . . . In waging their political fights, the Conservatives always associated their cause with that of the Divinity. Ultimately, they profaned the name of Christ. . . . Those people taking up the banner of religion confused, or found it expedient to seem to confuse, the purely political actions of the government with the universal principles of religion.[2]

José Manuel Groot, a conservative intellectual of the past century, interprets events from an opposite point of view:

> Peace and harmony could have been established then [in 1830], but the uncurbed passions of the anticlerical, liberal forces did not permit this, and the unhappy consequences have continued to plague the country, bringing discord, combat, and revolution. . . . The truth is that the ecclesiastical and political life of our nation had been always so intertwined that religion was necessarily the vital element of all our civilization and progress.[3]

It was in Mexico that the struggle between Church and state reached a peak of bitterness, doing much to shape the character of Mexican history throughout the national period. The intensity of partisan emotions which this dispute evoked is suggested by the statements of two Mexican historians. The liberal Alfonso Toro declares:

> The clergy had made of colonial society an assembly of hypocritical and subservient human beings. The priests made the Mexicans as ignorant as they were, as dirty, immoral and lazy as they were. Accordingly, the reformers have always tended to root out these vices, seeking to reduce the clergy to its proper role and to deprive it of the property it has collected and monopolized to the disadvantage of the people.[4]

At the opposite extreme Félix Navarrete maintains:

> The detractors of the Church pretend that grounds have existed for a struggle between the Church and the civil power since the earliest period of the discovery of Mexico, and that this fight has always been provoked by the Church. I say that grounds for this struggle have existed in Mexico only since 1833, the year in which Masonry provoked it so as to bring

[2] *Pascual Bravo: los partidos politicos en Colombia* (Medellín, 1938), pp. 53, 251.
[3] *Historia eclesíastica y civil de Nueva Granada* (Bogotá, 1953 edition), V, p. 515 and I, p. 7.
[4] *La iglesia y el estados en México: estudio sobre los conflictos entre el clero católico y gobiernos mexicanos desde la dependencia hasta nuestros días* (Mexico, D.F., 1927), p. 43.

an end to the influence of the clergy and even to the clergy itself. From that time on the Church has only defended itself against attacks.[5]

Because of the seriousness of the dispute between Church and state in Mexico, two fairly substantial selections, included in the reading material about Latin America's first century of independence, relate to that country. Although written in the 1930's, these selections are characterized by impassioned, emotional disagreement over the interpretation of events that transpired between 1854 and 1876. That the conflict between Church and state can be discussed in a calm, detached, and scholarly manner rather than in terms of the struggle between good and evil is revealed by the Francis M. Stanger article describing the issue in Peru, and above all by the excerpt from the writings of J. Lloyd Mecham, summarizing the results of the clericalism vs. anticlericalism rivalry of the first century of the national period.

Brazil, because it remained a monarchy for sixty-seven years after declaring its independence from Portugal, maintained intact many aspects of the administrative institutions fashioned during the colonial period. The relationship between Church and state was not altered essentially, and the battles that marked the dealings of churchmen with political leaders in the Spanish-American republics were largely absent from Brazilian development. In part, this was because Brazilian Catholicism had developed a greater flexibility and spirit of compromise than Hispanic-American Catholicism. It is notable that in 1810 a Portuguese-English treaty extended rights to the British to build a Protestant church in Rio de Janeiro, although it had to look like a private house and could not use bells to summon worshippers. The Bishop of Rio, José Caetano, strongly favored this concession to Protestant believers. It is difficult to imagine a similar response from a Spanish prelate in the year 1810.

The remarkable figure of Fr. Diogo Antônio Feijó also imparted an unusual character to Church-state relations in the early years of Brazilian independence. Fr. Feijó, regent of Brazil from 1835 to 1837, was a pious priest and at the same time the leader of anticlerical forces who demanded the superiority of civil over ecclesiastical authority, and the confiscation of the wealth of the religious orders. Moreover, Fr. Feijó abandoned the wearing of his clerical garb and led an unsuccessful campaign for legislation to permit the clergy to marry.

The most dramatic and consequential Church-state clash in nineteenth-century Brazil erupted in 1872, and involved the attempt of two

[5] *La lucha entre el poder civil y clero a la luz de la histórica* (El Paso, Texas, 1935), p. 230.

bishops to promulgate and enforce instructions from the Vatican that had not been officially cleared by civil authorities. Although the dispute left unpleasant memories on both sides, it did not generate the sort of bitterness that prevailed in several of Brazil's sister republics of Latin America. When the monarchy was overthrown and Brazil became a republic in 1889, Church and state officials were able within a short time to reach an amicable agreement upon separation of the two powers.

The liberal movements in nineteenth-century Latin America had, in many instances, been led by members of the aristocracy. When the liberal cause triumphed, little if any social upheaval occurred. Around the turn of the century, however, new middle groups began to emerge in the more advanced countries of Latin America. In the overwhelming majority of instances, these new groups were comprised of urban elements, depending for livelihood on commerce, manufacturing, or other business operations of a non-agrarian nature. Basically, the clergymen tended to be suspicious of, if not actually hostile to, the emerging middle class. They feared that the alleged materialism of the new capitalist class would threaten the supremacy of the spiritual values upon which the Church insisted. Traditionally, moreover, the Church in Latin America had prospered best when allied with the owners of the huge landed estates. Its ability to retain temporal power, or to reacquire it in those countries where it had been diminished or totally suppressed, seemed to depend upon the continuing strength of the landed aristocracy, and upon the preservation of a semi-feudal social structure in which neither the masters nor the serfs would oppose a privileged position for the Church. The rise to power of a new urban group, over which the Church had virtually no control, threatened the supremacy of an established order in which the Church was strongly entrenched.

In spite of hostile Church attitudes, new middle groups began to acquire political power in the more advanced Latin American republics at different periods in the twentieth century. Throughout the area their strength is growing, and in some republics they exercise the dominant political power. The men who make up these new groups have realized that in general the clergy has viewed them with hostile eyes. They have, therefore, been predisposed to continue and sometimes to intensify the struggle against the Church initiated in the previous century.

Although events in the nineteenth and twentieth centuries altered the traditional pattern of relations between Church and state in most Latin American countries, traditionalism remained largely unchallenged in regard to one important aspect of the social structure. While new middle groups were achieving positions of social, economic, and political importance, almost nothing was accomplished toward incorporating the vast lower mass into society. This fact constitutes the principal source of existing and potential political conflict involving the Church in contemporary Latin America.

The lower mass in Latin America is no longer docile, patient, and fatalistically resigned to a life of perpetual poverty. Crowding into the cities in a remarkable demographic shift that has seen the percentage of rural inhabitants decline rapidly, millions of former peasants have swelled the ranks of the urban proletariat. Able now to view the opportunities for material advance that life in the modern city can bring to those who are actual participants in society, they have become discontented with their role as nonparticipants in the economic and political life of their nations. The nature of future developments in Latin America depends to a great extent upon the type of leadership that the masses receive in their effort to join in the life of the twentieth century.

During recent generations churchmen have had little direct contact with the masses. In many Latin American countries the poverty of the Church and the scarcity of priests would have made this contact difficult to achieve, even when the desire for it existed. A contributing factor to this situation was the fact that the religious life of the lower classes seemed to present no immediate practical problem to the Church. Although most generally not practicing Catholics, and although usually startlingly ignorant about the faith, the great majority of the masses had at least an overwhelming predisposition toward Catholicism. More important, they had no alternative to being half-formed Catholics.

Today the masses have an alternative. Those who have flocked into the cities can join the Protestant churches that have been established in Latin America in mounting number. They can also join overtly antireligious movements, and they can become communists. Moreover, the role of Indian peasants in demanding radical land reform in Bolivia in 1953, the massive unrest among the northeastern Brazilian peasants and their support of the leftist Francisco Julião, and developments in Cuba since the inception of Fidel Castro's Sierra Maestra campaign in December, 1956, reveal the potentially favorable disposition of the rural masses toward Marxian expedients.

In the mid-twentieth century, then, the Church has had to concern itself with the masses. More and more its prelates have begun to speak out in favor of social justice. However, as has been true so often in the past, the Church is divided. Social justice has divergent meanings to different churchmen. To one group it means preserving the stratified, closed society. Men of this persuasion believe that if charitable work is expanded and paternalistic measures are more conscientiously applied, the masses will once again become content to remain in their place and will abandon any thought of challenging their superiors. The material by Jorge Iván Hübner included here demonstrates this approach to the social problem. The views of Hübner are in accord with those of many conservative Catholics throughout Latin America. On the other hand, numerous Catholics contend that the old social structure is doomed and that paternalism and charity will never suffice to keep the masses in line. They envision the emergence of genuine social pluralism in which all classes and functional interest groups will have the power to protect their essental rights and to compete on a basis of relative equality of opportunity for the advantages the nation has to offer. Latin America's Christian Democratic movement, especially in Chile where it has attained its greatest strength, urges this approach to the social problem. This fact is clearly revealed in the excerpts from two of the books of Eduardo Frei, for many years the leading figure in Chile's Christian Democratic Party.

How has the new interest of churchmen and of the Catholic laity in the social problem renewed the Church-state conflict? Whatever their differences of opinion as to what constitutes the ideal social system, churchmen and the practicing Catholic laity are convinced that a just social order can exist only if it is based upon the moral teachings of the Church. Therefore, they firmly believe that the Church must speak out boldly on the social problem, propose solutions, and insist upon the attempt to apply these solutions. This belief is expressed in the writing reproduced in this book of the archbishop of Guatemala. Conflict arises because the supporters of most twentieth-century reform moves that have come to power in Latin America or aspire to attain it are anticlerical and secular in orientation. Such men, whose anticlericalism is often attributable to the fact that they come from the new middle sectors once resolutely opposed by clergymen, are not disposed to allow the Church a role in helping to formulate social change.

The issue of whether or not the Church should share in devising and implementing social reform programs helped lead to the sharp conflict between ecclesiastical leaders and Juan Perón in Argentina. This conflict, as viewed from the anticlerical position, is described in the excerpt from the Perón speech and from an editorial of an official Peronist journal which are included in this book. As a result of the Argentine dispute, a bishop and a canon of the Buenos Aires Cathedral were exiled, the president of the republic was excommunicated, and several churches were burned.

The social justice issue has contributed to renewed political controversy involving religious questions in Mexico. The official party and the dominant political force in that country is the anticlerical Revolutionary Institutional Party (*Partido Revolucionario Institucional*), or the PRI, as it is called by Mexicans. The PRI has begun to express resentment over the criticism of the opposition Party of National Action (*Partido de Acción Nacional*), known as the PAN. The excerpt included from a 1960 publication of its youth organization shows that the PAN has been upbraiding the PRI for its alleged inattentiveness to social reform and for allowing large-scale communist infiltration. PAN members, who are beginning to refer to themselves as Christian Democrats, also argue that only the implementation of Catholic principles can lead to a just social order. The concluding selection in this book, an excerpt from a book by Robert E. Scott, suggests that the official Mexican Party, the PRI, has made steady political, economic, and social progress. The implication is that there may be little need for the type of improvement, purportedly Christian in nature, which the PAN insists only it can introduce.

Elsewhere in Latin America, signs of Church-state tension have begun once more to appear. The separation of Church and state in Chile, effected in 1925, has produced generally harmonious relations between the two powers. In September of 1962, however, the Chilean ecclesiastical hierarchy issued a pastoral letter lamenting the social injustices that were said to be glaringly evident throughout the country. The hierarchy further contended that a capitalistic system based upon the classically liberal concepts of unfettered economic individualism could not produce a just society. Almost at once Chile's Liberal Party, one of the country's most powerful political groups, began to issue indignant denunciations of the Church's alleged interference in political matters.

Centering in Chile, Colombia, Venezuela, and Costa Rica, but existing also more weakly throughout the Latin American republics, is a movement aimed at the organization of Christian trade unions which base their programs largely on the social teachings of the Catholic Church. To coordinate the efforts of these national associations, the Latin American Confederation of Trade Unionists (referred to generally by its Spanish initials, CLASC) has been established, together with a rural branch known as the Latin American Federation of Farm Laborers (FLAC). Early in 1963, after completing a tour of Latin America, Auguste Vanistendael, secretary general of the International Federation of Christian Trade Unions, stated: "Christian trade unions will be the dominant social-political groups in Latin America within a few years." This statement may exaggerate the influence that the Christian trade union movement is likely to have, for it is opposed even by many practicing Catholics who are scrupulously intent upon avoiding what might be even remotely construed as the interjection of the religious issue into areas considered by many to be purely political. Still, those who exercise governing power south of the Rio Grande, who are often accustomed to having tight control over labor organizations, can be expected to distrust and even to be hostile toward any new labor movement which looks to the social doctrines of the Catholic Church for inspiration rather than to national political programs.

The issue of Church and state and the social problem is complicated still further by the presence of Catholic reform advocates who regard the way of Christian Democracy as being too mild and traditionalist. In northeastern Brazil, for example, Father Antônio Melo Costa leads the Catholic Peasant Movement, which has come to include more than forty separate unions. He approves some of the objectives of Communism and "Fidelism," regarding them as compatible with Christianity, and has expressed certain doubts that adequate social reforms can be achieved through traditional processes of so-called democracy as they presently operate in Brazil. Should government officials decide that Fr. Melo Costa is becoming too troublesome a critic of their policies, Church authorities might have difficulty in deciding whether to support the zealous clerical reformer or the state.

As the social problem in Latin America becomes increasingly acute, a new variant in the conflict between Church and state could become a major issue—especially if the power of Marxism continues to mount among influential groups. The future status of Church-state relations will depend largely upon the ability of churchmen and middle-class policical leaders, precisely those groups which in the past have frequently demonstrated mutual antagonism, to find a basis for cooperation in responding to Latin America's social crisis.

In what must be taken as a criticism of the past record of middle-sector political groups, Stanford University's John J. Johnson has expressed the hope that the rising influence of Christian democracy "could provide a moral fiber in political life that the political parties themselves have not produced." The majority of Latin America's politicians might not agree that they lack a moral fiber which could be provided by Christian democracy. On the other hand, how many of the southern continent's Church leaders would agree with the statement made by the University of Virginia's John J. Kennedy at a 1962 conference on "Explosive Forces in Latin America."

> Too often churchmen seem to be the prisoners of their own statistics. The national census reports that about ninety-eight per cent of the population is Catholic; in reality, only twenty to thirty per cent may be active Church members. . . . Open acknowledgement of the fact that not all Latin Americans are practicing Catholics could, however, be an important first step in creating an atmosphere where the Church's legitimate interest in social reform could be exercised in conjunction with other reform interests with a minimum of conflict.

The conflict between Church and state is too deeply imbedded in the historical tradition of Latin America to disappear altogether within the foreseeable future. Along with such controversial matters as the role of the military, the value of democracy, and the applicability of Marxian economic analysis in newly emerging republics, it will continue to be a consequential issue. If not the principal theme in the future of Latin American development, it is likely to remain a distinctly audible obbligato accompaniment to that theme. To students in the United States, the heirs of a historical tradition that differs vastly from that of Latin America, the Church-state issue South of the Border will not cease to be a source of perplexity and puzzlement—until its centuries-old evolutionary process is painstakingly analyzed.

*The Force of the Church** | JOHN J. KENNEDY

During World War II, it was reported that the late Joseph Stalin dismissed the possibility of consultation between Allied leaders and the Papacy with the cynical question: "The Pope—how many divisions does he command?" In strictly military terms, of course, the question required no answer. Questions about the force of the Church are, however, normally stated in other terms, and the answers may reflect a wide variety of interests. The theologian offers answers of one kind; the canonist, of another, the doctrinal apologist of still another; while the historian of religion may present something quite different from all the others. To duplicate here the answers of any or all of these specialists would be pretentious. Rather what is assumed to be at issue is the question of the social power of the Catholic church in Latin America; an assessment of that power in terms meaningful to students of politics and international relations will be undertaken here.

A fundamental preliminary in this evaluation is some rudimentary identification of the nature of the church in Latin America. One body of opinion, too extensive and too erudite to be dismissed lightly, has seen the Latin American Church as an anachronistic survival of organ-

* Reprinted from *Explosive Forces in Latin America*, edited by John J. TePaske and Sydney Nettleton Fisher, published by the Mershon Center for Education in National Security of the Ohio State University as Number 2 in the series "Publications of the Graduate Institute for World Affairs." Copyright © 1964 by the Ohio State University Press. Used by permission of the author, the editors, and the publisher.

ized superstition in an age of reason and enlightenment.[1] In another view, the Church is essentially an instrument used by the economic and social elite to control and, on occasion, to oppress the masses. Another characterization has won increasing popularity of late, especially in the United States. In this view the Latin American Church can be regarded, hopefully, as a mighty, if cumbersome, weapon against international communism, which not only threatens social elites in Latin America but is also a great nuisance to North America. None of these characterizations, however, is of much help for present purposes. They do less to explain the force of the Church than they do to explain it away.

[The best possibilities for analysis probably lie in regarding Catholicism simply as a religion that commands the loyalty of large numbers of human beings who live under widely diverse conditions and who are committed to a creed which seeks to account for man in the universe.] The creed, moreover, provides for a Church that claims the authority to define and apply the principles of the creed itself in order to present man with the opportunity to gain salvation, not in this world, but in eternity. All of this may seem rather elementary. It is; but if it were not for these elements of belief, commitment, and authority, the Church would present no problem—at least no basic problem—to students of politics.

[The problem begins to take shape with the consideration that, if the goals of the Catholic religion are not of this world, the Catholic church has rarely hesitated to involve itself in the affairs of this world. Involvement has generally been on one of the two following bases: (1) In this world the Church must be assured of an unhampered sphere of action for the fulfilment of its mission.] While the Church will not insist that this sphere be everywhere and always uniformly defined, it will zealously seek to keep the area of operation one of its own choice and definition and will resist any efforts of other parties to establish its limits. The church-state conflicts, which fill so large a part of the modern history of the West, have in last analysis frequently turned on this point. These conflicts have resulted in various kinds of resistance on the Church's part. Its general attitude, however, was stated by Pope Leo XIII who emphasized that as the Church pursues "by far the noblest of ends, so is its authority the most exalted of all authority, nor can it be looked upon as inferior to the civil power, or in any way dependent upon

---

[1] Francisco Bilbao, *La América en peligro* in *Obras completas* (Santiago, Chile, 1897), 2, 5–121. This passage offers an extended statement of this view. See especially pp. 31–36 in which the situation of Latin America is contrasted with that of the nations that have moved out of the "shadow of Rome."

it."[2] (2) ⌊If human life has its goal in eternity, the conditions of life in this world should be consistent with that goal and conducive to it.⌋ The conditions are primarily to be determined by the integrity and dignity of mankind and the individual. ⌊The Church may not claim of itself competence to create these conditions or the responsibility for maintaining them, but it will, again and again, insist on a self-defined right to inspire and influence the course of events that may produce them.⌋

There is a temptation to say that the history of the Church in republican Latin America can be told in terms of selection and rejection between these two bases. In the first century after independence, the Church acted largely on the first; now emphasis is being shifted to the second. This idea has the attractiveness of simplicity and would seem to suggest an explanation of the apparent difference in behavior on the part of churchmen in the two periods. The one appears to be marked by the prevalence of church-state tensions arising from the efforts of churchmen to keep the sphere of ecclesiastical activity one of their own choice. The other is distinguished chiefly by the social concerns of the Church.

This, however, is too simple a view. It involves an assumption that the pattern of church-state relations is no longer a serious question for the Church—or for the State—an assumption which is not generally warranted. This is not to deny that there are signs of a shift in emphasis, but the evidence suggests other factors to be investigated before attributing change to abandonment of a traditional position. The increasingly urbanized character of Latin American society obviously presents to the Church a different complex of problems from that which a predominantly agricultural society once produced. The Latin American Church existed for centuries in a society where communities were isolated one from the other. This separation determined in part the basic patterns of ecclesiastical activity. Isolation has not everywhere vanished, but its force has been broken to a considerable extent by the appearance of technological factors in society, such as radio communications and mechanized transportation. These and a myraid of related factors have obviously modified the task of the Church. In examining specific modifications in its general task, however, one should bear in mind that the basic interests of the Church do not change.

All that has been laid down so far has been in terms of the general and the ideal. Reality has on occasion marred the ideal. Certain church-

---

[2] *Great Encyclical Letters of Pope Leo XIII* (New York, 1903), pp. 112–113. The excerpt quoted is from *Immortale Dei*.

men in Latin America, as elsewhere, have demonstrated more zeal for temporal concerns than for the eternal. Others have abused their authority. Moreover, the record of bad performance has not been limited to the ranks of the ordained. Conspicuous violation of principles of the Catholic laity has not been entirely unknown in Latin America. [In attempting to evaluate the social force of the Church in Latin America, one must acknowledge this divergence between the ideal and the real, but it is also necessary to recognize two related considerations. One is that the long-range significance of the Church has to be found in terms of the ideal. The other is that the gap between the ideal and the real is often a narrow one and sometimes non-existent.] Appraisal also requires recognition of what has been suggested above, namely, that if the Church faces a changing task in an evolving society, the concern and interests that the Church pursues are permanent and unchanging. Against the background of these considerations it is pertinent to evaluate the Church today within the scope outlined by the three following categories: (1) the current state of civil-ecclesiastical relations; (2) Church influences on social change; (3) some consequences of the factors considered under the above two headings for the position of Latin America in world affairs, especially within the inter-American system.

In connection with the first, there seems to be a new public image of the Latin American Church. Feature writers in newspapers and pictorial magazines give North Americans the impression of a new progressive Church whose leaders are anxious to scrape the barnacles off the old vessel and render her shiningly new and modern. This attitude means, among other things, that the new Church will assign secondary importance, or even less, to the question of how the state regards the Church. The suggestion is that the Church is no longer genuinely concerned about whether it has an official position, a recognized position, a neutral position, or whether its position is a matter of indifference to public authority. The further suggestion is that the happy day of complete separation of church and state is about to dawn, and no group will greet this news more eagerly than North American Catholics who have found the attitudes of their co-religionists in Latin America incomprehensible, not to say embarrassing, on this point as on so many others.

Eagerness along these lines had best be restrained. It will largely meet with disappointment. [Separation of church and state in the North American fashion is not possible for most of Latin America in the forseeable future.] The use of the North American model can only continue to provide, as it has in the past, a misleading standard for comparison. It is true that legal separation has been constitutionally established in many countries: in Mexico, nearly a century ago; in Brazil and Cuba, with the advent of the republic; and in Chile and Uruguay, more than a generation ago. In few, if any, of these countries, however, does the situation resemble that in the United States. Church and state have parted company, but they have often been unable to go their separate ways. Religious issues survive in politics. Conflicts occur, and occasionally they are bitter, as in Mexico in the 1920's. This is not to suggest that the conflicts can be resolved by reverting to the pre-separation status, a most unrealistic consideration. What is important is the acknowledgment that separation has not necessarily eliminated conflict.

But, it can be asked, is the situation any more disadvantageous for society in the foregoing countries than it is in the countries where the two authorities have not had separate courses assigned but where their overlapping interests and jurisdictions are frankly acknowledged? Examples are found in Colombia, where the acknowledgment is made through a concordat, or in Argentina, where it is made through constitutional stipulation. Have not these two countries been the scene of more political-religious tension in the past two decades than Mexico or Chile? The answer to this question, however, must take into account the survival of regalism in most countries where chruch and state are not completely separated. Moreover, the spirit of regalism may be re-enforced by that of nationalism which gives rise to suspicions of the "foreign" or cosmopolitan character of a universal Church. In the name of nationalism the state may seek guarantees that control of the Church be placed in the hands of its own citizens, as the Colombian government sought and obtained in the 1942 revision of the Concordat. In general, in countries with a strongly asserted regalistic tradition, the central question of Church patronage appears to be one that neither side desires to raise in any drastic or final way. Indeed, in Argentina each party seems to wish to meet the other half-way in the maintenance of that curious camouflage that always surrounds the exercise of patronal claims.[3]

Certain dedicated Catholics have been known to argue that the whole regalistic arrangement imposes so many liabilities on their Church that sacrifice of official status would be a small price to pay for getting rid of the arrangement.[4] The argument has so far failed to persuade

---

[3] John J. Kennedy, *Catholicism, Nationalism and Democracy in Argentina* (Notre Dame, Ind., 1958), pp. 12–23.

[4] José Manuel Estrada, *La iglesia y el estado* (Buenos Aires, 1929). First published in 1871, the book was omitted from the 12-volume edition of Estrada's works published in 1899. It was published again in *Hechos e Ideas*, Año 16, Tomo 27, Nos. 134–135 (June–July 1955), 581 ff. There is much in Estrada's later writings to suggest that after 1884 he no longer upheld the position taken in 1871.

the various national hierarchies, who apparently prefer to suffer disadvantages they have learned to live with than to risk experimentation. Even if Church authorities could bring themselves to accept the hypothesis, there would, however, remain the problem of convincing the civil authorities. In most countries of the regalistic tradition, the latter task would probably prove harder than the former.

This whole problem of church-state relations would certainly be different if Latin America possessed a genuine diversity of creeds and churches. While there has been a notable expansion of Protestant groups in certain countries in recent years, the development is not yet of a proportion to provide a new perspective for the church-state picture.

In summary, the church-state problem in Latin America continues. It is too firmly emplanted in the inheritance of the area to be eliminated in a generation or two. It is evident both in the tensions that appear from time to time and in the accommodations between the two parties. New social attitudes in the Church may mean that new and different accommodations will be forthcoming; but it is difficult, if not impossible, to envisage any arrangements that will isolate church and state, one from the other.

Within the second category of evaluation, Church influence on social change, general interest seems to center on the question of what role the Latin American Church will play in the future that it has not played in the past. At the present time this question will probably produce more speculation than definitive answers.

It is reasonable for speculation along these lines to anticipate some innovations on the part of the Church. It would, however, be quite unreasonable to expect any influence or support from the Church that would run counter to well-established orthodoxy in doctrine or practice.

This may appear a superfluous affirmation, but it is stressed because certain original and creative personalities within the Latin American Church have sometimes been regarded, at least in the United States, as being in fundamental disagreement with their fellows. Bishop Miguel de Andrea in Argentina or Father Alberto Hurtado in Chile are good examples. Andrea, especially, is often presented as though he had spent his life in a continual battle against other bishops. Then, when it is argued that men of his kind speak for the future of the Church, the implication is that in the future the Church will put less stress on orthodoxy. Bishop Andrea undoubtedly had a keener sensitivity to social trends than many other churchmen. This sensitivity made him a champion of social reform, and it is for this reason that his name has importance. But one has only to dip into his religious writings to realize that the bishop was not only orthodox but even conventional in his piety.[5] His work indicates that vigorous support of social reform is possible from the Church, but there is nothing in it to suggest that such support involves a departure from orthodoxy.

A second consideration is that while the Church seems to take a generally sympathetic regard for social legislation—and this regard indicates support for measures dealing with land reform, labor conditions, public housing, and public health—the Church cannot be evaluated solely as a militant social reform organization. The Church has an advantage in this connection because it can appeal to the conscience of the believer in terms of social obligation. It is significant that for many Latin Americans the Church is the most effective channel of appeal to provoke the desired response. But not all Latin Americans are believers. Nonbelievers bent on social reform may welcome the support of the Church. Collaboration of this sort is not entirely new or unprecedented. Twenty years ago in Argentina, Bishop Andrea and the Socialist leader Alfredo Palacios could both endorse, within the confines of a single book, certain advancements in labor legislation.[6] In such collaboration, however, each party has its own basis for action, and these bases will not necessarily be identical. By and large, the difference between them need not produce any great problems, but there is a possibility that in certain areas it may.

In terms of its own doctrinal interests, the Church is especially sensitive in the areas of the creation and maintenance of the family and in the education of youth. Here, conflicts are possible, even probable, in certain cases. In present circumstances it probably can be assumed that there will be a search for various ways to resolve such conflicts, but there should be no expectation that the Church will retreat from its doctrinal positions. There would seem to be a promise of minimizing conflict, however, if the Church could be persuaded to take one genuinely innovating step. This move would be the frank recognition of the presence of numerous unbelievers in Latin American societies. Too often, churchmen seem to be the prisoners of their own statistics. The national census reports that about 98 per cent of the population of

---

[5] See *La hora de la caridad* (Buenos Aires, 1934). The tone is not lacking in works where the primary emphasis is social: for example, *Conferencias* (Buenos Aires, 1931).

[6] Carlos R. Desmarás, *Ley del trabajo a domicilio comentada*, Prólogo del Dr. Alfredo L. Palacios, nota preliminar de Mons. Miguel de Andrea (Buenos Aires, 1942).

a particular country in Latin America is Catholic; in reality only 20 to 30 per cent may be active Church members. Churchmen are keenly aware of the difference, but they have long demonstrated a reluctance to admit it, and this reluctance has sometimes led them into difficult, not to say unrealistic, attitudes toward public policy. In defense of these same churchmen, it can be pleaded that their awareness extends also to other matters that must be considered here. Foremost among them is the fact that the 98 per cent figure does represent the baptized, and, generally speaking, those baptized in the Church are to be regarded as members of the Church unless by deed or word they specifically separate themselves. To limit pastoral responsibility to the 20 to 30 per cent of practicing Catholics is to attribute to the Church an exclusiveness which is incompatible with both its purpose and its history.

It does not involve any challenge to pastoral responsibility, however, to point out that the 20 to 30 per cent are responsive to pastoral authority in a way that the others are not. To ask ecclesiastical authorities to recognize this fact and to take account of it in their plans and work is not to ask the Church to sacrifice any doctrine. Nor is it to suggest that the Church be restrained in its efforts to expand the number of practicing members. Open acknowledgment of the fact that not all Latin Americans are practicing Catholics could, however, be an important step in creating an atmosphere where the Church's legitimate interest in social reform could be exercised in conjunction with other reform interests with a minimum of conflict.

If the possibility of conflict deserves some attention, it is no less important to note that in many parts of Latin America, tradition supports the concept of a working harmony between the Church and various elements in society. It is an oversimplification to say that in the past this harmony was dependent upon a political party, generally a conservative one, on the one side and the Church hierarchy on the other. Nevertheless, it is true that in certain countries, notably Chile and Colombia, the Conservative party was popularly regarded as the Church party, although elsewhere, notably Argentina, the conservatives were not so identified. By and large, however, the identity of Catholic with the conservative seems to be disappearing. At the same time, new political parties have emerged under the general designation of Christian Democracy, and the designation itself is an indication of, at the very least, strong sympathy with values the Church has sought to uphold.

For the student of Latin American government and politics, the obvious question is this: In the future, will an identity between Catholic and Christian Democrat be established as there was in the past between

Conservative and Catholic? A definitive answer is probably not possible
at this time, but the indications are to the contrary. Christian Democratic
leaders generally profess a personal adherence to the Church, but so
do leaders of other groups. Christian Democratic leaders claim the social
doctrine of the Church as their particular source of inspiration, but
they emphasize the absence of any organizational connection between
their parties and the Church. In most countries the movements are of
relatively recent origin, and it may be too early to undertake an appraisal
of their impact. Their ideological commitments, however, suggest that
traditional Christian teachings are adaptable to new situations, and in
this connection the movements may reflect the abiding force of the
Church.

Another significant facet of this general topic requires a brief examination of Latin American Catholicism in connection with the international
relations of the countries of the hemisphere and with the future of
the inter-American system. This has some implications both for the internal harmony of the system and the effectiveness of inter-American
co-operation against challenges from international communism.

Inter-American co-operation to date certainly demonstrates that only
an impoverished and stereotyped thinking can find potentially disrup-
tive issues between a "Protestant" Anglo-American and a "Catholic"
Latin America. Nevertheless, one should note an attitude that has developed among many Latin American Catholic intellectuals since World
War II. An anti-materialist spirit has been for many of them a logical
consequence of their religion. The spirit has led them to assert that
materialism rules equally in Moscow and in Washington and that all
that these two symbols stand for must be equally opposed. Naturally,
this view has not prevailed in all Church circles, but where the distortion
has been maintained vigorously, it is somewhat ironic that it originates
among dedicated Catholics. Greater exposure to the realities would seem
to be the only way of eliminating this concept.

At the same time the student of Latin American politics must acknowledge that common language, tradition, cultural factors, religious inheritance can give to the Latin American countries a kind of unity from
which the United States has to be excluded. In recent years, certain
Catholic spokesmen in Latin America have emphasized this unity and
have given it international implications. The Venezuelan leader Rafael
Caldera has stressed the concept of "two powers": the United States
in the north; and south of the Rio Grande, "one single people divided
in different states."[7] Mario Amadeo of Argentina has drawn attention

---

[7] *El bloque latinoamericano* (Santiago, Chile, 1961), p. 45.

to the values inherent in Ibero-America and urged a regionalism appropriate to them.[8] Neither of these gentlemen is the kind of naive opponent of the United States described above. Of their good will toward the United States and toward inter-American collaboration, there can be no doubt; and North Americans may be surprised to find so independent an attitude in these prominent Catholic spokesmen. The surprise, however, can also be a wholesome reminder that continental collaboration and harmony can be constructed on bases other than those proposed by North Americans.

On a different level, it may also seem to the North American observer that Catholic attitudes in Latin America display an exasperating ambivalence toward communism. Certain prominent persons, clerical and lay, declare their opposition, but in other Catholic circles the protests are muted. Certain Christian Democratic spokesmen assert that they cannot refrain from fighting a particular injustice merely because local Communists also fight the same particular injustice. At least one prominent Christian Democratic leader in Chile, Eduardo Frei Montalva, has asserted that he cannot be expected to lead a fight against communism simply for the purpose of defending the existing order.[9]

Naturally, none of this is intended to suggest that Catholicism supports pro-communist movements. It does, however, indicate that a revitalized, socially conscious Catholicism in Latin America is not necessarily an automatic support for United States policy objectives in the area.

Labor in Latin America * | VICTOR ALBA

There is much talk these days about the Latin American middle class, about students, intellectuals and oligarchs. But, except when there are strikes, little talk about the industrial working class.

There are some 15 to 20 million industrial workers in Latin America and labor unions exist in every country, even under the dictatorships. Latin American labor legislation is, generally, advanced (and as often as not, not carried out).

[8] *La encrucijada argentina* (Madrid, 1956), pp. 205–206.
[9] *Sentido y forma de una politica* (Santiago, Chile, 1951), p. 64.
* Victor Alba, "Labor in Latin America," *Dissent*, Vol. 9: No. 4 (Autumn 1962), pp. 387–392.

The industrial workers must cope as best they can with a multitude of complex problems stemming from industrialization, rapid urbanization and the prospect of automation. Their interests as workers force them to consider such problems as agrarian reform, inflation and the planning of economic development.

Nevertheless, it is the middle-class parties that spell out the orientation, study the problems, and propose the solutions. The labor movement as such rarely voices an opinion on these general questions. It is satisfied to fight for wages and working conditions. Only recently have any attempts been made to give the labor movement a voice of its own.

This has not always been the situation and it probably will not remain so in the future. But at present it may be said that the destiny of Latin America is taking shape without the decisive intervention of the industrial working class. To understand this we must briefly examine the character of the Latin American working class and the history of its labor movement.

a) *A considerable percentage of illiterate workers and, perhaps still worse, a great number of people whose formal education does not go beyond knowledge of the ABC's, who have no interest whatever in any cultural activity, and who are impervious to and suspicious of complicated explanations.* Such is the reality, and any program of workers' education must take this into account. This low educational level helps stir up differences within the working class. It creates castes of better educated workers, it establishes a hierarchy of wages and weakens trade-union solidarity.

b) *The peasant origin of the huge majority of industrial workers.* In a period of economic crisis or unemployment, they return to their villages where they are at least assured of food and shelter. In many areas workers abandon their work during protracted village festivals and at harvest time; hence there is a constant fluctuation of manpower, as well as of union strength. Educating these workers becomes a problem as does training them to fill skilled and specialized jobs.

c) *Persistence of an isolated, peasant mentality in the city worker.* He is often mistrustful, uninterested in social problems, and indifferent toward culture. A special study alone would be required to explain the influence this has on the psychology of the Mexican worker in his work and in his union, as well as his attitude toward his children, home and pleasures. We would find no doubt that alcoholism, use of harmful herbs, emotional and family instability stem largely from the peasant's failure to adapt to urban life.

d) [*The Latin American worker is in a transitional stage between artisanship (work performed in small workshops) and rationalized assembly-line work.* This creates problems of psychological adaptation which are reflected in his attitude toward his union.]

e) *Women scarcely take part in industry.* One out of 233 among Mexican women as compared with one out of 153 in the professions and with one out of 213 among university students. This disproportion also leads to friction in work and home and frequently provokes union injustices.

f) [*The great number of children who work before reaching the legal age at which they are permitted to.*]

g) [*General lack of interest in social problems and the absence of documentation*] (*magazines, libraries, books, lectures, workers' study circles, etc.*), *in virtually all of Latin America.*

Basic needs in Latin America are so pressing that there is neither time nor possibility for disguising them in idealism. [The workers are satisfied to fight for immediate aims.] Exploitation is so blatant that any theoretical explanation is useless. While the European labor movement, particularly at the beginning, was preoccupied with the future, the labor movement in the New World concentrated exclusively on the improvement of existing conditions without bothering about tomorrow. Hence, its weakness in theory.

Toward the middle of the 19th century a few dreamers imported European socialist utopias. In Argentina, Esteban Echevarria founded the Association of May in 1838 and wrote the *Socialist Dogma.* In Chile, in 1850, Francisco Bilbao created the "Society of Equals." Two poets in Mexico, Pantaleon Tovar and Juan Diaz Covarrubias, propagated utopianism, while in Brazil a Frenchman, Taudonnet, began to publish the *Socialist Review* in 1845. In Colombia the first socialist clubs were organized.

The old guild corporations of the colonial period disappeared or adopted a trade-union form. This development took place more rapidly when it received the help of the European immigrants already familiar with trade unionism. That is why Argentina, with its mass immigration, experienced working-class struggles first.

The first union in Latin America was created in Buenos Aires in 1853. The *Union Grafica* (Printers' Union) won a ten-hour work day for newspaper shops in 1878, the first limitation of the working day accomplished by strike action. Nine years later the railwaymen went on strike to protest a foreman's mistreatment of one of their men.

It was the socialist *emigrés* who, after the Paris Commune, led the way to coordination of the until then scattered unions. Several sections—French, German, Spanish and Italian—of the First International were established at Buenos Aires. Their members exercised influence in various trades so as to found the General Workers' Union of Argentina on May first, 1890.

This organization disappeared in 1896, weakened by a conflict between authoritarian and anti-authoritarian elements. In 1901 the Argentine Regional Workers' Federation (FORA) was organized. Exclusively trade-union elements left this in 1902 to found the General Workers' Union (UGT). In spite of a law permitting the expulsion of *emigré* agitators, the unions were very active. In 1902, 1904 and 1905 there were three general strikes, and in 1910 the Argentine Regional Workers' Confederation (CORA) was established. CORA and FORA merged in 1914, but split a year later. By the First World War the normal work day was ten hours (16 hours, however, for commercial employees), and wages kept up with price increases.

By 1918 FORA had 70,000 members and UGT had 80,000. Then, in 1929, after vain efforts to unify the unions, the General Confederation of Labor (CGT) was started. FORA remained independent. Trade-union cooperatives, certain of which lend economic support to strikes, have developed on a wide scale. In Uruguay and Paraguay similar movements developed.

As for Chile, thanks to foreign loans it was one of the first Latin American countries to become industrialized. British capital, followed by North American investments, built the railroads and worked the nitrate and copper mines in the inhospitable Northern regions. The working class developed rapidly, migration from the country into the cities was constant, contributing to the creation of a more democratic regime. The landed oligarchy was forced to permit universal suffrage in 1874, without any condition but literacy.

The nitrate region of Antofogasta, first exploited by combined Anglo-Chilean investments in 1866, saw thousands of peasants become miners. The solidarity which grew up among them was such as one rarely sees on the continent. The first strikes in the country were by the *salitreros* of Tarpaca in 1890 who wanted to be paid in cash, not in company-store vouchers. Jose Maria Balmaceda, president of the Republic, refused to act against the strikers and went so far as to suggest nationalizing the mines as well as the railroads. But in 1891 an oligarchical rebellion ended Balmaceda's regime and he committed suicide.

Chile today is still the country with the most highly developed cooperative movement. As early as 1900 there were 240 cooperatives. Starting in 1905, the anarchist movement organized the first groups and so energetic was their action that by 1907 a law establishing Sunday rest was promulgated. In 1910, out of 3,200,000 inhabitants listed by census, 55,000 were affiliated to 433 groups. A year later a large number of them had formed the Greater Workers' Federation of Chile (FOCH). The mass of workers affiliated in the north rapidly gained control and weakened the influence of the anarchist unions affiliated with the IWW. In 1921 the Federation constituted itself along industrial council lines, abandoning organization according to profession. Thanks to mutual-help organizations which it had created at the start, FOCH was able to sustain prolonged strikes such as the 1921 coal strike which lasted two months and which won an 8-hour day in the coal pits. After 1923 political events forced the FOCH into a crisis. The railroad workers' union split away from it and a number of other unions followed. Until 1936, when the Chilean Workers' Confederation (CTCH) was established, FOCH led a rather monotonous existence; independent unions conducted the principal struggles.

In 1924 a military government was established which decreed, for demagogic reasons, a Labor Code giving legal recognition to the unions and to joint industrial committees. It also abolished night work for women and children, made health insurance obligatory and set minimum wages. In 1925, Arturo Apessandri issued a constitution recognizing the right of union organization and setting a 48-hour week.

Bolivia's first trade union made its appearance in 1906 and was called the Workers' Social Center. In 1912 the FOI (International Workers' Federation), changed to the FOT (Workers' Labor Federation) after 1918, was set up. This organization and the FOL (Local Workers' Federation—an anarcho-syndicalist movement) often form united fronts. In Peru also, anarchists were the initiators of the labor movement, taking leadership of the Confederation of Artisans ("Universal Union") which existed since 1884. The union instituted several agrarian communities for artisans. The CGT came much later and was dissolved, together with the "Universal Union," by the 1930 military dictatorship, at the moment when the APRA movement, founded in 1924 by Victor Raul Haya de la Torre, began to develop. In 1922 Ecuador had its first union. As in the other countries, the central trade unions changed according to changes in the working-class ideologies and as the Communists formed their party—here by splitting with the socialists; or, as in Brazil, from anarchist groups.

In Central America the labor movement came late and has little influence. Costa Rican unions were unified only in 1943; in Guatemala two movements merged to form the Workers' Federation for Labor Protection; the Guatemalan Confederation of Workers was created in 1944.

By contrast, labor struggles in Cuba early acquired importance. In 1812, the Negro Juan Aponte led a slave uprising of 20,000 with the aim of establishing a Black Republic; in 1813 the *vegueros* refused to plant tobacco unless their wages were increased. In 1831, the copper mine workers rebelled and, in 1868, during the first war of independence, a group of Spanish anarchists founded the Society of Tobacco Workers. The work day then lasted 16 hours. In 1892 a Regional Workers Congress met to demand the 8-hour day. After independence from Spain, unions were rapidly formed and in 1925 joined together in a national Confederation which was successively dominated by the Communists and by democrats, then subjected to Batista from 1952 to 1959. Under Castro it is used to raise productivity and control the workers.

There are three different stages in the development of the Latin American labor movement:

a) *The period of origins:* Anarchists or socialists create unions, they have a life of their own, import European ideas and, without becoming political, take part in national problems.

b) *The period between the two world wars:* A withdrawal from active politics, but the unions become a battleground for Communists, socialists and anarchists. They rarely take part in the anti-imperialists' struggles except when these are conflicts with foreign enterprises (the most important being those in the Colombian banana plantations in Santa Marta in 1929, the Chilean mine strikes and, in 1938, Mexican oil).

c) *The post-war period:* The unions become completely unpolitical in their activities, while splitting into anti- and pro-Communist groupings.

Several major conclusions may be drawn from this sketch of the Latin American labor movement.

First, the Latin American proletariat is numerically weak. In recent years, as a result of industrialization, it has increased in size, but its consciousness remains undeveloped and non-political. Except for Chile, the once powerful socialist and anarchist influence has vanished. Communist influence has always been slight, although during certain periods such as the Popular Front days and after the Second World War, Communists directed the central unions of a majority of Latin American countries. At present, Communism influences primarily intellectuals, students and the middle class. The Communists often succeed in making use of the working class, but have failed to obtain appreciable results in recruiting.

A majority of the labor movement is led at present by elements of the popular and revolutionary democratic parties (Peru, Venezuela, Bolivia, Costa Rica), by a Socialist-Communist alliance (Chile and a section in Ecuador), by a Peronist-Communist alliance (Argentina), and by leaders who are to all intents state functionaries (Brazil). Within all these movements a very active struggle between democratic and Communist tendencies goes on. The outcome of these struggles depends more upon the leaders' personal popularity than upon their ideological views. In Chile, Venezuela, Colombia and Ecuador, the Christian-Democrats have begun to gain a measure of influence.]

In the second place, the labor movement has lived in a state of isolation from other social forces. It has almost never collaborated with peasant organizations in the few countries where they exist. There is even the example of the "Red Battalions" formed by Mexican workers during the 1910–1917 Revolution which helped the city forces crush the insurrectionary peasantry. Although on several occasions the unions have attempted to organize peasants, they have rarely succeeded. The same indifference is found with respect to the problem of the Indians. The unions have neither a program nor a viewpoint to help in the solution of this problem despite its considerable importance for the labor movement, one reason being that Indians are easily mobilized as strikebreakers. It is only recently that in a few countries—Peru, Venezuela—the unions have shown an active interest in the agrarian question.

This isolation sometimes takes on a politically reactionary character. Since industrialization takes place almost everywhere without any prior or parallel agrarian reform, it is the peasants who must pay for it. Thus, to a degree, the working class becomes a parasitic class living off the peasantry. Even without a conscious realization of this, the unions have often sided with the feudal oligarchy against the peasantry or have become the latter's accomplice through indifference toward the peasants. Suffice it to recall that the Cuban unions did not participate in the anti-Batista struggle. It is only lately that the unions, almost without exception, have taken a stand in favor of land reform. But even then it is only a platonic position which leaves to the popular and middle-class movements the brunt of the struggle against the *latafundists*.

Finally, such isolation creates very marked tendencies in the labor movement toward bureaucratization, the perpetuation of "leaders" in their posts, a fiction of democracy at meetings.

The result of this isolation and bureaucratism is the indifference of the unions toward important national questions. Not only a lack of interest in the agrarian and Indian problems, but no participation in planning where it exists, no struggle against dictatorships with the exception of some groups in Venezuela and Peru, no support to cultural activities, no help in the forming of workers or popular universities despite the fact that forty years ago such schools were common in Latin America and, particularly those under anarcho-syndicalist leadership tied to the labor movement.

Despite these shortcomings, the labor movement has a part to play in Latin American life. Growth of Latin America's economy and politics requires that the unions participate.

It seems clear that the Latin American "revolution" about which everyone talks is nothing but a typical bourgeois revolution. It seems also clear that the weak and politically inexperienced Latin American proletariat, lacking any doctrine, can play only a subordinate and secondary role in this revolution. But if it cannot lead the revolution, it does have sufficient weight to limit to some extent the freedom of movement of the bourgeoisie which itself is still in process of formation. Limits to exploitation can be established to prevent the repetition in Latin America of the worst characteristics of industrialization in Europe and the United States. Particularly, the labor movement ought by its action to prevent the bourgeoisie and the forces that support it (the technicians and the younger army people who possess a rather developed sense of efficiency) from attempting to force the nation's development by non-democratic means; that is, to prevent overexploitation of labor according to the Soviet model. This model, moreover, has a greater attraction for the bourgeoisie and the young military men and technicians than for the working class which mistrusts the Communists.

Very likely the major task of the unions at present is to win the right to actively participate in the economic planning about which everyone now talks and which the United States has finally come to accept. The cultural and technical level of the Latin American trade-union leadership is generally rather low. To prepare leaders, to renew the union teams by infusions of young blood, to attract intellectuals, students, technicians and especially young workers into the unions, to support the organizing of peasants and to help Indian groups become modern without losing their identity are among the many phases of union activity which still remain unexplored. Latin American labor needs to reform itself, needs to fall into step with the evolution of Latin America and make a reality out of the workers' movement's old slogan: to make itself the representative of all of society's interests precisely because it represents the interests of the workers.

(*Translated by* STANLEY PLASTRIK)

Latin America's Secular Labor Movement*

ROBERT J.
ALEXANDER

Historically, the labor movements of Latin America have been overwhelmingly secular and non-Catholic, in spite of the supposedly preponderant position of the Catholic Church in the area. This has been due as much to the fact that until recently the Church took little interest in labor affairs as to the political, social, and religious attitudes of those who did play the key roles in the founding and development of Latin American labor organizations.

The Latin American labor movement was in a real sense the child of the revolutionary convulsions of Europe in the middle of the nineteenth century. The ideas that were then acquiring popularity among the new European working class were carried to the New World, both by those who had participated in these early European struggles and by Latin Americans who had observed them.

The revolutions of 1848 had their impact on Latin America, as they did on the United States. In at least two countries, Argentina and Chile, important national intellectuals participated in these movements and were impregnated with the ideas that motivated them. Francisco Bilbao in Chile and Esteban Echeverría in Argentina were both profoundly influenced by the Utopian Socialist philosophies that were one of the motive forces of the 1848 revolutions, and, after the failure of these movements, they came back to their homelands to propagate the ideas they had learned in Europe.

Out of these Utopian Socialist beginnings grew some of the first efforts to establish a working-class movement in Latin America. Both in Argentina and Chile, the Utopians turned their attention to two efforts—the organization of mutual-benefit societies among artisan groups, and adult education among these same elements. The mutualist societies, which are still important in Chile, began then, and the establishment of the first Argentine trade union, the Unión Tipográfica of Buenos Aires, can be traced to the influence of the Utopian Socialists.

* Robert J. Alexander, "Latin America's Secular Labor Movement as an Instrument of Social Change," in William V. D'Antonio and Frederick B. Pike (eds.), *Religion, Revolution and Reform* (New York: Frederick A. Praeger, Inc., Publishers; London: Burns & Oates, Ltd., 1964), pp. 145–160.

Even more important were the First International of Marx and Bakunin and the Commune of Paris of 1871. Immigrants belonging to both the Marxist and Bakuninist wings of the International found their way to the New World particularly after the fall of the Commune, and there they established local branches of the International in Argentina, Uruguay, and Brazil, as well as in Mexico, Colombia, and perhaps in one or two other Latin American countries.

These local units of the International, often torn between the Marxist and anarchist elements, had stormy histories. However, their members played important parts in the establishment of the first solid trade-union movements in the east coast countries of South America, as well as in Mexico.

The first labor movements to be firmly established were those of Argentina and Mexico. In the latter case, however, the very promising beginnings that organized labor had in the 1870's and early 1880's were finally suffocated by the increasingly tyrannical dictatorship of Porfirio Díaz, and did not reappear with any force until the years immediately preceding the Mexican Revolution of 1910.

In Argentina, in contrast, the labor movement was put on a firm footing in the 1880's. A number of Argentina's presently existing labor organizations can trace their history back to that period. Most of these early unions—among restaurant workers, shoemakers, ship repair workers, and artisans of various types—were under anarchosyndicalist influence.

However, one Argentine union that dates from this same period of the 1880's had quite different origins. In 1885–86 one of the United States railway brotherhoods—no one is now quite clear as to which one—sent a delegation to Argentina and Chile to try to organize similar groups of railway and locomotive workers there. Out of their efforts came La Fraternidad in Argentina and the Federación Santiago Watt in Chile.

In 1890 the first attempt was made in Argentina to establish a central labor organization. As a result of the country's first May Day meeting, held in that year, the Federación Obrera de la República Argentina (FORA) was established. During the following decade this group, which was predominantly Socialist in its political orientation, led a somewhat fitful existence, having to be reorganized upon various occasions.

It was not until 1901 that the FORA was finally established on secure foundations and was able to maintain a continuous existence. In 1903 it was captured by the anarchosyndicalists who, a year later in the Fifth Congress, changed its name to *Federación Obrera Regional Argentina*, and adopted a consitution that proclaimed the ultimate objective of the FORA to be the establishment of "anarchist Communism."

The first decade of the present century was the "heroic" period of the Argentine labor movement. Those dominating the FORA were stanch believers in direct action and were strongly against signing collective agreements with employers because they considered that to be "class collaboration." They followed the procedure of presenting demands to employers, and if these were not immediately accepted, of going on strike forthwith. Nor would the anarchosyndicalists maintain paid officials in their unions, because they considered that any worker who lived from the dues collected from his fellows was "exploiting" them. Trade-union leadership was a purely voluntary endeavor, the only compensation for which was the joy of seeing one's fellows' lot improved, and the belief that one was forwarding the cause of the somewhat mystic "revolution."

However, the anarchosyndicalists were not completely without rivals during these years. In 1905 the Socialists established the Unión General de Trabajadores, which in 1909 was converted into the Confederación Obrera Regional Argentina (CORA), and passed under the influence of syndicalist elements, who patterned their organization and tactics on those of the CGT of France at that time.

The attitude of the government during these years was one of unmitigated hostility toward organized labor, of whatever color. Strikes, both partial and general, were met by highly repressive actions on the part of the police, and sometimes of the army. Labor leaders were arrested and sent to concentration camps in the southern part of the country,

Anarchosyndicalist influence in the Argentine labor movement re-

or they were deported, if they were foreigners.

mained dominant until 1910. In that year the FORA leaders announced their intention of sabotaging the ceremonies arranged by the government to celebrate the first centenary of Argentine independence. In reprisal the government organized bands of civilian toughs who turned Buenos Aires and some of the provincial towns into veritable battlegrounds. These gangs burned the headquarters of the FORA, the CORA, and the Socialist Party, destroyed the anarchist and Socialist printing presses, and beat up and even killed many of the workers who tried to defend these institutions.

The FORA suffered most from this persecution and for about two years was virtually driven underground. When it emerged in 1912, it had lost control of the labor movement to the more moderate syndicalist and Socialist elements in the CORA, and the anarchists never again succeeded in gaining predominance in Argentine organized labor.

While all of this was transpiring in Argentina, somewhat similar events were taking place in several of the other Latin American countries. Across the river in Uruguay, anarchosyndicalist elements organized the Federación Obrera Regional Uruguaya (FORU), which, while somewhat more moderate than its Argentine counterpart, was basically of the same orientation. A similar organization, Federación Obrera Regional Paraguaya (FORP), was established in Paraguay.

In Chile the early 1900's were also a "heroic" epoch for the labor movement. Around the turn of the century numerous "resistance societies" were organized, most of them under anarchosyndicalist inspiration, among the artisans of the principal cities, as well as among seamen and the nitrate workers of the northernmost provinces. There were violent strikes in Valparaíso in 1903, and in the nitrate *pampas* in 1907, the latter resulting in the shooting of hundreds of unarmed workers by soldiers in the city of Iquique, an event still vividly recalled in that part of the country.

The first central labor group in Chile was established in 1909, the Gran Federación Obrera de Chile (GFOC). Interestingly enough, it was launched at first by a conservative lawyer who saw in it a means of forwarding his own political career. However, it was soon penetrated by more radical elements, and, in 1916, the GFOC was captured by members of the Partido Socialista Obrero (PSO), which had been organized a few years before by a printing trades leader, Luis Emilio Recabarren.

In Brazil, too, the labor government got well under way in the years before World War I. Here again, the anarchosyndicalists were the principal political group to take leadership in the unions. In 1909 they established the country's first central labor group, the Confederação Operaria do Brasil (COB). The Brazilian anarchists were much more moderate and pacific than their Argentine counterparts, and were more inclined toward collective bargining, and early admitted the usefulness of having full-time trade union officials paid by the unions themselves. The COB, however, was faced with extraordinarily great difficulties as a result of the tremendous distances between the principal centers of labor activity, Recife, Bahía, Rio de Janeiro, Santos and São Paulo, and Porto Alegre, and the fact that the only means of transport among most of them was by sea.

In Cuba the organized labor movement grew with some rapidity in the early years of the new republic. The tobacco workers, the railroaders, and the maritime workers were among the first groups to establish solid organizations. These were under both anarchosyndicalist and Socialist influence.

Finally, in the case of Mexico, the re-establishment of the labor movement slightly preceded the outbreak of the Revolution of 1910. In the years immediately prior to 1910, there were important strikes in the Canaea copper mines and in the textile factories of Puebla. At the same time, the Partido Liberal, an anarchosyndicalist-inclined political group headed by the Flores Magón brothers, carried on an active propaganda for the establishment of a national labor movement. Interestingly enough, the influence of the Industrial Workers of the World (IWW) of the United States was of considerable significance at this time, particularly among the *braceros*, workers who then as now came North looking for jobs in the United States.

During World War I, the labor movements of Latin America increased in numbers and influence. Wartime circumstances stimulated the rapid development of industry and, at the same time, there was a rapid increase in prices. These factors made the labor movement both militant and effective.

In Argentina, the FORA and the CORA merged in 1914, but split again the following year over the old problem of whether the organized labor movement should be pledged to the achievement of "anarchist Communism." The majority argued that it should not become known as the FORA of the Ninth Congress; the minority felt that it should receive the sobriquet FORA of the Fifth Congress. Both groups grew rapidly in membership, and there were several important strikes, including a national railway walkout in 1917. The relatively friendly attitude of the Radical Party government of President Hipólito Irigoyen, which came to power in 1916, was an added stimulus to the growth of organized labor.

In Uruguay and Brazil, too, the economics of the war aided the development of the labor movement. Important strikes among maritime workers and textile workers in Brazil, and among the dockers and various other groups in Uruguay were the high lights of this period.

In Chile, the capture of the Gran Federación Obrera de Chile by the Socialists signified the general radicalization of the labor movement. The name of the group was changed in 1917 to Federación Obrera de Chile (FOC), and it adopted a centralized form of organization and a close alliance with the Socialists. Meanwhile, a Chilean offshoot of the United States IWW was established (using the same initials) with particular strength among the maritime workers and others in the ports up and down the country's attenuated coastline.

The Mexican labor movement grew rapidly during the revolution. Under Francisco Madero the first central labor group, the Casa del Obrero Mundial, was established. With the renewal of civil war after Madero's death, the Casa made an alliance with the forces of Venustiano Carranza, whereby it was given freedom to conduct its activities behind the Carranza lines in return for raising troops to fight in Carranza's army. The Casa's "red battalions" became an important element in Carranza's "Constitutionalist" army.

When Carranza gained dominance over most of Mexico, relations became somewhat estranged between the "First Chief of the Revolution" and organized labor. As the result of an electricity strike in Mexico City in 1916, several leading labor figures were sentenced to death, including Luis Morones, but none of them was executed. From then on, the labor leaders enjoyed the protection of Carranza's most powerful lieutenant, Alvaro Obregón. In 1918 they established the first truly national labor center, the Confederación Regional Obrera Mexicana, the famous CROM. Interestingly enough, the lingering anarchist strain in Mexican labor thinking was shown in the name of this group, copied as it was from the FORA of Argentina.

During World War I the labor movement began to grow in a number of countries in which it had previously been of relatively little consequence. Thus, in Peru the Federación Obrera Regional del Peru was organized. In 1918 it won the enactment by the government of a national eight-hour-day law as a result of a general strike. In Bolivia the Federación Obrera de Bolivia was established under anarchosyndicalist influence, and gained some following among artisan groups in La Paz and other centers. The first beginnings of a labor movement were to be seen in Colombia and in one or two of the Central American republics, although in these most of the organizations were of a mutual-benefit rather than trade-union variety.

The 1920's were generally a period of retrogression for the labor movements of the more important Latin American countries. The impetus for industrialization was relaxed, with the return of manufactured goods from Europe and North America to Latin American markets. Furthermore, the governments of many of the countries were particularly reactionary and dictatorial during these years. Finally, there were important divisions along political lines in several countries.

In Argentina, the labor movement was badly split during most of the 1920's. Although an effort was made to unify the two FORA's in 1922, the FORA of the Fifth Congress finally refused to participate in the new Unión Sindical Argentina (USA), which ended up weaker than the old FORA of the Ninth Congress since the railroad workers' organizations also refused to become affiliated with it. In 1926 two railroad workers' unions, La Fraternidad and Unión Ferroviaria, took the lead in establishing a third central labor group, the Confederación Obrera Argentina (COA), while in 1929 the Communists launched still another organization under the name of Comité de Unidad Clasista.

It was not until after the revolution of September 6, 1930, that a movement back toward unification of Argentine labor began.

The Uruguayan labor movement reflected pretty much the events in Argentina. A Unión Sindical Uruguaya (USU) was established in 1922 under syndicalist and Socialist influence, although the old anarchist FORU continued to exist. The Communists, after trying to get control of the USU and failing, withdrew in the late 1920's to establish a central labor organization of their own.

In Brazil, the organized workers were also divided, with the Communist Party, which was formed in 1922 by young anarchist labor leaders, struggling with their former comrades for control of the labor movement. The governments of this period were particularly hostile to the labor movement.

Although the organized workers had much to do with electing the Liberal Party candidate Gerardo Machado to the Cuban presidency in 1924, their alliance was short-lived. In 1924 the first national central labor body, the Confederación Nacional Obrera Cubana was established, at first under anarchist influence, but shortly falling under Communist control. Anti-Communist elements established a rival group, the Federación de Trabajadores de Cuba. Both labor groups were persecuted by the Machado regime, as it degenerated into the cruelest dictatorship that Cuba had had up until that time.

The Mexican labor movement of the 1920's was an exception to the decline that seemed to prevail elsewhere. With the ouster of Carranza by General Obregón in 1920, and the latter's assumption of the presidency later in the year, the CROM was in a particularly favored condition. It was strongly backed by the Obregón government, and many of its top leaders were given government jobs, through which they were able to finance the CROM with a certain munificence. Under President Plutarco Elías Calles, Luis Morones, Secretary General of the CROM, served, after 1924, as Minister of Labor and was one of the strong men of the regime.

During this period of close relations between the government and the CROM, there came into existence several dissident and smaller labor groups. One of these was the Confederación General de Trabajadores, which claimed to be loyal to the anarchosyndicalist ideas that had originally animated many of the leaders of the CROM. There also came into existence a Catholic labor group, which never gained any great importance. Both of these minority groups in the labor movement felt the heavy hand of the government from time to time.

The palmy days of the CROM lasted until late 1927. At that time, President Calles decided to change the constitution so as to permit the re-election of his predecessor, General Obregón. Luis Morones and the rest of the CROM leadership opposed this, since they felt that Morones himself should succeed to the presidency. As a result of this fight, the benevolent attitude of the government toward the CROM changed, and in the years that followed, the CROM was racked with one split after another, most of them fomented or encouraged by state governors or ministers of the national government acting in accord with the regime's general policy of weakening and dividing the labor movement.

The Mexican Government was not the only one in Latin America that adopted a prolabor attitude at one point or another during the 1920's. The government of President Arturo Alessandri in Chile began a policy that was to be followed by almost every other national government in Latin America in the two or three ensuing decades, when it gave, for the first time, legal recognition to the organized labor movement.

Alessandri, generally known as the first middle-class president of Chile, had been elected with the support of the organized workers in 1920. One of his first acts had been to commission the writing of a Labor Code, and this document was presented to congress in 1922. However, it was not until two years later in the midst of a constitutional-military crisis, which ultimately brought the downfall of Alessandri in September, 1924, that most of the elements of the Labor Code were written into law.

The labor laws passed on September 8, 1924, were far-reaching. Not only did they provide factory legislation and the beginnings of a social-security system, but they also provided for the legalization of trade unions and for an orderly system of collective bargaining. Prerequisites were established before a union could obtain legal recognition, and theoretically only a duly recognized union could thenceforward engage in collective bargaining. A system of conciliation and arbitration tribunals was set up to facilitate the bargaining process.

These laws were put into effect after the return to power of President Alessandri in March, 1925. Although he fell once again six months later, the process of establishing legal unions throughout the country was continued by Carlos Ibáñez, who became the dominant figure and finally the dictator of Chile, and who remained in power until the middle of 1931.

Prior to the passage of the 1924 labor laws the dominant political elements in the Chilean labor movement had been the anarchosyndicalists and the Communists—Recabarren's Partido Socialista Obrero having been converted into the Communist Party at the end of 1922. Both of these elements opposed the legalization of unions under their control, fearing, quite rightly, that with government recognition would come government direction over the unions. However, in spite of this opposition during the 1925–31 period, the great majority of unions in manufacturing, the mines, the maritime trades, and among white-collar workers sought and obtained legal recognition.

Quite understandably, the leadership of these legal unions was in conflict with the political groups that led the old "unlegal" organizations. It was from these latter groups that the core of the new Socialist Party was to come in the post-Ibáñez period. During the Ibáñez dictatorship, the legal unions were brought together in two central groups, the Confederación Nacional de Sindicatos Industriales and the Confederación Nacional de Sindicatos Profesionales, which soon after the fall of Ibáñez were to merge to form the Confederación Nacional de Sindicatos Legales.

During the 1930's a number of governments followed the Chilean lead by enacting extensive labor legislation and establishing a system for legal recognition of the labor organizations. This trend reflected the growing importance of the organized labor movement both in numbers and as an element in the process of revolutionary change that was already under way throughout the hemisphere. The labor movement, as well as reflecting this change, had become a basic element in pushing it forward.

During the 1930's, too, the political leadership of the labor movement changed. The defeat of the anarchosyndicalists became definitive, and the struggle for control of organized labor centered upon the Communists and a variety of other parties that advocated fundamental changes in the economic, social, and political life of their respective countries.

The defeat of the anarchists in the labor movement reflected, it seems to me, the changed nature of the Latin American urban labor force. The extreme individualism of the anarchists tended to appeal to the small artisan who had hopes of becoming the owner of a small shop someday himself. However, it had relatively little appeal to workers in factories, where relations with the boss were more impersonal, where there was relatively severe discipline, and where the need for the kind of law and order in relations with the employers that could be provided by collective bargaining was obviously necessary. Furthermore, few factory workers ever dreamed that they might themselves become factory owners.

Under these changed circumstances, leadership of the unions passed to political groups which, although they wanted to use the unions for their own purposes, accepted the idea of collective bargaining and more or less orderly handling of relations with the employers. After some hesitation, the Communists did accept collective bargaining, as did the other parties that became their principal rivals in the labor movement. But there was no room for the free-wheeling, direct-action tactics of the anarchosyndicalists.

During the 1930's, the labor movements of Latin America grew apace. As a direct result of the Great Depression, the industrialization of the area proceeded rapidly, and, with labor's increase in size, its political importance also mounted. Increasingly, the labor movements won laws that not only provided for legal recognition of unions, but also forced employers to deal with legally recognized labor groups.

In Argentina, the Confederación General del Trabajo (CGT) was established only a few weeks after the military coup of September 6, 1930, through the merger of the old COA and USA. Although the USA broke away again five years later, the CGT came to contain the great majority of the organized workers of Argentina, who by the advent of the Juan Domingo Perón regime in 1946 numbered perhaps 300,000 to 350,000. However, until 1943, no government had taken much interest in the welfare of the workers, and Argentina lagged behind the rest of the area in terms of labor and social legislation, thus paving the way for the able and agile demagoguery of Perón.

In Brazil, the Revolution of 1930, which brought Getulio Vargas to power, marked the beginning of a period of real economic, social, and political change. It represented the passing of power over the nation as a whole from the rural landlords to the cities, and Vargas was very aware of the fact that the workers made up an important element of the urban population.

Early in 1931 the Vargas regime passed the first law providing for legalization of the unions. Although both Communists and anarchists fought the implementation of this law, several thousand unions were legalized within the next three or four years. During the first five years of the Vargas administration, the various radical elements continued to dominate most of the labor organizations, but after the failure of a left-wing attempt, led by the Communists, to seize the government by force in November, 1935, Vargas cracked down ruthlessly on all left-wing elements in the unions. After he proclaimed the fascist-modeled New State regime in November, 1937, the labor movement was completely reorganized, being absolutely submitted to the control of the Ministry of Labor. Collective bargaining was eliminated in favor of a system of labor courts that dealt not only with requests for wage increases but with individual workers' grievances. This system endured until after the ouster of Vargas in October, 1945.

The Mexican labor movement was reunified in 1936 during the administration of President Lázaro Cárdenas. At that time most of the existing central labor groups were merged to form the Confederación de Trabajadores de Mexico (CTM). Like its predecessor, the CROM, the CTM was closely associated with the government. It has continued to be so until the present day. It remains the largest of the now numerous central labor groups in Mexico.

The Cuban labor movement enjoyed a short period of freedom of action immediately succeeding the fall of the Machado dictatorship in August, 1933. However, by 1935, the new dictatorship of Colonel Fulgencio Batista had largely broken the labor movement. It was not revived until 1938, when, as a result of a deal between Batista and the Communist Party, Batista allowed the Communists to establish under their control a new central labor group known as the Confederación de Trabajadores de Cuba. It remained under Communist control as long as Batista ruled, but after the election of a government of the Auténtico Party in 1944 it passed under Auténtico control.

In Chile the political and trade-union situation remained chaotic for some time after the fall of dictator Carlos Ibáñez in August, 1931. The Stalinist Communists revived the Federación Obrera de Chile. It had a powerful rival in the Confederación Nacional de Sindicatos Legales, while the anarchists and the Trotskyite Communists controlled a number of independent unions outside of either of the national confederations.

In June, 1932, a short-lived Socialist Republic, under the leadership of Colonel Marmaduque Grove, founder of the Chilean air force, rallied the backing of all of the labor groups except the Stalinist Communists and their FOC. In elections that followed the fall of the Socialist Republic, Grove ran for the presidency against Arturo Alessandri and several other nominees. He again had the backing of most of the labor movement. Early in 1933 the parties that had backed Grove in his unsuccessful campaign against Alessandri merged to form the Partido Socialista.

During the rest of the 1930's the Socialists dominated the Chilean labor movement. In December, 1936, the FOC and the Confederación Nacional de Sindicatos Legales merged to form the Confederación de Trabajadores de Chile (CTC), with a Socialist as Secretary General and a Communist as his assistant. The CTC formed a part of the Popular Front, which won the elections of 1938 and placed its candidate, Pedro Aguirre Cerda, in the presidency.

During the three-year regime of President Aguirre Cerda, the labor movement grew more rapidly than at any previous time in its history. Virtually all of the organizable workers in Chile were brought into the labor movement, including those in manufacturing, the mines, transport, government employment, and even the banks and larger commercial establishments. Collective bargaining became the rule of Chilean labor relations. Throughout this period the Socialists remained the largest element in the labor movement, with the Communists and others being of secondary importance. The anarchosyndicalists continued throughout the period to maintain their own separate organization, the Confederación General de Trabajadores.

During World War II the Communists reached the apogee of their influence in the Latin American labor movement as a result of various factors. For one thing, during the period from June 22, 1941, until the end of the war, the Communists followed a policy of discouraging all labor militancy, and of having cordial relations with all employers and with any government that was sympathetic to the cause of the Soviet Union and its allies. As a result, employers and governments were much more willing to deal with the Communist union leaders than with those of other political parties, who were more concerned with the welfare of their own particular followers than with the problems of the U.S.S.R.

This attitude was particularly useful to the Communists in those countries dominated by dictatorships. In Peru, Nicaragua, and Cuba, dictators favored the Communists while refusing to allow democratic trade-union leaders to function freely. For a short while even Generalissimo Rafael Leonidas Trujillo of the Dominican Republic gave free rein to the Communists.

In the second place, the cause of the Allies was popular among workers and the general public in the Latin American countries. The Communists of the various countries claimed full credit for themselves for the Russian victories at Stalingrad and elsewhere, and some of the general aura of victory rubbed off on the Latin American Communists, at least for a short period.

In some cases, moreover, the influence of the principal opponents of the Communists declined during the war, thus helping the growth of Communist influence in the trade-union movement and in general public opinion. This was particularly the case in Chile, where successive splits in the socialist ranks after 1940 greatly weakened that party.

Finally, the influence of the only existing international labor group in the Latin American area, the Confederación de Trabajadores de América Latina (CTAL), was thrown on the side of the Communists. Vicente Lombardo Toledano, the Secretary General of the CTAL, sided consistently the the Communists in disputes with their opponents in the various national labor movements, and used his influence to get various governments, particularly those headed by dictators, to take the same attitude.

After World War II, the Communist influence in Latin American organized labor declined precipitately. The close association with the Soviet Union, which had helped them during the War, was a handicap when the Cold War began. The Communists thus lost out in the labor movements of Mexico, Colombia, Uruguay, and, for a while, Chile. Furthermore, in the wake of World War II, several of the Latin American dictatorships were overthrown, and anti-Communist popular parties achieved legality, and in some cases came to power. As a result, the Communists lost control of the labor movements of Cuba, Venezuela, Peru, and Costa Rica.

The influence of the United States labor movement was also thrown against the Communists in the postwar period. The AFL named Serafino Romualdi as its Latin American representative, and he began a job of organizing the anti-Communist forces in the various national labor movements. The establishment of the Confederación Interamericana de Trabajadores in 1948, and of its successor, the Organización Regional Interamericana de Trabajadores (ORIT) in 1951, is to a very large extent the result of his work. Since its foundation, the ORIT has included within its ranks the majority of the organized workers of Latin America.

In addition to helping counteract Communist influence in Latin America's organized labor, the United States trade unionists have helped labor movements become much more effective in their work of collective bargaining. Through extensive advice and aid in establishing a wide variety of leadership training courses in the United States, Puerto Rico, and Latin America itself, United States unions have helped to strengthen the democratic elements within Latin American organized labor.

After Fidel Castro's rise to power in Cuba, it seemed possible that the Communists would be able to recoup some of the influence that they had lost in the labor movements of Latin America during the 1950's. When it had not as yet fallen into the hands of the Communists the Cuban labor movement under Castro made a "defensive-offensive" alliance with the Confederación de Trabajadores de Venezuela, and for some time after the Communists took over the CTC, the alliance remained in effect. Under Communist influence, the CTC launched a campaign to establish a "revolutionary hemispheric confederation of workers," and at first it looked as if its leaders might succeed in lining up considerable support for such an organization.

However, as the Communist nature of the Castro regime became increasingly clear, and as the Castro government's control over the Cuban labor movement became more obvious, the enthusiasm for the new Latin American labor confederation declined. When its founding congress was finally held in Chile in September, 1962, it included only one national labor center that had not been in the Communist-controlled Central

Unica de Trabajadores de Chile, which had been in the hands of the Communists since its establishment in 1952.

The Communists today remain a minority group in the labor movement of most of the Latin American countries. They dominate the principal central labor groups of Chile and Ecuador, although they actually control only a minority of the unions belonging to them. Elsewhere, they control only a fraction of the labor movements, at best.

In Mexico, most of the existing unions are closely allied with the government of the Partido Revolucionario Institucional. In Venezuela, Bolivia, Peru, and the Dominican Republic the labor movements are controlled in their majority by national revolutionary parties, and in Costa Rica the same kind of party is of major importance. In Colombia and Honduras the Liberal parties are the dominant element in organized labor, while in Argentina the Peronistas and independents are the principal political groups with power in labor.

In Brazil, most workers look upon the late Getulio Vargas' Partido Trabalhista Brasileiro (PTB) as their political representative. However, the PTB is a very heterogeneous party, which does not operate as such in the trade unions. In some areas, notably the states of Pernambuco and Guanabara, it has been seriously infiltrated by the Communists. Thus, although the Communists as such remain a minority group in Brazilian organized labor, they have been able to gain considerable influence in the trade unions. They are generally considered to dominate two of the country's five national labor confederations, and to have decisive influence in a third. Two remain outside of their control.

In several countries the Christian Democratic parties are of growing importance in the national labor movements. In Chile, the Christian Democrats represent the single largest political element in the Central Unica de Trabajadores, but are faced with a united front of other parties under Communist leadership and control. In Venezuela, the Christian Democrats are probably the second most important political group in organized labor, after the Democratic Action Party. In Brazil, the Christian Democrats are also gaining some strength, although their penetration of the labor movement is of comparatively recent origin.

Thus, in most Latin American countries, the labor movements have shown a high degree of immunity to penetration by totalitarian forces. Although they retain a revolutionary force, using their influence to bring about basic economic, social, and political changes, they seek to bring about these changes through democratic means. The control of the labor movements of most of the Latin American nations by democratic elements is a strong factor favoring a democratic solution to the deep crisis through which the whole region is passing today.

The University Student* | K. H. SILVERT

The profundity of change and the immense differences among coexisting groups in Latin America, both inside and outside the university, are what make of most political disagreements an intense and sometimes total clash. Rural Latin America is occupied by persons living in hunting and fishing cultures, in stable isolated agricultural towns, and in fiefs; there is also the small rural aristocracy professing the religious universalism of the medieval upper class. Urban Latin America, by and large, is inhabited both by traditionalists who respect hierarchy, oppose change, and judge all social action by religious precept, and by very different persons of modern temperament and relativistic ideas who are willing to accept some compromise on social issues and are ideologically committed to at least a limited secularism.

University students represent many but not all of these social segments. They are recruited overwhelmingly from urban centers. They are not by definition a modernizing element; indeed, they may form part of broader social groups whose strength powerfully inhibits development. But whatever the students' basic value commitment, they are in a world of disagreement more profound than explicitly ideological division. Two ways of life, two ways of thought, oppose each other in the Latin American city, and the accommodations tenuously lacing them can be only temporary, and adjustment forced by the need to maintain the mechanics of urban and quasi-national life. In the absence of a single national community to which all citizens unequivocally belong, Latin Americans are split into qualitatively different kinds of loyalty patterns. Villagers are concerned first with family and tribe, traditionalists with family and church and friendship commitments, and modernizers with building the impersonal mechanisms of national, industrial society. Given this situation, no single set of criteria of legitimacy can provide the consensus from which flows the power necessary for stable public institutions. The Latin American university student must make a relatively conscious choice from among a set of worlds, for he cannot merely fit himself into an already established and coherent community embracing all his peers.

good

* Reprinted from *Continuity and Change in Latin America*, edited by John J. Johnson, with the permission of the publishers, Stanford University Press. © 1964 by the Board of Trustees of the Leland Stanford Junior University. (Footnotes in the original version have been omitted.)

Mediterranean traditionalism can coexist for relatively long periods with some degree of modern social and economic organization. Indeed, all of Latin America's more economically developed states offer persistent demonstration that the payment of the privileges of the old for the benefits of the new can be deferred for quite a while. But the price of this indulgence is a weak institutional structure, unable to guarantee either continuity or predictability and thus inhibitive of contained and ordered change.⟦The power that Latin American student groups have demonstrated since the first decades of this century is, then, in inverse relation to the strength of governments and the efficacy of the university administrations themselves. The relative influence of organized student movement must be heightened by the essential fragility of societies in transition toward modern nationhood.⟧

CLASS AND THE NATURE OF STUDENT POWER

Weak social institutions make more salient the power of any organized group, whether composed of students, military officers, or clergy. The nastily sharp class distinctions of all Latin America also serve to protect rebels against the established order if they enjoy the power of high social status. The Latin American university traditionally has served to certify the elite position of the sons of the upper class. Access to higher education is still so restricted for the general population that one might reasonably conclude that the student selection process in most Latin American countries still effectively excludes the economically underprivileged. The educational pyramid narrows so abruptly that such a conclusion is inescapable. As recently as 1950, for example, 49 per cent of the population over 15 years of age in Latin America had no primary schooling at all or had failed to complete the first year; 44 per cent had more than a year of primary education, but only 8 per cent had completed it. Six per cent had some secondary school training, and 2 per cent had graduated; only 1 per cent of the population over 15 had attended an institution of higher learning. This steep decline in school attendance was expressed graphically in the Mexican ten-year educational plan submitted to President Adolfo López Mateos on October 27, 1959:

> According to recent information (1956), of every thousand children who manage to put their feet on the first rung of primary school [on the same base, 460 more never get even that far], only one reaches the last grade of the professional school. . . . During the course of the first six grades . . . no fewer than 866 are left on the road. Only 59 get to the threshold of secondary education; but of these, 32 drop out during the three scholastic grades of secondary, pre-vocational, and special educa-

tion, who added to the previous ones give us the figure of 973. Only nine arrive at the *bachillerato,* vocational education, and the professional cycle of primary normal instruction, of whom three drop out in the two or three grades involved . . . , with whom the total of desertion rises to 994. And, finally, only six get to higher education, but of these five drop out. . . . In summary, through the course of the sixteen grades that comprise a complete educational scale, 999 abandon their studies and only one finishes. . . . [To this we must add] the alarming circumstance that 471 abandon school . . . in the first grade.[1]

The survey adduces reasons for non-attendance and abandonment that are a direct function of class position: it estimates that at the time the report was prepared, 600,000 children then of school age had never attended school, and that an additional 366,000 had abandoned school for economic reasons, while 175,000 were out of school because of illness. Because the Mexican data are certainly not atypical, we may reasonably conclude that despite important differences in primary- and secondary-school attendance between, for example, Haiti at one extreme and Argentina at the other higher education as such remains the privilege of the few. The favored, moreover, come largely from families in the middle and upper-middle occupational categories in the national capitals; a somewhat smaller group comes from the same occupational levels in smaller cities; and a still smaller element is from the homes of higher-level workers and artisans, almost invariably from the capital. Numerous studies confirm the generality of this pattern, despite a few variant situations, mostly in provincial areas. For example:

> The group that receives higher education is naturally very much smaller than the "middle sectors," but in all the Central American countries it is observed that the majority of university students—as well as secondary school students—come from those urban middle sectors comprised of professionals, businessmen, and white-collar employees; and an important minority from artisan or worker groups.[2]

A 1961 survey of the law students in the University of Panama showed that about a third of the sample had fathers in the ranks of skilled, semi-skilled, or unskilled labor. It is worth adding here that only in Argentina, Chile, Cuba, and Panama, of all the Latin American republics, is the modal point of the educated population among those who have completed from four to six years of primary education. To put it another way, it is only in these four countries that there is a sufficiently broad base of persons with primary education to provide some social

[1] As quoted in Mexican news accounts of Oct. 28, 1959.
[2] Marshall Wolfe, "Las Clases medias en Centroamérica; Garacterísticas que presentan en la actualidad y requisitos para su desarrollo," CEPAL, Comité de Cooperacíon Económica del Istmo Centroamericano, Oct. 18, 1960, p. 29 (mimeo).

heterogeneity to the student body passing through secondary education into the university—a fact that goes far toward explaining the relatively high percentage of persons of lower occupational origins in the Panamanian law school.

There should be no presumption, however, that the Latin American university in general serves as an important group-mobility channel for lower-class persons. Students from working-class families rarely attend the most prestigious faculties or complete the full course of study. Further, it is probable that students with "worker" fathers have a life style characteristic of the lower-middle classes. The situation at the University of Chile accurately reflects the general state of affairs:

> The University's 13,000 students constitute no more than 1.5 per cent of the young people between 17 and 25 years of age in Chile, and the sons of working-class families have little hope of reaching any of the major professional schools. But this is not because of anything inherent in the University itself but rather is a reflection of general economic conditions and the desperate poverty of Chile's rural and urban masses. . . . The University remains a stronghold of Chile's middle class, many of whom themselves are hard pressed by need and are able to stay in the University only with great sacrifice.[3]

Student leadership also reflects this class influence. The only large-scale empirical study of student leaders in Latin America, an inquiry into the Chilean Student Federation (FECH), unequivocally establishes the middle-level occupational origins of those student leaders since 1920. The relatively large numbers of leaders coming to the capital from provincial cities, however, suggests that we should look to physical mobility as a probably significant element in the more general social picture.

The well-advertised interest of some Latin American university students in practical politics is a direct consequence of the introduction of new middle elements into full social participation in the more developed countries after the turn of the century. The symbol of their emergency is the Córdoba Reform of 1918, a declaration of academic independence and political intent. Wherever stimulated by the Argentine initiative, the Reformists adopted a populist tone reflecting the identification of newly integrating groups with all alienated elements, in a pattern not unlike the all-embracing national spirit of the French bourgeoisie in their own revolutionary day. The Reform created an elaborated body of doctrine that has been in constant use throughout Latin America ever since.

The traditional elitist social function of the university was by no means in direct contradiction with the thoughts of the newly mobile, who had

---

[3] Frank Bonilla, "The Student Federation of Chile: 50 Years of Political Action," *Journal of Inder-American Studies* (July 1960), p. 313.

assumed the responsibility of assisting their less fortunate fellows. The politics of the situation, however, were violently wrenched. Instead of producing only leaders of stasis, the university also began to create leaders of change. Within their academic environment the two elements mingled in fashions quite like those of the new strata developing in society as a whole. Rightists, forced into activism to maintain their positions, fomented the importation of new ideologies of conservatism from Europe, partially accounting for the Nazi and Falangist strains in the politics of Chile, Brazil, Argentina, and many other countries in the 1930's and 1940's, and still in full bloom in Argentina. Meanwhile, leftists seized on the traditions of elitism to justify a tutelary stance in anticipation of the reality of the victory of populist democracy.

Eduardo Frei, leader of the Christian Democrats in Chile and a leading exponent of "government by technician" in Latin America, provides this contemporary expression of the university as an agency for training elites:

> The University cannot isolate itself from this historical process [of modernization]; and in its fashion it can be a decisive factor in its orientation. Is it prepared for it, or does youth follow one set of paths, the University others, without giving them any reply? Is it only a machine to produce professionals who, on leaving the university, feel themselves frustrated . . . ?
>
> . . . The University is a social force and a great moral reserve. . . .
>
> It is now time for the University to provide ideas and cadres of responsible men capable of recognizing and stating the truth in an objective manner, and capable of elaborating and utilizing formulas that do not rest on intuition or on ambition disguised as "ability." . . .
>
> The University can provide the governing elites for this decisive historical crossroads, giving them a vision of the world and of our own America.[4]

The conscious acceptance of direct social responsibility by the new university students is an implicit identification of themselves as actual or aspirant members of an expanding elite. If there is some negative correlation between group size and elitist attitudes, then the exclusiveness of higher education in Latin America would seem to contribute importantly to the psychology of leadership. In the mid-1950's there were in all Latin America only about 350,000 registered students in institutions of higher learning, both state and private. Of this number, 40 per cent were registered in Argentine institutions, and almost half of them matriculated in one university—the National University of Buenos Aires. And once again it should be recalled that the drop-out rate is extremely high, so that very few of even these small numbers will ever be graduated.

[4] Eduardo Frei Montalva, "La Universidad, conciencia social de la Nación," *Prólogo* (Oct.–Nov. 1962), pp. 8–11 and passim.

There is some disagreement about these figures, for criteria concerning which institutions and which students should be considered of university level vary widely among countries and experts. Some estimates, for example, exclude schools of fine arts and theology, and other schools dedicated solely to the humanities. The student count is also a problem, for in many countries the central national university has some administrative responsibility for the college preparatory work in the secondary school system, and sometimes the universities either run the entire system or maintain one or more prestigious secondary schools. In any event, the highest enrollment figures given do not exceed 550,000 for 1960, still a very small figure when compared with that for the United States (four million students in higher education on approximately the same population base), and of course made even smaller by the high drop-out rate. On a percentage basis, the above figure is very small, especially when viewed against the large urban populations of many Latin American countries. Yet in absolute numbers it is large enough to cover a broad social spectrum including significant middle elements and some marginal upper-lower ones. Relative smallness and objective largeness justify ideologies of planned development, reinforcing the students' view of the university as a training center for the future holders of the power they expect at least partially to create for themselves.

THE STUDENT IN THE LARGE
STATE UNIVERSITY

Available information is much too sparse to permit a detailed discussion of differences between students in private and religious institutions and those in the state-operated universities. [With few exceptions the only student organizations that historically have had important roles in political life are those of the major national universities in the capital cities] However, where regional universities do experience student convulsion, they, too, are almost always within the state system. The State University of São Paulo, for example, has been consistently involved in national politics, and contributed not a few martyrs to the anti-Vargas cause during the early days of his experiment in authoritarian populism. Other cases could be cited of significant student activities in the regional public universities of Argentina, Chile, Peru, and Mexico, but even so, their effect on national life is usually indirect. This generalization holds true even though it was the regional university of Córdoba that played host to the delegates who promulgated the Reform of 1918. The ideal of the academic republic promulgated on that occasion had more profound ideological effect outside Argentina than within it. Nevertheless, even there the influences of the Reform were felt more strongly in other parts of the national university system than in Córdoba. As one Argentine authority summarized the results of the Reform in his country: "In truth there was no such reform, for the structure of the university, substantively as well as legally, was maintained. There were, on the other hand, statutory reforms, all tending toward seeing that the universities acquire a more flexible and efficacious rhythm of life."

The same author points out that within twenty years the national university system doubled in size, while administrative reform promoted a fresh academic spirit of freedom and innovation. The point here being made is that only the politics of national integration and development have stirred significant student action in this century. This ideological commitment behind student action explains why it is that both secular and religious private institutions are of little importance in general student movements, and why only major national issues have served to arouse students of the regional universities.

Of all Latin America's universities, the University of Buenos Aires is by far the largest, having something over 70,000 students. This number comprised about one-fifth the total university enrollment in Latin America less than a decade ago, and is still probably no less than 15 per cent of the total. This institution particularly merits discussion here not only because of its mammoth size, but also because the Student Federation of the University of Buenos Aires (FUBA) has long been politically active as well as formally participant in the administration of the university. Many of the generalizations hurried travelers make about Latin American universities and students are in reality but extensions of impressions of the famous case of the University of Buenos Aires.

Exactly 58,684 students were tallied in the census of October 1958 of the University of Buenos Aires, from which the following statistical profile is derived. (The number now is estimated at more than 70,000.) Seventy-five per cent of the student body was male, although the ratio varied widely from school to school within the university. In Philosophy and Letters, which embraces the education program, the sex ratio was reversed, while only two per cent of the engineering students were female. Ninety per cent of the students were below 30 years of age, the modal age being 20 years for the university as a whole, 21 in Engineering, 22 in Medicine, and 19 in Philosophy and Letters. These figures are not significantly different from those for any large United States university, and cast some doubt of how many "professional students" there actually are in at least this Latin American university. Ninety-one per cent of the students held Argentine citizenship, four per cent were from other Latin American countries, and the rest were resident non-citizens. Seventy per cent of the students were born in Greater Buenos

Aires and 13 per cent in the surrounding provinces. Only 2.2 per cent were born in towns of less than 2,000 population. The secondary school record of the students makes the urban nature of the student body even more apparent, for 80 per cent completed high school in Buenos Aires. Seventy-five per cent attended public secondary schools, while only 11 per cent were graduated from secondary parochial schools; the remainder were from secular private schools. As a group, then, the students were of normal university age, urban origin, and secular training.

Over 85 per cent of the students were single; 90 per cent had no children, and only 3 per cent had two or more children. Ninety per cent of them lived in a family situation, with either parents or a spouse. Thirty per cent were supported entirely by the family, a figure rising to 52 per cent in Medicine and 58 per cent in Dentistry. There were also 514 members of the armed forces registered. Only .6 per cent of the student body were employed in blue-collar occupations!

Twenty-seven per cent of the students' fathers and 33 per cent of their paternal grandfathers had been or were in employer positions; 10 per cent of the fathers and 5 per cent of the grandfathers had been or were professional. But only 5.4 per cent of the fathers and 8.3 per cent of the grandfathers had been or were of the laboring group.

Few of these students will ever receive their degrees. Approximately 30 per cent were in the first year of study at the time of the census, though this figure varied considerably by faculty. In Law, the freshmen were 49 per cent of the total. With 58,684 enrolled students, the university granted only 3,324 degrees in 1958. Normally the proportion of degrees awarded to freshmen registered is about 15 per cent. Drop-out rates for recent years vary from as much as 80 per cent in Architecture to 64 per cent in Law and 44 per cent in Medicine.

[In terms of party affiliation and attitudes toward the university, the students seem close to the Argentine national norm.] A poll taken in 1957 in the Faculty of Letters (often considered quite leftist) indicated that over 50 per cent of the students clustered about the center; 7 per cent said they were Communist, 8 per cent chose one or another of the conservative parties, and 22 per cent did not reply. Only 1 per cent avowed themselves Peronists. This student body has consistently returned reformist (center and left) student delegates to office, but only Exact Sciences has in recent years elected frankly Marxist student officers. Indeed, in the last two student elections the choice in the majority of faculties has fallen to the center and the right, and the reformist left and center-left have been forced to support moderate candidates in order to retain some power in the university administration. [In short, the University of Buenos Aires reflects all the political schisms of the upper and middle groups in Argentina. It is hardly surprising that Peron-

ism, a lower-class political movement, finds few supporters in this haven
of the middle- and upper-class Argentine.

Although the usual majority grouping of students calls itself reformist,
in deference to the Córdoba Reform, splits for electoral purposes are
common, and there is even striking evidence that some of the basic
academic tenets of the Reform are now being rejected by the Buenos
Aires students. Democratization of the university and its establishment
as a kind of autonomous academic republic governed by students as
well as faculty remain the goal of most students and professors. But
apparently there is much backsliding from some of the pedagogical
precepts implicit in these ideals. Only 1 per cent of the student body
receives scholarship assistance, for example, and certainly the scramble
for grades and academic advantage in Buenos Aires is as heated as
in many United States universities. On the crucial question of whether
the university should have entrance examinations (strongly opposed by
orthodox reformists), fully 70 per cent of the students supported some
kind of entrance examination or qualifying year of studies. Significantly,
in the most "popular" or socially least prestigious school, Economic Sciences, 47 per cent opposed any entrance requirement beyond the requisite secondary schooling.

FUBA has been politically restrained for the past several years, because of the general political instability of the country and the consequent threat of military intervention to force the government to oust
the elected university administration and appoint a new rector and
deans. The last major political student action of a public nature was
a massive demonstration in 1958 against permitting Catholic universities
to confer legally valid degrees. FUBA lost, and Argentina now has three
more or less regularly functioning clerical universities, two in Buenos
Aires and one in Córdoba. Otherwise, the fairly close collaboration between majority faculty and student groups has thus far prevented major
incidents and saved the university from intervention.

There is logic and relevance to the drift by reformists into a more
professional attitude toward the university and into politics of coalition
and limited compromise, activist but not narrowly fanatical. A recent
survey conducted among freshmen, seniors, and graduates of the Faculties of Economic Sciences, Medicine, and Exact Sciences shows unmistakably that there is a strong correlation between those students taking
a modern view of society (and who also are likely to be reformists),
and those accenting the vocational and technical aspects of learning.

> Taken as a whole, about a third of each sample [from Medicine] favored
> education for good citizenship and the building of a national spirit [the
> view of the old aristocracy as well as of the Reformists of 1918, although
> with a changed ideological substance], while the remainder favored a more

vocational and general cultural orientation. The figures as taken by mobility . . . indicate that with fair consistency the upwardly mobile tend to
respect more highly the practical and vocational functions of education,
as do those who rank highly on the national identification scale [the measure of modernism]. Low scorers on the national identification scale are
consistently above average in their desire for the formation of good citizens
and the national spirit.[5]

These correlations held constant through the Faculties of Economic
Sciences and Exact Sciences as well. It is only reasonable that technological change, the necessity for a high degree of specialization, and emphasis on economic development should lead modernizing Argentines to
insist upon improvement of vocational training at the university level,
even if at the apparent expense of some cherished notions of the "popular
university." This attitude explains a seeming contradiction in the literature concerning Latin American student movements. John P. Harrison,
for example, states in an article on the "political university" that "while
all of the aims of the reform movement mentioned above touch directly
upon the university as an institution, it is readily apparent that none
of them is concerned with curriculum revision or in improving the professional training of the student." Several pages later the author points
out, however, that reformism and curricular improvements are not necessarily mutually exclusive. "There has been, if anything, even less interest
in reforming university curricula and professional training to meet mid-
twentieth-century needs in those universities that closed their doors to
the reform movement than in those where it found fertile ground."

[Several interim conclusions would seem justified at this point: first,
that the Reformists of 1918 inherited the elitist notion of the university
from their predecessors; second, that because of their class origins and
general changes in the political environment, they imbued their assumption of an elite role with a populist and nationalist ideology vastly different from the ideals of their traditionalist predecessors; and third, that
with the passage of time the traditionalists have continued to conceive
the university's role as that of forming citizens in the Greek sense, while
the reformists have begun to value the quality of education as indirectly
contributory, through broader social processes, to nation-building. In
an important sense, then, the innovating student is approaching the
prevailing view of academicians in developed lands, while still continuing to place a greater weight on the immediate applicability of learning]
This view was given strong expression by Risieri Frondizi, brother of
ex-President Arturo Frondizi and rector of the University of Buenos
Aires from 1957 to 1962:

---

[5] Tentative findings are reported in Silvert and Bonilla, *Education and the Social
Meaning of Development:* A Preliminary Statement (New York 1961) Part II.

The Argentine university has wasted much of its energies in the search for ingenious solutions to administrative questions, without becoming aware that the problems of the university are of a pedagogical nature. . . . [It seems not to] matter that the university does no research, that one turns one's back on the needs of the country, that there are no professors fit to teach many courses, that the students still keep on repeating by rote the worn-out notes of past years . . . that there is no university life. . . . The university . . . should not be at the orders of a governor—or of a political party or an ideology—but rather ready to serve society, the people, who maintain it: not to give it what this or that person demands through his political spokesman, but what it [the society] needs for its progress, enrichment, and material and spiritual elevation.[6]

STUDENT POWER
AND POLITICAL ACTIVISM

The ascription of great political influence to student organizations implies that these organizations are surrogates for other interested social groups. It also suggests that if young persons can gain sufficient influence to change, on occasion, the course of national political life, then, as already noted, other power centers must be in such disarray as to elevate the relative power of any organized group. This argument has often been advanced to explain the prominence of the military's role in Latin American politics; it holds as well for student groups.

The following propositions may serve to explain relative student political strength in a more specific and functional sense:

1. All Latin American countries, with the possible exception of Cuba, are still in a pre-national state. Government is thus by definition weak; it can count on little anticipatory adjustment to law and thus, by the same token, has few means for the unequivocal imposition of regulation and sanction.

2. Instability and disorganization are characteristic not only of governments, but also of all interest and occupational associations. But because not all fall into disarray—or the same degree thereof—at the same time, the significance of and the relative power generated by the very fact of group organization vary from time to time and place to place.

3. The very explicitly defined class divisions, reinforced by tradition and custom, promise the university student an elevated chance of success in life. He comes from a middle- or upper-class family; he is acquiring the social certification of achievement and status. Even though he may be disappointed and fall into the "intellectual proletariat," his life chances are still very high, and he is realistic so to consider them. The

<hr>

[6] Risieri Frondizi, "La Universidad y sus misiones," *Comentario* (Oct.–Nov.–Dec. 1956), pp. 309 and passim.

following views expressed in the previously cited study of Panamanian law students imply that [at least some students use politics to bolster their already high chances of attainment]

> Their [the Nationalists'] expectation of success is high, and they seem to have a stronger motivation toward achievement than do the Moderates—radical nationalism may thus have been embraced because the success of the movement would mean the expansion of socio-economic opportunities, and because the Nationalists have projected their drive for achievement onto the nation as a whole.[7]

4. Traditional as well as modern persons place great stress upon the need for adequate leadership in Latin America; [the university is viewed as a necessary element in the training of leaders, and within the university, the faculty of law continues to produce the greatest number of political figures.] As we might expect, during the Aramburu government in Argentina (1955–58) 95 per cent of all high policy-making government officials were graduated from either a university or a military academy, and this figure rose to 100 per cent in 1960. Even during the quasi-populist Perón regime (1945–55), about 85 per cent of the policy-makers had higher degrees. Over half the persons at this level in 1960 were lawyers, and even during the Aramburu military interregnum, the career officers outnumbered the lawyers by only 14 to 12 in the top positions.

5. Youth is a relative concept to a certain extent. The exclusiveness of the university, coupled with strong family and class identification, makes of students apprentice professionals from the moment they matriculate. Thus the word *universitario* denotes anyone connected with the university, whether student, teaching assistant, professor, or graduate. The Latin American student is, then, not considered so callow as his North American counterpart and may be trusted with public power at an early age. For example, eight years after a revolution in which law students had played an important role, the Congress of Guatemala was still composed of deputies half of whom were 35 or below. Only six of 54 deputies were over 50 years of age.

6. [The strong desire for development on the part of major urban groups in Latin America has created a demand for a new socioeconomic ideology. The university is the natural site for the *pensador* and for the diffusion of his ideas]

7. The needs of Latin America's new industries have already impelled curricular revision and expansion in many Latin American universities

---

[7] Daniel Goldrich, *Radical Nationalism: The Political Orientations of Panamanian Law Students* (East Lansing: Bureau of Social and Political Research, 1962), p. 19.

in such fields as business administration and the sciences. But at least as important have been the effects of governmental commitments to partially planned procedures of economic growth, which are now given formal approval as an announced requirement of the Alliance for Progress, but which have been a long-standing administrative practice in such countries as Uruguay, Costa Rica, Mexico, and Chile. Economic planning has naturally force-fed the growth of faculties and departments of economics, but has also been felt in engineering, sociology, and public administration. Increased demand for technicians has fortified the power of the universities in these areas and has at the same time increased the student's certainty of success. The invitation to early manipulation of public power is quite explicit.

8. These circumstances, taken in sum and added to the social propinquity of the university situation, provide the conditions for the creation of student organizations that parallel the national parties. Wherever students have been studied for their politics, only a minority (albeit usually a large one) of students are found to "belong" to national parties in any positive sense. Student leaders, however, usually have some party coloration if not a firm identification, and factions within universities have at least a tenuous identification with national parties.

> To say that the student organization is "captive" or riddled with political factions is not to say that it is a passive instrument of more powerful and experienced politicians. The FECH [the Student Federation of the University of Chile] is really in the hands of students with strong political convictions who have a firm sense of dedication and allegiance to their parties. The University political groups enjoy considerable independence within the broad framework of basic party policy and organization. They are able to influence party decisions through their dominance of youth sections and by allying themselves with sympathetic elements in the party hierarchy. They ordinarily experience no conflict between their loyalty to party and their responsibilities to fellow students because they believe their parties offer the only acceptable solutions to the problems of youth and the nation.[8]

9. Latin America has always been a hearty consumer of European ideas and practices, and the university has long played a vital part in the process of importation, adaptation, and propagation. The present search for ideology, technique, and science has broadened the university's role in the mimetic process. Even though this imitation means that "much research is accomplished by waiting for the mail," as several Latin American university administrators have sarcastically put it, the

---

[8] Bonilla, "Student Federation of Chile," p. 330.

postman brings ideas that increase the power of the university establishment.

The nine above propositions suggest the basic reasons for the inherent institutional strength of Latin America's universities in relation to other social groupings. Not all students, however, attempt to use institutional power for public ends, nor do all activist students agree on how best to use it. Attitudes toward the proper use of power vary widely.

In the study of Argentine students already cited we find, for example, that medical students engage in little overt political activity. Well over half of them report that they argue politics with friends and acquaintances, but only 6 per cent of the freshmen and 8 per cent of the seniors attest to any party activity, and only 20 per cent of the former and 15 per cent of the latter attended a student association meeting in the six months prior to the interview. Only 17 per cent of the practicing physicians reported attending a professional association meeting during the same period. Students in the Faculty of Exact Sciences take a much more active part in student organizations than those in Medicine, but levels of participation and involvement in politics are not much higher. A strong sense of school identification and the familiarities fostered by small enrollments help to explain this higher level of student-oriented political activity.

The most surprising findings of all relating to political activity concern the numbers of students who participated in some sort of street rally or demonstration during the six months prior to the interview. For the three groups in Sciences (freshmen, seniors, and graduates), the percentages were 39, 11, and 12 respectively; for Medicine 16, 15, and 10; and for Economics 14 per cent among freshmen and 18 among graduates. The time period covered was one of quite intensive national political activity, and an affirmative answer may have meant only that the respondent listened to political speeches in a public plaza.

The study appears to show that few students participate extensively in both university and public political activities, that normally at least half in all the groups examined are passive, and that between one-quarter and one-third of the students constitute an "immediately available public," ready to be tapped for special occasions. This potential for action is paralleled in the community at large. It is estimated, for example, that at least 250,000 persons in Buenos Aires demonstrated in favor of religious higher education in 1958, with another 300,000 appearing later to oppose it. That half a million persons in a city of approximately seven million demonstrated on the church-state issue, in a period of only normal political tension, indicates the large reservoirs of readiness to respond to the leadership of university students and professors of Catholic as well as secularist persuasion.

THE EFFECTIVENESS OF STUDENT
POLITICAL ACTION

To this point we have sought to describe the nature of student political activity and to link student power with social organization and the institutional nature of the university.

Unless the unique historical development of each country is taken into account, however, attempts to categorize the range and effectiveness of student participation in politics may appear simplistic. For example, the location of the national university in Nicaragua outside Managua, the capital city, certainly has something to do with the relatively little one hears of Nicaraguan students. The much more important case of Brazil is strongly conditioned by the very late start that country had in higher education, which only came with the inauguration of several professional schools in the nineteenth century. The Reform was already two years old when the Brazilian government decided to merge existing schools of medicine, engineering, and law to form the nucleus of the University of Rio de Janeiro. In 1937 the University of Brazil finally emerged, a combination of the University of Rio de Janeiro and an embryonic Federal Technical University, and by 1959 Brazil had twenty universities plus some private institutes. This delayed development clearly affected the growth of a student political tradition.

Still, it should be possible to derive a set of categories sufficiently flexible to give realistic play to each unique case, yet precise enough to be meaningful. We know that students have been important in recent political events in Cuba, Colombia, Venezuela, and Guatemala—in all of which they have participated in the overthrow of dictatorial regimes. In the same countries, the students subsequently lost whatever decisive power they may have had. Probably the most realistic appraisal is that the students were in no case the decisive element in the overthrow, but rather participants in a broad national movement involving the military, the clergy, businessmen, industrialists, and labor groups. The ouster of Perón is a case in point. The intellectual community, including the students, provided the rationale for action, but the physical power to overthrow constituted authorities lay elsewhere. The effectiveness and the potential results of student action may be judged broadly according to the following scheme:

SITUATIONS OF STABLE TRADITIONAL SOCIETIES In very rudimentary, almost bi-class social structures, necessarily governed under crude dictatorial forms, students normally play a very limited role in innovation and political activity. This was the situation in the colonial era, and present-day Nicaragua, Haiti, and Paraguay fall into this category.

SITUATIONS OF BEGINNING MODERNIZATION AND DISARRAY   As the city begins to grow, as an industrially oriented middle class emerges, and as
the politics of change begin to operate, students assume a most important role in the importation and adaptation of ideology, in the organization of power as well as ideas, and in government itself. Factionalism
is one of the earliest signs of modern pluralism. El Salvador, Guatemala,
Ecuador, Peru, the Dominican Republic, and Panama are currently in
this state. Here, more than in any other social milieu, the student, representative of aspirant elites, finds a situation sufficiently simple for him
to exercise relatively great power over political events.

MORE MATURE SITUATIONS OF TEMPORARY RESOLUTION   When the social
structure is relatively complex, politics turbulent, and at least interim
political decisions made with the immediate future in mind, student
groups are usually very active, but limited in their role by other established interests. In such situations, student activity can still be of great
importance in defining issues and in precipitating incidents or even full-
scale revolts. But usually the university as an institution begins to turn
inward, preparing to meet the demand for professionalism that always
arises in times of rapid economic and political development. Colombia,
Venezuela, and Bolivia, for varying historical reasons, all fall into this
category.

SITUATIONS OF INSTITUTIONAL COMPLEXITY AND RELATIVE STRENGTH
Where the student finds himself in a plural interest structure and
complex class system, his relative power becomes even more limited.
The Mexican experience is a useful case in point. For some time the
Mexican student has had little organized voice in national affairs. The
bus strikes of 1958, which broke a peace that had lasted almost a generation, had little significance. Only the Technical University—the "poor
man's University of Mexico"—has given the authorities much difficulty,
and then only on matters having principally to do with the school's
internal administration. The strength of the Mexican government, the
ideological weight of the Revolution and the institutional expression
of this ideology by the state, the single governing party, and the intellectual community all combine to strip from the students much of their
political reason for being. To take another example, active as the Cuban
students were against the Batista regime, they are now contained by
the ideological as well as military strength of Castro's modern dictatorship. Even amidst Argentina's present institutional disarray, the massive-
ness of Buenos Aires, the strength of the competing interest structure,
and the complication of motivations and values impede pointed and
effective student action in public affairs. In these situations the students
may and usually do have much influence over university policy and

affairs, but their role in national politics must of necessity be one dependent on other, more primary, definitions of interest. Brazil, Mexico, Argentina, Uruguay, Costa Rica, Chile, and Cuba are all within this category.

Ideological orientation, too, will vary with the kind of developmental problem the country faces and with the particular student body involved. Ideologies of nationalism are felt but weakly, if at all, by the public at large in the least developed countries of Latin America. But the intellectual and modernizing student caught in the midst of the disorder of rapid change may indeed become impregnated with nationalistic views. Only certain students and student groups, however, will embrace exclusivism, impersonalism, anti-imperialism, and other of the more extremist views implied by nationalist ideologies. Students in Catholic and other private universities tend toward conservatism; i.e., they are opposed to the nationalism, secularism, and impersonalism of modern society. They may be anti-American as well, hostile to both capitalism and Protestantism as Latin conservatism traditionally has been. The state universities, leading in the modernization of the traditional academic disciplines along with a growing dedication to the physical sciences and empiricism, attract the innovators—and thus the nationalists—in much greater measure than such schools as the Catholic University of Chile or the Javeriana (Jesuit University) in Colombia. This political array is common to some degree throughout Latin America, describing students as much as other politicized groups. The nationalistic student of the state university draws more attention to himself than any other non-party group of ideologists, since he is also the innovator, the modernizer, the politically concerned, and likely to be pursuing studies closely involved with the developmental process. This constellation of attitudes and practices accompanies modernization everywhere, for wherever economic and social development has occurred, the nation-state has been its political vehicle.

SOCIAL CHANGE AND THE STUDENT

A complex mythology of the Latin American student has grown up in the United States, in large measure a result of the excited findings of observers scurrying to make up for irrevocably lost time. We hear that the Latin American student is a radical, uninterested in study, the pawn of professional agitators, the persecutor of his professors, and the bane of responsible university administrators. Some students are all these things. Others are serious and questioning young people working well and serenely in rapidly improving faculties and departments. Still others are apathetic playboys, or yearners after the glories of National Socialism, or social climbers thirsting to become oligarchs, or desiccated youths who aspire to no more than the routine life of the bookkeeper. Probably the majority of students in the state universities are more secularist than not, more nationalist than not, more middle-class than not, more center and left-of-center than not, and more worried about individual fortune than the fate of the state. They form the reservoir of modern men and women upon whom the nation can draw for its development, susceptible to national leadership and willing to take the risks demanded when societies break from one world of thought and action into another.

The Latin American university student is the child of his parents. To assume that the student is but a hot-eyed revolutionary is to presume that somehow registering in a university is sufficient to cut family ties, break class and other group identifications, and produce a special kind of creature divorced from his society. The intellectual community can be "ahead" of society as a whole, but it must have identifications with some sectors of the community, and can pull along only those people susceptible to its particular suggestions or prodding. To single out the Latin American student for special disdain is to forget that it is truly debatable whether he is more irresponsible, rapacious, corrupt, and foolish than his elders on the farm, in the government, in the bank, or in the trade union. Indeed, there is some reason for advancing the thesis that the student is at least temporarily a better citizen than his elders.

The simple fact of youth also crucially distinguishes the Latin American student from his parents. He still remains free to believe in and to attempt to apply the long-held ideals of the old liberal aristocracy—those desires for freedom, dignity, growth and progress so often honored in the breach since Independence. With whatever ideological superficiality, misplaced enthusiasm, and youthful conviction of ultimate right, the reformists have preserved and modernized these ideals, and often have displayed a courage and selflessness in their defense that merit admiration rather than contempt or condescension.

> Over and above nationalistic feeling and the commitments to party, there exists a set of canons governing and inspiring student action. In Chile these are not often articulated but they are recognized as going back to the very beginnings of the student federation. . . . They include the courage to hold and defend a point of view on fundamental issues, a readiness for self-sacrifice, loyalty in friendship, love of country, hatred and distrust of the military, a sentimental identification with the working classes, and solidarity with the youth of other Latin American countries. Students have been a force of progress within the university; their dedication to democratic ideals, their readiness to protest injustice, and their resistance to political repression have helped keep Chile politically moderate.[9]

[9] Bonilla, "Student Federation of Chile," p. 315.

The university is a propitious place for demonstrating the relationship between freedom and development. For long the reformist and neo-reformist students have instinctively linked the two in their hatred for authoritarianism on the one hand and their search for modernization on the other. If they have been tempted to adopt ideologies that the Western world rejects as totalitarian, it may well be that they have been offered no other seemingly viable alternative, have heard no objective and authoritative voices reaffirm the convictions of 1918, and have seen corruption and dictatorship blessed with international respectability. To leave the university and to grow up means to accept measures of conduct in contradiction with those avowed social ideals the student has been taught in civics texts, the speeches of his leaders, and the writing of the *próceres* (Founding Fathers). Rarely indeed is the gulf between ideal and real behavior so broad as it is in Latin America. But a major reason for hope lies precisely in the insistent presence of those concepts of free inquiry whose routine application must be a part of the modern university if it is to accomplish its pedagogical and research functions. There will always be tension between Academia and the public so long as the bold pursuit of ideas is hampered by cultures that fetter minds with archaic measures of hierarchy and demand ultimate commitment to unchanging standards of the good.

The Emergence of Modern Political Parties in Latin America*

ROBERT J. ALEXANDER

Latin America is growing up politically. One of the indications of this maturity is the emergence of modern political parties. The traditional *caudillismo* of the region is declining. Politics is becoming increasingly a clash of interests, programs, and ideas and less a mere struggle for power among conflicting charismatic leaders.

At least in part, the emergence of modern political parties in Latin

* Robert J. Alexander, "The Emergence of Modern Political Parties in Latin America," in Joseph Maier and Richard W. Weatherhead (eds.), *The Politics of Change in Latin America* (New York: Frederick A. Praeger, Inc., Publishers, 1964), pp. 101–125. Reprinted by permission.

America is a reflection of the basic economic and social changes that have taken place during the last two generations. With the development of important middle groups in society, politics is no longer, as it was during the first century of independence, merely a game played among rival cliques of a small ruling class.

Today, Latin America is characterized by increasing industrialization, urbanization, and population. The old social molds, built in an era when all wealth, education, and political power were the monopoly of a small landed and commercial aristocracy, are cracking or, in a few countries, have been swept away already.

As a result of these changes, the organized urban workers, rapidly growing professional classes, students (who come more and more from the middle ranges of society), the new industrialists, and, in some countries, even the peasantry are now playing a part in political life. Each of these groups has concrete objectives that it is seeking to obtain through political activity. Each seeks to mold the process of change in its own way. At the same time, conservative elements remain strong. They seek to resist the process of change altogether or to cede before it as little as possible. Finally, the whole process of social and economic transformation of Latin America has created fertile ground for political ideas and philosophies from abroad.

The political parties mirror these changes. They show the influence of various interest groups, reflect the clashes of political philosophies, and take a wide variety of points of view concerning the basic issues of social and economic change. There has emerged a type of party that is itself an integral part of this change.

THE TRADITIONAL PARTY PATTERN

Latin America has had political parties, at least in name, since the early days of independence. Almost every country had its Conservatives and its Liberals. The former generally stood for ultramontanism, opposition to free trade, and a highly centralized form of government; the latter faithfully reflected the liberalism of Europe in being both anticlerical and Manchesterian, and in addition often favored some form of federalism, at least in theory.

These parties held the stage until World War I. They fought out the great issue of nineteenth-century Latin America, the struggle over the secular power of the Church. In most cases, the Liberals won at least a qualified victory. However, it is a commentary on the politics of the time that if the great masses of the people had been consulted on this issue, it would in all likelihood have been decided in favor of the Church.

In the main, the Conservative and Liberal parties of the nineteenth and early twentieth centuries were political organizations of a special sort. They involved only a minute fraction of the population, they engaged in little day-to-day activity, and generally the party was a great deal less important than the man. Within the parties of both types there arose *caudillos*—more often than not, military men or civilians-turned-soldiers. They were the real binding force around which politics ebbed and flowed. Often there would develop a group within one of the parties, a subdivision specifically devoted to the interests of a particular *caudillo*. Sometimes such a personalist group would develop entirely outside the structure of the traditional party.

The armed forces played a crucial role in this process. The *coup d'état* (*golpe de estado*) and even civil war were more or less normal extensions of everyday political activity. The armed forces themselves were usually organized around particular military-political leaders. Frequently, they were a kind of federation of armed bands of regional *caudillos*, united for a longer or shorter time around a single national chieftain. The military training of such armies was low, their personal devotion to a particular leader high.

In Argentina, Brazil, and Chile, there were variations of this general pattern. These countries were characterized by a degree of political stability unusual for the area, and the rule of the landed and commercial aristocracy as a group was more important than the individual. The game of personal rivalries was generally channeled within bounds that most politicians agreed to and understood. As a result, the resort to force in these countries was much less frequent. Nevertheless, in the ABC countries, too, politics remained the monopoly of a small group belonging to or associated with the dominant economic and social oligarchy.

THE NATURE OF THE MODERN PARTIES

The kind of political party that has evolved in Latin America since World War I differs fundamentally from the parties of the first century of independence. It is an organization with reasonably well-defined programs and ideologies. The various parties represent the widest spectrum of political philosophy. Often they are organizations representing or seeking to represent the interests of particular groups within the evolving society. It is upon the basis of their ideologies, platforms, and programs, and their appeals to special interest groups, rather than on the grounds of allegiance to a particular political leader, that they recruit their membership.

The new political party in Latin America also has a much more intensive internal life than did the older kind. It has local organizations throughout the country conducting activities of their own most of the year and not merely on the eve of an election or in the morning after a *coup d'état*. They hold periodic membership meetings. They gather for regular local, regional, and national conventions, and they do so even when no election or other change in government is in the offing.

These parties involve relatively large numbers of citizens drawn from various classes. They often carry on organized activities within the ranks of labor unions, professional associations, and other nonpolitical groups. Many support a variety of periodicals and publish pamphlets and even books. Some have organized groups within them to carry on a continuous study of the economic and social problems of their countries—regardless of whether they are, at the moment, in the government or in the opposition. These studies may form the basis for policy and be published. Sometimes, though by no means always, the parties collect dues from their members and issue membership cards or other means of identifying those who belong.

Finally, the new parties are *civilista*. Although they have certainly not completely eschewed political cooperation with groups among the military (including participation in *coups d'état*), such contacts tend to be circumstantial and temporary, and their attention is centered on political action in the civilian field. Generally they seek, at least in principle, to keep the military out of politics.

TYPOLOGY OF PARTIES

There are many possible ways of analyzing the types of organizations that we have included under the heading of "new" or "modern" political parties in Latin America. We shall divide them here into three basic groups, each with its own subgroupings.

There are, first of all, the old traditional parties, which have been able to adapt themselves and their programs to the changing circumstances, the Conservatives and the Liberals.

Secondly, there are the parties of more recent origin following or seeking to follow European models. They include the Radicals, Socialists, Christian Democrats, Fascists, and the Communists and their splinters.

Finally, there are what may be called the indigenous parties of change, which have developed in recent decades. This type may be subdivided into what we shall call the national revolutionary parties and the personalist revolutionary parties.

Obviously, any attempt to put into nice categories all of the important political parties of Latin America is beset with serious difficulties. One may quarrel with the categories themselves, or one may doubt the validity of assigning a specific label to a particular party. Nevertheless, we feel that, for purposes of analysis, there is something to be gained by establishing some sort of system in what at first glance appears to be a confusing conglomeration of organizations with peculiar and often meaningless names. We believe that there is some discernible rhyme and reason to the political parties of Latin America and that they are among the most important phenomena in the process of revolutionary change in the area.

THE TRADITIONAL PARTIES

In most of Latin America, the traditional parties of the nineteenth century have ceased to be a major factor in political life or have disappeared altogether. In Mexico, El Salvador, Costa Rica, Venezuela, Peru, and the Dominican Republic, the Liberals and Conservatives no longer exist. In Guatemala, Cuba, Bolivia, and Brazil, their political weight is slight. In Haiti, they may be said never to have existed at all, since, until recent years, politics in that country has defied all description except in terms of rivalries among competing *caudillos* played against a background of permanent tensions between mulattoes and full-blooded Negroes.

Only in Honduras, Nicaragua, Colombia, and Uruguay are the traditional parties still the dominant competitors for power, and even in these nations, as we shall see, the Liberals and Conservatives have greatly changed in character. In Panama, Ecuador, Chile, Argentina, and Paraguay, they still have an important role in national politics, but they share the stage with more recent parties.

In countries where the traditional parties have maintained a foothold in the political arena, they have done so at the cost of a radical change in outlook. They have adapted themselves to changing circumstances by appealing to particular interest groups and by modifying their programs and methods of action.

THE CONSERVATIVES   Where the Conservatives continue to be a factor of importance, they are, in most cases, the party of the large landowning class engaged in a rear-guard struggle to maintain its privileges, or, as the Partido Blanco in Uruguay, the spokesmen of the rural areas against the encroaching power of the cities. Their voting strength in Ecuador and Chile comes largely from the ability of landlords to march their tenants and agricultural workers off to the polls to vote for Conservative Party candidates.

However, even in the Conservative parties, the "winds of change" have not failed to leave things untouched. Generally, the Conservatives are no longer distinguished principally as supporters of the secular power of the Church. Dissident groups have arisen under the banner of Social Catholicism, in direct and sometimes bitter opposition to the Conservative Party, as in Chile, or in cooperation with the old guard, as in Ecuador. In Argentina, the Conservatives have been profoundly shaken by the Peronista experience, with some of their leaders attempting to appear as more fervent advocates of social reform than Perón himself.

In Colombia, Paraguay, and Uruguay, the Conservatives probably owe their strength to the traditional appeal of party labels to their followers. In these countries, the active membership in the Conservative parties tends to cut more generally across class lines than in most of the other nations.

In Nicaragua, the Conservatives have, in recent years, played a unique role as the principal legal opposition to the dictatorship of the Somoza family. As a result, they have tended to attract many people of advanced ideas more anxious to fight the tyranny than concerned with problems of political tradition or ideology.

THE LIBERALS   With the exception of Chile and Nicaragua, the Liberal parties have become the spokesmen for important new segments of the population that have arisen in the wake of the economic and social revolution in Latin America. Thus the Liberal parties of Colombia, Honduras, and Ecuador are the principal political vehicle for the urban workers employed in factories and modern transportation, public utility, and agricultural enterprises. In Colombia and Honduras especially, the influence of the Liberal politicians is extensive within the organized labor movement itself.

The Argentine Radical Party (Unión Cívica Radical), which, in spite of its name, holds the same position in Argentina as the Liberal parties in other Latin American countries, has from the beginning differed from its counterparts in other nations. From the 1890's on, it has been the principal representative of the urban and rural middle classes, drawing much of its voting strength from the city workers. However, there has always existed within the Radical Party an element from the landowning aristocracy. The struggle for pre-eminence between this element and the more middle-class leadership had been partly responsible for the first major split within the Radical ranks in the 1920's between the so-called personalistas, led by Hipólito Irigoyen, and the antipersonalistas, led by Marcelo T. de Alvear. During the 1930's, the antipersonalistas shared control of the government with the Conservatives in a thinly veiled dictatorship backed by the military.

Since the advent of the Peronista phenomenon, the Radical Party is more clearly a middle-class party. The majority of both the urban and the rural working classes has come to regard the Peronistas as its chief defender and spokesman. Consequently, there has been a sharp division of opinion among the Unión Cívica Radical leaders as to what approach should be taken to the Peronistas, a division that in part led to the split of the party late in 1956 into the UCR Intransigente (more inclined to work with the Peronistas) and the UCR del Pueblo (more definitely anti-Peronista). However, even the Intransigente Radicals have been unable to exert any real influence in the organized labor movement.

Although recent years have been marked by much confusion in Argentine politics in general, and Radical affairs in particular, rough lines of political loyalty of various classes are fairly clear. Taken together, the Radicals may be said to represent the great bulk of middle-class folk, the Peronistas to speak for the majority of the wage workers; while the many smaller parties have minority followings among these two major classes and among the old aristocracy.

One of the most remarkable examples of adaptation to a modern environment by a traditional Liberal Party has been that of the Partido Colorado of Uruguay. Early in this century, under the leadership of José Batlle y Ordóñez, the party became the principal vehicle for social, political, and economic change in that small republic. Not only did it carry out the nineteenth-century program of separation of Church and state, but it also established some of the country's first social security and labor protective legislation. Under its leadership, Uruguay was the first Latin American country to establish a policy of economic nationalism as a means of achieving economic development and diversification. Finally, the Colorados sponsored the experiment in a multiple executive that has been one of the few serious attempts to deal with the Latin American tendency of converting a strong executive into a dictatorship.

The Chilean and Nicaraguan Liberal parties are exceptions to the general picture. In Chile, the Liberals have continued to represent a fraction of the traditional ruling class, and if anything have become more conservative than the Conservatives. They have joined with the Conservatives in the battle against agrarian reform and more equitable distribution of wealth. In Nicaragua, their survival is due partly to the fact that they have been the chosen political instrument of the Somoza family, which has run the country's affairs for more than a quarter of a century. The fate of the Liberal Party, once this clan has been ousted from power, is difficult to predict. Even under the Somozas, the Liberal Party has had support among some segments of the urban working class. This element may eventually assert control over the party in the post-Somoza period. Or the Liberals may, by that time, have become so discredited by their long association with the dictatorship that they will disappear.

EUROPEAN-PATTERNED PARTIES

Many of the newer-style political parties which during the last two generations have challenged the Conservatives and Liberals were patterned after European models. These include at least one Radical Party roughly similar to the Parti Radical Socialiste of France, various Socialist parties, the Christian Democrats, the Fascists, and the Communists of various shades.

The emergence of European-patterned groups reflects the impact of Old World ideas on Latin America. In not a few cases, immigrants from Europe sought to establish in their new countries the kind of political organizations with which they had been familiar at home. As was perhaps inevitable, most parties took on their own characteristics. At times they moved far from the original European pattern.

THE RADICALS The oldest of these European-oriented parties is undoubtedly the Partido Radical of Chile. It was established in the last decades of the nineteenth century as a left-wing offshoot of the Liberals. Like its counterpart in France, the Radical Party of Chile has been the typical expression of the middle class. At first a favorite among artisans and small shopkeepers, it subsequently became the party of the white-collar class, particularly the government bureaucracy.

Like the French Radicals, too, the Chilean party has oscillated violently in political philosophy and orientation. At times proclaiming themselves as socialists, they have at other times participated in Conservative government coalitions. Although they consider themselves to be of the left, they have more truly been the fulcrum of national politics, determining at any given instant whether the left or the right was to have the majority in Congress and even in public opinion.

For all their oscillations, the Radicals have played an important role in the modernization of Chile. They participated in the early 1920's in the government of President Arturo Alessandri, which was largely responsible for enacting the country's basic labor and social laws a decade before such legislation became popular in most other Latin American countries. In the early 1940's, Radical presidents headed governments that encouraged the almost universal unionization of urban workers and developed a program of economic development, making Chile one of the four most industrialized nations of Latin America.

The Radicals may well play a decisive role in determining whether Chile launches once again a program of democratic reform in the 1960's or falls into the arms of totalitarians. A great deal depends upon their willingness to form a center coalition with the Christian Democrats and other groups for the 1964 election. Their willingness or lack of it will probably determine whether changes of vital importance, like agrarian reform, can be carried out democratically, or whether the totalitarians will be faced with a divided opposition, permitting them to convert Chile into the first Latin American nation voluntarily to adopt the Communist path to social change and economic development.

THE SOCIALISTS   The Socialists were among the first political groups on the Latin American scene to advocate a fundamental transformation of their economies and societies. During the 1860's, 1870's, and 1880's, numerous immigrants who had been active in the First International and the first European Socialist parties found their way to America. They established small groups, and some of them sought affiliation with the International. Although most of them remained relatively isolated from the political life of the Latin American countries, a few became nuclei around which Socialist parties were organized.

The claim to be the oldest Socialist Party in Latin America is disputed between the Chilean Democratic Party, which appeared in the 1880's but subsequently gave up all pretense of belonging in the Socialist camp, and the Argentine Socialist Party, founded in 1896. During the decades before World War I, Socialist parties appeared also in Uruguay, Brazil, Mexico, and Cuba. In this period, they generally disputed control of the organized labor movements with the anarcho-syndicalists. In most cases, the parties were organized by immigrants from Europe. Although they quickly gained local adherents and even leaders, they regarded themselves as American counterparts of the Social Democratic parties in the Old World. In philosophy they were Marxist.

The Brazilian, Mexican, and Cuban parties disappeared during or soon after World War I. The Chilean Socialist Labor Party and the Uruguayan Socialist Party joined the Communist International. In Chile, a new Socialist Party did not appear until 1933. In Uruguay, Emilio Frugoni, the party founder, withdrew from the Communist ranks and re-established the Socialist Party in 1922.

In the 1930's and 1940's, a number of new Socialist parties were organized in Peru, Bolivia, Panama, Brazil, and Ecuador. In the 1950's an attempt was made by the Socialist International to associate all of these in the International. A Latin American Secretariat of the International, with which most of the parties did become associated, was established in Montevideo. The only actual members of the International, however, were the parties of Argentina and Uruguay, and the Uruguayan party withdrew in 1960.

[Unfortunately, most of the Socialist parties of Latin America have abandoned the camp of Democratic Socialism. In some cases, they have been heavily infiltrated or influenced by the local Communist parties. In most instances, they have adopted xenophobic nationalist positions that have made them violently anti-United States and pro-Soviet.] Only the Argentine Social Democratic Party and the Ecuadorean Socialist Party have remained more or less loyal to the ideas they originally espoused.

THE CHRISTIAN DEMOCRATS   The Christian Democrats are a relatively new type of party in Latin America. [They reflect the emergence of a more socially conscious wing of the Roman Catholic Church, a phenomenon produced largely since World War II.] Although the Uruguayan Unión Cívica and the Chilean Falange Nacional antedate the war, all of the others have emerged subsequently.

The Christian Democrats find their philosophical inspiration in the principal papal encyclicals on social problems: *Rerum Novarum, Quadregesimo Anno*, and *Mater et Magistra.* [Although their main constituency is found among the middle class, they have in a number of instances successfully sought to gain influence in the organized labor and peasant movements.] They are strong advocates of basic social and economic change. The quality of their leadership is generally high. They include among their ranks some of the outstanding intellectuals of the region, particularly those of the younger generation.

The three most important Christian Democratic parties are those of Uruguay, Chile, and Venezuela. The first of these was formed between the two world wars. It is unlikely to become one of the major Uruguayan parties, but it has an assured place in that country's political spectrum. It has mainly a middle-class following.

The Falange Nacional of Chile was established in the 1930's in the wake of a revolt of the Young Conservatives against their party. Although in the beginning its democratic orientation was the subject of some conjecture, the party evolved into one of the strongest supporters of the democratic traditions of Chile. Very early it began to seek support in the labor movement, and it has had considerable success in that direction. In the August, 1962, congress of the nation's principal central labor body, the Central Unica de Trabajadores de Chile, the Christian Democrats had about 35 per cent of the delegates. They represent the principal challenge to Communist control of the country's trade unions.

In the late 1950's, the Falange Nacional merged with a number of smaller groups of more or less the same orientation to form the present Christian Democratic Party. It is one of the six major parties of Chile and has a fair chance of electing one of its members president in 1964.*

The Venezuelan Christian Democratic Party, known as the Partido Social Cristiano (Copei), was established in 1946. It brought together a group of young intellectuals under the leadership of Rafael Caldera. Between 1946 and 1948 it was the country's second largest party. During the dictatorship of General Marcos Pérez Jiménez from November, 1948, to January, 1958, the party lost most of its more conservative elements because of its opposition to the regime. In 1958, it emerged as a strong advocate of basic social reform.

With the inauguration of President Rómulo Betancourt in 1959, the Copei entered the government along with Betancourt's Acción Democrática and the Unión Republicana Democrática (URD). The Copei remained after the URD withdrew in November, 1960. With the Acción Democrática, it bore the responsibility for carrying out a program of rapid industrialization, agrarian reform, educational expansion, and general transformation of Venezuelan economic and social life.

Although the Copei emerged from the Pérez Jiménez dictatorship proportionately smaller than it had been in 1948, it made slow but steady progress after 1958. It has achieved some influence in organized labor, and considerably more in the peasant movement. Its strength is still concentrated (as it was in the 1946–48 period) in the three mountain-states of Táchira, Mérida, and Trujillo, but it has succeeded in broadening its base both geographically and socially.

In addition to these three parties, Christian Democratic groups have appeared since World War II in Argentina, Peru, Bolivia, Paraguay, Brazil, Cuba, the Dominican Republic, Haiti, Puerto Rico, Nicaragua, Guatemala, and El Salvador. Generally, they are on the moderate left, although their exact position in national politics has varied with the general alignment of forces in a particular country.

---

* Eduardo Frei, the acknowledged leader of Chilean Christian Democracy, was elected President in 1964 [ed.]

The Latin American Christian Democrats regard themselves as counterparts of the European parties of the same name. They all belong to the Christian Democratic International. In a congress of the International in Santiago de Chile in August, 1961, the Venezuelan and Chilean parties sponsored a successful resolution urging a general alliance between Christian Democrats and other parties of the democratic left in Latin America.

THE FASCISTS   The European totalitarians have had counterparts in Latin America as well. There were Fascist parties in a number of Latin American countries, particularly in the 1930's and 1940's, when fascism was at its apogee internationally. In Brazil and Chile, the Fascists, known respectively as Integralistas and Nacistas, were for some years parties of considerable consequence. They had all the trappings of their European brethren, including uniformed storm troopers and anti-Semitism. With the international defeat of fascism, the Chilean Partido Nacista disappeared, but the Brazilian Integralistas transformed themselves into the Partido de Representação Popular, which in its new form has tried to eschew its Fascist past.

The most alive member of the Fascist International in Latin America is the Falange Socialista Boliviana. Formed in the late 1930's on the model of the Spanish Falange, the FSB remained a small group until 1952. Then, because it had not been discredited by participation in the regimes that preceded the national revolution of the year, the Falange became the principal focus of the forces opposed to the revolution. In the presidential elections of 1956 and 1960 and the congressional elections of 1958 and 1962, it received most of the opposition votes, and elected several members to Congress. For a while, a splinter of the government party known as the Partido Revolucionario Auténtico threatened to displace the Falange as the principal opposition group, but an alliance between the two was formed in the middle of 1962.

There have been Fascist parties in Argentina, Mexico, Peru, and perhaps one or two other countries, without, however, any significant role in the political life of these nations.

THE COMMUNISTS AND THEIR SPLINTERS   Among the European-patterned parties there are, finally, the Communists. There is now a Communist Party in every Latin American country. Some of them date from the early years of the Comintern, others arose in the 1940's and 1950's. Generally, the Latin American Communist parties follow the pattern of such organizations in other parts of the world. Over the years they have had two basic objectives: to serve the purposes of the Soviet Union and to establish the when and where of possible dictatorships of their own parties. They have followed faithfully the zigs and zags of the international Communist line.

The nature of the Communist appeal has varied from time to time. Generally, they have sought to picture themselves as the only real advocates of social change in Latin America and as the only true defenders of the working class. They have consistently pointed to the Soviet Union and other Communist countries as models that the Latin American nations should follow, first in terms of social revolution and more recently in terms of rapid economic development. In recent decades, they have sought to make the utmost use of nationalism and to turn it especially against the United States.

Until the advent of the Castro regime in Cuba, the Communists in most Latin American countries were little more than nuisance groups. Since 1959, however, they have achieved new importance. Their support of Castro has opened wider fields of contact with other political groups and has removed them from their almost complete isolation of the 1950's. The Castro phenomenon has also made the Communists more willing to use methods of violent insurrection and guerrilla war than they had been during most of their history. Moreover, the Cuban Revolution has sharpened the issue of social and economic revolution in Latin America. Thus, it has created a wider audience for the Communists' propaganda that only their particular totalitarian way would provide the kind of rapid change that the situation demanded.

The Communists have since acquired new allies in the Fidelista parties and groups in various countries. These Fidelistas have not formally joined the international Communist movement, but they have been willing to work openly with the Communists. They have been more anxious than the Communists themselves to engage in what the latter have called "putschism," that is, armed conflict with the supporters of the *status quo* or the advocates of peaceful change.

Although the Communists and Fidelistas have become allies, it is by no means certain that they will always remain so. Should the conflicts between Soviet and Chinese Communists come more clearly into the open and the various national affiliates of the international Communist movement be forced to align themselves with one or the other, it seems likely that most of the Communist parties will side with the Russians, while the Fidelistas might throw in their lot with the Chinese.

Previous splits in the international Communist movement have not found much echo in Latin America. The only exception has been the Trotskyites. At one time or another, there have been Trotskyite parties in Mexico, Peru, Bolivia, Chile, Argentina, Uruguay, Brazil, and Cuba.

The only member of this group to achieve any real significance in national political life has been the Trotskyite party of Bolivia, the Partido Obrero Revolucionario (POR). For a few years in the late 1940's and early 1950's, the members of the POR achieved considerable power in the trade union movement, and for a few months after the beginning of the Bolivian National Revolution in 1952 it controlled the Central Obrera Boliviana. However, their insistence that President Víctor Paz Estenssoro was going to play the role of Kerensky as against their own Lenin in the Bolivian Revolution incurred the enmity of the Movimiento Nacionalista Revolucionario, which was leading the revolution. It also caused disillusionment among most POR trade union leaders, with the result that the POR quickly lost its influence. Today it is reduced to two small groups of little significance.

THE INDIGENOUS PARTIES OF CHANGE

In additon to the parties that derived their ideological and programmatic inspiration from Europe, there are two groups of parties that have grown out of the changing situation in Latin America itself: the national revolutionary parties and the personalist revolutionary parties.

THE NATIONAL REVOLUTIONARY PARTIES The single most important group of democratic political parties in Latin America are the national revolutionaries. They have grown out of the particular circumstances of their countries. Because of the similarity of problems in various Latin American nations, however, they have tended to adopt broadly similar ideologies and programs. They include the Acción Democrática of Venezuela, the APRA Party of Peru, the Liberación Nacional of Costa Rica, the Movimiento Nacionalista Revolucionario of Bolivia, the Febrerista Party of Paraguay, the Partido Revolucionario Dominicano, and the Partido Popular Democrático of Puerto Rico. The Partido Revolucionario Institucional of Mexico might also be placed in this category.

These parties present in their platforms a program for the democratic transformation of their particular countries and of Latin America as a whole. They advocate an agrarian reform adapted to the specific needs of their respective nations. They favor extensive social and labor legislation and the development of strong trade union and peasant movements under democratic leadership. They are nationalist without being xenophobic. They seek to bring the key elements of their countries' national economies into the hands of local citizens or the national government. While not rejecting foreign investment, they seek to establish conditions for its entry that will not compromise their national sovereignty. They favor mixed economies, with the government performing the key function of stimulating and directing rapid economic development. Above all, they stand for the firm establishment of political democracy.

In recent years the national revolutionary parties have borne the responsibility of government in Mexico, Bolivia, Venezuela, Puerto Rico, the Dominican Republic, and Costa Rica. To be sure, conditions have varied considerably in each case. In general, however, these nations have been in the vanguard in Latin America because of their insistence on effecting basic social revolution through democratic means. Whether or not Latin America can achieve a solid basis for democracy depends to a very considerable degree on the ability of the national revolutionary parties to carry forward with sufficient rapidity the social transformation and economic development essential for making democracy the rule rather than the exception.

The Mexican Partido Revolucionario Institucional has been in charge of the conduct of the Mexican Revolution for a quarter of a century, and it has almost become synonymous with it. Unlike its kindred parties, the PRI came into being after, rather than before, the country was well started on the revolutionary path. It was established some eighteen years after the beginning of the Mexican Revolution. Through the PRI, a pacific method has been evolved for solving the perennial problem of the presidential succession, with Mexico enjoying an unusual degree of political stability. The PRI has also shown remarkable ability to adapt the pace and direction of the revolution to changing circumstances. Although other parties do function legally in Mexico, with considerable freedom of speech and the press, the machinery of government is fully in the hands of the PRI.

The Movimiento Nacionalista Revolucionario of Bolivia has led a revolution with many similarities to Mexico's PRI. It has attempted to incorporate the Indians into the nation by granting them land, the vote, and arms and by trying to bring as rapidly as possible education, medical care, and other social services to the Indian areas. It has at the same time pushed a program of economic development that is at last beginning to bear some fruit. It has sought to strengthen the nation's control over its own economy, principally through expropriation of the three largest tin-mining enterprises. The momentum of the revolution and the popular support of the government have given the country the most stable regime in its history.

For almost a quarter of a century the Venezuelan Acción Democrática has likewise been urging a fundamental revolution in the country's economic, social, and political affairs. When it was first in power between

1945 and 1948, it sought to obtain the largest possible return for the nation from the exploitation of its main export industry, petroleum, by foreign companies. And it tried to invest this return in the diversification of the economy, the development of education, and the improvement of living standards for large parts of the population.

Since 1959, the Acción Democrática has again been principally responsible for the conduct of government under President Rómulo Betancourt. Its regime started an agrarian reform that, by the time Betancourt went out of office early in 1964, provided 100,000 peasant families with land. It has doubled the number of students in school. It has sought to bring basic public services such as electricity, sewage, and water supply to virtually every town and village in the country. It has energetically pushed a program of agricultural and industrial development in which both government and private enterprise have played essential roles.

But the Acción Democrática regime since 1959 has had to face a degree of opposition from the extreme right and the extreme left unequaled in any other Latin American country. Remnants of the military clique that traditionally ran the country have been relentless in their efforts to overthrow the Betancourt government. At the same time, Betancourt has been the chief target of the Communists and the Castro government of Cuba, who are fully aware that his regime represents a clear negation of their claim that rapid economic development and drastic social reform are possible only under totalitarian tyranny.

The Puerto Rican government of the Popular Democratic Party under Governor Luis Muñoz Marín has operated under very different circumstances. But like the governments in Mexico, Bolivia, and Venezuela, it has pushed a land redistribution effort, a vast program for agricultural diversification, and industrialization under government inspiration and orientation, albeit largely through private firms. It has also succeeded in putting virtually every child of primary-school age into the classroom, and it has carried out public-health measures that have given the island one of the world's lowest death rates.

The Partido Revolucionario Dominicano was organized in exile, under the leadership of Juan Bosch, a distinguished literary figure. When dictator Rafael Trujillo was assassinated in May, 1961, PRD leaders returned home to establish grass-roots units of the party. It won the presidential election in December, 1962, putting Juan Bosch in the chief executive post; since taking office in February, 1963, the PRD government has launched a program of social reform and economic development—now again in jeopardy since the overthrow of the Bosch government in the fall of 1963.

In Costa Rica, the Liberación Nacional governments of Presidents José Figueres and Francisco Orlich have had perhaps the easiest task of any of the national revolutionary regimes. Social problems in Costa Rica have been less critical than elsewhere. But the Liberación Nacional governments have successfully initiated programs of industrialization and electrification of rural areas. They have encouraged the class of small landowners and assured it of adequate markets and credit facilities. At the same time, they stimulated the rise in urban living standards and the passage of sound, progressive labor and social legislation. In Costa Rica, too, the government has sought to increase the nation's return as a catalyst for economic development and social reform.

The national revolutionary parties of Peru, Paraguay, and the Dominican Republic have not as yet had an opportunity to show what they can do in government. However, the APRA Party, the first of the national revolutionary parties to come into existence, has contributed very considerably to developing a body of ideas shared by all of them. Several times it was kept out of control of Peru by force (the latest instance was in 1962).

All the national revolutionary parties recognize a kinship among themselves. On several occasions they have held international conferences. They have joined with some of the more advanced liberal parties to establish an Institute of Political Education in Costa Rica for the training of second-rank leaders, and they have lent moral support to one another in moments of great crisis.

PERSONALIST REVOLUTIONARY PARTIES The second category of indigenous parties consists of two organizations, the Partido Peronista of Argentina and the Partido Trabalhista Brasileiro (PTB). These two parties are similar in origin and are likely to evolve in somewhat similar directions in the years immediately ahead.

Both were organized by socially minded dictators, Juan Perón and Getúlio Vargas. In both instances, they were designed as vehicles for organizing working-class support for the dictators and their tenure in power.

Since the disappearance of their founders—Perón is in exile and Vargas committed suicide—the parties have seemingly taken different directions. Yet, there is good reason to believe that they may both end up in the camp of the national revolutionary parties.

During the 1950's, the Partido Trabalhista Brasileiro was the refuge for a large number of opportunistic politicians, who tried to use it as a means for sinecures and nepotism. It had been founded ten years earlier by trade union leaders and Ministry of Labor officials loyal to Vargas. But by the mid-1950's, the PTB had no important trade union figure in its top leadership. True, the urban workers continued largely to look upon the Partido Trabalhista as "their" party, but it had no identifiable philosophy or program. This state of confusion allowed pro-Communist elements to infiltrate the ranks of the PTB in several states.

When President Jânio Quadros resigned in August, 1961, the head of the PTB, Vice President João Goulart, became President of Brazil. However, this had relatively little effect upon the PTB as a party. The important currents at work within it were far removed from the national capital of Brasília.

In recent years, new forces within the PTB have come to the forefront in a number of states. They seek to clean out the more blatantly opportunistic elements and forge a program similar to that of the other national revolutionary parties, favoring planned economic development, agrarian reform, and vigilance against party subversion by corruption and Communism. The renovators have indeed seized leadership of the party in the states of Bania and Paraná. In Rio Grande do Sul, a similar movement under the leadership of Fernando Ferrari has sought to take control of the party from "orthodox" elements.

To be sure, the PTB is still a very heterogeneous grouping. In the city of Rio de Janeiro, it is led by pro-Communist xenophobic nationalists. In some other states, the opportunists are still dominant. However, if the grass-roots movement for cleansing and rebuilding the party on the basis of a genuine program of the democratic left gains national momentum, it is likely to convert the PTB into an ideologically consistent national revolutionary party.

The problem within the Peronista Party is of a somewhat different order. When Perón left the country, the work of reorganizing the party fell largely to its trade union members. They looked upon the party as a vehicle for the political expression of the organized labor movement. In general, they did not seek a return to Perón's kind of dictatorial regime. The ex-dictator himself, however, has made no secret of his desire to return to absolute power. In that case, he has assured the nation, "heads will roll." Most Peronista leaders have remained personally loyal to Perón, and as long as he is alive, there remains the constant danger that the Partido Peronista may be used as a vehicle for re-establishing his particular type of dictatorship. Without Perón, the political movement he began may well be incorporated into the democratic life of Argentina as a group of the moderate left, supporting a program not unlike that of the national revolutionary parties elsewhere. . . .

THE PARTIES AND THE LATIN AMERICAN REVOLUTION

. . . The often-cited "revolution of rising expectations" has had a tremendous impact upon the people of Latin America. They are fully aware that poverty is not supernaturally created; and they know that the landlord class has no God-given right to keep the great mass of the rural population landless. They have become convinced that if living standards are to be raised, the land must be redistributed and the economies diversified and industrialized.

Nationalism is virtually universal in Latin America. The same masses that seek social change and economic development also want to see the control of their national economies in the hands of their own citizens, and they are demanding this from those who control their governments.

The democratic parties of Latin America are committed to a program of social reform, economic development, and nationalism. Only the future can tell whether or not these parties will be able to carry out such a program on the basis of political democracy. This is today the great problem in Latin American politics. And the fate of the hemisphere rests upon its solution.

Dilemmas in the Study of Latin American Political Parties* | JOHN D. MARTZ

The rapid increase of popular participation in the Latin American political process has been reflected by the growing importance of its parties. One leading Latin Americanist has written that he would commend this field "to a whole generation of prospective graduate students in political science." Yet there have been relatively few serious efforts

* John D. Martz, "Dilemmas in the Study of Latin American Political Parties," *The Journal of Politics*, Vol. 26: No. 3 (August 1964), pp. 509–531. (Footnotes in the original version have been omitted).

to follow this advice. As another acute student of the area has observed, "Latin American political parties are outstanding in that very little research has been done on them." Thus, most of the existing studies have tended to reflect disciplinary deficiencies by emphasizing the legalistic and historical rather than analyzing the dynamics and inner processes.

In some cases the traditional approach has been unavoidable. The personalistic, particularistic nature of Latin American parties historically has rendered them difficult subjects for scholarly examination and precise, meaningful evaluation. All too seldom has it been feasible to deal with a party truly qualifying as such in the accepted context of a Western democratic political *milieu.* Currently this condition is in a state of flux, with the gradual emergence of formally structured national parties having identifiable doctrine and ideology derived from a history of evolution and development. Even so, what Latin Americans sometimes call political parties are often regarded by North American political scientists as factions, pressure groups, or fraternal organizations.

Methodological advances in the study of comparative politics have developed an awareness and recognition of distinctions between Western and non-Western countries. Those who have toiled most earnestly in this cause would admit to the elusive nature of Latin American processes, and the dilemmas of finding an appropriate conceptual framework are several. It behooves all Latin Americanists to examine and study at length the pioneering work of Almond and Coleman, whether or not its basic premises are fully accepted. A strong argument can be posited that regards as questionable the inclusion of Latin America with other areas termed "developing." There is no eschewing the fact that a dualistic arrangement as characterized by modern and by emergent political cultures is oversimplified. Likewise, the presence of certain features in all political cultures leads to the widely-accepted view that all are to some degree mixed.

The student of Latin America is deeply impressed with the impossibility of a dichotomy, for patterns of social and political institutions and behavior are diffuse and often illogical. Many of the countries in the region reflect an ethnic and cultural experience quite foreign to the Western. On the other hand, many European institutional characteristics have been inherited. To use the terminology of a somewhat modified discussion, elements of what may be called pre-industrial and partially-Westernized systems can be identified.

The present disciplinary state of Latin American studies demands that such problems be grappled with. The awareness that both modern and emergent, both pre-industrial and partially-Westernized characteristics are evident, is but a preliminary step. Further consideration suggests that the inclusion of Latin America by Almond and Coleman may have obscured as much as it illuminated. Certainly the related categorization of "new states" by Shils is also of limited value to the Latin Americanist. The terms of his discussion permit the classification of states as political democracies, tutelary democracies, modernizing oligarchies, totalitarian oligarchies, and traditional oligarchies. The relevance to Latin America is no more than mildly suggestive.

The foregoing is not to deny the overall significance of existing methodological studies of the developing areas, but provides a warning that all paths lead through the thorniest of briarpatches. Difficulties will inevitably be encountered; another meaningful sign lies in the brilliant contribution by Blanksten to Almond and Coleman's volume. This chapter contains a number of perceptive remarks about the parties without seriously proposing new tools or techniques. It is not surprising that existing works on the study of foreign political parties have centered largely on the European parliamentary framework. Yet such efforts offer rather few observations presently transferable to the Latin American context. For those who turn to the literature of stasiology, the result is a diet of European- or North American-oriented research that yields minimal nourishment.

A definition of political parties believed representative of this literature is that of Neuman, who views a party as "the articulate organization of society's active political agents, those who are concerned with the control of governmental power and who compete for popular support with another group or groups holding divergent views." There is no reason for students of Latin American parties to quibble with this definition, but it sheds little light on the organizations of the region. Duverger also gives small comfort; at one point he explicitly excludes all reference to the area, claiming that it "may be neglected because the frequent and effective interference of the government in both polls and parties denatures the whole system."

If such problems exist within the general framework of comparative political studies, narrower dilemmas also exist, one of which is perhaps impossible of present solution. This revolves about the feasibility of electoral analysis and the potential for useful statistical evaluation. Illustrative material can be taken from this writer's research on Venezuela's Acción Democrática (AD). Efforts were made to establish tentative hypotheses concerning the relative impact on that party of organization, ideology, and personalism. Impressionistic, indeed almost intuitive conclusions were the only ones possible, for the Venezuelan experience is not yet extensive. Such are the inadequacies that the utility of election returns over an extended period of time is an obvious but often effective road that cannot be employed in seeking meaningful generalizations here. Even with the 1963 elections, Acción Democrática had participated in but five sets of national polls; of these, three were conducted in less than three years during the 1940's when significant party opposition was non-existent. The other two came more than a decade later, with general conditions and electoral ingredients so diverse that substantive conclusions were little short of foolhardy.

Circumstances will not always be thus, to be sure; in Chile, for example, electoral figures derived from many years' experience can be used. In contemporary Latin America, however, there are in this special sense fully as many Venezuelas as Chiles. And one must not forget today's increasing disciplinary commitment to the use of quantification. This is not the place to debate the merits and shortcomings to this kind of technique; what is pertinent is the fact that raw data and information are still in short supply for the Latin Americanist, so much so that he finds it well-nigh impossible to proceed through the use of such analytical instruments. There is no disposition here to make light of efforts to quantify where it can be meaningfully done. Our present knowledge of Latin America, however, has not yet reached the point where major reliance can rest on such efforts.

Perhaps the single most obvious fact is that many roads lead to heaven; there is no justification for dogmatism, and nothing written here should be so construed. In this discussion, three kinds of analysis will be considered: party systems, legal and institutional prescriptions, and intra-party structure and programmatic schema. Each of these broad rubrics bears further research, although it will be argued here that the third is far more likely to be rewarding than the first two.

Classification and analysis of a given *party system* can be undertaken at two different levels. One deals with the degree of competition, the other with the number of parties effectively active in the system. A variable that can either be used separately or, instead, to tie together the two, is that of a democratic or authoritarian orientation. A party system, then, can be viewed as fully competitive, non-competitive, or semi-competitive. It can also be one-party, one-party dominant, two-party, or multi-party. A modification proposed by Almond in effect combines features of competitiveness with the number of participants. Thus he suggests four headings: authoritarian, dominant non-authoritarian, competitive two-party, and competitive multi-party. Misgivings about this scheme will be implicit in the comments that follow. It is held that the competitive and/or the numerical lines of approach, although having some value, threaten to become taxonomic exercises containing

undue fascination for their own sake.] The convenience with which most
of the twenty Latin American republics can superficially be pigeon-holed
is not automatically paralleled by its intrinsic value.

Analysis following the lines of competition demands a careful and
precise usage of the terms of reference. Most electoral systems contain
certain restrictions. These may well be necessary safeguards, yet they
create problems as to where the line is drawn between competitive
and semi-competitive or between semi-competitive and non-competitive
systems. A few examples will suffice. In the Venezuelan elections of
1963, an estimated 10 per cent of the electorate was affected by the
ban on participation of the Partido Comunista de Venezuela (PCV)
and the Movimiento de la Izquierda Revolucionaria (MIR). In view
of the irresponsible terrorism actively fomented by both, the governmental restriction was justifiable. This, however, does not make clear
whether the Venezuelan system of 1963 was competitive or semi-competitive. In all probability, the understanding for the need of such a
ban would lead sympathetic observers to regard it as effectively
competitive.

Turn then to the case of Argentina. There the military-controlled care-
taker government first reformed the half-century-old electoral system
embodied in the Sáenz Peña law, then drafted a series of executive
decrees aimed at the curtailment of *peronista* organizations. Again the
question is not the need or efficacy of such a measure, but the resulting
classification of the party system. At least 20 per cent of the electorate
was influenced by the restrictions. If Venezuela is competitive, should
a line be drawn between the ruling barring 10 per cent of the electorate
there and the 20 per cent in Argentina, thus making of the latter a
semi-competitive system? The answer may be difficult; it does not seem
significant.

Certainly Argentina is different from Venezuela. If it is termed semi-
competitive, then it must stand as comparable with contemporary
Nicaragua, where the electorate surely had less freedom of choice in the
February 1963 elections than did the Argentines. The Somoza dynasty,
already more than a quarter-century old, was perpetuated through the
controlled election of René Schick. Although the anti-Somoza Conservatives had splintered into three factions, the most popular and effective
group had been left with little choice but to announce its abstention
before the vote was held. According to the present typology, either
Nicaragua and Argentina must be classified similarly—which is misleading—or else the former slips down a peg and is called non-competitive.
This does not remove the dilemmas of the scheme, however.

The fully dictatorial states, notably Haiti and Paraguay, are obviously non-competitive, while the degree of repression is far greater than that of Nicaragua. In February 1963 the Paraguayan voter was manipulated even more than the Nicaraguan, and the Haitian case is far worse. The notoriety of François Duvalier's post-facto announcement of re-election in May 1961 is hemispheric, although scarcely an untoward manifestation of Haiti's political *milieu*. Nicaragua, Paraguay, and Haiti are placed in the same slot despite evident differences in degree of party competition. To escape this dilemma is to create a new category—but to what purpose? If Nicaragua is non-competitive, perhaps Haiti is "more" non-competitive; or the latter is "repressive" non-competitive while the former is "permissive" non-competitive. The morass gets deeper.

The classification of systems by degree of competition is therefore of limited value. There is a need to know the facts on which such a taxonomic effort rests, but the label itself is of little assistance. The twenty systems do not naturally fit into the four suggested categories, and a proliferation of categories confounds rather than clarifies. Casual usage of these four phrases provides a rough rule-of-thumb means of ordering the systems, but is of little utility to the knowledgeable researcher seeking new insights. Some would prefer to rely on the number of organizations in a given system. For years, stasiologists the world over have used this method, and it has cast its shadow upon Latin Americanists as well. Still again, however, much is left to be desired.

The belief here is a conviction that the essential regional pattern is one of multi-partism, while minor qualifications are precisely that—reservations, not contradictions. This is predicated upon the explicit assumption that all such numerical schemes are appropriately applied only to essentially democratic systems. "Essentially democratic" is itself imprecise, but the meaning should be sufficiently evident. The very study of parties, of their activities, attitudes, ideology, functioning, and relationship to the people—all these facets of stasiology depend upon a degree of representative government and democracy. Therefore, Haiti, by dint of the total absence of party activity, is in effect lacking in a party system. Calling it a one-party system is not conducive to fruitful study, for within the usual terms of reference no party exists, not even the amorphous kind of shock troops employed by Duvalier. Meaningful discussion of a party system must rest upon at least a minimal degree of participation and representation. Thus, a return and revival of organized activity by the *febreristas* in Paraguay would mean the operation of a party system. As it is, that country's so-called one-party system is a misnomer.

Often the category of "one-party dominant" is included as a means of providing for Mexico. Thus the position of the Partido Revolucionario

Institucional (PRI) has sometimes been likened to the Democratic Party in the southern United States. This category does not recommend itself as useful so long as the PRI is unique in the hemisphere, however. No real insight into the Mexican Revolution and the political organization it begat will come from "one-party dominant." Should another party assume a comparable posture, there would be justification in reviving the term. Until that time, the PRI will stand as one of a kind, and is more aptly held to be a singular variant to the multi-party pattern.

Both the "one-party" and "one-party dominant" labels have now been discarded. As for bi-party arrangements, it has long been customary to cite the cases of Colombia and Uruguay as important examples contrasting with the numerical domination of multi-party systems. Even these two may be questioned, however; both can be described as bearing a fundamental resemblance to bi-partism. In Colombia the historic confrontation of Liberals and Conservatives has stood out as an uncommon example of party survival, contradicting the usual phenomena whereby the gradual amelioration of basic issues over Church and State as well as centralism versus federalism led to a splintering of both groups. Colombia's oligarchical elements came to dominate both, with the masses largely proscribed from political participation. Occasional ideological or personalistic groups, such as the Communists and the Socialists, or—in the mid-1930's—the Acción Nacionalista Popular (ANP) and the Unión Nacional Izquierdista Revolucionaria (UNIR) were ineffective or fleeting groups that failed to win national importance.

Today the situation has taken a different shape. In 1957 Colombia adopted a constitutional alteration in which the two traditional parties agreed upon absolute equality of representation at all levels. The resultant *Frente Nacional*, now moving through its second administration, is an artificial creation that, some believe, has failed to end bitter partisanship and develop a national feeling and understanding of the processes of democracy. Moreover, the constitutional provisions make it virtually impossible for a third party to break the Conservative-Liberal monopoly of power. Yet others have come to life, vitalized by the inadequacy of the *Frente* to the needs of immediate social reform, and the present impossibility of gaining power by constitutional means has not discouraged them.

A prominent group is the Movimiento Revolucionario Liberal (MRL) of Alfonso López Michelsen, which has gained a number of congressional seats. Great activity also comes from the MRL de La Izquierda (MRLI), a *fidelista* group that broke away from its parent organization in the spring of 1963. Economist Luis Valencia and his wife Gloria Gaitán, daughter of the assassinated reformist political leader Jorge Eliécer

Gaitán, head a semi-clandestine pro-Castro band known as the Frente Unida de Acción Revolucionaria (FUAR). Even the discredited Gustavo Rojas Pinilla, from 1953–57 a dictator of uncommon ineptitude, has formed the right-wing Alianza Nacional Popular (ANP), which is nothing if not noisy. Besides the proliferation of parties in the face of constitutional barriers, the traditional parties themselves have been deeply divided into dissident wings. Conservative unity was allegedly achieved after a decade of rivalry by March 1963 agreement between leaders of the *ospinista* and *laureanista* wings, but the durability of the agreement has yet to be tested. The Liberals remain divided. All this seems to buttress the view, expressed in early 1961, that the generations-old devotion to the two-party system is much in doubt. Continuing attacks on the constitutional mechanics of bi-party control give proof "of the kaleidoscopic political picture now prevailing in Colombia and of the degree of fractionation which characterizes the party scene."

In Uruguay the situation is more complex, but the overall system also bears the earmarks of multi-partism. The historic division between Colorados and Blancos had, until the 1958 victory of the latter, followed a pattern of Colorado domination that led Fitzgibbon to suggest the arrangement was effectively one-party. Colorado strength in Montevideo for years assured the party its primacy, with the major opposition guaranteed minority representation and even a specific portion of the bureaucratic spoils. Yet it was true that the electoral system was the hemisphere's most elaborate, one that seemed "to breed parties and factions at election time as rapidly as a chain reaction. . . ." The Blanco upset in 1958, if anything, encouraged the growth of political organizations as the winners themselves were divided into warring factions of nearly-equal strength, those headed by the aging party chieftain Luis Alberto del Herrera and the recently-organized Unión Blanco Democrática (UBD). The Colorados continued to be separated into what can roughly be regarded as relatively liberal and conservative wings, and disunity further spiced by a strong dash of *caudillismo* and personal rivalry.

Uruguay also has a trio of small ideological parties that have survived over a long period of time. Oldest of these is the Socialist party, which can be traced back to the mid-nineteenth century. The Communists have been active in the labor field, with the existence of diplomatic relations between Uruguay and the Soviet Union making it an important agency for hemispheric activities of international communism. Finally, the Unión Cívica is a christian democratic party that is nearly a century old. None of these has a realistic chance of attaining power, but together they add to a political culture in which diverse interests are represented by a number of parties or factions that combine into a mosaic of exceptional complexity.

In presenting the view that multi-partism dominates, one more possible two-party contradiction might be cited—Honduras. The Conservative-Liberal clash so characteristic of nineteenth-century Central America carried over to the modern period, although political controversy has until recently been more realistically described in terms of factions, with ideological or programmatic distinctions viewed as artificial. In 1923 the creation of the Partido Nacional Hondureño (PNH) in effect reconstituted the bearers of the "conservative" banner, and its partisans came to power ten years later under the *caudillista* leadership of General Tiburcio Carías. Opposition was stifled throughout his rule, and freedom of political participation came only with the presidency of Juan Manuel Gálvez in 1949.

The latter proved one of the few truly democratic and able executives in Honduran history, and a notable concomitant was the resuscitation of partisan debate and a widening of the political spectrum. Despite a dictatorial interlude under Julio Lozano Díaz, party activists continued to increase. The present government of Rámon Villeda Morales is Liberal, but his PLN is opposed by the Conservative PNH and also the Movimiento Nacional Reformista (MNR), which is far more nationalistic than reformist. Of some influence in the nation's political process is the Frente de Juventud Democrática Hondureña (FJDH), which espouses the cause of the extreme left and is outspokenly pro-Castro.

The foregoing contributes to the contention that the regular pattern for contemporary Latin American party systems, given a relative degree of freedom and participation, is multi-party. Neither a numerical analysis nor classification in terms of competitiveness permits much more than a careful description. It is, of course, possible to pursue the multi-party arrangement further; this bears more research than has yet been undertaken. One scholarly proposal is a division into "working" and "immobilist" multi-party systems, with the former typified by Scandinavia and the Low Countries, the latter by France and Italy. This may not be applicable to Latin America. However, if meaningful indicators of directions for deeper research are to be found in this general area, perhaps they will be connected with a dissection of the region's multi-partism.

Matters of statutory mechanisms are always fair game for the stasiologist, and attention can be channeled along the lines of *legal and institutional prescriptions*. Once again there is a temptation to place overreliance on the efficacy of the approach. It is, for example, all too easy to link a multi-party system with proportional representation or a second-ballot simple majority, and a bi-party system with a simple majority ballot, as critics of Duverger's European-based study have observed. This criticism is symptomatic of Duverger's tendency to reject multicausality in favor of the basic formative power of electoral procedures. It is appropriate to bear in mind Wildavsky's cautionary concern that "the utilization of surface factors such as the number of parties, the type of ballot, and the type of party structure do not appear to provide the kind of propositions which would aid in the development of such a theory."

Properly put on guard, the student of parties can then pursue his subject under the twin banners of constitutional and electoral engineering. Constitutional structures vary, notwithstanding the general regional commitment to presidential systems characterized by a dominant executive. Indeed, the more prominent deviations from the presidential norm have come largely from a revulsion toward the several evils of personalism and paternalism in government. Among the prominent examples are present-day Uruguay, Cuba under its Constitution of 1940, Brazil in the months after the resignation of Jânio Quadros, Colombia since its 1958 constitutional revisions, and Chile before and after the Constitution of 1925. The best-known case is Uruguay.

The aversion of José Batlle y Ordóñez to presidential paramountcy and his personal observation of Swiss government-by-council early in the century encouraged him to espouse far-reaching reforms not fully adopted until the Plebiscite of 1951. In oversimplified form, it provided for a nine-member National Council of Government in which the electoral victors received six seats, the runners-up three, and the presidency rotated annually among majority members. The individualistic scheme, combined with the intricate party system alluded to previously, has contributed to a political process whose operations have been far from fully explored.

The Cuban Constitution of 1940 was another effort to remedy the ill effects believed—rightly or wrongly—the result of presidential government. The semi-parliamentary form advocated by the jurist José Manuel Cortina sought a strengthening of stability, improvement of the bureaucracy, and the restoration of public faith in the workings of government. While the President was elected by direct vote, a Prime Minister and Council of Ministers were appointed by him to assist in the administration of government. Further electoral rules encouraged multi-partism in legislative contests, with coalitions needed to pass legislation proposed by a Prime Minister not necessarily appointed from the stronger parties. Congress was given the power of interpellation as well as the vote of no-confidence which could topple one minister or the entire council. Additional provisions added to an arrangement that was interesting in concept but flawed in execution.

The recent Brazilian experiment in parliamentary government was equally ill-starred and short-lived. Resembling the Cuban attempt in general outline if not in certain specifics, its efficacy was undermined at the outset by the patently political motivation of constitutional amendments. The resignation of President Quadros seven months after taking office brought the succession of João Goulart, whose past record of opportunism engendered suspicion on the part of influential political sectors. Four new chapters were added to the constitution, stripping the presidency of its powers while holding the Council of Ministers responsible to the Chamber of Deputies. Presidential acts had to be countersigned by the head of the Council—unofficially the Premier—while the Chamber was empowered to overthrow the Council by means of a no-confidence vote. With authority in the hands of the Premier and the legislature, the latter rendered immobile by the partisanship of nine different parties, responsible decision-making was impossible through the diffusion of accountability and general inexperience with the arrangement. A plebiscite subsequently returned Brazil to its customary constitutional form.

An additional variant deserving of careful and searching research is the constitutional enthronement of two-party government in Colombia. The 1957 restoration of freedom was followed by an exercise in constitutional engineering based on the Pacts of Benidorm and Sitges. Principles of *alternación* and of *paridad* were approved through a national plebiscite and were framed by the congress. The result was the dictated alternation of Liberal and Conservative presidents until 1974, with the two parties equally represented from national down to local and municipal levels. Somewhat contrary to some expectations, the artificial structure has survived its first change in government and has seen the Conservative Valencia follow the Liberal Lleras Camargo. It nonetheless remains a delicately-wrought creation whose underpinnings are untrustworthy, while the *Frente Nacional* has moderated but slightly the bitterness of party strife and is viewed increasingly as an alliance of the Colombian elite to maintain its historic hegemony.

Chile provides a final case, contrasting its parliamentary system from 1891–1925 with the regime created by the Constitution of the latter year. The Balmaceda suicide in 1891 ushered in a period of congressional omnipotence during which time government reached its nadir. Ministerial instability, administrative corruption, and electoral manipulation became the order of the day. Not until the advent of Arturo Alessandri in the 1920's did conditions change, with events leading inexorably to the 1925 charter and the restoration of a strong executive. The political process was affected and the party system altered through the adoption of proportional representation, separation of congressional and presidential elections, and the congressional choice of the president in the absence of an electoral majority. Reestablishment of a presidential system left ministerial instability still the norm, as parliamentary interference gave way to the equally undesirable interference of many party leaders. Stevenson noted that the constitutional change represented a "structural restoration; it did not carry with it the restoration of the dominance of a given socio-economic class."

In each of these instances, the nature of the legal framework and of subsequent amendments influenced the setting within which political parties necessarily operated. Further study of these might well suggest new insights in the search for valid hypothesis. Much the same can be inferred from an examination of electoral systems, where several forms of statutory prescription stand out. Several have already been cited, and need not be repeated here. Uruguay comes to mind at once, as does Mexico, with its restraints upon the registration and participation of minor parties in elections.

Argentina's Sáenz Peña law not only created an unusual electoral form in that country, but encouraged and legalized an historic change in the course of Argentina politics. The impact of the Radical surge to power in 1916 was profound. Presently, the course of affairs has again been affected by executive revision of the electoral law that contributed to the victory of Arturo Illía and the Popular Radicals on July 7, 1963. Argentine use of an electoral college for presidential elections has been an additional feature to stand out, contrasting with the more customary regional reliance upon the D'Hondt system of PR for congressional elections. Various forms of electoral quotients have been used throughout the hemisphere while women have won the suffrage in recent years, although illiterates are still proscribed in some countries. This last issue remains sharply controversial.

The choice of but a few of the existing paths for research is a basic dilemma for many. At least limited use can be made of the approaches already sketched. For the present, however, perhaps the most fruitful lie within the area subsumed under the title *intraparty structure and programmatic schema.* The narrow orientation can be toward organizational and structural questions or, on the other hand, to ideological and programmatic ones. Almond and Coleman refer to the latter in terms of party "style," and distinguish pragmatic; *Weltanschauung* or ideological, and particularistic or traditional parties. One can examine these separately, but they are so linked together that anything approximating a thorough and searching study must consider them as related parts of the whole. A fascination with the dissection and ordering of organizational data must not permit the placing of exclusive emphasis on formal structure. Neumann has argued succinctly that

> Added depth to party analysis may be derived from another approach which has gained momentum in recent years: the study of ideological forces . . . In order to make the study of ideologies useful for political analysis, we must move beyond doctrinal or formal party program analysis into the area of party behavior . . . Ideologies are the key to an understanding of the long-range strategy behind the day-to-day tactics of political movements.

Limiting ourselves for the moment to organizational matters, attention goes to such facets of structure as leadership composition and mobility, interest representation, membership recruitment, organizational hierarchy, member participation, discipline, and political education. Each of these has relevance. One of the problems is that of arranging such data so that a logical sequence and pertinent interrelationships are shown. It need hardly be added that the overall image of a party depends upon the merging of all such aspects. The challenge of arranging such information is underlined by the difficulties encountered by Duverger in just such a matter.

It is not wholly a digression to comment on the categories the French scholar has proposed. This has been cited in Wildavsky's critical analysis, embracing fourteen separate criteria by which a party may be classified. This is not the place for complete reproduction, but it should be noted that the fourteen are by no means satisfactorily tied together. A cursory examination suggests that clarification would come by grouping the several points of study into several broader categories. Perhaps obvious but nonetheless practical groupings would be leadership, membership, organization, and articulation. Programmatic and doctrinal matters are still being excluded.

Both the examination of leadership and of membership follows parallel lines. Composition, class background, recruitment, and mobility are all relevant. Party leadership should be understood in terms of individual biographies, geographic and class background, educational training, political experience, and occupational representation. The leadership as a unit should be analyzed in terms of its mobility and flexibility, interchangeability of party responsibilities, and the degree of representation of relevant sectors of the given society. Leadership unity and disunity

---

[1] Sigmund Neumann, "Toward a Theory of Political Parties," *World Politics* Vol. 6: No. 3 (July 1954), pp. 554–555.

are also deserving of attention. Comparable information on the party rank-and-file is not as readily accessible. Composition, class background, and educational training are far more difficult to ascertain with precision, even where a broad intuitive assessment may seem possible. The number of members, their enthusiasm, and the degree of intraparty participation are aspects somewhat more easily determined.

Where the leadership may be examined in terms of flexibility, unity, and disunity, the membership is subjected to the study of its discipline, and from internal order it is a short step to organization itself. The overall structure, the chain of command and flow of party directives, internal communication, relative degree of centralization and decentralization, and the operations of basic organizational units must be scrutinized. A sometimes less tangible but clearly significant phase of party organization is the relevance of statutory directives to practical considerations. Explicit organizational declarations may be more myth than reality, and it behooves the researcher to determine and assess party operations. For example, Venezuela's Acción Democrática declares in its statutes that the supreme party organ is the Convención Nacional; its leaders regard the Comité Directive Nacional as dominant, while the membership holds the general impression that the Comité Ejecutivo Nacional is the most significant organ of leadership.

A fourth major area is somewhat blurred but cannot be overlooked: articulation. This embraces party activity in political education, the range of interests effectively represented, and the breadth of popular participation. Political education is becoming an increasingly vital function for parties and interest groups in the emergent nations. A party's articulation of various interests and demands is an important aspect of the political process in such countries, and the degree to which ordinary citizens may be brought into the mainstream of national life, leading to the beginning of a national consensus, is particularly crucial.

Political education may be carried out in a variety of ways, with the touchstone being broad participation. Ideally a large number of meetings will conduct a continual effort to draw forth the citizen, his attention and eventually his personal commitment. This may take the form of weekly discussion meetings, an organized local *fútbol* league, or community self-help projects in which partisanship is minimal. Propaganda and publicity are not to be omitted, and the party is well-advised to make available—if possible, *gratis*—copies of official or semi-official weeklies and dailies. Radios are also of use in more remote communities.

Among the more meaningful ways of studying Latin American parties is to examine the attempted incorporation of the citizenry into the society of the nation. Those republics with a sizable Indian population are especially close to the matter. The *apristas* of Peru and Bolivia's MNR have made concerted efforts to reach the Indians. By way of contrast, Guatemala and Ecuador have done little. There is no denying the deep-rooted social, economic, and cultural obstacles that exist but, from the standpoint of the parties, political education can most usefully be directed at these segments of the population.

Such are the four categories under which intraparty organization and operations can be grouped. Nothing has yet been said at length about ideology and program. Terminology becomes important, for an "ideological" party in one sense would be marxist, communist, or perhaps fascist. More broadly, however, when speaking of a party in terms of both organization and ideology, the latter work implies a program or platform. For the present, "programmatic" will be employed, with "ideological" indicating a strong doctrinal current. So stated, it becomes the programmatic aspect of party analysis that Neumann discussed in terms of "ideologies useful for political analysis." Moreover, it is the programmatic factor that has been the strongest single element in existing efforts to classify Latin American parties one-by-one.

Among the more recent attempts to design a typology of this sort was that of Alexander, in which all Latin American parties are placed under one of ten labels: Personalist, Conservative, Liberal, Radical, Christian Democrat, Socialist, National Revolutionary, Jacobin Left, Communist, and Fascist. Certainly the programmatic—if not necessarily the ideological—nature of the parties leads to this sort of classification. Beyond its relative simplicity and convenience, however, such an ordering has severe limitations. Once again it can be said that students familiar with the material will learn little that is new, while the layman may be unduly confused. Non-specialists can easily be misled by apparent contradictions in nomenclature.

In Brazil, Alexander points out that the Social Democratic Party (PSD) is Conservative, the National Democratic Union (UDN) is Liberal, while the Brazilian Socialist Party (PSB) is Socialist and the fragmented Brazilian Workers Party (PTS) belongs to the Jacobin Left. In Uruguay the Blancos (National Party) are Conservative and the Colorados are Liberal, while in Paraguay the Colorados are regarded as Conservative. The Dominican Republic offers its own confusion with the Dominican Party (PD) listed as Personalist while the Dominican Revolutionary Party (PRD) and the Dominican Revolutionary Vanguard (VRD) are both National Revolutionary. A nascent party system such as Guatemala's, although changing rather rapidly, offers such titles as the National Democratic Movement (MDN), which is Personalist; the Revolutionary Party (PR), which is National Revolutionary; the Authentic Revolutionary Party (PRA), of the Jacobin Left; and the Guatemalan Labor Party (PTG), which is Communist.

The plethora of names and multiple labels is inherently confusing. It is no criticism of Alexander to point out this fact, to which he would doubtless agree. There is, furthermore, a degree of mobility that makes such typologies somewhat temporary. This is inevitable, especially where party systems are evolving and passing through endless permutations. Without for a moment denying that such classification has some intrinsic value, it must be said that it does not lead much further. The dictates of logic suggest the possibility of grouping these ten categories under a few broader headings that would permit worthwhile generalization.

To make the effort in terms of programmatic direction would imply some form of a left-right spectrum; a different procedure would group the parties as ideological (marxist, etc.), pragmatic, and personalist; additional possibilities also exist. Whether the exercise is justifiable can hardly be determined until it is undertaken. There is bound to be some distortion if parties are judged purely in terms of program and doctrine. In the long run, relevant aspects of both organizational and programmatic party life must be examined before a sophisticated party typology can truly push back the bounds of our knowledge and understanding.

Such is the nature of the inquiry into political parties that no single conclusion or stopping point is visible; nearly the same can be said of this essay itself. A number of approaches have been proffered, the final ones of which seem to promise greater short-run rewards. In any event, it can but be repeated that there are no royal roads to ordered, meaningful knowledge and to theories of general applicability. We are all under an obligation to pursue the possibilities that lie before us. If many prove fruitless, at least a few will yield up some of the insights that may contribute to the development of a theory of Latin American political parties.

	MAJOR
Part 4	*POLITICAL*
	ISSUES

This section is devoted to an analysis of some of the major political issues in Latin America: agrarian reform, nationalism, communism, and the Alliance for Progress.[1] Also included is an examination of the attitudes of leaders of the armed forces toward some of these issues. Treatment of these topics in a somewhat isolated manner tends to hide what may well be the single overriding issue, that is, the development of a modern nation-state.

In recent years a great deal has been written about political development, but almost all authors concentrate on the new nations of Asia and Africa, and neglect those of Latin America. Given the lack of serious research in this area, it is necessary to start virtually from scratch in attempting to analyze Latin American political development.[2] What follows is an attempt to begin to rank the Latin American nations as to their degree of political development and to determine what developmental characteristics are most prevalent in this area of the world.

It is, needless to say, quite difficult to determine—with any degree of assurance—just what are the characteristics of a modern political system, and even more difficult to determine the degree in which these characteristics are present in any given polity. This problem has abated

[1] The selection of issues to be covered was based at least as much on the availability of scholarly works as on the editor's concept of what issues are presently of greatest importance.
[2] There are almost as many definitions of political development as there are works on the subject. The discussion below is based on the concept of political development as "the organization of political life and the performance of political functions in accordance with the standards expected of a modern nation-state." For a discussion of this definition and several others see Lucian W. Pye, *Aspects of Political Development* (Boston: Little, Brown & Company, 1966), pp. 33–45.

somewhat with the publication of *A Cross-Polity Survey*,[3] which includes evaluations of 57 "raw characteristics" for each of the world's 115 independent polities. Twenty of these characteristics, which appear to be components of a modern nation-state, have been scaled against the 20 independent polities of Latin America. These characteristics are:

a.   a modern bureaucracy
b.   a stable political party system
c.   a fully effective legislature
d.   significant interest aggregation by political parties
e.   a generally stable government since World War II
f.   at least moderate interest aggregation by the legislature
g.   no more than moderate interest articulation by institutional groups
h.   infrequent interest articulation by anomic groups
i.   at least moderate interest articulation by associational groups
j.   effective horizontal power distribution
k.   at least moderate interest aggregation by the executive
l.   political neutrality of the military
m.   limited or negligible interest articulation by nonassociational groups
n.   non-elitist or moderately elitist political leadership
o.   the lack of executive dominance
p.   no more than occasional press censorship
q.   a competitive electoral system
r.   present regime of at least partly polyarchic character
s.   at least moderate interest articulation by associational groups
t.   freedom of political organization for autonomous groups

On the scalogram the presence of each of the characteristics is represented by a plus sign on the "highly developed" side of the scalogram; their absence is represented by a plus on the "underdeveloped" side. A circle indicates the absence of reliable data.

With few exceptions, the rankings of polities by the scalogram is just about what one might have expected. Most persons would agree that Uruguay, Chile, and Costa Rica belong at or near the top, and that Guatemala, El Salvador, Paraguay, Nicaragua, and Haiti deserve their low ranking. The most questionable rankings are probably those of the Dominican Republic and Cuba. The high position of the former is almost certainly due to an overly optimistic view of the administration of Juan Bosch (which was in power at the time of the publication

---

[3] Arthur S. Banks and Robert B. Textor, *A Cross-Polity Survey* (Cambridge, Massachusetts: The Massachusetts Insitute of Technology Press, 1963).

A SCALOGRAM OF POLITICAL DEVELOPMENT IN LATIN AMERICA

nation	scale type		highly developed												underdeveloped							
		a	b	c	d	e	f	g	h	i	j	k	l	m	n	o	p	q	r	s	t
Uru	18	o	+	+	+	+	+	+	+	+	o	+	+	+	+	+	+	+	+	o	+
Chi	15	+	+	+	+	+	+	+	+	+	+	+	+	+	+	o	+	+	+	+	+
C R	14	+	+	+	+	+	+	+	+	+	+	+	+	+	+	+	+	+	+	+	+
D R	11	+	+	o	+	+	+	o	+	+	+	+	+	+	+	+	+	+	+	+	+
Mex	10	+	+	+	+	+	+	+	+	o	+	+	+	+	+	+	+	o	+	+	+
Ven	10	+	+	+	+	+	+	o	+	+	o	+	+	+	+	+	+	+	+	+	+
Col	10	+	o	o	+	+	+	+	+	+	+	+	+	+	+	o	+	+	+	+	+
Bol	10	+	+	+	+	+	+	+	+	+	+	+	+	+	+	+	+	+	+	+	+
Arg	8	+	+	+	+	+	+	+	+	+	o	o	+	+	o	o	+	+	+	o	+
Pan	8	+	+	+	+	+	+	+	+	+	+	+	+	+	+	+	+	+	+	+	+
Bra	7	+	+	+	+	+	+	+	+	+	+	+	+	+	+	+	+	+	+	+	+
Per	7	+	o	+	o	+	+	o	+	o	+	+	+	+	+	+	+	o	+	+	+
Ecu	6	+	+	+	+	+	+	+	+	+	+	+	+	+	+	+	o	+	+	+	+
Hon	4	+	+	+	+	+	+	+	+	+	+	+	+	+	+	+	+	+	+	+	+
Gua	2	+	+	+	+	+	+	o	+	+	+	+	+	o	o	o	+	o	+	+	+
E S	2	+	+	+	+	+	+	+	+	+	+	+	+	+	+	+	+	+	+	+	+
Nic	1	+	+	+	+	+	+	+	+	+	+	+	+	+	o	+	+	+	+	+	+
Par	1	+	+	+	+	+	o	+	o	+	+	+	+	+	o	+	+	+	+	+	+
Cub	0	+	+	+	+	+	+	+	+	+	+	+	+	+	+	+	+	+	+	+	+
Hai	0	+	+	+	+	+	o	+	o	+	+	+	+	+	+	+	+	+	+	+	+
errors		0	1	0	1	1	0	0	1	5	1	1	0	2	0	1	1	0	0	3	0

CR = .95   CS = .79

of *A Cross-Polity Survey*). The extremely low position accorded Cuba is more difficult to explain. It may be that the characteristics used here as components of a modern nation-state are in reality the components of a modern *non-communist* nation-state, and hence are not reliable indicators of the political development of a communist polity.

Turning from the ranking of polities to the ordering of characteristics, one can readily observe that the number of polities in which any given characteristic is present varies tremendously. With the exceptions only of Haiti and Cuba, autonomous groups are everywhere free to organize politically, while at the other end of the scale none of the Latin American nations has a truly modern bureaucracy. It might be noted that of the six characteristics present in two or less polities, four pertain to political parties or legislative assemblies. In other words, the components of a modern nation-state most notably absent in Latin America are stable political parties that are able to aggregate interests to a signif'cant extent and effective legislative bodies capable of at least moderate interest aggregation.[4]

---

[4] For a more complete discussion of the use of scalogram analysis in studying political development see Peter G. Snow, "A Scalogram Analysis of Political Development," *The American Behavioral Scientist*, Vol. 9: No 7 (March 1966), pp. 33–36.

The Land Reform Issue in Latin America*

THOMAS F. CARROLL

The land reform issue, which only a few years ago was under a sort of taboo in Latin America, has rapidly moved to occupy a key position among the policy problems of the region. The Cuban land reform, introduced in 1959 as one of the main props of the revolution, has dramatized both the necessity for overhauling existing land tenure systems and the ideological and power struggle inherent in such changes. Nowadays, land reform problems are vigorously debated throughout Latin America and there is a proliferation of projects and proposals in almost every country. While the issue is extremely complex and has many political aspects, the principal interest of economists has centered on the relationship between land reform and development. The purpose of this essay is more modest: it is to sketch with broad strokes the agrarian situation that calls for changes, to review some of the recent attempts at reforms or those currently in progress, and in the light of past experience to advance some ideas on how continued pressure for land reforms is likely to affect policy-making in Latin American countries.

Amidst all of its inherent complexity, the core of the land reform problem is relatively simple and can be stated in straight-forward terms: The existing pattern of land tenure (i.e., ownership and control over land resources) is such that it corresponds neither to the aspirations of the rural population nor to the requirements of rapid technological progress. What this usually means in action is redistribution of landed rights in favor of the cultivator, and greater social control over land resources. Such changes are now being advocated both by politicians wishing to capitalize on growing popular sentiment and by intellectuals interested in modernization of their countries' institutions. Economic developers are becoming increasingly aware of the key role of agriculture in Latin American economic growth and there is a tendency to look more closely at the land tenure system as a major factor in the stagnation

* Thomas F. Carroll, "The Land Reform Issue in Latin America," in Albert O. Hirschman (ed.), *Latin American Issues: Essays and Comments* (New York: The Twentieth Century Fund, 1961), pp. 161–201. (Footnotes in the original version have been omitted).

423

of the farm sector. What gives the land reform issue its peculiar fascination, however, is the income redistribution aspect. Land reform, if it is seriously done, implies a drastic rearrangement of property rights, income and social status. In some ways, therefore, every reform is revolutionary.

AGRARIAN STRUCTURE

In looking at the agrarian structure in Latin America what is most striking is the great concentration of ownership in relatively few large units, and the vast number of very small units at the other end of the scale. While it is difficult to generalize for so large and varied a region, the tenure systems have much in common in most countries. Broadly speaking, the main features of the agrarian structure are: (1) the importance of *latifundios*, or very large farms; (2) the large number of *minifundios*, or very small farms; (3) the special situation of the *communidades*, or communal holdings; and (4) the peculiar form of farm labor known as the *colono* system. A knowledge of the principal features of each system and the main problems it represents is essential in order to understand what is supposed to be "reformed."

The latifundio

Let us first consider the large farms and their importance. As practically all the statistics are in terms of management units (*explotaciones*) rather than ownership units (*propiedades*), the degree of concentration is usually even greater than the data indicate. A few figures will illustrate this concentration. In Guatemala 516 farms (0.15 per cent of all farms) represent 41 per cent of the agricultural land. In Ecuador 705 units (0.17 per cent) include 37 per cent of the farm land. In Venezuela 74 per cent of the farm acreage, comprising 6,800 units (1.69 per cent of all farms), is in holdings of over 1,000 hectares. Half the farm land in Brazil is in the hands of 1.6 per cent of the owners. In Nicaragua 362 owners have control over fully one-third of the agricultural acreage. The most extreme concentration could be observed in Bolivia prior to the land reform; there 92 per cent of the land was in fewer than 5,500 units, representing 6.4 per cent of all farms.

These figures, based mostly on census data, are of course not exact, yet they give a good indication of the magnitude of land concentration. If it were possible to calculate cultivated or cultivable land by farm sizes, the index of concentration would diminish, as many of the large units include mountain, desert or swampland of doubtful value. On the other hand, it is generally acknowledged that for historic reasons the *latifundios* include the best land in most of the countries, a fact which from the standpoint of quality tends greatly to increase the land monopoly. Census counts, moreover, are usually short in the small-farm category, so that the *minifundios,* worked frequently by squatters and migrant cultivators, are underestimated. Therefore, the true percentage position of the large units is likely to be even greater.

A rapid summation of the available data yields the figures shown in Table 1 for Latin America as a whole. Roughly 90 per cent of the land belongs to 10 per cent of the owners. This degree of concentration is far greater than that in any other world region of comparable size.

Much has been written about the historic origins of the *latifundio* system. Basically, it reflects the organization of society in Spain and Portugal at the time of colonization, and the super-imposition of this pattern on native cultures through large land grants. The *latifundio* pattern has two main variants: the *hacienda* type of extensively cultivated estates, and the intensively worked plantations. They give rise to quite different problems and call for different measures of reform.

The *hacienda* is typically a livestock-cereal operation, with very low capital investment and labor applied per unit of land area. Ownership is often of the absentee type and labor is provided by the *colono* system or one of its variants. While there are notable exceptions, the *hacienda* system is a paragon of inefficiency both on the firm level and nationally. Output per man and per land unit is low. The plantation, on the other hand, generally shows a high capitalization combined with stricter labor organization and controls. As a result, output per land unit is generally high and farm efficiency is above average. However, both systems embody monopoly elements, both result in extreme maldistribution of income, and in social conditions which have often been described as deplorable. The plantation problem is complicated by some foreign ownership and management, especially in the Caribbean area. But perhaps the worst feature of land concentration is the resulting concentration of power which in innumerable ways infuses the whole structure of society. It is against this concentration of power that most of the fury of popular land reforms has been directed. It is the destruction of *latifundismo* rather than other more positive goals, such as "family farming" or better land use, that provides the emotional and political mainspring of future reforms.

TABLE 1. ESTIMATED PERCENTAGE DISTRIBUTION OF
LAND HOLDINGS IN LATIN AMERICA, AROUND 1950

SIZE OF FARMS (HECTARES)	PER CENT OF FARMS	PER CENT OF LAND AREA
0–20	72.6	3.7
20–100	18.0	8.4
100–1,000	7.9	23.0
Over 1,000	1.5	64.9
Total	100.0	100.0

Source: Based on the very helpful regional summary provided by Oscar Delgado in his *Estructura y reforma agraria en Latinoamerica*, prepared for the Sociedad Económica de Amigos del País, Bogotá, 1960 (mimeographed).

The minifundio

Now let us look at the other end of the scale. The great majority of the farms are small, often so small that at the present levels of technology these *minifundios* cannot give the farm family an acceptable minimum level of living. In Guatemala 97 per cent of all farms are in units of less than 20 hectares. The corresponding figure for both Peru and Ecuador is 90 per cent, for the Dominican Republic it is 95 per cent, for Venezuela 88 per cent and for the private sector of the Mexican farm economy 88 per cent. In Colombia some 325,000 farms average ½ hectare, and a further half a million farms average 2½ hectares.

The gravity of the *minifundio* situation is increased by fragmentation, by illegal occupancy (squatting) and by shifting cultivation. In many areas (especially in the Andean mountains) these small holdings have become subdivided as a result of population pressure into tiny plots, often only a few feet wide. Métraux reports, for example, that in the Conima region on the eastern shore of Lake Titicaca there is not a single holding that is not broken up into fifteen or twenty plots. Many of the smallest units are operated by squatters on either public or private land who hold no title and whose farming operations both from the point of view of security and use of resources are extremely unsatisfactory. Finally, there is the problem of migrant or shifting small-scale agriculture, practiced in vast areas of usually forested land in the tropical belt, mostly accompanied by burning and other wasteful methods. The vast majority of *minifundios* represent a hand-to-mouth type of farming and are outside the market economy.

The origin of the *minifundios* also goes back to colonial times, when land grants were "bestowed on the lower order, the conquering armies or upon civilians of humble rank." Some of the more recent ones are homesteads conferred upon or sold to colonists who settled in frontier regions. Some are the result of simple occupancy, which may or may not have been confirmed legally. The extraordinarily rapid growth of population in recent decades has aggravated the *minifundio* problem both through further subdivision by inheritance and through spontaneous migration into new areas. The owners or occupants of small plots of land are beset by many problems. Many are at the margin of the market economy and represent neither a producing force of farm commodities nor an effective demand for industrial products. They generally lack not only land but other inputs necessary to raise productivity. Their plots are frequently exhausted and eroding. Institutional services, schools, roads, hospitals, are conspicuously lacking in *minifundio* areas. The peasants are at the mercy of unscrupulous tradesmen, money lenders, lawyers and petty officials.

It should be emphasized that the *minifundio-latifundio* patterns are not independent, but are often closely interrelated. Large estates are surrounded by many small *ranchos, chacras, huertas, hijuelas or sitios,* drawing seasonal labor from them and in many ways contributing to the maintenance of the system. The *latifundios* exercise an influence far beyond their own boundaries, and they are frequently a limiting force on regional development. More importantly, perhaps, the system acts as a barrier to social mobility, participating citizenship and the emergence of a broad base for upgrading the quality of human effort, which is a prerequisite for dynamic development.

The comunidad

The third major type of land holding in Latin America is the *comunidad,* far older in origin than the *hacienda* or the plantation. The Incas, Mayas and Aztecs all held land in collective fashion, and the survival of the system is today localized in areas of native Indian populations, mostly in the Andean areas. The number of Indians living on the plateaus and in the valleys of the Andean chain between northern Argentina and Ecuador has been estimated as between 5 and 6 million. The Indian *comunidad,* while being slowly eroded away, is a remarkably durable institution. Its base is the aggregation of extended families, who together have claim over a specific land area. The territory of the community is deemed non-transferable, but the proprietary rights of the several families are recognized and every individual is free to dispose of his land within the group. In modern times many communities have *de facto* subdivided and individualized their land holdings, but in most there is a periodic reallocation of land among members. Much of the work is performed collectively on an exchange basis. Sociologists and anthropologists have given considerable attention to the Indian *communidades* and have viewed them as heirs to the Inca *ayllus.*

A throwback to the *comunidades* is the Mexican *ejido,* product of the revolutionary land reform. Half the farmers in Mexico today are *ejidatarios.* Although the *ejido* system is much more closely connected with the social and economic mainstream of the country than are the geographically and culturally isolated *comunidades* of Peru, Bolivia or Ecuador, it suffers from very much the same economic ills. These communal arrangements, while embodying the seeds of cooperative economics, are excessively rigid and inhibit developmental forces. Members of the Andean communities are not able to obtain credit. There are no incentives for talented or ambitious individuals, and the system is not conducive to the emergence of effective leaders or group action in behalf of greater productivity. Capital investment by individuals is not encouraged. Thus the system in its present form represents a stagnant type of agriculture. Its main justification is on sociological grounds. For that part of the agricultural population which cannot be absorbed by the commercial farming sector or by urban occupations it offers perhaps a more secure and satisfactory way of life than that of the *colonos* or *peones.*

There has been considerable speculation about the possibilities of transforming the *comunidades* into modern cooperatives or true collectives, but apart from a few isolated cases, this has never been attempted on any meaningful scale. Several of the most recent land reform proposals (notably in Peru and Ecuador) contemplate such a transformation. While the obstacles are formidable the basic idea is intellectually attractive and challenging. Why wait until small independent owners can be organized into cooperatives, when the basic cultural framework may permit skipping such an intermediate stage? Yet it seems a long way from the communal *fiestas* to the bookkeeping system of a modern cooperative.

The colono system

The last major feature of the Latin American tenure system worth recording here is the pattern of agricultural labor. In a region where the majority of farm people are not owners of land, the systems of farm labor have a decisive influence on productivity and levels of living. In spite of its importance, this is a greatly neglected field. The available information on farm labor, and its multiple combination with sharecropping and tenancy, is conspicuously deficient.

In general, only a small fraction of workers in the countries are paid on a cash basis. Most have the status of tenant laborers, a typical arrangement that assumes many names and variants throughout Latin America. This is known as the *colono* system, in which the worker is paid in the temporary or traditional usufruct of a parcel of land and certain other privileges. In return, the *colono* must serve a specified number of days on the estate and fulfill other customary obligations, such as making available members of his family for certain tasks in the field or in the owner's household. This system is often combined with sharecropping or with tenancy on a cash rent basis. Most of the resident labor force on the *hacienda* is made up of *colonos*. They have different names in different countries: *yanaconas* in Peru, *inquilinos* in Chile, *huasipungos* in Ecuador, or *conuqueros* in Venezuela. Basically, all these represent similar arrangements.

The *colono* pattern is regarded as inefficient and as a poor base for economic development. The duality of the structure with its quasi-security aspects is not conducive to production incentives for the *colonos*, thus compounding the debilitating effects of landlord absenteeism.

In countries that have introduced land reforms the *colonos* were the first and most important beneficiaries of the programs. In Bolivia, for instance, the major immediate effect of the reform was to confirm the possession of the tenant workers who have been occupying and working small plots on the *haciendas*.

In contrast with other world areas, tenancy in its pure form does not loom large in the agrarian structure of Latin America. Important exceptions are Argentina and Uruguay. In Argentina, commercial tenancy is numerically more important than owner operation. In Uruguay, about one-third of the land in farms is managed by tenants. In the rest of the countries the degree of tenancy is relatively low. Contracts are generally of very short duration, and are verbal more often than not. Few of the norms of equitable and forward-looking tenancy arrangements are observed.

This review of the agrarian structure, brief and sketchy though it is, clearly shows the inadequacy of tenure institutions throughout the region. Units of production are either too large or too small, ownership and occupancy are often precarious, the communities are tradition-bound and inflexible, farm labor conditions are not many steps removed from serfdom, land as a resource does not freely exchange hands but is hoarded and unavailable to the small cultivator. There is no "tenure ladder" in the sense that a landless person could gradually work his way into the ownership class. Owners and non-owners of land are frequently separated by strict racial and cultural class barriers. The system reinforces the status quo and confers power upon those with inherited position and wealth. Farm investment is low, demand for consumer goods restricted, and large segments of the population are held at the margin of the economic mainstream in the countries. Political democracy and social mobility are greatly circumscribed. For brevity and simplicity the picture described is based only on land tenure conditions. If one were to superimpose the effects of the other institutional factors—which in addition to what may be called "access to land" include access to capital and access to markets, the tax structure, education, local government and other related aspects—the situation would appear even darker. . . .

COLONIZATION SCHEMES

Land settlement programs have been of two types. One involves the opening up of new or virgin lands or the creation of new settlement opportunities through large-scale irrigation, drainage, forestation and other land development measures. Such settlement is normally on public land. The other type includes the purchase, development and subdivision of privately owned farms in the already cultivated or "old" areas. Both programs are strictly limited by the amount of money available for land purchase and development.

In most cases, land settlement programs in Latin America can be regarded as little more than pilot schemes. This should not detract from their value. Indeed, these programs and the accumulated knowledge of the institutions which plan and execute them represent a most significant experience on which more comprehensive land reforms could draw in this difficult field.

While practically all the countries have some sort of land settlement policies and programs, the most notable are the activities in Uruguay, Chile, Colombia, Venezuela and Ecuador. The customary form of organization for land settlement is a semi-autonomous body created especially for the purpose. In Uruguay, for instance, a National Institute of Colonization was established in 1948. The basic law which created the Institute gives the following main objective: "To promote the rational subdivision of the land and its adequate utilization, in order to achieve the growth and improvement of agricultural production and the settlement and welfare of the rural worker." The main task of the Institute has been the purchase and redistribution of inadequately utilized large farms. Because of meager appropriations, in twelve years only about 1,300 new units have been established. However, the new settlements cover an area of 225,000 hectares and as they are being intensively cultivated with horticultural and industrial crops they are making an important contribution to agricultural output. The Institute has acquired an additional 210,000 hectares which it has not yet been able to distribute.

In Chile the instrument of land settlement is the Caja de Colonización, whose basic legislation was created as far back as 1928, although in its modern form it has operated only since 1935. As is true of its sister agency in Uruguay, the Caja's orientation and legal equipment are on the whole well conceived and workable. But the noble aims which brought the Caja into being have been frustrated by the well-known Chilean inflation, or perhaps more precisely, by the unwillingness of subsequent governments to put the Caja's appropriations and operations on a hard-money basis. In retrospect it can be seen that lack of effective pressure by the potential beneficiaries allowed the Caja to die a slow death. The result is that in almost twenty-six years new farms have been set up to the benefit of only some 3,300 families, many of whom were not bona fide landless cultivators.

Recently the Caja was given a new lease on life by a series of decrees which readjusted its finances and assigned to it for distribution the lands of a number of large government-owned farms of about 300,000 hectares. In addition, between the lands already held by the Caja and other public lands likely to be assigned to it, another one million hectares will soon be available for redistribution. (Half a million of this represents unimproved pasture land in the southernmost province of Magallanes where the Caja is assigning roughly 3,000 hectares per family unit.) While thus the rate of land settlement is likely to be accelerated considerably, it appears doubtful that under the existing circumstances the Caja can make significant improvements in the position of Chile's over 200,000 landless rural families.

A National Colonization Institute was recently established in Ecuador. It has suffered from poltical birth pains under changing administrations. Up to now it has concentrated its efforts on a single pilot project, which involves a little over 100 families. The first big project of the Ecuadorian Institute will be the subdivision of state farms. This program is now being studied with the help of the United Nations Special Fund. About 133,000 hectares are likely to be affected. As there are extensive government lands in Ecuador, it is hoped that the rhythm of land settlement can be stepped up greatly without the need of expropriation.

Brief mention should be made of the land settlement efforts of Venezuela, prior to the land reform. The outstanding fact about this program was its very high cost and the meagerness of the results achieved. Enormous investments were made in such things as roads, houses, machinery and irrigation, which considering the number of people benefited and alternative opportunities for social investment, seem extravagant and misdirected. The model villages created were designed for a level of living which far exceeded that prevailing in surrounding areas. Another point which is frequently criticized in the Venezuelan colonization is the paternalistic attitude adopted by the settlement agency (Instituto Agrario Nacional). Everything was being done for the settlers, and in many cases they were even given prolonged cash subsidies. No attempt was made to develop individual or community initiative or to put the projects on a sound economic basis. There is some evidence that the present administration is well aware of these past errors and that the new projects under the land reform law are being planned more realistically.

Land settlement agencies similar to the ones in Chile and Uruguay are also operating in a number of other countries, including Paraguay, Brazil, Peru and Colombia. Some of them have good programs, but their total impact on the land tenure problem has been small.

In Colombia, for instance, the Caja Agraria administers a settlement program on public lands, and is also subdividing some private holdings. For 1959–60 this involved only about 1,000 families, but more resources will become available in future years. In 1959 a special law ordered the investment of 10 per cent of all savings deposits in bonds of the Caja for purposes of land redistribution. The Development Loan Fund and the Export-Import Bank have concluded a loan agreement for $70 million, of which about $33 million has been earmarked to support land settlement programs. By the end of 1960, plans were under way to resettle 50,000 families in five years.

LAND TAXATION

Thus far we have dealt mainly with what may be called a "direct" attack on land tenure problems. There is a body of theory with a considerable following among economists which holds that land reforms could be brought about by indirect methods, thereby avoiding the large social costs of drastic programs and the injustices implicit in radical redistribution of resources. Foremost among these indirect approaches is land taxation. For this purpose, land taxation would assume a double role;

in addition to fulfilling a legitimate fiscal function, a properly adjusted and graduated land tax would gradually force the owners of estates either to intensify cultivation or to dispose of part of their holdings.

The experience with land taxation in Latin America is not encouraging. Colombia is the best example. As in other Latin American countries, land taxes in Colombia are extremely light and in many ways favor the large operators who have non-agricultural investments. The standard rate is 0.4 per cent.

Although the International Bank for Reconstruction and Development is generally reluctant to touch the controversial problems of land tenure, one of the principal recommendations of its missions to Colombia in 1950 and 1956 was the imposition of a graduated land tax based on potential land use. The first of these missions recommended (in what became known as the Currie Report) a graduated land tax which called for a rate of 0.4 per cent for well-utilized lands and higher rates for poorly used lands. The 1956 mission suggested assessing agricultural land based on optimum rather than current use and subjecting owners of speculative holdings to an income tax based on a presumed net return of between 3 and 5 per cent of the value of land and capital assets.

In 1957 governmental Decree 290 made a variant of these ideas into law, providing an elaborate system of tax incentives and deterrents designed to improve land use practices. The key provision required owners and tenants with more than fifty hectares to cultivate part of their land at least once a year. The cultivation requirements varied with the type of land, according to a classification to be made by the Geographic Institute. Non-compliance was to be punished by a progressive land tax based on cadastral value. There was no attempt in this decree to expropriate unused or underused private land whose owners did not comply with the cultivation quotas. The key to this whole procedure was the rapid completion of the land classification. A special ownership and use survey based on a questionnaire was also necessary to put the law into effect.

As of this writing, the penalties prescribed by Decree 290 for inadequate land utilization have not been applied. True, the Geographic Institute classified almost a million hectares, mostly in areas already fairly well developed. The low cultivation quotas posed no serious problem for farmers in these areas, and even where additional classifications have been available the provisions of Decree 290 have been inoperative. A land ownership and land use questionnaire was sent out in early 1958 but answers were incomplete and of questionable validity; in any event, the results have never been tabulated. This left the government without any basic data for the effective administration of the law, and no further attempts have been made to enforce it. However, this has not discouraged Colombian policy-makers from their determination to design some kind of land tax proposal. During the last two years a number of projects incorporating a graduated land tax have been elaborated and presented to the legislature. The over-all land reform bill prepared at the end of 1960 also involves tax incentives and penalties, although it relies upon other means to reform the agrarian structure. The Colombian experience shows that little can be achieved through a land tax if there is no effective enforcement machinery.

Similar attempts have been made in other countries, notably Chile, but here again the assessment machinery has been deficient. Moreover, the law fixes the global tax base at ten times the arbitrarily calculated "rental income" of agriculture in the base year. Changes in the evaluation from year to year cannot be greater than ten times the calculated changes in "rental income" from the previous year, nor can they be negative so as to reduce assessment below that of the previous year. Rental income is estimated by a special commission, which opens the way for further manipulation of the tax base. For example, in 1957 the commission's final determination of rental income for tax assessment purposes was only about one-fourth of the total agricultural income estimated by the Chilean Development Corporation.

The general impression one gets is that while the progressive land tax idea as a means of agrarian reform is theoretically attractive, in practice it runs afoul of the same power situation it is supposed to remedy. Certainly a graduated land tax cannot be easily implemented without cadastral surveys and a reasonably accurate land classification. But more importantly, there are the problems of political opposition and local enforcement which thus far have been the major obstacles to tax reform. The powerful landowning groups seem to be unwilling to submit to a graduated land tax which is of sufficient magnitude to mobilize the land market and improve the tenure distribution. By the time the balance of power has shifted away from them it is too late for such evolutionary and gradual measures and the pendulum invariably swings over to expropriation and confiscation.

NEW REFORM PROPOSALS

Plans are at present under way to introduce more or less important tenure reforms in a number of countries. Special mention should be made of projects in Peru and Colombia. A Peruvian commission on land reform and housing, which was established in President Prado's first governmental decree of August 1956, has, after four years of work, submitted the draft of a comprehensive agrarian law in September 1960. Pedro Beltrán was head of the commission before he became prime minister.

The general approach of the law is a "gradualistic" one. It aims primarily at a more effective utilization of Peru's land resources and an evolutionary transformation of the land tenure system without undue disturbance. While the law provides for a large number of important measures in such fields as land and water development, colonization, the Indian communities and rural labor, it touches the problem of the present distribution of farm property most gingerly. The plantation-type irrigated estates on the coast would not, on the whole, be subject to expropriation. However, uncultivated *latifundios* in the mountain areas may be acquired by the government for redistribution. In the tropical lowlands, systematic resettlement programs are envisaged.

All told, it is estimated that the law would affect approximately 25 per cent of the country's farm land, including 100,000 hectares on the coast and 3.5 million in the *sierra*, of which about half a million hectares represent land under cultivation and 3 million in natural pasture. The land would be acquired by a newly created Institute of Agrarian Reform through adequate compensation and payments over a period of five years. Land acquisition would be governed by a very complex rule, with different criteria applying to different parts of the country.

Perhaps the heart of the new law is the provision in which it assigns annually 3 per cent of the national budget to land reform over a period of ten years. Additional funds are to be made available for the opening up of new areas in the tropical lowlands and for land development in general. In this connection, it is worth mentioning that in July 1960 the Export-Import Bank and the Development Loan Fund authorized a loan of $52.5 million to Peru. Of this amount, $32.6 million is earmarked for the construction of penetration roads and $10 million for financing the establishment of colonists. A graduated land tax would produce additional revenue. The law has many other interesting provisions and is one of the most comprehensive on record. It contains 294 articles organized into 33 chapters.

Another interesting land reform project was prepared in Colombia by a special national agrarian committee in October 1960. This law, the outcome of considerable social pressures and the interest of President Lleras, goes far beyond the previous taxation proposals. It declares the necessity "to reform the agrarian social structure through procedures designed to eliminate and to prevent the concentration of rural property . . . and to grant land to those who have none." The proposal would exempt from expropriation the first 300 hectares of estates, and would partially exempt an additional 500 hectares up to an absolute limit of 800. Expropriations would be made at market value, partly in cash and partly in bonds. It remains to be seen if the Peruvian and Colombian proposals will mature into law, and if so, how they will be carried out.

A most recent land reform bill was prepared by the state government of São Paulo in Brazil and approved by the state legislature during the last days of 1960. The law provides for two types of programs: (1) subdivision and settlement of unutilized lands (giving preference to state property), and (2) creation of graduated land taxes to intensify land use. Expropriation can be effected after one year's grace if owners fail to cultivate their lands in accordance with certain criteria or to apply minimum standards to farm labor.

By the end of 1960, the following countries were reported to be considering some kind of land reform legislation and to have bills in preparation: Ecuador, Honduras, Nicaragua and Panama. An interesting plan by the state government of Buenos Aires in Argentina was shelved after the 1960 provincial elections.

CONCLUDING COMMENT

The foregoing does not pretend to cover all aspects of the complex problems of land tenure reform. Notably, policies introduced to benefit small farmers in the field of farm credit, marketing, price supports and social services have not been discussed, although many people refer to them collectively as "land reforms." It is the conviction of the writer that these and similar measures represent the focus not of land reform but of agricultural development, and that they are most effective where a healthy land tenure situation exists.

To put it in another way, land tenure improvement and agricultural development must go hand in hand. Past investments without land reforms have shown that the benefits are not shared by the large masses of farmers but go to a few big landowners and to those who monopolize the markets in farm products. Land reform without supporting measures of development—which has been the pattern so far—produces poor economic results and undue delays in raising levels of living. But on the basis of "first things first," more equitable tenure relations rate the highest priority and are a prerequisite for other types of action.

Vast land reserves are still available in Latin America for development and settlement. While the amount and accessibility of this reserve varies greatly from country to country and its quality is largely unknown, it can be said that Latin America is one of the few remaining world regions where an "agricultural frontier" still exists. Most of the frontier is in the tropical belt and the lands involved are state property.

There is a tendency to think of these new lands as the main solution for the region's land problems. Frequently it is asked: As the governments are the biggest landowners, why all the fuss about privately owned lands? True, these reserves offer opportunities to relieve the pressure in many areas, especially in the Andean highlands, where the population density is most acute. However, the public land reserves offer neither a quick enough nor a full enough solution to the present tenure problems. Experience of all countries that have settlement programs has shown that it is difficult to move large numbers of people into new areas, and that such an operation is extremely costly. Agricultural economists have repeatedly pointed out that in terms of potential production increases, the already established areas offer a much greater, more immediate and less expensive possibility. Social overhead facilities are already available in these areas which are close to the population and market centers.

This does not mean that land settlement in new zones cannot be an important factor in the agricultural development of Latin America. As a matter of fact, these new areas offer great opportunities, not only for new production, but also for the establishment of a healthier type of tenure, less encumbered by the traditional forms. Yet the colonization of far-off lands is too often used as a diversionary tactic by those who are opposed to land reforms. Settlement on public land is, of course, politically inoffensive. But even if the present rate of colonization were to be doubled or tripled, it is not likely to take the steam off the unrest and agitation in crowded areas. The bulk of the tenure problems must be resolved and the needed additional production opportunities can be found in the already settled areas.

With respect to land reform proper, the goals of tenure policy and the new institutions which would promote the frequently announced aim of economic development are only dimly visualized. The emphasis is on tearing down the old structure (principally the *latifundio* complex). Frequently there is no exploration of alternative models, beyond a vague concern with "family farming," an essentially north European and North American concept. It is doubtful, however, if the North American model in its fully commercial form is realistic for Latin America in more than a portion of the area. The medium-sized market-oriented farms in Latin American countries almost never operate with family labor alone. Even small units frequently have a *patrón* who manages and some *colonos* or *peones* who do the work.

There is little exploration of possible cooperative or communal types of tenure (the *ejido* was a very special Mexican solution). While the preoccupation with breaking up the existing system (and with it the bonds of a paternalistic and rigid class structure) may be far from wrong, there is real danger of aggravating the *minifundio* problem in the process.

Perhaps the Puerto Rican experience with what is known as the proportional-profits farms may be relevant. This arrangement is carried out under the island's Land Law of 1941. Sugar cane areas expropriated in excess of the constitutional limitation of 500 acres (applying to corporations) are operated by the Puerto Rico Land Authority, a public corporation, and farmed by unionized workers. These workers receive, in addition to their wages, part of the profits, distributed in proportion to the work done during the year. This arrangement seems to have maintained productive efficiency and is one way to distribute rights in land without excessive subdivision of the land itself. There are many possible variants of such an arrangement. The search for viable alternative tenure systems that strike an appropriate balance between social equity and productive efficiency is perhaps the most important and urgent task of land reform experts.

The preoccupation with "legalism" and with legislative details is striking. Land reform laws are invariably long, complicated and detailed. This makes their implementation very difficult. Only a fraction of the laws have actually been carried out (Bolivia is a prime example). In addition, the many detailed provisions are not only hard to implement, but are equally hard to change if they prove unworkable. The tendency to complicated laws resulted frequently in a veritable jungle of previous legislation which must be cleared away. Most of the legislative detail has of course very little meaning when it comes down to the peasants. In Bolivia, for instance, few of the illiterate Indians understand the land reform law, even though it has been translated into their native languages.

A key issue, and perhaps the most controversial one, is the expropriation procedure. With the exception of oil-rich Venezuela, no major land reform provides for acquisition of land at going market values. The exact conditions of compensation are dictated by the current conception of social justice and the relative power position of the various groups involved. Where inflation has accompanied reforms, the real value of compensation has been greatly reduced. The reforms could be placed on a self-financing basis if the landlords accepted compensation of a magnitude which was within the repayment capacity of the average beneficiary, but none of the land reforms thus far carried out has been self-financing in this sense. The basic dilemma of expropriation is how to minimize the injustices inherent in a land distribution program, which by definition goes against present market forces and pretends to change the prevailing distribution of wealth. Given overwhelming political power, a government such as Cuba seems to have no difficulty in nationalizing property. But where power is more delicately balanced, the problem of how much to pay for land and on what terms becomes more crucial.

One word about implementation. With land traditionally the basis of power, political and economic, there is an almost irresistible tendency to let personal favoritism, political influence and outright bribery intrude upon the land-granting process. The land settlement programs of most countries, on however modest a scale, have been traditionally important means for the rewarding of political favors by the ruling party. Thus land frequently does not get to the people who need it most and who are legally entitled to it. This is a further reason to justify a more drastic approach in which the peasants themselves can take an active role. Unfortunately, the framers of even revolutionary land programs seldom appreciate the necessity to make the cultivators participate actively in the land reform process. There is a tendency to manage the whole program from the top. This not only dissipates the potential contribution of the peasants to community development and self-help projects but causes great delays and frequent hardships in the distribution process itself.

It is the conclusion of this paper that, as a consequence of economic and social pressures, the central focus of land reforms in Latin America has been and will continue to be a substantial redistribution of rights in land in favor of the masses of cultivating farmers, and a corresponding shift in power and income-producing capacity. Developmental measures, such as credit, education and market assistance, must accompany tenure reforms *but are not substitutes for them.* The bulk of the reforms will take place in the already cultivated areas and will involve thorny problems of expropriation. Land settlement programs on public land and such indirect measures as land taxation can be an important complement to land tenure reforms but cannot replace them.

What are the chances for "peaceful, democratically planned reforms"? The available evidence is not encouraging. In fact, on the basis of past experience alone, an outlook of pessimism is warranted. With the possible exception of Venezuela, policy tends to polarize on one side in a "do nothing" attitude and on the other in a radical, revolutionary stance. The former group may tinker with some land settlement or tax reforms, and is likely to appoint commissions to "study the problem." It may even pass some laws—which, however, are likely to remain on the books.

With this group, in general, the hope is that the problems will go away. Where, on the other hand, land reforms have been imbedded in violent revolutions, there is either a nearly complete neglect of the technical and developmental aspects (as in Bolivia) or a tendency toward political excesses (as in Cuba) which not only involve a very high social cost but may eventually cancel out the possible benefits and may even (as in Guatemala) lead to a reversal of the whole process.

Yet the picture is not without hope. An important outside factor is the future attitude and aid policy of the United States. The Act of Bogotá represents a significant new line of thinking in this respect. For the first time, an important policy document speaks of the need for "land tenure legislation and facilities with a view to ensuring a wider and more equitable distribution of the ownership of the land." It is possible that the resources to be devoted to land reform under the new Special Fund for Social Development and other technical assistance will provide exceptional opportunities to support new and effective programs.

Moreover, the spectacle of Cuba dispossessing not only the wealthy upper classes but also the middle income groups has profoundly affected the attitude of many of the ruling elements in the rest of Latin America. Meanwhile the *campesinos* have in a number of places made their voice heard, either through the ballot box (as in Chile in the last election) or, more commonly, through agitation, occupancy of *haciendas* and general rural unrest (Colombia, Peru).

This conjunction of events may eventually lead to meaningful land reform over wide areas of Latin America.

*Nationalism in Latin America** | K. H. SILVERT

Strong nations and social progress are synonymous terms for modernist Latin Americans. Both youth's rebelliousness and maturity's revolutions carry the banners of national integrity, economic development, and social

* K. H. Silvert, "Nationalism in Latin America," *Annals of the American Academy of Political and Social Sciences,* Vol. 334 (March 1961), pp. 1–9. (Footnotes in the original version have been omitted.)

justice. The entire revolutionary package also includes such other standard components as the growth of industrial cities, the proliferation of science and secularism, and a drastic broadening of the base of political participation. In their very nature, contemporary revolutionary movements in Latin America are not only nationalistic, but also populist in emotional overtone and in the ideological planning of the functions of the state.

This "massification" of nationalism in Latin America, as well as in many other underdeveloped lands, forces us to an amendment of classical thinking about the manner in which nationalism, middle classes, capitalism, and democracy may link themselves. Because nationalism bears an inevitable relationship to the development of a complex class structure—including middle groups, of course—many Latin-American revolutions of the past have been easily labelled as merely transplanted repetitions of that most classical bourgeois uprising of them all, the French Revolution. New factors, however, are now operating to make of Latin America's present wrenchings an epic of special and particularly absorbing interest. Ideologies of violence, mass communications, and a highly complex and productive technology are combining to speed the rhythm of change and to stamp a new nature into the process of social development. True it is that certain necessary characteristics define modernization anywhere and at any time. Just as in the France of 1789 to 1848, development still involves at least a certain degree of impersonal loyalty to fellow citizens, a necessary minimum of empiricism and secularism, an extended array of occupations and, thus, a complicated class structure, and an extension of the range of political participation. But wherever fundamental change has firmly begun in Latin America, special ideological as well as merely administrative solutions are needed to govern the rapidity of the direct jump into mass organization forced by the new techniques and communications and translated into a political imperative by the revolution of expectations.

THE MATTER OF DEFINITION

The study of nationalism is a particularly useful strategy not only for lacing the past to the present, but also for comparing certain families of current happenings. The concept explains at least one way of using the past to justify what we do today; it defines the new powers of old political units in such areas as Latin America; and it assists the social scientist toward prediction, because its presence implies certain necessary correlatives among the persons and institutions involved in what we have been loosely calling modernism and development. A greater definitional precision than has been customary is required for these purposes best to be served. But precisely because nationalism is one of the fundamental social values of the Western, developed world, its manifestations in such societies impregnate all levels of behavior and evoke many partial definitions as a substitute for the complex and pervasive whole.

Although definition is not the purpose of this article, we cannot proceed without converting nationalism from amorphous word to objective term. This duty is not so easily discharged.

> Nationalism is so much with us, plays so large a role in shaping the setting of our daily lives, that it is often taken as a simple matter about which we know more or less as much as we need to know. In fact we do know a great deal about it, but what we do not know or have taken for granted without adequate evidence adds up to an impressive body of ignorance and uncertainty which is all the more dismaying because of the frequent failure to face up to the limitations of our knowledge. It is a far more complex and elusive matter than it is usually given credit for being. . . .
> . . . there is no real agreement as to what a nation is. No one has succeeded in devising a definition which is watertight in the sense that without opening up a number of leaky "ifs" and "buts," it enumerates the constituent elements of the nations we know in such fashion as to distinguish them satisfactorily from other types of communities in which men have intensely lived their lives through the ages. . . .[1]

From the copious writings on nationalism, despite their seeming confusions and contradictions, a coherent series of statements can be abstracted to serve at least the purpose of establishing grand categories and dimensions. The following paragraphs offer a proposed set of subdivisions of the many senses in which the word nationalism is used, with suggestions for their significance within the Latin-American context.

Nationalism as patriotism

[Nationalism as partriotism refers to the love of country and national community, on the one hand, and, on the other hand, to the collection of symbols expressing this love] Glorification of the race, military pomp and ceremony on the occasion of national holidays, martial anthems, and homage to the symbolic baggage of the nation are celebrated on many occasions in Latin America. These evocations of a national spirit were the custom of small upper groups imitating European practice

[1] Rupert Emerson, *From Empire to Nation: The Rise to Self-Assertion of Asian and African Peoples* (Cambridge, Mass.: Harvard University Press, 1960), pp. 89–90.

long before Latin-American governments could, in fact, even dream of claiming to represent nationally conscious peoples. [The transfer of the feelings of local and neighborhood, *barrio,* identification still remains totally unaccomplished in many rural and depressed urban areas.] There is even an objective shortage of national symbols in most countries, despite the solemn ceremonials, not only because the process of social integration has been completed nowhere, but also because of a relative shortage of war heroes, great exploits, and glittering conquests, the raw material of national mythology. The best known of all attempts to evoke a glorious past to serve as anchor for a justification of the future are the various *indigenista movements*—and especially those of Mexico and Peru—which seek to find in the romance of past Indian greatness hope for a national flowering.

Indirect demonstration of the incompleteness of nationalist movements in Latin America may be found in the large numbers of historians to be found everywhere busily searching for cultural roots, as contrasted with the relatively tiny number of studies seeking justification out of contemporary happenings. This problem of the search for symbols is common in underdeveloped areas, as the following statement by an African demonstrates by implication:

> For young and emergent nations there is no study as important as that of history; the reasons are clear enough. Our past is very much a part of our present and as we comprehend that past so will the probems of the present be illuminated. Most great and far-reaching movements have begun with a romantic appeal to the past. History is full of examples of nations and communities, who in the hour of their resurrection looked back to their ancestors, their culture, for guidance and inspiration.[2]

There can be no doubt that not resurrection but, rather, the creation of myth is the way of the historian in the new nationalism. But the need to think in these terms appears universal, as the German Romanticists demonstrated to a shuddersome extreme.

Nationalism as social value

[Nationalism as a social value refers to the norm defining the loyalty due to fellow citizens and to the secular state as the ultimate arbiter of all conflicts of public interest.] This aspect of nationalism is the crucial one, for [a broad loyalty to fellow citizens and a fitting set of functional institutions is the critical social factor permitting the organization of the high degree of specialization—and, hence, interdependence—to-

seems to be accept of St. authority - in Simon's sense

[2] K. Onwuka Diké, "African History and Self-Government: 3," *West Africa* (March 21, 1953), No. 1882, p. 251.

gether with industrial urbanization which we call economic development.]
This feeling is at the core of such a definition as the following:

> Nationalism is a state of mind, in which the supreme loyalty of the
> individual is felt to be due the nation-state. . . . Formerly, man's loyalty
> was due not to the nation-state, but to differing other forms of social
> authority, political organization and ideological cohesion such as the tribe
> or clan, the city-state or the feudal lord, the dynastic state, the church
> or religious group. . . .[3]

Social psychologists and sociologists have frequently used such terms
as identification, national consciousness, consensus, and even legitimacy
which can be somewhat equated with the value referred to here. The
essential difference in the construction of the concept, however, is that
[the idea of nationalism is here defined as a social psychological concept
with its particular institutional referent, the state,] rather than as an
attitude in itself without regard to the power factors which support
it and through which it expresses itself. Consider the following statement
from a recent volume concerning the Middle East, in which the term
"empathy" is used to indicate essentially the same loyalty toward fellows
which we hypothesize as being a part of the very definition of a nationally integrated society:

> . . . empathy [is] . . . the inner mechanism which enables newly mobile
> persons to *operate efficiently* in a changing world. Empathy, to simplify
> the matter, is the capacity to see oneself in the other fellow's situation.
> This is the indispensable skill for people moving out of traditional
> settings. . . .
> . . . high empathic capacity is the predominant personal style only in
> modern society which is distinctively industrial, urban, literate, and
> *participant.* . . .[4]

Empathy, then, as it is structured in patterns of loyalty toward fellow
citizens, legitimated in terms of an apposite set of symbols, and enforced
and mediated by the state, is the essential measure of whether any
particular Latin-American country is a nation-state in more than appear-
ances. Although no Latin-American society can be counted as mature
in this sense, Uruguay, Argentina, Costa Rica, and Chile are probably
farthest along the road to national integration. In Costa Rica, the phenomenon of a landed peasantry, and, in the other countries, the striking
urbanization, relatively advanced degree of industrialization, and
absence of ethnic disparities, all contribute to an ease as well as a necessity of national co-operation. In Mexico, Colombia, Brazil, Venezuela,
and Cuba, ruling groups and significantly large portions of a relatively

---

[3] Hans Kohn, *Nationalism: Its Meaning and History* (Princeton, N.J.: Van Nostrand,
1955), p. 9.
[4] Daniel Lerner, *The Passing of Traditional Society* (Glencoe, Ill.: The Free
Press, 1958), pp. 49–50.

well-developed middle group are in agreement about the desirability of effective nationhood, but there is still too much ethnic disparity, too great a divorce between city and country, to harsh divisions among social classes, and in Colombia and Cuba, too much political turmoil to permit this consensus to universalize itself. In such lands as Peru, Bolivia, Guatemala, Ecuador, El Salvador, and Panama, the small national groups are moving with one or another degree of speed and one or another ideological commitment toward their version of nationalism, but the response is sluggish in a social body not yet prepared for a complex level of national identification. Slow rates of movement among all groups characterize Honduras, Paraguay, Nicaragua, the Dominican Republic, and Haiti.

The recent political experiences of Cuba and Bolivia should warn us that slipping from one to another category is not such a difficult procedure when a strong motor force is provided by the changing ideological commitments of elite groups. The social ratification of and later participation in these commitments, dependent as these actions are upon really fundamental change in the structure of society, demand outside help, patience, and knowledge if the process is to be accomplished with a minimum of pain and a maximum of simple human decency. In the long run, these changes will come anyway, of course.

Nationalism as ideology

[Nationalism as ideology involves those explicit bodies of thought employing the symbols of nationality in order to promote actions intended at least partially to glorify the nation as a good in itself.] The ideologies of nationalism are the most discussed of all the aspects of the subject, not only because of their visibility, but also because they touch on the delicate subjects of expropriation, racism, xenophobia, anti-imperialism, and political extremism. The possible range of ideologies in any given situation depends upon such other factors as the stage of development of the society concerned, the relationships among social classes, the condition of the international marketplace of ideologies, and the availability of given types of political leaders and party and interest group structures. The ideologies of nationalism, varying widely in their content as a function of other conditions, may take some of the forms discussed below.

In the early stages of national development, when a small socioeconomic and intellectual elite usually holds power, ideology may be expected to be aristocratic in tone and hortatory, rather simplistically imitative of other examples and but dutifully exclusivistic. The cases of Honduras, Nicaragua, El Salvador, Paraguay, and Ecuador come immediately to mind. And despite *aprismo* in Peru and the Arévalo-Arbenz leftist period in Guatemala, these two countries have probably not emerged from this family of ideological occurrences.

[When the nation is in swift process of change as the result of the full commitment of the leadership in combination with rapidly growing middle groups, with mobility pressures high and public problems gross and uncomplicated, nationalistic ideologies tend to be strongly exclusivistic, economically protectionist, romantic, and as universal in appeal as possible.] Left and left-center politics are certain to exist; conservative politics are, of course, impossible, Bolivia, Venezuela, and Cuba clearly fit this category, as probably does Brazil.

[Once a fairly high, fruitful, and unthreatened level of national integration has been achieved, ideological appeals can become more rational and flexible.] The necessity for continued interdependence serves to promote continued communications among the now more complex social divisions. Chile, Argentina, Uruguay, Colombia, Mexico, and Costa Rica are varying distances from this level; the process has not as yet reached a stable culmination anywhere.

A state of arrested national integration at any one of the three stages given above can lead to ideological excess and politics of violence. Such extremist ideologies as the *justicialismo* of Perón may arise in answer to a situation of twisted growth in which important parts of the functionally national body social are deprived of institutional access to the seats of power and prestige. Another type of response may well be one of ideological emptiness, highly characteristic of Colombia, which vented its impotence in a tragic letting of blood from 1948 to 1958; Chile, which has been in economic depression for the last six years; and Guatemala, which has not yet been able to find a new politics of development after the revolution of 1954.

The development of nationalism within a context of growing democracy would seem to be favored by a steady movement as unhindered by uncontrollable inhibitions as possible. And yet there appears a strong likelihood in Latin America that there are inherent cultural brakes to an even social development.

OTHER DEVELOPMENT

Available statistics exist to demonstrate clearly that not all of Latin America is by any means an undifferentiated desert of the underdeveloped. In addition, we have readily at hand completely conventional theory to point out to us what "should" be the relationship between

socioeconomic development and nationalism. A standard line of reasoning runs as follows: in developing countries, new occupational groups
arise to operate the new machinery; a change in occupational structure
leading to higher productivity must be supported by extended educational systems and a greater penetration of the communications apparatus; new measures of prestige and political power thus develop which,
together with the economic shifts, produce a changed class structure;
this new social class system containing "middle groups" demands values
of social cohesion different from, let us say, feudal norms, so that continuity and predictability may be built into the more complex and interrelated society. In its political expression, this new value is nationalism,
as we have said. In order, then, to be able crudely to infer what likely
degree of nationalism we may find in the Latin-American republics,
we might employ statistics concerning occupational stratification, industrialization urbanization, the production of consumers' goods, and so
on.

We should not be deceived by the appearance of rigor which the
use of statistics in this case might seem to afford. A recent attempt
to relate economic indices to democracy in Latin America demonstrates
clearly how difficult it is to go beyond a simple two-way split of the
countries by the use of such data. Employing historical analysis, this
study first divides all the Latin-American countries into two camps:
one, democracies and unstable dictatorships and, two, stable dictatorships. In the former are Argentina, Brazil, Chile, Colombia, Costa Rica,
Mexico, and Uruguay, and in the latter are all the rest. A consistent
tendency naturally appears for the democracies and unstable dictatorships to enjoy higher per capita incomes, higher educational levels, and
the like than the others. Even though the averages hold up well enough
to demonstrate the undeniable trend, the range of the figures allows
for such an overlap as to create many marginal cases not at all adequately handled by this method of demonstration. For example, the
spread of annual per capita income for the more democratic is from
112 to 346 dollars, while the less democratic roam from 40 to 331 dollars.
The literacy range for the former is from 48 per cent to 87 per cent
and for the latter from 11 per cent to 76 per cent. Not only do all
the figures demonstrate this great overlap, but even in one most significant case, enrollment in primary schools, the less democratic come off
seemingly more advantageously than their more libertarian brethren.

Figures concerning occupations, which should be very indicative for
our purposes, leave us with the same problems of grossness. Let us
assume that all persons except those at the lower levels in primary occupations form a potential universe of modern persons because of their

⎮incomes and the fact that they are engaged in urban occupations. This assumption is crude and open to much objection, especially at the lower levels of urban service occupations, but it must be remembered that we are speaking of an immediately potential universe only. By the use of this device, the Latin-American nations rank themselves as follows:

TABLE 1. PERSONS ENGAGED IN
SECONDARY AND TERTIARY
OCCUPATIONS PLUS HIGH
OCCUPATIONAL CATEGORIES
IN PRIMARY OCCUPATIONS
IN LATIN AMERICA—1950

RANKING	COUNTRY	PERCENTAGE
1	Argentina	80.9
2	Chile	71.1
3	Venezuela	62.6
4	Cuba	(59.4)
5	Costa Rica	53.6
6	Colombia	53.4
7	Ecuador	48.9
8	Paraguay	47.1
9	Panama	46.5
10	Brazil	39.5
11	Mexico	39.3
12	Guatemala	39.1
13	El Salvador	37.4
14	Nicaragua	(31.6)
15	Bolivia	27.4
16	Honduras	16.9
17	Haiti	15.4

The most obvious difficulty with this chart as an indicator of development is the relatively low positions of Brazil and Mexico. The figures are averages, of course, which means that the large peasant populations of those two countries depress their rankings. If the statistics treated of only the non-Indian population in Mexico and of the southeastern part of Brazil, then the developed parts of both countries would take the high positions which they do, in reality, occupy. If we make these corrections and aid our interpretation with other figures, then the dividing line appears to fall between Colombia and Ecuador, and our common sense remains unviolated. What we learn with some objectivity is that the countries of the top half of the list—Argentina, Chile, Venezuela, Cuba, Costa Rica, Colombia, Mexico, and Brazil, but not in that order—

have a greater capacity and social need for national coordination than the others. What we do not explain is why Bolivia has committed itself to a nationalist-populist solution while Paraguay has not, or why Mexico has had a gaudily revolutionary past while Brazil has been content so far with softer solutions.

Such statistics are still so rudimentary for our purposes as to gain significance only through such other research as historical analysis, case studies of power distribution, attitude testing, and careful assessment of ideological currents. Let us briefly look elsewhere for an at least interim understanding.

SPECIAL NATURE

No other economically retarded part of the world has for so long been so intimately tied to Europe by language, religion, custom, and ethos. That the silver cord is connected with Iberia rather than with Scandinavia or the United Kingdom is, of course, a fundamental working concept of all persons connected with Latin-American affairs. We must ineluctably consider this relationship once again in the case of Latin America's national revolutions, for by such measures as technological advance, access to world intellectual currents, and intensity of commercial traffic with the United States and Western Europe, certain portions of Latin America might have been reasonably expected by now to have arrived at a reasonably stable national existence. Instead, we find Argentina still pimpled by barracks revolts and other stigmata of classbound politics, Chile unable to digest her post-war industrialization, Uruguay wandering in an ideological desert, and even Mexico in an unexpected stasis with respect to full integration of lower class and Indian groups. As for such truly economically retarded countries as Paraguay, Honduras, and Nicaragua, all rates of movement are remarkably slow for this part of the century. The fitful nature of change, the long periods of quiescence, the recurrent fascination with solutions of force, even in the most advanced countries, need more explanation than we can give them here.

A kind of social psychoanalysis is an intuitive and often employed stratagem of explanation. We are told that Latin Americans are individualists, romanticists, that they bear the mark of a feminine ethos, that they have never recuperated from the imprint left by the *hidalgo*, that the *conquistadors* who sired the generations are unwilling to dirty their hands. However true these explanations may be, the easily ascertainable fact of the matter is that everywhere the development of impersonalism, science, empiricism, and pragmatism has lagged. But, at the same time, great cities have arisen with astounding speed; impressive factories sell their products through television; and admirable personal sacrifices have been made in the name of man's dignity and freedom. In a modern world, these currents are contradictory, for science and technology must be mutually supportive; and, in a democratic world, these currents are contradictory, for individualism and nationalism must also be mutually supportive if the strength of national organization is not to flow to totalitarian solutions. The firm decision to build these relationships has not yet been generally made in Latin America. The great cities, thirsty hopes for higher standards of living, and brave aspirations for political freedom cannot be supported in the presence of landless peasants, Byzantine aristocrats, feckless intellectuals, and ravenous merchants.

The peculiarity of nationalism in Latin America is that nowhere, even in the most advanced countries, has there been an irrevocable and hard decision to renounce the advantages of traditionalism and an oversimplified universalism—a renunciation which is in itself the price of social development. The Latin American is taught to jump from loyalty to family and small group to transcendental identifications. He does not recognize the functionalism of an intermediate level of loyalty to impersonal community, and so he makes difficult the establishment of the only processes which can supply the material things for which he is clamoring so loudly. Like it or not, there is a metaphysical price to be paid for modernism.

Intensive economic assistance, technical advice, and educational interchange can help to reduce the difficulty of the adjustment to a sane national integration, but they are no guarantee of libertarian results. Style, ideology, and ethos can convert the new economic and social power thus created into monopolistic, repressive, and fraudulently humanistic molds. If one's experience in Latin America is based on Mexico, he will probably be optimistic; if on Argentina, then he may well be pessimistic. In any case, however, the recognition must be clear that the growing national power of the Latin-American states is not yet securely devoted to democratic principles and that at least one major reason for this irresolution is that the nation-state has not yet been accepted merely as a social device or artifact, but is still seen either as a vicious and un-Christian evocation of original sin or as a pristine god to be worshipped for itself alone.

The New Latin American Nationalism*

JOHN J. JOHNSON

The most important single phenomenon in Latin America today is the rapid growth of nationalism. The nationalist ferment there, as in other developing areas, reflects the passionate efforts of millions of people to create something for themselves and to attain greater status in the world. Neither all the people nor all the twenty republics in Latin America are approaching those goals at the same pace, but nearly everywhere—from huge Brazil to tiny Panama—the movement is underway, and the tempo of the advance is quickening.

In some ways it is surprising that this nationalist fervor should have developed so late, for as long ago as the period between 1810 and 1825, when independence was achieved in Latin America except for Cuba and Panama, there was a flood of writing in praise of nationhood. Yet for a century after that, antinationalist sentiments ordinarily inhibited those attitudes that might have propelled nationalism beyond the bounds generally associated with mere patriotism. Strong class distinctions were partial barriers to national unity, and in several countries, the political and intellectual elites of European background looked down upon their fellow nationals of Amerindian and African origin. Furthermore most Latin Americans, regardless of class or ethnic origins, were essentially parochial in their loyalties. There were several reasons for this. For one thing, the resources of the central governments were so meager that they had little to offer in return for the allegiance of rural people. Throughout the nineteenth century, no national administration in Latin America was able to secure the firm loyalty of the municipalities and states, as the United States government was able to do successfully; they could not afford to give subsidies to railroads, pensions to veterans, or land to small farmers and to colleges. As a consequence [the first century of political independence in Latin America was full of struggles that sacrificed national unity to provincial loyalty.] In Ecuador the contest between Guayaquil and Quito still goes on, as it has for a century and a half.

Unlike certain of the countries of Western Europe the Latin American

* John J. Johnson, "The New Latin American Nationalism," *The Yale Review,* copyright Yale University, Vol. 104: No. 2 (Winter 1965), pp. 187–204.

republics did not have a proud military history around which to rally their people. Only Chile won notable military victories over its neighbors following independence, and none of them, except perhaps Mexico, the Dominican Republic, and Ecuador, had "hereditary enemies" across their borders.

It was the desire for political freedom rather than the urge to protect or preserve racial or cultural peculiarities that produced the ferment which brought freedom to the republics. And after independence was achieved, racial enmities were kept at such a low level that they could not be used to exploit prejudice or to gain personal or group advantage, as they so often could be in Europe. In addition, the Catholic Church was preeminent in education, and its teaching favored cosmopolitan rather than nationalistic interests. Intellectuals lived with their feet in America but with their eyes turned toward Europe, and particularly toward France. Even Alfonso Reyes, who avoided the European influence more successfully than many, observed that although Mexican nationality was rooted in the Mexican soil, it was "naturally" internationalist. The Mexican Independence centennial in 1910 was little more than a gaudy tribute to the non-Mexican character of the life of the Mexican elite.

The twentieth century has provided much better conditions for the growth of Latin American nationalism, and, in spite of individual differences among the nations, the pattern of development has been remarkably similar throughout the area. Everywhere it has passed through two principal stages, which might be called aristocratic and popular nationalism.

Aristocratic nationalism, which was uncoordinated and provided elaborate safeguards for individualism, was shortlived. It flourished immediately after the First World War but was already becoming anachronistic by 1930, when the world-wide depression struck. It was fashioned by intellectuals who were dismayed to learn that the war had brought about the decline of France as a military power and made the United States, instead of Great Britain, the undisputed financial center of the world and the principal trader with Latin America. Historically France had been the cultural homeland of the intellectuals; now, along with their countries, they were being drawn irresistibly into the orbit of the United States, and this was something that many of them distrusted, resented, and even despised. In desperation they decided that the best defense was to attack, and so they defended their own cultures by verbally attacking their acknowledged enemy, the United States.

Ammunition was close at hand. As early as 1900, José Rodó, the Uruguayan man of letters, had set the tone for antipathy toward the United

States in his essay *Ariel*, in which he warned the youth of Latin America against being seduced by the materialism of the United States, whose "prosperity is as immense as its incapacity to satisfy even a mediocre view of human destiny." Shortly thereafter the Venezuelan Rufino Blanco Fombona, in his attacks upon "the Caliban of the north," went far beyond the frontier opened by Rodó. In 1922, as apprehension over cultural penetration by the United States was mounting, Gabriela Mistral, the future Nobel prize-winning poetess from Chile, warned her readers that all of Latin America was vulnerable to the "spike of steel and gold" wielded by the United States. Two years later the widely respected Argentine thinker and socialist politician, Alfredo Palacios, reminded his contemporaries that "the United States, like Faust, had sold its soul in exchange for riches and power." The Mexican philosopher José Vasconcelos and the Argentine sociologist José Ingenieros repeatedly cautioned their countrymen against being attracted by the superficial glitter of "Yankee" culture, and they were joined by a host of lesser figures who built their reputations on an ability to denigrate the United States and its way of life.

Other intellectuals were concerned less with cultural and more with political domination. They spoke of the "imperialistic designs" of the United States on Latin America, and their catalog of complaints was long, beginning with United States aggression against Mexico in 1846 and ending with United States domination of the Pan-American Union. The Peruvian Francisco García Calderón sarcastically described Latin America's role in the Pan-American Union as that "of a Grand Eunuch, distinguished, but of scant influence." In between were the "attack on Spain" in 1898, "the rape of Panama," Theodore Roosevelt's "big stick policy," Wilson's "meddling in Mexico," gunboat diplomacy, and finally "economic penetration as a prelude to political control." To this enumeration of charges against the United States as a nation were added resentment against United States businessmen and diplomats who refused to accept Latin Americans as equals. In part, it was to counter the real and imagined pressures from the United States that the Latin American republics initially gave the League of Nations warm support. But by 1930 Latin Americans had decided that the League was of little use to them, and nationalism won an important victory at the expense of internationalism.

The intelligentsia's tactics were understandable, and perhaps even appropriate for a while, but they could not succeed in the long run. The men of letters had set themselves the impossible task of justifying a culture that could not be justified on at least three fundamental counts. In the first place, that culture was not original. Many of its features

were little more than cheap borrowings from the cultures that had
evolved in Western Europe and the United States under the impact
of liberalism and its concomitant individualism, and often they had little
relevance to the realities of Latin American life. In the second place,
the culture the intellectuals sought to justify they shared with almost
no others except the political and landholding elites, and the landholders'
strong orientation toward overseas trade tended to make them interna-
tionalists rather than nationalists. This was clearly the situation in Brazil,
where throughout the 1920's the government was guided by spokesmen
for the export-minded coffee barons. (But Brazil was in some respects
something of an exception. As early as the first decade of the century,
under its able foreign minister Rio Branco, Brazil began a reorientation
of its foreign policy away from Europe and toward the United States,
which already had become the most important buyer of Brazilian exports.) Finally the culture that the Latin American intellectuals were
defending did not provide for a national fabric into which the life of
the masses could be woven; it would have left a vast majority of the
people to vegetate more or less permanently on the outskirts of
civilization.

In such circumstances, intellectual rebellions against the United States
or attempts to create a national ethos by using local history, folklore,
and music could not possibly arouse widespread nationalist sentiment.
Intellectuals could protest, but they could not reform things. Most of
them were incapable of giving the Indians a sense of personal identification with their countries because they knew nothing about the Indians.

But by 1930 nationalism in Latin America had begun to acquire the
populist quality which has since remained its trademark. In Mexico
this development was a by-product of the social revolution of 1910.
Elsewhere, it was a logical derivative of secularizing and modernizing
processes which dated from the late nineteenth century, and which by
the 1920's had already shifted the more advanced republics (Chile, Uruguay, Argentina, and to a lesser extent Cuba) well away from feudal
agrarianism toward urban industrial life.

One major consequence of this transformation was a political revolution that greatly strengthened the new urban middle sectors—entrepreneurs, managers, professional men, and bureaucrats—at the expense of
the traditional landholding elites. But since the land oligarchs could
at first depend on the influence of the Catholic Church and the military
establishments, the political spokesmen for the new urban middle groups
were driven to seek out electoral support among those who were emerging from the lower classes—laborers, dock workers, and miners who
were sufficiently literate to satisfy suffrage requirements. This reliance

on a small but potentially powerful industrial proletariat determined not only the middle sector's political tactics and the kinds of programs they sponsored but also the character of the nationalism they favored.

The new nationalism contrasted sharply with the aristocratic nationalism which it was replacing. Since the worker's entrance into the political arena had made him an *homo economicus,* ⌈popular nationalism played⌉ upon social and economic urges rather than upon cultural ambitions⌋. It stressed the needs and aspirations of society, and in so doing it struck a hard blow against the liberal tradition and the "inactive" state inherited from the nineteenth century and still defended after the First World War by the intellectuals. Implicit in this stand was a conviction that the central government should possess not only the administrative, technical, and financial capabilities to regulate national development but also the power to impose its will on all persons and corporations within the nation, including foreigners and foreign companies. And unlike the old nationalism, which lacked political appeal, the new nationalism was quickly enriched with political slogans and then converted into an ideology which was institutionalized in the state.

By enhancing the status of the worker, who was ordinarily from the *gente de color* (people of color), the proponents of popular nationalism placed themselves under two major obligations: to establish that the laborer was worthy of his new role, and to demonstrate concern for his welfare. Mexico, where the first serious efforts of this sort were made in the 1920's, set the pattern. Scholars who could accept the new view, and, too often, propagandists posing as scholars, discovered in ancient art the Indian's hidden talents and potential. Others made a virtue of his simple peasant life and associated his destiny with that of the nation. Thus the artist Diego Rivera and the anthropologist Manuel Gamio, to mention only two of a host of "Indianists," sought to convert the still unassimilated tribesman into a "noble rebel," the symbol of true Mexicanism.

Since the population of Mexico and more than a dozen other nations was predominantly European-American or European-African, a natural extension of the new favorable judgment of the working man was to upgrade persons of mixed blood. The racist theories of LeBon and Gobineau and certain schools of positivism, especially those in Argentina and Peru, which had lingered on from the nineteenth century, were finally laid to rest. They were replaced by the theory that the crossing of native American blood with that from Europe produced a better human specimen than the offspring of either strain alone.

⌈The mestizo thus came to hold the key to spiritual and cultural attainment.⌋ In Mexico, José Vasconcelos prophesied that mestizo nations would fulfill the great dream of a human synthesis, a harmonious fusion of two opposite worlds. In Brazil, the sociologist Gilberto Freyre played upon the same theme but in a lower key. A new world, vibrant and changing, was to supersede the old one, which had lost its orientation and cultural dynamism in the time of Louis Napoleon. In Mexico, the historian Silvio Zavala declared that the cities of Latin America "'change their skins every ten years," and are thus representative of youth, life, and progress, while European cities bear witness only to old age and paralysis.

[Meanwhile there appeared an impressive body of "nationalist" legislation designed to keep the common man voting for the new urban middle-sector leadership.] Fledgling labor groups were brought under the "protection" of the state and incorporated into pro-administration, broad-front political movements. Central authorities, in theory at least, assumed responsibility for a wide range of health and education programs. Several republics (notably Uruguay, Chile, and Mexico) strengthened their laws requiring the central government to promote industry and commerce as a means of conserving foreign exchange, to protect citizens against breakdown in international trade resulting from depressions and wars, and to provide jobs for those entering the labor market for the first time.

[Legislation against foreigners proliferated.] The Brazilian constitution of 1934, for example, proposed to protect the worker by placing restrictive quotas on the admission of European and Asiatic immigrant groups who might supplant Brazilian nationals in their jobs. Elsewhere foreign operatives of banana and sugar plantations, mines, transportation companies, public utilities, and manufacturing and commercial enterprises were instructed to hire more nationals and to guarantee them equal pay for equal work. Colombia's so-called "ten-twenty-thirty law" of 1936 stipulated that in large enterprises, whether foreign or domestic, aliens could not constitute more than 10 per cent of the wage workers or 20 per cent of the salaried employees, and that no more than 30 per cent of total salaries could be paid to non-Colombians.

[With increasing determination, the republics asserted their sovereign right to control and exploit their own natural resources.] A country that does not develop its own resources loses them, declared José Vasconcelos. To increase the prestige of local institutions of higher learning, professional men who were nationals but had taken their training abroad were required upon their return to complete additional courses in their specialties before they could practice.

[But popular nationalism was more than an artifice for wooing the worker with promises of utopia, and more than an ideology useful for promoting the political influence of the new urban leadership. It offered something to all groups, and most of all it seemed to supply the only acceptable guidelines for future development. Consequently, as the 1930's wore on, public opinion was increasingly quick to overlook the drawbacks of nationalism and to give added weight to its positive values.

why?

Thus the impulses generated by nationalism, in one country after another, induced central governments to assume the responsibilities that could give them a truly national character. Important among these was providing firmer leadership in rural areas and provincial centers. This was a vital step, although not the final one, in overcoming the urban bias of Latin American culture, in shifting the locus of patriotism away from regional communities, and in making the inhabitants of various regions conscious of and dependent upon one another.

why "thus'?

If, as was true, nationalist demagogues played upon the economic hopes and fears (and even, sometimes, on the greed) of the urban laborer, their ideology often gave him his only feeling of belonging to a group; and group security in turn gave him some of the courage he needed to turn his back on traditional institutions and relationships before new fundamental steps and standards had been decided upon.

Before the Second World War, popular nationalism from time to time produced a hypersensitivity to any slight, real or imagined, to cultural or economic autonomy—as in Mexico in 1938, when foreign-owned petroleum properties were expropriated. But it also provided targets for the anxieties and frustrations generated by the difficulties through which the republics were passing.

By the end of the Second World War, Latin American nationalism had drawn heavily upon fascism and Naziism, particularly in Argentina under Juan Perón and in Brazil under Getulio Vargas. This can be taken to mean that nationalist ideology was not producing specifically Latin American solutions to the area's problems, and that is true and significant. But it is equally important that nationalism, whether under the influence of Naziism and fascism or not, was evoking emotions that gave the citizens of a number of countries a feeling that the need for change was urgent. And if those emotions, sometimes exaggerated and overdramatized, fired some men to pursue goals and ambitions that could not be realized, it drove others to constructive action.

Since the Second World War popular nationalism has taken on important new dimensions. Never as oriented toward the past as European nationalism has been, now it turns less and less to local history for its symbols. No longer worried, even remotely, about United States territorial designs upon the Hemisphere, nationalists in countries like Chile, Peru, and Ecuador have themselves become aggressive. They now press for national control over adjacent waters and submerged lands, often far beyond the limits recognized by international law. They insist that Latin America can never be completely sovereign as long as a European colony remains in the Hemisphere; they oppose colonialism in any form and in all quarters, and they make a point of demonstrating their own "non-imperialialism."

[The new nationalism less often seeks respectability in the world arena, and more often stresses domestic problems.] One consequence of this attitude is that most of the republics express an intense desire to participate in international decision-making but also insist that internal problems require all their resources and become reluctant to share the cost of implementing the decisions they help to reach. In the United Nations, the Latin American states constantly request more committee posts and greater representation in the General Assembly while continually calling for lowered UN assessments and regularly voting against increases.

Since 1945 new leaders have transformed Brazil, Argentina, and perhaps Panama into strong, self-willed republics. Theirs is essentially an economic nationalism. Whereas their predecessors stressed the conservation of unreplenishable resources, the production of consumer goods and semi-durables, and the defense of workers from foreign exploitation, they have pointed to the "collective humiliations" accompanying economic dependence, which they associate with production of raw materials. In this regard ex-President Juscelino Kubitschek of Brazil once said, "We want to be on the side of the West, but we do not want to be its proletariat." As a corollary the new economic nationalists demand the industrial capacity to produce capital goods; they have chosen to make the integrated iron and steel plant and the petrochemical factory the marks of their countries' developmental aspirations and the showcases of their national achievements. Belching smokestacks may lack economic justification, but one can hardly question their startling psychological impact. The Paraíba Valley in Brazil is now proudly called the "Valley of the Chimneys."

Economic nationalism fathered xenophobia, whose most legitimate heir to date has been neutralism. For Mexico, neutralism has already become an all-embracing passion, manifested on several occasions in its refusal to be coerced into radically altering its original stand on Castro's Cuba. (In Brazil during the administrations of Jânio Quadros and João Goulart, who was overthrown on April 1, 1964, the current of neutralism became stronger almost by the day.) The other republics, besides being encouraged by these "declarations of independence" by Mexico and Brazil, know that the United Nations—where each state has one vote, and all member states proclaim the right of self-determination—is on their side; and they, too, are on their way to making neutralism the cardinal principle of their foreign policies.

Neutralism, meanwhile, is many things to many people. Particularly in the smaller republics, it is the hostile reaction to all slights: "to being taken for granted," "to being run by other nations," "to looking to Washington for inspiration." For the more modern republics, neutralism may mean discarding United States influence, not out of hostility but from a genuine desire for freedom of action. It is also a way of satisfying a growing urge for esteem and prestige within the community of nations, of substantiating claims to an equal and independent place in the world. Neutralism in Latin America is also keeping up with the international Joneses, who are in this case the new nations of Africa and Asia that claim complete independence of action in their foreign relations.

For some, neutralism represents equality, and for others it reflects deep personal convictions that their countries suffer from being allied with either side in the present worldwide ideological struggle. Neutralism is a quest for a third position in the East-West conflict. Yet in international affairs Latin American neutralists have not joined the neutralist bloc, although any and all of them may vote with that bloc on some issues.

The Quadros administration in 1961 used the alleged advantages of a third position to justify reorienting Brazil's foreign policy in the direction of neutralism. To emphasize his point, Quadros argued that since the United States had abandoned its traditional position as a neutral or "honest broker" between quarreling factions in Europe and Asia to assume the leadership of an ideologically committed group of states, Brazil no longer had an uncommitted nation in which it could have confidence and to which it might look for guidance. In these circumstances Brazil, according to Quadros, was compelled to develop an independent foreign policy. Neutralism is also a useful vehicle for rationalizing closer relations with the Soviet and Communist Chinese blocs. The Communists of either bloc, dedicated as they have been to building up suspicions of and hostility toward the United States, obviously regard neutralism in Latin America as a victory in their campaign to control men's minds and loyalties.

Neutralism can, of course, provide techniques for needling the United States, or the USSR, or both. It can even be a means of engaging in international blackmail, as Egypt, India, Yugoslavia, and Indonesia have occasionally been accused of doing. It is undoubtedly true, as Albert Hirschman has said, that the realization that they can maneuver between the Eastern and Western blocs must be exhilarating to neutralists.

But to assume that blackmail is the essence of Latin American neutralism, or that it is only a political gimmick, is to miss a most important point. Neutralism, above all, is Latin America's way of saying that it is entering a new era in its basic relationships with the United States and the rest of the world. Neutralism represents at least as sharp a break with the past as the one that came after the First World War. At that time developments quite beyond their control required that the republics loosen their ties with Western Europe and align themselves so closely with the United States that in several cases they became little more than satellites of their more powerful neighbor. The present break, in contrast, is free and deliberate.

Many hypotheses have been offered to explain the changed direction of popular nationalism since the Second World War. The one most generally advanced in the United States is the growth of Communism in the area—a development that was given a great boost by the launching of the first Russian satellite in 1957, and which has been strengthened, in some circles, by the Kremlin's defense of the Castro regime in Cuba when it has been under extreme pressure from the United States.

[There is no denying that Latin American Communists have embraced nationalism, and with good reason. Drawing support from all sectors of society as it does, nationalism provides the Communists with a cloak of respectability; and in its anti-foreign manifestations nationalism is directed most often against the United States] Communist support of nationalism thus wins considerable sympathy from persons who have no commitment to Communist ideology. In defying the United States, the Communists win at least the covert, and sometimes the open, support of those nationalists, including some intellectuals, who sincerely believe that United States influence is the greatest menace from which the area suffers. The Communists also benefit from the fact that in Marxism they have a ready-made vocabulary which attracts men who would hurry their nations toward their theoretically inevitable fate. In a region not particularly noted for its promotional and managerial capabilities, the Communists often provide the expert organizational skills that are needed to bring together the special interests held by the nationalists.

But popular nationalism of a decidedly radical nature probably would have asserted itself without the stimuli of Communism and Castroism. In the first place,[the urban middle-sector leaders who originally raised nationalism to the level of a political ideology in the 1930's lost control of it almost as soon as they came to power] They discovered as office-holders that nationalism directed against the outside made good campaign material; but they also learned that given the prevailing attitudes

abroad and particularly in the United States, it was incompatible with
domestic policies that could be implemented only with financial and
technical assistance from the United States and Western Europe. In
power these leaders had to urge moderation, thereby exposing themselves to the same sort of charges that a decade earlier they had leveled
against their predecessors in office.

[So the urban middle-sector leaders were often burned by the very
fires they had lighted.] They made foreign policy a national issue that
could no longer be determined behind closed doors by professionals.
With foreign policy subject to popular debate and increasingly conditioned by popular attitudes, Latin America has become much like the
United States, where foreign policy may be determined by legislators
who are elected to office on the basis of narrow local issues and then
become experts on world affairs.

The middle-sector politicians had also rapidly broadened the electoral
base—Brazil's electorate, for example, increased 35 percent between
1958 and 1962—with the result that voters were swept into the political
arena faster than they could be absorbed by established political groups
and much faster than their minimal demands could be satisfied within
the existing social, economic, and political systems. [Many of the newly
enfranchised, as a result, succumbed to the blandishments of nationalists
promising simple solutions to complex problems.]

The emergence of a domestic industrial class had the indirect effect
of driving still other workers into the arms of those who were providing
the blueprints for radical nationalism. So long as a significant number
of industrial enterprises were controlled from abroad and foreigners
were the prime employers of skilled and semi-skilled labor, officeholders
could enthusiastically support the workers in their demands for improved
conditions on the grounds that they were serving as protagonists against
"foreign rapacity." But to the extent that nationalist economic policies
fulfilled expectations and domestic capitalists displaced foreign ones as
employers, politicians were obliged to make decisions concerning labor
problems in economic rather than political terms. The stronger the industrialists became, the more inclined were the workers, whose leaders
did very little to impress upon them their social responsibilities, to listen
to the "outs." The "outs," meanwhile, took advantage of labor discontent
to associate the "ins" with men who could often be accused of having
gained their fortunes by cooperating with foreigners.

The political leadership also lost ground to radical nationalist groups
in the universities. Historically, students in Latin America have always
chafed under the restraints of their elders, even when circumstances
have been relatively favorable. This has been true in part because they

have learned in the classroom about the problems in their societies, and about the distressing lack of sustained attention given to those problems by political leaders in power. Students have also been known for an exalted sense of patriotism that is easily translated into the conviction that their countries would be stronger except for constant "victimization" by foreign nations, especially the United States.

The world has most recently been made aware of the Latin American student mentality by the Panama riots of January 1964, but the potential for nationalism in the universities had been mounting for several years— Vice President Nixon's confrontation with the students of San Marcos University in Lima, Peru, and of Venezuela's Central University in Caracas revealed the possibilities. There were and are understandable reasons for this student attitude. Despite considerable economic expansion and the extension of welfare activities, private and public bureaucracies upon which students in the nonscientific fields have come to rely heavily for employment have absorbed a steadily decreasing share of those completing their courses in institutions of higher learning. Students of the humanities and law have been especially hard hit. They, like nearly all university students in Latin America, have a healthy regard for their own worth and a feeling that they are entitled to positions commensurate with their intellectual attainments. Dim prospects for the future, and a search for quick answers to what they see as both personal and social dilemmas, have turned many of them (although relatively few in terms of the total university population) toward noisy, aggressive nationalism.

Students have thus proved to be major allies of the ultranationalists. In each of the more advanced countries, the students are one of the few groups organized on a nationwide basis; Brazil's 80,000 to 100,000 university students, for example, are welded together in a single major national organization. As nationalist propagandists students have still another advantage: the high station accorded them in their culture permits them to engage in agitational politics with greater immunity from police intervention than any other group from which the extreme nationalists draw their mass support.

[Mass communications media are employed constantly by the Communists and ultranationalists to feed the rising spirit of nationalism and assure that nationalist issues are kept current. They use the press and television, but most of all radio:] Brazil has more than 700 radio stations and 7,000,000 receivers, many of which are public (in bars, plazas, etc.). In their scramble for an ever larger public, the mass communications media, representing all shades along the political spectrum, direct much of their attention to the expanding groups of urban workers. It is through the press and radio that the worker receives his introduction to the vocabulary of national politics. It is through the press and radio that he learns about domestic achievements and about groups accused of impeding national progress and impugning national sovereignty. Many workers take what they hear at face value and then, with the assistance of professional organizers, convert it into ammunition for the face-to-face nationalist debates that have kept most of the republics, and especially the more modern ones, in a state of almost continual turbulence.

There is no doubt that nationalism will continue to flourish in Latin America. As in the rest of the developing world, radical nationalism in Latin America is essentially an urban phenomenon, and the major cities of the Hemisphere are growing at an annual rate of 5 percent or more per year, compared to approximately 3 percent for the population as a whole. Again, the modern social revolution is everywhere a national adventure; but in Latin America, where it is still gaining momentum, it has been mainly the urban workers, the fastest growing socioeconomic group, who have given social upheavals their nationalist and adventurous flavor. [Furthermore nationalism tends to inhibit or delay the sort of open conflicts among interest groups that industrialization encourages; this means that it often will be kept alive by politicians who feel that they stand to lose from any airing of differences between traditionalists and modernists.]

There are several ways in which nationalism, even of a virulent sort, could prove to be an essentially positive force. First, the people of Latin America will continue to feel at times that their sovereignty is being threatened by other nationalisms, as well as by imperialistic capitalism. On such occasions nationalism can act as a countervailing influence and provide a sense of security. This is clearly the case in Argentina, where nationalism is at least in part a reaction to the growing strength of Brazil. Second, no Latin American republic—except Mexico, where after 1917 a social revolution gradually took on a mystique that has survived largely intact to the present—has ever developed a "true faith" which it has felt compelled to propagate at all costs. Nationalism, especially in the form of neutralism, might become the cement that will give cohesion to widely divergent social elements. And if this should happen, it might produce the almost messianic zeal needed to overcome the inertia and reaction that have so far hindered modernization and reform. Third, nationalism might mobilize the working classes for constructive action. As yet they have not permanently attached themselves to any leadership group or ideology and, for the moment at least, nationalism appears more capable than democracy (although the two are

by no means incompatible) of catching the imagination of the articulate
elements. When and where this is true, nationalism may, by guiding
the new elements into acceptable activity, provide the unity and the
time required to create roots for the new societies that are forming.
Furthermore, it could conceivably inspire the decision-making groups
to organize new institutions of sufficient size and viability to cope with
the sweeping social changes that will be necessary if the many are
to escape from their past. Traditional democracy has not produced such
institutions anywhere in Latin America, nor has the Alliance for Progress;
and the extreme Left in Latin America has not yet shown that it can
achieve what the Center-Left has failed to accomplish. But if nationalism
can somehow move Latin America ahead at a reasonable even if erratic
pace, then the inhabitants of the republics could be expected to gain
self-confidence, as the Mexicans have; and this self-confidence could conceivably be reflected favorably in their relations with non-Latin American peoples.

There are however many circumstances that could make nationalism
a negative force in Latin America. There is the ever-present danger
that nationalism will become little more than an unconscious substitute
for the charismatic leader, the man on horseback, who beguiled his
followers with promises of utopias and who, incidentally, could retain
his following for prolonged periods of time only by resort to force and
violence. In similar fashion, irresponsible men could use nationalism
to widen the gap between ideologies and realities. In Bolivia, for example, the ideology of labor leader Juan Lechín dictates that the tin
mines must continue to produce and that the miners' benefits must be
greatly increased. The reality is that the mines are almost exhausted
and that production will continue its headlong decline unless the
ideology bends enough to allow heavy foreign borrowing and prolonged
foreign technical control of the operation.

There is also the prospect that nationalism could create difficulties
simply by encouraging citizens to look to the economically advanced
countries for example and inspiration. This attitude could imply a grudg-
ing recognition of inferiority vis-à-vis the inhabitants of other nations,
and if so, it could lead a people to direct their frustrations against
the very culture they would like to emulate. Without going into the
complexities of the situation, this would seem to be what has been
happening in Cuba since 1960.

Nationalism thrives best as an instrument of central authority. In Latin
America however, direction from above has repeatedly discouraged the
growth of public responsibility and political sophistication at the local
level, and such a growth is desperately needed. Furthermore nationalism,

while good at destroying or weakening older alliances and loyalties, may not generate the degree of unity essential to the functioning of modern states. Thus far in Latin America, only in Mexico has nationalism proved capable of holding disparate groups together for sustained periods of time. Cuba may provide a second case.

Finally, nationalism could prove to be little more than antiforeignism, as it often has in the past. Anti-foreign nationalism sows the seeds of its own destruction because to the extent that it succeeds in reducing foreign "dangers" its appeal as a rallying point declines; and what is worse, if the nation then fails to find domestic issues capable of attracting a wide range of interest, it may well ignite class warfare. Also, if anti-foreign nationalism is not understood by those against whom it is directed, it will almost certainly weaken even further the front that the Hemisphere presents in international organizations.

It is no longer a question of whether or not there will be nationalism in Latin America; it is here and here to stay. It is only a question of who will give it direction. If this fact could be accepted within and without Latin America, then the banners of popular nationalism might be wrested from the spokesmen of the irresponsible left. Should such a recovery prove possible, there might be time to use nationalism as a constructive force in essentially democratic approaches to national reform and development.

The Alliance for Progress: Aims, Distortions, and Obstacles*

ALBERTO LLERAS CAMARGO

The documents that gave formal birth to the Alliance for Progress were signed at Punta del Este, Uruguay, on August 17, 1961. That date does not mark, however, the sudden commencement of a new stage in inter-American relations, but the culmination of a laborious process in which all the countries forming the Organization of American States (O.A.S.) took an active part.

* Alberto Lleras Camargo, "The Alliance for Progress: Aims, Distortions and Obstacles," *Foreign Affairs,* copyright © Council on Foreign Relations, Inc., New York, Vol. 42: No. 1 (October 1963), pp. 25–37.

Notwithstanding this, even today the multilateral character of the Alliance is not clearly perceived. Ask any American from, say, the Middle West what the Alliance is, and he will tell you, if he happens to be exceptionally well informed, that it is a policy of the United States toward Latin America which imposes new burdens on him as a taxpayer but which, properly handled, may serve to stop the Latin Americans from falling under the power of Communism, as Cuba fell. To what extent is this extraordinary distortion the work of those who have had an interest in making the movement attractive? To a great extent, certainly. The truth is that such misinterpretations and oversimplifications were powerful enough to make the very authors of the policy lose sight of its original meaning, its importance, its direction.

For, as should be known, the Alliance for Progress was the crowning confirmation of a Latin American policy seeking to effect a change in the traditional postures of the United States of America with regard to the southern portion of the hemisphere, and, in particular, with regard to the possibilities for the latter's development. It was, at the same time, the imposition of a new way of looking at the Latin American governments' obligations to their peoples. When it began to be disfigured, so that it appeared as merely another phase of the policy of the United States toward Latin America, the governments and peoples south of the Rio Grande felt that they were absolved from doing their share and that from then on they were to wait for the United States to carry out its part of the undertaking alone. So remarkable a change— which took place between the birth of the Alliance and a year and a half later—was facilitated and, I dare say, even characterized by North America's instruments of mass communication—press, radio and television—and by the international news agencies that are fed from United States sources. A great deal of the responsibility for this distortion of the aims of the Alliance also lies at the door of government officials—not excluding those of the United States—charged with the duty of issuing information about it. Nor were matters mended by the attitude of the Latin American governments which found fault with the United States for being too slow in getting the Alliance under way, as if they themselves had no part in launching what might and did seem to be just another one-way apportionment of foreign aid.

But, happily, a few months ago an excellent reaction set in—a movement back toward the historical and, if you like, the philosophical origins of this multilateral policy. There are records of those origins. The documents which were signed two years ago have very few precedents in the history of international relations. The aims and purposes of the Alliance for Progress are so wide-reaching and complex, and penetrate so deeply into what the Charter of the United Nations terms the "domestic jurisdiction" of the states—beyond trespass by that organization or any other—that, as commitments between nations, they are exceptional if not unique.

Neither the Charter of Punta del Este nor the Declaration to the Peoples of America, which preceded it, nor any of the annexed resolutions, has the formal character of ordinary international agreements, covenants and treaties. Following the best tradition of inter-American diplomatic procedure, the whole of this process—which might well prove decisive for the history of the hemisphere—rests merely on a booklet of declarations and commitments which require no ratification and whose duration depends entirely on the good will of each state. The governments bind themselves, not so much to the other signatory nations as to their own peoples, to carry out a policy which will, in effect, be the product of the closest international collaboration. Any of the 20 states may, without previous notice, withdraw from the Alliance simply by communicating the fact. Any state, moreover, may renounce the economic, political and social principles agreed upon in the various documents. The Punta del Este agreements, then, are no mere diplomatic instruments, but the final adoption of a great conjoint policy which is itself the result of a deep collective conviction.

In the political field the first move in this new direction is rightly attributed to the President of Brazil, Juscelino Kubitschek. In August 1958, in an aide-mémoire addressed to the other American presidents, he proposed that the governments should all pledge themselves to a joint effort to fight against Latin American underdevelopment. Kubitschek received from his colleagues the most stimulating response in favor of Operation Pan America. In September of the same year a new aide-mémoire defined in vigorous terms the probable objectives of the Operation. In this second memorandum one can already observe the influence of the Economic Commission for Latin America (ECLA) which, under the direction of the Argentinian economist, Raul Prebisch, had been trying to break the closed circle of underdevelopment with new ideas—ideas that were regarded with hostility or reserve by people in financial circles in the United States and in the World Bank. The second memorandum outlines the conception of development and underdevelopment and the possibilities of progressing from one to the other. It makes clear not only the advantage but also the method of estimating the growth of Latin American countries and of setting a specific goal for development in terms of a specified rate of growth. It asks for an indication of the probable fountainheads of international resources and the extent to which they would have to be drawn upon in order to complement national efforts. It considers it essential to examine the factors chiefly responsible for strangulations of the Latin American economy with a view to eliminating them by collective or individual action. Most important, the memorandum, besides accepting and expressing the spirit of the studies carried out by ECLA and the Inter-American Economic and Social Council, uses even the ECLA technical terminology which is henceforward to predominate in all the inter-American resolutions on economic coöperation.

In that same month of September 1958, an informal meeting of ministers of foreign affairs, gathered in Washington on the invitation of the Secretary of State, gave rise to the creation of the fruitful Committee of Twenty-one, which was to have its first meeting in December of that year at the Pan American Union. The chairman was one of the greatest figures on the American scene, Colombia's former President Alfonso López, who, though sick, lent vigor and direction to undertakings which undoubtedly were decisive factors in the success of the Committee. Various task groups were formed, embodying what were to be the central themes decided on at the Punta del Este Conference almost three years later. One of them worked on and finally drew up the initial statutes of the International Development Bank, previously rejected by the United States as an instrumentality of no value in promoting the economies of Latin America. Another group tackled the problem of basic products arising from the constant and disheartening imbalance in the terms of exchange between the United States and the Latin American nations—an imbalance aggravated just at that time by the striking fall in the prices of principal exports. Still another group examined the possibilities of regional markets, and pioneered in the creation both of the Central American Common Market and of the Latin American Association for Free Trade. And, finally, another team worked on the problems of technical coöperation.

The Committee of Twenty-one met again in April and May 1959. In January that year the Cuban Revolution had triumphed. Up to then the leader of the movement, Fidel Castro, seemed disposed to coöperate with the other Latin American countries and with the United States in the drive for development, which was already assuming a categorical definiteness with something of the same character and almost the identical terms that were finally to be adopted at Punta del Este. Castro was present at the 1959 meeting and delivered a speech which, though long and confused, was not more recriminatory than that of any of the more impatient delegates. It is said that, while speaking and on being asked to assess the amount the United States would have to contribute as foreign aid to the development program, Castro read

aloud a figure which one of his economists had passed on to him—
$30,000,000,000. That was taken to be a *boutade* of the bearded chief-
tain. It turned out to be not very different from the figures that were
finally arrived at and agreed on at Punta del Este.

But there is no truth in the rumor about the influence Castro is supposed to have exercised on the United States—through the excesses
of his revolution—to change its policy toward Latin America. The fact
is that the Government of the United States, as Dr. Milton Eisenhower
has recently shown in his book, "The Wine Is Bitter," had for some
time been evolving a modification of the orthodox principles hitherto
considered appropriate for the economic development of Latin America.
It had come to the conclusion that only through unorthodox means
and only through joint action—which would necessarily imply structural
changes in the social and economic life of the southern republics—would
it be possible, if not indeed to achieve development, at least to prevent
the disorganization and the economic and political collapse of that
quarter of the world. The effect of events in Cuba, such as expropriation
and the trend toward Communism, has been to give greater urgency
to the intentions of the United States that led to the Charter of Bogotá
and Punta del Este; it did not, however, engender a new policy, but
was merely a factor in urging—chiefly on the Latin American governments—the adoption of such a policy.

The Committee of Twenty-one, known technically as the Commission
for Studying the Formulation of New Measures for Economic Coöperation, had its last meeting in Bogotá, where the whole anterior process
of study and discussion culminated in a series of resolutions which ought
to be regarded as the basis of the policy that was to be subsequently
incorporated into the Alliance for Progress. There now appeared, without
any resistance from the United States, but rather with its unequivocal
support, certain theses that had been impugned both there and in Latin
America as excessively radical. Thus it was acknowledged that economic
development could not by itself bring about the desired social welfare
in time, and that it was necessary to engage simultaneously in a movement for the improvement of living conditions of the Latin American
peoples in order to avert tremendous social upheavals among vast masses
of the population sunk in misery.

The Act of Bogotá was, among documents of its kind, the first to
proclaim the need for structural reforms—above all in the systems governing taxes, tenure and use of land, and education—in order to set on
foot a great effort directed toward endowing the population of Latin
America with shelter, schooling, employment and health, by means of
the most wholehearted mobilization of domestic resources and a consid-

erable contingent of foreign aid. In consequence of these declarations, the Act of Bogotá recommended the creation of a Special Fund for Social Development which should contribute, on flexible terms, to the exertions of such Latin American countries as might propose to undertake or amplify action in the fields mentioned. Later on, the United States gave the Fund $500,000,000 of which $394,000,000 was to be administered by the Bank for International Development, $100,000,000 by the United States Government, and $6,000,000 placed at the disposal of the Pan American Union for such research as the new policy might require.

In the discussions on these matters the United States assumed an attitude of readiness to yield to Latin American pressure; it revealed its broad-mindedness and its increasing abandonment of its traditional policy; it sometimes even went so far as to urge the acceptance of certain bold schemes presented by others, and to insist, for example, on the advisability of carrying out agrarian and tax reforms. It was obvious that none of the Latin American countries—not even Mexico after 50 years in the climate of social revolution—could compare in social gains and just distribution of land and taxes with their powerful northern neighbor. But it was equally obvious that in order to promote similar conditions in the nations of the south the United States had to jettison a number of ideas which had traditionally weighed on its relationship with Latin America, and which had failed. Such was the idea that most important and decisive collaboration for the development of Latin America could and should proceed from North American private capital—an idea that was to be superseded by the conviction that such collaboration ought to come mainly from public funds. Such, too, was the notion that economic development would, unaided, produce social change quickly enough to satisfy the anxious masses of Latin America; this in turn gave way to a sense of the urgent need to undertake, again with public funds, campaigns for social welfare and even for human rehabilitation.

In place of another outworn conception it came to be recognized that any loans made to Latin American governments for the purposes of economic development and social welfare should be on easy and flexible terms, both as to time and as to interest, so as not to impose an intolerable burden on their already weakened position with respect to balance of payments. It was equally recognized that the law of demand and supply, in its application to Latin America's basic commodities, was causing an imbalance in the terms of exchange, which in turn was steadily impoverishing the nations of the south. But more than this, the United States recognized that it was necessary to come to the rescue, with such artificial measures as agreements on specific commodities, in order to avoid even more alarming consequences. The same spirit of comprehension led to the approval of existing regional common markets—or the creation of them—in an effort to accelerate the economic advancement of the Latin American states. And, crowning all these heterodox initiatives was the fact—without which the new stage would have been impossible—that the American States endorsed the theory of planning.

All these new ideas and undertakings are the principal points that mark the radical change in the Latin American policy of the United States—a change effected by two Administrations, representing each of the two great parties. They were arrived at and carried out in a period extending from the last months of the Eisenhower Administration to the first two years of Mr. Kennedy's Presidency. A curious parallel is to be found in recent American history. It was President Hoover who initiated the policy of non-intervention and good neighborliness toward Latin America; yet it remained for Roosevelt to christen, launch and steer it with admirable decision and energy, to such a degree, indeed, that even in the memory of Latin Americans and, quite naturally, in the memory of his fellow citizens, the fact of continuity is lost sight of. It is forgotten that in this respect there was no distinction of substance, but merely of style, between the Roosevelt Administration and that of his predecessor.

Most of the initiative in the present policy has been due to certain persons in Latin America, nearly all of them belonging to a new school of economists. The governments, however, that set their seal on the policy at Punta del Este were not fully aware or convinced of its ultimate implications. In Latin America, perhaps more than anywhere else in the world, political leaders have a habit of carrying revolutionary statements beyond the point to which they are really prepared to go. That practice does not generally have any serious effects on internal politics. But international politics is quite another thing, since every word is reckoned, or ought to be reckoned, at its face value. We can, then, be reasonably sure—as indeed the event has proved—that when the governments pledged themselves to change fundamentally certain traditional structures in the political, social and economic life of Latin America—as in the case of agrarian reform—they were not yet absolutely determined to carry all this out. The unwarrantable delays which later on took place, and which did not give the Alliance for Progress a chance to make the impact on the Latin American peoples that was hoped for, clearly indicate that when Punta del Este witnessed the signing of the most broadly sponsored and socially advanced document in the common history of our hemisphere, not all the signers understood its scope or divined its depth and gravity.

The declarations and pledges of Punta del Este were profoundly logical and consistent. The structural reforms announced were strictly indispensable if the Latin American states seriously intended to pledge themselves simultaneously to economic development and immediate social rehabilitation; the latter implied in great measure not only an increase in consumption, but also a natural decline in the capacity to save money for the promotion of the former. The Soviet Union had lived through 40 long years of austerity, privation and even misery in order to push its economic development. However, we in the Western Hemisphere proposed to achieve a similar aim, while at the same time procuring better living conditions, though we knew this meant artificially enlarging our capacity to acquire good dwellings, get sufficient schooling, enjoy better health and increase earnings. All this could be accomplished because it would be possible to finance part of the enterprise with foreign aid.

The basic and almost elemental problem of Latin America is the vertiginous increase in population which threatens to drown any rhythm of economic growth and overflow any capacity to improve living conditions. This problem was examined with a certain tactful and calculating discretion at Punta del Este, and it figures implicitly or prominently in every study in which the future of these countries is considered. Here is the reason why agrarian reform is one of the vital needs in our development. For there is no sort of economic expansion, however swift or successful, that can assimilate both the rural masses who cease to live by agriculture and the new surplus hands, whether in the town or in the country, who come year by year to glut the labor market. Nor must we forget that agrarian reform is needed from the point of view of equity, as another means of distributing patrimony and income more justly among the Latin Americans. It is all the more necessary because up to now such distribution has been sought mainly through systems of taxation which bite hardly at all into capital and income associated with land.

We must likewise expect this reform to result in a greater productivity of property neglected by inactive landowners, who prefer to derive profit from appreciation of land values rather than wrest it from the raising of crops and cattle with considerable toil and risk. But agrarian reform also has to be a hope and incentive for millions of peasants who are being displaced by the appearance of rural mechanization, and whose numbers in relation to the land are far in excess of what modern economics considers advisable. Those peasants, quite unprepared for industrial life, will become, if they go to the great towns, denizens of those hovels and slums which constitute a dismal but characteristic blot on the contemporary Latin American city—transformed, as it has been during the last 20 years, from a distinctive, progressive and inviting place into a sinister, proliferating farrago, hideous with sudden and uncontrolled contrast between old and new forms of wealth and with the blight and fester of rampant misery.

But among the conditions laid down by the Alliance for Progress, agrarian reform is not the only one that upsets people in Latin America. There is also tax reform. To indicate how outlandish this situation is, it is enough to say that not a single Latin American, whether of high standing or of the underworld, has ever been imprisoned for not paying his taxes or for sending in a fraudulent income tax report. In all that vast area it is unthinkable that deceiving or defrauding the state in this matter of taxes should be considered a crime, and what is more, the law does not consider it as such. As a result, tax evasion is widespread. But apart from this, symptomatic as it is, the systems of taxation are in themselves quite benevolent. In some countries taxes are very low or exemptions are large. Where tax collection is well organized, the brunt falls on the great industrial incomes—whether foreign-owned or national—and the earnings of employees, for these are precisely the sources which can most easily be checked. But there are many extremely well-to-do and even very rich people who pay no taxes; they have recourse to all sorts of anachronistic though still legal loopholes. For example, agriculturists and cattlemen are protected under the pretext that, if they were taxed, they would have to raise the prices of their produce and would thus cause an increase in the cost of living. A number of countries allow discounts on individual and mercantile incomes when these are accompanied by losses in farming activities; since this arrangement can hardly be controlled by the state, it easily lends itself to falsification of facts.

Now, if the countries that signed the Punta del Este agreement are to carry out what they said they were going to carry out—that is, an authentic revolution in their way of life and a sudden speeding up of economic expansion—they will need tax reforms, which in some instances will have to be drastic. But the classes necessarily affected by such measures have offered and will continue to offer strong resistance, first to the reforms themselves, and afterwards—for obvious reasons—to the Alliance for Progress. Hence the echo of dissatisfaction which is now heard everywhere in Latin America, in congresses and assemblies where the cattleman, the landlord and the great evader of taxes abound and have been silently and effectively representing their interests all through the successive and superficial political changes that have occurred.

In general those voices are the very ones that have been clamoring, in a heart-rending nationalistic strain, against outside interference in the political life of each country, in order to defend the status quo in taxation and landownership. In the past no Latin American nation has effected or even attempted either of these reforms without having to face tremendous opposition and embroilment. To try to carry out the two at the same time, throughout the hemisphere, looks like madness. But whose madness? Let us remember that the governments themselves, seemingly of their own accord, yielded to the gentle suasion of the economists who had been advocating these measures as a prerequisite to improvement in Latin America's precarious situation. Where, then, the madness?—especially since the situation certainly cannot be remedied by less radical means.

But there is still another obstacle, and it is quite a big one, for it contributes to the *mañana* attitude commonly imputed to Latin America. This is the grievous lack of technical training for the preparation and accomplishment of the early stages of any project, whether of legislation, engineering or social betterment on any important scale. Several countries have no trustworthy statistics. When, as happens in planning, work is undertaken on schemes that attempt to assess the present with a view to a distant future, the results are uncertain and highly questionable. But even for such concrete projects as a dam, an industrial plant or a power station, the financial basis cannot be accurately calculated— for lack of special technical knowledge. Sometimes a project after having been accepted is held up because the detailed blueprints of the concrete work are not forthcoming. All of which does not prevent certain voices in Latin America from attributing the delay in Alliance projects wholly to the bureaucratic machinery of the United States.

For here indeed is the source of the Alliance's great error in procedure. Inter-American organs were set up to study and prepare plans for national development, but it was left entirely to the United States' initiative not only to find the way in which its contribution should be made available, but also to arrive at some standard of judgment as to how and when and to whom support should be apportioned for carrying out Alliance plans. The result was to create a pattern of bilateral operation which, on the one hand, set the tone of the discussions between the United States and each separate Latin American nation for each particular case; on the other hand it caused an unending series of misunderstandings, resentments, conflicts and—though quite exceptionally—opportunities for scoring in the political game. How distant and different from the spirit and intention of the Alliance for Progress! President Kubitschek and I, on being called in to furnish an opinion on the functioning of the Alliance, both agreed—which was hardly remarkable—that the Alliance must be given back its original character and that this should be accomplished by establishing an inter-American body to administer the Alliance. Such a body could really be entrusted with the responsibility of scrutinizing the extent to which each country, including the United States, fulfills the commitments it assumed at Punta del Este. But if a single nation, however rich or powerful, should try to take that responsibility on itself, its action would be interpreted as an attempt at unwarranted invasion of each state's internal jurisdiction—in short, as an instance of imperialism.

It would not, then, be right nor in keeping with the spirit of Punta del Este for the United States to engage alone in the enterprise of Latin American development. The newly formed Inter-American Development Committee may be the means of solving the existing misunderstandings which harass and hinder the march of this policy and counteract its beneficial effects on the hemisphere. But it is not right, either, to place the whole burden of carrying out this great undertaking upon President Kennedy, who has had to assume responsibility for the Alliance whenever it has been abandoned by its Latin American partners, and has also had to join issue with his own compatriots who, though well aware that there is as yet no other way, strive to block the path of his policy.

The Congress of the United States approves of the Alliance and extols it—mark you—as a *policy* of that nation. Individually, Senators and Representatives follow the same line, converted as they are into jealous guardians of the social and economic transformation of Latin America. On the other hand, their fault-finding, usually based on unsound information, can scarcely be said to help to make the program acceptable. But what is seriously harmful is their manifest itch to slash the figures of the budget when it is laid before them; and although they may later on repent of having yielded to the temptation, the wrong has been done, and the whole of Latin America has interpreted their action as a lack of good will on the part of the United States toward the Alliance. It is already being pointed out that when the moment came to give the Alliance the necessary financial support the United States failed in precisely that part of the joint undertaking which it pledged itself to perform. For of what use would the Alliance for Progress be if its only result were that United States Senators should tell Latin America when and how to enact its agrarian and tax reforms? It was understood from the very beginning that to carry out this gigantic enterprise would require sufficient foreign financing for Latin America to solve, above all, its balance-of-payments problem created by the incipient stages of industrialization. It would deform the great undertaking if that contribution were to be scrimped and instead we were offered counsel and warnings about the revolution that will break out in Latin America unless we hasten to effect the reforms called for by the Charter of Punta del Este.

President Kennedy has grasped the meaning of this policy far better than most of his fellow citizens. He knows it is necessary, and he knows why. He realizes all the dangers that exist for this part of the world if its governments do not enter upon a thorough and far-reaching social transformation. He understands also the difficulties they will come up against; politician that he is, inured to conflicts with the legislative branch, he knows quite well that there will be wrangles, delays and setbacks in many legislative bodies before all the countries embark, as is now inevitable, on a great reform.

On their side the Latin Americans, and especially their rulers, ought to comprehend and sympathize with the impediments President Kennedy often finds in dealing with a Congress that cannot or will not always follow a pure line of international politics, without deviating toward the tastes and misconceptions of the electorate. Whenever the occasion arises to show the citizenry how advisable a policy like the Marshall Plan or the Alliance for Progress is, it seems necessary to explain it in extravagant terms and present it as if it could have been conceived only for the good and profit of the United States. The arguments thus employed are soon taken up and repeated by the Communists and the foreign beneficiaries—friendly governments and peoples to start with—who are then able to reason that there has been at bottom neither generosity nor disinterestedness, no real altruistic sentiment, no defense of common principles, but only an indirect pursuit of direct mercantile advantages for the United States.

Some day it will be necessary for a president of that country—it might well be Mr. Kennedy himself—to tell his people that foreign policy does not always have to produce direct material benefits, and that it is not manoeuvred in the sole interest of merchants, industrialists and taxpayers; but that it may be conducted as a sort of long-term investment, extending perhaps through several generations, at great risk, without any guarantee of success, but serving in the long run, and in the widest and highest sense, the interest of the nation. It was in this spirit that the last three wars were fought. Did anybody explain then that the profits would be quick and solid on the money poured out to maintain American soldiers in France, afterwards throughout the world and later still in Korea? Seriously, nobody was demanding such an investment. And nobody in the United States, not even the greatest reactionary, would protest because now, at last, it is Latin America's turn to receive foreign aid, when it needs it most for its defense and development. What may be an error is to try to convince the people of the United States—quite unnecessarily—that the Alliance for Progress is a policy that really seeks to open markets for them and to get back the $1 billion that were lost in Cuba.

The Alliance and Political Goals*

JOSÉ FIGUERES

Twice in my lifetime I have heard the news: "The United States has joined! The U.S. has entered the war!" Those were anxious moments, first during World War I and then during World War II. On both occasions a world already embattled heralded the entry of a new fighter, young and vigorous, as the assurance of victory for the cause of freedom.

The Alliance for Progress may be considered as the third entry of the United States into an embattled world. In this struggle the theater of war is the Western Hemisphere. The battles are of a different nature. Once again, however, the appearance of the new fighter in the battlefield assures victory for the cause of freedom.

THE CAUSE OF MISUNDERSTANDING

How little we know about the back of the moon, our closest neighbor in space! How little the North American public knows about the war that has been waging in the southern half of this hemisphere during the last few decades—the war that the United States is now joining!

"Ignorance," in the original meaning of the word, "not knowing," "not being aware of," is still the main cause of misunderstandings in the

* José Figueres, "The Alliance and Political Goals," in John C. Dreier (ed.), *The Alliance for Progress: Problems and Perspectives* (Baltimore: The Johns Hopkins Press, 1962), pp. 66–88.

era of communications. Ignorance still prevails in all countries. I once met an African student who admired Abraham Lincoln, "that wonderful chief who conducted the war of the United States against South America." Presumably Lincoln also preserved the unity of the hemisphere as one great nation.

I knew a lady in Latin America who would like somebody to explain exactly what the difference is between the United States and the United Nations. And I know a radio and television commentator in Miami who said a few weeks ago that the Latin Americans have been engaged, up to the time of the present Cuban crisis, in a cops and robbers game.

Yet for those who have been in it, this game of cops and robbers happens to be our Second War of Independence. It is also the war in which the United States now participates through the Alliance for Progress.

Sovereignty without freedom

Our First War of Independence, between approximately 1800 and 1825, separated the present Latin American republics from Spain and Portugal. We became sovereign nations. Unlike the citizens of the United States, however, the citizens of many of our sovereign nations did not become free men. All our constitutions were democratic, but many of our governments were dictatorial. It took a century of education, a thousand trials and errors, and a Second War of Independence to establish democratic governments.

The Second War of Independence has been waged during the last fifteen or twenty years. Tyrannies have fallen one after another, giving way to progressively representative governments. Whatever the shortcomings of some of the new regimes, they do constitute steps forward. Only three of the twenty-one Latin American countries are still ruled by the old-time dynasties and cliques. Peaceful means are now being sought to bring that era of suffering to an end.

The Latin American liberal movement of recent decades has established liberty over sovereignty; it has also laid the foundation for economic and social development. In sporadic actions at the beginning, followed by more co-ordinated efforts at the end, this movement has written an important page of our history, which is generally unknown in the United States.

It was only when one of our operations backfired—when one of the several groups which fought the Cuban dictatorship of Batista and assured the victory of the Cuban Revolution, had defected against the democratic forces to join the cold-war enemy in Havana—that many

North Americans realized that the curtailment of freedom anywhere in the hemisphere constitutes a danger everywhere.

The delusion prevails in the United States that the present Cuban tragedy is the first communist attainment of power in the New World. Nothing is further from the truth. My own little country, Costa Rica, was the first American victim of the World Communist Revolution, from 1940 to 1948. It took a sacrifice of two thousand lives to overthrow a pro-communist government which had destroyed the electoral institutions in order to stay in power. Our struggle against communism was, unfortunately, launched at a period when the United States was a wartime ally of Soviet Russia.

The second case was Guatemala, where a communist-dominated regime was overthrown in 1954, this time with some co-operation from the United States.

Cuba is the third communist adventure, not the first. All the same, for my generation of Latin Americans the present struggle in Cuba may be regarded as the twentieth, since we admit no distinction between tyranny of the left and tyranny of the right. We have devoted our life-long efforts to protect the angel of freedom, and it matters not to us from what direction the poisoned arrows come.

The U.S. should know

We are not embittered or vindictive on account of the frivolous treatment given by the world press to a saga in which our generation of fellow Latin Americans has played an important role. Yet it is necessary for many North Americans to know that their new ally, Latin America, is the only continent that has been fighting vigorously and conscientiously for individual freedoms and representative government during the last quarter of a century. Some countries have fought for national defense and others for national sovereignty. We have fought for personal liberty and for the survival of the democratic political system.

It would be difficult to recount the number of deaths, prison years, exiles, and torture sessions that the men and women of my generation have endured. Comparing the personal histories of many of my comrades-at-arms with mine, I am ashamed to remember how short my prison terms and how mild my years of exile have been. I am grateful to recall how good my fortune was in combat. I am moved to observe how benevolent my fellow countrymen are when they shower on me so many of the distinctions that were due others who are no longer here.

As a non-Cuban, I hold the unique honor of having been in Batista's jails, and of having later confronted Fidel before his own applauding crowds. As a Costa Rican, it has been my privilege and my sorrow to participate, during the period between 1948 and 1955, in four successive actions which constitute the first breach of peace in our country in over a hundred years, and the first armed clash with the communist movement in the American Hemisphere.

Other Latin Americans have done much more. It is not my desire to exalt myself nor to praise my fellow countrymen. Rather I want to assure you North Americans that when you enter this Alliance for freedom, this Alliance for economic solidarity, this Alliance for general well being, you are *not* entering a game, and you are *not* associating yourselves with either cops or robbers.

A *realistic alliance*

Why is the United States joining in Latin America's Second War of Independence? For the same reason that the United States joined in World War I and then in World War II: because the instinct of the nation saw, yesterday and the day before as well as it sees today, that the moment had arrived when her own national freedom and prosperity were endangered.

For years we Latin Americans have wanted the United States not merely to help us, but to join in the fight against dictatorship and poverty. It is a Darwinian principle that no being and no species and no nation can be expected to act for the exclusive benefit of others. Self-defense comes first, or simultaneously.

Yet realism is no negation of idealism. They both walk hand in hand. North Americans who participated in the two World Wars, or who may take part in this new kind of war which is the Alliance for Progress, might be personally moved by the ideals of freedom and human solidarity. But the nation as a whole must be realistic. Its first concern must be the security of its own citizens. Its noble idealism must be channeled to the attainment of this realistic goal.

We Latin Americans consider this new Alliance to be realistic as a defensive move of the United States government. This is all we expect. This is all we ask for. Ever since Bolivar's time we have known that the well being of the Americas is indivisible. If the United States enters the fight with a view to the protection of her own freedoms, with an eye on the long-range interests of her own commerical growth, in the spirit of an investment and not of an expense, we are satisfied. We know that the sower is not the man who wastes his seeds in feeding the wild birds.

In the course of our Second War of Independence, for a long time the United States appeared to regard the attack on our freedoms as a Latin American concern alone. On this assumption the government of the United States ignored our plight. The people of the United States did not learn of our sufferings. The press of the United States disdained our achievements.

Under a policy of "business as usual" the investors of the United States were inclined to deal, and to induce their government to deal, with whoever was in power. Liberty and law, or tyranny and lawlessness, were unimportant. Neutralism ruled the day. When it was necessary to find out on which side some North Americans were neutral, often it turned out that they were neutrals on the side of "stability," which was a euphemistic allusion to the prevailing despotism.

There was a time in the United States when it required unusual courage, even heroism, for a North American in public life to stand for freedom and decency in the Latin American controversies. The sudden popularity of young Congressman Charles O. Porter in our continent and the lasting gratitude that my liberated fellow-countrymen feel for him are the result of his courageous support of our democratic forces at decisive moments. Now history is proving him right.

ECONOMIC SHORTCOMINGS

The author of the previous chapter, Dr. Raúl Prebisch, our greatest economist, represents several generations of Latin American scholars who have long stressed the need for economic programs and who have actually formulated such programs for the development of our southern republics. The Alliance for Progress is a tribute to their life-long studies and services.

Dr. Prebisch, whose learning knows no bounds, has, in his discussion, invaded the field of political analysis, permitting me, therefore, to invade the field of economics. Admitting that I do not know how to draw the line between economics and politics, I intend in a constructive spirit to comment on five economic shortcomings of the Alliance—which may be premature because these views are based on only a few months of observation.

EMERGENCY MEASURES FIRST There seems to be insufficient realization that the Alliance is a belated effort. If it had come at an earlier date—for example, ten years ago—when the export prices of Latin American commodities were at a relatively satisfactory level, and when dictatorships were falling without being replaced by the communists, then the introduction of programming and the orderly supply of deficit capital from outside would have been decisive in starting or accelerating the process of peaceful growth. In 1962, however, after a long period of decline in export prices and of new political turmoil, the situation in most countries is so grave that they need *emergency measures first*, and then, or simultaneously, the application of economic programs. We are prescribing a wholesome diet to people in acute physical pain who urgently need a sedative. By the time we finish our examination and apply the sedative, if we apply it at all, the patient will have lost his faith if not his life.

Lend Lease was not conducted this way, and it won the war. The Marshall Plan took deficiencies and waste for granted, and it saved Europe. Is Latin America once more going to be the ugly duckling? No political stability and no permanence of democratic governments can be expected in Latin America today without immediate emergency measures of economic assistance. In fact, it is almost impossible to recapture the time lost. I respect researchers, analysts and bankers. But my instinct seems to tell me that on occasions we call on them at the wrong time. At this moment of belated efforts, we cannot take the risk of treating as a banking business what is really a war. This *is* war!

EXISTING BUSINESS   There is neglect of existing private business in the Latin American economies under the "terms of reference" of the international financing institutions. You may find credit for new projects, but seldom for the ordinary and mounting needs of thousands of reputable established firms. The advantages of the modern concept of "projects" are undeniable. But we seem to have gone too far to the extreme of what is now called "projectitis."

Some private U.S. banks have a more practical approach. They prefer to lend to established borrowers. But, (a) they have no satisfactory mechanism for obtaining guarantees rapidly; and (b) they do not go into the medium- and long-term credits that Latin American businessmen need. There is little realization in the United States that the poorer nations have practically no stock markets and no diversified savings which the enterprisers can tap. They are forced to use long-term credit. And banking resources for this credit are scarce in those countries, for the very same reasons.

When we speak of developing a country, or a continent, the assumption seems to be that we are going to start from scratch: an overall plan, plus shiny new projects. This sounds beautiful to the theorist, but it so happens that underdeveloped countries already have a functioning economic machinery. In fact those countries are underdeveloped partly because the existing machinery of established firms needs oil and fuel. Under the "terms of reference" of international banking institutions, our most urgent need, the need for refinancing, has become taboo. To those who lack understanding of our local circumstances, a firm that needs refinancing is considered to be in bad shape. You must have new "projects."

The next step in this direction would be to recommend to those countries that they discard the automobiles and trucks that they presently have in service, because, after lengthy studies, a few efficient Cadillacs will be shipped in.

THE MAGIC THERMOMETER. The International Monetary Fund would be an even better institution than it is, if it were accompanied, as Lord Keynes is said to have wanted at Bretton Woods, by an international commodity fund. Since bankers have in our society and in our conferences all the influence that they should have, and since bankers deal in currencies and not in commodities, we got out of Bretton Woods with a good currency fund and without any commodity institution. This may have been the most fatal mishap in recent economic history. Probably underdevelopment would be a minor problem today if an appropriate institution had watched international commodity prices as effectively as the International Monetary Fund has looked for currency stability.

I knew a peasant who used to look at the thermometer and marvel at the magic power of such a small instrument to influence atmospheric temperatures. In our international business today, we expect the value of currencies to be the cause, instead of the consequence, of economic stability. Instead of preventing the price of coffee from dropping, as we rightly protect the price of wheat, we technically recommend austerity to the democratic government of Colombia, "to stabilize the currency."

Newspapers speak of political unrest in Brazil as "the cause" of currency devaluations. Actually devaluations and unrest are both effects of the ignorance of our era in the field of international terms of trade. At this very moment, international coffee agreements are being reached which, largely because of our own faults as Latin Americans, are sure to constitute a true stabilization of hunger. Austerity does not mean a little less butter for the people who have never been able to afford butter. Austerity imposed upon Latin America for monetary purposes usually means aggravated social tensions, loss of prestige for democratic governments, chaos, and eventual dictatorships from right or left.

You may say that this is a dismal picture and there is no solution in sight. Unfortunately that is nearly right. The Alliance for Progress will not find stable solutions until a thorough study is made of the commerce between the industrialized and the less developed nations of the West. This is not only a problem of commodity prices. It embraces the whole relationship between the poor and the rich countries, which is as inadequate today as was the internal relationship between labor and business in Britain in the 1850's.

Marx prophesied that the gap between the "exploited" and the "exploiters" would continually widen until the Revolution would close it. He would have been right if the economic tendencies had not been checked and channeled by the growing forces of political democracy.

In the eventful year of 1848 John Stuart Mill announced that the distribution of incomes is a matter of political decisions and not of economic laws. Political decisions, and not automatic adjustments, have established social justice internally in the advanced democracies of today. As an unexpected corollary, an ever-expanding market has brought about an ever-expanding production. The same process will have to be repeated in the relation between the proletarian and the industrial countries of our time. International justice will have to be established to the advantage of our countries by enlightened political action and not by blind economic forces.

This will call for a great deal of knowledge. Barbara Ward and other scholars are working in this field. We Latin Americans are obliged to give our contribution. An analysis must be made of the international phenomena that constitute important causes of underdevelopment in the world of today. In the meantime, the programs of the Alliance for Progress are in order, and the emergency measures that the accumulated evils call for are imperative.

SOCIAL REFORM   The Alliance for Progress calls for reform in the social structures of Latin American countries. No advice could be wiser. No recommendations could better help the political groups to which I myself belong. Democratic social change has always been the basis of our struggle. Yet at this critical moment I would recommend some caution. In many countries the same social groups that have traditionally prevented change, with the approval and solidarity of the industrial nations, are still in power. Remember the Russian saying: "for centuries you have trained the goats to eat the cabbages; do not now suddenly expect the goats to guard the cabbage patch."

Under our circumstances, social justice primarily means higher wages. Higher wages in turn mean increased consumption. Increased consumption for our poor peoples does not mean enjoying a room in one of the palaces of the few rich. Rather, it means a little more food and clothing, and medicine, and small battery radios in the thatched huts. Much of this comes from abroad, and it has to be paid for in foreign currency. Are we prepared to meet the added burdens to those lean balances of payments?

Not to be misinterpreted, I must say that my party in Costa Rica has adopted a policy of increasing wages and salaries in accordance with the rising productivity of the economy. From 1953 to 1958, during our second term of office, we succeeded in elevating personal incomes to the level of productivity of the moment. Unfortunately since then the export prices of coffee, bananas, and cocoa dropped. I do not want to tell you of the hardships and the possible chaos that Costa Rica faces now. We are paying a high price for having anticipated the Alliance for Progress by five years in an act of faith in international stability and solidarity.

No measures of the Alliance for Progress can greatly improve the living standards of our countries until our dependence upon exports is considerably reduced through industrialization, which will take a long time, or until exports are stabilized at a fair level, which will take a long struggle.

Some of our countries may and should distribute land, which they have. All of them should enforce tax collection. But I seriously doubt if there is as much meat to distribute, as some North Americans believe, in the body of our tiny, privileged minorities.

The liberal parties of Latin America (and mine is one of them) are all for fair distribution as long as there is something to distribute. But we are not social agitators. We are engaged in economic development as a means to popular well being. Therefore, we have to encourage capital formation: not luxury, not waste, but indispensable capital formation, which inevitably means some degree of consumption sacrifice.

TAXATION We do not believe that our general system of taxation is as bad as some outside observers say. Whatever its obvious defects, our systems lay emphasis on consumption of nonessential goods, which is economically desirable. I feel a compelling need to tell North Americans that our consumers pay a $1,700 import duty on a Volkswagen, $2,200 on a Chevrolet, and over $200 on a small refrigerator or a television receiver. In some countries of South America these duties are even higher.

You North Americans disburse the bulk of your personal taxes at a government office, based on your paychecks. We pay at the store where our check is spent. What difference does it make? Whatever our reputation as tax evaders, and your reputation as tax avoiders, the store is certainly a place where no one can cheat.

Through these high consumption duties, overall taxes in my little country, Costa Rica, gather 20 per cent of the total national income. This is approximately the same proportion as you pay in the United States in different ways.

It is not the taxes that make the big difference between you and us. It is what you and we have left after taxes. Both your average and your minimum net income are around ten times the income in countries like mine, which is in the medium levels of the twenty-one Latin American Republics.

It is not my pleasure to express these observations. I am acting as the Devil's advocate. Those of us who have long struggled for something like the Alliance must now watch for its success. Perfection is the enemy of goodness. Government is the art of continuously choosing the smallest of several evils. Accordingly, let not our ideals of social well being conduce us to any situation in which we might have to share Omar Khayyam's regrets: "Indeed the idols I have loved so long have done my credit in men's eyes much wrong."

I confess that something strange seems to be happening to me and to some other Latin Americans directly engaged in the fields of production, social improvement, or politics. We must be color blind, because we see red traffic lights where our colleagues, North and South American, who work in the more technical fields of economics here in the United States, see green.

I know most of the economists in inter-American activities. For years they have been my friends, giving me their valuable technical advice while I have given them my modest political support. These scholars, notably those stationed here in Washington during these cherry blossom days, must think that I have become an alarmist on the Latin American situation, after having been a sanguine crystal-ball gazer a few years ago, when dictators were falling without being replaced by communists and when our foreign commerce was comparatively sound. I sense a strange feeling when conversing with my friends, whether they be North Americans or Latin Americans. It would appear that we look at things in different ways. Everything is fine in Argentina, except that an austerity government fell. Colombia is growing at a satisfactory rate, with a stable currency, though two weeks ago half a million members of the Liberal Party voted pro-Castro. Things are going well in Peru, under a decent government, yet everybody is jittery about how peaceful this June's elections will be. The economic growth of Mexico is phenomenal, but, in spite of great social efforts during a half-century of Revolution, two-thirds of the people are as badly off relatively as they were in 1910. Costa Rica is a stable little country, yet after six years of crops sold at low prices, 40 per cent of bank debtors cannot meet their obligations; hospital employees are not being paid; unemployment is rampant; and the next government faces a deficit of one-half a year's income.

There seems to be no end to the number of economic studies. Oftentimes you know where your shoes are tight and where they need stretching, and every week you get a new recommendation for a thorough analysis of the anatomy of your feet.

Things are quieting down in Venezuela, presumably of their own accord, though perhaps if it were not for Rómulo Betancourt, the Venezuelan oil wells might have been by now in Russian hands. Brazil is a giant, slowly and surely plowing its way with little to worry about; but to some of us it looks like a gigantic powder keg. The financial situation of Ecuador is normal, though the overall picture is as hopeless as the price of cocoa.

I have visited countries where there is too much credit according to the technicians, while industries and farms are laying off needed workers because they cannot meet pay rolls. I can tell you of countries where there is not enough food, supposedly because of inflation, and of countries where the currency is sound but the goods are unavailable. Never have I been so confused. This situation reminds me of the patient who was thoroughly examined by good doctors from head to foot, with the conclusion that everything was all right except his health.

Oh Lord, please make me wrong! I believe that the way to go about the hemispheric situation, if it were politically possible—which is a great "if"—would be the following:

a. Full-scale emergency measures, at the cost of some degree of efficiency, in the spirit of Lend-Lease and the Marshall Plan.
b. Long-range development programs and social reforms.
c. A thorough revision of international commerce, which will require a great deal of study, and which, I believe, contrary to some people's opinion, will still be necessary in the future, after the Latin American economies have been diversified.

THE PROBLEM IS POLITICAL

Many of you will be surprised if I say that the economic problem of financing world development is small, while the political problems are almost unsurmountable. When the European vacuum had to be filled after the Second World War, the economy of one industrial country alone, the United States, then half as large as it is today and having been strained by the cost of a great conflict, was strong enough to supply the deficit capital needed to rebuild the Old World. There never has been such a large or such a wise investment in prosperity and security for all. Today the combined economies of Western Europe, the United States, and perhaps Japan, could easily supply the development needs of the less developed non-Soviet world.

I could fill this book with figures to prove this contention, which is shared by the scholars who specialize in this field. One-tenth of the current unused industrial capacity of the West could produce the trucks, tractors, and factories that would start the wheels turning in all the retarded nations of today. One-half of one per cent increase in the overall output of the developed countries would produce all the outside push that is needed for the "take-off" of the world's incipient economies. It is not judicious to disparage scientific achievements, though it is provocative to observe that the cost of sending a man to the moon may be the equivalent of the capital needs of the whole underdeveloped world for a period of five to ten years.

Money and bookkeeping are useful inventions, yet when we lose sight of physical things and look exclusively at their symbols we soon get confused in words, mental habits and prejudices, and, even worse, in political entanglements. It is not dollar bills, nor bank drafts, nor the taxpayer's money that are needed to help industrialize other countries. What is needed are concrete mixers, bulldozers, and power plants—the things that can be readily produced by the developed nations at a small additional burden to their industrial plants, probably helping to stabilize their own economies at the same time.

The major problem is: How can you make people understand? This is primarily a political problem—in the United States, in Europe, in Latin America, in the entire world.

Latin American politics

The political difficulties that Latin America presents to the Alliance for Progress and to the general understanding between the Americas may be partly traced to this: our countries, though widely differing among themselves, are still the type of societies common before the Industrial Revolution—an elite at the top and a large majority at the bottom, with a relatively small middle class.

In times of normality or stagnation the elites may well express the feelings of their nations. Whereas in times of change or crisis, the elite minorities become more and more disconnected emotionally from the impoverished majorities. They lag ten to twenty-five years behind. Yet they continue to be the spokesmen of their countries in their relations with the outside world. Their members travel abroad, and at home they receive the visitors from the richer countries. It is practically impossible for most visitors to penetrate the "barrier of isolation" of our ruling class. Speaking with taxi drivers, who are an encyclopedia in most countries, is not enough. They are over-sophisticated. Domestic servants are under-sophisticated. It is not surprising therefore to find foreign journalists, foreign diplomats, and foreign businessmen making the same mistakes in their appraisal of a situation. In good faith they speak the language of the local oligarchy, and they repeat its errors.

Neither is it surprising that U.S. labor, through its international officials, has been generally right in its evaluations of Latin American political leaders and forces. On most of our issues your organized labor has been on the side of the angels, doing much to save the prestige of the United States.

A few professors called the Latin Americanists, a few liberals who are members of entities like the "Inter-American Association for Democracy and Freedom" or the "Friends of the United States of Latin America" (FUSLA), and some exceptional individuals, have turned out after years of being considered along with some of us as troublemakers, to be the true precursors of the Alliance for Progress. The bulk of North Americans, on the other hand, have had an interchange of ideas almost exclusively with people who are either inactive in politics or who belong to the small conservative parties. These parties, generally speaking, cannot be expected to carry out the reforms recommended in the Alliance for Progress.

Almost in every country we have reform-minded leaders and political groups who are not communist, but who are simply unwilling to sacrifice the pro-communist vote. In the past these coalitions have led to different kinds of results. In the late sixties they can only lead to communist-dominated governments. Such parties and such governments will definitely oppose the Alliance for Progress.

Latin America's liberal parties

There are organized currents of public opinion in Latin America that have received scant notice in the United States and which seem to be a good expression of the democratic trends of the time: the liberal parties.

Political parties in general seem to play a larger role in Latin America and Europe than in the United States.

When President Kennedy announced the Alliance for Progress in a historic speech, twenty-three political parties sent him a joint message of appreciation and solidarity, which I had the honor of presenting to the President. These liberal groups, whether in government, in the opposition, or in exile, are the true representatives of Latin America, if Latin America is going to follow social development along democratic lines. Democratic labor is a part of this movement. So are some intellectual circles, most of the young professional people, and a large proportion of the technocrats. In some countries one-third of the entrepreneurs help the liberal movement while the rest of the business community is either indifferent or allied with the oligarchies.

Our parties have organized a small Inter-American Institute of Political Education in Costa Rica, to train young leaders in the answers of democracy to the problems of our time. I am a member of this Institute. We receive economic help from some liberal groups in the United States. We train 60 students at a time, which is all we can do, instead of 6,000 which is what we should do. We also publish a magazine, "Combate," which attempts to be a voice for the social-democratic thinking of the day, particularly in the inter-American field.

I believe that this liberal movement of Latin America, which is friendly to the United States, despite certain understandable resentments, is the logical vehicle for the political action of the Alliance for Progress. Belated as the Alliance is, it comes at a time when the generation of Latin Americans who have fought for freedom is still active in politics. If we fail to deliver economic development democratically, the new generation now at the universities will try economic development at any political cost.

In recommending the liberal movement, I am prejudiced and I am grinding my own ax. But I am willing to change over if someone can find a better tool to hack out a path for the progress of the Alliance.

United States political problems

Perhaps the major political problems of the Alliance for Progress will be found in the United States. The government of this country faces the dilemma of simultaneously leading a contented people at home, who tend to be conservative because they have a great deal to conserve, and a number of malcontented, allied peoples abroad, who tend to be revolutionary because they have a great deal to change.

The people of the United States are still oriented toward Mother Europe, which is commendable, and not to Sister Latin America, which is lamentable. This country inherited the English language, a great deal of the English political wisdom on internal affairs, and some of the English disregard for the Spaniards. Latin America inherited the language, the chivalry and the anarchy of the Iberian Peninsula, and some of its distrust for the British, who speak English.

Foreign aid is opposed in this country today on the same grounds on which higher wages and social improvements were opposed in 1900. The historic experience that a better distribution of the national income has made industry richer, and not poorer, is still not easily applied in the minds of most people to the distribution of world income. Although slavery and cheap labor internally have long been proved to be expensive for a free nation as a whole, cheap raw materials and services from the poor countries are still assumed to be inexpensive for an industrial nation as a whole. As a result, the citizens of rich countries are requested to compensate as taxpayers, through foreign aid, what they should be paying directly as consumers of foreign goods and services through regulated international trade.

The remedies for these long-entrenched and almost invisible defects of foreign commerce are not yet clearly established. In the meantime underdeveloped countries have to be helped with the transitory measure called "aid," if world tensions are to be kept within control.

The leaders and many of the scholars of the United States have a clear view of these problems, and recognize how small they are economically by comparison with the output of the free industrial world. But it will take time, even under today's diffused education, for the majority of the citizens of any great nation to become sophisticated in this field. Meanwhile the press and the Congress of this country, with increasingly numerous and praiseworthy exceptions, represent the average level of public opinion. This understandably makes the work of your leaders in international affairs an almost impossible task.

Western Europe's part

Western Europe should share in the responsibility of Latin American development. Historic ties, culture and trade link our republics with Europe as much as with the United States. Although we have direct relations with the mother countries, the good offices of the United States are essential, especially in co-ordinating the efforts of what is really a triangular economy.

LOOKING TO THE FUTURE

The success or failure of the Alliance for Progress depends on our ability to meet political difficulties in all our countries. The problem is up to the wisdom of our peoples.

Two equally unhappy things may happen if the Alliance should fail. Stagnation is not one of them. One may be the communization of the Latin American continent, following the pattern of continental China. This would call for increased military protection of North America and Western Europe. The United States' bookkeepers would have to write off, among things of greater consequence, $12 billion worth of investments. We Latin Americans would have to surrender 150 years of struggle for freedom.

The other thing that may happen is the "Balkanization" of Latin America. Our continent may be divided in two political camps resembling a geographical mosaic, like Germany and Berlin, or Korea or Viet-Nam. For the time being the division of the hemisphere resembles China, with Cuba playing the role of Formosa.

You may think that I am trying to frighten you. I am! I am worried myself and I am not in bad company. Dr. Milton Eisenhower has said that the communist movement is spending $100 million a year in education and propaganda in Latin America. I ought to know what that means.

Let me say, in passing, that any course that Latin America may take, other than the road chosen by the Alliance for Progress, will cost the United States an amount imcomparably greater than the Alliance in money, in human resources, and perhaps in more serious sacrifices. Moreover, the cost of any other alternative will mean, for the United States, an expense, a bleeding, whereas the cost of the Alliance will mean a profitable investment.

How are the Latin American liberal forces going to behave in this final phase of our Second War of Independence? Here I must be brutally frank. We are happy and honored to have the United States as an ally, but please do not take us for granted!

Other politicians can be taken for granted, but not those of us who have already sacrificed so much in suffering. I myself am convinced that the hardships of my friends and companions who are now in the Cuban dungeons and the plight of the Cuban people at large would have been lighter, in spite of a communist government, if the opposition to the Castro regime had not been so vociferous, so persistent, so heroic, and, unfortunately, so futile.

I understand the reasons why the Hungarian patriots and the Cuban invaders were not supported. And please understand why I am not inclined to encourage our peoples to engage in suicidal resistance in those countries where worse may come to worst. Tyranny is not merely an exercise in cruelty; it is a means to an end. The communist revolution has its objectives. Its repressive measures of cruelty must be roughly proportional to the amount of opposition that it faces.

Sufficiently it has been my lot to send friends on voluntary missions from which they might not return, when my conscience told me that the sacrifice was justified. I have paid too many calls of bereavement on soldiers' widows and mothers to look at heroism lightly.

After the original experiences of the communists in Costa Rica and Guatemala, where they were defeated, probably no country that falls in their hands in the future will be liberated by its own people without a torrent of blood. This is a world struggle, and not the struggle of any one of the Latin American republics. Though I have not lost my fighting spirit, it is not in my nature to recommend disproportionate sacrifices.

UNITY OR FAILURE

It is not out of unkindness but out of a sense of urgency and anxiety that I say these things. The writing on the wall is "Unity or Failure." Never could I be unkind at a moment like this, when my soul is filled with reminiscenses of an inspiring address on unity or failure delivered in Washington by one who could inspire; when I hear replayed inside me the melodies of a symphony which is all kindness and love; when the air is full of notes from Lincoln's Second Inaugural Address.

If, because of God's inscrutable designs, the North American people are not prepared to support their leaders in this great conception of the Alliance for Progress, and to make it possible for them to build the bulwark of Christendom and democracy that the Western Hemisphere should be; if it is Latin America's fate to remain poor or to adopt a heathen culture; then the Latin American peoples who have given costly contributions to the democratic system should not be expected to go into further sacrifices and to die for a civilization that the North enjoys and the South only craves.

On the other hand, if it is God's desire that the New World should be united in prosperity and liberty; if this fortunate nation joins the Alliance with a full decision of the heart, and her citizens share the greatness of her leaders; if we work together with a minimum of expediency and a maximum of principle; if loyalty is reciprocal; then, undoubtedly, we shall all be on duty, and the entry of the United States will be heralded as it was in the First and the Second World Wars as the final assurance of victory for the cause of freedom.

No sacrifice will then be spared. And no smallness of the spirit will deter us from sharing your glory, if your Kennedy achieves what our Bolivar envisaged.

*Who Are the Communists?** | ROLLIE E. POPPINO

The Communist parties of Latin America claim to be the vanguard of the proletariat. The primary purpose of the party, in the Communist view, is to awaken the political consciousness of the proletariat, to inspire it to political action, and to lead it to political power. The Communists maintain incessantly that only they understand and care about the grievances of the lower class and are capable of forming a government that will satisfy these grievances. It is in the nature of things, according to the Communists, that the upper class and the middle class exist only by exploiting the proletariat. Thus, with rare exceptions, members of the upper and middle classes can not appreciate and will not alleviate the plight of the lower stratum of society. Any real improvement in the lot of the masses must be accomplished by the masses themselves, working through and in support of their Communist party. This is the line that recurs constantly in propaganda and recruitment campaigns of the Latin American Communist parties.

The implication in the Communist claims and reasoning is clear. The Communist party is, and must be, composed overwhelmingly of members drawn from the working class. This implication is highly misleading when not completely erroneous. It has never been more than partially true anywhere in Latin America.

The fiction that the communist parties are predominantly of, as well as for, the proletariat is one that the Communists have assiduously sought to preserve. They have done so largely for reasons of practical politics and ideological conviction. But, in addition, they have perpetuated the fiction at least in part because they want to believe it. Marxist-

* Reprinted with permission of The Free Press from *International Communism in Latin America* by Rollie E. Poppino. Copyright © 1964 by The Free Press of Glencoe, a division of The Macmillan Company.

Leninist doctrine holds that the proletariat is peculiarly endowed with the characteristics required of all good Communists. Understandably, those party leaders and members with other social backgrounds have been reluctant to acknowledge that they are perhaps less qualified to be Communists than their lower-class compatriots.

At times they have gone to ridiculous lengths to demonstrate their proletarian prolivities. In the 1920's, for example, the intellectuals and other middle-class members of the Brazilian party affected the habits, mannerisms, and characteristic garb of the city working class in a dramatic effort to show that they were proletarian at heart, if not in origin. A somewhat more sophisticated manifestation of this attitude is the requirements, expressed formally in the statutes of the various parties, that all party members must belong to and participate actively in a trade union, a peasant society, or another appropriate mass organization. If the parties were as proletarian in character as the Communists have insisted, this requirement would seem to be superfluous.

Despite the exaggeration and self-deception evident in their claims, the Communists are sincere in the desire to build the party on a predominantly proletarian base. This was not always the case. In the early years of the movement in Latin America most Communist party leaders plainly held a low opinion of the political level of the working class as a whole. They deliberately sought to create an elite party, separate and distinct from the masses it presumed to lead. This attitude has gradually changed, however, as the lower class has demonstrated a growing capacity to play an active role in national politics. The Communists are more determined than ever to establish the primacy of the party among the lower class, for they recognize that the proletariat is potentially the dominant political force in Latin America. They are still bent on maintaining the party as an elite organization, but they are convinced that it must be clearly identified with the common people. They have found it easy to attribute past mistakes and setbacks to the low level of proletarian consciousness among party leaders or to the party having lost touch with the masses. This line of reasoning has led them to the conclusion that the party must attract a higher proportion of members from the proletariat. Thus, the Communists consistently direct their strongest appeals to the working class of Latin America, particularly to the factory, transport, and maritime workers, who constitute the "true proletariat" in the Marxist view.

Heavy concentration on the urban working class is by no means restricted to the Communists of Latin America. The urban workers were the first to be organized into trade unions and, however reluctantly, to acquire the habit of paying dues. For decades organized labor has been a prime target of most of the political parties, since the party or individual who gains control of the trade unions gains both an important source of funds and a strategically located mass following that can be manipulated for partisan purposes.

The Communists have competed vigorously, and, on the whole, effectively, for positions of leadership in the labor movement. Frequently they have taken the initiative in establishing unions and federations among unorganized workers. Invariably, their objective has been to convert the labor organization into a political appendage of the party and to exploit it to the advantage of the party. In order to achieve this goal, Communist labor leaders have generally been careful to serve the immediate material interests of the union membership. By and large they have proved highly successful in securing the wage and contract benefits demanded by their labor following. They have often been even more effective in claiming responsibility for benefits granted by the government or extracted by labor leaders of other political persuasions. In these ways the Communists have lent credence to their claim that the party is concerned primarily for the welfare of the proletariat.

The response of the Latin American workers to the appeals of communism has varied from time to time and from party to party. As a general rule, during periods of open political activity the parties have absorbed relatively larger numbers of recruits from the working class than from other sectors of the population. On the other hand, these proletarian members have been among the first to drift away when the party has been repressed. Over the years, however, the proportion of working-class members in the Latin American Communist parties has gradually risen. It is probable that wage earners of all categories now constitute the majority of the rank and file in the Latin American communist movement as a whole. Total party membership, nonetheless, has never represented more than a small fraction of the entire labor movement in any country of Latin America.

Although the Communists might, in theory, prefer to limit their active labor following to the "true proletariat," as practical politicians they have made no serious attempts to do so. They have concentrated heavily on organizing workers in the vital food and service industries in the larger cities, since they recognize that the power to cause or avert strikes in these industries greatly enhances their bargaining position. To facilitate dissemination of the party line, particularly when they do not have open access to the press, radio, and television, the Communists have made a special effort to enlist recruits in the fields of communications and entertainment. These areas have consistently accounted for a disproportionate share of the total party membership.

Some of the most militant working-class supporters of the Communist party have been drawn from outside the urban labor force and from sectors that might not qualify as proletarian in a strict Marxist interpretation. The miners, plantation workers, and petroleum workers in much of Latin America are included in this category. The Communists were among the first to appreciate the political potential of such groups and, although they have not been able to hold all of their original gains, the party is still generally strong in these sectors. The Mexican communist artist David Alfaro Siqueiros organized and led the Miners' Federation of the State of Jalisco in the 1920's, while the nitrate miners of northern Chile have been a bulwark of the Communist party since the days of Luis Emilio Recabarren. Communist labor organizers were the first to win the sympathies of banana-plantation workers in Costa Rica and of oil-field hands in Venezuela. In nearly every other country of Latin America the Communists have drawn support from comparable groups. Despite the range of occupations represented, all these groups share common characteristics that make them attractive to the party. In organization, outlook, and aspirations they resemble the urban proletariat far more than they do the traditional rural lower class. Although they are usually located at some distance from centers of population, they are accessible and are concentrated in relatively large numbers. They receive wages and so are included in the money economy. In the great majority of instances they are employed by foreign companies, principally firms with headquarters in the United States. Thus, they have an identifiable, alien employer who is easily transformed in Communist propaganda into an enemy of the nation and exploiter of the local populace. It is significant that the Communists have generally not been permitted to make important gains among the employees of oil industries owned by the state or of mines and plantations owned by local capitalists. In Cuba, where such enterprises have been nationalized, Communist labor leaders subordinate the interests of the workers to those of the state.

Another of the myths that the Communists are now seeking to convert into reality is the long-standing claim that the party represents the peasants of Latin America. Since the day of the feeble "worker-peasant blocs" in the mid-1920's, Communists have been proclaiming their intention to establish governments of workers and peasants, implying that the two groups are of equal stature in the eyes of the party. In fact, however, during most of its history the Communist movement in Latin America has shown little interest in the rural lower class. The Communist party, like most other parties in the area, was overwhelmingly urban in composition and outlook. Its leaders were neither able nor willing to sustain the effort required to surmount geographical and psychological barriers separating them from the peasantry. The principal obstacle was their inability to communicate with the illiterate and apathetic rural masses, who played little if any role in national politics and whose expectations for change were even lower than their standard of living.

In the two decades before World War II the Communists of Latin America had an excellent opportunity to build a peasant following, for few other political groups were paying any attention to the rural masses. Yet, only for a brief moment in El Salvador, and in Mexico where indigenous revolutionary groups had already aroused the hopes and political awareness of the peasantry, did the Communists encounter even temporary success in creating a peasant-party apparatus. In the rest of the area their indifference and inability to comprehend the peasant mentality prevented them from generating enthusiasm for the party among the rural lower class.

Since the second world war several factors have coincided to bring about a gradual change in the condition of the peasants and the Communist attitude toward them. Considerable improvements in transportation and communications have served to reduce the physical and intellectual isolation of many rural communities, while in most countries parties of the center and left have launched competing campaigns to incorporate the rural inhabitants into the political life of the nation. Within the Communist movement a few prominent figures were inspired by the victory of the peasant-based Communist party in China, and suggested that the Latin American parties might well draw valuable lessons from the Chinese experience. The Guatemalan Communists sought openly to create a Chinese-style armed peasant force in the latter days of the Arbenz regime, and the Brazilian party began sending a few organizers into rural districts at about the same time. On the whole, however, the Latin American Communists remained largely indifferent to the rural masses until the success of Castro's revolution in Cuba.

The Cuban example demonstrated to the satisfaction of Communists and other leftists throughout the area that a revolutionary movement using guerrilla tactics and appealing to the recently aroused aspirations of the peasants could come to power against overwhelming odds in Latin America. The fact that peasants did not play a decisive role in the essentially urban, middle-class revolt against Batista was widely ignored, inasmuch as Castro initially claimed—and was believed—to have led a successful agrarian-based revolution. In any case, it quickly became evident that the promise of wholesale land reform and a dramatic rise in social status have an almost irresistible appeal to the landless throughout Latin America. The ease with which the Cuban Communist party seized credit for and substantial control over the Cuban revolution gave the Latin American Communists a tremendous psychological boost. Since 1959, inspired by what they believe the Cuban model to be, Communists in most of the region have been sustaining a concerted drive to win a mass rural following, attempting to take over existing peasant organizations and to establish new ones.

In the present situation, therefore, the party has both a genuine interest in the peasants and an appeal certain to excite their expectations. But the opportunity to pose convincingly as the only saviour of the downtrodden-peasant masses has passed. After generations of neglect the peasants may now choose among a broad range of parties, all employing virtually the same demagogic approach. This situation may facilitate Communist penetration of peasant groups organized by other parties, but it hampers Communist recruitment efforts in the rural areas. Under the circumstances, in spite of the attention the Communist party belatedly lavishes on them, peasants still account for only an insignificant minority in the Latin American Communist movement.

In Communist demonology the middle class—the despised *bourgeoisie*—is the first and foremost enemy of the people. The Latin American Communists have consistently echoed the approved Marxist-Leninist preachments on the evils of the middle class, haranguing against "bourgeois mentality," ridiculing "bourgeois morality," satirizing middle-class concern for the rights of the individual, and denouncing "bourgeois greed for profits" at the expense of the proletariat. Since the movement began in Latin America the publications of every Communist party and the public statements of every prominent Communist spokesman have been riddled with such phrases. Yet, virtually every Communist party in Latin America has drawn most of its effective leaders and its most militant members from the very class that it professes to hold in contempt.

This obvious disparity between theory and application causes the Communists little public concern. The same Marxism-Leninism which teaches hatred for the *bourgeoisie* has supplied the formulas for rationalizing inconsistency between word and practice. In the first place, it is accepted that class origin per se does not bar an individual from membership in the party. Any person, regardless of social background, may be qualified to become a Communist, provided he is capable of placing the interests of the masses above his class interests and personal welfare. Within the broad limits of Marxist-Leninist doctrine, moreover, the expression "bourgeoisie" is subject to somewhat elastic interpretation. In response to practical situations that have faced Communist parties everywhere, international Communist theoreticians have found it necessary and convenient to refine and re-define the term to meet the political exigencies of the moment. Contempt and suspicion of the middle class remain a central tenet of Marxism-Leninism, but some sectors of the middle class are clearly more contemptible than others. In practice the individual Communist parties in Latin America are allowed considerable latitude in recruiting from and cooperating with segments of the *bourgeoisie,* as immediate circumstances dictate.

The Latin American Communists tend to classify the various sectors of the *bourgeoisie* primarily according to size and source of income. In general, the higher the income, the higher the level of resistance and opposition to the party, but when further distinction must be drawn the source of an individual's wealth is more significant than the amount. A middle-income landlord, for example, might well be more hostile to the party than the owner of a large manufacturing plant.

In the Communist view the *petit bourgeois* white-collar workers are the most attractive, or least suspect, sector of the middle class. This sector includes employees in commercial firms, school teachers, bank workers, medium- and low-level bureaucrats, and others whose income is derived from modest salaries rather than from property. The *petit bourgeoisie* is regarded as the middle-class element closest to the masses—and therefore extremely susceptible to communist appeals—because it suffers from the same economic pressures that oppress the proletariat. This group appears to provide the bulk of the middle-class membership in the Communist parties of Latin America.

Comparable in economic status but much less reliable politically, from the Communist point of view, are the small shopkeepers and artisans whose clientele is drawn chiefly from low-income groups. For although this sector's standard of living places it on substantially the same level with wage earners and low-salaried employees, it is capitalistic in that its livelihood depends on profits. In most respects it shares the economic plight of the proletariat and can be expected to endorse at least some of the political objectives of the Communist party. In a few of the smaller parties, such as those of Central America, this lower–middle-class element accounts for a significant portion of the total membership.

Artists, intellectuals, professionals, and higher-level bureaucrats comprise a separate small sector of the *bourgeoisie* that has always been a prime target of the Latin American Communist parties. The individuals in this group ordinarily have several occupations and sources of income, including private practice, university professorships, positions in government agencies, and investments in real estate. Thus, they are capitalists by definition, but their income is seldom derived directly from what the Communists call "monopoly capitalism." In Communist eyes they have the great advantage of being deeply concerned with questions of social justice, economic development, and national sovereignty, while their lack of ties with large national and foreign enterprises permits them to view national problems "realistically." Relatively more individuals from this group than from any other sector of the middle class are responsive to the appeals of communism. The bulk of these remain outside the party but participate actively in Communist-front organizations. The select few who become party militants account for much of the leadership of every Communist party in Latin America. As a general rule, at least half the Communist leadership is from this group, and the proportion is higher in the smaller parties.

The Communists divide the remainder of the Latin American middle class into two broad categories, distinguished by attitude toward "imperialism" rather than by economic status. The first, which they call the "national *bourgeoisie*," is comprised largely of owners and managers of firms that compete against foreign imports and foreign-owned enterprises in Latin America. The Communists regard this "patriotic" sector as at best a temporary and vacillating ally, since it is opposed to any significant change in the condition of the proletariat. It can ordinarily be expected, however, to support ultranationalistic campaigns and demands for expanded trade with the Soviet bloc. This sector contains a large percentage of the anonymous "friends of the party," who are an important source of funds for the Communist movement, but it provides few active sympathizers and virtually no recruits to the party anywhere in Latin America.

The second group is the *entreguista* middle class, so-called for its alleged willingness to "hand over" the resources and sovereignty of Latin America to "Yankee imperialism."[1] In the Communist analysis of Latin America society, this minority group shades imperceptibly into the "reactionary" upper class of bankers, large industrialists, merchants in the import-export trade, and large landowners. On occasion it is possible for the party to take advantage of "secondary contradictions" between elements of this group and their imperialist allies, but on the whole it is regarded as the implacable enemy of the party and of the masses. Even this group, nonetheless, includes friends of the party, who seem to look upon contributions to the Communist movement as a form of insurance.

It is significant that a sector which has supplied much of the leadership of the Latin American Communist parties is rarely described by Com-

---

[1] The expression *entreguista*, used in both Spanish America and Brazil, is derived from the verb *entregar*, to hand over or surrender. As employed by Communists it has a highly derogatory meaning tantamount to treason.

munists in terms of class origin or social status. This sector is comprised of university students, one of the most articulate and politically alert elements of Latin American society. Although students in Latin America are drawn preponderantly from upper- and middle-class families, the Communists assume, on the whole correctly, that during their student years their political attitudes and actions will not be determined primarily by financial or class interests. Rather, their highly developed nationalism, their sensitivity to social and economic injustice, and the long tradition of student participation in politics will make them prone to use political action to change the *status quo*. In the Communist view, while they are students they are opponents of the classes from which they come. This characteristic sets them apart, if only temporarily, from the rest of society and gives them an importance to the Communists on a par with that of workers and peasants.

In actual fact, only a small minority of the university-student body in Latin America has ever subscribed fully to the Communist program for social, economic, and political change. This small group, however, has consistently been large enough to serve as a reservoir of potential Communist party leaders throughout the area. At least half the current leaders of the Latin American parties first entered the Communist movement in their student days.

The Latin American Communists have an ambivalent attitude toward the armed forces, whom they regard as another special group outside the usual class structure. They regularly describe the military establishments as organs of repression in the service of the state, even while insisting that these could become "progressive" forces in the "democratic struggle for national liberation." The Communist press is quick to denounce traditional militarism, but praises all indications of military sympathy for the aspirations of the people. In general the Communists feel that the army is the military service closest to the masses and thus most susceptible to the appeals of the party. The victory of Castro's guerrilla forces over the professional army in Cuba has not reduced Communist efforts to attract members from the armed forces in the rest of Latin America.

Through their campaigns against "imperialism" and for "national emancipation," the Communists appeal to the professional concern of military officers for the defense of national sovereignty and expansion of the national economy. A significant number of ultranationalistic officers in several countries has temporarily, and sometimes inadvertently, made common cause with Communists in "anti-imperialist" propaganda campaigns involving demands for an "independent" foreign policy, nationalization of public utilities and natural resources, or acceptance of

Soviet assistance for economic development. A much smaller group, made up chiefly of retired army officers, has long been conspicuous in the leadership of a broad range of international Communist-front organizations. Nevertheless, with a few major exceptions, as in El Salvador and Brazil during the 1930's and in Venezuela since 1960, the Communists have failed to persuade commissioned or noncommissioned officers to join them in revolutionary adventures.

Women comprise only a small segment of the total membership of the Latin American Communist parties. This is a matter of continuing concern to party leaders, who emphasize the desirability and need to attract more women into the Communist ranks. Most of the parties maintain several special-interest front organizations designed to appeal to housewives, working women, female students, and women in the professions. Nearly every party has a sprinkling of women in the leadership and, wherever possible, includes women among its candidates for public office. This tendency has been most highly developed in Argentina, Chile, Uruguay, and Brazil, where the participation of women in politics is widely accepted. Even in these countries, however, no more than 10 to 15 per cent of the Communist party members are women.

The foregoing groups and classes of society supply the leaders, members, and sympathizers of the Communist movement throughout Latin America. Thus, even though no two parties are identical in the number or proportion of members from the various social categories, the composition of the movement is remarkably uniform from country to country. The parties are overwhelmingly urban. With rare exceptions the top leadership is comprised of men of middle-class origin and men who have risen to middle-class status. In nearly every instance the great bulk of the membership is drawn from the lower middle class and the upper strata of the working class. Without exception the peasantry contributes only a small percentage of the Communist party rank and file.

The rank-and-file Communists in all parts of Latin America have several basic attitudes in common. They are sufficiently ambitious to be dissatisfied with their lot. They have enough education and awareness of the world around them to realize that their social and economic conditions can be improved. As a result they are impatient for immediate and sweeping change in the *status quo*. These attitudes, of course, are shared by millions of Latin Americans who do not become Communists. The motivations and avowed objectives of Communists and non-Communist leftists are often indistinguishable. The characteristics that set the Communists apart are their complete loss of faith in the democratic process as known in Latin America and their readiness to destroy the established order to achieve their objectives.

Above all, the Communists are a dedicated minority. To a considerable extent their numerical weakness is offset by their high degree of dedication to the cause, willingness to submit to rigid discipline, and subordination of everything else to the party. These qualities make them unique in Latin America. No other party in the area is so demanding of its members or is able to instill in them such a great measure of loyalty and confidence in ultimate victory. In their faith and fanaticism the unreligious Communists are more like members of a zealous missionary order than are the followers of other Latin American political parties.

These qualities, required of all Communist militants, are reinforced at every turn by the party. Every Communist is expected to make communism his way of life, and the demands upon his time and energies are usually such that he must comply or leave the movement. Each Communist, regardless of his position in the party, is expected to be an active member of a cell in his neighborhood or place of employment. In addition, he is expected to contribute dues regularly, to buy and read the party press faithfully, to take part in a continuing round of Marxist-Leninist study groups, and to give unstintingly of his time whenever called upon to perform any of a myriad of party tasks, such as distribution of propaganda leaflets, painting of wall slogans, attendance at public rallies, or participation in street demonstrations, riots, and the like.

It is evident from the Communist record that these high standards have never been fully met by all of the rank and file. Exhortations against apathy and inertia among the members have been a recurrent theme in the party press since the early days of the Communist movement in Latin America. For a variety of reasons the great majority of the recruits that have joined the party in the past four decades have proved unable to sustain the required level of enthusiasm for the Communist cause over a long period of time. There has been a fairly steady loss of members who drifted away out of boredom, because of refusal to follow a sudden reversal of the party line, or to avoid the disadvantages of party membership during the periods of repression. Although attrition has been heaviest among the rank and file, it has affected all levels of the party to a greater or lesser degree. By and large such losses have been compensated by the addition of new members whose hopes and illusions have not yet been dimmed, but over any ten-year period the turnover in party members throughout Latin America has been on the order of 60 per cent. In times of crisis it has been even higher in individual parties. As a result the Communist movement in Latin America is marked by a predominance of young, enthusiastic, and relatively inexperienced members.

Even during periods of extreme repression, a portion of the members has remained constant to form the hard core of the party. These are the Communist militants whose dedication and loyalty have been established beyond question, often in the underground or in exile. They constitute a separate, elite group within the membership and are formally recognized as such in the statutes of some of the parties. The existence of the militant hard core accounts in large part for the accordion-like capacity of the Communist parties to expand or contract rapidly in response to the circumstances of the moment.

The proportion of militants to total membership varies according to the conditions under which the party operates. Ordinarily, when the Communists have legal status or freedom of action, militants represent from one-third to one-tenth of the total. On the other hand, during times of repression, they may account for virtually the entire membership. The experience of the Cuban party is typical in this respect. In the last years of World War II, when the party was claiming some 150,000 followers, only 25,000 were considered militants. By 1958, after serious reverses and five years of illegality, the party was reduced to about twelve thousand active members, practically all of whom qualified as militants. The bulk of those hard-core members who had been jailed, exiled, or otherwise neutralized during the second Batista regime, appear to have resumed active status when party fortunes improved in 1959. This same pattern has recurred in all of the Latin American Communist parties that have exerted even marginal influence in national politics.

In contrast to the continuous process of renewal of rank-and-file members, there has been remarkable continuity in Latin American Communist leadership. The top leaders are predominantly "old" Communists, both in years and experience. The majority of the party presidents, Secretaries-General, and key Central Committee members have been active Communists for twenty-five years or more. In at least six of the parties—those of Argentina, Brazil, Costa Rica, Cuba, Paraguay, and Venezuela—the same individual or clique has held sway for over a quarter of a century, and in Uruguay party-founder Eugenio Gómez dominated for thirty-four years before his ouster in 1955. The record for longevity is shared by Victorio Codovilla and Rodolfo Ghioldi, both of whom in 1963 still led the Argentine party they had founded forty-five years earlier. Other party founders who hold key positions in their organizations are Obdulio Barthe, of Paraguay; Gustavo and Eduardo Machado, of Venezuela; and Manuel Mora, of Costa Rica. These men, and David Alfaro Siqueiros, titular head of the Mexican party, all entered the Communist movement in the 1920's. A listing of Communists who have played leading roles in the party since the 1930's includes Luiz Carlos Prestes, the Brazilian Communist chief; Luis Corvalán Leppe, Secretary-General of the Chilean party; Gilberto Vieira White, of Colombia; Blas Roca, of Cuba; and Uruguayan party leader Rodney Arismendi. Most of the remaining Latin American Communist leaders rose to prominence in the party during or soon after the second world war.

The disparity between the long tenure of the top leadership and the comparative youth and inexperience of members at lower levels of the party—characteristic of the Communist movement throughout Latin America—is pointed up in the report of the Fourth National Congress of the Communist Party of Brazil. In a sense this Congress, held in November 1954, was a meeting of the party elite, for it excluded all members of less than two years standing and those who did not hold office above the cell level. Yet, even within this select group fewer than one-third of the delegates had been party members for over ten years. The proportions were reversed among Central Committee members, where more than two-thirds had been active in the party for a decade or longer, and well over half had been Communists for at least twenty years. The median age of the delegates was thirty-six years; that of Central Committee members was at least ten years higher. The age gap between leaders and followers has tended to widen since 1954, as many of the members of the Central Committee at that time continue to occupy high posts in the Brazilian party.

The Communist movement in Latin America has attracted leaders of somewhat different backgrounds and widely varying personalities. An indication of the range of diversity among them may be seen in the careers of Victorio Codovilla, Luiz Carlos Prestes, and Blas Roca. Codovilla, an Italian who migrated to Argentina before World War I, was the first important figure to emerge as a leader of Latin American communism. His reputation stems as much from his activities in the international Communist bureaucracy as from his role in the Argentine party. Codovilla appears to have had no profession or occupation other than that of a paid party official since 1917. His facility for anticipating shifts in the Soviet power structure and for currying favor with the dominant faction in the Kremlin has not been surpassed by any Communist leader in Latin America or elsewhere. As head of the earliest and largest Communist organization in the Western Hemisphere, he soon became the principal Latin American adviser to the Comintern. He was a member of the first Latin American Secretariat in Moscow and Treasurer of that body when it was transferred to Buenos Aires, as the South American Bureau, in 1928. Codovilla went into exile when the Argentine party was suppressed in 1930. He remained out of the country until early in 1941, serving for several years on the Comintern staff in Moscow and as a Comintern agent in Spain during the civil war in that country. In 1940, on his return to Latin America, he is reported to have conveyed Soviet directives for the expulsion of Mexican Communist leaders, Valentín Campa and Hernán Laborde. Following the revolution of 1943, Codovilla was again exiled—this time to Chile—but returned to Argentina in 1945. In the postwar period Codovilla has usually represented the Argentine party at international Communist gatherings. Probably because of his frequent absences, he has not held the office of Secretary-General of the party for many years, but continues on the party's Executive Bureau.

Luiz Carlos Prestes, of Brazil, is unique among Latin American communist leaders in that he has military background and had earned a national reputation as a revolutionary before he became a Communist. Born in 1898, the son of an army captain who died shortly thereafter, Prestes was raised in poverty. He graduated from the military academy with honors in 1918 but did not attract public notice until 1924, when he led a rebel column on a prolonged campaign through the Brazilian hinterland seeking to inspire a popular revolution. Although he failed in his objective and went into exile in 1927, Prestes gained nationwide fame and the sobriquet Knight of Hope, which he carried with him into the Communist camp three years later. Refusing an offer of amnesty by the new Brazilian government, in 1931 he went to the Soviet Union, where he remained for about four years being groomed for his future role as head of the Communist movement in Brazil. He returned to Brazil in 1935 to direct the left-wing National Liberation Alliance and the ill-fated uprising against the Vargas regime in November of that year. Prestes was captured and sent to prison, where he languished for nine years, until he was released under a general amnesty in 1945. During the two years that the party enjoyed legal status, Prestes supervised its highly successful recruitment drive and was largely responsible for attracting half a million votes for party candidates in the elections of 1945 and 1947. He won the only Communist seat in the Senate, which he held until January 1948, when the mandates of all Communists in public office were canceled. Prestes then went underground for a decade but maintained close control over the clandestine party and represented it periodically at international Communist meetings. When he emerged from obscurity in 1958 to lend support to a flagging electoral campaign, it was soon evident that his popular appeal had waned. Within the party, however, he has retained full authority and the loyalty of the rank and file. Opponents who challenged his leadership in 1957 and 1960 have been systematically isolated and expelled. There are indications that over the years Prestes has had somewhat more freedom than other Latin American Communist leaders to modify Soviet directives to meet local conditions. Nonetheless, he has never pursued a course opposed to current Soviet foreign-policy objectives, regardless of the immediate impact on the Brazilian party.

Blas Roca is one of the few top Latin American Communists drawn from the proletariat. He was born Francisco Calderío, of a working-class family in Manzanillo, Cuba, in 1908. He joined the Communist party before 1930 and distinguished himself as a labor activist. He took the name Blas Roca—his favorite alias in the Communist underground—before becoming Secretary-General of the party in 1934. Roca's elevation to the highest post in the party at age twenty-six appears to have been arranged by Fabio Grobart, the Comintern agent delegated to purge the Cuban Communist organization following its poor showing in the 1933 revolution. His rapid rise in international Communist circles was marked in 1935 by his appointment as an alternate member of the Comintern's Executive Committee. In Soviet eyes he apparently ranked with Rodolfo Ghioldi—the only other Latin American among the alternate members—next to Luiz Carlos Prestes, who was a full member of the Executive Committee. An excellent organizer and flexible tactician, Roca has proved worthy of Soviet confidence. In the three decades of his reign he has converted the inconsequential Communist party into a cohesive political force through rigid discipline and timely cooperation with Cuban strong men Fulgencio Batista and Fidel Castro. Communist gains during the first Batista regime—legal status, control of organized labor, and a voice in national affairs—have now been overshadowed by the success of Roca's policy of apparent subordination to Fidel Castro. With the incorporation of the party into Castro's United Party of the Socialist Revolution, Roca has formally surrendered leadership of the Communists to the Cuban dictator. He remains, however, on the directorate of the new political body and a prominent spokesman for Cuban communism in international Communist circles.

The similarities between the Latin American Communist leaders are more striking than the characteristics that distinguish them from each other. Without exception the leaders of the Latin American parties are professiosal Communists in the full meaning of the expression. They have been trained in the Soviet Union, and many of them have served for prolonged periods as officials in the international Communist bureaucracy in Latin America or Europe. They are steeped in Marxist-Leninist doctrine and have learned to interpret every political development affecting their country or the party in Marxist-Leninist terms. For the sake

of their political convictions they have endured oppression, imprisonment, and exile from their native land. More significantly, they have
survived drastic purges and dramatic reversals and counterreversals of
international Communist policy. They occupy positions of leadership
because they have proved adept at anticipating and rationalizing Soviet-
dictated departures from past Communist policies and at making such
departures palatable to the rank and file. Within the limits of Marxist-
Leninist doctrine, as formulated at any particular time by the head
of the Communist Party of the Soviet Union, the Latin American leaders
have shown themselves to be completely flexible— so much so that their
enemies accuse them of an absolute lack of political principles. Yet,
they have been inflexible in refusing every opportunity to reject Soviet
tutelage or to withdraw from the international movement, even when
such actions appeared to serve the immediate interests of the local party.
In short, their careers are fully identified with the international Communist movement as directed by the Soviet Union.

Conditions Favoring the Rise of Communism in Latin America*

ROBERT J.
ALEXANDER

Communism breeds on discontent. Discontent is the historical background for the Communist movement in Latin America. Conditions of
life in most countries south of the Rio Grande are still backward, poor,
and in many cases oppressive. Wages are low; chances for advancement
are limited; class and racial barriers are high. Yet this pattern is changing, and changing rapidly. For more than a generation there has been
a widespread revolt against traditional conditions. The Industrial Revolution and social revolutions come hand-in-hand. It is this movement of
revolt that the Communists have tried to exploit.

Latin America is still a predominantly agricultural region, in spite
of the tremendous strides towards industrialization which have been
taken since World War I. In many regions, agriculture has been truly

* Robert J. Alexander, *Communism in Latin America* (New Brunswick, New
Jersey: Rutgers University Press, 1957), pp. 3–17.

feudal in its landholding patterns, and class differences have been intensified by a racial distinction between the landlord class and the tenants
or peons.

Medieval methods of exploitation of land and labor have been particularly prevalent in the Indian countries: Peru, Ecuador, Bolivia, Guatemala, and Mexico. In the first two countries, these conditions still exist,
though in the other three, more or less thorough moves have been made
in recent years to abolish them.

In these countries, where Indians make up the great mass of the
agricultural tenants and peons, there has been a struggle, ever since
the Conquest, between white or mestizo (half Indian-half white) landlords and Indian agricultural communities, a battle in which the Indians
have been generally the losers. The Indian has had little standing in
the courts of law, and although in colonial times the King and, to a
lesser degree, the Church sought to afford him some protection, the
instruments of government have been largely in the hands of the Indian's
oppressors. As a result, it was for centuries a comparatively simple procedure for the landlords to steal, bit by bit, the holdings of the Indian
communities.

Those Indians who came under the control of the white and mestizo
landlords were as good as bound to the soil. They were granted a bit
of land upon which to grow their corn and beans, but in return for
this were obliged to till the soil of the landlord gratis. Until recent
years, the Indians of Bolivia were obliged to spend six days a week
thus laboring on the lands of their "patrons."

In these Indian countries and in most others, the personal relations
between the landlord and his tenants and laborers were those of master
and servant. It is still true in much of rural Chile that tenants and
laborers must take off their hats in the presence of their employer. Any
attempt to argue about the conditions under which they labor is regarded as "subversive." Much the same conditions obtain in rural Brazil,
and until recent years were widespread in Argentina.

The income of most of the agricultural workers and tenants in Latin
America has been hopelessly low. Most of the population of Latin
America is still "out of the market"; that is to say, they receive little,
if any, money income with which to purchase the output of manufacturing industries, native or foreign.

They live in more or less self-sufficient communities, where they grow
most of their own food supply—a food supply which leaves most of
them victims of malnutrition and the diseases which it breeds. They
build their own huts of mud and wattle, or clapboard or sometimes
stone; often they produce all or part of their own clothing. Such food

and clothing as they cannot produce for themselves, they get in the local village, where purchase is often by barter rather than cash.

Most Latin Americans have little acquaintance with those material things which have become necessities in more advanced countries. Many, if not most, of them have never seen a moving picture. Scarcely any agricultural workers own radios, though in some cases they have become familiar with them through public loud-speakers in the village.

Until recent years, few rural workers of Latin America had travelled more than a few miles from their native village. Medical attention is still minimal, and incantations and local herbs have been the only protection against or cure for disease. Although scourges such as plague, yellow fever, smallpox, and more recently malaria have given way before growing public health services, many, if not most, of the rural workers and tenants of Latin America still suffer more or less constantly from diseases caused by intestinal parasites and undernourishment.

Of course, there have been exceptions to this state of affairs. The workers in the more modern forms of agricultural activity, particularly those producing commodities for sale in the world market, have lived under better circumstances. In the sugar fields of Cuba, Puerto Rico, and the northern part of the Pacific coast of South America, employers have been forced to pay their labor money wages, and have found it to their own advantage to provide the health services which will assure healthy workers, who can do a full day's labor. In Cuba and Puerto Rico, too, strong labor movements have grown up, which have greatly modified the ancient subservience of the agricultural worker to his employer.

The great plantations of the United and Standard Fruit Companies of Central America and the West Indies have also brought a different way of living for agricultural workers. They have not only provided excellent health services, they have built houses which are a considerable improvement over the huts from which these workers originally came, and are good even when compared with the habitations of the average Latin American city worker. These agricultural workers, also, have come into closer contact with the amenities of modern civilization: plumbing, schools, motion pictures. These companies have, however, found it hard to learn to treat their people as anything more than children who must be housed, fed, doctored, and entertained.

In recent years many agricultural workers have sought liberation by fleeing to the cities. The cities of Latin America have grown phenomenally in the last three decades. Mexico City, for instance, has more than quadrupled in size since the beginning of the Mexican Revolution in 1910, and has doubled since the middle 1930's. São Paulo has grown almost as fast and has become the biggest city in Brazil and the second largest in South America.

This tremendous increase in the population of Latin American cities has occurred in exactly the period during which the countries concerned have cut off immigration from abroad, so all the increase in urban population has come by reason of migration from the countryside. The East Coast countries of South America have, as a result, been faced with a serious shortage of agricultural workers.

Although the move of the Latin American worker from the countryside to urban industry has not as yet brought him a standard of living comparable to those of the workers of the more advanced industrial nations, it has brought him new social and economic freedom. The Latin American urban worker does not have the servile attitude of the agricultural tenant or wage worker. He is a man, a citizen, and often a trade union member, not a serf. With this improved status and greater freedom has come a desire to improve his position still more.

Insofar as the story of the Communists in Latin America is concerned, this increased independence and feeling of unrest of the urban workingman is more important than his actual low standards of living, and much more important than the lower standards of his rural brothers. For the movement of social unrest and revolt which has swept Latin America since World War I has been, with some few exceptions, an urban development.

The city has been in revolt against the chains which custom, history, and the law have imposed upon it. Conscious of its increased economic power, it has been unwilling to be content any longer with a secondary role in the life of the nations of the continent.

The social classes which have been particularly active in the Latin American social revolution have been the working class, both the white-collar and the manual workers, and the growing industrial (and to some degree commercial) middle class. It was their voices, their votes, their money, and their strong right arms, which, upon occasion, broke the crust of the landholder-dominated, semifeudal Latin American society of the days before World War I.

The Latin American social revolution has had four basic components: nationalism, economic development, change in class relationships, and political democracy. The Communists have tried with greater or less success to use each and all of these factors in their propaganda and organization.

As nationalism has spread in the modern world, Latin America has caught the infection. Generally, the growing nationalism of Latin America has taken the form of a desire to be "free" from real or alleged subservience to certain of the Great Powers. This has often led to a feeling of unity among the Latin Americans themselves, and perhaps helps to explain why growing nationalism has not more often been turned against Latin American neighbors.

Latin American nationalism has been largely "anti-imperialism." During World War I and the post-World War I period, it centered on the struggle against United States interference in the internal affairs of the Latin American countries, against United States invasions of Nicaragua, Mexico, the Dominican Republic, Haiti, and other countries, and against evidences of Latin American subservience to the United States, such as the infamous Platt Amendment to the Cuban constitution.

With the Good Neighbor Policy, and the agreement by the United States to recognize the juridical equality of all of the American nations, the emphasis shifted from opposing overt intervention by the United States Government to resisting what many Latin Americans conceived to be the intervention by United States private business interests in the internal affairs of their nations.

There developed a widespread resentment toward foreign ownership of key elements in the Latin American economy. Expropriation of United States agricultural and petroleum interests in Mexico and of American petroleum interests in Bolivia before World War II, as well as repatriation of British and French investments in the public utilities and railroads of Argentina, Uruguay, and Brazil after World War II, were evidences of this feeling.

The two World Wars and the Great Depression undoubtedly fed the fires of nationalism in Latin America. During World War II, in particular, the Latin Americans were actively courted by both sides. They also were impressed with the importance to the Allied war effort of their provision of key raw materials and supplies. The importance of their role was even more evident to the citizens of Brazil and Mexico, because of the participation of their forces in the victorious armies.

The wars and the depression particularly aroused economic nationalism. The Latin American countries, whose role in the world economy had been largely that of producers of agricultural and mineral raw materials, became painfully aware of the dangers of an economy based on one or two such products.

In both wars and the depression, the Latin American countries had difficulty both in selling their mineral and agricultural products and in obtaining the manufactured goods which they needed from the industrial nations of Europe and North America. Those experiences convinced most thinking Latin Americans that their nations must become more self-sufficient. They became eager to diversify their countries' economies, and in particular to develop manufacturing industries.

This drive for economic development has become an integral part of the Latin American social revolution. Since the early 1930's, it has become almost an article of faith. Few politicians in the region would dare openly to proclaim opposition to industrialization and economic diversification. Virtually all of the countries have provided protection for infant industries, either through old-fashioned tariffs or through more newfangled exchange control devices. Many of the countries have established development banks or corporations, which have brought the government into active participation in the process of economic development.

The net result of this growing economic diversification has been to strengthen the urban against the rural elements in the economic and political life of the Latin American nations. It has also hastened the demands for fundamental redistribution of power in the economies and politics of the Latin American nations.

This class realignment is the third fundamental feature of the Latin American social revolution. It has taken two principal forms: a demand for agrarian reform, and moves to strengthen the position of the urban worker by organizing him for his self-defense and writing legislation on his behalf.

With the exception of Mexico, agrarian reform has at first been urged and promulgated by city folk. However, it has been the means of involving the agricultural worker and tenant in the civic and economic life of his community and nation. It is likely that pressure will come, increasingly, from the agricultural worker himself for an extension of agrarian reform in such parts of the region as it has not yet encompassed.

The growth of the trade union movement and of protective legislation has also been an integral part of the realignment of classes. It has been closely associated with the nationalist drive, since the first large conglomerations of wageworkers were usually those employed by foreign enterprises—railroads, public utilities, mines, factory farms, and manufacturing enterprises—and labor organization thus took on a patriotic coloration. Union organizations, strikes, and other movements aimed against foreign-owned enterprises were often able to enlist a general sympathy in the community which they probably never would have aroused had the firms involved been owned and operated by nationals.

Labor legislation and trade unionism have been surprisingly advanced for the type of economy which Latin America has possessed. By the end of World War II there was virtually no nation in Latin America which did not have its Labor Code—detailing the treatment of labor in factory legislation, social security, regulation of collective bargaining, and support and control of trade unions.

In virtually every nation the great majority of "organizable" workers—

those on railroads, docks, and ships, in factories, in public utilities, even in many factory farms—are now in trade unions. These workers' organizations are still weak, being too dependent upon the good will of a political party or the State, but they have succeeded in arousing the working class to its possibilities and, in a more limited way, to its responsibilities.

The growth of strong middle and working classes has had profound effects on the social, economic, and political structure of Latin America. In Mexico and Chile power over the State passed from the landholding aristocracy to the urban middle and working masses—though in the latter case, the city folk had not dared even by the 1950's to attack the aristocracy in its rural strongholds and carry out an effective agrarian reform.

In other countries, too, political power changed hands. The Vargas Revolution of 1930, despite all the subsequent vagaries, effectively took control of the national government out of the hands of the rural landholders, though there, as in Chile, the new political forces did not dare attack the aristocracy on its own home ground. The Perón Revolution, whatever else it brought, ended once and for all the control of the rural landlords and cattle barons over the destinies of Argentina.

The 1952 Revolution in Bolivia signalized the end of the feudal era in that country. Events since the death of Juan Vicente Gómez in 1936 have greatly undermined the position of the rural landholding element in Venezuela, though that unfortunate country had not by 1957 been able to throw off the century-old curse of military domination of political affairs.

In all the countries in which the shift in class power has begun, it is a continuing process, in most cases still far from completion. Even in Mexico, the Revolution which began in 1910 was still 45 years later a living and evolving phenomenon.

In some countries the shift in class relations had not occurred by the early 1950's. In Peru it lagged behind, the alliance of the military with the traditional landowning and mercantile classes keeping a firm if uneasy grip on the nation. Central America was still largely controlled by large landowners and military men. The dictatorship of Generalissimo Rafael Leónidas Trujillo had converted the traditional system of the Dominican Republic into a personal monopoly of power and wealth.

The shift in class relationships was accompanied by a struggle for political democracy. This is the fourth element in the Latin American social revolution.

The desire on the part of the masses of the people of Latin America for greater participation in the affairs of their government, and for the fundamental freedoms associated with political democracy, was profound indeed. However, the great danger in the Latin American social revolution has been that it might be diverted from democratic channels, that democracy might be sacrificed to achieve the other objectives of the revolution. This certainly occurred in Argentina under Perón. The Communists, too, have constantly sought—though frequently using democratic slogans—to direct the revolution into courses which would result in the establishment of their own particular brand of totalitarianism.

The Communists have consistently attempted to use all the slogans of the Latin American social revolution for their own propaganda. They have striven especially hard to portray themselves as ardent nationalists of the particular countries in which they were operating.

The Communists have embraced "anti-imperialism" with a vengeance. During most of their history they have been violently opposed to the United States' economic, political, and social influence in Latin America. Only during the late 1930's and the second part of World War II, when their "anti-imperialist" propaganda was directed against Axis influence in Latin America, have they modified their "anti-Yanquism."

During the 1920's and early 1930's the Communists had some success in enlisting Latin Americans in their world-wide campaign against "imperialism." Many Latin American intellectuals, including Haya de la Torre, people who were later active in the Venezuelan Democratic Action Party, and other non-Communists, were among the delegates to the World Congress Against War and Imperialism of 1928. Many of them continued to be active in the League Against Imperialism founded at the 1928 meeting and in the several Anti-War and Anti-Imperialist Congresses held in America.

Since World War II the Communist campaign against the United States in Latin America has been renewed with increased intensity. Campaigns "for peace" and "against Yanqui imperialism" became the principal preoccupation of the Latin American Communists.

In spite of the Latin American Communists' attempt to portray themselves as true-blue nationalists, it has been too obvious, in many instances, that their basic orientation was Russian, not Chilean or Brazilian or Argentine. This was particularly true during World War II. In the beginning they adopted a violent "anti-imperialist" position, aimed against the Allies and against the United States, and in some instances even bordered on anti-Semitism, so violent were their sympathies for the Axis.

Then, with the entry of the Soviet Union into the war, the Communists of Latin America, as everywhere else, adopted an equally violent pro-war attitude. So extreme was their position of "support for the United Nations," that they used their influence in the labor movement throughout the continent to put a damper on virtually all attempts at strikes and other movements upon the part of the organized workers. Frequently, such movements were denounced by the Communists as being of Nazi inspiration or worse.

During the war, too, they were less cautious about hiding their association with the Soviet Union. They tried to use the widespread sympathy for the Soviet Union's bitter struggle against the Nazis to aid their own positions in their respective countries. This tended to rebound upon them in later years, when popular sympathy for the Soviet Union had to a very considerable degree turned into hostility.

The Communists also have attempted to make use of the strong drive for economic development in the Latin American countries. This often fitted in very well with their opposition to the United States. They spread widely the idea that the United States was purposely trying to hold back the development of the Latin American countries. They were ardent advocates of the industrialization of Latin America and at the end of World War II went so far as virtually to advocate "calling off" the class struggle for a longer or shorter period of time, so as to form an alliance between the labor movements they controlled or influenced and the national employers' groups. At various times they toyed with the idea that the national employers were a "progressive" element in the economies of the various countries of Latin America, and sought to enlist their support in the campaign against United States influence in Latin America.

Of course, the Communists have attempted to take the leadership, when the opportunity presented itself, in upsetting traditional class relationships in Latin American countries. Their own doctrine has naturally made them seek a leading position in the trade union movements, and in some countries, such as Peru and Guatemala, Brazil and Cuba, they have attempted to develop support on the basis of appeals to suppressed racial groups—Indians in the first two instances, Negroes in the latter two.

From the early days the Communists have included in their programs demands for agrarian reform and other fundamental shifts in class and social relations in the Latin American countries. Only in Mexico and Guatemala have they had any real opportunity to take part in carrying out such changes, and in the former case they played only a very minor role.

At various times the Communists have attempted to theorize concerning the class changes which have been going on in Latin America. Their theories have varied with changes in the party line. Usually, however, they have urged that a bourgeois revolution of "national liberation" was the next step in the development of these countries; this was their line in Guatemala after World War II. However, they have also talked about a revolution which would result in the establishment of a "popular democracy" on the pattern of the early post-World War II regimes of Eastern Europe. This has been the line in Brazil and was adopted in Guatemala in the last months of the Arbenz regime. During the "Third Period" of the late 1920's and early 1930's the Communists tended to skip over the interim stages and seek the immediate establishment of an avowedly Communist regime. This was their line in Cuba, for instance, right after the fall of the Machado dictatorship in 1933, when they had the slogan of "Build the Soviets!" and actually attempted in some areas to establish their own governments on a local scale.

Finally, the Communists have attempted to capitalize on the fourth factor in the Latin American social revolution and depict themselves as supporters of democracy. There is no doubt that they have been severely persecuted by various Latin American governments from time to time, and they have pictured campaigns in defense of their own group as crusades for the general principles of political democracy and civil liberties. They laid particular stress on this role as defenders of the cause of democracy during World War II.

The Communists have thus attempted to use the rising tide of the Latin American social revolution as a means of bringing themselves to power. They have tried to seize the control of the revolutionary currents, and to divert them in the Communist direction. The surprising thing is not that they have occasionally succeeded in doing so, but rather that, in spite of the very profound feeling of revolt and change which has swept Latin America since World War I, the Communists have made comparatively little progress.

One of the key reasons why the Communists have not been more successful is that there have been other movements, of native Latin American origin, which have been able to seize and keep the leadership of the revolution in various countries. It is a very obvious fact that in any country in which there is another strong mass movement, the Communists have fared badly. Thus, in Peru, the Communists have never succeeded in getting any really wide base of support, and what importance they have had has come from the backing they have received from successive dictatorships. This has been due to the fact that the Aprista movement gained and held the support of the great masses of the people, who might otherwise have been influenced by Communist ideas and organization.

In Venezuela, too, the rise of the Democratic Action Party completely checked the progress of the Communists, and again the Communists' influence was largely something engendered by the dictators to act as a check on the influence of Democratic Action. In Cuba, the Auténtico movement had the same effect; in Costa Rica, the rise of the Liberación Nacional movement of José Figueres cut the very base out from under the Communists. In Puerto Rico the rise of the Popular Democratic Party of Muñoz Marín has undoubtedly prevented the Communists from getting a significant following.

Even in Argentina this same phenomenon has been repeated. The appearance of the Peronista movement in the middle 1940's undoubtedly had the result of checking the growing influence which the Communists had been enjoying inside and outside of the labor movement for about half a decade before the Peronista Revolution of 1943.

Chile and Guatemala further illustrate the fact that the best check for the Communists in Latin America has always been a native social revolutionary movement. The Communists in those two countries have been able to get real rank and file support and to wield tremendous influence on all aspects of the countries' life because of the lack of any such rival movement. In Chile such a movement existed in the decade of the 1930's, in the Socialist Party. However, as a result of a variety of circumstances the Socialist Party crumbled away, and the Communist Party gained an opportunity of which it made full use. Consequently, Chile was by the late 1940's one of the few countries in which the Communists had been able to build up a really substantial group of followers, who looked upon them as the only true defenders of the working class and the social revolution.

In Guatemala, the case was somewhat different, but equally informative. There, no rival social movement existed. As the result of peculiar circumstances, no leader and no party appeared able firmly to support and push forward the social revolution, but equally firmly reject Stalinism and all its works. As a consequence, in Guatemala the Communists achieved a degree of power which they probably have not obtained in any other Latin American nation and were able to build up a sizable body of popular support in the cities and in the countryside.

Those Latin American governments opposed to the social revolution have not infrequently worked with the Communists, in order to undermine the indigenous social revolutionary movements. This has been notoriously true of Peru and Venezuela. In the former country the Communists worked successively with the Sánchez Cerro, Benavides, Prado, and Odría dictatorships. In the elections of 1939 and 1950 Communists were elected to the dictator-controlled congress on the official ticket of the dictator. The Dictator-President Prado backed the Communists' bid for control of the labor movement, and General Odría in the late 1940's and early 1950's gave considerable help to the Communists in the labor movement.

In Venezuela, too, the dictatorial regimes opposed to the revolution worked with the Communists. While the democratically controlled trade unions were virtually destroyed after 1948, Communist-dominated unions continued to function with but little interference. Large public meetings were held by Communist trade unions, and they were allowed to hold regularly scheduled conventions. The work of the dictatorship was to turn control of a large part of the Venezuelan trade union movement over to the Communists.

Dictator Anastasio Somoza, of Nicaragua, and Dictator Generalissimo Rafael Leónidas Trujillo, of the Dominican Republic, both worked with the Communists during a short period in the middle 1940's, using them to bolster up their tottering dictatorships. In both of those countries the Communists got their first real chance as a result of this coquetting with the dictators.

The prevalence of dictatorial regimes in Latin America led to the development of a policy which may or may not have been consciously planned by the international Communist leaders responsible for the operations of the Communist Parties in Latin America. The widespread use of this new tactic, which was adopted in the late 1940's and early 1950's, makes it appear to be a well-designed, centrally directed move.

The tactic consisted of having more than one Communist Party in dictator-controlled countries. One party, usually the "official" one, engaged in more or less bitter opposition to the dictatorship; the other, "unofficial" but nonetheless, in actuality, just as official, supported the regime. This tactic was adopted in Argentina, Peru, Venezuela, and Cuba. In Mexico, more than one Communist Party was used, but for reasons which seem to be quite distinct from those in the other countries mentioned.

In Argentina the Communist Party had some difficulty making up its mind concerning what position to take in regard to Perón. At first, so long as World War II was on, they bitterly opposed Perón, coining the term "Peronazi" to describe his followers. However, after the war was over, and after Perón had been elected President of the Republic, they faltered. The official Party adopted a position of "critical support"; while a dissident faction broke away to form the Movimiento Obrero Comunista, under the leadership of former Politburo member Rodolfo Puiggros, which placed itself frankly in the Peronista ranks. In subsequent years, in spite of certain twistings and turnings, the official Communist Party tended to continue to regard itself as part of the Opposition, while the Movimiento Comunista was accepted as a fulfledged member of the Perón camp and came to have considerable influence in the inner circles of the Perón regime. It tried both to influence Perón and his followers in the Communist direction and to build up organizational strength in the Peronista trade unions.

In Peru the coming to power of the Odría dictatorship in 1948 resulted in the splitting of that country's Communist Party. The "official" group led by Secretary General Jorge del Prado, was outlawed and went into opposition to the Odría regime. Another element, led by the Party's principal trade union figure, Juan P. Luna, allied itself with the Odría regime, formed a Workers Independent Electoral Committee, and won a senator and various deputies in the Odría congress.

In Venezuela the split in the Communist movement was older, dating from the middle 1940's, when the Communist Party split over the question of relations with the Medina Angarita dictatorship. Two separate parties were formed, one usually called the Red Communists, the other, the Black Communists. With the Army *coup d'état* in November, 1948, which ousted the Democratic Action government, the Black Communists adopted a policy of friendship towards the resultant military dictatorship and, as a result, were allowed to function quite openly, maintaining a significant hold on the country's trade union movement. The Red Communists, on the other hand, adopted a position of strong opposition to the military dictatorship and sought to work with the Democratic Action Party.

In Cuba the same tactic was used, but with a somewhat different twist as a result of General Batista's *coup d'état* in March, 1952. After a short period of hesitation, the Communist Party officially took a position of opposition to the dictatorship. However, a significant number of Communist trade union leaders withdrew from the party and joined the "Labor Bloc" of Batista's own Partido Acción Progresista. The P.A.P. was weak in labor support and welcomed them with open arms. The "unofficial" Communists were able to make some progress in rebuilding the Communists' trade union strength, which had been completely destroyed during the democratic administrations of Presidents Grau San Martín and Carlos Prío Socarras.

The split in Mexico has been of a somewhat different nature. It originated in considerable part from the prima donna attitude of Vicente Lombardo Toledano. During the 1940's Lombardo Toledano became the kingpin in the Communists' trade union activities in Latin America, but he refused to join the official Communist Party of Mexico, with whom he had fought many bitter battles in past years. Instead, he organized his own Partido Popular in 1947, which did not apparently lessen his position vis-à-vis the top leaders of the international Communist movement.

There is no doubt that, in some cases, democratic governments have also given aid and comfort to the Communists and have helped them to gain positions of importance. During World War II this tendency was widely prevalent. The Communists at that time were more pro-United Nations than the United Nations themselves, and their weight was welcomed in the fight against Naziism and Fascism both inside and outside of Latin America. The Communists won more freedom of operation, and not infrequently actual aid, from the governments of Latin America during that period than during any other part of their history.

In particular cases, democratic leaders have worked with or used the Communists. This was true of President Lázaro Cárdenas of Mexico during the 1930's. He was in the midst of a severe struggle to carry forward agrarian reform and other aspects of his revolutionary program, and he welcomed any support he could get. The Communists were allowed to occupy important posts in the government-sponsored and oriented labor movement, the Confederación de Trabajadores de Mexico. During subsequent administrations the Communists lost most, if not all, of the ground they had gained during the Cárdenas period.

In Guatemala, too, the history of the late 1940's and early 1950's is one of the democratic government leaders working with and giving strong support to the Communists. Such instances have occurred, as well, in Chile under González Videla in 1946–47; in Ecuador on various occasions; in Colombia during the late 1930's and early 1940's, in Costa Rica during the administrations of Presidents Calderón Guardia and Teodoro Picado, to mention but a few examples.

One other factor has played a certain part in whatever success the Communists have had in Latin America—sympathy for the Soviet Union. It was to a very considerable extent admiration of the Russian Revolution which led to the founding of the Latin American Communist Parties. The Anarchists of Brazil were very sympathetic, and out of their ranks came the Brazilian Communist Party; the Socialist parties of Uruguay and Chile went over as such to the Communist International, largely because they wanted to be ranged alongside the "first workers' republic."

In the early years picturing the successes of "building socialism" in the Soviet Union was a very important part of the propaganda of the Latin American Communist Parties, and aroused a good deal of sympathy, perhaps more among the intellectuals than among the manual workers.

The great era of the Soviet appeal, however, was during the second World War. At that time the sympathy of the workers and the middle-class people of Latin America was overwhelmingly with the Allies, and there was very widespread admiration for the way in which the Red Army first stood off and then rolled back the armies of Hitler.

The Communists capitalized to the utmost upon this wartime sympathy for the Soviet Union. They became almost the principal spokesmen for the Russians—or at least seemed to be regarded as such by many in the Latin American countries. They urged closer relations with "our great ally," the Soviet Union, and various Latin American countries during this period recognized or re-recognized the Soviet Union. Relations were close between the new Russian embassies or legations and the Communist Parties of the various countries. There was little or no attempt to hide the close relationship between the Communists of Latin America and those of the Soviet Union. On the contrary, every attempt was made to capitalize upon this relationship.

The tide of sympathy for the Soviet Union ebbed after the War, a feeling of hostility developed in many parts as a result of the intensification of the Cold War, and the close relation of the Communists with the Russians lost its appeal. They became less ostentatious about it, and it seems likely that distrust arising from this relationship was a considerable factor in alienating a large part of the Latin American working class in the postwar years. Local Latin American nationalisms were ruffled by the professed adherence of the Communists to the Soviet Union.

In the early 1950's the Communists used their Soviet connections in still another way. Although they never ceased to picture the beauties of life in the Soviet Union, they began to lay emphasis on a somewhat more practical aspect of the subject. Resentment was widespread in many Latin American countries against the great dependence of their economies on that of the United States. The Communists, of course, helped in any way they could to stir up this resentment. One of their most potent arguments was to picture trade with the Soviet Union, Eastern Europe, and China as an answer to this excessive dependence on the United States.

The Chilean Communists were using this argument as early as 1946–47, when the González Videla government recognized the Soviet Union, a Soviet Embassy was established, and rumors flew that González was willing to negotiate with the Russians concerning the export of the country's copper output—which at that time was still selling at a low price fixed by United States authorities.

Later this became a theme exploited throughout the hemisphere. The success of some of the countries of Western Europe in negotiating limited trade treaties with the Soviet Union contributed to a widespread belief that such trade accords could be reached by Latin America. The negotiation of a treaty between Argentina and the Soviet Union in September, 1953, for the exchange of about $150,000,000 worth of goods each way further contributed to the popularity of this idea.

The Communists, naturally, did their utmost to publicize the virtues of the Communist countries as trading partners. In Bolivia they suggested such trade as a possible solution to the pressing tin problem. In Guatemala they encouraged the government actually to undertake negotiations with the Communist countries. Various Latin American groups attended the Moscow Economic Conference in 1952, though no concrete results seem to have been achieved by them there, and some of the delegates, at least, returned without any great enthusiasm.

Such success as the Communists have had in Latin America has been due, then, to three principal factors: their ability to exploit the Latin American social revolution; help which they have received from various governments, dictatorial and democratic; and their more or less close connection with the Soviet Union.

On the other hand, their chief stumbling blocks in the area have undoubtedly been indigenous social revolutionary movements which have been able to capture the imagination of the people of the various countries and to lead these people down the road to social, economic, and political change without making them instruments of international Stalinism and the Soviet State; and the ability of the United States and other non-Communist countries to demonstrate to the Latin American peoples that they can offer Latin America more effective aid in achieving its goals of higher living standards, more equitable distribution of income, and political democracy than can the Communists.

The Thinking
of the Military   JOHN J. JOHNSON
on Major National Issues*

Granting that the armed forces, either directly or indirectly, are constantly affecting decision-making at the national level in nearly all of the republics, it becomes essential to determine something else: how institutionalization, professionalization, and the social-regional back-

* Reprinted from *The Military and Society in Latin America* by John J. Johnson, with the permission of the publishers, Stanford University Press. © 1964 by the Board of Trustees of the Leland Stanford Junior University.

ground of the officers have been reflected in the positions they have taken on such major issues as public education, industrialization, state capitalism, nationalism, communism, and agrarian reform. This can be done by comparing the attitude of the armed forces with that of the currently dominant civilian elements.

Unlike the historian Carl Becker, who considered democracy an economic luxury, the political leaders of Spanish America have almost universally associated working democracy with education. They have publicly proclaimed their faith in public education even when they have had neither the will nor the resources to improve it, and while sending their own children to private schools. Since World War I the new owners of industry and commerce have clamored for public schools that would provide trained personnel needed to operate their plants efficiently. Thousands upon thousands of classrooms have been constructed, thousands upon thousands of teachers have been trained, and the illiteracy rates have dropped to about 55 per cent for the area as a whole; but there are more illiterates than there were in 1950 simply because the spread of education has been unable to keep pace with population growth.

The armed forces have caught the spirit of the civilian leadership. Ask any officer what his country's most serious problem is, and seven times out of ten he will say "insufficient education." But on the basis of past experience, there is even less reason to expect a military government to act decisively in the field of education than to expect it from a civilian regime. No military government in Spanish America, unless one chooses to call Lázaro Cárdenas's government in Mexico military, has ever had an outstanding record in the educational field. Perón, it should be noted, built schools and trained teachers first of all to peddle propaganda, not to disseminate learning. In those republics historically dominated by the military, literacy rates are lower than in the republics where civilians have had a greater role in government. Thus in Haiti, Bolivia, and Venezuela, each with a long history of military domination, the literacy rates stood at 10.5 per cent, 30.1 per cent, and 48.9 per cent respectively in 1950; on the other hand, Costa Rica, which has been relatively free from military control for 80 years, had a literacy rate of 78.8 per cent in 1950, and Uruguay, which shook off the incubus of militarism early in this century, had a literacy rate of 80 per cent. Mexico, which was plagued by military government for a century after its independence but which has had reasonably responsible government for four decades, still has not been able to raise its literacy rate above 57 per cent.

In the field of higher education, there is a strong tendency toward regression in military-dominated governments because students are likely to be the leaders of the civilian opposition and, as such, subject to attack by officers. Pérez Jiménez closed institutions of higher learning repeatedly in the hope that he could quell the student opposition to his dictatorship. In Cuba, the National University was in recess a large part of the time under Batista, who ruled with the armed forces at his back.

Military governments have probably been more favorable to Catholic schools than have the civilian regimes, but this is something that is extremely difficult to measure. The revolutionary generals who dominated Mexico from 1920 to 1946 sporadically struck hard at Catholic education, but they did not permanently cripple it. And as of 1963, when Mexico had been under middle-sector leadership for a decade and a half, more children were attending Catholic schools than at any time in the nation's history. Perón broke with the Church at the end of his regime and vented his spleen upon the Catholic schools, but this was to no avail, and the Church's influence on education is as great as it was when he came to power. But under Pérez Jiménez, Catholic educational institutions uniformly were given a relatively free hand, and teachers from various reactionary Spanish Catholic orders flooded the country's cultural institutions. Certainly there was no diminution of Catholic influence in Colombian education under the military dictator Rojas Pinilla. The Catholic Church has also held a strong position in the weak educational system of Peru, where the military has been always close to the center of government; but it has been weak in Costa Rica and Uruguay, where the military men are as nonpolitical as any in Spanish America.

Although the armed forces show relatively little sympathy for education per se, they have made a significant contribution to the civilian sector by providing it with technically trained personnel. Commissioned and non-commissioned officers with technical skills easily move into nonadministrative posts in the civilian area. In Argentina, for example, the services have considerable difficulty keeping men trained in electronics and communications from leaving their posts in favor of civilian jobs. Every country in Spanish America with an air force knows, as is known in the United States, that the national air force is the principal, if not practically the sole, source of pilots and navigators for commercial air lines. In republics like Ecuador, where the labor movement is underdeveloped, commissioned officers and non-commissioned officers with technical training move freely into service in the merchant marine. In Venezuela the low level of academic training and the high pay and benefits that military men receive have combined to discourage Venezuelan armed forces personnel from actively seeking civilian employment.

Professionalization and social background appear to be the important determinants in the attitude of officers toward education. They may espouse the ideas of intellectuals regarding public education, but they do not have a clear understanding of what they mean. The army, which is ordinarily the branch most active in the civilian area, is still so non-technical that the educational requirements of the common soldier are nil. At the present stage of their development, the armies can use an illiterate conscript almost as effectively as they can a literate one. Then, too, the armed forces, despite their declarations to the contrary, have not considered representative democracy a primary objective, so they have not felt the same need as have many civilians for educating the masses.

The attitude of the officers toward Catholic education can be explained in terms of their social environment. As noted above, an important percentage of officers come from "well-established small-town families" and families recently migrated to America, especially from Italy and Spain. These groups are the hard-core Catholic elements in the republics, and the available evidence indicates that the military bureaucracy is at least as Catholic as the civilian bureaucracy or the middle sector as a whole. When we add to these considerations the fact that historically the Catholic Church often has been the only organized group that would readily spring to the support of a military government, the professional soldier's approval of Catholic education is understandable.

The urgent need for greater industrialization is accepted as self-evident in Spanish America. As might be expected, however, there are differences of opinion as to the degree of urgency. These differences exist both between countries and between social-economic groups within a given country. The attitude of the armed forces vis-à-vis that of the civilian elements toward industrialization is determined almost solely by the extent to which military professionalization has been carried out, and the social background of the officers does not seem to be a factor one way or another. In general, it may be said that in the technically lesser-developed countries, and also where professionalization is not advanced, the officers are less concerned with industrialization than are the urban middle sectors. In the more developed countries, like Argentina, the armed forces are in the forefront of those most concerned with the desirability of industrial growth.

The Honduran army does not think in terms of industrial development of the nation. Soldiers' clothes and shoes come almost entirely from abroad, and their officers have no serious interest in changing this situation. "We will buy where we can get the most for our money," was the stand taken by one colonel. Nor are the Honduran armed forces any more concerned than civilians with the development of the country's transportation system. "We do not want easy access to the Nicaraguan border," said one highly placed officer.

The Ecuadorian armed forces take much the same position that the Honduran services do. In the words of a senior air force officer, "We have tried to work with local industry but have been unsuccessful. It is cheaper to import." It was evident that the policy of the armed forces was hurting when in mid-1960 Ecuadorian newspapers carried numerous accounts of the efforts of local business interests to force the military to buy more domestically produced goods, such as clothing and shoes.

The Venezuelan armed forces have moved one step beyond those of Honduras and Ecuador. They buy locally for enlisted men but the officers outfit themselves from abroad. At this time there are only scattered suggestions from the officers that the nation should manufacture anything more than the simplest material requirements of the services.

At the other extreme from Honduras and Ecuador is Argentina. There the armed forces feel that their responsibilities give them every right to be a party to decision-making when industrial development is involved. They strongly favor the expansion of the iron and steel and petroleum industries. They also feel that the nation should manufacture a wide variety of the requirements of a modern military establishment. They have therefore pushed for the manufacture of heavy equipment; at one time under Perón's rule they even attempted to produce airplanes. They actively supported Perón's program to develop Argentina's merchant marine and national air lines, and the army has since favored the expansion of land transportation to the south and to the west toward the Chilean border.

In those countries where the armed forces are actively promoting industrialization, the primary area of dispute is the extent to which foreign capital should be permitted to participate. Although since the overthrow of Perón influential elements in the Argentine forces have favored foreign participation in the development of the nation's petroleum industry, the evidence seems to indicate that under normal circumstances they would be as quick to take a stand against foreign participation in basic areas of the economy as would the *peronistas*.

In other of the more sophisticated republics there is a latent opposition to foreign capital, but the armed forces are in general no more opposed to foreign economic penetration than are civilians. The Chilean armed forces, for example, have never seriously challenged foreign control of the nation's copper industry, and in 1963 they were less inclined than a majority of the civilians to advocate expropriation. Under the military dictatorship of Pérez Jiménez, foreign capital was more vigorously solicited than most Venezuelan civilian elements would have preferred. And as of 1960 the Honduran armed forces would have offered foreign capital better terms than would the civilian group in control of the country.

There is a direct link between industrialization and state interventionism in Spanish America. State intervention in the economic sphere first came about as a result of the desire to hasten economic expansion. It is now justified on the basis of three widely held beliefs: (1) Industry cannot survive without protection from outside competition, and only the state can provide that protection; (2) since the accumulation of domestic private capital is slow, the state, with its ability to accumulate capital fairly rapidly through taxation and foreign loans, must intercede in the industrial sphere in order to maintain the highest possible rate of development; (3) solicitude for the working groups requires that the state exercise some control over the prices of necessary commodities.

Although statism is properly associated with middle-sector leadership, there is no doubt that the more professionalized armed forces have for several reasons given the ideology their blessing. Being bureaucrats themselves, officers do not find bureaucratic control of economic resources objectionable. Coming as they do from essentially non-industrial families, they are not disturbed by state rather than private control of industry. The interest of officers in public economic and welfare projects stems also from a desire to manage them, which is a way in which they can exercise financial power of the kind that they could never hope to achieve themselves. Furthermore, state intervention has hastened industrial development, or so it is believed in the area, and the armed forces welcome this. More specifically, the state has assumed responsibility for the development of those basic economic sectors—notably transportation and power—which domestic and foreign private capital has shunned, but which are vital to the armed forces. Finally, state control and regulation of natural resources have the approval of the armed forces, whose future obviously depends on a continuing supply of certain raw materials.

Throughout Spanish America, nationalism—of a kind that "seeks equality and someone else to blame" but is free of aggressive intentions toward neighboring countries—has been raised to the level of a major ideology. Although it may be given a cultural, economic, or juridical emphasis, depending upon the country and the moment, its essence is always that Spanish American civilization, which is now threatened from all sides, is unique because it was built upon Christian values inherited from Spain and because those values give a primacy of the spiritual against the materialistic. So firmly is this belief held that it may be going too far to say that it dominates the subconscious Spanish American mind. In more concrete terms, however, nationalism has such political appeal that civilians vie against civilians (and against the state) for the privilege of championing it and the armed forces strive to sharpen their image as its true defenders.

Nationalism in its broadest sense is manifested in such a variety of ways that it would be impossible to determine with certainty whether civilians or the armed forces (which are at all times likely to have militantly nationalistic elements) are the more nationalistic. At a somewhat lower level certain generalizations can be made. Cultural nationalism, for example, is practically a civilian monopoly. Economic nationalism is ordinarily shared by civilians and the armed forces, with the latter, often responding more to emotionalism than reason, becoming particularly concerned when the control or depletion of natural resources is a consideration or when foreign investment is involved in "strategic" areas of the economy. Juridical nationalism, which for our purposes may be taken to mean a concern over direct or indirect threats to the national sovereignty, is in the final analysis the preserve of the armed forces.

As in the case of industrialization, it is generally true that the more institutionalized and professionalized the military establishment is, the greater is the possibility that it will be strongly nationalistic. Thus the Argentine armed forces are the most nationalistic in Spanish America (although others may at times be more chauvinistic). With them it is an article of faith that Argentina has the human and material resources to become a sort of second United States, at least in a Latin American sphere of influence. But even in Argentina, the navy, which has historically had strong ties with Great Britain and the United States, is considerably less nationalistic than the army, whose ties before World War II were with Germany and Italy. And it should be pointed out that Germany and Italy were, in the minds of the Argentine military, "the adversaries of those countries exploiting Argentina." As one Argentine naval officer stated the navy's position, "We spell *nacionalismo* (of the army) with a 'z'" (*nazionalismo*).

In Honduras, which represents the other extreme from Argentina, "officers are by education and profession incapable of thinking in the abstract," and display few nationalistic tendencies. In Venezuela the armed forces feel that they are "the only group to preserve the national heritage," but a priest in Caracas came closer to presenting the civilian consensus when he said, "Officers are strongly nationalistic at first, then corruption takes over." In Quito, Ecuador, a banker stated the prevalent opinion in and out of the armed forces when he said, "There is very little nationalism here; there is a problem with Peru." In Peru there are officers of all ranks who strongly advocate nationalization of oil and mineral properties.

Chilean civilians agree with the armed forces that politicians exploit nationalism more than do the armed forces, who, it is said, "cannot conceive of a situation that would lead to war with a neighboring country." A story illustrating this point was making the rounds of Santiago in mid-1960. It was that Chilean politicans had so incensed the public over Argentine claims to small "Chilean" islands in the straits area that the Chilean navy was obliged to move out of Valparaiso as if to sail south to protect the national interests; in fact, the story ran, the vessels did not have enough fuel to make the trip, so they were simply moved beyond the horizon and kept there until the public calmed down, whereupon they returned to Valparaiso.

When the armed forces do choose to become active spokesmen for nationalism, they have working in their favor three important considerations. First of all, "their swords are consecrated to the national will," and they are charged with the defense of the nation's honor. Second, unlike soldiers of an earlier era whose loyalties were to a *jefe*—and unlike politicians who even today cannot see beyond the borders of their own states or the interests of their parties—officers can claim to react as true national patriots, as Argentines, Chileans, or Mexicans. This image is encouraged by the fact that the armies, navies, and air forces are rapidly replacing the Catholic Church as a symbol of unity on national holidays, a development which took place in the United States at least by 1930, except that in the United States the armed forces replaced the politician who wrapped himself in a religious mantle. This "national" image of the armed forces permits them, on those occasions when they seize power, to maintain that they are interpreting the desires of the people disgruntled with the narrowly conceived if not actually anti-national objectives of the politicians. Third, in several of the republics—such as Argentina, Peru, El Salvador, and Guatemala—the military is the country's best-organized institution and is thus in a better position than political parties or other pressure groups to give objective expression to the national will when the fatherland is confronted with a challenge to its power, position, or prestige. Mexico offers an important exception to this generalization; there, not the armed forces but the PRI is the best organized institution, and the party rather than the armed forces has been the unifying force at the national level.

Communism and *fidelismo* have become the principal catalysts that keep the political cauldron boiling in Spanish America. They may be expected to win added support before they decline in favor, if that is their destiny. There is no assurance that they are so destined. Having demonstrated in Cuba that a small group of determined men can take over a government and achieve power by offering a quick way to end "economic imperialism," the communists and *fidelistas* now threaten to fill the power vacuum created by the shift of the middle-sector leadership to the right of the political spectrum, which has occurred in some countries. The communists' potential is enhanced by the fact that despite their successes, the current dominant leadership has refused to take communism seriously. There are four principal reasons for this. First, the leaders are so preoccupied with the internal problems of their countries that they have not developed an emotional involvement in cold war politics. This allows them to feel that the United States is trying to lead them in a great crusade against communism rather than trying to help them meet their real and pressing social-economic problems and political requirements. Second, they are so accustomed to expecting the United States to make the final decisions in the Hemisphere that they are sure, despite what has occurred in Cuba, that if the United States seriously intended to root out communism in the Hemisphere, it could somehow do so. Third, the leaders are convinced that were it not for the evidence of communism in their midst the United States would not be so concerned with the development of the area. Fourth, they feel (for reasons quite difficult to explain) that if communism takes over they would be able to divest it of the worst features of its international connections and mold it to serve the specific requirements of their people.

It can be stated categorically that as a group, armed forces officers are more noisily anti-communist, if not necessarily more effectively anti-communist, than all but a very few civilians. One may say further that without the armed forces, but with all other things being equal, every republic in Spanish America except Uruguay, Costa Rica, and Cuba would stand politically to the left of where it is now; it would only be a question of how much further left. But having said that, much remains unsaid. The military's enmity toward communism often seems more emotional than reasoned; and while sincere, it ordinarily appears not to have been accompanied by a real understanding of communist strategy and tactics on the international or domestic scene. The anti-communism of the armed forces has tended to result in actions that circumscribe communist activities but do not simultaneously effectively combat the conditions that breed more communism.

The communists are untried, and this in itself is enough to cause concern in an institution like the military, which has an inherent distrust of political change. But the communists do not always suffer at the hands of the military. Because the armed forces, when they seize power, must seek civilian support wherever it can be found, they can easily end up in alliance with the communists, whose opportunism and short-range objectives can be served by working with the opposition. It was the search for public approval that drove the Venezuelan military dictator Pérez Jiménez to outlaw the communists and then to work with them so that he might, through them, claim a semblance of support from organized labor and offset Democratic Action influence. And when Batista seized power in 1952 he gave the communists a relatively free hand in the labor movement, and in return the communists kept labor in line until Batista fled before Castro's forces. When the Organization of American States voted sanctions against Rafael Trujillo, who as dictator of the Dominican Republic for a quarter century had represented himself as the principal anti-communist in the Hemisphere, he blandly announced that he might be forced to collaborate with the communists.

More recently, between July 1962 and January 1963, the Peruvian junta (which seized power after a disputed presidential election) favored the communists, who in turn cooperated with the military regime. Communist-controlled unions backed the junta when Aprista Party workers called a strike and in return the communists were given influential positions in government ministries. Communist-controlled labor federations, such as the Civil Construction Federation and the Chauffeurs Federation, were granted official recognition. The government newspaper, *El Peruano*, praised communist union officers as "authentic" leaders of the working class and branded the Apristas as "under political control." A month after taking over the government, junta co-presidents Pérez Godoy and Torres Matos, accompanied by officials of the labor ministry, inaugurated the communist-directed Maritime Congress held at Callao. Finally, in January 1963, the junta began to root out the communists, presumably because of their success in inciting the Indians of the Andes to rebel against the large landholders, who have a long record of irresponsibility and gross mistreatment of the Indians. But as late as April 1963, the junta was unwilling to crack down on communists and intellectuals sympathetic to communism who had found their way into the government.

The Honduran armed forces are probably so completely devoid of ideological bias that it may well be true that they do not distinguish between communist and democratic doctrine. According to one well-placed Honduran, "If you were to ask an officer what his political indoctrination is, he would say 'What's that?'" The Chilean armed forces "know their ideologies," being by Latin American standards quite professionalized, but even they would be reluctant to jeopardize their status by moving against an extreme leftist government that was freely elected and seemed content to work within the framework of the constitution.

Finally, although all the professional armed forces have thus far taken a stand against communism, it should not be concluded that all officers are anti-communist. There may well be a few communists or communist sympathizers in the armed forces of every Spanish American republic. What is more important, however, is that there are some who ignore communism or who might opt for communism if it appears to be the winning side in national politics. These elements do not appear to constitute a serious threat at the moment, but they may be dangerous in the near future, when officers drawn from the working sectors of society and from the cities choose to compete for power with their seniors in the military hierarchy.

Agrarian reform has been given top priority in a number of republics and has been made one of the major objectives of the Alliance for Progress, but so far achievements have not been impressive. Vastly more complex than simple land redistribution, agrarian reform impinges upon every major area of Spanish American civilization. In the social sphere, agrarian reform cannot ignore the fact that almost everywhere family, clan, and village ties discourage large-scale relocation of the landless peasants to isolated frontier regions where public lands are often available. Thus the Indians of Ecuador will not willingly go in large numbers to the tropical Amazon drainage basin unless conditions are made far more attractive than they are at present. In the economic area agrarian reform involves creating incentives to production, granting credits, training technicians by the hundreds, developing hybrid seeds, improving livestock strains, and importing farm machinery, to mention only a few of the more important tasks. In the political sphere, the problem is to satisfy the deserving and restless but economically and politically unsophisticated peasants without disturbing unduly the economies of the countryside or driving into militant opposition the reactionary landholding element, which, through family ties, often shares many interests with the urban financial elites.

Like the current middle-sector leadership, the armed forces have been ambivalent in respect to agrarian reform. The question "what is the single most serious problem your country faces?" was put to several dozen officers interviewed in Honduras, Ecuador, Chile, Argentina, Brazil, and Venezuela; not one mentioned land reform. In pursuing this subject with them, it was obvious that they are only passively favorable to agrarian reform. A Venezuelan colonel might have been speaking for a vast majority of them when he said, "I support orderly agrarian reform," which in effect meant reform, including land distribution, that would proceed only as rapidly as the state could or would allocate scarce resources to agrarian reform rather than to alternative and competing needs. As late as 1963, nowhere in Latin America except in Venezuela had an agrarian reform program predicated upon such a premise given more than a glimmer of hope that the over-all agricultural problem might be resolved in the foreseeable future, to say nothing of satisfying the impoverished peasants' demands for "land now."

The armed forces' stand on agrarian reform, including land redistribution, derives from a complex of circumstances, some with historical roots and some of recent origin. The historical ones are the military-landholding-Church alliances and the personal interests of officers with family ties linking them to the landholding elite. These circumstances have relevance, but they do not seem to be controlling. In the first place, the old military-landholding-Church alliance is no longer meaningful in several of the republics (Chile, Venezuela, and Argentina, for example), yet in those countries the armed forces would as quickly look askance at revolutionary agrarian reform as they would in Colombia, where the alliance still persists. In the second place, as we have said, at no time since the Independence period have a significant share of officers come directly from the landholding elites.

More recent and more relevant developments determining the attitude of the armed forces toward agrarian reform include the effects of institutionalization and professonalization, the officers' economic views, and above all their growing political ties with the urban middle sectors. Institutionalization has made bureaucrats of officers, and as the Mexican novelist Mariano Azuela has remarked, "The bureaucrat represents the force of inertia." Officers simply do not see what they have to gain from rapid change, particularly when all the evidence they have indicates that rapid agrarian reform probably would be accompanied by decreases in foreign exchange earnings, which was desperately needed for modernization. And to officers, modernization has become synonymous with technological modernization; they support the building of smokestacks rather than haystacks. Their professionalization makes them gradualists and thus distrustful of disorder and social ferment, which are inherent in any revolutionary movement.

To the extent that officers have had a comprehension of the workings of private capital, it has ordinarily come through having invested private capital in real estate. They can associate a farm with family ownership much more quickly and meaningfully than they can an impersonal factory, and their sympathies, consequently, may be easily enlisted by the embattled landholder but not by the industrialist or man of finance. Retired Ecuadorian officers, for instance, have shown great interest in possessing their own banana plantations, no matter how small the plantations may be; it is tempting to speculate that for them the landholder, astride his horse and issuing orders which are accepted without question, combines at a rather primitive level the individualism they were deprived of in the service and the discipline and respect they were trained to expect during their professional careers.

Historically, land meant power in Latin America; today, it is associated with affluence and security. The urge to own a plot of land and a home on the outskirts of the overcrowded cities is shared by civilians and military men alike. And as long as officers can look forward to satisfying their desires "to get away from it all," they will be inclined to share with the more financially secure civilian elements the distrust of legislation designed to circumscribe the landholder's freedom of action.

One of the most persistent and widely held misconceptions regarding the armed forces is that they remain aligned with the landholding elite. The conception is not only untrue but pernicious, for it often leads to dangerously wrong conclusions. The military no longer reflects the thinking of the landed elites in Mexico, Cuba, Costa Rica, El Salvador, Venezuela, Bolivia, Chile, Argentina, and Uruguay; in several of those countries, the historical alliances were dissolved decades ago. That group of countries not only contains approximately 70 per cent of the area and 69 per cent of the population of Spanish America, but it includes the five best-developed countries of the area—Mexico, Costa Rica, Chile, Argentina, and Uruguay. In Portuguese Brazil, which must be ranked with the five more highly developed Spanish American republics, the alliance between the military and the landed elite collapsed before the end of World War II; when we add Brazil to the others, it is apparent that at least 80 per cent of all of Latin America by area and 72 per cent of the region's population is not subject to rule by landholders and officers. The remaining countries, Colombia excepted, constitute the most backward and least influential part of the Hemisphere.

This is not to say that since World War I the armed forces have not fought to keep the old elite in power; they have done so on several occasions, as in Peru, where officers have seldom reflected the interests of the groups from which they come. It is to say rather that the armed forces are sufficiently flexible and opportunistic to accept change once it occurs. Thus when middle-sector leadership took over in Uruguay (1903), Argentina (1916), Chile (1920), Mexico (1946), and Costa Rica[1] the armed forces joined them, except that in Argentina the military returned the landed elite to power in 1930 and kept them there by force for thirteen years, when an anti-landed elite element within the officers corps seized control of the government. The military coup of 1945 gave the Venezuelan middle sectors their first opportunity to govern, and while the coup of 1948 negated all the gains made by the civilians, the armed forces after 1958 provided President Betancourt with the strength he needed to maintain his precarious control of the nation.

The attitude of the officers is more explicable than is the reasoning of those who refuse to see what has happened to the military. In the first place the armed forces up to now have come from essentially the same economic groups as have the middle-sector leaders—from that small but growing class standing between the very rich and the miserably poor. It was thus understandable that as soon as the middle sectors established their political capabilities the armed forces might, as they actually did, align with them. Middle-sector government is bureaucratic and modernizing, as are the armed forces. Furthermore, officers' families are well represented in the civilian bureaucracies. Middle-sector governments have expanded public spending enormously, and this has meant larger budgets for the armed forces. Finally, the middle sectors and the armed forces are in basic agreement on most major issues—industrialization, state capitalism, nationalism, and agrarian reform. It bears repeating at this point that the military ordinarily would broaden the political base more slowly than the middle sectors have found expedient, and that the officers would take a tougher stand on communism than the civilian politicians have been willing to take thus far.

If the civilians and the armed forces can work together harmoniously, the question naturally arises, "Why have the civilian sectors rather than the armed forces seemed to be innovators?" To begin with, the civilians have not always been the innovators, as witness the transformation that took place under Carlos Ibáñez in Chile during the late 1920's and in Argentina under Perón in the 1940's. But in the vast majority of cases in which civilians have been innovators it is probably because the various military establishments have been saddled with seniority systems. Seniority, whether in an African tribe or a Spanish American military establishment, is an inescapable recipe for extreme conserva-

---

[1] Authorities differ on when the middle sectors, in this case a rural middle sector, achieved control in Costa Rica, but most would agree that the shift took place sometime before 1920.

tism.[2] As long as the seniority system remains, military decisions will be made by men in their late fifties, their sixties, and their seventies, men who have theoretically had a minimum of contact with civilians. At the same time, three out of four civilians are under 35 years of age, the average voter is 36 years of age, and a large share of those elected to high public office are in their thirties and forties. Therefore, serious differences of opinion will inevitably arise between civilians and the military as to what should be altered and how rapidly the alteration should take place. This assumes that officers are going to remain involved in politics and decision-making, a warranted assumption as long as officers think like the Venezuelan colonel who said in August 1960, "Since 1958 we have given civilians all the authority they need to run the country."

One cannot be sure what the outcome would be if it were decided to retire all officers in Spanish America promptly at age 45 (and the increased cost of retirement benefits would be negligible); but it is generally agreed that majors and lieutenant colonels have been on the side of those civilians anxious for "progress" more often than have full colonels and generals. Furthermore, since the tendency in the armed forces is toward ever greater technical preparation, early retirement would serve to narrow the gap between the technically more competent junior officers and their superiors.

The point, again, is simply that officers from middle-class families have been able to cooperate successfully with the civilian urban middle sectors once those groups have beaten the traditional landed elite at the polls. Today in several of the republics the officers have come to support the interests and aspirations of the urban propertied groups; the conservatism of the officers is of the same nature as that found in the urban middle sectors, and not, as is sometimes contended, the conservatism of the rural, landholding elite. From this two important conclusions may be reached: (1) now that officers are coming increasingly from the lower middle sectors and the working masses, the armed forces may be expected to be more inclined than formerly to gravitate toward positions identified with popular aspirations and to work with the representatives of the popular elements, such as the Frente de Acción Popular (FRAP) in Chile, on those occasions when they attain power legally; and (2) any Latin American politician who complacently expects the armed forces to hold off the mob power of the left for an indefinite period faces not only a rude awakening but risks an irreparable loss in influence.

[2] Ibáñez and Perón, it should be noted, were middle-ranking officers when they achieved power.